Letters of
Benjamin Rush

MEMOIRS OF THE

AMERICAN PHILOSOPHICAL SOCIETY

HELD AT PHILADELPHIA

FOR PROMOTING USEFUL KNOWLEDGE

VOLUME 30, PART 2

Letters of

BENJAMIN RUSH

EDITED BY L·H·BUTTERFIELD

Volume II: 1793-1813

PUBLISHED FOR

THE AMERICAN PHILOSOPHICAL SOCIETY

BY PRINCETON UNIVERSITY PRESS

1951

Printed in the United States of America
by Princeton University Press at Princeton, New Jersey

IV.

The Greatest Battle:
Rush and the Yellow Fever
1793-1800

1793 August-November. Great epidemic of yellow fever in Phila-
       delphia; BR attacked twice or thrice; his sister and three of
       his apprentices die.

1793 Nov. 5. Resigns from College of Physicians on account of
       disagreement over treatment of yellow fever.

1793 Nov. 12. Mrs. Rush and the children return to Philadelphia.

1794. Publishes *An Account of the Bilious Remitting Yellow Fever
       ... in the Year 1793*. The fever reappears in Philadelphia
       this year.

1795 January. Serves as president of national convention of aboli-
       tion societies in Philadelphia.

1796. Assumes duties of chair of theory and practice of medicine
       at the University in succession to Dr. Adam Kuhn. (Formally
       appointed to this additional chair in 1805.)

1797 Nov. 27. Appointed treasurer of the United States Mint by
       President John Adams.

1797. Establishes a country residence at "Sydenham," north of the
       city.

1797. Renewed epidemic of yellow fever. In retaliation for attacks
       by William Cobbett, BR enters a libel suit against him which
       is protracted until December 1799.

1797-1801. Vice-president of the American Philosophical Society.

1798. Publishes *Essays, Literary, Moral & Philosophical*.

1798. Renewed epidemic of yellow fever.

1799. Publishes *Three Lectures upon Animal Life*.

1800 February-April. Cobbett's attacks on BR in the *Rush-Light*.

1800. Begins his autobiography ("Travels through Life").

Julia Stockton Rush. Portrait by Charles Willson Peale

Part IV. *The Greatest Battle:*
Rush and the Yellow Fever
1793-1800

To Elizabeth Graeme Ferguson?[1]

My dear Friend,   Philadelphia, January 18th, 1793

Your friendly letter, accompanied by the poetical address, came safe to hand.[2] I thank you for them and have only to lament that the latter is so little merited. The poetry is excellent, and no wonder —considering Waller's reply to Charles 2d, "that poets succeed best in fiction."[3]

For some days past the conversation of our city has turned wholly upon Mr. Blanchard's late aerial voyage.[4] It was a truly sublime sight. Every faculty of the mind was seized, expanded, and captivated by it. 40,000 people concentrating their eyes and thoughts at the *same* instant, upon the *same* object, and all deriving nearly the *same* degrees of pleasure from it, added greatly to the novelty and originality of the scene. I cannot think that an invention in which so much ingenuity and fortitude have been displayed was intended only to amuse gazing cities and countries. It is no uncommon thing for the most useful inventions to be progressive in their nature, and for the first hints which produce them to sleep for centuries before they are brought to perfection. The loadstone served only to *amuse* for 1,500 years before it was applied to the purposes of navigation. The first command to man to "subdue the earth,"[5] like every other divine command, *must* be fulfilled. The earth certainly includes water and air as well as dry land. The first and the last have long ago yielded to the dominion of man. It remains for him only to render the air subservient to his will. This I conceive will sooner or later be effected by the improvement and extension of the principles of balloons.

I have destined them to be employed as remedies where a sudden and extensive change in the body is required. Pure air, exercise, and above all a hundred conflicting emotions in the mind will concur to produce this change. Perhaps they may carry astronomy so far beyond the gross air which lies near our globe as to enable them to make immense discoveries of the nature and number of the heavenly bodies. Perhaps they may increase and facilitate the connection between distant countries by means of commerce. Above all, who knows but they may be the vehicles which shall convey the inhabitants of our western world to Jerusalem to pay their annual homage to the Saviour of the World during the period of the millennium? Should this be the case, the 8th verse of the 60th chapter of Isaiah will be intelligible.[6] I refer you to the whole of the chapter, particularly to the verses which succeed the above, in which there seems to be an evident relation to the conversion and ingathering of the inhabitants of this western part of our globe. The persons who are to carry their gold and silver with them are probably the Jews, for their property in all countries has always been personal, thereby more easily to favor their return to the city of their ancestors.

I have only to add to this letter that humanity and reason are likely to prevail so far in our legislature that a law will probably pass in a few weeks to abolish capital punishments in *all cases* whatever.[7] This triumph of truth and Christianity over ignorance and Judaism will mark an era in the history of mankind. It will I have no doubt soon be followed by a change in all our systems of religion which exhibit the Deity as delighting in or even consenting to the eternal execution of any of his creatures.

We have a Benjamin in our family[8]—a stout, healthy, noisy fellow of 2 years old, so that there is now no impediment to your kind wishes to Mrs. Rush, who joins in love to you with, my dear madam, your very affectionate friend,

BENJN RUSH

P.S. Have you read Winchester on the Prophecies? He has performed a voyage of circumnavigation around the Old and New Testaments. He has examined passages, verses, and even words with a microscope. In short, he appears to be a theological Newton.

MS: Historical Society of Pennsylvania, Gratz Collection.

[1] There can be little doubt that this letter was written to Mrs. Ferguson. A penciled note in a modern hand on the MS states that it was so directed, but we need not rely on this statement. Mrs. Ferguson was BR's affectionate friend, his principal feminine correspondent (except for Mrs. Rush), and a writer of the kind of poetry that he here acknowledges.

[2] Neither the letter nor the "poetical address" to BR has been found.

[3] Dr. Johnson relates that when Charles II asked Edmund Waller (1606-1687) how it happened that his panegyrical poem on Cromwell was so superior to that on Charles himself, Waller (who was a courtier as well as a poet) replied, "Poets, Sir, succeed better in fiction than in truth" (John-

son's *Lives of the English Poets*, ed.
G. B. Hill, Oxford, 1905, I, 271).

[4] On 9 Jan. 1793 Jean-Pierre Blanchard (1753-1809), "the celebrated
French aeronaut," ascended in his hydro-
gen balloon from the yard of the Walnut
Street Jail in Philadelphia to make the
first aerial voyage in the United States.
He was in the air forty-six minutes,
landed near Woodbury, Gloucester co.,
N.J., and returned the same evening to
the city in time to pay his respects to
President Washington, who had witnessed the ascension in the morning. BR
had lent Blanchard a pulse glass in
order to ascertain the effect of height
above the earth on the pulse. Some days
after this letter was written Blanchard
took tea with BR, who afterwards
recorded various other information on
aerial travel in his Commonplace Book.
See Penn Mutual Life Insurance Company, *The First Air Voyage in America*

..., *Together with a Fac Simile Re-
printing of the Journal of My Forty-
Fifth Ascension by Jean Pierre Blan-
chard*, Phila., 1943; Jeremiah Milbank,
Jr., *The First Century of Flight in
America*, Princeton, 1943, p. 23-9; BR,
Autobiography, p. 303-4.

[5] See Genesis 1:28.

[6] This verse reads: "Who are these
that fly as a cloud, and as the doves to
their windows?"

[7] On BR's connection with this reform movement, see his letter to John
Coakley Lettsom, 16 Aug. 1788.

[8] Benjamin (1791-1824) was BR's
sixth son and tenth child; he was later
apprenticed to William Waln, a merchant
and shipowner, sailed to many lands,
and died unmarried at New Orleans
(Biddle, *Memorial*, p. 242; BR, *Autobiography*, p. 270; frequent allusions in
BR's letters to John Adams, 1810-1812).

To the Humane Society of Massachusetts[1]

Sir,   Philadelphia, 9h March 1793

I am directed by the Humane Society of Philadelphia to return
you their thanks for your acceptable publications delivered to them
by Colonel Pickering. We rejoice to find that your endeavors to
disseminate knowledge upon the important subject of preserving
human life have been so successful in your state. We enclose you two
publications[2] which have been circulated in the neighborhood of
this city, and we hope with good effects. The paper enclosed No. 2
was pasted up at all the public parts of our city; from the influence
of the publications we have reason to believe many lives have been
saved in our city. Some years ago it was common for twenty or
thirty people to perish in a summer from drinking cold water while
they were heated by labor. But in the course of the two last summers
we have lost only two citizens from that cause. It is extremely agreeable to observe the directions of the Society upon that subject so
generally and so carefully complied with by the most illiterate of
our citizens. It proves that there is no knowledge essential to the
life or happiness of our fellow creatures that may not be made to
produce its intended effects, provided that industry and means
suited to those great ends be employed for that purpose. These

means I conceive are of so simple a nature that they might be made as familiar objects of knowledge in all our schools as they now are in the closets of philosophers. We teach our children many things that are much more difficult, and few things of half the consequence to them that such articles of knowledge would be in their future pursuits and business in life.

Signed &c., B Rush

MS (draft, only partly in BR's hand): Library Company of Philadelphia, Rush MSS.

[1] The "humane society" movement, the primary objective of which at first was the resuscitation of victims of drowning and asphyxiation, began on the European continent in the 1760's. The Royal Humane Society was organized in London in 1774, one of its most active sponsors being BR's friend John Coakley Lettsom. It still flourishes, and the present secretary, Mr. A. Axson, has kindly sent me from the Society's early *Annual Reports* a number of references to BR's work in resuscitation of the apparently dead. In 1807 BR was named by the Society an "Honorary Guardian of Life"; one other American, Bishop James Madison of Virginia, appears with him on the Society's list. Offspring of the London Society were soon founded elsewhere in the British Isles, in Philadelphia (1780), and in Boston (1786). Following the parent society's lead, the Philadelphians placed drugs, medicines, appliances for restoring respiration, with directions for their use, at the ferries and other places of public resort on both sides of the Schuylkill and Delaware Rivers; they also offered rewards for life-saving and for essays on new methods of restoring life in cases of suspended animation. BR was early an honorary member of the Massachusetts Society, among whose founders were his friends Benjamin Waterhouse and John Warren. (Abraham, *Lettsom*, p. 140-50; Mease, *Picture of Philadelphia*, p. 240-1; Scharf & Westcott, II, 1477; M. A. DeW. Howe, *The Humane Society of the Commonwealth of Massachusetts*, Boston, 1918, ch. I, and p. 302.)

[2] One of these was certainly "Directions for Recovering Persons Who Are Supposed to Be Dead from Drowning, also for Preventing and Curing the Disorders Produced by Drinking Cold Water or Other Liquors, and by the Action of Noxious Vapours, Lightening, and Excessive Heat and Cold————— Published by Order of the Humane Society of Philadelphia." This was published in *Poor Richard Improved . . . for . . . 1790* (unpaged) and signed by BR and others as "Managers of the Society." BR told Pickering in a letter of 21 Sep. 1789 that it was composed by himself (Pickering and Upham, *Pickering*, II, 430). Doubtless these "Directions" were the same as those posted as handbills by the Society during the summer months at public pumps and in taverns (*Moreau de St. Méry's American Journey*, transl. and ed. Kenneth Roberts and Anna M. Roberts, Garden City, 1947, p. 323; Scharf & Westcott, II, 1477). In the first volume of BR's *Med. Inq. & Obs.* (1789), p. 129-32, is "An Account of the Disorder Occasioned by Drinking Cold Water in Warm Weather, and the Method of Curing It."

To Thomas Smith[1]

Philadelphia, March 14, 1793

Your niece Mrs. Blodget put a letter into my hands a few days ago in which you request my opinion of Mrs. Smith's case.[2] I am sorry to inform you that I think her in a critical situation, but I do not despair of her recovery, provided she immediately begins to use the only remedy that is radical in complaints of the breast, I mean *riding on horseback*.[3] Take her with you to all your courts. The more she roughs it on these journeys, the better. Bring her to Philadelphia in the spring. The seashore must not be visited, for the sea air is hurtful in all cases of diseases of the breast. Let her nag be a gentle one and his gait a pace. She should begin with short stages and never ride after she is fatigued. Her diet should be regulated by the state of her pulse. When it is full or tense, she should live on milk and vegetables. But when it is weak and quick, she may eat animal food in moderation. She should wear flannel moistened with soap liniment next to her breast. The feet should be preserved with great care from the cold. If a milk and vegetable diet does not reduce her pulse when full or tense, she should lose a few ounces of blood occasionally, and if a troublesome pain in her side should at any time occur, it should be removed if possible by a small blister to the part affected. If a troublesome cough should at any time prevent her sleeping, it should be composed by laudanum or asthmatic elixir.

I repeat it again that my hopes of her recovery hang chiefly upon her *riding on horseback*. She should, like the ancient Tartars, live on horseback. Short excursions from home will not do. She must perform journeys, and they must be repeated during the whole of the present spring and approaching summer. She must avoid only riding in damp weather and in the evening air, and, I repeat it again, never, never ride after she is fatigued.

I have done all that I could to promote the wishes of our trustees respecting our College, but I fear all to no purpose. General Irvine has proposed a visit to Mr. Penn[4] to obtain a lot from him. I shall accompany him, and from Mr. Penn's former character for liberality I do not despair of our success.

Printed (in part): Thomas F. Madigan, *The Autograph Album*, December 1933, p. 99-100.

[1] The addressee has been identified from internal evidence, but this is sufficient, for Thomas Smith (see BR's letter to him of 26 Feb. 1790) was Rebecca Smith Blodget's uncle, was a judge, and was a trustee of Dickinson College.

[2] Smith's wife was named Letitia; she lived until 1811 (Smith, *Smith*, II, 523).

[3] BR's standard prescription for consumptive patients; see BR to Lettsom, 15 June 1790.

[4] John Penn (1729-1795), grandson of William Penn, and the last colonial governor (his title was lieutenant governor) of Pennsylvania, 1763-1771, 1773-1776; after the Revolution he lived a retired life at his estate of Lansdowne on the Schuylkill (DAB).

To James Abercrombie[1]

Dear Sir,   22d April 1793

During my residence in London in the winter of 1769, I was introduced, by our worthy countryman Mr. West,[2] to Sir Joshua Reynolds, who favored me a few days afterwards with a card to dinner. At his table I met a group of authors, among whom was the celebrated Dr. JOHNSON.[3] The day was to me one of the most memorable I passed while abroad, on account of the singular display which I witnessed both of talents and knowledge. Dr. Johnson came late into company. Upon his entering the room, he found Sir Joshua consoling one of his guests[4] under the pain he felt from having been handled very severely by the reviewers. "Don't mind them," said Johnson to the complaining author. "Where is the advantage of a man having a great deal of money but that the loss of a little will not hurt him? And where is the advantage of a man having a great deal of reputation but that the loss of a little will not hurt him? You can bear it."

At dinner I sat between Dr. Johnson and Dr. Goldsmith. The former took the lead in conversation. He instructed upon all subjects. One of them was drunkenness, upon which he discovered much of that original energy of thought and expression which were so peculiar to him.

The *anemone maritima* was named by one of the company, about which naturalists have disagreed whether it belonged to the vegetable or animal kingdom. "It is an animal," said Dr. Johnson, "for its ashes have been analyzed, and they yield a volatile alkali, and this we know is the criterion of animal matter as distinguished from vegetable, which yields a fixed alkali." I was much struck with this remark; for I did not expect to hear a man whose studies appeared, from his writings, to have been confined to moral and philological subjects decide so confidently upon a controversy in natural history.[5]

A book which had been recently published led to some remarks upon its author.[6] Dr. Goldsmith, addressing himself to Dr. Johnson, said, "He appears, Doctor, from some passages in his book, to be one of your acquaintances." "Yes," said Johnson, "I know him." "And pray, what do you think of him?" said Goldsmith. "He is well enough—well enough," said Johnson. "I have heard," said Goldsmith, "he is much given to asking questions in company." "Yes, he is," said Johnson, "and his questions are not of the most interesting nature. They are such as this—'Pray, Doctor, why is an apple round, and why is a pear not so?'"

During the time of dinner, Dr. Goldsmith asked me several questions relative to the manners and customs of the North American Indians. Dr. Johnson, who heard one of them, suddenly interrupted him and said, "There is not an Indian in North America who would have asked such a foolish question." "I am sure," said Goldsmith, "there is not a savage in America that would have made so rude a speech to a gentleman."

After dinner he was drawn into a dispute with a citizen of London about the riot which had taken place a short time before, in St. George's fields, and the well-known steps that were taken by the British government to quell it.[7] The citizen condemned the conduct of government in very harsh terms, and said that Colonel ———[8] had declared he would have suppressed the riot without firing a gun or killing a man. "That may be," said Dr. Johnson. "Some men have a knack in quelling riots, which others have not, just as you, sir, have a knack in defending them, which I have not."

I regret that I cannot gratify you by detailing the whole of the Doctor's conversation during the course of the day. I should not have ventured, after the lapse of nearly four-and-twenty years, to have given you the above from my memory, had they not been impressed upon it by my having occasionally related them since among my friends.

I concur with you in your partiality to the genius and writings of Dr. Johnson; and, after making some deductions from his character on account of his ecclesiastical and political bigotry, I am disposed to consider the single weight of his massy understanding in the scale of Christianity as an overbalance to all the infidelity of the age in which he lived.[9]

With great regard, I am, dear sir, your sincere friend,

BENJAMIN RUSH

Printed: The Port Folio, iv (1804), 393. Also a transcript made by Abercrombie and sent to Boswell in 1793, owned by Lt. Col. Ralph Isham, New York City, 1948; now in the Yale University Library.

[1] James Abercrombie (1758-1841), a graduate of the College of Philadelphia, 1776, and D.D., College of New Jersey, 1804, was assistant minister of Christ Church and St. Peter's, 1794-1832, conducted the Episcopal Academy for some years, published sermons and other works, and was long a well-known figure in Philadelphia literary and social circles. Possessing strongly tory inclinations, it was with difficulty that he reconciled himself to living in America, and after 1800 he became notorious for his anti-Jeffersonian sermons. To compensate for having to live in a republic, he idolized the memory of Dr. Samuel Johnson, collecting his works, furnishing James Boswell with materials for the great *Life*, and issuing, about 1811, a prospectus for "a more complete collection of [Johnson's] writings, than has ever yet been published." (This last project did not materialize.) The genesis of the present letter is explained by the following note "To the Editor" which precedes the letter as printed in the *Port Folio*:

"Sir,

"The following interesting communication was made by me to Mr. Boswell, a short time before his death; Dr. RUSH having politely committed to paper, for that purpose, at my request, the information, casually given, some time before, in the course of conversation. Mr. Boswell received it with many thanks, and intended to insert it in his third edition of the life of his illustrious friend, Dr. Samuel Johnson. He lived not, however, to execute that intention; I have, therefore, solicited, and obtained Dr. Rush's permission to hand it to you: a literary journal, like the Port Folio, being the most proper channel to convey to the admirers of Dr. Johnson, any anecdotes, respecting him, or any of his sentiments, which have not yet been given to the world.

"Yours, &c.

"JAMES ABERCROMBIE.

"Philadelphia, Nov. 23, 1804."

See also note 9, below. On Abercrombie see Sprague, *Annals*, v, 392-9;

Univ. of Penna., *Biog. Cat. of Matriculates*; bound collection of Abercrombie's works, including prospectus for an edition of Johnson's *Works*, in Hist. Soc. Penna.; Boswell, *Letters*, ed. C. B. Tinker, Oxford, 1924, II, 454. BR's letter has been edited, with a full account of its background, by L. H. Butterfield in *Benjamin Rush's Reminiscences of Boswell & Johnson*, privately printed, Somerville, N.J., 1946.

[2] Benjamin West, R.A. (1728-1820), the first American artist to win a European reputation, was the friend and teacher of many young Americans who sought out his London studio; West and BR corresponded desultorily for many years, and in 1810 BR presented the painter with a souvenir of Penn's Treaty Tree, which West had made famous in an early painting (DAB; BR's *Autobiography*, p. 58; BR to Robert Barclay, 9 May 1810). West's letters to BR are in Rush MSS, XXIII.

[3] BR's high esteem for Johnson as a guide to moral conduct is outlined in *Benjamin Rush's Reminiscences of Boswell & Johnson*, 1946, cited in note 1.

[4] Undoubtedly Oliver Goldsmith; this was a typical exchange between Johnson and his wayward friend.

[5] Concerning *anemone maritima* and the test by which Dr. Johnson rendered his decisive verdict, Dr. Edwin Grant Conklin, of Princeton, has stated in a communication to the editor: "Combustion was not understood until the work of Lavoisier and Priestley some time later than 1769, but there is a difference in animal ash as compared with that of plants, and it is an illustration of Johnson's omniscience that he knew of this. Of course this test is not now used as a diagnostic test, but the presence of cellulose in plants and its absence in animals is diagnostic, and this probably leads to differences in the ash of these two. . . . There is no doubt that sea anemones are animals of the phylum Coelenterata and the class Actinozoa."

[6] That is, James Boswell, an identification which could be easily conjectured and which is confirmed by Boswell's being named in the account of this occurrence in BR's *Autobiography*, p. 59.

The name was naturally suppressed in a letter being transmitted to Boswell.

⁷ According to BR's *Autobiography*, p. 59, the London citizen was Heaton (called "Eaton" by BR) Wilkes (1727-1803); he was a brother of the celebrated agitator John Wilkes. The popular demonstration in St. George's Fields, 10 May 1768, was in the interest of John Wilkes, who had been jailed, and it was bloodily suppressed by a detachment of Foot Guards. (Horace Bleackley, *Life of John Wilkes*, London, 1917, genealogical chart and p. 199-200.)

⁸ Unidentifiable.

⁹ This paragraph, suppressed by Abercrombie when he communicated the letter to the *Port Folio*, derives from the MS copy he sent to Boswell in 1793. The copy was found in 1940 among other Boswell papers in Malahide Castle, Ireland, and later came into the possession of Col. Isham, by whose kind permission it is here first printed. In his acknowledgment to Abercrombie, Boswell singled out this passage of BR's letter for special praise (*Letters*, ed. C. B. Tinker, Oxford, 1924, II, 454).

To John Coakley Lettsom

Dear Sir,   Philadelphia, April 26, 1793

Your long political letter, referred to by you in your short letter by the *Wm. Penn*, came safe to hand.¹ I deplore with you the death of the late King of France.² His execution was unjust, unconstitutional, illegal, impolitic, and cruel in the highest degree. From the private history of his life and the public history of his death, I am disposed to believe that he was the best king in Europe and the honestest man in the French nation. Ninety-nine of our citizens out of a hundred have dropped a tear to his memory. He was the father of the freedom and independence of the United States.

But one wicked act does not justify another. We deplore and reprobate likewise the interference of Great Britain in the dispute between the French nation and their late king. What can she expect to gain by it, equal to the loss of an hundred thousand men and a hundred millions of pounds? She must at last acknowledge the independence of the French Republic and submit to negotiate with her Convention; for the noble cause in which she is engaged, though much disgraced by her rulers, must finally prevail. The infidelity and cruelty of the French nation do not militate against this opinion, for they are qualified in a peculiar manner by both to be the scourge of nations as wicked as themselves.

I beg you would present my most respectful thanks to Mr. How³ for his elegant present of Lady Rachael Russel's *Letters*.⁴ He could not have sent a book that would have been more acceptable in my family, for my wife had read it hastily some years ago and had long wished to possess a copy of it. I have inscribed on the inside of the cover of it: "Julia Rush, presented by Richard How

of England, 1793." It is an invaluable work, and the public will long owe a debt of gratitude to Mr. How for giving it to the world.
    I am, &c.,

BENJAMIN RUSH

Printed: Pettigrew, *Lettsom*, II, 441-2.

[1] Lettsom's two letters, of 6 Nov. 1792 and 6 Feb. 1793, respectively, are in the Rush MSS, XXVIII.

[2] Louis XVI was guillotined on 21 Jan. 1793.

[3] Richard How brought out an edition of Lady Russell's *Letters* (see following note) that I have not identified.

[4] Rachel, Lady Russell (1636-1723), was the wife of the patriot-martyr William, Lord Russell, and tried unsuccessfully to save him from the block; she corresponded with Archbishop Tillotson, and her letters were edited by T. Sellwood, London, 1773 (DNB; *Brit. Mus. Cat.*). There were numerous later editions, but I have not connected Richard How (who is said in Lettsom's letter of 6 Feb. 1793 to have prepared the edition sent) with any of them.

To John Nicholson

Dear Sir,   August 12th, 1793

Nothing could be more opportune than your kind offer to the poor Africans. They had nearly despaired of being able to complete their church. The person who once offered to lend them money was Colonel Cox.[1] Finding that you had anticipated him in that benevolent act, he followed your kindness by bequeathing to them one hundred pounds. From their numbers, their increasing prosperity, and their punctuality in all their engagements, I have no doubt but your interest will be paid to a day every quarter. The lot and building amply secure the principal. In all my intercourse with the blacks, I have found them affectionate and grateful. You will find them more so, for you have greater demands than I have ever had upon their gratitude and affections. I find they have allotted a pew for each of us, on different sides of the pulpit of their church. On Saturday next they purpose to raise their roof, after which they are to have a dinner under a tree at a private house in the Neck, about a mile from town.[2] I hope I shall have the pleasure of meeting you there, for they intend to invite you with two or three more of their white benefactors. I wish to suggest to you an idea of offering 10,000 or more acres for sale on moderate terms, and on a credit for a few years, to *Africans only* who have been brought up as farmers. The attraction of color and country is such that I think the offer would succeed, and thereby a *precedent* be established for colonizing, in time, all the Africans in our country.[3]

[636]

Adieu, my dear friend. May Heaven prosper you in all your great and extensive pursuits, and may you long continue to enjoy the highest and only rational pleasure that wealth can confer—I mean the luxury of doing good. From yours sincerely,

BENJN RUSH

Printed: Pennsylvania Magazine of History and Biography, VI (1882), 113-14.

[1] Among the numerous Philadelphia Cox's and Coxes, it is not possible to say with certainty which one made this benefaction.

[2] For an account of these proceedings, see BR to Mrs. Rush, 22-23 Aug. 1793.

[3] For BR's fully developed plan of a Negro farm colony, see his undated letter to the Abolition Society, printed below at the end of 1794.

To Mrs. Rush

My dear Julia, Philadelphia, August 21, 1793

To prevent your being deceived by reports respecting the sickliness of our city, I sit down at a late hour, and much fatigued, to inform you that a malignant fever has broken out in Water Street, between Arch and Race Streets, which has already carried off twelve persons within the space which has been mentioned.[1] It is supposed to have been produced by some damaged coffee which had putrefied on one of the wharves near the middle of the above district. The disease is violent and of short duration. In one case it killed in twelve hours, and in no case has it lasted more than four days. Among its victims is Mrs. LeMaigre. I have attended three of the persons who have died with it, and seven or eight who have survived or who are I hope recovering from it.

As yet it has not spread through any parts of the city which are beyond the reach of the putrid exhalation which first produced it. If it should, I shall give you notice, that you may remain where you are till you receive further advice and information from me. The influenza continues to spread, and with more violent symptoms than when it made its first appearance. I did more business in 1780 than I do at present, but with much less anxiety, for few of the diseases of that year were attended with any danger, whereas *now* most of the cases I attend are acute and alarming, and require an uncommon degree of vigilance and attention.

August 22. Marcus[2] has been ill with the influenza but is now better. Richd., Ben, and all the rest of the family are in good health.

I have just received a letter from Dr. B. Young in which he has the following paragraph: "I have just seen Mr. Woolstonecraft.[3] He does not like your lands, and that for the most childish reasons. He says that he saw but *one* flight of pheasants, *three* fishy ducks, and *not one* woodcock on the whole creek, and that he will never settle anywhere where he cannot support himself by his *gun*." So much the better! I have received since you left town conveyances for nearly all the lands I sold to the New England men. They *adjoin* the lands sold by Robt. Morris to the French Company,[4] who are about to improve them in the most extensive manner next spring. *All* is for the best, and *all will end well.*

A son of Dr. Priestley[5] has just arrived in this city from France. He gives a most distressing account of the affairs of that country. But let us not despair. Chaos existed before the order and beauty of the Universe. The devil who is the present tenant of our world,[6] will not quit his hold of it till he has done the premises all the mischief that lies in his power, but go he must sooner or later, with all his family of nobles and kings.

Adieu. With love as usual, I am, my dear Julia, yours affectionately,

BENJN RUSH

P.S. John should come home as soon as his vacation expires. [*On cover*:] Your letter is just come to hand of August 21.[7]

Addressed: Mrs: Julia Rush at Richd Stockton's Esqr: near Princeton New Jersey.
MS: Josiah C. Trent, M.D., Durham, North Carolina.

[1] BR had treated sporadic cases of what might have been yellow fever during the first two weeks of August, but his suspicions were first aroused by the case of Catherine, wife of the West Indies merchant Peter LeMaigre, who died on 20 Aug. She lived in Water Street between Race and Arch, "nearly in a line with" Ball's Wharf, where lay the damaged coffee to which BR attributed the infection; see Powell (cited below), p. 11-12, and map in Drinker, *Not So Long Ago*, p. 18. There is a vast body of writing about the epidemic of 1793 that so profoundly affected BR's career and reputation. Among contemporary sources the best are BR's own *Account of the Yellow Fever in 1793* and Mathew Carey's *Short Account of the Malignant Fever*. (When Carey's work is cited below without specific page, the reference is to the list of the dead at the end of the book.) BR's long and almost unbroken sequence of letters to his wife, from 21 Aug. to 11 Nov., provides a graphic day-by-day record of the epidemic. The numerous later accounts are now superseded by J. H. Powell's recent and admirable study, *Bring Out Your Dead*, Phila., 1949.

[2] A Negro servant, whose devoted conduct during the epidemic won BR's heartfelt praise; see letters of 14-15 and 17-18 Oct. 1793.

[3] Charles Wollstonecraft (d. 1817), brother of Mary (Wollstonecraft) Godwin, who paid for his passage to America in 1792; he lived for a time at

Wilmington, Del., with the Irish expatriate A. H. Rowan, and in 1798 entered the army, attaining the rank of brevet major in the artillery, 1815 (William Godwin, *Memoirs of Mary Wollstonecraft*, ed. W. C. Durant, London and N.Y., 1927, p. 47-8, 155-6, 300-1, 304-5; F. B. Heitman, *Historical Register and Dictionary of the United States Army*, Washington, 1903, I, 1053).

⁴ The Asylum Company, organized in 1793 to establish a retreat for émigrés from Revolutionary France; the settlement of "Azilum" was near present Towanda, Penna., on the upper Susquehanna (Elsie Murray, *Azilum: French Refugee Colony of 1793*, Athens, Penna., 1940).

⁵ All three of Priestley's sons migrated to America in 1793; they were followed by their father the next year (DNB).

⁶ So punctuated in the MS. BR's meaning would probably be clearer if the passage were corrected as follows: "The Devil, who is the present tenant of our world, will not," &c.

⁷ Since none of Mrs. Rush's daily letters to her husband during the yellow-fever epidemic survive, we can only conclude that she herself disposed of them.

To Mrs. Rush

My dear Julia,   Philadelphia, 22nd August [17]93

This day agreeably to invitation I dined a mile from town, under the shade of several large trees, with about an hundred carpenters and others who met to celebrate the raising of the roof of the African Church.¹ They forced me to take the head of the table much against my inclinations. The dinner was plentiful—the liquors were of the first quality—and the dessert, which consisted only of melons, was very good. We were waited upon by nearly an equal number of black people. I gave them the two following toasts: "Peace on earth and good will to men," and "May African churches everywhere soon succeed to African bondage." After which we rose, and the black people (men and women) took our seats. Six of the most respectable of the white company waited upon them, while Mr. Nicholson, myself, and two others were requested to set down with them, which we did, much to the satisfaction of the poor blacks. Never did I witness such a scene of innocent—nay more—such virtuous and philanthropic joy. Billy Grey in attempting to express his feelings to us was checked by a flood of tears. After they had dined, they all came up to Mr. Nicholson and took him by the hand, and thanked him for his loan of money to them. One of them, an old man whom I did not know, addressed him in the following striking language: "May you live long, sir, and when you die, may you not die eternally." The company broke up and came to town about 6 o'clock in good order, few or perhaps none of them having drunken more than 3 or four glasses of wine. To me it will be a day to be remembered with pleasure as long as I live.

In order that my other class of friends, the criminals in the jail, who overheard or witnessed the raising of the roof of the church, might sympathize a little in the joy of the day, I sent them about one o'clock a large wheelbarrow full of melons with the following note: "Dr. Rush sends herewith a few melons for the persons who are suffering in the jail for their offenses against society. He begs that while they are partaking of this agreeable fruit they will remember that that BEING who created it still cares for them, and that by this and other acts of kindness conveyed to them by his creatures, he means to lead them to repentance and happiness."[2]

Adieu. In consequence of my absence only two hours from town, my business increased so much as to keep me employed till after 10 o'clock. The malignant fever is stationary, and the influenza as violent as was mentioned in my letter of yesterday. The family through divine goodness continue well, and none of them now more so than yours sincerely,

BENJN RUSH

P.S. Love as usual. Read this letter to your Mama. She belongs to *our* African Church.

August 23rd. We continue *all* well.

Addressed: Mrs: Julia Rush at Richard Stockton Esqr: near Princeton New Jersey.

MS: Mr. Lloyd W. Smith, Madison, New Jersey.

[1] A similar but less detailed account of this occasion will be found in BR's *Autobiography*, p. 228-9.

[2] The prisoners had been able to witness the raising of the roof because the jail was at Walnut and Sixth Streets, and the new church was on Fifth be- low Walnut. BR frequently sent gifts of watermelons to the jail, with similar notes; see his *Autobiography*, p. 238, 253. A quaint answer from the prisoners on one of these occasions, 16 Sep. 1800, will be found in the Rush MSS, XXI, 7.

To Mrs. Rush

My dear Julia,   Philadelphia, August 25th, 1793

Since my letter to you of Friday, the fever has assumed a most alarming appearance. It not only mocks in most instances the power of medicine, but it has spread through several parts of the city remote from the spot where it originated. Water Street between Arch and Race Streets is nearly desolated by it. This morning I witnessed a scene there which reminded me of the histories I had read of the plague. In one house I lost two patients last night—a respectable young merchant and his only child. His wife is frantic this evening with grief. Five other persons died in the neighborhood yesterday afternoon, and four more last night at Kensington. The College of Physicians met this afternoon to consult upon the means of checking the progress of this dreadful disease. They appointed a committee to draw up directions for that purpose. The committee imposed this business upon me, and I have just finished them.[1] They will be handed to the Mayor when adopted by the College, and published by him in a day or two. I hope and believe that they will be useful.

After this detail of the state of the fever, I need hardly request you to remain for a while with all the children where you are. Many people are flying from the city, and some by my advice. Continue to commit me by your prayers to the protection of that Being who has so often manifested his goodness to our family by the preservation of my life, and I hope I shall do well. I endeavor to have no will of my own. I enjoy good health and uncommon tranquillity of mind. While I depend upon divine protection and feel that at present I live, move, and have my being in a more especial manner in God alone, I do not neglect to use every precaution that experience has discovered to prevent taking the infection. I even strive to subdue my sympathy for my patients; otherwise I should sink under the accumulated loads of misery I am obliged to contemplate. You can recollect how much the loss of a single patient once in a month used to affect me. Judge then how I must feel in hearing every morning of the death of three or four!

I shall confine John and Richard to the house and oblige them to use precautions against the disorder. My mother and sister are so kind and attentive as to prevent all our wants and wishes.

My love to your uncle and aunt and all the children.[2] I am afraid you will burden our good relations. No!—this cannot be. They love you, and they love to do offices of kindness and humanity. Adieu. From your sincere and affectionate

BENJN RUSH

P.S. "Seekest[3] thou great things? Seek them not, for behold I bring evil on all flesh."[4] What powerful antidotes are war and pestilence to pride, vanity, and ambition!

August 26. I am still preserved, and in good health. What a blessing!

Addressed: Mrs Julia Rush at Samuel W: Stockton Esqr: Trenton New Jersey.
MS: Josiah C. Trent, M.D., Durham, North Carolina.

¹ BR's autograph draft of these directions, signed by Shippen as vice-president and Griffitts as secretary, is in the archives of the College of Physicians; they may be read in BR's *Account of the Yellow Fever in 1793*, p. 21-4. BR recommended marking the houses of the sick; clean and airy sickrooms; a hospital for indigent patients; the abolition of the tolling of bells for funerals; avoidance of the sun, fatigue, and intemperance; and disinfection by gunpowder, vinegar, and camphor.

² Mrs. Samuel W. Stockton was the former Catherine Cox, or Coxe (Stockton, *Stockton Family*, p. 53).

³ MS: "Seeking."

⁴ Jeremiah 45:5.

To Mrs. Rush

My dear Julia,   Philadelphia, August 26th, 1793

The boys have discovered so much apprehension of being infected by my clothes, and I think so justly, that I have concluded to send them to Trenton. If our uncle's house is too crowded already to receive them, perhaps they may be accommodated at Mr. Armstrong's.¹ Do attend to their reading something useful every day during their absence from town. I dread very much their contracting habits of idleness. All the schools in town are either broken up by design or moldering away by the daily desertion of scholars into the country. It is indeed a serious time. Dejection sits upon every countenance. Tomorrow the directions of the College of Physicians will be published. I hope they will do good, but I fear no efforts will totally subdue the fever before the heavy rains or frosts of October.

Five persons died this morning in Water Street, and five more are expected to die tonight, among whom is Mrs. Duncan's son, the merchant.² He lies in 2nd Street near the corner of Walnut Street.

After a busy day, I continue to enjoy good health. Help me to thank the divine Preserver of Men for it. Adieu. From, my dear Julia, yours sincerely,

BENJN RUSH

P.S. August 27th. *Still* in good health, though called out of bed at ½ after five o'clock. Keep the boys from exposing themselves to heat, cold, dampness,³ and fatigue. Again adieu. The boys will give many anecdotes of Ben. He is in fine health, and everybody says has grown handsome. He is as much devoted to Aunty Wallace as he used to be to his Mame Teen.⁴ I enclose you a half-joe for contingent expenses.

Addressed: Mrs Julia Rush at Saml W: Stockton's Esqr Trenton.
MS: Josiah C. Trent, M.D., Durham, North Carolina.

[1] Rev. James Francis Armstrong (1750-1816), a graduate of the College of New Jersey, 1773, and a trustee from 1790; for many years pastor of the Presbyterian Church in Trenton (John Hall, *History of the Presbyterian Church in Trenton, N.J.*, 2d edn., Trenton, 1912, p. 179-227; Princeton Univ., *Gen. Cat.*, 1908).

[2] Probably John Dunkin, merchant; Ann Dunkin, widow, presumably his mother, lived at 96 South Second St. (*Phila. Directory* for 1793; Carey, *Short Account*).

[3] MS: "damness."

[4] Evidently Ben's name for Betsey Steen, a governess or servant in the family, who was with Mrs. Rush in New Jersey and who is frequently mentioned in the following letters.

To Mrs. Rush

August 27, [17]93
Tuesday night, 10 o'clock

My dear Julia,

I feel very much for the safety of both the boys. They are both indisposed with the headache and by no means in a condition to travel in the night, but of two dangers I believe they have chosen the least. I have advised them to go to bed as soon as they reach Trenton, and by no means to expose themselves to cold, heat, or fatigue during their absence from town.

The disease spreads, and a most alarming apathy as to exertion prevails among our citizens. Our neighborhood will be desolate in a day or two. Dr. White's, Mr. Chew's,[1] and Mr. Lewis'[2] families are all on the wing. Young Mr. Duncan died this afternoon, much beloved and lamented by all who knew him.

Adieu. In mercy to my fellow citizens and family, my life, so long and so often forfeited to divine justice, is *still* preserved. My love to each of the children. For some days past, my mind has been so occupied with the immense objects now before me that I had almost forgotten them. Tell them all that the best proof they can give of their affection for their Papa is to pray for his health and life, and to be dutiful to their Mama and kind to each other.

From your affectionate

BENJN RUSH

Addressed: Mrs: Julia Rush Trenton Richd Rush.
MS: Josiah C. Trent, M.D., Durham, North Carolina.

[1] Benjamin Chew (1722-1810), president judge of the high court of errors and appeals; he lived at 110 South Third St. (DAB; *Phila. Directory* for 1793).

[2] William Lewis, the lawyer? See BR to Mrs. Rush, 3-4 Sep. 1793, and note 2 there.

To Mrs. Rush

My dear Julia,   Philadelphia, August 29th, 1793

Your letter dated yesterday came safe to hand.

I am pleased with your situation at your good aunt's. *⟨I will enable you to settle with her once a week, provided my life be spared —for to live a week now in Philadelphia as I now live is to be the subject of a miracle.⟩*[1] Be assured that I will send for you if I should be seized with the disorder, for I conceive that it would be as much your duty not to desert me in that situation as it is now mine not to desert my patients. I have sent Becky[2] with Ben to Mr. Bradford's[3] farm this afternoon. They were most affectionately received by Betsey Johnson.[4] Mrs. Wallace furnished them with tea, coffee, sugar, and sundry other things to render them less burdensome to our good friends. The disease has raged with great virulence this day. Among the dead are Woodruf Sims[5] and Mr. Stiles[6] the stonecutter. The last exhibited signs of the plague before he died. I have seen the same symptoms in the hospital fever during the late war. They have however greatly increased the terror of our citizens, and have excited an apprehension that this is in reality the plague, but this I am sure is not the case, although it comes nearer to it in violence and mortality than any disease we have ever before had in this country. Its symptoms are very different in different people. Sometimes it comes on with a chilly fit and a high fever, but more frequently it steals on with headache, languor, and sick stomach. These symptoms are followed by stupor, delirium, vomiting, a dry skin, cool or cold hands and feet, a feeble slow pulse, sometimes below in frequency the pulse of health. The eyes are at first suffused with blood, they afterwards become yellow, and in most cases a yellowness covers the whole skin on the 3rd or 4th day. Few survive the 5th day, but more die on the 2 and 3rd days. In some cases the patients possess their reason to the last and discover much less weakness than in the last stage of common fevers. One of my patients stood up and shaved himself on the morning of the day he died. Livid spots on the body, a bleeding at the nose, from the gums, and from the bowels, and a vomiting of black matter in some instances close the scenes of life. The common remedies for malignant fevers have all failed. Bark, wine, and blisters make no impression upon it. Baths of hot vinegar applied by means of blankets, and the cold bath have relieved and saved some. Mrs. Chaloner owes her life to the former remedy. She caught it from her husband,[7] who caught it in Water Street near the place where it originated. He too is upon the recovery. This day I have given mercury, and I think with some advantage. Dr. Wistar and myself consult much together, and I derive great support and assistance from him in all my attempts to stop the progress of this terrible malady. He is an excellent man, and rises in his humanity and activity with the danger and distress of his fellow citizens. I have advised all the families that I attend, that can move, to quit the city. There is but one preventative that is certain, and that is "to fly from it."

Johnny Stall[8] sleeps and eats with us, and thereby relieves me very much. My mother and sister are a part of the means that providence employs to preserve me from the infection. They are very kind. Mrs. Wallace has contrived a small mattress on some chairs, on which I rest myself by lying down every time I come into the house. Adieu—with love to your Mama, your aunts, the children, and all friends, I am, my dear Julia, your faithful and affectionate

BENJN RUSH

August 30th. Another night and morning have been added to my life. I am preparing to set off for my daily round of duty, and feel heartily disposed to say with Jabez, "O! that the hand of the Lord may be with me,"[9] not only to preserve my life but to heal my poor patients. Betsey's relations are all well.

Addressed: Mrs Julia Rush to be left at Saml: W: Stockton's Trenton.
MS: Josiah C. Trent, M.D., Durham, North Carolina.

[1] This passage of three lines in the MS was heavily scratched out by BR, apparently before posting the letter. The present reading is somewhat conjectural.

[2] Either a servant or, more likely, a relative. BR's brother Jacob had a daughter Rebecca, who was fourteen at this time (Biddle, *Memorial*, p. 229).

[3] Doubtless William Bradford, at this time chief justice of Pennsylvania. He was currently living at his father-in-law's place, Rose Hill, in the Northern Liberties; see BR to Mrs. Rush, 20-21 Oct. 1793.

[4] Unidentified.

[5] Wooddrop Sims, merchant, 155 South Water St. (Carey, *Short Account*; 1791 *Directory*).

[6] William Stiles, South Third St.; his wife and son were also among the victims (Carey, *Short Account*; 1793 *Directory*).

[7] John Chaloner was an auctioneer in North Third St. (1793 *Directory*). He had served in the Philadelphia militia in the campaign on the Delaware (BR, *Autobiography*, p. 127).

[8] John F. Stall, an apprentice, who paid for his devotion to duty with his life in September. BR afterwards sent Stall's mother a silver cup in memory of her son (BR to Mrs. Stall, 5 Feb. 1794). See also BR's *Account of the Yellow Fever in 1793*, p. 347-8, and Powell, *Bring Out Your Dead*, p. 120.

[9] Compare I Chronicles 4:10.

To Mrs. Rush

My dear Julia,   Philadelphia, September 1, 1793

In the language of good old Dr. Sproat's prayer, I am enabled yet to thank God "that I am alive, while others are dead." Two persons have died at Mrs. Lewis',[1] next door to Peter Baynton's, with the malignant fever, viz., two of the Misses Mifflins.[2] A woman has died with the same disorder in Dock Street near Mr. Eke's,[3] and her husband will probably follow her before tomorrow morning. Thirty-eight persons have died in eleven families in nine days in Water Street, and many more in different parts of the city. Funerals are conducted agreeably to the advice of the College of Physicians. It is indeed truly affecting to see a solitary corpse, on the shafts and wheels of a chair, conducted through our streets without a single attendant in some cases, and with only 8 or 10 in any instance, and they at a small distance from it on the foot pavement. This evening I fear I shall lose a son of Joseph Stansbury,[4] a sweet youth, a little older than our Richard. It has been peculiarly fatal to young people. I rejoice that our boys escaped from the city. I hope they avoid fatigue, heat, and cold, for if they carried the smallest portion of the infection out of town with them, it may be excited into action by either of the above-mentioned means. I have received a kind letter from Miss Rachel Bradford full of inquiries after the state of the disease and of solicitude for my preservation. May her unmerited goodness return fourfold into her own bosom! It is painful to look back upon what we have seen, but more distressing to look forward. I fear we have seen only the beginning of the awful visitation. I find in a small record which I kept when an apprentice of the yellow fever in the year 1761[5] the following paragraph, which I read with anticipating horror: "It began in August and prevailed in September, October, November, and December, carrying off for some time twenty persons in a day." In confirmation of this note, Mr. Duche tells me that he frequently at that time buried twelve persons in a day in Christ's and St. Peter's churchyards. But I fear I shall tire you with tales of woe. I cannot help it.

> "Of comfort *now* let no man speak.
> Let's talk of graves, of tombs, of epitaphs.
> Make dust our paper, and with rainy eyes,
> Write SORROW on the bosom of the earth."[6]

[646]

No part of your last letter pleased me more than your determination to be more thankful for the mercies of God hereafter, and more faithful in improving them to the purposes of his glory and your eternal happiness. O! the littleness of greatness! Thrones, titles, splendid and even commodious houses, wealth, friends—what are they all when viewed through the medium of a relentless and desolating fever? Help me, my dear Julia, by your prayers to "be always ready." I have cut out much work for my divine master, to be performed in months or years to come, but if he means to have it completed by other hands, "his will be done." I can truly say I am more anxious to be pardoned and to be delivered from the guilt, dominion, and punishment of my sins than to be preserved from the present pestilential fever. If I survive the present dangers to which I am exposed, what offering of gratitude will ever equal the infinite weight of my obligations to my gracious deliverer? You must help me to be more humble, more patient, more devout, and more self-denied[7] in everything. Adieu. With love as usual, I am, my dear Julia, yours sincerely,

BENJN RUSH

September 2. I have just received your letter and am satisfied with all your arrangements. I enclose you 20 dollars. Do write to the boys to take care of themselves and to avoid the worst of all infections—the vices of the College. I have been four times interrupted by different calls since I sat down to write this postscript. Adieu. Love to dear Mrs. Cox[8] and all your uncle's family.

Addressed: Mrs: Julia Rush to the care of Saml W: Stockton's Trenton.
MS: Josiah C. Trent, M.D., Durham, North Carolina.

[1] Sarah Lewis, widow, 54 Walnut St. (1793 *Directory*).

[2] Sarah and Hester, daughters of Charles Mifflin (Carey, *Short Account*).

[3] John Peter Eck, grocer in South Third St. "by the dock"; Eck himself died of the fever later this month (Rush MSS, Account Books; BR to Mrs. Rush, 24-25 Sep. 1793; 1793 *Directory*; Carey, *Short Account*).

[4] Joseph Stansbury (1742-1809), china dealer and loyalist poet, is principally remembered as one of Benedict Arnold's intermediaries in 1780. He was able to return to Philadelphia after the Revolution, his treasonable activities not becoming known until recently. The son mentioned by BR died soon afterward. (DAB; BR to Elias Boudinot, 30 Jan. 1781, note 4; Carey, *Short Account*.)

[5] Error for 1762.

[6] Approximately quoted from Shakespeare, *Richard II*, III, ii, 144-7.

[7] Thus in MS.

[8] Probably Samuel Stockton's mother-in-law.

To Nicholas Belleville[1]

Philadelphia, September 3d, 1793

In compliance with your request communicated to me by Mrs. Rush in her letter of this day, I set down with great pleasure to inform you that the fever which has ravaged our city from some weeks past is at last arrested in its fatality. The medicine which has performed this kind office is *calomel*. I was led to give it by finding salts and cremor-tartar ineffectual to open the bowels. From 10 to 20 grains, with an equal quantity of jalap, are a dose.[2] The patient should drink plentifully of chicken water or water gruel and lie in bed during the operation of the physic, for it generally sweats as copiously as it purges. It moreover sometimes pukes when it finds bile on the stomach. From dissections it appears that the liver is either inflamed or obstructed, and the bile much vitiated in the gall bladder or in the small bowels. The calomel expels the latter and opens the obstructions of the former. This mode of healing the disease has saved 9 out of 10 when applied in its early stage. The calomel and jalap must be repeated every other day if the disease continues, and infusions of camomile flowers, snake root, bark, wine, &c., on the intermediate days. In obstinate cases which resist these remedies, bark, clysters, hot and cold baths, according to the state of the system, must be applied to the skin. Blisters are of no service.

I am, dear sir, your friend and most obedient servant,

BENJN RUSH

P.S. Some of our physicians condemn the above practice, but it is those only who have seen but little of the disease. Those who have seen most of it have adopted it. Dr. McElvaine[3] probably owes his life to it. Three of the faculty besides him are confined with the disorder, viz., Drs. Hutchinson, Wistar and Carsan.[4]

MS (copy, not in BR's hand): College of Physicians of Philadelphia.

[1] Dr. Nicholas Belleville (1753-1831), born in Metz, France, accompanied Pulaski to America, 1777, and afterwards settled in Trenton. Esteemed for his social qualities, he had a lucrative practice and attended Joseph Bonaparte when the latter lived at Bordentown. (Wickes, *Hist. of Medicine in N.J.*, p. 142-5.) The original of the present letter has disappeared; according to a note of transmittal with this copy in the College of Physicians Library, the copy was made for Elias Boudinot.

[2] This is the first announcement of BR's mercurial purge, which he regarded as an infallible specific for yellow fever and which became notorious as "Rush's ten-and-ten." He has himself provided a full and dramatic report of how he came to decide that powerful purges were the true means of curing

the fever; see his *Account of the Yellow Fever in 1793*, p. 197-203, where he tells of the encouragement for purging he found in the famous Mitchell MS and his recollection of Dr. Young's successful use of a compound of calomel and jalap in the army hospitals. BR improved on Young by adding a larger proportion of jalap "to carry the calomel through the bowels" more rapidly (so that his formula was actually 10 and 15); met with immediate success in the cases in which he ordered the purges; and announced his discovery of a cure to the College of Physicians on the day the present letter was sent.

[3] William McIlvaine (1750-1806), M.D., Edinburgh, 1771, practised at Bristol, at Philadelphia for some time prior to 1793, and afterwards at Burlington; member of the College of Physicians, 1791 (Wickes, *Hist. of Medicine in N.J.*, p. 326-9; Ruschenberger, p. 246).

[4] John Carson (1752-1794); M.D., Edinburgh, 1776; founding member College of Physicians, 1787; trustee of the University of Philadelphia, 1794 (*New Engl. Hist. & Geneal. Reg.*, XLII [1888], 161; Ruschenberger, p. 215-16).

To Mrs. Rush

My dear Julia,   Philadelphia, September 3, 1793

Another day through divine goodness has been added to my life, and I feel as if I had survived a battle. I have had five new calls today, all to patients in the yellow fever. Of the twelve to whom I was called yesterday, eight are out of danger, from the powerful operation of the medicine I mentioned in my letter of yesterday.[1] I have sent an account of it to Dr. Belville. Mr. Lewis[2] is in a safe way, but our neighbor Mr. Hawkins[3] is infected. His boy, who yesterday and last night was in the delirium of a fever, today is downstairs and entirely free of danger. But this success has been checkered, for I have lost two patients whom I attended in consultation, one of them Stevens[4] the saddler, who makes the 6th of his family that has fallen a victim to this disease.

September 4th. I am still alive and in health. "Thy mercies are new unto me, O Lord, every morning!" Great is thy goodness to me and to my dear family. I am now waiting with great anxiety for my breakfast, having had a call from my bed. I was too much fatigued to fill my paper last night, and too much hurried this morning. I lose not a moment. The bed my kind sister provided for me in the back room lies unoccupied all day. Adieu. Love to all. "Brethren, pray for us."[5] Hark! a knock at the door! Alas, it is called[6] to Mrs. Boggs[7] at Bishop White's. Again adieu. The delay of a minute seems a year to a patient after a physician is sent for. From yours sincerely,

BENJN RUSH

P.S. Keep the boys out of the College, and impose a system of reading on them.

Addressed: Mrs Julia Rush at Richd Stockton Esqr: Princeton New Jersey.
MS: Josiah C. Trent, M.D., Durham, North Carolina.

[1] Apparently missing, for in BR's letter to his wife of 1 Sep., with postscript of next day, the new cure is not mentioned. It was BR's habit to write at night a full account of the day and then to add a few lines in the morning before the letter was posted. There is thus a gap for 2-3 September in the sequence.

[2] Mentioned as "the lawyer" in BR's *Account of the Yellow Fever in 1793*, p. 203, and hence identifiable as Judge William Lewis (d. 1819), of 82 South Third St. Richard Rush prepared for the bar in Lewis' law office. (1793 *Di-*rectory; Martin, *Bench and Bar*, p. 8, 287; Powell, *Richard Rush*, p. 6; BR to James Madison, 5 Dec. 1801.)

[3] Probably John Hawkins, cordwainer, 66 Walnut St. (1793 *Directory*); Carey's list of the dead includes a John Hanskins, shoemaker, who is probably the same person.

[4] John Stephens, saddler and cap maker, 72 Chestnut St. (1793 *Directory*).

[5] I Thessalonians 5:25.

[6] Thus in MS.

[7] Not further identifiable.

To Mrs. Rush

My dear Julia,   Wednesday, September 4, 1793

The post is on the wing. I can only inform you that I put a letter into the post office for you directed to Princeton—this morning. I shall, if well, write to you again this evening. After a busy morning, I am, thank God, still in good health. Dr. Hutchinson is not dead, but in great danger. The disease spreads, but its mortality is much less in proportion to the number who are affected. The jalap and mercury cures 9 out of 10 of all who take it on the day of the attack. Adieu.

BENJN RUSH

Addressed: Mrs Julia Rush at Saml W: Stockton Trenton.
MS: Josiah C. Trent, M.D., Durham, North Carolina.

To Mrs. Rush

My dear Julia,   Philadelphia, September 5th, 1793

Still alive and in *good health*, after having visited and prescribed for nearly one hundred patients. The disease continues to spread, but with no more mortality than a common bilious fever in the hands of those physicians who use the mercurial antidote. I now save 29 out of 30 of all to whom I am called on the first day, and many to whom I am called after it. Fewer deaths have occurred I believe this day than on several days last week, and yet many hundred people more have the fever now than had it last week. Some of my brethren rail at my new remedy, but they have seen little of the disease, and some of them not a single patient. Most of the publications in the papers come from those gentlemen. They abound in absurdities and falsehoods. This night will probably end the busy life of Dr. Hutchinson. He continued to object to taking my medicine, and was supported in his obstinacy by two young doctors who had obtruded themselves[1] upon him. Dr. Kuhn is better. Dr. McIlvaine is well, and my invaluable friend Wistar is out of danger. Poor Bill Bache[2] was almost heartbroken during his master's indisposition. Pet. Baynton[3] is infected; Mrs. Baynton, Kitty, and Mrs. Bullock[4] are all in a safe way. I have had 12 new calls today and have not lost a single patient since the night before last. I have found lately, I hope, a preventative of the disease as well as a cure. It consists (not in drenching the stomach with wine, bark, and bitters) but in keeping the bowels gently open, for in them the disease first fixes its poison. I owe these discoveries, as well as my preservation, to the prayers of my friends.

September 6th—6 o'clock in the morning. Blessed be God, my life, health, and reason are still preserved to me. I forgot to mention that one of my pupils, Washington,[5] has got the disease. He lies at Mrs. Ceronio's,[6] a mile from town, where he is so much ashamed of being visited by me that I heard of his illness by accident only from Johny Stall. I shall try to see him, though I fear from the violence of his symptoms and the progress of the disease that he will not recover. John Cox[7] has become active and useful to me. He is very intelligent on the subject of the disorder and knows no fear. Dr. Mease[8] has taken charge of all Dr. Hutchinson's public patients and is to divide the profits of attending them equally. If the Doctor survives, the partnership is to be perpetual. But this is improbable, for though I have just heard that he is still alive, yet I hear that he has a symptom which none (at least of my patients) have survived. Adieu. The box of clothes, with a letter from my sister, were sent this morning by the stage, committed to the care of Mr. Sayre.[9] I paid the freight of the box here. Adieu. My love to all the family at Morven. Do oblige the boys to read systematically and to avoid cold, fatigue, and heat, also intemperance in eating, for each of those exciting causes has produced the disease when the body has been infected. There is no certainty that they did not carry the infection from town. It lies from 1 to 16 days in the body, and the fever may be excited at any time within those days.

Adieu again. Yours—yours—yours,

BENJN RUSH

Addressed: Mrs Julia Rush at Richd: Stockton Esqr: Princeton.
MS: Josiah C. Trent, M.D., Durham, North Carolina.

[1] MS: "himself."

[2] William Bache (1773-1818), grandson of Benjamin Franklin, graduated at the College or University, 1790, and obtained his M.D. at the University, 1794; studied abroad; married Dr. Wistar's sister Catharine, 1797; practised in Philadelphia and in Virginia (Univ. of Penna., *Biog. Cat. of Matriculates*; Richard W. Davids, *The Wistar Family*, p. 7; Bache MSS, Princeton Univ. Libr.).

[3] MS: "Banyton." Baynton recovered. His wife was Elizabeth Bullock, sister of the Joseph Bullock mentioned in BR's letter to Mrs. Rush of 31 July 1791; see also Barratt, *Old St. Paul's*, p. 200, note. Kitty was doubtless their daughter.

[4] Mrs. Joseph Bullock was the former Esther Baynton, sister of Peter mentioned in the preceding note (Barratt, *Old St. Paul's*, p. 200, note). In the following letters there are frequent allusions to this family, which lost a son and a daughter in the epidemic (Carey, *Short Account*).

[5] Warner Washington, an apprentice from Virginia (BR's MS List of Apprentices). BR announced his death in a letter to Mrs. Rush of 12 Sep. 1793.

[6] Catharine (Hicks) Ceronio, wife of Stephen Ceronio, a merchant who had moved to the East Indies (Keith, *Provincial Councillors*, p. 456).

[7] John Redman Coxe (1773-1864), an apprentice who was to enjoy a long and distinguished career. Grandson of Dr. John Redman, he studied abroad after graduating M.D. at the University of Pennsylvania, 1794; practised in Philadelphia from 1796, edited the *Phila. Medical Museum*, 1805-1811; published an *American Dispensatory*, frequently cited in these notes, Phila., 1808, and numerous other medical works; professor of chemistry, 1809-1819, and of materia medica and pharmacy, 1819-1835, at the University of Pennsylvania; collected a famous library dispersed at his death. Coxe's family connections and his brave conduct during the epidemic of 1793 assured him of BR's friendship, which was warmly and steadily reciprocated. A valuable group of Coxe's letters to BR written while studying abroad is in Rush MSS, XXVII; BR's side of the correspondence is largely in Hist. Soc. Penna., Dreer Coll. (DAB; Mary C. Coxe, "A Biographical Sketch of John Redman Coxe, M.D.," Univ. of Penna., *Medical Bulletin*, XX [1907-1908], 294-301.)

[8] James Mease (1771-1846), M.D., University of Pennsylvania, 1792, became a prolific author and compiler of works in many fields besides medicine. Mease was one of the few physicians who supported his former teacher's treatment of yellow fever, and at the height of the epidemic BR entrusted to Mease all his notes on it, for arrangement and publication in case BR died. To Mease we also owe the fullest medical account of BR's death, written to J. C. Lettsom after reading Lettsom's erroneous account. (DAB; BR to Mrs. Rush, 4-5 Nov. 1793; Pettigrew, *Lettsom*, III, xxi-xxix; see also Introduction, above, p. lxi.)

[9] Not clearly identifiable; there were numerous New Jersey Sayres.

To Mrs. Rush

My dear Julia,   Philadelphia, September 6, 1793

This day my new calls have been only six or seven. I hope the disease is not pausing to take breath. The new medicine bears down nearly all opposition. Out of 100 persons who have taken it from me *on the first day*, not one has died. The deaths which now occur are chiefly of poor people who have no doctors, or of respectable people who are in the hands of quacks or of the enemies of mercury. Your letter of today would have alarmed me more did I not know you were in possession of the new and successful mode of treating the disorder. Should it spread among you, I shall send John Cox to carry into execution my mode of treating it. He is master of the symptoms of the disorder as well as of the remedy, and has cured several persons whom I have never seen. Still, however, keep out of the way of it. The contagion affects across a street and perhaps much further. This evening Dr. Hutchinson breathed his last. It is remarkable that he denied the existence of a contagious fever in our city for above a week after it appeared among us, and even treated the report of it with contempt and ridicule. The reason, I fear, was the first account of it came *from me*.[1]

I shall write a few lines to Emily this evening.

My friend Wistar is not so well tonight as last night. Upon my mentioning my surviving the present epidemic as a conditional event, he kindly said last evening, "You cannot die now, Doctor. The pleasure of your discovery must like a cordial keep you alive." Indeed it has infused a vigor into my body and mind which has contributed very much to support me under my present great exertions. Dr. Griffitts has adopted mercury in his practice and is popular and successful. We consult together every day. Dr. Mease is appointed one of the inspectors of sickly vessels in the room of Dr. Hutchinson. He thinks his fortune made for life.

Several of our physicians are said to lie by, under various excuses, to avoid infection. But I hope it is not true. Dr. Kuhn is certainly indisposed. Dr. Parke[2] attends him. Dr. Jno. Morris[3] in Pear Street is ill. A Mr. Hayes[4] died opposite to him this afternoon.

I have found hundreds to be infected who have used bark, wine, vinegar, &c., as preventatives. I rely chiefly upon cleanliness, a temperate and chiefly vegetable diet, and a very small portion of porter, and I have observed people who live most simply, and who avoid fatigue, heat, and cold, to escape more generally than others who pursue a contrary mode of living. I have been called to many

[653]

in whom the disorder was brought on after a full meal. This was the case in [*i.e., with*] Dr. Hutchinson after dining with Mr. Jefferson in the open air on the Banks of Shuilkill.[5]

For the first week of the prevalence of the disease, I advised my patients and friends to fly from the city. I now advise them to remain where they are, to avoid going out of their houses, and to send for a *mercurial physician* as soon as they are affected. No other metal in a physician's head will do any good now, not even gold any more than lead. My medicine has got the name of an *inoculating powder*, for it as certainly and as universally deprives the yellow fever of its mortality as inoculation does the smallpox.

September 7th. Still a debtor to divine goodness for another day of health and life. I have offered you all up to God this morning in my prayers, before 6 o'clock. The psalm I read in order was the 52nd. I could not help connecting it with the melancholy event of Dr. Hutchn's [*Hutchinson's*] death. Poor fellow! He died as well as lived my enemy. But this between ourselves. Adieu. Love to all friends. Dr. Smith must not be forgotten. Your ever affectionate

BENJN RUSH

P.S. Let me know how your influenza is. The yellow fever has chased it and nearly all[6] other diseases from our city. It is a monarchical disorder. You will see by this day's paper what my African brethren have done for the city.[7] No one of them has died with it, and I suspect none have been infected. They furnish nurses to most of my patients. I enclose you 20 dollars.

Addressed: Mrs: Julia Rush at Richd: Stockton Esqr: Princeton.
MS: Josiah C. Trent, M.D., Durham, North Carolina.

[1] See BR's *Account of the Yellow Fever in 1793*, p. 15-21.

[2] Thomas Parke (1749-1835), a Quaker of Chester co.; M.B., College of Philadelphia, 1770; studied afterward in London and Edinburgh; physician to the Pennsylvania Hospital, 1777-1823, where he succeeded BR in the care of the insane patients; a founder and 4th president of the College of Physicians (Ruschenberger, p. 132-4; Whitfield J. Bell, "Thomas Parke, M.B., Physician and Friend," *Wm. & Mary Quart.*, 3d ser., VI [1949], 569-95).

[3] John Morris (1759-1793), a privately trained Quaker physician; founding member of the College of Physicians; died on 8 Sep. 1793 (Ruschenberger, p. 251; BR to Mrs. Rush, 8-9 Sep. 1793).

[4] A Jacob Hays is listed among the dead in Carey's *Short Account*; he is not in the 1793 *Directory*.

[5] Thus in MS.

[6] This word inadvertently omitted in MS.

[7] Believing that Negroes were immune to yellow fever (and being supported by earlier writers on the subject), BR had appealed through the news-

papers to his friends at St. Thomas' Church to provide nurses. Absalom Jones and William Gray notified Mayor Clarkson that they would undertake this work, and a notice to that effect appeared in the papers on 7 Sep. BR afterwards acknowledged his mistake about the Negroes' supposed immunity and paid high tribute to them for their services. (*Account of the Yellow Fever in 1793*, p. 95-7; letter to an unidentified correspondent, 29 Oct. 1793.) Because the notion of immunity persisted, Jones and Richard Allen undertook to refute it in *A Narrative of the Proceedings of the Black People, during the Late Calamity*, Phila., 1794.

To Mrs. Rush

My dear Julia,   Philadelphia, September 8th, 1793

It is indeed as I expected. The disease has awakened like a giant refreshed by wine. I have this day been called to more new cases than I have time to count. Two more of our doctors are sick, and Dr. Morris is numbered among the dead. I entered his room this morning just as he expired. His excellent mother[1] rushed from his bed into my arms, fell upon my neck, and in this position gave vent to the most pathetic and eloquent exclamations of grief that I have ever heard. I was dumb, and finding myself sinking into sympathy, tore myself from her arms and ran to other scenes of distress. Among my new patients are Mrs. Seargeant,[2] Mr. Ed. and Mrs. Fox,[3] and two women in Mr. Hammond's family.[4] One of the two last is highly infected. My chair was arrested in Arch and 3rd Streets, and I was dragged in the two places to six different and new applications. Mrs. Saml. Meredith[5] I suspect has a spice of the infection, but she is not confined. The blessings and good wishes that I received from the whole family last evening were very acceptable. Secretary Hamilton is ill. A Dr. Stevens of St. Croix is his physician.[6] Dr. Kuhn continues by his advice to oppose mercury and jalap, but he stands now nearly alone, for its most bitter enemy and calumniator has this day adopted it. 99 out of an 100 who take it on the *first* day recover, and all would recover probably, had I time to attend closely to them after the expulsion or extinction of the poison by the mercury.

I find I am remembered by more than my Princeton friends in their addresses to the throne of grace. Mr. Connelly,[7] the vendue master, took me by the hand this day in the street, and with a faltering voice and eyes overflowing with tears told me that he carried me on his heart to the footstool of his Maker. It was a cordial to my soul. Through infinite goodness, I am preserved not only in health but in uncommon tranquillity of mind, never elevated, and never but twice depressed, and each time by a sudden paroxysm of sympathy with the distressed. The fear of death from the disease has been taken from me, and I possess perfect composure in the rooms of my patients. Help me to praise God for this and all his other inestimable blessings to me. Let it be the business of our future lives (if we should be reunited here) to record and to celebrate the goodness of our God.

September 9th. Still alive and in good health after five hours' comfortable sleep. "Be merciful unto me, O God! be merciful unto me, for my soul trusteth in thee, yea in the shadow of thy wings do I make my refuge, until these calamities be overpast." Psalm 57th. Adieu, my dear Julia. I almost forget, in the distresses of my fellow citizens, my dear children and friends.

The colds taken at the great fire on Saturday has helped very much to increase the number of sick. It is remarkable that those who have it mildly rarely infect others, and this is the case with all who take mercury. Since the cool weather, the disease has put on in some cases an inflammatory appearance. I yesterday bled two patients, but not till they had been thoroughly purged. The medicine does not cure unless it produces *large, black,* or *dark*-colored evacuations from the bowels. *Sweating* generally follows these evacuations. Communicate this to Dr. Beattie.[8] [. . .][9] and Becky are well. Our whole family has been preserved in the very heart of infection. Washington is well. Fisher[10] complains, and I fear Jno. Cox will lie by this day, but they have seen so much of the efficacy of mercury in the disorder that they treat their complaints with as much indifference as a common cold. When I am called on the first day, I endeavor to compose the fears of my patients by telling them that they have "nothing but a yellow fever," and that mercury and jalap are as certain a cure for it as bark is for an intermittent. I have this moment been called to Thos. Willing, who believes himself to be infected.

Addressed: Mrs Julia Rush at Richd Stockton Esqr: Princeton.
MS (not signed): Josiah C. Trent, M.D., Durham, North Carolina.

[1] Margaret (Hill) Morris (1737-1816), of Burlington and Philadelphia, the author of a journal of some celebrity, several times printed, most recently as *Margaret Morris: Her Journal with Biographical Sketch and Notes*, ed. John W. Jackson, Phila., 1949.

[2] Presumably Mrs. Jonathan Dickinson Sergeant, the former Elizabeth Rittenhouse; she did not die of the fever, but her husband did (DAB, under her husband's name; BR to Mrs. Rush, 8-9 Oct. 1793).

[3] Edward Fox was a notary public on Chestnut St. (1793 *Directory*); both he and his wife evidently recovered.

[4] George Hammond (1763-1853), the British minister, who lived in South Second St. BR claimed to have cured four of Hammond's employees, only to have two of them die some time later under the care of "a French physician." (DNB; 1793 *Directory*; BR to Mrs. Rush, 11-12 Sep. and 18-19 Oct. 1793.)

[5] The former Margaret Cadwalader; she was one of BR's prize patients, for she took the powerful mercurial purges with good results, though she was "a lady of uncommon delicacy of constitution" (DAB, under her husband's name; BR, *Account of the Yellow Fever in 1793*, p. 253).

[6] A testimonial letter from Hamilton to Stevens, dated 11 Sep. 1793, was published in the newspapers; it is available in BR's *Account of the Yellow Fever in 1793*, p. 214-16. BR had himself gone to Stevens, lately of St. Croix, to learn the West Indies treatment, which consisted of bark, wine, and cold baths; but he found that three out of four of his patients died under this therapy (same, p. 194-5), and turned to the depleting methods described in letters that follow. On 16 Sep. BR published a long letter to the College of Physicians explaining his treatment and denouncing "violent evacuations" in a disease of "debility" requiring stimulants (same, p. 216-23). Edward Stevens (d. 1834) is an interesting but obscure figure. He was an intimate friend of Alexander Hamilton's from boyhood and attended King's College with him, graduating in 1774; M.D., Edinburgh, 1777; professor of the practice of medicine at Columbia, 1794-1795; special U.S. commissioner to San Domingo (Thomas, *Columbia University Officers and Alumni*, p. 32, 85, 103; Hamilton, *Works*, ed. J. C. Hamilton, N.Y., 1851, I, 1-2; *Amer. Hist. Rev.*, XVI [1910-1911], 64-101).

[7] Connelly & Co., vendue masters, are listed in the 1793 *Directory* at 78 South Front St.

[8] John Beatty (1749-1826), a graduate, 1769, and trustee, 1785-1802, of the College of New Jersey, served as an officer in the Penna. Line, 1776-1778, and was commissary general of prisoners, 1778-1780. He had been apprenticed to BR in 1770 and practised at Princeton from time to time, but eventually grew more interested in politics, serving as delegate to Congress, 1783-1785; N.J. assemblyman, 1789-1790; U.S. representative, 1793-1795; secretary of state, N.J., 1795-1805. (Alumni Records, Secretary's Office, Princeton Univ.; BR, MS List of Apprentices; J. M. Beatty, Jr., "Letters of the Four Beatty Brothers of the Continental Army, 1774-1794," PMHB, XLIV [1920], 193-263.)

[9] MS torn; the word "Ben" should doubtless be supplied.

[10] Edward Fisher, an apprentice from Virginia; M.D., Edinburgh, 1795; settled at Petersburg, Va., 1796; about ten years later moved to Columbia, S.C. During BR's illness Fisher was his principal attendant, and earned from his master the epithet of "an enthusiast in humanity." (BR's MS List of Apprentices; *New Engl. Hist. & Geneal. Reg.*, XLII [1888], 162; BR to Mrs. Rush, 11-12 Oct. 1793, and to John Redman Coxe, 25 May 1796; Fisher's letters to BR in Rush MSS, V.)

To Mrs. Rush

My dear Julia,   Philadelphia, September 10th, 1793

Hereafter my name should be Shadrach, Meshach, or Abednego, for I am sure the preservation of those men from death by fire was not a greater miracle than my preservation from the infection of the prevailing disorder. I have lived to see the close of another day, more awful than any I have yet seen. Forty persons it is said have been buried this day, and I have visited and prescribed for more than 100 patients. Mr. Willing is better, and Jno. Barclay[1] is out of danger. Amidst my numerous calls to the wealthy and powerful, I do not forget the poor, well remembering my dream in the autumn of 1780. Dr. Mease, Dr. Penington,[2] the two Glentworths,[3] and Dr. Parke have all adopted my mode of treating the disorder, and are all alike successful with me. Dr. Kuhn has set his face against it, and many follow him, and hence the continuance and mortality of the disorder. You will easily believe this when you recollect that my mode of treating the locked jaw has not to this day been adopted by many of the practitioners in this city. But all will be right bye and bye.

September 10th [*i.e., 11th*]. O! that it were October or November 10th! for I despair under present circumstances of the disease being checked till we have *frost* or *heavy rains*. Thank God! I am still in good health. "I will sing of thy power, O Lord, Yea, I will sing aloud of thy mercy in the *morning*, for thou hast been" and thou are still "my defense and refuge in the day of trouble." Psalm 59th, 16. It is now a little after 6 o'clock, and the knocker is in motion. My African brethren are extremely useful in attending the sick. I met a good woman of their society a few days ago at the foot of a pair of stairs. "Hah! Mama," said I, "*we black* folks have come into demand at last." She squeezed my hand, and we parted. Billy Grey and Ab. Jones have been very active and useful in procuring nurses. It is remarkable that none of the French exiles have taken the disorder.[4] Adieu. Continue to love and pray for your affectionate friend,

BENJN RUSH

P.S. I have found bleeding very useful since the weather has become cool, after the bowels are well cleansed, provided the pulse be *full* and *tense*.

Addressed: Mrs: Julia Rush at Richd Stockton's Esqr: Princeton.
MS: Josiah C. Trent, M.D., Durham, North Carolina.

[1] John Barclay, banker, alderman, and former mayor of the city, 1791-1792. Carey bestows high praise on Barclay for his conduct during the epidemic. BR also attended Mrs. Barclay, and both recovered. (Martin, *Bench and Bar*, p. 95; Carey, *Short Account*, p. 30, note; BR to Mrs. Rush, 17 Sep. 1793.)
[2] John Penington, M.D., College of

Philadelphia, 1790, died of the fever about ten days later (Penington's thesis [copy in *Coll. Phys. Phila.*]; BR to Mrs. Rush, 20 Sep. 1793).
[3] The brothers Glentworth were: 1. Peter Sonmans G., who seems to have had no medical degree and who died of the fever early in October. 2. Plunket Fleeson G. (1760-1833), who obtained

his M.D. at the College or the University, 1790, and was a fellow of the College of Physicians, 1792; he figured later in BR's quarrel with Cobbett. (Univ. of Penna., *Gen. Alumni Cat.*; Barratt, *Old St. Paul's*, p. 199, note, and 225; Ruschenberger, p. 227; BR to Mrs. Rush, 6-7 Oct. 1793, and to Brockholst Livingston, 5 Mch. 1800.)

[4] That is, the refugees from Cap François, San Domingo (Haiti), where a slave insurrection was in progress. Two thousand arrived before the end of August (Powell, *Bring Out Your Dead,* p. 5), undoubtedly bringing with them the cases of yellow fever that, with the cooperation of the *Aedes* mosquitoes in local marshes, produced the terrible epidemic. In his *Account of the Yellow Fever in 1793,* p. 94, BR remarked: "The refugees from the French West-Indies, universally escaped [the fever]. This was not the case with the natives of France, who had been settled in the city." He tentatively accounted for these circumstances by differences in diet.

To Mrs. Rush

My dear Julia,   Philadelphia, September 11, 1793

The pleasure of the Lord continues to prosper in my hands. I have this day visited and prescribed for upwards of 100 patients and have not had a single death among them. Four persons in the British minister's family will swell the triumphs of mercury, jalap, and bloodletting. This evening I have been called to Mr. Genet's.[1] Dr. Kuhn continues to oppose my method of treating the disorder, but it will not do.[2] The increasing number of my patients every hour refutes his objections to it. My health improves, and I endure labor with less fatigue now than I did three weeks ago. This is the more extraordinary, as I am unable to drink wine or malt liquors or to eat meat, and now live wholly upon milk and vegetables, and drink nothing but water.

September 11 [*i.e., 12*]. Alive and in good health after a most comfortable night's rest. "O! bless our God, ye people, and make the voice of his praise to be heard, which holdeth our soul in life, and suffered not our feet to be moved." Psalm 66, 8, 9. It is not yet five o'clock, and I have had seven calls already. This day my directions for curing and preventing the disease will be published in the newspapers.[3] They will save me much trouble in writing to country practitioners, and will moreover help the people to cure themselves, not only without but in spite of physicians who know nothing of the disorder. Adieu. My letters I fear will be shorter hereafter than they have been. Where are the children? I almost forget in public duties all my private ones. Again adieu. From, my dear Julia, your ever affectionate

BENJN RUSH

P.S. Write to me often. Don't mind postage. What pleasure can money give hereafter equal to that which arises from hearing from friends under present circumstances?

Addressed: Mrs: Julia Rush at Richd Stockton's Esqr: Princeton.
MS: Josiah C. Trent, M.D., Durham, North Carolina.

[1] Edmond-Charles-Edouard G e n e t (1763-1834), the newly-arrived minister of the French Republic to the United States, who resided at Twelfth and High (Market) Sts. (*Webster's Biog. Dict.*; 1793 *Directory*).

[2] A letter of Kuhn's dated 7 Sep. had been published in the papers; it detailed his method of treatment (bark, wine, and cool bath), with acknowledgments to Dr. Stevens and strictures on the use of emetics. To this BR publicly replied on the 11th, saying that Kuhn's method, "if persisted in," will result in "desolating three fourths of our city." (BR's *Account of the Yellow Fever in 1793*, p. 207-12.)

[3] See the following letter.

To His Fellow Citizens: Treatment for Yellow Fever

September 12, 1793

Dr. Rush regrets that he is unable to comply with all the calls of his fellow citizens who are indisposed with the prevailing fever. He begs leave to recommend to such of them as cannot have the benefit of medical aid to take the mercurial purges, which may now be had with suitable directions at most of the apothecaries,[1] and to lose ten or twelve ounces of blood as soon as is convenient after taking the purges, if the headache and fever continue. Where the purges cannot be obtained or do not operate speedily, bleeding may now be used before they are taken. The almost universal success with which it hath pleased God to bless the remedies of strong mercurial purges and bleeding in this disorder enables Dr. Rush to assure his fellow citizens that there is no more danger to be apprehended from it, when those remedies are used in its early stage, than there is from the measles or the influenza.

Dr. Rush assures his fellow citizens further that the risk from visiting and attending the sick, in common cases, at present is not greater than from walking the streets. He hopes this information will be attended to, as many of the sick suffer greatly from the want of the assistance of bleeders and of the attendance of nurses and friends.

While the disease was so generally mortal, or the successful mode of treating it only partially adopted, Dr. Rush advised his friends to leave the city. At present he conceives this advice to be unnecessary, not only because the disease is now under the power of medicine, but because the citizens who now wish to fly into the country cannot avoid carrying the infection with them. They had better remain near to medical aid and avoid exciting the infection into action, which is now in their bodies, by a strict attention to former directions.

Dr. R. does not believe it will be prudent for those persons who are in the country to return to town until after *frost* or *heavy rains* have taken place, both of which alike weaken or destroy the contagion of the yellow fever.

Printed: Federal Gazette (Philadelphia), 12 September 1793.

[1] In the issue of the *Federal Gazette* in which the present letter was printed, there began appearing advertisements by various chemists and druggists for "Doctor Rush's Mercurial Sweating Powder for the Yellow Fever, with printed directions for taking the same, prepared and sold by permission."

To the College of Physicians: Use of the Lancet in Yellow Fever

Gentlemen, September 12, 1793

As the weekly meetings of our College have become no longer practicable, I have taken the liberty of communicating to you the result of further observations upon the prevailing epidemic.

I have found bleeding to be useful, not only in cases where the pulse was full and quick, but where it was *slow* and *tense*.[1] I have bled in one case where the pulse beat only 48 strokes in a minute, and recovered my patient by it. The pulse became more full and more frequent after it. This state of the pulse seems to arise from an inflamed state of the brain, which shows itself in a preternatural dilation of the pupils of the eyes. It is always unsafe to trust to the most perfect remissions of fever and pain in this state of the pulse. It indicates the necessity of more bleeding and purging. I have found it to occur most frequently in children.

I have bled twice in many, and in one acute case four times, with the happiest effects. I consider intrepidity in the use of the lancet at present to be as necessary as it is in the use of mercury and jalap in this insidious and ferocious disease.

I lament the contrariety of opinion among the members of our College upon the remedies proper in this disease. This contrariety seems to arise from the yellow fever being confounded with the jail or hospital fever. The fevers of Breslau, Vienna, and Edinburgh, mentioned in some late publications, in which the cold bath was used with so much success, were of the latter kind. The two diseases are totally different from each other in their cause, seasons of prevailing, symptoms, danger, and method of cure.

From, gentlemen, your friend and brother,

BENJAMIN RUSH

Printed: Federal Gazette (Philadelphia), 12 September 1793.

[1] This, BR's fateful pronouncement of the necessity of bleeding in yellow fever, is of more biographical than scientific significance, but it is important to realize that BR believed that experience as well as theory sustained him. Having failed with stimulating remedies and having had remarkable success with depletion by purges, he turned to other depleting remedies. There was abundant testimony, even from professionals, that bloodletting *worked*; e.g., see Samuel P. Griffitts' letter, printed in BR's *Account of the Yellow Fever in 1793*, p. 273. BR furnished an exhaustive and extremely revealing analysis of his motives and results in drawing blood (same, p. 258ff.); using the lancet, he said, was equivalent to emptying the pockets of a man who is struggling to raise himself up. David Ramsay, who was among the best-informed medical men of his time, observed in 1813: "It is probable that not less than six thousand of the inhabitants of Philadelphia were saved from death, by purging and bleeding during the autumn of 1793." Ramsay also said, with more truth than he realized, that upon the role BR assigned to the lancet "his fame as an improver of medicine, in a great degree, must eventually rest" (*Eulogium*, p. 89-90, 79). For a modern appraisal of BR's therapy, see O. H. P. Pepper, "Benjamin Rush's Theories on Blood Letting after One Hundred and Fifty Years," Coll. Phys. Phila., *Trans.*, 4th ser., XIV (1946), 121-6.

To Mrs. Rush

My dear Julia,   September 12th, 1793. 6 o'clock in the morning

After a restless night I am still alive and preparing for the awful duties of the day. Yesterday exceeded any of the days I have seen for distress and death in our city. Two more of our physicians are laid up. Poor Washington[1] is no more. I send you these few lines only to let you know that I am still wonderfully supported in mind and body, but that I stand in greater need than ever of the prayers of all good people. Adieu. Adieu. Yours affectionately,

BENJN RUSH

Addressed: Mrs Julia Rush at Richd Stockton's Esqr: Princeton.
MS: Josiah C. Trent, M.D., Durham, North Carolina.

[1] Warner Washington; see BR to Mrs. Rush, 5-6 Sep. 1793.

To Mrs. Rush

My dear Julia,   Philadelphia, September 13, 1793

Alive! and though I slept but three or four hours last night, am still through divine goodness in perfect health. Yesterday was a day of triumph to mercury, jalap, and bleeding. I am satisfied that they saved, in my hands only, nearly one hundred lives. The disease has been said to have become more mild, but this is not true, for where the above medicines are not used, death follows more certainly than in the beginning of the disease, on the 3rd, 5th, or 7th days. Besides combating with the yellow fever, I have been obliged to contend with the prejudices, fears, and falsehoods of several of my brethren, all of which retard the progress of truth and daily cost our city many lives.

You had better go on to your Uncle Elisha's.[1] I do not believe it will be prudent for you to come to town for a month or six weeks to come. Every room in our house is infected, and my body is full of it. My breath and perspiration smell so strongly of it that a lady with more truth than delicacy complained to me of it a few days ago. My eyes are tinged of a yellow color. This is not peculiar to myself. It is universal in the city. Even the Negroes who do not take the disease discover that mark of infection in their eyes. On one day my face had for a few hours a yellow hue. Yet under all these circumstances, and upon a diet consisting wholly of milk and vegetables, I enjoy, as to my feelings and activity, a perfect state of health.[2]

"Blessed be the Lord who daily loadeth us with benefits, even the God of our salvation. He that is our God is the God of salvation, and unto the God the Lord belong *the issues from death*."[3]

Adieu. With love as usual, I am, my dear Julia, yours sincerely,

BENJN RUSH

P.S. I had forty or fifty new calls yesterday and the day before. Dr. Mease is ill. Griffitts, Gibbons,[4] Wistar, and Leib[5] are well or mending. Scarcely a family now escapes the disease.

Addressed: Mrs Julia Rush at Richd Stockton Esqr Princeton.
MS: Josiah C. Trent, M.D., Durham, North Carolina.

[1] Elisha Boudinot (1749-1819), of Newark, Julia's mother's brother; a lawyer; formerly commissary of prisoners for New Jersey; his second wife was Rachel, sister of BR's friends Thomas and William Bradford (Boudi- not, *Boudinot*, I, 33; II, 392). The Rush family did not go on to Newark.

[2] In a public communication of 16 Sep. BR recommended "a milk and vegetable diet" and "cooling purges once or twice a week" for those not yet

infected (*Account of the Yellow Fever in 1793*, p. 229). This was in accord with his view that the disease was an "inflammatory" one, requiring a treatment quite opposite to the stimulative therapy of Stevens and others.

3 Psalms 68:19-20.

4 John H. Gibbons (ca. 1759-1795); M.D., Edinburgh, 1786; member College of Physicians (Ruschenberger, p. 226).

5 Michael Leib (1759 or 1760-1822), apprenticed to BR in 1778, probably never took a medical degree; a surgeon in the Revolution, he became a member of the College of Physicians, 1788, and in later years was much more active in politics than in medicine, sitting in the state legislature, 1797-1798, 1815-1816, serving as member of Congress, 1799-1806, and as U.S. senator, 1809-1814. Leib is said to have "rocked the cradle of democracy" in the Northern Liberties, which is one way of saying that he was a principal founder and long one of the stalwarts of the Jeffersonian party in Pennsylvania. (BR's MS List of Apprentices; Ruschenberger, p. 242; *Biog. Dir. Cong.*)

To Mrs. Rush

My dear Julia,   Philadelphia, September 15, 1793

Life and health become every day more and more a miracle in persons who are constantly exposed to it. The disease spreads. Scarcely a family escapes it. I have this day visited above twenty families which have all from two to six persons in it confined to their beds, and many which have one. Poor Mr. Mervin![1] after dismissing me and sending for a French physician, sent for me again this morning. But alas! it was too late to help him. He was yellow, cold, and puking blood. "O! Doctor," said he, wringing his hands, "I was persuaded by my friends to employ the French physician. But help me, help me." I told him I would do my utmost for him, and with a heart wrung with anguish I hurried from his room. Many, many such scenes do I witness daily. For several days past I have sent 50 and 60 patients to other doctors. My old patients are constantly preferred by me. Kuhn's publication has done immense mischief. Many doctors will follow him, and scores are daily sacrificed to bark and wine. My method is too simple for them. They forget that a stone from the sling of David effected what the whole armory of Saul could not do. Many hundreds of my patients now walk the streets and follow their ordinary business. Could our physicians be persuaded to adopt the new mode of treating the disorder, the contagion might be eradicated from our city in a few weeks. But they not only refuse to adopt it, but they persecute and slander the author of it.

September 16. Since writing the above I have had an attack of the disorder,[2] but in consequence of losing blood and taking one of my purges I am now perfectly well—so much so that I rested better last night than I have done for a week past. Thus you see that I have proved upon my own body that the yellow fever when treated in the new way is no more than a common cold. I thought it proper to give you this information to prevent your being alarmed by reports concerning me. Don't think of coming to see me. Our city is a great mass of contagion. The very air in it is now offensive to the smell. If I should relapse, you shall hear from me. Mr. Stall and Mr. Cox are doing wonders in our city. They visit and cure all my patients. Adieu. Continue not only to pray for, but to give thanks for, my dear Julia, your ever affectionate

BENJN RUSH

P.S. I have sent to hire a hack[3] with which I expect in a day or two to[4] visit my patients. Converse with nobody now who comes from Philadelphia. Everything is infected in our city. Love as usual.

P.S. I have just received your letter. By all means go to Mr. Boudinot's.

Addressed: Mrs: Julia Rush at Richd Stockton Esqr Princeton.
MS: Josiah C. Trent, M.D., Durham, North Carolina.

[1] Miles Mervin, schoolmaster; both he and his wife were victims (Carey's *Short Account*; BR's letters of 18-19 and 20 Sep. 1793).

[2] For a more detailed account of this seizure, see BR's *Account of the Yellow Fever in 1793*, p. 343-4; from the data given there it seems most likely that the date at the head of the present letter should be September *14*. BR con-

sidered himself fully recovered by the 19th, but he was too weak to work as he had worked before.

[3] In a letter to the papers, dated 16 Sep., BR observed that it would be "an act of great humanity" for the city to provide all physicians and bleeders with horses and chairs (*Account of the Yellow Fever in 1793*, p. 230).

[4] This word omitted in MS.

To Mrs. Rush

My dear Julia,   Philadelphia, September 17, 1793

Through divine goodness I past a most comfortable night and was the first white person that rose in the family this morning. My young men are out among my patients, and like old General Harkemar[1] I am fighting the disease, through them, upon my stumps. Tomorrow I expect to go out in a close carriage to visit such as are in most danger. Having past through the disorder, I shall be less liable to take it hereafter than before, for though some have relapsed, none have taken it twice. By all means hasten to your

Uncle Elisha's with all the children. Our city, and above all our house, will not be pure till after frost or heavy rains. Bear up, my dear child, under the pain of our long separation, and be thankful that we are not separated forever. O! the dismal tales of dissolved unions of husbands and wives, and parents and children you will hear when you come to town! Nay more, you will hear of *whole* families being swept away by the present disorder and the West India remedies which have been used to cure it. Wigton and his wife,[2] Thos. Anthony, young Mr. Walker,[3] all in our neighborhood, are no more. Mr. and Mrs. Barclay, Dr. Mease, a son of Robt. Bridges,[4] Jos. Coates,[5] and many hundred others owe their lives to the new remedies. Mr. Stall is just now gone out to see Mrs. Meredith, who is now certainly infected. Forty and fifty now die every day. Adieu. My love to the dear boys. I rejoice to hear that they behave so well. My love, my tenderest love, to your Mama, sisters, and brother. My room is full.

Yours—yours—yours,

BENJN RUSH

P.S. Betsey Steen's clothes were sent by Betsy Currie[6] to Saml. Stockton's. Her sister at Mr. [...][7] has had the fever violently but is now perfectly recovered.

Addressed: Mrs Julia Rush at Richd Stockton's Esqr Princeton.
MS: Josiah C. Trent, M.D., Durham, North Carolina.

[1] General Nicholas Herkimer won the battle of Oriskany, in Aug. 1777, after receiving a mortal wound in the leg (DAB).

[2] John Wigton, a schoolmaster, lived in South Third St. (1793 *Directory*).

[3] Not certainly identifiable.

[4] Bridges was a sailmaker in Front St.

(1793 *Directory*).

[5] Josiah Coates, grocer, in Church Alley (same).

[6] Probably the same as Betsey Correy, a servant; see BR to Mrs. Rush, 23-24 July 1776.

[7] Name obscured by seal.

To Rachel Rush Montgomery

My dear Sister,   Philadelphia, September 18, 1793

Your affectionate letter[1] found me preparing to go out after a recovery from an attack of the yellow fever, rendered [light][2] by my previous regimen and by the use of the new remedies. I am [grateful] for the honor it has pleased God to [bestow] upon me by restoring me so soon to my duty to my fellow citizens. The disease still rages. One hundred persons died on Sunday and Monday last, but *more* by the West India mode of treating it than by the disease. Never did I witness such deep and universal distress. My indisposition was in part occasioned by a *last look* from a beloved friend[3] who had been killed by a [Frenc]h physician. I never can forget his [fran]tic cries to me in his last moments [of] "help —help."—I despair of the disorder [being] checked before frost or heavy rains. There are it is said 190 fresh graves in the Catholic [church]yard. For many days before [my sick]ness I visited and prescribed for above [. . . pati]ents. During this time I seldom slept more than two or three hours in the four-and-twenty, eat nothing but milk and vegetables, and drank nothing but water. Our streets are nearly deserted. Nobody is seen in them but persons hunting doctors, nurses, and gravediggers. Adieu! "Brethren, pray for us."[4]

From your affectionate brother,

BENJN RUSH

P.S. No part of this letter must be published. The truths contained in it will expose me [. . . .][5]

MS: Army Medical Library, Historical Branch, Cleveland.

[1] Not found.
[2] A fragment of the MS at the top of the inner margin of both pages has been torn away, rendering several words, here bracketed, doubtful.
[3] Presumably Miles Mervin; see BR

to Mrs. Rush, 15-16 Sep. 1793.
[4] I Thessalonians 5:25; II Thessalonians 3:1.
[5] Remainder of text missing on a page now lost.

To Mrs. Rush

My dear Julia,   Philadelphia, September 18th, 1793

I begin this letter in the back parlor with a patient sitting by my side waiting for advice. You cannot doubt therefore of my perfect recovery from my late indisposition. A worthy friend of mine is now gone for a chariot for me, in which I expect to visit a few of my patients in the middle of the day. Don't be uneasy about me. I shall run no unnecessary risks by undertaking too much business before I have regained my former strength. Poor Johnny Stall gave way last night, and he is now under the operation of the physic in our house. Fisher and Cox are faithful and attentive. The former attends Mr. Jos. Swift's family ten miles from town, where the infection was carried to them by one of his sons.[1] Mr. Meredith is well after three bleedings. Thinking people submit to my method of treating the disorder, but many, very many, follow that which was *dictated* by Dr. Shippen's learned and sagacious friend Dr. Kuhn. A son of Saml. Morris in 2nd Street has died under it.[2] Two other of his sons have recovered under my care by bleeding and purging.

Last night's *cold* I hope will give a check to the disorder. The heat of Sunday and Monday was very fatal to the sick. It aided the disease and the doctors in destroying not less than 100 people.

Dr. Kuhn is fled to Bethlehem, Dr. Stevens to New York, and Dr. Shippen is nobody knows where.[3] None of the doctors who have been ill are so far recovered as to be able to attend the sick except your husband. I am thankful for this great privilege. It is meat and drink to me to do my Master's will. He loved human life, and among other errands into our world, he came "not to destroy men's lives but to save them."[4] Adieu. Love as usual. Yours very affectionately,

BENJN RUSH

Addressed: Mrs: Julia Rush at Richd Stockton Esqr: Princeton.
MS: Josiah C. Trent, M.D., Durham, North Carolina.

[1] Joseph Swift was a merchant and alderman in South Front St. (1793 *Directory*).

[2] The son who died was also named Samuel, born 1775. His father (1734-1812) was a well-known merchant and sportsman; captain of the Philadelphia Troop of Light Horse, 1775-1786; member of Assembly, 1776-1777, 1781-1783. Capt. Morris was in New Jersey when the epidemic broke out, and stayed there; some heartrending letters to his children in Philadelphia, who were unable to leave because one or more of them were sick most of the time, have survived. (Moon, *Morris Family*, I, 320-56.)

[3] In October Shippen wrote BR, concerning the opening of the medical school, from Abington, then eight or nine miles north of the city (BR to Mrs. Rush, 11-12 Oct. 1793).

[4] Luke 9:56.

To Mrs. Rush

My dear Julia,   Philadelphia, September 18th, 1793

I have this day visited one family in the neighborhood on foot, and four at a distance in a carriage, and feel so well after it that tomorrow I expect to visit a dozen or twenty. My pupils have been very busy for me and have in general been successful. One or two[1] have dropped off from the want of sufficient bleeding. Our house continues to be crowded at all hours. For some days before my confinement, I refused from 50 to 60 patients a day. This was a most painful task. Many of them left me in tears. One man, a sailor, offered me £20 to visit his wife, but I declined it. In riding through town I was often stopped by half a dozen people all imploring me to visit a wife, a husband, a brother, or a child. Judge how I must have felt in tearing myself from them! for I could only visit a certain number, and by undertaking more than I could attend, some I knew would die from neglect. So great is the apprehension of death from the disorder that I have seldom visited a patient the *first* time without being met at the head of the stairs by some member of the family in tears. Good Mrs. Mease[2] took me by the hand the first time I visited her son and was dumb for some time with fear and distress. Another lady whom you do not know fell upon my neck and wept aloud for several minutes before she would let me enter her husband's room. They were patients of Kuhn's. They proposed a consultation, but I objected to it. I said I had a confidence in my remedies and that I must attend him alone or not at all. They consented to my proposal, and after three bleedings he recovered. On Sunday last, while I was under the first attack of my fever, Miss Morris, daughter of Saml. Morris, came weeping to me. She could not speak for some time. At last said she, "O, Doctor, come and see my brother Casper.[3] My brother Samey is dying in the next room to him under Dr. Kuhn's direction." I endeavored to comfort her by smiling in her face, "You see me here just taking the disorder, and yet I have no fear as to its issue. I hope I shall be able to cure your brother." I sent Mr. Stall to see him, and he cured him in two days. But this is only the background of the distress which pervades our city. Many die without nurses. Some perish from the want of a draught of water. Parents desert their children as soon as they are infected, and in every room you enter you see no person but a solitary black man or woman near the sick. Many people thrust their parents into the streets as soon as they complain of a headache. Two such exiles have taken sanctuary for half a day in our kitchen and shop. These scenes now cease to move me, but—the last *dying look* of good Mr. Mervin threw me back to more sympathizing times. I shall never forget the motion of his hands and his pathetic cries for "help—help!" To support me under these awful events which hourly pass before me, I hear from all quarters that the new remedies begin to force themselves into use. Mr. Fleming[4] called upon me this morning and informed me that he had found in visiting his congregation many people cured by following my printed directions without the advice of a physician. Mr. Helmuth called upon me soon afterwards and told me nearly the same thing. So universal is the contagion in our city that you meet no one in the street who has not a yellow eye and a dilated pupil. Nay more, there is scarcely any person in town who has not a preternaturally quick pulse. I have counted many this day in our back room in the wrists of persons who appeared to be in good health, and found them all except one to beat above 80 instead of about 66 strokes in a minute. My mother's pulse (though in good health) is 96. I ascribe my freedom from fatigue and my sleepless nights wholly to the stimulus of the contagion on my system, for I am so full of it that it is now become part of myself. It is not dangerous unless excited into action by heat, cold, fatigue, or high living. It takes 16 days to discharge it from the body after being removed from its action. I have kept faithful notes of every symptom and change in the disorder which (if it should please God to preserve me through my present scenes of danger) I shall give to the world, together with the history of the rise, progress, persecution, and final efficacy of the new remedies. Such is my opinion of them that I think, properly managed, they might be directed to cure the plague as certainly as the yellow fever.

Thus have I given you a long letter which I hope will make up for my late short ones. Tomorrow my hurry will begin again, after which my letters will be shorter. I received a most affectionate letter from Polly this morning and sent her a short answer to it. Do copy the facts relative to the contagion and send them to her, but *by no means* to be made public or even *copied* by anybody.

I have not heard of the death of Mr. Hare.[5] Among the late dead are our neighbor Thos. Anthony, Mr. Walker, Mr. Ketland's[6] friend, all Ross[7] the blacksmith's family, Corn. Barnes,[8] Henry Pratt's wife,[9] Mrs. Wigton, and Emily Bullock.[10] Near twenty persons have died in Pear Street alone. Mr. Helmuth told me that 22 persons were buried yesterday in the Lutheran graveyard alone. It is said there are 191 new graves in the Roman Catholic graveyard.

September 19th. In good health, blessed be God! Upon second thought you had better take Richd. with you to NewArk. He will be out of the line of hearing from any of us at Bordentown, and exposed to the contagion from our city. If he reads history at his uncle's, his time will not be misspent.

We lead a camp or wilderness life in our family. Mr. Cox slept with us last night as well as Mr. Fisher. I have had many new calls already this morning, but I now decline all except my *old* patients, to whom I consider myself as under a contract not to leave in the day of their adversity. It is the only line I have drawn in my duties to my fellow citizens.

Provisions have risen very much, and many people begin to dread the calamity of famine in addition to that of the pestilence.

I have hired Frederick to attend me every day with a chariot. This will protect me from the sun and night air, both of which are strong exciting causes of the disease.

Adieu, my dearest and kindest friend. You lie near my heart, and I shall never forget your great solicitude for me. Continue to "pray without ceasing," not only for me but for a distressed and desolating city. Some of the rich suffer, but the weight of the distress and mortality falls upon the poor. May God recompense to them double hereafter for their unparalleled sufferings here. Adieu. Love as usual. Yours most affectionately,

BENJN RUSH

P.S. I enclose you 30 dollars.

Addressed: Mrs: Julia Rush at Richd Stockton's Esqr: Princeton.
MS: Josiah C. Trent, M.D., Durham, North Carolina.

[1] Supply "patients."

[2] Esther (Miller) Mease (DAB, under the name of her son James).

[3] Three children of Capt. Samuel Morris (see note on preceding letter) are mentioned: Catharine (1772-1859), the only unmarried daughter in the family; Caspar (1764-1828), who recovered and carried on the family brewing business; and Samuel, Jr., who had died of the fever before this letter was written (Moon, *Morris Family*, I, 351).

[4] Rev. Francis A. Fleming, a Catholic priest who had come to the United States from Ireland in 1789; he fell a victim of the fever two weeks later (Powell, *Bring Out Your Dead*, p. 237; 1793 *Directory*; BR to Mrs. Rush, 6-7 Oct. 1793).

[5] Probably Robert Hare, the elder (1752-1812), speaker of the Pennsyl-vania Senate, 1796-1800; Hare was a well-to-do brewer and father of the famous chemist of the same name (Edgar Fahs Smith, *Life of Robert Hare*, Phila. and London, 1917, p. 2-3; Martin, *Bench and Bar*, p. 181; Keith, *Provincial Councillors*, p. [129]).

[6] Thomas Ketland, merchant, South Third St. (1793 *Directory*).

[7] Hugh Ross, blacksmith and tavern keeper, 69 Walnut St.; his wife and son constituted his family (same; also Carey, *Short Account*).

[8] Cornelius Barnes, merchant, Bread St. (1793 *Directory*).

[9] Pratt was a merchant in South Water St.; he also lost a child (same; also Carey, *Short Account*).

[10] Not named in Carey's list of the dead.

To Mrs. Rush

My dear Julia,   Philadelphia, September 20th, 1793

The distress of our city increases, and the shafts of death fly closer and closer to us every day. Poor Dr. Penington is no more. His death was occasioned by his going out too soon after his recovery. Mr. Strawbridge[1] likewise, our old neighbor, is dead. Mrs. Mervin has followed her husband to the grave. Johnny Stall continues ill, and Fisher is poorly and confined in our house. Johny Alston[2] is abed at Mrs. Wilson's,[3] and Jno. Cox is drooping. Through the prayers of my friends, purified and accepted through the mediation of a gracious Redeemer, I am again in good health and possess my usual tone of mind. Be thankful that you are alive and out of town. Be thankful that you are in health. Be thankful that death has as yet made no breach in our little flock—nay, be thankful that you are not called to witness the distress which passes between 8 and 9 o'clock in our entry every morning, exclusive of the still more accumulated distress from pain, fear, grief, poverty, solitude, famine, despair, and death which pervades nearly every house in the city. Adieu. Fly to NewArk with all the children. There patiently and humbly wait for the deliverance of our city and the life and health of your affectionate husband,

BENJN RUSH

Addressed: Mrs Julia Rush at Richd: Stockton's Esqr Princeton.
MS: Josiah C. Trent, M.D., Durham, North Carolina.

[1] John Strawbridge, merchant, 98 North Fourth St. (1793 *Directory*); he is not entered in Carey's list of the dead.
[2] John Alston, or Allston (1772-1793), of South Carolina, who had been apprenticed to BR in 1792; he died four days after this letter was written

(BR's MS List of Apprentices; BR to Mrs. Rush, 24-25 Sep. 1793; *Inscriptions in St. Peter's Church Yard*, p. 509).
[3] Half a dozen Widow Wilsons are listed in the 1793 *Directory*.

To Mrs. Rush

My dear Julia,   Philadelphia, September 21, 1793

I continue through divine goodness perfectly well of the fever, but I suffer a little from a sore throat brought on by the mercury I took to cure the fever. I yesterday paid 25 visits in Frederick's chariot and was rather invigorated than fatigued by the ride. I prescribed besides for above 25 more patients, chiefly poor people, in my back room, and I am sorry to add was forced to decline 38 fresh applications. I sent them all to Drs. Leib, Porter,[1] and Annan[2] (my old pupils), who are the only physicians (Dr. Griffitts and perhaps one more excepted) who have adopted the new mode of practice. The rest continue to murder by rule. Nor is this all. They have confederated against me in the most cruel manner and are propagating calumnies against me in every part of the city. Dr. Currie[3] (my old friend) is now the weak instrument of their malice and prejudices. If I outlive the present calamity, I know not when I shall be safe from their persecutions. Never did I before witness such a mass of ignorance and wickedness as our profession has exhibited in the course of the present calamity. I almost wish to renounce the name of physician. Even the nod of Dr. Kuhn in his lurking hole at Bethlehem commands more respect and credit from my brethren than nearly 1,000 persons in different parts of the city who ascribe their lives to the new remedies. Our neighbor Davidson[4] died yesterday under the use of bark, laudanum, and the cold bath administered by the hands of Dr. Currie. Indeed the principal mortality of the disease now is from the doctors. Our house continues to be a hospital. Jno. Stall is stationary after 5 bleedings. Fisher was so ill as to require a 3rd bleeding in the middle of the night. My sister is drooping. Cox is better and does duty with a spirit that he never showed before. Marcus has not, like Briarius, a hundred hands, but he can turn his two hands to a hundred different things. He puts up powders, spreads blisters, and gives clysters equal to any apothecary in town. Adieu. Take care of yourself, and continue to pray for our poor devoted and desolating city. Indeed I have thought that all good Christians should *sit, walk, eat,* and even *sleep* with one hand constantly lifted up in a praying attitude to the Father of mercies to avert his judgments from us. O! that for his elect's sake he would cause the time of our sufferings to be shortened. Tell the whole village of Princeton to pray fervently and constantly for us. I have just now been sent for to visit a woman who has lost a husband, two children, and three apprentices with the fever. Adieu. Yours sincerely,

BENJN RUSH

Love as usual. Ben and Becky are well.

Addressed: Mrs: Julia Rush at Richd: Stockton's Esqr: Princeton.
MS: Josiah C. Trent, M.D., Durham, North Carolina.

[1] John Porter, physician, 91 North Sixth St.; he had been apprenticed to BR in 1778 (1793 *Directory*; BR's MS List of Apprentices). A letter from Porter to BR of 17 Sep. 1793 testifying to the effectiveness of "the new method" of treatment is printed in BR's *Account of the Yellow Fever in 1793*, p. 236-7.

[2] William Annan (d. 1797), 348 South Front St.; apprenticed to BR in 1787, he became a fellow of the College of Physicians in 1796 (1793 *Directory*; BR's MS List of Apprentices; Ruschenberger, p. 208).

[3] William Currie (1754-1828), privately trained, served as a surgeon during the Revolution and was a founding member of the College of Physicians; he had a good professional standing and wrote several medical tracts (Kelly & Burrage, *Dict. Amer. Med. Biog.*). The latter brought him into collision with BR. In the *Federal Gazette* for 20 Sep. appeared a letter from Currie declaring that there were few cases of yellow fever in the city and that most of the supposed victims suffered only from a non-infectious "common remittent fall fever." For this disorder, he went on, BR's treatment was proper, but for genuine yellow fever it was "certain death" (BR's *Account of the Yellow Fever in 1793*, p. 230-3; see also Powell, *Bring Out Your Dead*, p. 82-4, and *passim*). Currie renewed his attack some weeks later (see BR to Mrs. Rush, 1-2 Nov. 1793), and he was to figure prominently in BR's quarrel with Cobbett (BR's *Autobiography*, p. 101, and note).

[4] Probably James Davidson, shopkeeper or merchant, 84 South Third St. (1793 *Directory*; Carey, *Short Account*).

To Mrs. Rush

My dear Julia,   Philadelphia, September 22, 1793

Hitherto I have suffered by sympathy only with the distresses of my fellow citizens. But sickness and distress have at last reached our family. Jny. Stall is almost below hope. From the beginning of his disorder he has objected to taking medicine and has deceived all around him in his accounts of its operation. Fisher, who lies in the front room, is I hope a little better, but he has been in extreme danger. But our afflictions do not cease here. This morning Marcus yielded to the disease. He has been twice bled and well purged. The disease, although it occurs frequently among the blacks, has not proved fatal in a single instance under my care. Marcus lies in the shop. Jno. Alston is very ill at Mrs. Wilson's. My mother and sister both complain. We have two black nurses in the house who attend the apprentices. Peter[1] is to us now a little host. He is not only useful to us in the family but has this evening visited two patients for me. I predicted this two weeks ago to Mr. Meade when he called upon me to consult with two other physicians. I told him that one doctor was enough for one patient now, for "that the time I feared would come when the people would be glad to receive a visit from my little black boy Peter." I expected this evening to have made my own bed, but my mother has relieved me from that trouble. In this afflicting situation I hope I have not sinned nor charged God foolishly.

[674]

"If to correct me, be his will,
I'll bear it, with submission still,
A tender father, sure he proves,
And but corrects, because he loves."[2]

Two of Mrs. Hamilton's[3] maids are dead next door. Two persons will probably die at Jno. Hawkin's tonight. His wife is one of them. Mr. Lea,[4] Mr. Shippen's son-in-law, and Major James Moore,[5] my universal friend, died this day. Dr. Johnson[6] of the Dispensary died two days ago. Three and thirty were buried in the Potter's field[7] before 3 o'clock this afternoon. Thus you see that the striking passage of the funeral service of the Episcopal Church is reversed in me. In the midst of death, I am in life. But O! by how tender a thread do I now hold it. I feel as if I were in a storm at sea in an open boat without helm or compass. My only hope and refuge thou knowest, O! God, is in thee! Miss Sproat[8] the younger is said to be dying. Mrs. Hutchinson[9] and child are both living. She recovered under my care, deserted by all her husband's political and medical friends. Her expressions of gratitude to me for attending her indicated a strong and delicate mind.

I have this day kept the house, owing to the extreme heat of the weather, for I have no complaint but weakness and a little sore mouth from the mercury. But I have not been idle, having pre-scribed in the back parlor for crowds of sick people. Tomorrow I expect, if the weather be cool, to visit a few patients.

Betsey Steen's sister was very ill but is now well. I have heard nothing of Isaac Wikoff's[10] son lately. Hundreds die that we do not hear of for days afterwards.

September 23. Johnny Stall is still alive, and Mr. Fisher and Marcus are better. Alston is very ill at his lodgings. Deaths since yesterday: Miss Hartley,[11] sister to Mrs. Burdeaux;[12] B. Poult-ney;[13] Mrs. Heatley;[14] and Mrs. Young, the bookseller's wife.[15] The two last killed by bark and laudanum. All my old medical friends, except Griffitts, have deserted me in my practice. Currie, Ross,[16] Barton, and even Wistar and Johnson[17] (of the Dispensary) are disciples of Dr. Kuhn.

Adieu. I am in perfect health through unmerited divine good-ness, and am preparing to visit Alston and one or two more patients in the neighborhood. Mrs. Clymer has been confined but is better. Love as usual. Yours—yours,

BENJN RUSH

Addressed: Mrs Julia Rush at Richd Stockton Esqr Princeton.
MS: Josiah C. Trent, M.D., Durham, North Carolina.

[1] A Negro servant boy; he later caught the fever but survived; there are numerous references to him in the following letters.

[2] Source not traced.

[3] Abigail (Franks) Hamilton, widow of Andrew Hamilton, lived at 80 South Third St., which was presumably on the corner of Walnut (Keith, *Provincial Councillors*, p. 136; 1793 *Directory*). BR lived at 83 Walnut, one house from the corner of Third.

[4] Thomas Lea, a merchant who lived in South Fourth St. (1793 *Directory*; Carey, *Short Account*).

[5] A livery-stable keeper in Lombard St. (same, twice).

[6] Robert Johnson, 68 Chestnut St. (same, twice).

[7] The "Potter's Field" in Philadelphia had, since 1706, been in the open ground at Sixth and Walnut Streets later converted into Washington Square (Jackson, *Encyclo. of Phila.*, IV, 1018). In his letter of 21-22 Oct. 1793, BR mentioned seeing a tent erected for the accommodation of gravediggers in the Potter's Field, where "Upwards of 1000 persons have been buried . . . since the 1st day of August."

[8] Anne (or Nancy) Sproat, daughter of Rev. Dr. James Sproat; BR reported her death in his next letter (Carey, *Short Account*).

[9] Dr. Hutchinson's second wife, Sidney (Evans) Howell Hutchinson (DAB, under Hutchinson's name).

[10] Isaac Wikoff (d. 1814) was a merchant, 217 South Second St. (1793 *Directory*; *Inscriptions in St. Peter's Church Yard*, p. 60). His son evidently survived.

[11] Susanna Hartley (Carey, *Short Account*).

[12] The widow Burdeaux, in Spruce St., had at various times been a patient of BR's (Rush MSS., Account Books).

[13] Benjamin Poultney, probably of Poultney & Wistar, ironmongers (1793 *Directory*; Carey, *Short Account*).

[14] Harriot, wife of Charles Heatley, attorney in North Second St. (same, twice).

[15] Agnes, wife of William Young, a Scot who came to Philadelphia after the Revolution and whose shop was at 52 South Second St. (same, twice; also *Hist. Cat. St. Andrew's Soc. Phila.*, II, 372-3).

[16] Andrew Ross (d. 1823), 6 Pruan (Prune) St.; he was a founding member of the College of Physicians, but little is known of him. He was to be involved, unpleasantly if accidentally, in BR's quarrel with Cobbett. (1793 *Directory*; Ruschenberger, p. 262; BR, *Autobiography*, p. 101, note, and 369).

[17] This is curious in view of BR's mention earlier in this letter of Johnson's death.

To Mrs. Rush

My dear Julia, Philadelphia, September 23, 1793

This day at half after 12 o'clock my dear and amiable pupil Johnny Stall breathed his last. His mind for weeks before he died seemed to be prepared and composed for his fate. Upon my telling him at breakfast a few days before he was taken sick, that I did not forget him in my prayers, he modestly said, "Nor do I you, sir, in mine." He died in the highest acts of benevolence to his fellow creatures, doing his Master's work—healing the sick and relieving the distressed. Thousands who witnessed his zeal and boldness in rushing into danger lament his death. You may conceive of my opinion of his and Coxe's judgment in the present disease when I add that as soon as I was seized with the fever, I committed myself wholly to their care and charged them if I should be unable to prescribe for myself, to prescribe exclusively for me. Dr. Griffitts was at this time confined, for he is *fully* in the new opinions and practice in the prevailing epidemic.

Mr. Fisher is I hope out of danger. He is as patient in sickness as he is pleasant and kind in health. Marcus is well. I have this day visited about a dozen patients in Frederick's carriage. Two of them were Mr. B. and Mrs. Sims[1] in the country, who are infected by a maid that went out to them from their town house. They both met me in tears. Mr. Sims fell on my neck and cried aloud like a child. I soon composed their fears by assuring them that they were in no danger and by concealing from them, as far as was prudent, that they were tinctured with the disorder. Another scene of much more tenderness passed between me and a respectable Quaker family this afternoon. I passed from the front door upstairs to the bedroom of the master of this family through a train of children weeping and blessing me as I went along. I found him on the 4th day of the disease and in great danger. He had been bled by Dr. Parke only three times, and purged but once or twice. I ordered a 4th bleeding and gave him some strong mercurial purging pills which I carry with me in my pocket. I left the family with a *hope* only of his recovery. This at that time was enough. They seized the word as if it conveyed a kingdom to them.

September 24th. Thank God not only for my life and health this morning, but for the appearances of the weather. An equinoctial gale with rain would do more for our city than a thousand physicians. The disease spreads. Though all our citizens are not ill, yet no one *now* is well, for they all breathe an air nearly alike charged with the contagion. A giddiness in the head, sickness at stomach once or twice a day, pain in the back or sides are almost universal complaints in people who walk the streets or follow their usual work. O! that the time of our calamity might be shortened! The poor— the poor are everywhere the principal sufferers. I dare not complain, for all I suffer from weakness, labor, sympathy, persecution, &c., is trifling compared with what others suffer and with what I have merited. In all things, at all times, and in all places, I endeavor to give thanks. Miss Sproat is no more. Jos. Tatem[2] died in the Jerseys a few days ago. He carried the infection with him from town. Mrs. Hawkins has revived and may recover. Jno. Alston is in great danger.

Dr. Ruston has come forward with a long publication[3] on the prevailing disorder, reprobating my practice and thereby weakening the confidence of the public in the new remedies that are *generally* successful, for no more die who use them than die of pleurisies who use bleeding, or of the smallpox who submit to inoculation. It is strange that the essays upon our disorder should have come chiefly from itinerant and fugitive doctors, or from a dull and profligate usurer who has not seen a sick man these seven years.

Adieu. Love as usual. I am, my dear Julia, yours affectionately,

BENJN RUSH

P.S. I have just heard that my dear friend Dr. Griffitts is again confined. Alas! our devoted city! The followers of Kuhn still live to administer poison to our citizens. Dr. G. was a Joab in the present disease.

Addressed: Mrs Julia Rush at Richd Stockton's Esqr Princeton.
MS: Josiah C. Trent, M.D., Durham, North Carolina.

[1] This seems to be intended for a Mr. and Mrs. B. Sims, whom I am unable to identify.

[2] Joseph Tatem, tailor, 82 South Second St. (1793 *Directory*).

[3] The article by Ruston (on whom see BR's letter to him, 29 Oct. 1775) appeared in the *Federal Gazette*, 23 Sep. and was entitled "An easy method of curing the present fever prevailing in this city." Ruston's "cure" was to administer tartar emetic and tamarind water. As for bleeding in this type of fever, said Ruston, "you may almost as well, clap a knife at once, to the throat, as present a lancet to the arm of your patient."

To Mrs. Rush

My dear Julia,   Philadelphia, September 24, 1793

The post which brought your letter left town too soon after I received it to admit of my answering it by him. Since I have heard of the precautions taken at Trenton to cut off an intercourse with our city, I feel less anxious to have you at NewArk. Take lodgings at Princeton or Trenton or where you please for yourself and the children. I can advise you no further, but be assured I shall be satisfied with whatever you do. To direct your conduct, situated as we both are, would be like Kuhn, Ruston, and Logan[1] writing treatises on the yellow fever in their closets for the instruction of men who have gained a knowledge of it at the hourly risk of their lives for four or five weeks.

This day at 2 o'clock my dear boy Alston expired. I saw him but three times in a disease which required three and thirty visits. He refused to be bled for nearly a whole day because I was unable to visit him, and life and death often turn upon the application of a remedy at an hour or a moment in this ferocious disease. He caught it at his lodgings, chiefly in attending Miss Wilson,[2] to whom he was attached. He had visited but four or five patients for me in the whole course of the prevalence of the disease.

September 25. Through divine goodness I slept more last night than I have slept any one night for six weeks, and am in as good health as is compatible with the weakness of the most extreme old age. Alas! our hopes of an equinoctial storm are blasted! The sun shines, and the weather has again become warm. But God's will is done on earth as much by pestilential contagion and ignorant physicians as it is by the songs and praises of saints and angels in heaven.

Richd. must go to Mr. Frazier's[3] and submit to all the rules of his house and school. The disease increases, but as the help of man is now at an end, it is to be hoped the hour is not distant when God will make bare his arm for our deliverance. Many die now from the want of bleeders as well as doctors. Even the apothecaries begin to shut up their shops, and many are unable to procure the mercurial purges when they are prescribed as soon as is necessary. I visited a few patients yesterday and expect to visit a few this day, but O! you cannot conceive with what difficulty I climb a pair of stairs. I carry a vial of Lisbon wine with me in my pocket, and when I am faint wash my mouth with a spoonful of it. It acts as powerfully on my whole system in that way as a pint of wine in my stomach would have done at any other time. Adieu. With love as usual, I am yours sincerely,

BENJN RUSH

Deaths
Dr. Morris's widow.[4]
Mrs. Clow.[5]
Mr. Eke [*Eck*], our neighbor.
Mr. Jno. Smith and two children[6] in Chestnut Street next to Saml. Howells.[7]
Mr. Christ. Kucher and son.[8]
Dr. Linn[9] is supposed to be dying. Upward of 100 it is now be-

lieved are buried every day. *Despair* now, as well as the want of doctors, bleeders, nurses, and necessaries, carry off many.

Addressed: Mrs Julia Rush at Richd Stockton Esqr Princeton.
MS: Josiah C. Trent, M.D., Durham, North Carolina.

[1] George Logan (1753-1821), of Stenton; M.D., Edinburgh, 1779; Quaker politician, patron of agriculture, friend of Franklin and Jefferson; best remembered for his volunteer diplomatic missions in 1798 and 1810 to prevent war between the United States and foreign powers (DAB). An article by Logan on the fever appeared in the *Federal Gazette*, 23 Sep.; Logan's recommendations were not very different from BR's, though he expressed doubt about venesection.

[2] Not clearly identifiable.

[3] Rev. William Frazer (1743-1795), Scottish-born Anglican clergyman; preached in several rural New Jersey parishes from 1768; rector of St. Michael's Church, Trenton, 1788-1795, and kept a boys' school there (Hamilton Schuyler, *History of St. Michael's Church, Trenton*, Princeton, 1926, p. 133-7). Richard Rush entered this school in May 1794 to prepare for Princeton

(BR, Notes on Continental Congress, &c., vol. 3).

[4] Abigail Dorsey, widow of Dr. John Morris (Moon, *Morris Family*, II, 585-9).

[5] Presumably Mrs. Andrew Clow, wife of a merchant in South Front St. (1793 *Directory*); she is not entered in Carey's list of the dead, but Andrew Clow is.

[6] John Smith, Sr., and his son John and daughter Sarah are entered in Carey's list of the dead; he is not in the 1793 *Directory*.

[7] Samuel Howell, merchant, 54 Chestnut St. (1793 *Directory*).

[8] Christopher Kucher, sugar refiner, or "sugar baker," 88-90 North Second St., and his son Philip (same; also Carey, *Short Account*).

[9] John Linn, or Lynn, physician, 35 Walnut St. (same, twice). BR announced his death in a letter of 25-26 Sep. 1793.

To Elias Boudinot

My dear Friend,   Philadelphia, September 25, 1793

The sympathy contained in your most affectionate letter of yesterday[1] was a cordial to my soul.

HERE will I meet my *Ebenezer*,[2] for thus far hath the Lord preserved and helped me. Hitherto I have endeavored to have no will of my own as to my surviving the present calamity. I can truly say that no anxiety for my family has produced for a moment a wish for life. The widow's husband and the orphan's father I am sure will take care of them.

The disease continues to spread. In short, though all our citizens are not confined, yet from the general diffusion of the contagion through every street in the city, nobody is perfectly well. One complains of giddiness or headache, another of chills, others of pains in the back and stomach, and *all* have more or less quickness of pulse and redness or yellowness in the eyes. No words can describe the distress which pervades all ranks of people from the combined operations of fear, grief, poverty, despair, and death. More tears have been shed in my entry and in my back parlor within the last month than have been shed perhaps for years before in our city. Never can I forget the awful sight of mothers wringing their hands, fathers dumb for a while with fear and apprehension, and children weeping aloud before me, all calling upon me to hasten to the relief of their sick relations. But this is but a faint picture of the distress of our city. My labors in combating the disease have been great, and before I was precluded from a *close* and *vigilant* attention upon my patients, they were successful in 99 cases out on 100, but my principal exertions have been created by the pride, ignorance, and prejudices of my medical brethren. From the dull Dr. Kuhn down to the volatile Dr. B. Duffield[3] (Dr. Griffitts and five or six others, chiefly my old pupils, excepted), they have all combined to oppose, to depreciate, and even to slander the new remedies. Colonel Hamilton's letter[4] has cost our city several hundred inhabitants. I have not heard of a single person having recovered by the use of the West India remedies since Kuhn left the city, from which we now infer that [. . .]'s[5] family and all Kuhn's patients had nothing but common remitting fevers from *cold* instead of the malignant *contagion*. Kuhn's last printed letter[6] has added much to the mischief of his first absurd publication. But why complain of the ignorance or malice of my brethren? They are a part of the instruments of the divine displeasure against our wicked city.

> "When obedient nature knows his will
> A Doctor, or Disease, alike can kill."[7]

It is computed that 100 persons upon an average have been buried every day for the last eight or ten days. The sick suffer from the want not only of physicians, bleeders, nurses, and friends, but from the want of the common necessaries of life. Five physicians, four students of medicine, and three bleeders have died of the disorder. But the mortality falls chiefly upon the poor, who by working in the sun excite the contagion into action. Whole families have been swept away by it. Some of the wealthy are at last affected. Mr. Vanberkle,[8] Mr. Powel,[9] Mrs. Blodget, and Mr. Clymer are at present confined by it. Vanberkle is in danger. By the help of a banister I contrive to climb up about a dozen pairs of stairs every day. My milk and vegetable diet (for I loathe meat and fermented liquors), an obstinate wakefulness for nearly a week before my late indisposition, profuse night sweats, my disease, my remedies, and above all my constant labors, have reduced me to the weakness of an old man of 80. Nothing scarcely is left of what I was two months ago but my voice and my usual spirits. But in my present debilitated state my divine Master still honors me to work for him. In my parlor, on my couch, and even in my bed I prescribe for 50 to 100 people, chiefly the poor, every day. Adieu, my dear friend. Give my love to my dear aunt and to all our dear friends, and continue to pray for our distressed and desolating city as well as for your sincere and affectionate

BENJN RUSH

P.S. Tell the whole village of Elizth: town to lift up their hands and hearts to heaven "without ceasing" for us.

Addressed: Elias Boudinot Esqr: Elizabeth town New-Jersey.
MS: Historical Society of Pennsylvania, Society Collection.

[1] This letter has not been found.

[2] See I Samuel 7:12.

[3] Benjamin Duffield (1753-1799); A.B., College of Philadelphia, 1771; completed medical courses at the same, 1774; founding member, College of Physicians; attended at the Bush Hill emergency hospital, 1793; lectured privately on midwifery and other subjects, 1793-1799. BR declared that Duffield was "Kuhn's principal trainbearer," and in his *Autobiography* cited him as a shameful example of the ingratitude of pupils. (Ruschenberger, p. 221; Packard, *Hist. of Medicine in U.S.*, I, 130, 141, 337; BR to Mrs. Rush, 29-30 Sep. 1793, and to John Redman Coxe, 19 Dec. 1794; see also Powell, *Bring Out Your Dead*, p. 72-3.)

[4] Hamilton's name has been taken out of the MS with ink eradicator, but can be faintly read; the letter referred to is one of 11 Sep. praising Dr. Stevens' method of treatment (printed in BR's *Account of the Yellow Fever in 1793*, p. 214-16).

[5] This name has also been eradicated and cannot be read.

[6] A public letter of 13 Sep. to Mayor Clarkson, in which Kuhn asserted that yellow fever was still uncommon in Philadelphia, Kuhn having seen only seven cases (BR, *Account of the Yellow Fever in 1793*, p. 213-14).

[7] Source unknown.

[8] Pieter Franco van Berckel, who in 1787 succeeded his father (Pieter Johan van Berckel, first minister from the Netherlands to the United States) under the title of resident (A. J. van der Aa, *Biographisch Woordenboek der Nederlanden*, Haarlem, 1867-1878, II, 352). In the 1793 *Directory* he is listed as Francis Van Berckell, minister resident from the United Provinces, 258 High (Market) St.

[9] Samuel Powel (1738-1793), a graduate of the College of Philadelphia, 1759, and trustee, 1773-1793; traveled and lived abroad, accompanying John Morgan on his tour of Italy; mayor of Philadelphia, 1775, and again in 1789; speaker of the Pennsylvania Senate, 1792-1793; much interested in scientific agriculture, he had a country place, called Powelton, west of the Schuylkill (Moon, *Morris Family*, II, 460-86). For his death a few days later, see BR's letter of 29-30 Sep. 1793.

To Mrs. Rush

My dear Julia,   Philadelphia, September 25, 1793

Another day has been added to my life, for which I desire to be thankful. I have tottered up about a dozen pairs of stairs and prescribed for a great number of people in our back parlor. After answering letters and emptying my memorandums into my diary or journal of the disorder, I have sat down for two evenings past and employed an hour or two before bedtime in putting up medicines for the poor. This is a new and humble employment for me, considering how many more important duties I am called to perform, but I take great delight in it. "The poor," said Dr. Boerhaave, "are my best patients, because God is their paymaster." I wish at all times to be under the influence of this heavenly and benevolent sentiment.

September 26th. The day lowers! O! that the windows of heaven might be opened and floods of rain be poured upon our city. It would at least *weaken* the contagion of the fever which now fills every street in the city. Perhaps nothing but frost (without an extraordinary interposition of divine power) will finally and totally *destroy* it. I received a most comfortable letter from our Uncle Elias Boudinot yesterday, to which I have written an answer to be sent to this day's post. One praying and believing friend at the present juncture is worth a city full of friends who know not God and obey not the gospel. I am just preparing to set off for Mr. Meredith's, who is alarmed with the fear of a relapse. I shall take Mr. Vanberkle in my way, who is very ill. He neglected himself till the 5th day, believing from Kuhn and Currie's publications that he had nothing but a common fever. Hundreds have been sacrificed by this mistake. We have but *one*, we cannot have but *one* fever in town. The contagion of the yellow fever like Aaron's rod swallows up the seeds of all other diseases. We might as well talk of two suns or two moons shining upon our globe as of two different kinds of fevers now in our city. Young Cattle[1] from the Jersey College is very ill at Mrs. McCall's.[2] It is unfortunate for him that he left the Jersey College to come into one of the most infected streets in town. Good Dr. White stands to his post, as does Dr. Blackwell. Mr. Pilmore is everywhere where there is sickness or distress. Old Mr. Cottringer[3] died this morning. Few old people survive the disease, even with the best attendance from nurses and physicians. Dr. Linn died yesterday—under the care of bark and wine doctors. James' master, Mr. Chandler,[4] who lived in the house with him, is infected. I prescribed for him last night in my back parlor, but if the first remedies do not cure him, I fear he will be very ill, and I cannot attend him at his lodgings. Mr. Fisher continues to mend. He was five days in the maw of the Lion. Five copious bleedings and large doses of the purging medicine saved him. I have heard since the death of Alston that the puking which terminated his life was occasioned by his drinking a pint of cold water immediately after taking a dose of medicine. Before this, Mr. Coxe says, he was in little danger. Such accidents must often happen where the sick are nursed by blacks ignorant of their business and frequently asleep or out of the room. Marcus continues to mend. I have just seen the sexton of the Quaker meeting, who assures me that he [thinks?][5] upwards of an 100 have been buried daily for some time past throughout the city, and that the mortality increases. O! that God would rend the heavens and come down! and save our guilty city from utter desolation! for vain—vain now is the help of man. The Negroes are everywhere submitting to the disorder. Richd. Allen, who has led their van, is very ill. If the disorder should continue to spread among them, then will the measure of our sufferings be full. Adieu. Continue to pray for us, and for none more earnestly than your ever faithful friend,

BENJN RUSH

P.S. Love—love—love as usual to friends, relations, and the dear children.

Addressed: Mrs Julia Rush at Richd Stockton's Esqr Princeton.
MS: Josiah C. Trent, M.D., Durham, North Carolina.

[1] I.e., Cattell. He recovered. There is no record of his attending the College at Princeton.
[2] Lydia, widow of George McCall, importer, at 107 Walnut St.; she was Cattell's grandmother (1793 *Directory*; *Hist. Cat. St. Andrew's Soc. Phila.* [1],

238-9; BR to Mrs. Rush, 3-4 Oct. 1793).
[3] John Cotringer (Carey, *Short Account*).
[4] Not further identified.
[5] Obscured by seal.

To Mrs. Rush

My dear Julia, Philadelphia, September 26, 1793

This day at 12 o'clock my last apprentice, Jno. Coxe, went home with the prevailing fever, and at 2 my poor dear sister, overcome with fatigue and anxiety, retreated to her bed, where she is very ill. My mother cannot long keep up. She left me early in the evening to pass three or four gloomy hours in the back parlor by myself. Marcus is now sitting dull and silent with me. I take up my pen to chase away melancholy, but O! a thousand distressing scenes crowd upon me and offer themselves as subjects for my letter. O my! —— But I will not infect you with any portion of the gloom which now oppresses every power of my soul. It is the Lord—let him do what seemeth him right. *Shall a living* man complain for the punishment of his sins.

Dr. Redman this day yielded to the disorder. He had adopted the new remedies and used them with success in one of his old families. I paid him a visit this morning and think him in great danger.

Mr. Powel is ill over Skuilkill. I visited him this afternoon. Mrs. Powel is at her brother Richard's,[1] from whence she sends expresses twice a day to inquire after her husband. This is but one of many, many instances in which this savage disease has separated man and wife. Mr. VanBerkle is I hope better.

September 27. The sky again lowers, and a few drops of rain have fallen. Thousands revive at the sight. I have been much comforted by reading the 121st psalm this morning, and hope I shall be strengthened by it for the labors of the day. My poor dear sister continues very ill. I now see clearly the reason why providence has confined me so much by sickness and weakness to my house. Hundreds more, especially of the poor, have been relieved by my advice at home whom I could not have visited and who would otherwise probably have died. Dr. Wistar has published a history of his recovery.[2] It is (if not designed) yet certainly *calculated* to injure me and to create doubts as to the efficacy of the new remedies. You see I am in the situation of the French Republic, surrounded and invaded by new as well as old enemies, without any other allies than a few of my old pupils, who are too little known to give credit to any innovation in medicine. But I am unmoved by the dull and wicked confederacy, having resolved to stick to my principles, my practice, and my patients, through divine support, to the last extremity. It is possible they may drive me from the city if I survive the present calamity, but I hope I can now be happy anywhere or in any employment, wielding the plow with as much composure of mind as I now wield the lancet, or teaching a country school with as much pleasure as I have formerly taught medicine. With love as usual, I am, my dear Julia, yours sincerely,

BENJN RUSH

Addressed: Mrs: Julia Rush at Richd: Stockton Esqr: Princeton.
MS: Josiah C. Trent, M.D., Durham, North Carolina.

[1] Elizabeth (Willing) Powel (1742/1743-1830) and her brother Richard Willing (Moon, *Morris Family*, II, 486-7; Keith, *Provincial Councillors*, p. [90]).

[2] In Bache's *General Advertiser*, 26 Sep.; Wistar "believed many persons had been supposed to have been cured of the disease, who had never had it," and he concluded without deciding which remedies were best. BR in a letter of 4 Oct. charged Wistar with failure to give proper credit to the mercurial purges Wistar himself had taken, and the latter defended himself in a reply dated 4 Nov. (BR, *Account of the Yellow Fever in 1793*, p. 235-6; Rush MSS, XXXVI, 116-18). Frequent references in the following letters make it clear that BR considered Wistar's conduct peculiarly treacherous and unkind.

To Mrs. Rush

My dear Julia,   Philadelphia, September 29, 1793

I fear you have suffered some anxiety in consequence of not hearing from me by yesterday's post. It was occasioned by my being hurried over Skuilkill to see poor Mr. Powel early in the morning—the *time* I had allotted to write to you. I found him very ill. The neglect of a 4th bleeding by the young doctor who attended him had produced delirium and a train of alarming symptoms. Yesterday was spent in trying to recover him by Dr. Griffitts and myself, but alas! to no purpose. This morning at 6 o'clock he expired in a small room in a small farmhouse with nobody with him but Dr. Griffitts, the young doctor who stayed constantly with him, and an old Negro coachman of Mr. Hill's.[1] Mrs. Powel is at her brother Richard's.

My poor dear sister continues in extreme danger. She had the disease three days before she would take a dose of medicine or submit to be bled. This infatuation with respect to the existence or danger of the disorder seems to be one of its most characteristic symptoms. I fear the issue of this night. She is perfectly composed and prepared for her dissolution. O! the pain which attends under all circumstances the rupture of the ties of nature! I hope I shall be supported under this heavy affliction, if it should please God to try me with it. My mother I fear would not survive it.

I have this day paid one-and-thirty visits and feel myself no ways weakened by them. On the contrary, the exercise of my body and mind in the duties of my profession adds daily to the vigor and activity of both. Never was the healing art so truly delightful to me! and never had I more reason to be thankful than I now have for the honor God has done me in giving me health enough to renew my intercourse with my patients.

Dr. Redman is better. He has been cured by the new remedies. John Cox, after two bleedings and two purges, this day visited several patients for me. Ed Fisher has taken his seat at our table and in a day or two expects to enter upon duty. He is perfectly well and in good spirits. Dr. Say[2] is still in danger but with some favorable symptoms. Dr. Harris[3] and Dr. Saml. Duffield[4] are confined. The former uses the new, the latter Dr. Kuhn's remedies.

Mr. VanBerkle I hope is in a safe way after seven bleedings. Young Cattle is still ill but has no bad symptoms. I have bled him twice this day.

The mortality on Friday and Saturday last was less by one half than it had been for 10 days before, owing I believe partly to the more general use of the new remedies. The people rule here in medicine as well as government. They have by their clamors forced even Ben Duffield to adopt them. This man has spent whole weeks in abusing those remedies and their advocates in every part of the town. He is Dr. Kuhn's principal trainbearer. Dr. Parke has adopted the new remedies and has since saved many lives. The most unkind attacks I have had from my brethren, however, have come from Dr. Wistar and Dr. Currie, formerly my most cordial friends.

September 30th. My poor sister is still alive, and I hope with some symptoms which are favorable. The disease is indeed a most formidable one in all its forms. No wonder it requires medicines that possess the strength of Hercules to subdue it. I continue to mend, and through divine goodness even to thrive upon labor, care, persecution, and a milk and vegetable diet. The sky again lowers. O! that that God who created winds, rain, and hoar frost would send them among us to chase away or destroy the pestilential contagion. Adieu. Love as usual. Yours sincerely,

BENJN RUSH

Addressed: Mrs: Julia Rush at Richd Stockton Esqr: Princeton.
MS: Josiah C. Trent, M.D., Durham, North Carolina.

[1] Perhaps Henry Hill (see BR to Montgomery, 10 Dec. 1784); but there are numerous Hills listed in the 1793 *Directory*.

[2] Benjamin Say (1755-1813); said to have been trained at the University of Pennsylvania; a founding member of the College of Physicians; active with BR in numerous humanitarian causes (DAB).

[3] Robert Harris (d. 1815), on whose training I have no information; military surgeon and founding member of College of Physicians (Ruschenberger, p. 232).

[4] Samuel Duffield (1732-1814), M.B., College of Philadelphia, 1768; a founding member of the College of Physicians, and an active member and officer of the Philosophical Society from 1768 (Ruschenberger, p. 221).

To Mrs. Rush

My dear Julia,   Philadelphia, September 30, 1793

You write like a spectator only of the distresses of our city. What is a little furniture, a few clothes, a whole city, or even the globe itself compared with one human life? Had I believed that certain death would have been the consequence to myself and the whole family of taking Johnny Stall and Ed Fisher into the house, it would have been my duty to have done it. Neither of them had any other home, for Mr. Stall[1] (where Fisher lodged) had fled into the country, and had I shut my doors upon them, they must have perished in the streets. Remember, my dear creature, the difference between the law and the gospel. The former only commands us "to love our neighbors as ourselves," but the latter bids us love them *better* than ourselves. "A *new* commandment I give unto you, that ye love one another, even as I *have loved* you."[2] Had I not believed in the full import of that divine and sublime text of Scripture, I could not have exposed myself with so little concern, nay with so much pleasure, for five weeks past to the contagion of the prevailing fever. I did not dare to desert my post, and I believed even *fear* for a moment to be an act of disobedience to the gospel of Jesus Christ.

My poor dear sister, after having hung over the grave by the single thread of a cobweb for twenty-four hours, is I hope this evening a little better, but far, very far, from being out of danger. My mother still complains, but will not be bled or take the mercurial purges. John Cox is well and has visited several patients for me this day. Ed. Fisher expects to take the field again in two or three days. Dr. Redman is out of danger, and my much-beloved and *tried* friend Dr. Say, after lying for two days nearly as low as my sister, this day has exhibited very hopeful signs of recovery. Wm. Hall's[3] only son has escaped death by *six*, and Master Jno. Adams[4] at Mr. Ketland's by *seven* bleedings. The latter asked politely two days ago for you and John and Richard, and concluded by saying that "he should always love me like a father." Four of our neighbor Cresson's[5] family owe their lives under God to the free use of the new remedies. They are full of affection and gratitude to our family. In short, to tell you of all the people who have been bled and purged out of the grave in our city would require a book nearly as large as the Philadelphia directory. Two of Thos. Bradford's sons[6] are ill and will, to use a Scotch phrase, swim for life. His father-in-law, Mr. Fisher,[7] is no more. Jno. Hawkins died this evening, suffocated with the noxious effluvia of a small room in which four persons besides himself were ill with the fever at the same time with himself. His wife, who was ill under more favorable circumstances of air and nursing, recovered.

I have this day paid three and thirty visits. One of them was to Eb. Hazard,[8] who is very ill but I hope in no immediate danger. I gain strength every day, but I use it with caution. I walk to no patients but to those who are in the neighborhood.

October 1st. My dear sister is still alive. Her recovery is barely possible. The sky again lowers, but alas! I fear we shall have no rain. The mortality yesterday was very great. O! that God would arise and for his great, great name's sake shorten the days of our calamity. What a bitter thing must *sin* be to deserve even such a punishment as a destroying pestilence! But how many more awful punishments have been inflicted upon and await it. Adieu. Love as usual. Yours affectionately,

BENJN RUSH

Addressed: Mrs: Julia Rush at Richd: Stockton's Esqr Princeton.
MS: Josiah C. Trent, M.D., Durham, North Carolina.

[1] Probably John Stall, who kept a boarding house at 72 North Third St. (1793 *Directory*).

[2] Matthew 5:43, &c.; John 13:34.

[3] William Hall (1752-1831), 51 High (Market) St., one of the proprietors of the *Penna. Gazette*; his wife, mentioned a few days later, was the former Jane Trenchard (1793 *Directory*; *Hist. Cat. St. Andrew's Soc. Phila.* [I], 188-90; BR to Mrs. Rush, 3-4 Oct. 1793).

[4] Not further identified.

[5] James Cresson, lumber merchant, 70 South Third St. (1793 *Directory*; BR's *Account of the Yellow Fever in 1793*, p. 267).

[6] Thomas Bradford had three sons, none of whom died in the epidemic; one of the sons who was infected was Thomas, Jr. (BR to Elias Boudinot, 2 Oct. 1793), who became a well-known lawyer (S. S. Purple, "Genealogy of . . . William Bradford," *N.Y. Geneal. and Biog. Rec.*, IV [1873], 187).

[7] Samuel Fisher, hatter, 27 High (Market) St., father of Mary, with whom BR had been in love in earlier days (1793 *Directory*; Carey, *Short Account*).

[8] On his case and its outcome, see letter to Mrs. Rush, 3-4 Oct. 1793 and note; also 7-8 Oct. 1793.

To Mrs. Rush

My dear Julia,   Philadelphia, October 1, 1793

This day at 3 o'clock my dear sister breathed her last. She spoke yesterday with great joy of the love and goodness of God, and repeated several passages from the Psalms suitable to her situation. Her last words to me last night at 10 o'clock were: "A thousand and a thousand thanks to you, my dear brother." Soon after this she became delirious and said little that could be connected or heard. She has died a martyr to the cause of humanity. Hundreds will remember her zeal, her sympathy, and her tears who have come to me for relief. A few weeks ago it was proposed to her to leave town. "No." said she. "My life is of no consequence to me or the public. I will stay here and take care of my brother. His life may be useful to many." Never did kindness, affection, or friendship rise higher than hers have done to me during the whole of our late connection with each other. She invigorated me by her conversation and rendered my evenings a contrast to the gloomy labors of the day. The separation was indeed a most painful one. But it has pleased God to support me under it. In half an hour after she died, I got into my carriage and visited several patients, for the King's business requires fidelity as well as haste. She was buried this evening in Dr. Sproat's churchyard near her two children. Marcus and Peter, with I believe Billy Grey, followed the hearse to the grave. The coffin was a very plain one, for we had all agreed in case of our deaths to be buried without expense and to give the difference between a plain and a mahogany coffin to the poor. Hereafter (if I survive the present calamity), when we have less distress from poverty in our city and I have the command of more cash, I will preserve her name and her virtues by a handsome tombstone.[1] In mentioning the name of cash, I cannot help adding that great distress pervades our city from the want of it. Provisions are high, and no service can be procured for the sick but at an immense expense. The price of bleeding is 7/6, and of nursing three dollars and three and a half a day. A man of an handsome income whom I advised a few days ago to send to the apothecary's for a dose of the mercurial medicine told me that he could not do it from the want of money, and begged I would send him a dose of it from my shop. Friendship is nearly banished from our city. A few (Quakers chiefly) act upon a forlorn hope as committee men to provide for the poor at Bush hill.[2] They have performed wonderful exploits of fortitude and humanity, and hitherto none of them that I have heard of have submitted to the disease.

My mother droops, but not so much as she did yesterday. She bears the death of my dear, dear sister with great resignation and fortitude. Ah! why did I mention her name again? My heart has flown into the coffin with her.

October 2nd, 1793. Through divine mercy, I am in good health after a comfortable and refreshing night's sleep. The sky lowers and the wind blows. My heart revives at the prospect of a change in the weather. Yesterday was a very mortal day. Pray now, my dear Julia, not only for my life, but that I may be firm, unshaken, immovable, and always abounding in the work of the Lord. I enjoy uncommon peace and composure of mind, for which I desire to be very thankful. Adieu. God reigns, let the Earth rejoice [. . .][3] is an administration of love and mercy for it [. . .][4] and died for all the [*Remainder of page torn off.*]

Addressed: Mrs: Julia Rush at Richd: Stockton's Esqr: Princeton.

MS (signature and portion of text missing): Josiah C. Trent, M.D., Durham, North Carolina.

[1] BR copied his very fitting epitaph for Mrs. Wallace's tomb into his Commonplace Book; see *Autobiography*, p. 235.

[2] Bush Hill, north of the city (now at Spring Garden between Seventeenth and Eighteenth Streets), was the imposing residence of William Hamilton, where Vice-President Adams had been living and which was appropriated by the city (Hamilton being absent) for use as a hospital during the emergency (Jackson, *Encyclo. of Phila.*, II, 354-6, with cut of the mansion). J. H. Powell, in *Bring Out Your Dead*, gives detailed and highly interesting accounts of affairs at the Bush Hill hospital and of the heroic work of Mayor Clarkson's emergency committee.

[3] MS torn; two words missing.

[4] Six or seven words missing.

To Elias Boudinot

My dear Friend,   Philadelphia, October 2, 1793

May heaven reward the piety and benevolence of your fellow citizens at Elizabeth town! Perhaps it may be difficult to convey your charity in the form of provisions to our poor. A little cash sent to the Mayor or to the setting committee of the city would be much more acceptable. Hundreds suffer from the want of it, and I am sorry to say that most of the former sources of charity in cash are dried up or carried into the country. There is little credit given now for anything. Every service to the sick is purchased at a most extravagant price. The price of bleeding is 7/6, and nurses' wages are 3 and 3½ dollars per day. Families who lived by the daily labor of journeymen or day laborers suffer greatly from the death of the persons by whom alone their daily wants were supplied. My heart has been rent a thousand times in witnessing distress from that cause as well as from sickness. I have in vain endeavored to relieve it. The resources of a prince would not have relieved one half of it.

To my labors out of my own house it hath pleased God to add a heavy domestic affliction. Yesterday my dear Sister Wallace breathed her last. She had previously weakened her constitution (naturally delicate) by great fatigue in nursing me and waiting upon the poor who crowded my house at all hours of the day and night. She had moreover been indisposed three days before she would consent to be bled or to take medicine. Her illness was short but very violent. She died as she had lived for nine years past, believing and rejoicing in God her Saviour. Her last words to me were: "A thousand and a thousand thanks to you, my dear brother." The separation was indeed a most painful one. She was my friend, my nurse—nay more, she was to me a kind of guardian angel. Her tenderness and solicitude for my health and life, and her exertions to preserve both, exceed all description. *My heart descended into the grave with her.*

Continue, my dear friend, to bear me in your mind in your addresses to the throne of Grace. My labors and my distresses would be severe indeed did I not feel them as coming from the hand of a friend who sticketh closer than a brother or a sister. My health improves, and I daily pay between 30 and 40 visits to sick people. The disease still spreads and (from the ignorance or want of physicians, nurses, &c.) with very great mortality. We look and pray with great anxiety for rain or frost, from both of which we expect relief. Two of T. Bradford's sons have been very ill. One of them, Thomey, is I hope out of danger. Eb. Hazard is in jeopardy. Mr. VanBerkle is safe after seven bleedings, so are Mr. Saml. Meredith and Mrs. Clymer after four. Colonel Hamilton's remedies are now as unpopular in our city as his funding system is in Virginia or North Carolina. But alas! there are not physicians or bleeders enough in our city to apply the new remedies to a tenth part of the people who require them in *time* or *manner* to do effectual service.

Adieu, my dear friend. With love to my dear aunt and Cousin Susan, I am yours very affectionately,

BENJN RUSH

Addressed: Elias Boudinot Esqr: at Elizabeth town New Jersey.
MS: Historical Society of Pennsylvania, Society Collection.

To Mrs. Rush

My dear Julia,   Philadelphia, October 2nd, 1793

From the derangement of the post office, I do not receive your letters now until two or three days after they are written. Yours of the 27th comforted me very much, as it discovered a mind resigned to the divine will and faith in God's promises. Your account of my dear John gave me great pleasure. Give my love to him, and tell him to continue to merit the character you have given him. I dare not think much of the children; hence I seldom mention their names. At present they have no property in me, and I scarcely dare to call them mine. Ah! will the time ever come? But I am done. To me belongs now nothing but the present moment. Nor do I repine at it. On the contrary, I wish to rejoice in the honor God has conferred upon me in making me in any degree useful to my fellow creatures. My account of the efficacy of the new remedies is strictly true where patients are well attended, nursed, and accommodated, but this alas! is *now* seldom the case. The declaration has done good.[1] It begat confidence and has saved many thousand lives. Dr. Currie has recanted in this evening's paper and gives full credit to bleeding and purging in the *yellow* fever.[2] His and Kuhn's mistakes have cost our city many hundred lives.

My dear mother has passed a tolerable day, more composed than I expected. In riding up Arch Street this morning, I cast a look at the grave of my dear, dear sister. If I survive the present calamity, I will adorn it with healing plants and water them with my tears. She died in the highest acts of kindness and benevolence to her fellow creatures.

October 3rd. Here will I erect my Ebenezer. Hitherto hath the Lord preserved me. The last six weeks of my life include the mercies and miracles of a century in other times. My health improves daily, and I now walk up a pair of stairs without halting to rest or without the aid of a banister. I have had no merit in any of my exertions, for I serve a Master whom I am afraid of offending and who has claims upon me infinitely beyond ten thousand lives. After this declaration I need not tell you how much I startle at the proposition of retiring from the present scenes of danger and distress. I have given you full credit for having never advised it. It would have lessened my respect for you forever. I yesterday received a kind letter from Susan, which I have answered. The sympathy and prayers of my relations have been very comfortable to me. Adieu. With love as usual, I am, my dear, dear Julia, yours very affectionately,

BENJN RUSH

Addressed: Mrs: Julia Rush at Richard Stockton Esqr: Princeton.
MS: Josiah C. Trent, M.D., Durham, North Carolina.

[1] I am unable to determine which of BR's frequent communications to the papers this refers to; perhaps to a reply to Dr. Stevens, dated 17 Sep., which BR concluded by saying that, with proper therapy and nursing, the disease would soon be reduced, "in point of danger and mortality, to a level with a common cold" (*Account of the Yellow Fever in 1793*, p. 223-5).

[2] Currie's retraction was actually very equivocal; he approved BR's treatment for "the prevailing epidemic," but denied, by implication, that BR had been treating cases of *yellow fever* (same, p. 241-2).

To John R. B. Rodgers[1]:
An Account of the Prevailing Epidemic

My dear Friend,   Philadelphia, October 3d, 1793

In compliance with your request, I set down at a late hour and after a busy day to give you a short account of the origin, symptoms, and treatment of the fever which has prevailed with so much mortality in our city for the last six weeks.

I shall begin by observing that I have satisfactory documents to prove that the disease was generated in our city. To suppose, because the yellow fever is an epidemic of the West-Indies and because it seldom occurs in North-America, that it can exist among us only by importation, is as absurd as to suppose that the hurricanes which are so common in the West-Indies, and which occur here only once in twenty or thirty years, are all imported from that country.

The disease attacks in a variety of ways, according to the habit and predisposition of the patient or the nature and force of the exciting cause. It sometimes comes on in the form of a regular quotidian or tertian. Many are indisposed for two or three days with headache and pains in the back, sides, or bones, without much perceptible fever. But in a majority it attacks with chills, headache, sickness or vomiting, and severe pains in the limbs or back. The pulse in this state of the disease, since the 10th day of September, has generally been full and tense, the tongue whitish and moist, the eyes red, the pupils dilated, the urine high-colored, the thirst great, and the skin hot and dry. These symptoms remit every day

[694]

or every other day, and from the tertian type, which is its original and natural form, a recovery or death generally happens in acute cases on the 3d, 5th, or 7th days. It attacks all ages. Even young children are not exempted from it, but it is most acute and most mortal in young persons between fourteen and twenty-five.

Before the 10th of September, I found strong purges of calomel and jalap alone, given on the first day of the disease, sufficient to conquer it in most cases.[2] They brought away large quantities of green, dark-colored, or black bile of a most fetid and acrid nature. The pulse, which in the warm weather was weak and low, rose with every evacuation. The skin likewise, which remained dry under the most powerful sudorifics, became moist under the use of those active remedies.

Since the 10th of September, I have found bleeding, in addition to the mercurial purges, to be necessary in nineteen cases out of twenty. The pulse, the appearance of the blood, the spontaneous hemorrhages, and the weather (exclusive of the stimulus of the contagion) all indicated the use of the lancet. At first I found the loss of ten or twelve ounces of blood sufficient to subdue the pulse, but I have been obliged, gradually, as the season advanced, to increase the quantity to sixty, seventy, and even eighty ounces, and in most cases with the happiest effects. I have observed the most speedy convalescence where the bleeding has been most profuse, and as a proof that it has not been carried to excess, I have observed in no one instance the least inconvenience to succeed it.

I have bled in three cases where I have seen incipient petechiae,[3] and in each case with success. I was warranted in this bold practice, not only by the tension of the pulse, but by a precedent for it which I recollected in the works of Dr. De Haen[4] of Vienna.

I bleed not only in the exacerbations of the fever, but likewise in its remissions and intermissions, where I find a low, slow, but corded pulse. I have recovered two patients with this pulse in whom it beat less than 50 strokes in a minute.

On every day of the disease, after giving the mercurial medicine, I prescribe a purge. Castor oil, salts, cremor tartar, sulphur, and clysters answer in most cases, but in some I have been obliged to have recourse to calomel and gamboge in moderate doses.[5] I was led to purge every day, not only by recollecting the advantages of that practice in the yellow fever of 1762 in carrying off the re-accumulated bile, but by observing the disease in all cases to attack a weak or previously disordered part of the body. The purging creates an artificial weak part, which, by inviting a determination of the fluids to the bowels, prevents those effusions in the brain, stomach, bowels, liver, and lungs which bring on death.

I have in nearly every case for the three last weeks rejected bark, wine, and laudanum in the first stage of the disorder, even though the most perfect intermission of the fever took place.[6] Nor do I conceive those medicines to be necessary in the convalescent state of the disease. Mild and nourishing diet restores the strength much sooner than the most powerful tonics. I have reason to believe laudanum to be poison when given with an active or corded pulse in this fever.

The next articles to purging and bleeding in my materia medica are cool air and cool drinks. I often direct the head to be bathed and the hands and face to be washed with cold water. Toast and water, balm tea, lemonade, tamarind water, barley water, and apple water are the common drinks of my patients. The less they eat in the first stage of the disorder, the better. As soon as the pulse is reduced, I indulge them in wine whey, bread, or roasted apples, or mush in milk, chicken, beef, mutton, or veal broth, coffee and tea with buttered toast, and weak chocolate. I forbid the use of animal food until they are able to walk about. Cleanliness is advised in every stage of the disorder, with gentle exercise and country air to complete the cure.

In those few cases where the disease comes on with typhoid or typhus symptoms, I recommend the common remedies for those states of fever.

If sufficient bleeding and purging have been omitted in the beginning of the disorder, and hemorrhages, with petechiae, a low pulse, and a black vomiting, have come on, little can be done. The ceremonies of bark, clysters, and the cold bath may be performed in such cases, but I have heard of no instance in which they have done any service.

I think I have seen blisters afford relief in local determinations to the head, breast, and stomach, after sufficient evacuations have been used.

Where a troublesome vomiting does not yield to bloodletting, I know of no remedies equal to a tablespoonful of sweet milk given every half hour, or to weak camomile tea.

Where a dull pain in the bowels attends with a full or corded pulse, I have prescribed clysters of cold water with evident advantage. Where flatulency attends, I prescribe camomile tea or weak brandy and water, provided the pulse be sufficiently reduced.

By means of the remedies before-mentioned, I think I was the unworthy instrument in the hands of a kind Providence of recovering *more* than ninety-nine out of an hundred of my patients before my late indisposition. A number died during the few days of my confinement, from the want of well-timed bleeding and purging. Since my recovery, the disease has become more violent and obstinate, and some have died under my care from my inability, from weakness and occasional returns of my fever, to be early and punctual in my attendance upon them; for recovery often depends upon the application of the remedies, not only on a *certain* day, but frequently at a *certain* hour. The concentration of the contagion in every part of the city moreover has increased the difficulty of curing the disease, for it constantly counteracts the use of the remedies which are intended to abstract stimulus; hence we observe (other circumstances being equal) there is most mortality where there is most contagion. The delays in procuring bleeders, and the ignorance or neglect of nurses, added to some other circumstances too gloomy to be mentioned, have contributed very much of late to increase the mortality of the disorder. But with punctual and skillful medical assistance, good nursing, and airy rooms, I am still of the opinion that this disease is as much under the power of medicine as the measles or influenza.

The newspapers have informed you how much the opinions and practice I have delivered in this letter have been opposed by many of the physicians of our city. They first called the prevailing epidemic the jail fever. They might as well have called it the smallpox. They have declared that we have two distinct fevers in town— the one a putrid yellow fever and the other a common remittent. It would not have been more absurd to have asserted that we have two suns and two moons shining upon our globe. What makes this mistake the more inexcusable is, the common remitting fever, which has been confounded with the present highly contagious epidemic, has not been observed as usual in the suburbs or in the neighborhood of the city.

But the mistakes of some of my brethren have not ended here. Where the disease has made its chief impression on the head, it has been called the internal dropsy of the brain. Where it has attacked the throat, as it has done in some mild cases, it has been called an angina maligna. Where it has attacked the sides, it has been called a pleurisy, and in one person in whom it first affected the bowels, it was treated as a bilious colic. The disorder in this case terminated in a black vomiting and death on the third day.[7]

The success of the new remedies has at last created such a clamor in their favor that most of our physicians have been forced to adopt them. They bleed however as yet sparingly, and purge after the first day only with lenient physic. Some of them blend wine, bark, and laudanum with them. They might as well throw water and oil at the same time upon fire in order to extinguish it.

I must here pay a tribute of respect to the memory of my much-loved friend Dr. Penington, who adopted the new remedies as soon as they were mentioned to him. His expanded mind was not cast in a common mold. It vibrated in unison with truth the moment it came in contact with it. My excellent and judicious friend Dr. Griffitts was likewise an early and decided friend to plentiful purging and bleeding. Such of my former pupils as are settled in this city recommend them, and I hear from all quarters with great success.

It was extremely unfortunate that the new remedies were ever connected with *my* name. I have no other merit than that of having early adopted and *extended* a mode of treating the disorder which I had learned in the year 1762 from my first preceptor in medicine, Dr. Redman, and which is strongly recommended by Hillary,[8] Mosely,[9] Mitchell,[10] Kirby,[11] and many other writers upon this fever. In my first address to the public, I acknowledged that I received the first hints of the safety and efficacy of jalap and mercury in this disorder in the military hospitals in the year 1777, and from a description of a disease nearly related to ours in an East India publication.

In the use of all my remedies, I have in this disease repudiated names and been governed only by the CONDITION OF THE SYSTEM.

I am indebted to Dr. Sydenham,[12] as well as to my own observations, for the decided manner in which I have rejected the idea of a common remittent in our city. I have been told that by propagating this opinion I terrify my patients. Perhaps I do, but I save them by their fears, for I excite in them at once a speedy application for help and a faithful obedience to all my prescriptions. Universal truth is universal interest, and falsehood and misery always go hand in hand. The opinion which has been published by some of our physicians, that we have now a mild and a malignant fever in our city, has led all those people in whom the fever has come on in an insidious form to neglect themselves for several days under the idea that they had nothing but a common fall fever, and from this deception I believe hundreds have perished by the disorder.

I cannot conclude this letter without lamenting further that several publications from men who had never seen the disorder, or who had seen only a few cases of it, have contributed very much to distract the public mind—to lessen a confidence in mercurial purges and bleeding—and to produce an indiscriminate use of general remedies without any respect to the state of the system, and thereby to add to the mortality of the disease.

Adieu, my dear friend. I shall only add my prayers that your city may be preserved from the calamities which now afflict ours, and that you may never know, from experience, the labors, the anxiety, the deep domestic distress, and the calumnies which for six weeks past have been the portion of your sincere friend and former preceptor in medicine,

BENJAMIN RUSH

Printed: Federal Gazette (Philadelphia), 7 October 1793.

[1] John Richardson Bayard Rodgers (1757-1833) graduated at the College of New Jersey, 1775, and served as a military surgeon, 1779-1783; M.B., University of the State of Pennsylvania, 1784, and M.D., Edinburgh, 1785; a founding member of the College of Physicians; professor of midwifery at Columbia, 1792-1808; trustee of the College of Physicians and Surgeons, N.Y., 1807-1811, 1820-1822. BR was fond of Rodgers, who was not only an old pupil but the son of an old friend, John Rodgers, D.D. To Rodgers BR later directed his inquiry (see letter of 16 Oct. 1797) about a post on the Columbia medical faculty. Rodgers' letters to BR are in Rush MSS, xxv. (Alumni Records, Secretary's Office, Princeton Univ.; Ruschenberger, p. 261; Thomas, *Columbia Univ. Officers and Alumni*, p. 19, 22, 31, 81.) The present letter was written to relieve BR of the "large and frequent demands from country practitioners for information respecting the prevailing fever" (to Mrs. Rush, 3-4 Oct. 1793). It is the best available epitome of his theory and practice in the epidemic.

[2] Note by BR: "Each purge consists of ten grains of calomel and fifteen of jalap. One should be given every six hours until four or five large evacuations are procured from the bowels."

[3] "Red or purple spots on the skin, which frequently appear in the small-pox, &c." (*Quincy's Lexicon*, N.Y., 1802).

[4] Anton de Haen (1704-1776), a pioneer in the use of the clinical thermometer (Mettler, *Hist. of Medicine*, p. 312). BR quotes his *Ratio medendi in nosocomio practico*, Vienna, 1758-1773, in *Account of the Yellow Fever in 1793*, p. 271.

[5] Note by BR: "Each dose consists of two or three grains of calomel, and two grains of gamboge, made into a pill with a little flour and common syrup. A dose should be given two or three times a day, so as to procure large evacuations from the bowels."

[6] Note by BR: "The Bark has been recommended as a preventative of the fever. However proper it might have been during the warm weather, I am satisfied that it is not so now. So universally is the contagion diffused, through every part of the city, that out of a great number of persons in apparent good health, whose pulses I have examined, I have met with only two in whom they were not fuller and quicker than natural. In two old persons in good health, between 70 and 80, the pulse beat between ninety and an hundred strokes in a minute. I have found this preternatural fulness and quickness in the pulses of black, as well as of white people; also in a woman who had the yellow fever in 1762. This state of the pulse cannot be ascribed to fear,

for that passion *weakens* it. The only preventatives that experience warrants are a temperate diet, the loss of a little blood, and keeping the bowels gently open. To these should be added, great caution in avoiding fatigue, the hot sun, and the night air."

[7] Note by BR: "One of these gentlemen urged in a consultation as an objection to plentiful bleeding that there were only TEN POUNDS of blood in the human body."

[8] William Hillary, M.D. (d. 1763), student under Boerhaave, practised at Bath, in Barbados, and in London (DNB). He wrote *Observations on the Changes of the Air, and the Concomitant Epidemical Diseases in Barbadoes, with a Treatise on the Bilious Remittent Fever*, London, 1759, which BR issued, with notes, at Philadelphia, 1811.

[9] Benjamin Moseley, M.D. (1742-1819), physician at the Royal Hospital at Chelsea from 1788; author of *A Treatise on Tropical Diseases*, 1787, which was several times reprinted (DNB).

[10] John Mitchell (d. 1768), an English physician, naturalist, and cartographer, who lived at Urbanna, Va., for some years and was "for a time perhaps the ablest scientific investigator in North America" (DAB; T. Hornberger, "The Scientific Ideas of John Mitchell," *Huntington Libr. Quart.*, X [1946-1947], 277-96). In a letter of 24 Mch. 1790 to Samuel Griffitts, secretary, BR informed the College of Physicians that he had borrowed from Franklin a copy of a letter by Mitchell to Cadwallader Colden on the yellow-fever epidemics in Virginia a half-century earlier, and suggested that the letter be read at a meeting (Coll. Phys. Phila., Archives). It was this MS which BR came upon when he "ransacked" his library in the early weeks of the epidemic of 1793, and which prompted him to adopt a depleting therapy (*Account of the Yellow Fever in 1793*, p. 197-200). Mitchell's letter naturally became the subject of much discussion as the dispute over treatment of the fever continued,

and it was twice printed: partially, in the *Phila. Medical Museum*, I (1805), 1-21, and completely in the *Amer. Medical & Philos. Register*, IV (1814), 181-215; see BR to David Hosack, 15 Aug. 1810.

[11] Probably Timothy Kirby, author of a dissertation *De febre putrida maligna*, London, 1773 (Surg. Gen. Off., *Index-Cat.*, 2d ser., VIII, 734).

[12] Thomas Sydenham (1624-1689), "the English Hippocrates," whose name and authority BR reverenced above all others', at least in later life. For Sydenham's life, see DNB, and for a modern evaluation of his work, see C.-E. A. Winslow, *The Conquest of Epidemic Disease*, Princeton, 1943, ch. IX. Sydenham's fame rests on his contributions to descriptive pathology, but BR's admiration for him sprang from the fact that he could trace so many parallels between his own and Sydenham's professional views and career: Sydenham had held that one epidemic disease always swallows up another (a point of great importance to BR, whose successful cases were alleged by his critics not to be cases of yellow fever); Sydenham had advocated vigorous bloodletting and purges, or none at all; Sydenham had been cruelly persecuted for pursuing measures he believed right. In an introductory lecture "On the Character of Dr. Sydenham," delivered 9 Dec. 1793, BR told his pupils that the only perceptible flaw in the master's character was that he had sometimes yielded to others' opinions, in order "to avoid the imputation of . . . obstinacy." BR hoped his pupils would never so yield on any occasion (*Sixteen Introductory Lectures*, p. 62-3). BR's supreme rebuke to the College of Physicians, as he believed, was not his resignation, but his presenting that august body with a set of Sydenham's *Works* (see letter to John Redman, 5 Nov. 1793). BR named his country villa, acquired in 1798, "Sydenham," and in 1809 he published an American edition of Sydenham's *Works . . . on Acute and Chronic Diseases.*

To Mrs. Rush

My dear Julia,   Philadelphia, October 3rd, 1793

In addition to my public duties, I have large and frequent demands from country practitioners for information respecting the prevailing fever. To *read* their letters alone would be burdensome at *any time*, but it is much more so at present. To save the trouble of writing answers to each of them, I have this evening composed a short account of the origin, symptoms, and treatment of the disease which I shall address to Dr. Rodgers of New York in the form of a letter and publish in Mr. Brown's paper. My postage for letters frequently amounts to 7/6 a day.

I have this day paid between 40 and 50 visits. Mrs. McCall's grandson Cattle is out of danger; so is Master Adams at Mr. Ketland's. The three Roman clergy have all been ill. Two of them I hope are in a safe way. Mr. Hazard left me from an antipathy to bleeding as a remedy in his disorder.[1] Dr. Hodge[2] is now his physician. This man has seen a great deal of the disorder, but he is no more the wiser for it than the black nurses who attend the sick. He is, if possible, duller than Dr. Kuhn. Both Mr. Bradford's sons are well; so is Mr. VanBerkle, the latter after seven bleedings. He met Colonel Hamilton on his way to town, who advised him if he caught the fever to use Dr. Stevens' remedies and that Mr. Walcot[3] would furnish him with the directions how to use them. Mr. VanBerkle had heard so much of the credit of the new remedies before he was taken sick as to prefer them. But had he sent to Mr. Walcott, he would not have found him. He and his wife have fled, and I am now attending a servant[4] in his family in consequence of an order from him before he left town. I think it probable that if the new remedies had been introduced by any other person than a decided Democrat and a friend of Madison and Jefferson, they would have met with less opposition from Colonel Hamilton.

October 4th. The sky lowers, but alas! I fear we shall have no rain. My brother informs me that the grass is burnt up in the neighborhood of Reading. He expresses in a letter to me uncommon solicitude for my health and life. My mother is better, and Ed Fisher has again taken the field. He yesterday rode five miles in the country to see a son of Thos. Morris,[5] an old patient of Kuhn's, and who had lost a son by following Kuhn's mode of treating the disease. Yesterday there was great mortality in the city. Townsend Speakman,[6] Mr. Kay,[7] Clow's partner, and Jno. Todd the schoolmaster[8] are among the dead. Our cousin Parry Hall[9] is ill. Wm. Hall's *only* son is upon the recovery after six bleedings. This event has healed the wound which death made in his family last winter. Mrs. Hall is truly thankful. You know her character. I am often oppressed and even distressed with the kindness of my patients, and by few more than by Mr. Hall's excellent family. I observe with great pleasure an evident sense of the divine goodness to pervade all those families who have been delivered from death. Men now talk of God and of his providence who appeared scarcely to believe in either two months ago.

Adieu, my dear Julia. Not a ray of alleviation of the present calamity breaks into our city from any quarter. All is a thick and melancholy gloom. But God is not slack in fulfilling his promises. Continue to wrestle with him in your prayers. It is all right, and hereafter we shall behold our sufferings as the emanations not only of justice but of love. Again, adieu. I am, blessed be the God of my life, in good health, and acquire strength daily. Love as usual. Yours sincerely,

BENJN RUSH

Addressed: Mrs: Julia Rush at Richd: Stockton's Esqr: Princeton.
MS: Josiah C. Trent, M.D., Durham, North Carolina.

[1] Hazard's position is explained in a letter he wrote to Samuel A. Otis of Boston, 12 Oct. 1793, which also provides a lively picture of BR at work in the epidemic. Having advertised his mercurial remedy, says Hazard, BR now "prescribes *that*, and bleeding, *in all cases*, and boasts lustily of his success. At the same time, it is a fact that he has lost three of his apprentices, and his sister, out of his own family. He is a perfect Sangrado, and would order blood enough to be drawn to fill Mambrino's helmet, with as little ceremony as a mosquito would fill himself upon your leg." Called to a friend of Hazard's and thrice ordering purges and venesection, BR was rebuffed on the third day by the patient, who, according to Hazard, "having felt his own pulse, objected against bleeding, as unnecessary. The Dr. pronounced 'this opinion as one of the most dangerous symptoms in the case; the disorder was extremely insidious; the case extremely critical; not a moment to be lost; send for the bleeder directly. . . . You must be glystered to-day; but, if you are not *bled* to-day, I shall not be surprised to hear that you are *dead* to-morrow.' The patient declared he would lose no more blood; the Dr. declared he would no longer consider him as his patient, left him to *die*, and the man *got well*" (Mass. Hist. Soc., *Colls.*, 5th ser., III [1877], 334-6).

[2] Hugh Hodge (1755-1798), a graduate of the College of New Jersey, 1773; privately trained; surgeon in the Revolution; member College of Physicians, 1793; father of the well-known Princeton theologian Charles Hodge (Ruschenberger, p. 235; A. A. Hodge, *Life of Charles Hodge*, N.Y., 1880, p. 7). BR declared in November that "Dr. Hodge leads the van of my calumniators," and their quarrel was renewed in 1797 over the case of Dr. Nicholas Way (to Mrs. Rush, 7 Nov. 1793; to Ashbel Green, 10 Sep. 1797).

[3] Oliver Wolcott (1760-1833), of Connecticut; comptroller of the U.S.,

1791-1795, and a close friend of Hamilton's, whom he succeeded as secretary of the treasury; afterwards governor of Connecticut (DAB).

[4] See BR's letter to Wolcott of 8 Oct. 1793.

[5] Thomas Morris (1745/1746-1809), brother of Capt. Samuel Morris, was a well-to-do brewer in North Second St.; his son Anthony had died on 9 Sep.; his two other sons, Joseph and Thomas, were both infected but recovered (Moon, *Morris Family*, II, 393-6; 1793 *Directory*).

[6] Chemist and druggist, 8 South Second St. (1793 *Directory*).

[7] This name is not in either Carey's list of the dead or the 1793 *Directory*; for Clow, see note on BR's letter of 24-25 Sep. 1793.

[8] John Todd, Sr., who kept a school on Chestnut St.; his wife and son also died in the epidemic (1793 *Directory*; Carey, *Short Account*; BR to Mrs. Rush, 24-25 Oct. 1793).

[9] Parry Hall was the son of Jacob, brother of BR's mother; he was a printer, bookseller, and stationer at 149 Chestnut St.; BR announced his death in a letter of 1-2 Nov. 1793 (J. Hall Pleasants, "Jacob Hall," *Md. Hist. Mag.*, VIII [1913], 233; 1793 *Directory*).

To Mrs. Rush

My dear Julia,   Philadelphia, October 4, 1793

I concluded my letter this morning by informing you that I daily improved in my strength.[1] I ought rather to have said with St. Paul, in a physical as well as a spiritual sense, "When I am weak, then am I strong."[2] After paying a few visits in the neighborhood, I returned with a slight attack of my fever.[3] It went off in an hour or two with a gentle sweat, and I have passed the day at home in as much health and spirits as usual, prescribing constantly for such persons as I was unable to visit, particularly for the poor. This little indisposition was brought on by the fatigue of yesterday, for I was *forced* by the entreaties and tears of persons who stopped my carriage in the streets to visit many more people than I had intended when I left my own house. Mr. Coxe and Mr. Fisher have visited all my patients for me this day, and I hope to their entire satisfaction. I fear I shall lose good Mr. Fleming, the Roman priest, in consequence of my inability to visit him at the usual hour. The delay of a day, nay of a single hour, in administering the remedies proper in this disorder, is often attended with irretrievable consequences.

I informed you this morning that yesterday the disease was uncommonly mortal. Thirty-two were buried in the Potter's field alone. The disease affects as generally as the plague, and were it not for the new remedies, I have no doubt but it would have proved equally fatal to our citizens. Scarcely a family in town has escaped it, and in many families scarcely a child or a servant misses it.

October 5th. I rose at my usual hour this morning after a comfortable night's rest, for which I desire to be thankful. How precious is sound sleep in a city where thousands now pass wearisome and sleepless nights! How great is the gift of life in a place where upwards of an hundred fellow creatures die every day! Poor Peter yielded to the disorder last night. He and a child of two years old whom I saw at Jonth. Meredith's[4] store a few days ago were the only two gay things I have seen in Philadelphia for near seven weeks. The sight of the child smiling and crowing in my face reminded me of the Arab's child mentioned by Bruce smiling in the arms of its half-starved mother in the deserts of Nubia. It affected me in a manner which I cannot describe. We were last night flattered with the hopes of rain, but alas! the heavens are still as brass over our[5] heads. The *coolness* of the weather is, however, favorable to the sick, though I fear it increases their number by exposing people to take cold and thereby exciting the contagion into action. Since I sat down to conclude this letter, I have been interrupted not less than half a dozen times. Adieu. I shall visit only a few patients this day. My letter to Dr. Rodgers will not be published before Monday. The wages for nursing now are 4 dollars per day. The distress of our city from the want of money alone is very great. Adieu once more. From your affectionate [....]

P.S. My mother joins in much love to you and the children. Josey[6] informed me three days ago in the street that Ben and Becky were well.

Addressed: Mrs: Julia Rush at Richard Stockton Esqr: Princeton.
MS (signature cut out): Josiah C. Trent, M.D., Durham, North Carolina.

[1] MS: "strenth."
[2] II Corinthians 12:10.
[3] This was BR's second attack, as he believed, of the fever; for other details, see his *Account of the Yellow Fever in 1793*, p. 344-5.

[4] Jonathan Meredith, tanner, South Third St. (1793 *Directory*).
[5] This word omitted in MS.
[6] Probably a servant at Rose Hill, the Boudinot-Bradford residence north of the city.

To Mrs. Rush

My dear Julia,   Philadelphia, October 6, 1793

All your letters except the one sent by Mr. Webb[1] have come safe to hand. It is not in my power to answer them regularly, for they are often detained in the post office two or three days before I can get them. Confusion and distress pervade every branch of business at the present time in Philadelphia. You need not return the 20 dollars. I have or I can command enough for all my exigencies. You will probably soon require more, for alas! I know not when you will be able to come to Philadelphia—all is as yet a gloom before us. I shall be gratified with your and the children wearing mourning for my dear sister. I deplore her loss every hour of the day. So deep a rent was never made by death in my heart before.

Mrs. Harris' family[2] is still in town. I was this day sent for to visit one of her grandchildren, but was obliged to decline going, owing to my extreme weakness. I am unable now to attend even my old patients, so very weak-handed am I, and so multiplied is the sickness. My dear friend Dr. Griffitts is again ill. I have visited him twice today and have this evening ordered him to be bled a fourth time. Old Mr. Guest[3] died at 5 o'clock this afternoon. Jos. Harrison[4] and Dr. Peter Glentworth are likewise dead. Dr. White's coachman is very ill, and from the want of proper attendance will I fear sink under the disease. The zealous and the indefatigable Mr. Fleming died last night. My mother was much affected and gratified by your letter. She wept over it. You may depend upon her care of everything in the house. She has sent Ben his winter clothes long ago.

October 7th. Through divine goodness I passed a comfortable night after 1 o'clock, before which hour I was disturbed by successive knockings at the door. I expect to visit Mr. Saml. Meredith this forenoon, who is again indisposed. It is painful to do duty with a weak, tottering body, but I am kept from repining by recollecting that my divine Master performed many or perhaps most of his laborious acts of love to mankind with a much weaker body than mine. This is evident from several passages in the history of his life. They know but little of the extent of the obligations of Christianity who give such a worthless reptile as I am the least credit for any one exertion in the cause of humanity, for I profess to believe in and to imitate a Saviour who did not *risk* but who *gave* his life, not for his friends but his enemies. I enclose you a sweet little psalm by Dr. Watts which I cut out of a newspaper.[5] Though I have a most imperfect claim to the promises contained in it, yet it has pleased God to make it a cordial to my soul.

My dear mother sends a great deal of love to you and the children. Peter after two bleedings is better. He has been very much terrified with the fear of dying, and I have endeavored to improve upon his fears by setting before him his wicked life.

Adieu, my dear Julia. Love to all friends. Yours very affectionately,

BENJN RUSH

P.S. I desired Jno. Coxe last night to visit Mrs. Harris' grandchild. But I fear he has not done so, for he is full of business and not very well.

Addressed: Mrs Julia Rush at Richd Stockton's Esqr Princeton.
MS: Josiah C. Trent, M.D., Durham, North Carolina.

[1] Not identified.
[2] Not identified.
[3] John Guest, Sr., probably the father of the John Guest who kept a shop in South Second St. (Carey's *Short Account*; 1793 *Directory*).
[4] Harrison's death was reported by error (BR to Mrs. Rush, 8 Nov. 1793). He was not a Philadelphian, and I have been unable to identify him with certainty.
[5] Sealed on the first page of the letter is a clipping dated Philadelphia, 4 Oct. 1793, containing the four quatrains of Isaac Watts' version of the 41st Psalm, of which the first and last are as follows:

"Blest is the man whose bowels move,
And melt with pity to the poor,
Whose soul by *sympathizing* love,
Feels what his *fellow-saints* endure....

"Or if he languish on his couch,
GOD will pronounce his sins forgiven,
Will save him with a healing touch,
Or take his willing soul to Heaven."

To Mrs. Rush

My dear Julia,   Philadelphia, October 7, 1793

Among the dead of this day are Mrs. Coltman[1] and Major D. Franks.[2] The former died without a physician, not believing herself to be infected. The latter died at Mr. Kean's[3] under the care of a French physician, deserted by all his former friends—so much so that he was buried in the Potter's field. Upwards of an 100 persons more it is said have this day been conveyed to the grave. My publication of this evening[4] has met with a kind reception from my fellow citizens. I have only *named* the mistakes of my brethren. The public has been very liberal in applying harsh epithets to them.

Mr. Hazard *survived* the remedies of Dr. Hodge and is now out of danger. The mercurial purges and two plentiful bleedings which I gave him laid the foundation of his cure.

Mr. Seargeant[5] is very ill. He wished for me as his physician but heard that I was indisposed. I lament exceedingly that this was the case, for I take as much pleasure in going to old enemies as to old friends. He is attended by two French physicians, so that there are three chances against him to one in his favor—viz., a violent disease and two doctors. Mrs. Kepple[6] and Mrs. Math. Clarkson[7] are ill. They are bad subjects for the disease and unfortunately both my patients. Mrs. Blodget is well and a most zealous advocate for the new remedies.

October 8th. "Thy mercies are indeed new unto me, O Lord! every morning."[8] Great, very great are thy faithfulness and goodness to the most unworthy of all thy creatures. Seldom have I at any time enjoyed a more perfect night's rest. I even had dreams unmixed with wringing of hands, weeping eyes, coffins, biers, and all the other marks of distress and death. The respite even in a dream has revived me. A sudden call to a child of Colonel Pickering's[9] obliges me to conclude my letter sooner than I intended. Mrs. Bett[10] in our neighborhood is ill under my care, and my dear, dear friend Dr. Griffitts is not yet out of danger. O! what tugs are daily and hourly made upon my poor threadbare heartstrings! But hush! It becomes me at all times and in all places only to "GIVE THANKS." Adieu. Love to all the family. Yours sincerely,

BENJN RUSH

P.S. Jno. Coxe called at Mrs. Harris', but she had sent for another doctor.

Addressed: Mrs: Julia Rush at Richd Stockton Esqr: Princeton.
MS: Josiah C. Trent, M.D., Durham, North Carolina.

[1] Sarah Coltman, midwife (Carey, *Short Account*).

[2] No doubt David Salisbury (variously spelled) Franks, major and aide-de-camp to Gen. Arnold in the Revolution, vice-consul at Marseilles, 1784-1787, and at the time of his death assistant cashier of the Bank of the U.S. (Morais, *Jews of Philadelphia*, p. 38, 454-5; 1793 *Directory*; Carey, *Short Account*). BR contradicted the report of Franks' burial in the Potter's Field in a letter of 9-10 Oct. 1793. A well-documented biographical sketch by H. L. Zitt, "David Salisbury Franks, Revolutionary Patriot (c. 1740-1793)," appeared in *Penna. Hist.* XVI (1949), 77-95, after the present volume was sent to press.

[3] Not certainly identifiable; perhaps John Kean, assistant cashier of the Bank of the U.S., 74 Walnut St. (1793 *Directory*).

[4] The letter to Dr. Rodgers, printed above under 3 Oct. 1793.

[5] Jonathan Dickinson Sergeant; he died next day (BR to Mrs. Rush, 8-9 Oct. 1793).

[6] Wife of George Keppele, merchant, 98 High (Market) St.; her case proved fatal (1793 *Directory*; Carey, *Short Account*).

[7] Wife of Mayor Matthew Clarkson; her maiden name was Mary Boude (John Hall and Samuel Clarkson, *Memoirs of Matthew Clarkson . . . and of His Brother Gerardus Clarkson* [Phila.], 1890, p. 17). She recovered.

[8] Approximately quoted from Lamentations 3:23.

[9] This son died (Carey, *Short Account*).

[10] Not identified. BR gives her name as Betts in his letter of 10-11 Oct. 1793, announcing her death. She is not entered in Carey's list of the dead.

To Oliver Wolcott

My dear Sir,   October 8, 1793

Your girl,[1] whose case at first was not a violent one, *dies* from the inability of her mother to procure a bleeder for her till two days after bleeding was prescribed. Many now die from the same cause. In short, the distress of our city exceeds description.

I shall most cordially comply with your request,[2] provided I continue to enjoy tolerable health, but alas—I am so weak that climbing a few pair of stairs in a forenoon frequently unfits me for duty during the remaining part of the day.—Yours sincerely,

BENJN RUSH

MS: Connecticut Historical Society, Wolcott Papers.

[1] This was a servant; see BR to Mrs. Rush, 3-4 Oct. 1793.
[2] Presumably to continue to care for the Wolcott domestics.

To Mrs. Rush

My dear Julia,   Philadelphia, October 8th, 1793

I had almost written that I *rejoiced* in the addition that our sister has made to your brother's family,[1] but alas! I have nothing to do with *joy*, and I sometimes feel as if I never should smile or indulge a moment of gaiety again as long as I lived. This morning at 8 o'clock Mr. Seargeant breathed his last. I was mistaken in the account I gave you this morning that he wished for me to attend him. Before his illness he told one of his neighbors that in case of an attack of the disorder he would employ none but a French physician. The mortality of the disease has been worse this day than ever. Doctors Parke, Currie, Physic,[2] James,[3] Mease, and Griffitts are all confined—the last is still in great danger. Mr. Meredith is again ill. Fisher has gone out in a close carriage to see him. Danl. Offley,[4] the Quaker preacher, is below hope; so is Mr. Baldwin[5] the apothecary, Mr. Delany's[6] son-in-law. Miss N. Redman is in danger. She has been bled twice this day. Dr. Redman, whom I saw in visiting Nancy, is perfectly recovered. His every breath is full of praises to God and love to the whole human race. He begged to be remembered to you and your Mama and the whole family at Morven in the most affectionate manner.

There is not a single overseer of the poor nor a magistrate but Mr. Clarkson now in town. Judge of the distress of our city from

[708]

those circumstances! Mr. Fisher is just returned from Mr. Meredith's and, I am comforted in adding, left him much better.

I do not think it will be safe for you now to receive any article of dress out of our house. It is perhaps at present one of the most infected houses in town. Nearly an hundred people discharge their infected breath in it every day, for many people in the first stage of the disorder are able to walk about and to call upon a physician. Peter is mending, though very slowly, after three bleedings.

October 9th. I wept last evening in reading the 102nd psalm, but blessed be God, my sorrow was indeed of a night's continuance only. This morning my mind is composed. "Not my will, but thine be done." The calls have been numerous this morning, but I have declined them all. Mr. Fisher is indisposed from the fatigue of yesterday. The 100 dollars will be very acceptable from your brother. The carriage drains me of 6 dollars every day. I could *now* command any sum I pleased from *either* of the banks, but I had rather be under obligations to your brother than to any citizen of Philadelphia. Adieu. My love to all the family. Kiss your little newborn namesake for me. Again adieu. Yours very affectionately,

BENJN RUSH

P.S. I heard from Ben again two days ago by a line from Mr. Bradford. He says he has no Papa. [....][7] All Betsey Steen's friends are well.

Addressed: Mrs: Julia Rush at Richd Stockton Esqr: Princeton.
MS: Josiah C. Trent, M.D., Durham, North Carolina.

[1] This probably refers to the birth of Julia, daughter of Richard and Mary (Field) Stockton (Stockton, *Stockton Family*, p. 77).

[2] Philip Syng Physick (1768-1837), a student under John and William Hunter, and M.D., Edinburgh, 1792, was to become the preeminent figure in early American surgery; for his career, see DAB. Physick seems to have been firmly attached to BR from the time he settled in Philadelphia: the two were associated in the founding of the abortive Philadelphia Academy of Medicine; there are frequent allusions in BR's letters and papers to consultations with the younger man; and Physick was BR's own surgeon (BR to Ashton Alexander, 20 Feb. 1798; to John Adams, 20 Sep. 1811).

[3] Thomas Chalkley James (1766-1835), M.B., University of the State of Pennsylvania, 1787, studied obstetrics in London and Edinburgh; on staff of Pennsylvania Hospital, 1807-1832; professor of midwifery, University of Pennsylvania, 1810-1834 (obtaining his M.D. in 1811); an American pioneer in obstetrical science and one of the founders of the Historical Society of Pennsylvania (DAB; Gross, *Lives of Physicians and Surgeons*).

[4] Daniel Offley, anchor manufacturer and "public Friend," was a member of the citizens' committee to care for the indigent sick; Carey pays high tribute

to his services, which resulted in his death (Watson, *Annals*, I, 430; Carey, *Short Account*, p. 26, 29).

[5] Daniel Baldwin (Carey, *Short Account*).

[6] Probably William Delany, "chemist, druggist, and apothecary," 78 South Second St. (1793 *Directory*).

[7] One line has here been heavily scratched out.

To Mrs. Rush

My dear Julia, Philadelphia, October 9th, 1793

It turned out as I expected. Mrs. Kepple's gross habit and her delay in sending for me till the 3rd day of her disorder afforded a most unfavorable prospect of her recovery from the moment I saw her. She died this day at 5 o'clock. Mrs. Clarkson is still ill, but I do not despair of her. Mrs. Bett is below hope. Her habit was a bad one, and she too soothed herself, for several days before I saw her, with a belief that her complaints were the effects of an old chronic disorder to which she had been subject for many years. My invaluable friend Dr. Griffitts is I hope a little better. He has been bled seven times.

October 10th. After a comfortable night's rest I rose this morning at 7 o'clock and have ever since been in the midst of sickness and distress. All my meals are public. Frequently eight or ten people witness the simplicity of my diet, for I am still obliged to live wholly on bread and milk and coffee with bread and butter. Tea has become insipid and almost offensive to my stomach. *Where* and *when* this will end I know not, but I leave all to the disposal of my faithful Creator and Redeemer, in whose will I am enabled frequently to rejoice.

The new remedies prevail universally in *name*, but many of our doctors offer incense to the public mind by one or two bleedings or purgings, and then pour in their poisonous doses of bark and laudanum. I shall this day publish some extracts from Dr. Moseley which will cover them with confusion and show that they have been as deficient in *reading* as they are in *reasoning* and *observation*.

Excuse the shortness of this letter. My love as usual to all friends. Ed Fisher is better. He is a most affectionate and pleasant companion—and what is more, full of compassion for the sick. My mother keeps up wonderfully. Adieu. From, my dear Julia, yours sincerely,

BENJN RUSH

P.S. Major Franks was *not* buried in the potter's field. Honest Jno. Thompson,[1] the blacksmith with the wooden leg, who lives opposite to Mr. Kean's, prevented it and obtained a grave for him in Christ Church burying ground.

Addressed: Mrs Julia Rush at Richd: Stockton Esqr: Princeton.
MS: Josiah C. Trent, M.D., Durham, North Carolina.

[1] He is located by the 1793 *Directory* at 99 Walnut St.

To Mrs. Rush

My dear Julia,   Philadelphia, October 10, 1793

My letters contain such a dull repetition of melancholy events that I fear you will tire in reading them. The mortality this day has been very great. It still falls chiefly upon the poor and particularly upon servants. Mr. Clarkson informed me this day that he had documents to show that nearly 2,000 persons had died in our city since the first appearance of the disease, and *most* of them with the prevailing fever. Mrs. Betts died this morning—also another of the Catholic priests.[1] He was my patient till the late return of my fever, and I fear suffered from my being obliged to desert him. Nancy Redman is in a hopeful way, and Dr. Griffitts nearly out of danger.

October 11th. A return of my fever last evening[2] will confine me this day to the house. It belongs to the disease to end in an intermittent in many people. Mr. Meredith, Mrs. Clymer, and Mr. Willing have been much afflicted in that way, and what is unfortunate, it will not bear the bark.

Adieu. With love to each of the family and the dear children, I am, my dear Julia, your ever affectionate

BENJN RUSH

Love to Dr. Smith.

Addressed: Mrs Julia Rush at Richd Stockton's Esqr Princeton.
MS: Josiah C. Trent, M.D., Durham, North Carolina.

[1] Rev. Laurence Graessl, a Bavarian priest who had come to the United States in 1787 and in the summer of 1793 had been named coadjutor-bishop to Bishop Carroll of Baltimore (Powell, *Bring Out Your Dead*, p. 237-8).

[2] This was BR's third and most severe attack. He did not reveal its seriousness to his wife until a letter of 8 Nov. 1793, q.v. On 24 Oct. he addressed a letter to "My dear Sister," probably one of his sisters-in-law (Mary or Susan Stockton), then in New York, which survives only in a fragment (Hist. Soc. Penna.,

Gratz Coll., uncatalogued) and is not printed here. In it he says: "My dear Julia knows nothing of the violence of my late attack. Happily I had such intervals of ease as to write short letters to her every day. Conceal it from her and from our friends at Princeton." For other details on his seizure, see his *Account of the Yellow Fever in 1793,* p. 360-2.

To Mrs. Rush

My dear Julia,   Philadelphia, October 11, 1793

I have this day confined myself to the house and prescribed from the reports of the young gentlemen. I cannot say too much in favor of Mr. Fisher. He is an enthusiast in humanity, and he has discovered uncommon talents in his profession. Dr. Woodhouse[1] has been very useful to me in visiting a number of patients for me this day. Dr. Griffitts is out of danger, and I hope Mrs. Clarkson is in[2] a fair way of doing well.

I received a most elegant letter from Susan Baynton[3] two days ago—full of solicitude for her relations. I was happy in being able to inform her that death had made no breach among them except in Mr. Bullock's family.

October 12th. Blessed be God, I passed a quiet and comfortable night and have not a single complaint this morning but extreme weakness. I shall not go out today—nor perhaps for some days to come. My fellow citizens I hope will excuse me,[4] especially when they recollect how often my premature exertions have brought back my fever.

I received a letter from Dr. McIlvaine yesterday containing an offer of his house for 10,000 dollars or a lease of it for seven years at £250 a year. I received a letter from Dr. Shippen likewise (from Abington), proposing to me to advertise the lectures to commence on the 1st of December or 1st January.[5] Strange men! to propose contracts or undertakings to a man who is a "poor pensioner upon the bounties of an hour."[6] Dr. Young was once asked in a bookseller's shop in London, by a gentleman who met him there by accident, to dine with him the next day. "Tomorrow, sir," said he, "I expect to meet my God. Today is my own." The same spirit which dictated this speech should influence every man in my situation.

Adieu, my dear Julia. I have thought more of you and the dear children within these two days than I have done for six weeks, owing to my greater retirement from the hurry of business. Again adieu. I view you all at a distance on a safe and pleasant shore with your eyestrings pained in looking at me, paddling towards you in a boat shattered and leaky by many successive storms. But in every situation, let us praise the Lord for his goodness and his wonderful works to the children of men. With love as usual, I am, my dear Julia, your ever affectionate

BENJN RUSH

Addressed: Mrs Julia Rush at Richd Stockton's Esqr Princeton.
MS: Josiah C. Trent, M.D., Durham, North Carolina.

[1] James Woodhouse (1770-1809), a graduate of the University of the State of Pennsylvania, 1787, was apprenticed to BR in 1787, and obtained his M.D. at the College or the University in 1792; he held the chair of chemistry in the new University from 1795 and made notable contributions to that science (DAB). BR repeatedly praised Woodhouse's services in the epidemic of 1793, but later disapproved of his irreligious views and bad manners, and entered a very severe obituary notice of Wood-house in his Commonplace Book; see BR's *Autobiography*, p. 316.

[2] This word omitted in MS.

[3] Probably a sister of Peter Baynton and Mrs. Joseph Bullock, mentioned in BR's letter of 5-6 Sep. and elsewhere.

[4] This word omitted in MS.

[5] McIlvaine's letter has not been found; Shippen's, dated 11 Oct. 1793, is in Rush MSS, XXXVI.

[6] Edward Young, *The Complaint* (1742), Night I.

To Mrs. Rush

My dear Julia, Philadelphia, October 13th, 1793

I informed you in the close of my last letter that you and the dear children had occupied an unusual share of my thoughts within the last few days. The effects of this new train of thinking discovered themselves last night. I dreamed that I saw you at a distance at a window in a house in Coates Alley uptown, with a countenance healthy and pleasant, without the least tincture of that sallow gloom which pervades the face of every Philadelphian. I made signs to you that I would first go home and prescribe for my patients, and that I would come up to you in the evening. But ah!—I awoke soon afterwards, and that evening did not come.

I recollect now that we had an infant called by your name.[1] She was pleasant and smiled in my face the morning we parted. How does she do? How many teeth has she got? Does she yet articulate any words? John and James you say are with you. I hope they behave well. I have heard of Richd. and Emily by letters from each of them. Mary you say is at Mr. Armstrong's. Many, many thanks to him for affording her a shelter in our storm. I owe more gratitude to your dear Mama than I shall ever be able to pay for her frequent remembrances of me, more especially in her addresses to the great Arbiter of life in my favor. Your brother and sister have been friends indeed. May their goodness to you return an hundredfold into their own bosoms! You say nothing of Abbey.[2] I hope she is well. My love, my sincere, my increasing love to THEM ALL.

I have this day according to promise confined myself to the house and prescribed through the reports of my pupils. I have consented further to the advice of some of my most solid friends not to go into an infected room again until I am much better able to bear the action of the contagion on my system than I have been for some weeks past. I shall ride out, if I am spared, but it shall be into the country and only for the restoration of my own strength and health. I hope this conduct will not be offensive to my divine Master. He requires nothing unreasonable from his creatures, and to go further than I have done would be I fear to "tempt the Lord" to preserve me out of the ordinary means of his holy and wise providence. The first sick room I entered on the 4th of this month affected me so much that I was seized with a giddiness and sunk down upon a bed. I narrowly escaped a chilly fit after it. Such attacks are to be expected every day by a person in my weak state.

October 14th. Through divine goodness I passed a comfortable night without pain or fever and feel stronger today than yesterday. I am again able to relish tea and chicken broth. I cannot describe Mr. Fisher's kindness and attention to me. He seldom asks me how I am but his eyes seem to fill with tears. Our old neighbor Mr. Franks[3] died last night. Mr. Adgate[4] and Mr. Orton[5] died some time ago. Meyers Fisher is ill under the care of Robert, the new French doctor.[6] His treatment of him shows him to be equally a stranger to the disease and to the principles of medicine. Nancy Redman is on the recovery. Dr. Mease is again ill. Dr. Woodhouse has hopes of him. Young Maur. Rodgers[7] has been ill but is now well. He was attended by Dr. Woodhouse. Adieu, my dear Julia. From your ever affectionate

BENJN RUSH

MS: Josiah C. Trent, M.D., Durham, North Carolina.

[1] Julia Rush was less than a year old, having been born 22 Nov. 1792. She was BR's seventh child and third daughter to survive infancy. When she was twelve her father said she was "every-thing that the fondest parents could wish an only child to be. In point of interest she is the first of all my children." In 1820 Julia married Henry J. Williams, a Philadelphia lawyer; she

died without issue in 1860. (Biddle, *Memorial*, p. 257-8; BR to John Adams, 23 Mch. 1805.)

[2] Abigail Stockton (1773-1853), Mrs. Rush's youngest sister; later Mrs. Robert Field (Stockton, *Stockton Family*, annotated copy in Princeton Univ. Libr., p. 81; Hageman, *Hist. of Princeton*, I, 344-5).

[3] Presumably David F r a n k s (b. 1722), a wealthy Jewish merchant and land speculator, best remembered as the father of the celebrated Rebecca; uncle of David S. Franks, mentioned in BR's letter of 7-8 Oct. 1793; a tory, he had been obliged to leave Pennsylvania in 1780 (Morais, *Jews of Philadelphia*, p. 34-6; Sabine, *Loyalists*, I, 444-5; Carey, *Short Account*).

[4] Andrew Adgate, cardmaker in North Second St.; founder of the Uranian Academy, a musical society, 1787; mem-

ber of the citizens' emergency committee during the epidemic (1793 *Directory*; John T. Howard, *Our American Music*, N.Y., 1939, p. 109-11; Carey, *Short Account*, p. 29).

[5] Not identifiable; an Azariah Horton is entered in Carey's list of the dead but is not found in the 1793 *Directory*.

[6] This was "Citizen Robert" (first name unknown), who had just arrived in town from "Manillas in the East Indies" via Boston. He was reported to be both experienced and successful in treating yellow fever, and he had come on from Boston for the express purpose of putting his skill to use. (*Federal Gazette*, 11 Oct. 1793; reference kindly furnished by Dr. J. H. Powell.)

[7] Not identified. The spelling of the first name is uncertain; it is possibly "Maury."

To Mrs. Rush

My dear Julia,　　　　　Philadelphia, October 14, 1793

I have this day sent twice to the post office for letters from you, but could obtain none, owing to the crowd of applicants on the same business. The disappointment was the more painful as I received only one letter from you last week.

The disease continues to rage, with I fear unabating mortality. Mrs. Dr. Smith is ill and attended under my direction by Dr. Woodhouse and Ed Fisher. The poor Doctor alone remains with her. Mrs. Blodgett (who is well) and Billy are fled to Norristown. Wm. Hall and Mrs. Clarkson are out of danger. Dr. Mease is very low but not despaired of.

October 15th. Through divine goodness I continue to gain strength every day. My sleep last night was truly refreshing. Marcus has slept in the room with me for some time past, chiefly of late to hand me a little food in the middle of the night, for I have become so much a child, or an old man, in constitution that I am obliged to eat often or I become weak and fainty. My patients know this so well now that many of them hand me a glass of milk and a crust of bread as soon as I enter their houses, just as they hand other people a glass of wine. I cannot tell you how much we all owe to Marcus. His integrity, industry, and fidelity deserve great praise. I told you formerly how universal his talents were. I am sure with a little instruction he would exceed many of our bark and wine doctors in the treatment of the present fever. It has been a great alleviation of our distress that he has remained with us. Half the servants in the city have deserted their masters, and no wonder, for they were much exposed from the nature of their duty to taking the disorder, and when sick suffered and died by neglect or were sent to the hospital at Bush hill. You know I have always pitied this humble class of people, and I am happy in reflecting now that I never added by a bill to the distresses of any of them.

My mother is uncommonly well and more active than ever. We shall owe her much for her care of the house since the death of my dear, dear sister. Peter is well but very cross. He is so reduced that you[1] would hardly know him. My mother complains much of the expenses of housekeeping. As a sample of the advanced prices, I shall only mention that she pays 7/6 per dozen for washing[2] and 2/6 a half peck for apples. The diet of the family consists chiefly of milk, and our faithful Brindle has kindly supplied us with all we want.

The sky is overcast. O! that the great Jehovah would descend in mercy upon our city in showers of rain! All hearts now are faint, and all hope is now in God alone. Adieu, my dear Julia. Continue to pray for your ever affectionate

BENJN RUSH

P.S. Love as usual. I fear I have been deficient in not including good Dr. Smith among the friends at Princeton to whom I wished to be remembered.

Addressed: Mrs Julia Rush at Richd Stockton's Esqr: Princeton.
MS: Josiah C. Trent, M.D., Durham, North Carolina.

[1] This word omitted in MS.
[2] Thus in MS.

To Mrs. Rush

My dear Julia,   Philadelphia, October 17th, 1793[1]

Satisfactory accounts still arrive from all quarters that the disease evidently declines, but many have died this day, and many are yet very ill. Among the dead is a son of John Donaldson's,[2] and among those who are in danger is good old Dr. Sproat.[3] I informed you formerly of the death of his daughter. His son followed her a few days afterwards. Two of the old ladies at Mrs. Hodge's[4] it is said are no more. Janey Riddle's husband and his brother followed Janey to the grave a few days ago.[5] Two of Colonel Marsh's sons (Mrs. Josiah's brothers)[6] are dead, with many other valuable persons on the hill. None of the above persons were my patients. Geo. Bullock[7] is ill at Mrs. Bartram's[8] in Front Street. Dr. Woodhouse attends him for me. He was indisposed three days before Dr. W. saw him.

I have this day received a kind letter from Mrs. Fergusson.[9] She refers me for comfort and support to the 5th chapter of Job, from the 18th verse to the end.

October 18th. Not better, but perfectly well. Blessed be God for his goodness! Marcus proposes to feed me today with beef soup. I cannot tell you how much I owe to the fidelity and affection of our humble black friend. He has been a treasure to us in all our difficulties.

I have this morning received from Mr. Fergusson[10] of Dublin a large impression on *red* wax of that beautiful seal which he described in his letter of last year. It is admirably executed and has not suffered by crossing the sea. I have received many European letters within these few weeks, which at any other time would have afforded me great pleasure. One of them was from Granville Sharp,[11] authorizing me to draw for £14-14-0 sterling of contributions in London to the African Church of Philadelphia. Among the contributors I find the name of the Duke of Grafton for five guineas.

No one physician except Dr. Griffitts and Dr. Annan has sent to inquire after my health since my last confinement. The confederacy now is stronger than ever against me. Wistar is or will be at the head of it. He knows that he has injured me, and therefore he cannot forgive me. Many, many persons I fear are killed now by bark, wine, and laudanum to spite me. Their rancor has no bounds. They watch my patients with great solicitude, and console themselves under my numerous cures by declaring that my patients had nothing but the common fall fever. The few whom I lose they say died of the yellow fever and are all killed by mercury and bleeding.

Adieu. With much love as usual to all friends, I am, my dear Julia, your sincere [....][12]

Addressed: Mrs: Julia Rush at Richd: Stockton Esqr: Princeton.
MS (signature cut out): Josiah C. Trent, M.D., Durham, North Carolina.

[1] No letters for 15-16 and 16-17 Oct. survive. BR would surely have mentioned this hiatus if he had failed to write, and we may therefore conclude that one or two letters have disappeared.

[2] The son's name was Hugh; his father was a wine merchant at 22-24 Walnut St. (Carey, *Short Account*; 1793 *Directory*).

[3] His death is reported in BR's next letter.

[4] Doubtless Hannah Hodge, who kept a shop at 67 High (Market) St.; she was the widow of Hugh Hodge (1793 *Directory*; Conyngham, "Reminiscences," p. 195, note).

[5] James Riddle, his wife, and George Riddle are entered in Carey's list of the dead.

[6] Capt. James Marsh and brother are listed by Carey. Col. Marsh is not clearly identifiable. Mrs. Josiah was Elizabeth, the wife of James Josiah, the packet captain mentioned in BR's letter of 8 Nov. 1793 (*Penna. Archives*, 2d ser., VIII, 142; Rush MSS, Account Books).

[7] Son of Joseph, mentioned in BR's letter of 5-6 Sep. 1793; George's death is reported in BR's letter of 25-26 Oct.

[8] Perhaps the wife of Alexander Bartram, china dealer, 98 South Front St. (1793 *Directory*).

[9] This letter has not been found.

[10] Several letters, principally on medical subjects, from Hugh Ferguson of Dublin are in the Rush MSS, XXIII, but those mentioned by BR are missing.

[11] Sharp's letter, without date, is in the Rush MSS, XXVIII.

[12] A word or two has been cut away with the signature.

To Mrs. Rush

My dear Julia,   Philadelphia, October 18, 1793

Good Dr. Sproat finished his course this morning and was carried to his grave by eight of the members of the African Church this afternoon.[1] His son-in-law, Mr. Spencer,[2] is ill. Dr. Hodge is, I suppose, his physician. It is truly distressing to think of the desolation which has followed the footsteps of this man and of all the doctors who use bark, wine, laudanum, and hot or cold baths in this disorder. It is much more inflammatory than a common pleurisy, and who ever thought of using those remedies in that disease?

This morning I received a note from Mrs. Blackwell, written under great agitation of mind, informing me that the good Doctor[3] is ill with the fever at Gloucester. John Coxe flew to his relief. He bled him and gave him the mercurial purge. He expects to visit him every day, and from present appearances he entertains great hopes of his speedy recovery.

Dr. Griffitts with his whole family left the city this day. Dr. Mease mends, but very slowly. His head has been much affected by the disorder. Mrs. Miller,[4] his grandmother, is indisposed. Dr. Woodhouse attends her.

I am again employed in Mr. Hammond's family. After curing four of his servants, a French physician was sent for a few weeks afterwards to his steward and to one of his maids. They both died.

[718]

Mr. Fisher is now attending his groom. It is probable that Mr. Hammond was persuaded that my four cures in his family were only of the fall fever, because I did not put the yellow color of the disorder in their faces. I put it in a more suitable place by means of the strong but safe mercurial purges.

Good old James Craig[5] died a few days ago.

October 19th. Blessed be God, I continue to improve not only in health but in strength. I received a letter from Dr. Rodgers and another from your kind sister Polly yesterday urging me to leave the city.[6] I have written to Polly, and I hope shall satisfy her that such a step would be unwise and perhaps sinful.[7] I am still useful. I prescribe with success in my house, and my pupils under my direction save many, many lives every day. Three or four more rainy or *very* cold days would destroy all the contagion in the city, and such weather must come soon. In the meanwhile be assured that I will not go into an infected room to see a patient until I am as strong as I was before my confinement. I have already resisted two very pressing calls from old friends.

Adieu, my dear friend. My best love to all friends. From your sincere and affectionate friend,

BENJN RUSH

P.S. The disorder revived yesterday a good deal in consequence of the warmth of the weather.

Addressed: Mrs: Julia Rush at Richd Stockton's Esqr: Princeton.
MS: Josiah C. Trent, M.D., Durham, North Carolina.

[1] For a more detailed account of the death and funeral of BR's old pastor (whose family was nearly extinguished by the fever), see BR's letter of 20-21 Oct. 1793 and also Sprague, *Annals*, III, 126-7.

[2] Not further identified; his name does not appear in Carey's list of the dead.

[3] Robert Blackwell, D.D. (see BR to Mrs. Rush, 26 Aug. 1787); he recovered.

[4] Not further identified.

[5] James Craig, Sr., a native of Scotland; merchant at 161 South Second St. (1793 *Directory*; Carey, *Short Account*; *Hist. Cat. St. Andrew's Soc. Phila.* [1], 152).

[6] J. R. B. Rodgers' letter, 13 Sep. 1793, is in Rush MSS, XXXVI; the particular letter of Mary ("Polly") Stockton's here referred to cannot be located.

[7] BR's letter is also missing.

To Mrs. Rush

My dear Julia,   Philadelphia, October 20th, 1793

This day poor dear Mrs. Smith breathed her last.[1] She appeared and, Mr. Fisher says, was out of danger for two days, but sunk under the want of good nursing (being attended only by a black child of 14 years of age) and under deep depression of mind, brought on by the loss of her old friends in sickness, Mrs. Rodgers[2] and Mrs. Kepple, and perhaps too by hearing the sound of the bier at every hour of the night and day, passing by her door to the graveyards above her. Many have died from the above circumstances in spite of the most effectual medical aid. Danl. Offly's death has been ascribed wholly to his black nurse having fallen asleep and to having passed a whole night without drinks or food in the weak but convalescent state of his disorder. He was a patient of Dr. Mease's. The Doctor is out of danger. Dr. Phile[3] died yesterday morning. Major Sproat's widow[4] is no more. Mr. Pilmore is better. Dr. Annan (a bold practitioner) was one of his physicians. Dr. Blackwell was bled twice this day. Dr. Woodhouse is to visit him tomorrow with John Coxe. Geo. Bullock is still in great danger. None of his family visit him, although Mrs. Bullock's solicitude for his recovery is very great. The Reverend Mr. Turner[5] is ill. He preceded Dr. Sproat's corpse and exhorted at his grave, for contrary to the late custom of our city, 100 people, chiefly women, attended the good old man's funeral.

Dr. Griffitts and his whole family did not leave town till yesterday. He sent me a parting note containing kind expressions of friendship and prayers for my preservation. An extract from it in favor of plentiful bleeding will, I expect, appear in Mr. Brown's paper of tomorrow.[6]

Marcus has just now returned from Rose hill[7] upon a visit to Becky and Ben. They are both in good health. Ben's cheeks were like a rose. He thinks he has grown quite handsome. He was shy as to conversing with Marcus, but said he loved him. Marcus carried Becky sundry articles of diet.

Dr. Wistar's brother[8] has been recovered under the care of the Doctor and of Dr. Hodge, from extreme danger, by *three* bleedings in *one* day and by a strong dose of the mercurial medicine. This cure has transpired by accident, for pains have been taken to prevent its being known, especially to me!!!

October 21. A *cold* morning and a good night's rest call upon me with equal force to offer up my grateful praises to the Author of every public and private blessing. If the weather continues to increase in coldness, and above all if we should have a few days' heavy rain joined with it, the disease will be driven from the city in a few weeks. A few scattered cases may perhaps exist from carelessness or accident during the winter. I find by my notes of the disorder taken in the year 1762 during my apprenticeship that it continued (probably in that way only) during the months of November and December. From the contents or charges in Dr. Redman's daybook, it visibly and almost wholly declined about the 15 of October. Thus you see the most malignant and deadly contagion has its laws and its bounds as well as fire and water. Adieu. Yours most affectionately,

BENJN RUSH

Addressed: Mrs: Julia Rush at Richd Stockton Esqr Princeton.
MS: Josiah C. Trent, M.D., Durham, North Carolina.

[1] Rebecca, wife of Provost William Smith (see BR to Thomas Smith, 26 Feb. 1790). For an account of her death, see William Smith's letter to BR, 23 Oct. 1793, in Smith, *Smith*, II, 372-6.

[2] Hannah, wife of William Rogers, D.D., professor of rhetoric and belles lettres at the University (1793 *Directory*; Carey, *Short Account*).

[3] Dr. Frederick Phile, naval officer of the Port of Philadelphia, 1770-1771, 1777-1791 (Martin, *Bench and Bar*, p. 133; Carey, *Short Account*).

[4] Maria (ca. 1767-1793), wife of Maj. William Sproat (ca. 1757-1793), merchant in Vine Street; the Major was the son of Rev. Dr. James Sproat and had died of the fever ten days earlier (Sprague, *Annals*, III, 126; Timothy Alden, *Collection of American Epitaphs*, N.Y., 1814, I, 179; 1793 *Directory*; Carey, *Short Account*).

[5] Rev. Joseph Turner, described on his tombstone as "some time Rector of St Martins Marcus Hook and Assistant to the Rector of the Sweedish Churches in the state"; he recovered and lived until 1821 (1793 *Directory*; Barratt, *Old St. Paul's*, p. 231).

[6] An extract of Griffitts' letter, dated 19 Oct., is printed in BR's *Account of the Yellow Fever in 1793*, p. 273. It commends BR's therapy and concludes: "If my poor frame, reduced by previous sickness, great anxiety, and fatigue, and a very low diet, could bear *seven* bleedings in five days, besides purging, and no diet, but toast and water, what shall we say of physicians who bleed but once?"

[7] This is the first mention by name of the place where two of the children from the Rush household found refuge during the epidemic. Rose Hill was the property of Elias Boudinot; it was on the road to Frankford in what is now North Philadelphia at the junction of Cambria and Rosehill Streets. In 1793 it was occupied by Judge William Bradford, Boudinot's son-in-law. (*Brief of Title to the Rose Hill Estate*, Phila., 1868; Boudinot, *Boudinot*, II, 109; see also BR's letters of 29-30 Aug., 3-4 Nov., 12 Nov. 1793.)

[8] Thomas Wistar, merchant, 133 High (Market) Street; he was treasurer of Mayor Clarkson's emergency committee during the epidemic (1793 *Directory*; Powell, *Bring Out Your Dead*, p. 144, 205).

To Mrs. Rush

My dear Julia,   Philadelphia, October 21, 1793

The nearer falling bodies approach the earth, the greater the attraction they have to each other. The same may be said of husbands and wives that love each other, when they lessen the distance that parts them. I feel more united to you at Trenton than at Princeton. The time of our meeting is, I hope, not very far distant. The disease declines evidently every day. Should the weather be as cold as in former years, I think it probable that you will be able to come to town about the middle of November.

I rode out this forenoon—the first time since the 10th of this month. I found more people in the streets than before my confinement, and their countenances wore a more cheerful aspect. I observed a tent in the Potter's field in riding by it. It was erected for the accommodation of the gravediggers, who worked there day and night. Upwards of 1,000 persons have been buried in that graveyard alone since the 1st day of August.

Dr. Blackwell has been in great danger but has some hopeful symptoms this evening. Dr. Woodhouse has visited him twice this day, once with John Coxe and once alone, owing to Mr. Coxe being a little indisposed.

Geo. Bullock will hardly live till tomorrow morning. Dr. Woodhouse did not see him till the 3rd day of his disorder. His father sent him into the country for safety. He came into town without the knowledge of any of his family, and concealed his illness till it was too late to do him any service.

Your nurse Barry[1] visited us this afternoon. She and her sister have recovered from the fever under my directions without a visit from any of us. She and her mother and children were in great distress from the want of everything. We did not send her empty away. She begged to be remembered to you in the most affectionate manner.

Emely and Richard's letters came safe to hand. Richard falls off in his handwriting. I am glad to hear [such][2] good accounts of John and Julia.

October 22nd. I have only to add that I continue through divine goodness to gain strength by every night's rest, and that I am, with much love to Mr. Armstrong's and Uncle Saml.'s families[3] and to each of the children, your sincere and affectionate

BENJN RUSH

P.S. Mr. Fisher sends his most respectful compliments to you. He is a most amiable young man. The late distresses in our city have awakened uncommon talents and virtues in him. Betsy Steen's letter did not come to my care. All her friends I believe are well. I cured her sister at Mr. Fisher's.

Addressed: Mrs: Julia Rush at the Revd: Mr: James Armstrong's Trenton. *MS*: Josiah C. Trent, M.D., Durham, North Carolina.

[1] The 1793 *Directory* lists a Rebecca and a Margaret Barry, both widows.
[2] MS torn.
[3] MS: "Mr. Armstrong and Uncle Saml. families."

To Mrs. Rush

My dear Julia,   Philadelphia, October 23, 1793

I am sorry to inform you that the late moderate weather has so far revived the disease that the mortality is nearly as great as before the late rain and cold weather. 700 have died since the 11th of October. 3,400 have died since the first of August. O! that God would hear the cries and groans of the many hundred and perhaps thousand sick which still ascend to his throne every hour of the day and night from our desolating city! I feel the distresses of my fellow citizens the more from my being unable to assist them, and from my hearing constantly of some of them being murdered by large and ill-timed doses of bark and wine. But I must not arraign the conduct of divine providence.

> "When obedient nature knows his will,
> A doctor or disease alike can kill."

Dr. Blackwell is out of danger, much to the honor of Mr. Coxe. Geo. Bullock is still alive, and had he been properly attended by his nurse for two days past, Dr. Woodhouse says, might have recovered.

I received an affectionate letter from my sister Montgomery a few days ago.[1] She sympathizes tenderly with us in the death of our dear sister. All her letters to her since the commencement of the disorder (she says) were very pious and full of solicitude for my life. One expression in Mrs. Montgomery's letter to my mother pierced my heart. I cannot copy it, but it contained another proof that she willingly and cheerfully exposed and gave her life to save mine.

I have given you great credit everywhere for having never once advised me to leave the city. You will perceive by the paper of this evening that in my infirm and confined situation I have not been useless to my fellow citizens.[2] Many hundred people would subscribe similar certificates of being cured by my advice, or by my publications alone, without a visit from any physician. I am however best satisfied that the detail of those cures should be a secret till that great day when envy and calumny shall be able to detract nothing from them.

October 24. A clear and moderate day. But it is all just as it should be—wise, just, and good. "There is more sin," Dr. Priestly says, "in complaining of the weather than most people are aware of."

Adieu. With love to all surrounding friends, I am, my dear Julia, yours sincerely,

BENJN RUSH

P.S. My mother sent her cloak to Betsey Steen by mistake. She begs Betsey to take good care of it. All Betsey's relations are out of town or well in town.

Addressed: Mrs: Julia Rush at the Revd: Mr: Armstrong's Trenton.
MS: Josiah C. Trent, M.D., Durham, North Carolina.

[1] This letter has not been found.
[2] The *Federal Gazette* for 23 Oct. 1793 contains a letter to the editor from a William Young attesting the great value of BR's purging powders.

To Mrs. Rush

My dear Julia,   Philadelphia, October 24th, 1793

I move at present in so small a sphere, and see and hear so little of what goes forward in our city, that my letters will contain nothing hereafter that can interest you. I have not been out of the house this day and have prescribed to not more than half a dozen people. This sudden diminution of business is occasioned in part by the disease having left the heart of the city, in which I have generally practised, and by its being generally known that I am too weak to visit patients. My pupils are still busy, but it is chiefly in attending poor people.

My excellent friend Saml. Coates,[1] who has been an Anthony Benezet in every stage of our late distresses, called upon me this evening and kindly offered to lend me £50-0-0. I shall probably require it, for I have only a few dollars in the house, and this is not a time to ask for money from my patients. I have expended since the commencement of the disorder nearly £200 in cash and have contracted some debts. In what manner a part of it has been spent, I shall not mention. I regret only that it was not £2000.——*This*, only between ourselves.

I receive every day polite and friendly letters from the country. Some of them contain expressions which indicate a great degree of ignorance of the state of the public mind in our city. I am supposed to have created a great many friends and a large fund of gratitude among my fellow citizens. This is far from being true. The relations and patients of the physicians whose practice I have opposed have taken part with them in their resentments, and I am now publicly accused at every corner of having murdered the greatest part of the citizens who have died of the present disorder. These slanders must increase, for ignorance and error when detected and exposed can *never forgive*. Dr. Griffitts, Dr. Say, and my old pupils are the only friends I have left among my medical brethren. After what has passed between me and the rest of them, we can never consult or even associate together hereafter. Did New York offer a retreat to me, and with it a chair in their University, I should prefer ending my days there (if I survive the present calamity) to continuing in Philadelphia, where I see nothing before me but strife and misery.[2] One consolation I derive from the persecutions which have followed my late exertions in behalf of my fellow citizens, and that is, they nourish a humble hope that my labors have been accepted in heaven and that they will be owned hereafter by the impartial Judge of the Universe. John Todd[3] the lawyer died this afternoon. Thos. Hale[4] the carpenter, and Gerd. Vogles[5] died a few days ago—the last in jail, and it is said with hunger.

October 25th. We are all well. My good mother has recovered her health and spirits and is more active than she has been for several years. Adieu. Yours affectionately,

BENJN RUSH

Addressed: Mrs: Julia Rush at the Revd: Mr Armstrong's at Trenton.
MS: Josiah C. Trent, M.D., Durham, North Carolina.

[1] Samuel Coates (1748-1830), Quaker merchant and philanthropist; he was a manager of the Pennsylvania Hospital, 1785-1825, and president of the board of managers from 1812 (Morton, *Hist. of the Penna. Hospital*, p. 421-3). BR's letters to the managers were usually addressed to Coates, and the two seem to have been on uninterruptedly good terms.

[2] BR actually took steps in this direction in 1797; see his letter to J. R. B. Rodgers, 16 Oct. 1797.

[3] John Todd, Jr. (1763-1793), a Quaker lawyer resident in South Fourth St.; he had married Dolly Payne (later Mrs. James Madison) in 1790; his father and mother had died earlier; his infant son also died; and his wife nearly succumbed (Carey, *Short Account*; 1793 *Directory*; Maud W. Goodwin, *Dolly Madison*, N.Y., 1896, p. 30, 38-44).

[4] Identified as a "bell-hanger" in Carey's list of the dead.

[5] Not found in the 1793 *Directory* or in Carey's list.

To Mrs. Rush

My dear Julia,   Philadelphia, October 25th, 1793

This morning at 1 o'clock Geo. Bullock breathed his last. I paid a short visit to Peter Baynton's family this afternoon, who informed me that Mr. and Mrs. Bullock bear his death with composure. It was expected for several days, and nothing that could be done was omitted on the part of Dr. Woodhouse to save his life.

The mortality has been less this day than usual. Only one person has been buried in the Quakers' graveyard. From five to fourteen have been buried there every day for many weeks.

Dr. Blackwell is not so well as he has been. He has been attended and even nursed under great disadvantages compared with what he would have had in town and in his own house. The French physicians are everywhere getting into disrepute. They have, in conjunction with our bark, wine, and cold bath doctors, destroyed at least two-thirds of all who have perished by the disorder. The principal remedies of the French physicians are hot baths, clysters, niter, camphor, and cremor tartar. They seldom bleed, and all of them reprobate the mercurial purges. One of them (a Jew) does not even feel the pulse of his patients. Upon being offered a hand for that purpose by a Mr. Morrison,[1] he said, "No—no. I never feel the pulse—that is the way the Philadelphia physicians catch the disorder." This man died on the 3rd day.

My situation for some time past has been in some respects like that of the children of Israel in the wilderness, but it has differed from it in one particular very materially, and that is, my clothes have not waxed old. On the contrary, I have become so ragged that I am hardly fit to be seen in my own house. This evil at present is without a remedy, for there is scarcely a tailor or shoemaker who carries on business in town, their apprentices and journeymen being dead, or turned gravediggers, or having left the city.

October 26th. A warm and cloudy morning—God send a plentiful rain! We are all, through divine goodness, in good health. Our whole neighborhood has become pure, there being at present not a single sick person within a square of us.

Adieu. My best love to all our dear and invaluable friends at Trenton. I begin to count the weeks and days that interpose between our meeting, for I now begin to think that it will please God to bless us again as an unbroken family, my dear sister alone excepted from our number. Adieu. From yours affectionately,

BENJN RUSH

Addressed: Mrs: Julia Rush at the Revd: Mr Armstrong's Trenton.
MS: Josiah C. Trent, M.D., Durham, North Carolina.

[1] Four Morrisons or Morisons are entered in Carey's list of the dead.

To Mrs. Rush

My dear Julia,   Philadelphia, October 27, 1793

Yours of the 24th of this month came safe to hand yesterday morning, enclosing a letter to Betsey Steen's mother which shall be sent to her sister at Mr. Fisher's. I have hitherto been silent upon the subject of another house, because I considered myself as treading upon the brink of the grave. Since it has pleased God to check in a great measure the ravages of the fever and to restore my health, I have contemplated moving out of the house I now occupy *before* you come to town. Besides the reasons you mention for it, I have another. Mr. Hamilton[1] sent me a note on the 11th of September (a day ⟨*on which I visited upwards of an hundred of his fellow citizens at the risk of my life*⟩[2] of uncommon distress and darkness in our city) and raised my rent to £140 a year, and yesterday he sent another note demanding the rent of the last quarter. Such acts of insensibility to a man laboring and broken down as I was, have affected me so much that I wish all connection between us as landlord and tenant to be dissolved forever as soon as possible. This information must not be made public. I shall part with him in peace and without a complaint. I wish landlords would consider the wickedness of *rack* rents. They have been one of the procuring causes in my opinion of the late judgment of God upon our city. I have thought of taking the house in which Mr. Lea lived in 4th Street.[3] I prefer it to Mr. Mead's as being more retired. It will moreover be convenient to the lot we once viewed together, if God in his providence should enable us to purchase and improve it.

I cannot promise to visit and escort you to town. I still keep up a considerable share of business by means of my pupils—and what is more, I have reason to believe that I keep ignorance and error (in the present disease) in *constant awe* by continued extracts from the authors from which I have derived my principles and practice and which are published in the newspapers. The envy and hatred of my brethren have lately risen to rage. They blush at their mistakes—they feel for their murders—and instead of asking forgiveness of the public for them, vent all their guilty shame and madness in execrations upon the man who has convicted them of both.

My good friend Samey Coates called to see me this evening and informed me that there had not been a grave opened in the Friends' burying ground nor an admission or death *this day* in the hospital at Bush hill. Dr. Blackwell is still in danger.

October 28. Blessed be God for the change in the weather. We are all well. Adieu. With love to all our Princeton friends and to each of the children, I am, my dear Julia, your ever faithful friend,

BENJN RUSH

Addressed: Mrs Julia Rush at Richd: Stockton's Esqr: Princeton.
MS: Josiah C. Trent, M.D., Durham, North Carolina.

[1] This was presumably William Hamilton, of Bush Hill and The Woodlands (on whom see BR to Mrs. Stockton, 19 June 1787, note 3). He had very large property holdings, and it is known that BR rented from him at some period, for an undated request by Hamilton for a quarter's rent is in Rush MSS, VII.

[2] Scratched out by BR.

[3] This was a house at 98 South Fourth St. owned by Edward Shippen (father-in-law of the late Thomas Lea); BR occupied it from the end of 1793, or more probably the beginning of 1794, until 1796, and again from 1806 until his death (1793 *Directory*, under Lea; 1794-1796 *Directories*, under BR; BR to Mrs. Rush, 1-2 and 11 Nov. 1793, and to John Adams, 26 July 1809). An engraving of the house by C. A. Poulson, "from memory," is reproduced in Scharf & Westcott, II, 871; in Goodman, *Rush*, facing p. 326; &c.

To Mrs. Rush

My dear Julia,   Philadelphia, October 28, 1793

I have great pleasure in informing you that Dr. Blackwell is much better. He was bled five times. After the 3rd bleeding an old patient of Dr. Kuhn's went down to Gloucester and begged Mrs. Blackwell in the most pathetic terms not to consent to his being bled again. Mrs. Blackwell acted with firmness and propriety, and submitted to the subsequent bleedings with full confidence of their being proper, though advised only by Mr. Coxe. In this way have I been opposed and frequently defeated from the commencement of the disorder by the interference of the friends and followers of Dr. Kuhn.

The disease visibly and universally declines. But some worthy people still have it, among whom is our cousin Parry Hall, who is in great danger. Dr. Woodhouse and Mr. Fisher attend him.

Tomorrow we expect to move into the front parlor. Our little back parlor has resembled for two months past the cabin of a ship. It has been shop, library, council chamber, dining room, and at night a bedchamber for one of the servants. My mother has hired Betsey Correy at 7/6 a week to take charge of the kitchen, which will enable Marcus to clean and whitewash the house and to purify all the infected articles of furniture in it.

A new clamor has been excited against me in which many citizens take a part. I have asserted that the yellow fever was generated in our city.[1] This assertion they say will destroy the character of Philadelphia for healthiness, and drive Congress from it. Truth in science as in morals never did any harm. If I prove my assertion (which I can most easily do), I shall at the same time point out the means of preventing its ever being generated among us again. I am urged to bring forward my proofs immediately. To this I have objected—until I am able to call upon a number of persons for the privilege of using their names. To a gentleman who pressed the matter upon me this day, I said that the good opinion of the citizens of Philadelphia was now of little consequence to me, for that I thought it probable from present appearances that I should begin to seek a retreat and subsistence in some other part of the United States.

"Do all the good you can," said Mr. Westly [*Wesley*] to Mr. Pilmore when he entered into the ministry, "expect to be persecuted for doing good, and learn to *rejoice* in persecution."—A hard lesson to flesh and blood! but I hope it will please my divine Master to teach it to me.

October 29th. We are all well—thank God! Adieu from yours, with usual love and sincerity,

BENJN RUSH

Addressed: Mrs: Julia Rush at Richd: Stockton Esqr: Princeton.
MS: Josiah C. Trent, M.D., Durham, North Carolina.

[1] This was the beginning of a controversy that did not end with BR's death; the subject is dealt with in numerous letters below, and often in BR's publications. BR's mistaken insistence that yellow fever was wholly local in origin was almost as objectionable in some quarters as his depleting therapy was in others. Philadelphians were bound not to like it, and a good example of local sentiment is found in a letter from Richard Peters to Timothy Pickering, 22 Oct. [1793], which closes with this paragraph:

"I wish you would stop our Friend Rush's Cacoethes Scribendi. His Assertion that the Philadelphia Hot beds produced this deadly Plant is I believe unfounded & I am sure very mischievous. It is certainly an exotic. It is said that the Doctors advize the Citizens who are Fugitives not to return until a Month has expired after the Cessation of Hostilities between the Malady & its Victims. This is a mischievous Opinion at a Distance & will be eagerly caught at by the Anti Philadelphians. Stifle this Brat if you can" (Mass. Hist. Soc., Pickering Papers).

To Rachel Rush Montgomery

My dear Sister,   Philadelphia, October 29, 1793

Your affectionate letters drew tears from our eyes. Never did a brother feel more for the loss of a sister than I felt for ours. She was my friend and counselor in the difficult and distressing duties I was called upon to perform to my fellow citizens. She was my nurse in sickness. In short, she gave her life to save mine, for when she was advised to go out of town to escape the fever, she calmly said, "No, I will stay and take care of my brother though I were sure I should die with the disorder, for my life is of no consequence to anybody compared with his." During the prevalence of the fever she was active, intelligent, and useful among the patients who crowded my house at every hour of the day and at most of the hours of the night. No person ever wept in our parlor or entry (and many, many tears were shed in both) with whom she did not weep. Her whole soul was made up of sympathy and kindness. In her last illness she was composed and patient as an angel. She repeated several passages from the Psalms expressive of the love and goodness of God the day before she died. Her last words to me were, "A thousand and a thousand thanks to you, my dear brother, for all your kindness to me." She was buried near her two children. My whole heart descended into the grave with her. But it is time to quit a subject with which I could fill many pages. Our dear mother has had a light attack of the fever but is now in her usual health. On the 10th of this month I was a second time attacked by the disorder and for a day or two was in great danger, but it has pleased God to restore me again to life and health. I am still very weak and unable to do any business. My wife and children are in the Jerseys, where they have been for several months. The disease visibly and universally declines in every part of the town. It is expected that in two or three weeks we shall not have any more of it in the city.

With love to Mr. Montgomery, Miss Betsey, Mr. and Mrs.

Forster, and John,[1] in which our dear mother joins, I am, my dear and alas! now my only sister, your affectionate brother,

BENJN RUSH

Addressed: Mrs: Montgomery at Joseph Montgomery Esqr: at Harrisburgh.
MS: Josiah C. Trent, M.D., Durham, North Carolina.

[1] Miss Betsey was Elizabeth Montgomery (ca. 1770-1814), BR's niece, afterwards Mrs. Samuel Laird; John (b. 1771, date of death unknown) was her brother, said to have been postmaster at Harrisburg, 1791-1793; Mrs. Thomas Forster was the former Sarah Petit Montgomery (1768-1808), another niece of BR's (John M. Forster, *Sketch of the Life of the Rev. Joseph Montgomery*, Harrisburg, 1879, p. 47).

To ————[1]

Dear Sir, October 29th, 1793

Accept of my thanks for your friendly note and the interesting paper enclosed in it.

The facts which I have preserved during our late calamity relate only to the origin, history, and cure of the disease.

The only information which I am capable of giving you relates to the conduct of the Africans of our city. In procuring nurses for the sick, Wm. Grey and Absalom Jones were indefatigable, often sacrificing for that purpose whole nights of sleep without the least compensation. Richard Allen was extremely useful in performing the mournful duties which were connected with burying the dead. Many of the black nurses it is true were ignorant, and some of them were negligent, but many of them did their duty to the sick with a degree of patience and tenderness that did them great credit.

During the indisposition and confinement of the greatest part of the physicians of the city, Richard Allen and Absalom Jones procured copies of the printed directions for curing the fever, went among the poor who were sick, gave them the mercurial purges, bled them freely, and by these means, they this day informed me, they had recovered between two and three hundred people.

I was the more pleased with the above communication as it showed the safety and simplicity of the mode of treating the disease which you have politely said was generally successful.

From, dear sir, yours sincerely,

BENJN: RUSH

P.S. The merit of the blacks in their attendance upon the sick is enhanced by their not being exempted from the disorder. Many of them had it, but in general it was much milder and yielded more easily to art than in the white people.

MS: Pierpont Morgan Library, Signers Collection, Series III.

[1] In all likelihood the addressee was Mathew Carey, who quotes part of this letter in his *Short Account*, p. 63, and paraphrases the rest of it. See also Absalom Jones and Richard Allen, *A Narrative of the Proceedings of the Black People during the Late Calamity*, Phila., 1794.

To Mrs. Rush

My dear Julia,   Philadelphia, October 29, 1793

My letters of late have become so very uninteresting that I fear you will not think them worth their postage.

At 3 o'clock this afternoon I received a visit from Richd. Allen and Absalom Jones. They informed me that after most of the physicians of the city were confined, they procured the printed directions for curing the fever, went among the poor who were sick, gave them the mercurial purges, bled them freely, and by those means saved the lives of between two and three hundred persons. This information gave me great pleasure, as it shows the safety of the medicines I had recommended and that, with good attendance, the disease is as certainly under the management of art as the measles or influenza.

Dr. Blackwell continues to mend. I wrote a note to Mrs. Blackwell this morning, congratulating her upon the Doctor's recovery under the care of two young physicians and upon the triumph in his case of youthful reason and experience over gray-headed ignorance and error.

Our kinsman Mr. Hall is still in danger. His wife's sister is nearly gone. The disease in her fixed upon her brain and has induced a true mania, which will probably prove fatal before morning.

October 30th. In a former letter I mentioned to you that I had wept one evening over the 102nd psalm. Last night I felt great satisfaction in reading the 103rd psalm. I beg of you to read it over and over and to join with me in praising God for the wonderful deliverance he has wrought for me. You know as yet but *one quarter* of the dangers to which I have been exposed. "I have said (almost literally) to corruption, 'Thou art my father,' and to the worm, 'Thou art my mother and my sister.' "[1] The history of the circumstances under which life was preserved in me will form an interesting memoir in the account of the disease which I expect to publish as soon as I have strength and time enough for that purpose.[2]

I sometimes contemplate a ride to Princeton a week or two hence, but I can determine nothing positively as yet, for my presence in town is necessary to beget confidence in my pupils, and they have constantly from 20 to 30 patients under their care. I expect to take charge of the Hospital on Saturday. Adieu, my faithful and sympathizing friend. I am grateful for all the distress you have felt on my account. With love as usual, I am ever yours,

BENJN RUSH

Addressed: Mrs: Julia Rush at Richd: Stockton Esqr: Princeton.
MS: Josiah C. Trent, M.D., Durham, North Carolina.

[1] Job 17:14.
[2] This absorbing narrative was published as a supplement to BR's *Account of the Yellow Fever in 1793*, p. 339-63. In the 2d edn. of BR's *Med. Inq. & Obs.* (1805), it was given the title "A Narrative of the State of the Body and Mind of the Author, during the Prevalence of the Fever."

To Mrs. Rush

My dear Julia,   Philadelphia, October 30, 1793

The postmaster having at last provided a letter carrier, your letter of yesterday came to hand this day. It gave me great pleasure. John's letter[1] which accompanied it was equally satisfactory. The style and sentiments contained in it do him credit. Dr. Woodhouse, Mr. Fisher, and his Grandmama were charmed with it.

I am much obliged to Dr. Green[2] for an interest in his prayers. I have done him ample justice whenever I have heard his conduct blamed for leaving the city, and have openly declared that I advised him not to come to town at the time he proposed it. Dr. Ewing and Dr. Magaw receive no quarter from the public. The latter I have lately heard was indisposed in the country. I hope this is true. He is a good man and I think would not have left his flock, had his health permitted him to remain with them. Mr. Pilmore preached last Sunday, and this afternoon in walking by St. Paul's Church I saw him in the reading desk. Prayers have been offered up in that church twice a week ever since the commencement of the judgment of God upon our city.

Dr. Blackwell continues to mend. I received a most affectionate note from Mrs. Blackwell this evening by Mr. Coxe, in which you and the children are not forgotten. P. Hall is still in very great danger.

I have as yet visited no patient since my last confinement. I pass my time chiefly in reading and in adding to my notes of the *late* epidemic. Sometimes seated in your easy chair by the fire, I lose myself in looking back upon the ocean which I have passed, and now and then find myself surprised by a tear in reflecting upon the friends I have lost and the scenes of distress that I have witnessed and which I was unable to relieve. This evening I viewed a corner of the front room in which I sat in silence and darkness for half an hour at a time when the disease baffled the power of medicine. I felt over again all the horror and distress which the prospect of the almost or perhaps total desolation of our city at that time excited in my mind. I cast a look (I then thought most probably a final one) towards my dear family, for I had resolved to perish with my fellow citizens rather than dishonor my profession or religion by abandoning the city. I never can forget the anguish of soul with which in this awful situation I wrung my hands and I believe wept aloud. Soon afterwards——But why this painful retrospect of past troubles? "The winter is gone: the flowers appear upon the earth, the time of the singing of birds is come, and the voice of the turtle is again heard in our land."[3]

October 31. I am sorry to hear of your Mama's indisposition. Give my love to her and to all friends. Adieu, my dear friend. From yours sincerely,

BENJN RUSH

Addressed: Mrs: Julia Rush at Richd Stockton's Esqr: Princeton.
MS: Josiah C. Trent, M.D., Durham, North Carolina.

[1] In Rush MSS, XXXVI, dated 29 Oct. 1793.
[2] Rev. Ashbel Green, assistant to Dr. Sproat in the First Presbyterian Church.

On the circumstances of his absence from the city, see his *Life*, ed. J. H. Jones, N.Y., 1849, p. 272-5.
[3] Song of Songs 2:12.

To Mrs. Rush

My dear Julia,   Philadelphia, October 31, 1793

In dating my letter I am led to reflect that it is the last day of the month in which my dear sister died. I feel disposed to wish to arrest time at its present point, that I might still be within a month of the distressing day on which we parted. The nearer I can keep to that day, the nearer I feel my union to be to her and the less disposed I feel to consider her as gone forever.——Excuse this introduction to my letter. I shall never be able to review the melancholy scenes I have passed through, nor my sufferings from sickness and other causes, without feeling a revival of gratitude and affection to that dear woman which I never shall be able to express.

Our worthy kinsman Mr. Hall, Mr. Fisher thinks, is below hope. His wife's sister died this morning. The disease you see from these two cases is not deprived of its mortality. Many, I fear, will die with it in the course of the next month from ignorance or carelessness. The citizens are crowding into town every day. I wish they may not repent their coming in so soon. I have been called to two persons this day who came to town a day or two ago. Mr. Fisher hopes the complaints of the one we consented to attend are not from the contagion of the yellow fever. I ought to have mentioned above that Mr. Hall is dying of a relapse of the disorder brought on by extreme fatigue in sitting up three nights successively with his sister-in-law. How few people recover from fevers of any kind which are brought on by such strong predisposing causes! I shall lose a sincere friend in him. He visited me in my sickness, and I had great comfort in his pious conversation.

Envy and malice begin to be hoarse from their loud and long complaints against me. Dr. Wistar's friends alone are clamorous and unforgiving. He deserted me in the hour of danger and persecution. He *had given* the mercurial purges with success before he was sick. He had heard from his pupil Mr. Bache and from myself daily accounts of their wonderful efficacy; he had even *assented* to their success in curing the disorder by a very delicate but unmerited compliment which he paid me in his sickness for having introduced them into practice; and yet after all this, in his publication after his recovery, he says "he had not made up his mind" as to their efficacy. At this time the mercurial purges and myself were blasted in every part of the town for killing our citizens, and it was no longer safe or prudent to be *our* friend. Upon reading the Doctor's publication, I threw the paper from me and repeated the following lines from Shakespear:

> "This was the most unkindly cut of all.
> Thro' this, the well beloved Brutus stabbed,
> And as he plucked his cursed steel away,
> Mark how the blood of Caesar followed it,
> As rushing out of doors to be resolved,
> If Brutus so unkindly knocked or no—
> *For Brutus as you know was Caesar's angel.*"[1]

Dr. Wistar has heard of my having applied the above lines to him, and says I called him an assassin. I owned to the truth of the charge, but added that I had said much worse things of him than all that he had heard: that he had concealed the truth, that he had passed by a friend who was assassinating[2] by a set of ruffians without offering to assist him, and that by withholding his testimony in favor of mercury and jalap he had added to the mortality of the disorder.

November 1st. We are all well. Blessed be God for it and for the rain of yesterday and last night. Love as usual. Yours—yours—yours,

BENJN RUSH

MS: Josiah C. Trent, M.D., Durham, North Carolina.

[1] Approximately quoted from *Julius Caesar*, III, ii, 181ff.
[2] I.e., being assassinated; BR not in-

frequently used the present participle with the force of the passive.

To Mrs. Rush

My dear Julia,   Philadelphia, November 1, 1793

I concluded my letter last evening with an account of Dr. Wistar's desertion of his friend and, with him, of truth and humanity to his fellow citizens. I shall begin this letter by informing you that this day has produced a discovery of a letter from Dr. Currie to Dr. Hodge in which he has abused me in the most intemperate manner. Copies of this letter are circulating among the physicians and no doubt affords[1] them much consolation under the load of disgrace which their ignorance and blunders have brought upon them. One charge among many others brought against me is that I meanly introduced the mercurial purges to make money by the sale of them. The fact is as false, of my making money by them, as the motive is unkind to which he ascribes it. Nine-tenths of all the purges which went out of my shop before the apothecaries began to sell them were *given* away. My dear sister once offered me a dollar and an half which she received during my absence from home for some of them. I refused to take it, and she gave it to the first poor patient that came into the house afterwards. You may easily conceive of the number of those purges which I gave away when I add that I used three pounds of jalap and two and an half of calomel in the course of a few weeks, for after the 19th of September I sent everybody to the apothecaries for medicines of all kinds, except those poor people who had no money to buy them. You may conceive further of the demand for those powders and for advice when I assure you that my parlor and entry for several weeks were as crowded at all hours as ever you saw Holland's[2] or any other cheap shop in our city.

I expect to procure a copy of this letter, through the influence of Dr. Mease, which I shall immediately publish. It will show that I had a more formidable monster than the disease to contend with during the late calamity.

My dear kinsman P. Hall died last night. I have no doubt of his having entered into the joy of his Lord, and I have more than once this day fancied that I saw my dear sister running towards him to congratulate him upon his arrival on the coasts of bliss and to inquire of him after the health and comfort of her beloved brother.

I received a most friendly visit this day from Mr. Fitzsimons. He and his whole family have escaped the disorder.

November 2nd. Adieu, my dear Julia. I shall begin this day to make inquiries after Mr. Shippen's house. I hope to be in a condition to receive you all in two or three weeks, either in that house or in Mr. Mead's. With love as usual, I am yours most affectionately,

BENJN RUSH

Addressed: Mrs Julia Rush at Richd Stockton's Esqr: Princeton.
MS: Josiah C. Trent, M.D., Durham, North Carolina.

[1] Thus in MS.
[2] The 1793 *Directory* lists a Benjamin Holland, merchant, 3 North Front St.

To Mrs. Rush

My dear Julia,   Philadelphia, November 3rd, 1793

This afternoon Mr. Fisher drove me in the chair as far as Rose-hill, where I had the pleasure of seeing our son Ben in good health. My emotions upon his being brought near me (for I did not get out of the chair) may more easily be conceived than described. He has grown tall and handsome but still retains his sour countenance. Josey bid him laugh, which he did with great glee. His voice is as coarse as ever, but he speaks much plainer than he did when he left town. He says he wants to see you very much. Becky is impatient to bring him home, but I objected to it till we get into a larger and purer house. She sends a great deal of love to you.

After parting with Ben, we rode up to Captain Barry's.[1] The whole family came to the door and received us with a degree of joy that rose almost to acclamations. Suspected as we were of being infected, they would have dragged us from the chair into the house had we permitted them. They regaled us with sweetmeats and biscuit and offered us wine, but my stomach will not yet bear it. They inquired for you and gave you great credit for the fortitude and even heroism with which you had conducted yourself in my late perilous and distressing situation.

Colonel Hamilton is indisposed and has sent to New York for Dr. Stevens. He still defends bark and the cold bath in the yellow fever, and reprobates my practice as obsolete in the West Indies. A fact will soon come to light which will cover him and his physicians with confusion. It will appear in a few days that *two-fifths* of all the sick that were sent to Bush hill have died under the most favorable circumstances of accommodation and attendance.[2] Ben Duffield and a Frenchman[3] were their physicians. The new remedies were never used to[4] any of them. Under the most unfavorable circumstances of attendance from my own sickness, the sickness of my pupils, &c., I seldom lost more than one in twenty of all who passed through my hands.

Dr. Kuhn came to town last Friday. A man died on Saturday night who returned from the country a week ago.

November 4th. Adieu. Love as usual. Yours sincerely and affectionately,

BENJN RUSH

Addressed: Mrs: Julia Rush at Richd: Stockton's Esqr: Princeton.
MS: Josiah C. Trent, M.D., Durham, North Carolina.

[1] John Barry (1745-1803), the Irish-born American naval hero (DAB).

[2] Carey reported that of "about one thousand" admitted to Bush Hill between 16 Sep. and 30 Nov., "nearly five hundred are dead" (*Short Account*, p. 34).

[3] Jean Devèze (1753-1829), a French military surgeon who had come to Philadelphia with the other refugees from Cap François in the summer of 1793. As the principal physician at Bush Hill, where he instituted a therapy radically different from that of BR, he was awarded $1,500 by the citizens' committee. As J. H. Powell has shown,

Devèze was one of the principal heroes of the epidemic. Appointed surgeon-major of the military hospital established in Philadelphia by the French Republic, he stayed in the city at least through 1797. His *Recherches et observations sur les causes et les effets de la maladie épidémique qui a régné à Philadelphie* . . . , Phila., 1794 (French and English texts together), has a place in medical history because it first contended that yellow fever is non-contagious. Devèze wrote other works on the yellow fever after his return to France, where he served as one of the court physicians for many years. (*Biog. Univ., Supplément*;

Packard, *Hist. of Medicine in the U.S.*, I, 130-3, II, 1110-11; Surg. Gen. Off., *Index-Cat.*, 1st ser., III, 718; Powell, *Bring Out Your Dead, passim.*)
⁴ Thus in MS.

To Mrs. Rush

My dear Julia,   Philadelphia, November 4, 1793

Your letter of the 2nd of this instant gave me great pleasure. I have the deepest sense of your fervent and unabated affection for me, and in the midst of my dangers and distresses at all times derived consolation from reflecting that I lived every moment in your remembrance and was constantly carried by you to the throne of heaven for my preservation. I derived comfort in the near prospects of death likewise, from reflecting upon your extraordinary prudence, your good sense, and pious dispositions, all of which qualified you in an eminent degree to educate our children in a proper manner in case I had been taken from you. This idea, connected with an unshaken faith in God's promises to widows and fatherless children, sometimes suspended for a while my ardent and natural attachment to you and the children and made me at times willing to part with you, provided my death would have advanced the great objects to which I had devoted myself. Life was most desirable at one time only when I thought of the unfinished works I should leave behind me, and particularly a long and exact detail of my opinions and practice in the yellow fever. To render this detail in some degree useful in case I had died, I wrote all my notes in a fair, legible hand and committed the arrangement and publication of them to my dear pupil Dr. Mease.

I do not give up my hopes of being able to pay you a short visit. Can you provide me with a separate bed and room? And will you consent to receive me without the usual modes of salutation among long absent and affectionate friends? This must be stipulated before I can consent to comply with your invitation.

Mr. Fisher drove me out to Mr. Meredith's this forenoon. We were received with great kindness and pressed to stay to dinner. I declined it, but with a promise to spend part of a day with them some time in the course of this week.

I received a visit this day from Dr. Mease. He is a mere skeleton but retains his usual fine spirits.

November 5th. Marcus, Betsey, and Peter send their duty and love to you. I have this morning made Marcus very happy by giving him the suit of clothes I wore during the prevalence of the fever. I have in the stead of it put on my suit of black.

My mother joins in much love to you and the children and all friends.

Addressed: Mrs: Julia Rush at Richd: Stockton Esqr: Princeton.
MS (signature cut away): Josiah C. Trent, M.D., Durham, North Carolina.

To John Redman[1]

Dear Sir,   Philadelphia, November 5, 1793

I beg you would convey, by means of this letter, my resignation of my fellowship in the College of Physicians.

I request at the same time their acceptance of a copy of Dr. Wallis' edition of the *Works* of Dr. Sydenham.[2]

With the tenderest sentiments of respect for yourself, I am, dear sir, your sincere friend and the College's well-wisher,

BENJAMIN RUSH

Printed: Ruschenberger, *Account of . . . the College of Physicians of Philadelphia*, 1887, p. 58.

[1] The letter is addressed to Redman in his capacity as president of the College of Physicians.

[2] This was an edition of Sydenham's *Works on Acute and Chronic Diseases* annotated by George Wallis, London, 1788, 2 vol. For the significance of the gift, see note on BR's letter to J. R. B. Rodgers of 3 Oct. 1793, and also his *Account of the Yellow Fever in 1793*, p. 337.

To Mrs. Rush

My dear Julia,   Philadelphia, November 7th, 1793

Your letter of yesterday came to hand in the evening. You cannot be more impatient for our meeting than I am, but I dread the thoughts of seeing you in town till the city is more thoroughly purified from the contagion of the yellow fever. Many have sickened, and some have died, of the citizens who have come into town within these ten days. I will give you the earliest notice of the time when it will be proper to return, but a day of the month must not govern you while we are unable to foretell or to govern the changes in the weather.

I shall attend to your advice respecting my brethren. Indeed I never intended to begin a controversy with them. I have hitherto calmly contradicted their falsehoods. Dr. Hodge (stimulated by the Wistar family) leads the van of my calumniators. I gave him no other offense than declining to consult him, as I did latterly with all the wine and bark doctors. A Jew and a Christian attempting to worship in the same temple and by means of the same ceremonies is not a more absurd sight than two physicians meeting to consult about a disease on the cause and cure of which they differed as widely as light differs from darkness. I did not take this decisive step with my brethren till I made myself hoarse in trying to persuade them to adopt the new remedies, and until they had accused me in the newspapers of murdering my patients by bloodletting. The die with them is cast. I feel as if I were more than able through divine support to meet the gathering storm. Since it has been convenient and safe for the citizens to visit each other and to meet at corners, I have heard enough to satisfy me that I shall not be driven from the city. My old patients cannot desert me, for I did not desert them in the day of their adversity, and some of Kuhn's patients whom I cured have already declared that they intend to employ me. I was sent for to one of the wealthiest of them this morning.

Well might David prefer the scourge of a pestilence to that of the evil dispositions of his fellow men. I hope God will forgive my want of faith. I am now sure that he that hath in abundant mercy delivered me from the rage of the late pestilence will likewise deliver me from the scourge of tongues and the wrath of man.

Your Mama's letter was balm to my heart.[1] She gives you great credit for your proper and dignified behavior during the whole time of my sickness and dangers, but she has not added to my opinion of you. I have often said that you were an uncommon woman. I can now truly say that you are a GREAT woman, and it will always be my consolation and pleasure (for we should have *pride* in nothing) that in all the letters I have received from my wife and three of my children, not one of them contained a single request or even hint to me to leave the city during the prevalence of the late fatal epidemic. For such a wife and such children, I desire to be thankful.

I shall not write again until Saturday. My tenderest love to your Mama and to each of the family. Mr. Fisher sends his respects to you. He rises daily in my opinion for every quality that can adorn a gentleman or constitute a physician.

From your sincere friend,

BENJN RUSH

P.S. Dr. White's family is come to town, but they keep close house.

Addressed: Mrs: Julia Rush at Richd Stockton Esqr: Princeton.
MS: Josiah C. Trent, M.D., Durham, North Carolina.

[1] Mrs. Stockton's letter, dated from Morven, 3 Nov. [17]93, offers religious consolation to BR and praises the exemplary conduct of Mrs. Rush and John: "As to yourself, your monument is already erected in the hearts of every person of sensibility that has ever heard your name through out the reign of this awful pestilence. . . . New Jersey echos from all her shores the constancy, the courage, the benevolence, of the man that devoted himself living or dying to the comfort and health of his fellow citizens" (Rush MSS, XXXVI, 120).

To Mrs. Rush

My dear Julia,   Philadelphia, November 8th, 1793

I have this day received by Captain Josiah[1] from London a letter to you from Dr. Edwards,[2] accompanied with your silk gown which you committed to his care to be dyed. I have sent the letter by the post. I received a long and interesting letter from him at the same time, also a valuable medical book from Dr. Proudfit.[3]

The disease has declined again since the last rain. I have had no calls to patients in the yellow fever for two days past, but several to patients indisposed with other diseases. My applications for advice in my house have been considerable likewise, but from no person affected with our late epidemic.

That my letters may contain a faithful narrative of all that related to myself during the late calamities of our city, I may *now* venture to inform you that in the morning of October 10th, at one o'clock, I was attacked in a most violent manner with all the symptoms of the fever. Seldom have I endured more pain. My mind sympathized with my body. You and my seven dear children rushed upon my imagination and tore my heartstrings in a manner I had not experienced in my former illness. A recovery in my weak and exhausted state seemed hardly probable. At 2 o'clock I called up Marcus and Mr. Fisher, who slept in the adjoining room. Mr. Fisher bled me, which instantly removed my pains, and then gave me a dose and an half of the mercurial medicine. It puked me several times during the night and brought off a good deal of bile from my stomach. The next morning it operated downwards and relieved me so much that I was able to sit up long enough to finish my letter to you. In the afternoon my fever returned, attended with a sleepiness, which is always considered as an alarming symptom.

Mr. Fisher bled me again, which immediately removed it. I slept pretty well the next night, was very weak but free of pain the next day; but the night following I fell into just such a fainty fit as I had about the crisis of my pleurisy in the year 1788. I called upon Marcus, who slept in the room with me, for something to drink and afterwards for some nourishment, which revived me in a few minutes, so that I slept well the remaining part of the night. One or two nights afterwards he gave me something to eat, which prevented a return of the fainty fits. It was not till the 15th of the month I was able to set up, nor did I leave my room for many days afterwards. Mr. Fisher says he has seen no person more violently seized than I was. My recovery was under God owing to the *speedy* use of the new remedies. This second attack of the fever I now see was sent in mercy to me and my family. Had I not been arrested by it in my labors, my poor frame would probably have sunk, before this time, under nothing but weakness and fatigue.

I used to wish, when called to more patients than I could attend, that I had an hundred hands and an hundred feet. I now wish that I had an hundred hearts and an hundred tongues to praise the power, goodness, and mercy of my gracious Deliverer, to whom alone belong[4] the issue from sickness and the grave.

Strike out from the list of deaths in your letters Jos. Harrison and Jonth. Penrose.[5] Many people walk the streets now who were said to be dead during the prevalence of the disorder. Adieu. Love as usual. Yours sincerely,

BENJN RUSH

P.S. Marcus is constantly employed in preparing and purifying the house for your reception. I hope to be able to give you notice next week on what day you may return. I accord with all your propositions, for I expect to be more of your *boarder* hereafter than ever. I have much unfinished business to complete, and "Brethren, I say the time is short."[6]

Addressed: To Mrs: Julia Rush at Richd. Stockton Esqr Princeton.
MS: Josiah C. Trent, M.D., Durham, North Carolina.

[1] Identified in note 6 to letter of 17-18 Oct. 1793.

[2] Enoch Edwards (1751-1802), BR's earliest apprentice; served as a surgeon in the Revolution; member of the Pennsylvania ratifying convention, 1787, and of the state constitutional convention, 1789; associate justice of common pleas, 1791-1802. In 1793 he traveled in England and Scotland and called on many of BR's old friends. (BR's MS List of Apprentices; Edwards' letters in Rush MSS, IV, XXI, XXXVII; BR's *Autobiography*, p. 311-12; McMaster and Stone, *Penna. and the Federal Constitution*, p. 726-7.)

[3] James Proudfit, M.D., College of Philadelphia, 1790; continued his studies

at St. Bartholomew's Hospital, London (Proudfit's inaugural thesis [copy in Coll. Phys. Phila.]; letters from Proudfit in Rush MSS, XXVI).

[4] Thus in MS.

[5] Jonathan Penrose was a justice of the peace, 308 South Front St. (1793 *Directory*).

[6] I Corinthians 7:29.

To Mrs. Rush

My dear Julia,   Philadelphia, November 11, 1793

My business has increased so much with my strength within these few days, that I am forced unwillingly to relinquish the hope I had cherished of paying you a short visit at Princeton. My time of attending the Hospital moreover has commenced, and you know I am not accustomed to neglecting my duty to that institution. The lectures are to begin on the 9th of next month. Some preparation will be necessary for my course, for the late busy season which I have passed through has prevented my making myself master of several subjects on which I must decide in the course of the winter. I endeavor to console myself under my constant labors by recollecting a speech of Dr. Finley's on his deathbed. "I have," said he, "led a busy and laborious life. I was ashamed to take rest here. Eternity will be[1] long enough to rest in."

We had yesterday four deaths with the yellow fever, and some more are expected. Unless we have a few frosty nights this week, it will by no means be safe for you to return at the time formerly mentioned. My bed and the furniture of my room have been exposed for several nights, but as yet no frost has touched them. A woman died yesterday from the contagion lodged in a surtout coat which her son brought into the house. Have patience. As you said to me in one of your letters written a week or two before our marriage, "I long—yet dread to see you." Many people are crowding into town, and as yet but few have caught the fever, but recollect that none, or but few of them, come into infected houses or to an infected family. I am this day to meet Mr. Shippen at his son-in-law's, Mr. Burd's,[2] upon the subject of his house. You shall hear tomorrow of the result of our negotiations. Mrs. Clymer speaks in high terms of the house.

The slanders of my *old* brethren begin to subside a little. A catalogue of them would fill a sheet of paper. One among many is that I have not been sick, but I confined myself to avoid danger. Poor creatures! Where could I have met with greater danger than from the contagion in my own house? Until the 10th of October

I was confined only five days. My confinement since was the effect not only of a severe attack of the fever, but of such a degree of weakness, attended with a cough and occasional fever, as rendered me scarcely able at times to climb a pair of stairs.

I have this morning been rebuked, humbled, and comforted by reading the 37th psalm. I find I am a perfect Jew in unbelief. I desire to be humbled into the dust for it.

Mrs. Harrison, whom I visited yesterday as a patient at her son Mathias's,[3] inquired after you with great solicitude. She said that she had thought of you much oftener during the distress of our city than you had thought of her. You had, I find, the sympathy, and hereafter you will have the praises, of all who know you.

Adieu. My tenderest love to all the family. Yours—yours—yours, my faithful Julia,

BENJN RUSH

Addressed: Mrs Julia Rush at Richd Stockton's Esqr Princeton.
MS: Josiah C. Trent, M.D., Durham, North Carolina.

[1] Omitted in MS.
[2] Edward Burd (1751-1833), for many years prothonotary of the Pennsylvania supreme court, had married Elizabeth, daughter of Edward Shippen, 1778 (Keith, *Provincial Councillors*, p. [70-1]). He lived at 88 South Fourth St. (1793 *Directory*).
[3] Not further identified.

To Mrs. Rush

My dearest Julia,   Philadelphia, November 12, 1793

I want words to describe my emotions upon hearing that the dearest person to me upon the face of the earth is at last within three miles of me after a long and most distressing separation. A longer and colder ride into the country than usual this morning has so far exhausted my strength that I fear I could not bear a ride to Rosehill and afterwards—a first interview with you. I have moreover a patient ill with a disorder which cannot bear the loss of two visits a day at a *certain* hour without the risk of his life. For these reasons I have prevailed upon Mr. Fisher to convey you this letter, with a request to come into town with him or with an assurance that I will come out (if as well as usual) in the forenoon and spend the day with you tomorrow.

If you come to town, you shall have the front room (now the purest in the house) to yourself. I will sleep in the room adjoining you with the door open between us. Kiss Ben. But—ah—who will kiss my dear Julia? Her most affectionate husband,

BENJN RUSH[1]

Addressed: Mrs: Julia Rush at Rosehill Mr Fisher.
MS: Josiah C. Trent, M.D., Durham, North Carolina.

[1] This conclusion to the long series of letters written during the epidemic was a little studied. BR wrote: "Kiss Ben *(for me)*. But—ah—who will kiss *(you for)* my dear Julia *(your)* her most affectionate husband."

To James Kidd[1]

Dear Sir,   Philadelphia, November 25th, 1793

I sincerely congratulate you upon your appointment to a professorship in the College of Aberdeen and highly approve of your accepting of it. Your great attainments in oriental literature will render you useful in that station. In America Rabbi Robinson[2] himself would not command the least respect or even clothe himself by teaching the Hebrew language.

The present commotions in Europe appear to be the commencement of the third woe mentioned in the book of Revelations.[3] They will I hope usher in a glorious day of peace, liberty, and universal happiness.

The United States will not take part with France in her present struggle for liberty. We continue to prosper in all the arts of peace. The city of Philadelphia alone has experienced a sad reverse of situation since last spring, 4,000 of her citizens having perished in the course of three months with a bilious remitting yellow fever. The distress produced by this event, among all classes of people, was nearly equal to that which was produced by the great plague in London in the years 1664-5.

The language of heaven in the wars, famine, and pestilence which now prevail more or less all over the world seems to be "Seekest thou great things? Seek them not, for behold, I bring evil on all flesh."[4]

The conduct of the French Convention seems intended to prove that human reason alone in its most cultivated state will not make men free or happy without the aid of divine revelation and the influences of the Spirit of the Gospel upon the hearts of men.

If Dr. Beattie be living, do present my most affectionate respects to him, and tell him that I owe a great debt of gratitude to him for the instruction and pleasure I have derived from reading his excellent works.

From, dear sir, your sincere friend,

BENJN RUSH

Addressed: Mr: James Kidd Professor of Oriental languages, Marll: College Aberdeen. ⊕ the Wm Penn Capt Dale.
MS: Henry E. Huntington Library.

[1] James Kidd (1761-1834), born in Ireland, came to Philadelphia in 1784 and was employed as a tutor in the Latin or grammar school of the University, 1789-1790. He studied Hebrew privately and with great assiduity, went to Edinburgh to complete his theological training, and was appointed professor of Oriental languages at Marischal College, Aberdeen, just before this letter was written. Licensed by the Aberdeen Presbytery in 1796, Kidd preached for many years at a church there and became an extremely popular pulpit orator; D.D., Princeton, 1818; published many theological writings. (DNB; Univ. of Penna., Trustees Minutes, 1789-1790; Kidd's letters to BR in Rush MSS, IX.)

[2] Search and inquiry have failed to identify this person. BR apparently had in mind a British scholar but may not have remembered his name correctly.

[3] See Revelation 11:14.

[4] Jeremiah 45:5.

To Frances Stall[1]

My dear Madam,   February 5th, 1794

Permit me to request your acceptance of a small mark* of my esteem for your late excellent son and my much beloved pupil.

With great regard and unabating sympathy with you and your family, I am, my dear madam, your sincere friend,

BENJN RUSH

*A half pint silver cup, with the following inscription: "For Frances Stall, from Benjamin Rush, as a mark of esteem for her son John F. Stall, who died September 23, 1793, in the 19th year of his age."

MS (draft): Library Company of Philadelphia, Rush MSS.

[1] For the background of this letter, see BR to Mrs. Rush, 29-30 Aug. 1793, note 8.

To Horatio Gates

Philadelphia, 23rd March, 1794

An old friend who admires and prefers a republican form of government as much as he did in the year 1777, who wishes success to the cause of France while he laments the errors and vices of the National Convention, and who sincerely abhors all dramatic representations of royalty in the United States, is very happy in an opportunity of assuring General Gates of the continuance of his respect for his republican, and friendship for his private, virtues. The name of that old friend is

BENJN RUSH

Addressed: General Gates near New York.
MS: New-York Historical Society, Gates Papers.

To James Kidd

Philadelphia, May 13, 1794

Your letter of the 20th of January[1] came safely to hand. I shall take no notice of your inquiries after your family, for I take it for granted that they and you are again happy in each other's society. Nor shall I controvert your assertions concerning the Mountain[2] of Paris. I feel disposed to be still, in order that I may see the salvation of God. How mysterious at first sight, and yet how infinitely wise and just is it, that that land of Catholicism should banish superstition and tyranny in Europe, and one impostor overturn another in Asia. Thus do the potsherds of the earth smite each other. The United States continue to flourish in agriculture, arts, and commerce. France does not ask for our assistance in her present contest with despotism, and Great Britain, since the recapture of Toulon, holds out olive branches to our country. How kind is providence in every deluge, whether of water or of blood, to prepare an ark for the preservation of the poor human race.

I have just committed to the press a history of our late epidemic; it will contain nearly four hundred octavo pages.[3] Reverberate over and over my love to Dr. Beattie. I cannot think of him without fancying that I see Mr. Hume prostrate at his feet. He was the David who slew that giant of infidelity.

Adieu, from yours sincerely,

BENJ. RUSH

Printed: One Hundred Years of Temperance: A Memorial Volume of the Centennial Temperance Conference Held in Philadelphia, . . . 1885, N.Y., 1886, p. 25.

[1] In Rush MSS, IX.
[2] La Montagne, les Montagnards: the party of the extreme left in the revolutionary government of France.
[3] *An Account of the Bilious Remitting Yellow Fever, as It Appeared in the City*

of *Philadelphia, in the Year 1793*, Phila.: Dobson, 1794. This work quickly attained classic status, and the narrative portions still make excellent reading. A 2d Philadelphia edn. appeared late in 1794, and it is this edition, rather than the first, which (for reasons not apparent) is generally regarded as vol. III of the first collected edition of BR's *Medical Inquiries and Observations*; see *L.C. Cat.* The *Account* was thereafter reprinted in the several reissues of the *Med. Inq. & Obs.*, 1805, 1809, 1815, 1818. An Edinburgh edn. was published in 1796; a German translation (*Beschreibung des gelben Fiebers, welches im Jahre 1793 in Philadelphia herschte*) was issued at Tübingen in the same year (copy in Coll. Phys. Phila.); and a Spanish translation, with an extended commentary, followed in 1804 (see BR to David Hosack, 15 Aug. 1810).

To the Philadelphia Committee of Health

Gentlemen,   September 13, 1794

On the 29th of August I informed you that I had met with a number of cases of the yellow fever in our city. Since that time I have observed it to be *contagious* in several instances. I have since likewise heard of many cases of the disease in the city, which have been called by the less unpopular names of jaundice, bilious fever, and intermitting fever by the physicians who attended them. The remedies of bleeding and purging continue to be successful in every case in which they are applied on the first day of the disease; and could all the physicians of the city be prevailed upon to call it by its common or West India name and to treat it with copious evacuations, there would be no more danger to life nor injury to the credit of our city from it than from the measles or influenza.

Dr. Physick, Dr. Barton, and Dr. Dewees[1] (of New Street) have concurred with me in declaring the yellow fever to be in town. Dr. Barton assures me that he has seen one case in which it was contagious.

The best thing the Committee can do for the safety of the city is to make the above information public. It will excite the citizens to apply early for medical aid, and it will produce in the minds of such of the physicians as are unprejudiced an early suspicion of the presence of the disease in those cases where it comes on with its less obvious symptoms.

From, gentlemen, your friend and fellow citizen,

BENJN: RUSH

MS (draft): Library Company of Philadelphia, Rush MSS.

[1] William Potts Dewees (1768-1841) studied privately and attended medical courses at the University, practising for some years before obtaining his M.D., in 1806; a very successful obstetrician, he wrote important works in his field and briefly held the chair of midwifery at the University, 1834-1835 (DAB).

To John Redman Coxe

My dear Friend,   Philadelphia, September 19, 1794

This letter will find you I hope safely arrived in London and happy in the society of your English relations and friends.

In my last letter to your Papa[1] I informed him that I had met with a few cases of yellow fever in our city. I then supposed them to be sporadic, but it has since become epidemic among us, but with so few circumstances of terror or distress that scarcely anybody has left the city upon the account of it. Mercury, jalap, and the lancet have been adopted by most of our physicians, and hence the disease has been attended with mortality in very few cases. The Kuneans call it an inflammatory remittent and deny it to be the true yellow fever. Where a yellowness attends, they call it a jaundice. This conduct is necessary; otherwise they would be obliged to subscribe to the generation of the disease in our city and to the use of depleting medicines. Dr. Kuhn lost Caleb Emlen's eldest son[2] last week on the 5th day of a fever. He was yellow before as well as after his death. The Doctor called it a *putrid* fever. I did not hear what medicines he took, but he was not bled.

Drs. Physic, Barton, Annan, and Dewees openly support me in declaring the yellow fever to be in town. Two physicians who owned they had seen cases of it have since denied it. Such has been the clamor against me that a proposal has been made in a company of citizens to "drum me out of the city." I am not moved by insults nor threats, but persist in asserting and defending all my opinions respecting the disease. The only revenge I seek of my fellow citizens is to save their lives, and the only notice I take of the slanders of my medical brethren is to refuse to consult with them.

The same fever prevails at this time in Charleston, Baltimore, New York, and New Haven. Wherever the new remedies are adopted, the disease is reduced in point of danger and mortality to a level with the measles and smallpox. In two of the above places, the disease has been evidently the offspring of American heat and putrefaction. My success has been much greater this year than last, owing to my patients' being so much better attended and nursed. I have bled more freely in our present than in our late epidemic. From a newly arrived Englishman I took 144 ounces of blood at twelve bleedings in six days—four of those bleedings were in twenty hours. I gave him within the course of the same six days nearly 150 grains of calomel with the usual proportions of jalap and gamboge.[3]

I have taken full notes of the fever from the 9th of June to this day, and hope to give the public another volume upon it next spring.[4] It will contain a more extensive view of my principles and a fuller defense of bloodletting in fevers than my first volume upon this subject.

Give my love to my much-esteemed friend Mr. Fisher. I would write to him, but I know not where or how to address him. You both continue to retain a large share of my gratitude and friendship. The date of my letter brings fresh to my recollection scenes never to be forgotten, in which you were almost my only friends. May heaven bless and reward you for your kindness and sympathy! My dear Mrs. Rush and the children (who are still in town) join me in love to your honored parents, sister, and brothers, from, my dear pupil, your affectionate friend,

BENJN RUSH

Addressed: Dr John Redman Coxe to be left at Daniel Coxe Esqr: London By the way of Liverpool.
MS: Historical Society of Pennsylvania, Dreer Collection.

[1] Daniel Coxe (ca. 1741-1826), formerly an eminent lawyer in Trenton, who as a zealous loyalist had returned to England after the Revolution; BR had made Coxe's acquaintance on his return voyage from Europe in 1769 (BR, *Autobiography*, p. 74; E. Alfred Jones, *Loyalists of New Jersey* [N.J. Hist. Soc., *Collections*, x], p. 52-4). There are letters to BR from Coxe after the latter's return to England in Rush MSS, XXVII; but the other side of the correspondence has not been found.

[2] Caleb Emlen was a lumber merchant at 6 North Third St. (1794 *Directory*).

I have not identified his eldest son.

[3] According to Coxe's *American Dispensatory*, 1825 (p. 301-2), gamboge is the gum resin of a tree native to Siam and Ceylon: "*Medical use*—Gamboge evacuates powerfully both upwards and downwards; some condemn it as acting with too great violence, and occasioning dangerous hypercatharsis; while others are of a contrary opinion."

[4] This eventually appeared, with the "Defence of Blood-Letting," as vol. IV of BR's *Medical Inquiries and Observations*, Phila., 1796.

To John Redman Coxe

My dear Friend,   Philadelphia, November 4th, 1794

Accept of my thanks for your affectionate letter.[1] I rejoiced to hear of your safe arrival and of your happy interview with your family.

In my last I informed you of the revival of the yellow fever in our city. My decision upon the subject of its existence and generation a second time among us exposed me to more persecution than last year, owing to Dr. Kuhn's remaining in town and perverting and directing the public mind. His influence in our city and with our physicians is more extensive than ever. Wistar and Currie have apostasized from the use of jalap, calomel, and bloodletting in the yellow fever, and have given Kuhn's remedies in many cases. Currie acknowledges that he has lost 17 out of 23 patients in the disorder. Wistar and Kuhn have been nearly as unsuccessful, but they ascribe their numerous deaths to bilious and intermitting fevers, gout, dropsies of the brain, and half the diseases of Cullen's nosology. My success has been unparalleled in the history of my practice. Out of upwards of 120 of "strongly marked" cases, I lost but two where my prescriptions were followed in the first stage of the disorder. Many dishonorable arts were employed to shake the confidence of my patients in my remedies by emissaries from the idolaters of bark and wine. One while they were told that I bled people to death, then that I was a horse doctor, and where both these charges failed of their intention, the old slander of *madness* was slyly insinuated against me. In my publication next spring I hope to divert you with some anecdotes of our citizens and of our physicians that will show their folly, ignorance, and craft in a light that will expose them to the contempt of all wise and good men. Our mode of practice has been adopted in New Haven, Baltimore, and Charleston with almost universal success.

Dr. Griffitts, Dr. Physick, and Dr. Dewees (lately of Abingdon) have been my only supports this year. Griffitts has bled 7 times in four days, and Physick has in two cases saved his patients by drawing above 120 ounces of blood from them.

I yesterday gave an introductory lecture upon the connection of metaphysics with the study of medicine. It was well received. The prospects of large classes are considerable. Dr. Carson died a few days ago. The professorship of chemistry will be offered to Dr. Priestley.[2] What say you to qualifying yourself to succeed him? His age will prevent his discharging the duties of that chair more than eight or ten years.

Adieu, my dear friend. My best love to your worthy parents and to each of your brothers and sisters, in all which my dear Mrs. Rush joins most affectionately. Remember whose son and grandson you are. Be wise, just, and kind; otherwise you will break the charter of your family. Once more adieu! From yours sincerely,

BENJN RUSH

P.S. In my second volume on the yellow fever I shall ascribe the inflammatory constitution of the air for the two last years in our city to an unusual impregnation of it with oxygene. I have sent a copy of your thesis to Dr. Beddoes.[3] Your principles upon inflammation must prevail.

MS: Historical Society of Pennsylvania, Dreer Collection.

[1] Coxe's letters to BR from abroad are in Rush MSS, XXVII; they provide revealing glimpses of medical developments in London and elsewhere.

[2] BR's letters to Priestley (who had just come to America), urging him to accept the chair of chemistry in Philadelphia, are lost, but Priestley's replies (in Rush MSS, XXX) have been printed in his *Scientific Correspondence*, ed. H. C. Bolton, N.Y., 1892; see especially p. 139-41, 143-4, 144-5. He declined the post with regret.

[3] Thomas Beddoes, M.D., and medical writer (1760-1808), who established at Clifton a "Pneumatic Institute" for the treatment of disease by inhalation (DNB). In the Rush MSS, III, there is an interesting letter, without date, from Beddoes to BR on his progress in establishing the Institute.

To John Redman Coxe

My dear Friend,   Philadelphia, December 19th, 1794

Accept of my thanks for your letter by the *Pigon*. Your next, I hope, will contain all the medical news of Edinburgh.

We have nothing interesting here. A *syncope* has taken place in medicine in our University. Dr. Priestley has declined the chemical chair, and as yet no successor has been appointed to it. Dr. B. Duffield is giving a course of lectures on midwifery gratis—under the patronage of Dr. Shippen. The design of this volunteer course was to defeat Dr. Price,[1] who has merit and would otherwise have had a large private class. Actuated by resentment, the Doctor has written to a Mr. Steel[2] in London to come over to our city and to teach anatomy with him, thereby to lessen the reputation and class of Dr. Shippen. I doubt of the success of the measure. I have taken and shall take no part in the dispute.

B. Duffield seldom concludes a lecture without a phillipic against me. Dr. Kuhn delivered the two lectures upon the yellow fever a few days ago which you heard last year. His class smiled at him during the greatest part of the time he was employed in reading them. But low as he is with the students, he is still the Apollo of the College of Physicians.

Dr. Griffitts, Dr. Physick, and Dr. Dewees (late of Philadelphia County) continue to support my principles and practice in their utmost extent. Dr. Physick is rising into great business, more especially in surgery.

I have requested your Grandpapa to send you a copy of the

second edition of the first volume of my *Inquiries*.[3] The 2nd edition of the *Account of the Yellow Fever* has made its appearance in our city. It contains but few additions. I have reserved all the facts and opinions suggested by the disease this year for another volume to be published (if my health be spared) next summer.

I am preparing three or four clinical lectures upon the gout, to which I shall apply some of my principles.

Mrs. Rush, Mr. Alexander,[4] and all my little folks join in love to you and Mr. Fisher with, my dear friend, your affectionate preceptor,

BENJN RUSH

P.S. Our winter fevers are (as last winter) strongly marked with bile and require copious bleeding.

Addressed: Dr: John R: Coxe (of Philadelphia) now at the University of Edinburgh. By the way of London.

MS: Historical Society of Pennsylvania, Dreer Collection.

[1] Philip Price, M.D., 7 South Fourth St.; he is said to have lectured privately on theory and practice and on midwifery (1794 *Directory*; Packard, *Hist. of Medicine in U.S.*, 1, 337).

[2] Not further identified.

[3] *Medical Inquiries and Observations. ...Volume I, Second American Edition*, Phila.: Dobson, 1794. This is usually regarded as the first volume in BR's collective *Medical Inquiries*.

[4] Ashton Alexander (1772-1855) came of a prominent Virginia family, was an apprentice of BR's, 1794-1795, and graduated M.D. from the University of Pennsylvania, 1795; practised for many years in Baltimore, where he was a founder and the first secretary of the Medical and Chirurgical Faculty of Maryland, 1799, and provost of the University of Maryland, 1835-1850 (Kelly & Burrage, *Dict. Amer. Med. Biog.*; BR's MS List of Apprentices). There are nearly thirty letters from Alexander to BR in Rush MSS, 1, dating from 1796 to 1813, and these demonstrate the strongest kind of attachment between BR and his pupil. Only a few of BR's letters to Alexander have been traced.

To the President of the Pennsylvania Abolition Society[1]

Sir, [*1794?*]

It has long been a matter of regret among the friends of the free blacks that they are employed chiefly as servants and sailors, for which occupations many of them are but little qualified and in which they are peculiarly exposed to continue in the practice of such vices as have been contracted in slavery. Most of the black men who come to Philadelphia from New Jersey and the southern states are farmers. To obtain employment for them more congenial to their knowledge and former habits, it has been the wish of many of their friends to see them occupied in agricultural pursuits. In order to effect if possible this desirable end, I request the Abolition Society to accept of 5,200 [*acres of*] land in Bedford County. Its situation and quality are mentioned in the description of it.

For the settlement of it by the blacks the following plan has occurred to me:

1. That a tract of 400 acres in fee simple be given to an intelligent farmer who shall by his advice and influence assist in the establishment of the settlement.

2. That portions of lands be given in fee simple to each individual or family in proportion to their numbers not exceeding 50 acres, and that if more be required it be sold to them.

3. That one tract be reserved for the support of schools and places of worship.

4. That all farms which shall be deserted or become vacant by death without issue shall escheat to the Abolition Society.

5. That no sale shall be made of a farm by the owner of it but to a black and an actual resident or cultivator of the soil.

6. That the name of the settlement be *Benezet*, after the late worthy and indefatigable advocate of the freedom of the blacks, Anthony Benezet.

The difficulties and expenses of effecting a settlement upon the plan which has been proposed will I have no doubt be considerable. Should the attempt be successful, its beneficial consequences upon the safety and honor and prosperity of our country can hardly be estimated. It may probably lead to similar enterprises in the southern states.

But should the plan which has been mentioned appear at first view impracticable, or should it after trial prove unsuccessful, the lands are hereby given to the Abolition Society to be disposed of at such time and manner as they may deem proper, and the money arising from them to be applied for the emancipation and melioration of the condition of the blacks.

Benjn Rush

MS (draft): Library Company of Philadelphia, Rush MSS.

[1] The addressee has been assigned with some confidence (James Pemberton was at this time president of the Abolition Society), but the date is uncertain, and there is real doubt whether the letter here drafted was ever sent. It is now published because it unfolds a scheme highly characteristic of BR; indeed he had earlier proposed that John Nicholson initiate such a project (see letter to Nicholson, 12 Aug. 1793). The document is placed at the end of 1794 because BR had acquired 20,000 acres of land in Bedford co. in Feb. of that

year (Goodman, *Rush*, p. 303) and because he was most active in the work of improving the status of Negroes just at this time (see letter of 14 Jan. 1795). The Bedford co. records throw no light on this episode, nor do the MS minutes and correspondence of the Abolition Society itself as preserved in the Hist. Soc. Penna. Ten years later, when BR presented three small tracts of land in Cambria co. to the Society, his letter was spread on the minutes, and formal thanks were voted (MS Minutes, 1800-1824, p. 89). BR's draft of the later, more perfunctory letter of presentation, dated 1 June 1804, is in the Rush MSS, Box 10, as is the Society's letter of thanks, dated 28 Sep. 1804.

To the Pennsylvania Abolition Society[1]

Philadelphia, January 14th, 1795

The delegates from the several abolition societies in the United States, convened in this city, express to you with great satisfaction the pleasure they have experienced from the punctual attendance of the persons delegated to this convention, and that harmony with which they have deliberated on the several matters that have been presented to them at this time for their consideration. The benefits which may flow from a continuance of this general meeting, by aiding the principal design of its institution, the universal emancipation of the wretched Africans who are yet in bondage, appear to us so many and important that we are induced to recommend to you to send delegates to a similar convention which we propose to be holden in this city on the first day of January in the year one thousand seven hundred and ninety-six.

We have thought it proper to request your further attention to that part of the address of the former convention which relates to the procurement of certified copies of the laws of your state respecting slavery, and that you would send to the next convention exact copies of all such laws as are now in force and of such as have been repealed. Convinced that an historical review of the various acts and provisions of the legislatures of the several states relating to slavery from the periods of their respective settlements to the present time, by tracing the progress of the system of African slavery in this country and its successive changes in the different governments of the Union, would throw much light on the objects of our inquiry and attention, and enable us to determine how far the cause of justice and humanity has advanced among us and how soon we may reasonably expect to see it triumphant, we recommend to you to take such measures as you may think most conducive to that purpose for procuring materials for the work now proposed and assisting its publication, and to communicate to the ensuing convention what progress you shall have made towards perfecting the plan here offered for your consideration and care.

Believing that an acquaintance with the names of the officers of the several abolition societies would facilitate that friendly correspondence which ought always to be preserved between our various associations, we request that you would send to the next and to every future convention an accurate list of all the officers of your Society for the time being, with the number of members of which it consists. And it would assist that convention in ascertaining the existing state of slavery in the United States if you were to forward to them an exact account of the persons who have been liberated by the agency of your Society, and of those who may be considered as signal instances of the relief that you have afforded, and also a statement of the number of free blacks in your state, their property, employments, and moral conduct.

As a knowledge of what has been done, and of that success which has attended the efforts of humanity, will cherish the hope of benevolence and stimulate to further exertion, we trust that you will be of opinion with us that it would be highly useful to procure correct reports of all such trials and decisions of courts of judicature respecting slavery, a knowledge of which may be subservient to the cause of abolition, and to transmit them to the next or to any future convention.

It cannot have escaped your observation, how many persons there are who continue the hateful practice of enslaving their fellow men, and who acquiesce in the sophistry of the advocates of that practice merely from want of reflection and from an habitual attention to their own immediate interests. If to such were often applied the force of reason and the persuasion of eloquence, they might be awakened to a sense of their injustice and be startled with horror at the enormity of their conduct. To produce so desirable a change in sentiment as well as practice, we recommend to you the instituting of annual or other periodical discourses or orations to be delivered in public on the subject of slavery and the means of its abolition.

We cannot forbear expressing to you our earnest desire that you will continue without ceasing to endeavor, by every method in your power which can promise any success, to procure either an absolute repeal of all the laws in your state which countenance slavery, or such an amelioration of them as will gradually produce an entire abolition. Yet, even should that great end be happily obtained, it cannot put a period to the necessity of further labor. The education of the emancipated, the noblest and most arduous task which we have to perform, will require all our wisdom and virtue and the constant exercise of the greatest skill and discretion. When we have broken his chains and restored the African to the enjoyment of his rights, the great work of justice and benevolence is not accomplished. The newborn citizen must receive that instruction and those powerful impressions of moral and religious truth which will render him capable and desirous of fulfilling the various duties he owes to himself and to his country. By educating him in the higher branches of science, and in all the useful parts of learning, and in the precepts of religion and morality, we shall not only do away the reproach and calumny so unjustly lavished upon us, but confound the enemies of truth by evincing that the unhappy sons of Africa, in spite of the degrading influence of slavery, are in no wise inferior to the more fortunate inhabitants of Europe and America.

As a means of effectuating in some degree a design so virtuous and laudable, we recommend to you to appoint a committee annually, or for some other more convenient period, to execute such plans for the improvement of the condition and moral character of the free blacks in your state as you may think best adapted to your particular situation.

By a decree of the National Convention of France, all the blacks and people of color within the territories of the French Republic are declared free and entitled to an equal participation of the rights of citizens of France.[2] We have been informed that many persons of the above description, notwithstanding the decree in their favor, have been brought from the West-india islands by emigrants into the United States and are now held as slaves. We suggest to you the propriety as well as necessity of making inquiry into the subject and of effecting their liberation, so far as may be found consistent with the laws of your state.

Copies of our proceedings will be transmitted to you, and we hope that you will receive such satisfaction as will induce your early attention to the objects we have here recommended.

By order of the Convention,

BENJAMIN RUSH, President

Attest

Walter Franklin, Secretary

MS (copy, not in BR's hand): Historical Society of Pennsylvania, Minutes of the Pennsylvania Abolition Society, 1787-1800.

¹ BR was certainly not the principal author of this circular letter, for the style is heavier than his, but it contains ideas characteristic of him (e.g., the proposal of an annual anti-slavery oration) and epitomizes the aims and methods of the early abolitionists, among whom BR was a leader. See the preceding letter and also BR to Lettsom, 18 May 1787, note.
² This action occurred 4 Feb. to 11 Apr. 1794 (*Cambridge Modern History*, N.Y. and London, 1903-1912, VIII, 728-9).

To John Redman Coxe

My dear Friend,   Philadelphia, May 5th, 1795

Your long and instructing letter of the 22nd of December 1794 gave me great pleasure.

You have helped to reconcile me to the prejudices of my Philadelphia brethren by your details of the feeble and erroneous practice of the physicians in Edinburgh.

But courage, my dear pupil. New truths are slow; but they are sure in their progress. We have had a bilious remittent accompanied with pleuritic symptoms epidemic in our city during the last winter and the present spring. Many have died who were only *moderately* bled and whose bowels were not raked with calomel and jalap. From the great success of the opposite practice, Kuhn and Wistar have been forced to retreat to our remedies, and the disease under the depleting treatment, properly extended, has become less mortal even in their hands. Dr. Physick has become a champion for our remedies, and under the influence of the success of his practice (by their means) he has risen into extensive and profitable business. His old master, Dr. Kuhn, has been compelled to admit him into his consultations, and in one instance he has lately had the mortification of seeing his patient greatly relieved by a single bleeding in hydrothorax, after he had used digitalis and tonics for many months to no purpose.

During the last year I have cured five out of six cases of hydrocephalus internus by copious bleedings, and several cases of general dropsy by the same remedy. One of the latter was in the Hospital in the presence of all the students of the University.

In my 2nd volume upon the yellow fever I shall prove that *dissolved* blood is the effect of a tendency to palsy in the muscular fibers of the veins. It is the most vehement call of the system for a repetition of bloodletting. I have in one instance drawn dissolved blood by four successive bleedings from a young man, and afterwards obtained sizy blood from him in several successive bleedings.¹

We used the lancet under similar circumstances in 1793, but I did not then know that the dissolution of the blood was produced by a paralytic state of the veins, indeed by the excessive force of impression on the blood vessels. You will find, Mitchell[2] says, that blood drawn from the *arteries* was never dissolved, owing I suppose to their greater power of resisting in their muscular fibers the stimulus of the contagion of the fever. This idea suggests an advantage from *arteriotomy* in preference to venesection in all fevers which produce dissolved blood.

The young gentlemen in the shop all join in love to you, as do my dear Mrs. Rush and all my little folks. With respectful and affectionate regards to your honored parents and to your brothers and sister, I am, my dear friend (in grief and adversity, as well as in prosperity), yours sincerely,

BENJN: RUSH

P.S. May 22, 1795. Accept of my thanks for Darwin's *Zoonomia*.[3] It is a high treat to me. I find we think alike in many points, but not in everything. His metaphysics are erroneous and his phraseology often obscure or affected. But upon the whole it is one of the first works in medicine of the 18th century.

Addressed: Dr John R: Coxe (of Philadelphia) Student of Medicine Edinburgh. By the Diana Liverpoole. (Corrected in another hand to read: "Store Street hospital Tottenham Court Ro[ad] London.")

MS: Historical Society of Pennsylvania, Dreer Collection.

[1] On the diagnostic value of the appearance of the blood, see BR's "Defence of Blood-Letting," *Med. Inq. & Obs.*, 2d edn., 1805, IV, 291-2, 326-8; and O. H. P. Pepper, "Benjamin Rush's Theories on Blood Letting," Coll. Phys. Phila., *Trans.*, 4th ser., XIV (1946), 124-5.

[2] The MS seems to read "Mithell," but probably BR refers to the "Dr. Mitchell of Kentucky" who is mentioned in BR's "Defence of Blood-Letting" (*Med. Inq. & Obs.*, 2d edn., 1805, IV, 329) but who has not been further identified.

[3] *Zoonomia, or The Laws of Organic Life*, completed in two volumes, London, 1794-1796, was the work of Erasmus Darwin (1731-1802), British physician, botanist, and poet; chiefly medical, it ranges over many subjects and in some respects prefigures the evolutionary doctrine established by Darwin's more famous grandson Charles. BR thought it a brilliant if fallacious work, and Samuel Miller concluded a long exposition of Darwin's theories with the statement that "The most competent judges seem to concur in pronouncing it the ablest medical work of the eighteenth century." (DNB; BR to Currie, 26 July 1796, and to John Seward, 28 Dec. 1796; Miller, *A Brief Retrospect of the Eighteenth Century*, N.Y., 1803, I, 271-8.)

To the Earl of Buchan

Philadelphia, 25th June 1795

The name of Buchan is dear to every friend of science and humanity in the United States.

Mr. Sommerville's[1] recommendation by your lordship was considered by me as a demand of the payment of a debt in civilities which is due to you from strangers in every part of the world. He is pleased with our country and cannot fail of being happy in a settlement among us.

The United States continue to demonstrate by their internal order and external prosperity the practicability, safety, and happiness of republican forms of government and among a people too educated for monarchical principles and habits.

With great respect for your lordship's talents and virtues, I am, my lord, your lordship's most obedient servant,

BENJN RUSH

Addressed: The Right Honble: The Earl of Buchan Dryburgh Palace Scotland. To the care of Mr Pinkney.[2]
MS: Boston Public Library, Chamberlain Collection.

[1] Not further identified.
[2] Presumably Thomas Pinckney (1750-1828), of South Carolina, U.S. minister in London, 1792-1795, and negotiator of the celebrated treaty with Spain in the latter year (DAB).

To John R. B. Rodgers

Dear Sir,   Philadelphia, June 25, 1795

As you delight in all improvements that are calculated to lessen human misery, I know you will be pleased to hear that Mr. Benjamin Wynkoop,[1] a citizen of Philadelphia, has invented a MACHINE, which is moved by the constant motion of the sea in all weathers, for pumping water and foul air out of ships and thereby preventing a great source of the calamities to which seamen are exposed. The machine, I have been told, has been subjected to a faithful experiment and has afforded great pleasure and satisfaction to all who have seen it. In examining the model and description of this machine, I have had my attention fixed upon the great advantages which will arise to commerce from its preserving provisions and even the timber of ships from the corruption and decay to which foul air exposes them. But its chief advantage will consist in preventing the generation of those fevers which are produced at sea by the confinement of human and other effluvia in the holds of ships, and which in all countries have destroyed so many thousand lives.² The machine may further tend to lessen the inconveniencies of long sea voyages by enabling mariners to carry a large quantity of livestock with them; for domestic animals, in common with human creatures, become sickly and die when confined together in close apartments. This was experienced during the late war in an attempt that was made to transport hogs and sheep for the support of the British army in America. I congratulate you upon this discovery. It affords a fresh proof of the dominion of human reason over natural evil, and it may serve to nourish a hope that the time will come when, comparatively speaking, "evil there shall be none"³ upon the surface of our globe.

From, dear sir, your sincere friend,

BENJAMIN RUSH

Printed: New-York Magazine; or, Literary Repository, vi (1795), 448.

¹ Benjamin Wynkoop (1734-1803), entered as "gentleman," 151 South Water St., in the *Directories* of this period, was treasurer of the Rumsean Society, a group of financiers and patrons of science founded in 1788 for the promotion of James Rumsey's steamboat (Richard Wynkoop, *Wynkoop Genealogy in the United States of America*, N.Y., 1870, p. 66; James T. Flexner, *Steamboats Come True*, N.Y., 1944, p. 140, 175).

² In a report to Gov. Mifflin after the epidemic of 1798, the Academy of Medicine strongly advised that a law be passed compelling "every vessel . . . to carry and use a ventilator," Benjamin Wynkoop's being specifically recommended (Condie & Folwell, *Hist. of the Pestilence*, Appendix, p. xxii-xxiii). References elsewhere in the Condie & Folwell account indicate that Wynkoop's machine was actually used by the port authorities for cleansing ships that arrived during the summer of 1798.

³ Jeremiah 50:20.

To John Redman Coxe

Dear, [very?]¹ dear Sir,   Philadelphia, October 5th, 1795

Your letters continue to afford me both pleasure and instruction. The communications contained in your favor of the 17th of July are truly interesting. The fact from Dr. Clark² completes my theory of hydrocephalus internus. The membrane found in the trachea in the hives I believe to be the effect, like the one described by Dr. Clark, of inflammation, and not produced (as I once supposed) by indurated mucus. This opinion has led me to bleed more copiously than formerly in that disorder, and always with success.

I have lately adopted a new theory of mania. I suppose it in nearly all cases to be accompanied by inflammation in the brain.³

This, the water, blood, pus, and *hardness* found in the brain after death all demonstrate, for they follow inflammation in other parts of the body. The *hardness* is a real schirrus[4] analogous to schirrus in the liver. In consequence of the adoption of this theory, I have lately cured three deplorable cases of madness by copious bleeding (100 ounces in one case). It was aided afterwards by the cold bath.

The season is now sickly. Ten of my family have been confined with remitting fevers. 24 bleedings in one month have cured us all. I submitted to two of them in one day. Our infant of 6 weeks old was likewise bled twice, and thereby rescued from the grave. We have had several cases of yellow fever. One of them was saved by the loss of 160 ounces of blood in ten days. He was a young Englishman of 23 years of age.

Dr. Gibbons died yesterday morning of the apoplectic state of fever. His physicians, Kuhn and Wistar, called it apoplexy. He lost it is said but 35 ounces of blood by three bleedings.

I condole with you in the loss of Miss Benezet.[5] But keep up your hopes. Your education, talents, and the merit you have acquired in the year 1793 cannot fail of procuring you business, reputation, wealth, and a good wife in our city.

My dear Mrs. Rush and all the family join in love to you and all your Papa's family.——From yours sincerely,

BENJN. RUSH

Addressed: Dr: John R: Coxe at Daniel Coxe Esqr London.
MS: Historical Society of Pennsylvania, Dreer Collection.

[1] Obscured by a blot.

[2] Coxe had mentioned discussing in London a medical case with a Dr. Clark whom BR had cited in *An Account of the Yellow Fever in 1793*; but as BR there cites several treatises by Clarks and Clarkes (whose Christian names are not given), identification is impossible.

[3] "I shall now deliver an opinion, which I have long believed and taught in my lectures, and that is, that the cause of madness is seated primarily in the blood-vessels of the brain, and that it depends upon the same kind of morbid and irregular actions that constitute other arterial diseases. There is nothing specific in these actions. They are a part of the unity of disease, particularly of fever; of which madness is a chronic form, affecting that part of the brain which is the seat of the mind" (BR, *Diseases of the Mind*, p. 17-18).

[4] I.e., scirrhus.

[5] The announcement of Miss Benezet's approaching marriage, Coxe told BR in his letter of 17 July 1795, provided "no small occasion of unhappiness to me" (Rush MSS, XXVII). This was doubtless Maria Benezet, who married George Willing at Christ Church, 7 Oct. 1795 (*Penna. Archives*, 2d ser., VIII, 18).

To John Cowan[1]

Dear Sir,   Philadelphia, 11th October 1795

Mr. McCullough's[2] letter will give you the melancholy news of the death of your friend Mr. Grey.[3] He was well attended by Dr. Potter,[4] one of my former pupils. My numerous engagements, particularly to some families in the country, prevented my visiting him more than two or three times. But ample justice was done to him, and he appeared to die from obstructions or effusions which had probably taken place from the want of bleeding before he came to town.

I have heard with pleasure of your successful practice in the fever in New York. Do inform me immediately—what are your remedies? If bleeding and purging, to what extent do you use them? How many patients do you lose in a given number, and what is the practice of the other physicians in New York? An answer to these questions by the post (so accurate as to bear the public eye) will much oblige me and all the other friends of reason and of the lancet in Philadelphia.

Your Case Book shall be delivered to your order. It is full of new and extraordinary facts, but none of them are improbable or incredible to men who comprehend those secret laws of the animal economy which are developed in those hours when most of physicians consign their patients to the grave.[5]

From, dear sir, your friend,

BENJN RUSH

Addressed: Dr: John Cowan Physician at Mr. John Henry's Broker No. 57 Stone Street New York.
MS: Long Island Historical Society.

[1] John N. Cowan (d. 1801), a physician in New York, had sent over his case book to be transmitted to a Mr. Antony. Cowan's covering letter is dated 27 Oct., no year specified (Rush MSS, III); hence BR's letter should with little doubt be dated 11 *November*. John Henry, with whom Cowan lived, wrote BR after Cowan's death (letter dated 28 Mch. 1801, Rush MSS, VII).

[2] Numerous McCullochs and McCulloughs are entered in the Philadelphia *Directories* of this period.

[3] Cowan had inquired in his letter about a Mr. Grey and his family who were en route to New York.

[4] Nathaniel Potter (1770-1843), of Maryland, who obtained his M.D. at the University of Pennsylvania, 1796; settled in Baltimore, 1797; first professor of theory and practice in the Medical College of Maryland, 1807-1843; a prolific writer on medical subjects, Potter is best remembered for pioneering experiments proving the noncontagiousness of yellow fever (DAB). His relations with BR were very friendly: letters from Potter to BR are in the Rush MSS, XIII and XXXVIII, but only a few widely scattered letters from BR to Potter have been located.

[5] Whatever BR's deficiencies as a

Jeremy Belknap

Charles Nisbet

Ebenezer Hazard

A GROUP OF RUSH'S CORRESPONDENTS

Diploma of Membership in the Humane Society

THE
Rush-Light.

15th FEB. 1800.

CONTAINING

BY PETER PORCUPINE.

NEW YOKK:

Published by WILLIAM COBBETT, No. 141, Water-Street,
where all Communications to the Editor are requested
to be addressed, *post paid.*

clinical statistician may have been, he preached and practised the habit of keeping careful case records. See especially his lecture entitled "Observations on the Duties of a Physician" (1789), in *Med. Inq. & Obs.*, 2d edn., 1805, I, p. 401-2.

To John Redman Coxe

Dear Sir,   Philadelphia, December 8th, 1795

I am happy to find by your letter by Captain Eggar[1] that you are about to devote the approaching winter months to surgery and midwifery. They will be extremely useful to you in procuring you an establishment in our city. I have contemplated a berth for you in a lying-in dispensary which I hope will soon be set on foot among us. The more therefore you qualify yourself for this situation, the better.

I see no objection to your returning and commencing business in Philadelphia *next* spring. By remaining too long abroad, you may pass away from the memories of many people who knew you in 1793. Besides, you will learn more in one year by practising among the poor than in attending hospital practice for seven years.

Our classes are much crowded this season. Dr. Shippen has 100 pupils. Woodhouse upwards of 70. My class exceeds 100. Dr. Kuhn has his usual number of 35.[2] Dr. Griffitts has declined lecturing, owing to sickness and distress from the loss of a favorite child. It is expected he will resume the duties of his chair next year.

I have adopted and taught your doctrine of inflammation.

I have this year publicly rejected nosological arrangement and substituted in the room of it *states* of diseases. I have admitted 29 states of fever. The students have adopted this new mode of dividing diseases with great avidity.[3]

The fevers of the present season are generally attended with uncommon determination to the head, producing what I have called the *apoplectic*, the *paralytic*, the *hydrocephalic*, and the *maniacal* states of fever. They all require and nearly all yield to copious depletion. I drew 60 ounces of blood from a man in the maniacal state of fever in twelve hours and cured him in two days. But Dr. Physick has far exceeded me in this mode of reducing the system. He drew 75 ounces at *one* bleeding from Dr. Dewees in the apoplectic state of fever, and cured him thereby in a few hours. The lancet has at last become less unpopular in our city. It is introducing Griffitts, Physick, Dewees, Woodhouse and a Dr. Gallaher[4] rapidly into business. Griffitts and Physick are forced upon Kuhn in consultations only because they are believed to be acquainted with the most successful manner of using it.

My best respects to all your good family. All mine join in love to you and them. My son John is becoming enthusiastic in medicine. Adieu. From your ever affectionate friend,

BENJN: RUSH

Addressed: Dr: John R: Coxe to the care of Daniel Coxe Esqr: London. The Patty Liverpoole.

MS: Historical Society of Pennsylvania, Dreer Collection.

[1] Thomas Eggar, or Egar, ship-captain, of Almond St. (1794-1796 *Directories*).

[2] BR first wrote "25."

[3] For substantiation of this statement, see an extract from a letter written by Samuel Cooper to William Bache, 9 Jan. 1795, quoted in a note on BR's letter to Belknap, 6 June 1791.

[4] Listed as James Gallagher, doctor of physick, 239 High or Market St., in 1795 *Directory*.

To Ashton Alexander

My dear Friend,   Philadelphia, December 21, 1795

I sit down to discharge a double debt to you contracted by your two kind letters. My answer to them will be short, for I must meet my class in half an hour at the Hospital. The interval between my ordering Peter to get my chair and his bringing it to the door is, alas! the only time I can devote to you, though hours would be too few to inform you of all I wish to communicate to you.

My class consists of 106 pupils inclusive of my apprentices. It would have been larger had not Dr. Shippen persuaded several young gentlemen to attend Kuhn in preference to me. To effect this, he not only extolled Kuhn's learning and sagacity in strong terms, but spoke with great illiberality of my principles and character in medicine. It is thus he pays me for nearly curing his son of a pulmonary consumption by 25 bleedings after he had been deserted as incurable by Kuhn and most of the physicians of the city. I do not mention this anecdote with a view to complaining. On the contrary I consider Dr. Shippen's unkindness and ingratitude with pleasure, for slander and persecution and one part of my real estate. In this respect my enemies have unwillingly made me one of the richest men in the United States.

I have read my bulletin to my class upon the yellow fever of 1794. It was well received. It will be sent to the press in the spring.[1]

I have lately had many cases of the maniacal state of fever, both in the Hospital and in private practice. They yield to copious bloodletting. I discharged three patients in one day as cured of that deplorable malady about two weeks ago from the Hospital. As pulmonary consumption is the chronic state of pneumony, so madness is nothing but the chronic state of frenzy. From the continuance of the appetite and of muscular excitement, it requires more bleeding to cure the former than the latter state of that disease. My dear Mrs. Rush and all the children join in love to you with yours—yours—yours,

BENJN RUSH

P.S. I shall send you a printed copy of my *Syllabus*[2] of my lectures in a few days under cover of a letter from Mr. Blount.[3]

Addressed: Dr Ashton Alexander at Dumfries Virginia.
Printed: Autograph Letters and Autographs of the Signers of the Declaration of Independence in the Possession of George C. Thomas, Philadelphia, 1908, unpaged; text corrected from a photostat in the Historical Library, Yale University School of Medicine; original not located.

[1] It appeared in the fourth volume of *Med. Inq. & Obs.*, 1796.
[2] *A Syllabus of a Course of Lectures* *on the Institutes of Medicine*, Phila.: T. Bradford, 1795.
[3] Not identified.

To Horatio Gates

My dear Friend,   Philadelphia, December 26th, 1795

My whole heart reverberates every sentiment contained in your friendly letter.[1] Little did we think that the father of the discipline of the American army in 1775 and the conqueror of Burgoyne in 1777 would be overlooked in the arrangements of that government which owes its existence in part to his exertions. But to be passed by without notice is not the only punishment of true republicanism in our country. Many of us have been forced to expiate our sacrifices in the cause of liberty by suffering every species of slander and persecution. I ascribe the opposition to my remedies in the epidemic which desolated our city in 1793 chiefly to an unkind and resentful association of my political principles with my medical character. My enemies triumphed over me for a while, only because they had contracted no guilt by voting for or supporting the Declaration of Independence. I do not mention this fact by way of complaint. A kind and bountiful providence has showered a thousand blessings upon me which more than compensate for the losses and persecution I have incurred by my republicanism. I am easy in my circumstances, happy in my family, and since the year 1793 renovated in my constitution. Since the part I took in the establishment of the government in 1787, I have retired wholly from political life. You will believe my repentance of my public virtue to be sincere when I add that I have not read the treaty[2] nor a single essay in favor of or against it. Nay more, I have not and shall not even read Mr. Randolph's pamphlet.[3] Once only have I been in company with the President of the United States since he came to our city, and that was shortly after he arrived. But under these habits of retirement my principles have undergone no change. The word *Republic* is still music in my ears. I still abhor the substance and shadows of monarchy. I still love the common people with all their weaknesses and vices, both of which in our country I ascribe in part to the errors and corruptions of our government. Above all, I still unite with all good men in considering the fiscal systems as the seeds of all the discontents and commotions which have existed or which may hereafter exist in the United States. It is the epitome of all that is wicked in morals and government. But I must restrain my pen. I forget that I am a spectator only of men and things, and that I live in a foreign country. In one thing more I am unchanged. I still love and esteem my old friend General Gates. He was always dear to me. Do come and pass a few weeks in our city. Bring Mrs. Gates along with you. Let us feast once more, before we are parted by the grave, upon the republican principles and maxims with which our bosoms glowed in the years 1774, 1775, and 1776. We will fancy Richd. H. Lee and Saml. Adams are part of our company. Jno. Adams, who once took the lead in our republican conversations, shall not be of our party. We will still respect him for his integrity, while we deplore his apostasy from his first love. Adieu. My dear Mrs. Rush joins in respectful compliments to Mrs. Gates with yours sincerely,

BENJN: RUSH

MS: New-York Historical Society, Gates Papers.

[1] Dated from New York, 23 Dec. 1795; *Biddle Papers*, pt. i, No. 112; present location unknown.

[2] The treaty with Great Britain negotiated by John Jay in 1794. Considered a Federalist treaty and a diplomatic victory by Great Britain, its ratification occasioned bitter controversy in 1795; see McMaster, *Hist.*, II, 212ff. BR wrote of it a little later:

"The treaty with Great Britain, once reprobated by 19/20 of our citizens, is now approved of, or peaceably acquiesced in, by the same proportion of the people. Two reasons are given for this change of opinion. 1st, it is said upon further investigation to be less injurious to our country and more favorable to all its interests than was thought upon first reading it, and 2ly, it has been signed by the President of the United States, in whose *integrity* all confide and in whose *wisdom* a great majority of our citizens have still the most unlimited confidence" (to Samuel Bayard, 1 Mch. 1796; photostat in Rush Family Papers, deposited in Princeton University Library; original not located).

[3] *A Vindication of Mr. Randolph's Resignation*, Phila., 1795, a pamphlet issued by Edmund Randolph, who had resigned as secretary of state in Aug. 1795, following charges (instigated by the British minister) that Randolph had been guilty of incorrect relations with the French minister, Fauchet (DAB).

To John Redman Coxe

My dear Friend,   Philadelphia, January 16, 1796

I steal three minutes from the hurry of my winter engagements to thank you for your letter of the 22nd of October. I agree with you in believing that you had better return in the spring to Philadelphia and begin business in your grandfather's shop. You cannot have a better situation. Dr. Physick is established, owing in part to his situation in Arch Street and in part to his having adopted the new principles in medicine.

I have lately discharged six and cured eight patients of mania in our Hospital since the 1st of November. They were all recent cases. When the new building[1] is completed, I shall undertake the cases of chronic madness with which you know the Hospital abounds. My remedies for the recent cases were bleeding to oz.100 down to oz.30, strong purges, low diet, kind treatment, and the cold bath.

All is peace in our country. General Washington is still esteemed by a great majority of our citizens, and his treaty with Great Britain becomes less unpopular in proportion as it is understood. It will be disapproved of, it is thought, by the lower house of Congress, but they will notwithstanding, it is said, comply with its stipulations.

My dear Mrs. Rush and all our little folks join in love to you and your excellent parents and all their family with, my dear friend, yours sincerely,

BENJN RUSH

P.S. I have lately attempted the cure of cancerous external tumors by local bleeding with cups, and with some prospect of success.

Addressed: Dr John R: Coxe, to be left at Daniel Coxe's Esqr London. By the Prudence Capt: Miller. (Corrected in another hand to read: "No. 3 Browns Buildings St. Mary Axe City.")

MS: Historical Society of Pennsylvania, Dreer Collection.

[1] I.e., the West Wing, completed in Nov. 1796, for insane patients (Morton, *Hist. of the Penna. Hospital*, p. 78).

To John Dickinson

My dear Friend,   Philadelphia, February 16, 1796

Your friendly letter, with its interesting enclosure,[1] came safe to hand at a moment when the care of the Hospital, the labor of composing several new lectures upon a most difficult subject, viz., "the diseases of the mind," and the usual hurry of my private business prevented my paying that attention to the proposed publication I wished. I have since looked over it, but not with the care I had purposed. The manner, the matter, and the style are all equally interesting. It is calculated to arrest the *running* reader, and to awaken even the palled relish for moral and religious instruction. In this way only shall we counteract the infidel writers of the age. They seduce by the novelty of their manner and brilliancy of their style much more than by their arguments, for these are generally overlooked or soon forgotten. Paine's witty reflection upon the "drabcolored dress," &c., of the Quakers is more universally remembered and quoted than anything else in his absurd and impious *Age of Reason.*[2]

I return you the manuscript agreeably to your request. I expect to have the pleasure of introducing it into the world when you have made the purposed additions. All your directions respecting the choice of a printer, capitals, &c., shall be faithfully attended to.

I rejoice to find the vigor of your talents and benevolence still unimpaired. One of the Reformers who spent the evening of his life in composing books in defense of his principles was requested by one of his friends to spare himself and not to hasten his death by his severe studies. "What!" said the pious champion for truth. "Would you have my master come and find me idle?" May we both be actuated by a similar disposition to bring forth fruit in our old age!

I am now preparing a work for the press to be entitled "an attempt to explain sundry passages in the Old and New Testament by the principles of medicine and the laws of the animal economy."[3] It will contain many new arguments in favor of Christianity, and will I hope render infidelity, at least among physicians, as much a mark of ignorance as it is of impiety or immorality. Should it please God to bless this work to the benefit of any of his creatures, I shall be thankful. What an honor to be employed by HIM in any way, but chiefly in promoting the knowledge, the love, and the future enjoyment of HIMSELF.

My most respectful compliments await Mrs. Dickinson and my

old acquaintance Miss Sally, who I hear is wise in the things which are to be hereafter, as well as in human affairs. Miss Maria I hear is a fine sprightly girl, but as yet, she says, "no Quaker."

How I long to spend an afternoon or an evening in the society of your amiable family, in which I have been more happy than in any family in this country except my own!

My dear Mrs. Rush joins in love to all your fireside with, my dear friend, yours very affectionately,

BENJN: RUSH

MS: Historical Society of Pennsylvania, Logan Papers.

[1] Dickinson's letter, dated 15 Feb., is listed in the *Biddle Papers*, pt. i, No. 88; its present location is not known. From BR's letter of 5 Apr. 1796, q.v., it appears that the enclosure was the MS of a work by Dickinson issued anonymously later this year with the title *A Fragment*, an octavo tract of seventy-two pages introduced by the following note: "The following Essay is a Fragment, detached from a Treatise designed for the Instruction of Youth, which a weak State of Health will most probably prevent being completed." The essay is a teleological defense of theism.

[2] "Though I reverence their philanthropy, I cannot help smiling at the conceit that if a Quaker could have been consulted at the Creation what a silent and drab-colored Creation it would have been! Not a flower would have blossomed its gayeties, nor a bird been permitted to sing."—*The Age of Reason*, Part I (Paine, *Complete Writings*, ed. P. S. Foner, N.Y., 1945, I, 498).

[3] On this long-projected work, see BR's letter to Belknap, 5 Apr. 1791.

To Thomas Jefferson

Dear Sir,   Philadelphia, March 1st, 1796

The bearer of this letter, Mr. Weld,[1] a young gentleman of amiable manners and good education, was introduced to me by a letter from an old Scotch friend now settled in Dublin. In traveling through the United States he could not be satisfied without paying his respects to Mr. Jefferson.

What strange events have happened in our city since your retirement from public life! The late honorable treaty with Spain has revived your name among your Republican friends. Mr. Pinkney's success as a negotiator has been ascribed to information and instructions issued by our Executive at a time when your influence was felt in the councils of our country.[2]

We have been much struck lately by a public acknowledgment from a late officer of state of our obligations to Great Britain for many of the political institutions to which the United States owe their happiness. This acknowledgment has led some of the Republicans to inquire into the *nature* and *number* of those institutions. Upon an investigation of them, they are as follows: 1. Funding systems and perpetual debt. 2. A cruel and absurd system of penal laws. 3. A cruel and absurd code of laws with respect to debtors. 4. Oppressive religious establishments. 5. Imports and excise instead of an equal land tax. 6. Unequal distribution of property among the children of the same family. 7. Innumerable perjuries from the absurd mixture of oaths with all our revenue laws. Our judicial system alone derives some merit from our descent from and former connection with G. Britain, but it owes the obstinate stability of its present imperfections chiefly to the unfortunate association of the evil with the good parts of it.

You drew up the Act of Independence of the United States. The wishes and prayers of thousands are, that you may live to realize that Act by giving us the principles and habits of an *independent* people.

From, my dear sir, your sincere old friend,

BENJN RUSH

MS: Library of Congress, Jefferson Papers.

[1] Isaac Weld, Jr. (1774-1856), an Irish topographical writer, afterwards published *Travels through the States of North America and the Provinces of Upper and Lower Canada during the Years 1795, 1796, and 1797*, London, 1799. Not very flattering to Americans, the work was popular in Europe, was several times reprinted, and was trans- lated into French (DNB).

[2] The Treaty of San Lorenzo with Spain, negotiated by Thomas Pinckney in 1795, granted to Americans the right of free navigation on the Mississippi and the use of New Orleans as a port of entry and deposit (DAB, under Pinck- ney). The Treaty proved extremely popular in the United States.

To Griffith Evans[1]

Dear Sir,   Philadelphia, March 4th, 1796

Accept of my thanks for your friendly and interesting letter from Paris. I deplore with you the factions which have torn that country to pieces, but you and I believe that "all evil is good in disguise," and of course that the present distractions of France are nothing but the seeds of great and universal happiness.

The United States continue to exhibit proofs to the world that republics are practical governments. We are still peaceable and happy, and I have no doubt but we shall continue to be so for many, many generations to come.

Dr. Priestley has fixed his permanent residence in Northumberland town. He is now on a visit to our city, in which he is admired and caressed by all classes of citizens, and by the autocrats[2] for his *political* and by the aristocrats for his *religious* principles. He has preached three times in the Universal Church to crowded and respectable audiences. His sermons (one excepted) were very popular. The unpopular one gave offense only by detailing the vices of heathens in too gross language, in showing the necessity of the Christian revelation to correct and banish those vices from civilized society.

Mr. Winchester preaches on Sunday evenings to crowded audiences, but they are composed chiefly of the second and lower classes of our citizens. He is, as usual, eloquent, Scriptural, and irresistible in his reasonings upon all subjects.

The treaty with Great Britain, though not popular in the House of Representatives, will, it is expected, be supported by them. The treaty with Spain will, it is said, be ratified by a unanimous vote in the Senate. Thousands on the western waters already begin to shout its applause.

With best respects to Dr. Edwards, I am, my dear sir, your sincere friend,

BENJN: RUSH

Printed: Pennsylvania Magazine of History and Biography, VI (1882), 113.

[1] Griffith Evans (1760-1845), of Chester co., and later of Germantown, Penna., held minor state and federal posts for many years; his mission abroad may have been in connection with his work as secretary of the commission to adjudicate claims of British citizens under the sixth article of the Jay Treaty of 1794 (T. Ward, "Griffith Evans," PMHB, VI [1882], 342-3; Evans' "Journal" of Indian negotiations, 1784-1785, same, LXV [1941], 202-33). BR is replying to a letter from Evans, of 19 Aug. 1795 (Rush MSS, IV).

[2] This is neither sense nor sound construction. I suspect a slip of the pen or an error in transcription. The "and" following "citizens" should be omitted; and "autocrats" is an error (by BR or the copyist) for "democrats."

To John Dickinson

My dear Friend,   Philadelphia, April 5th, 1796

The additions and alterations to the "Fragment" to which you refer in your letter of yesterday,[1] were received and put immediately afterwards into the hands of Mr. Thos. Dobson.

Dr. Priestley is now delivering a course of sermons in our city upon the external evidences of Christianity. He has exhibited in the most striking manner the superiority of the Jewish and Christian revelations over the pagan religions in principles, in morals, and in ceremonial institutions. Next week he purposes to show the truth of Christianity from the miracles which accompanied its establishment. I mentioned to him a few days ago your zeal in the cause to which his late sermons have been devoted. He was delighted with the information and expressed a desire to be acquainted with you. I have promised him that pleasure the next time he visits Wilmington. Upon all subjects (two or three in divinity excepted) you will harmonize with him. I have never met with so much knowledge accompanied with so much simplicity of manners. You will be charmed with him.

Adieu. From, my dear friend, yours sincerely,

BENJN RUSH

Addressed: John Dickinson Esqr: at Wilmington State of Delaware.
MS: Historical Society of Pennsylvania, Logan Papers.

[1] Dickinson's letter of 4 Apr. 1796 is in Hist. Soc. Penna., Logan Papers; on Dickinson's *Fragment*, see BR to Dickinson, 16 Feb. 1796.

To John Redman Coxe

My dear Friend,   Philadelphia, 28th April 1796

All your letters afford me pleasure and instruction. It is some consolation to me to find that I am not so singular in my principles and practice in medicine as I am represented to be by my domestic enemies. I shall publish Mr. Blissard's[1] opinion of the cause of dropsy in my next volume, under the head of the *hydropic state of fever*. This volume is now nearly ready for the press, but an unusual share of business (chiefly among strangers) will not permit me to complete it. I hope however to put the last file upon it before the 1st of June.

My late success in the treatment of mania has brought me an increase of patients in that disorder. My remedies are frequent but moderate bleedings, purges, low diet, salivation, and afterwards the cold bath. I have lately received a polite letter from Dr. Willis[2] containing a short detail of his mode of treating madness. It accords in some particulars with mine, but differs from it materially in others. He does not seem to view the disease as a fever, and that it requires the same remedies as any other fever attended with local determination. I have supposed it to be to frenzy what pulmonary consumption is to pleurisy.

Dr. Barton has succeeded Dr. Griffitts as professor of materia medica in our University. Dr. James was opposed to him. He lost the appointment by three votes. Dr. Shippen was Barton's *open* friend, and the other professors (Woodhouse and myself excepted) did not oppose him—hence his success! I consider him as a recruit to the enemies of the new system of medicine, and that he will be supported in proportion as he barks at me.

Our diseases continue to wear a most inflammatory aspect. Dr. Kuhn bleeds by the quart, and Currie and Wistar have lately taken 103 ounces of blood from a man in a pleurisy. This obsequiousness to my practice has not lessened their hostility to me. On the contrary, the confederacy and malignity of the party is more close and more violent than ever. I long to be reinforced by you and Fisher. Your Grandpapa proposes to fix you in an office near to him in 2nd Street. This will be better than to live with him, for it will give you a chance of more *private* patients, who are the chief support of young physicians in all countries.

My dear Mrs. Rush and all my little folks join in love to you and your worthy parents with, my dear friend, yours sincerely,

BENJN RUSH

P.S. We shall have six graduates next month. Potter and Otto[3] are among them. The first writes upon arsenic, the second upon epilepsy.

For public news I refer you to the public papers. The British treaty will *finally* be adopted, it is said, by the House of Representatives. I have not read it, nor a single essay or speech in favor or against it. My whole business in the world now is to take care of my wife and children and to complete my system of medicine.

Addressed: Dr John Redman Coxe to be left at Daniel Coxe's Esqr: London.
MS: Historical Society of Pennsylvania, Dreer Collection.

[1] Probably William Blizard (1743-1835), surgeon to the London Hospital from 1780, where he founded a medical school; knighted 1803 (DNB).

[2] Francis Willis, M.D. (1718-1807), attended George III in his first attack of insanity, 1788 (DNB). Willis' letter to BR has not been found.

[3] John Conrad Otto (1774-1844), son of Dr. Bodo Otto; a graduate of the College of New Jersey, 1792, and apprenticed to BR the same year; M.D., University of Pennsylvania, 1796; member of BR's Academy of Medicine, 1797; fellow of the College of Physicians, 1819; on staff of Pennsylvania Hospital, 1813-1835, and of other institutions (Princeton Univ., *Gen. Cat.*, 1908; BR's MS List of Apprentices; Morton, *Hist. of the Penna. Hospital*, p. 501; Ruschenberger, p. 254).

To John Rush

Directions and advice to Jno. Rush from his father and mother composed the evening before he sailed for Calcutta, May 18th, 1796.[1]

We shall divide these directions into four heads, as they relate to *morals, knowledge, health,* and *business.*

I. MORALS

1. Be punctual in committing your soul and body to the protection of your Creator every morning and evening. Implore at the same time his mercy in the name of his Son, our Lord and Saviour Jesus Christ.

2. Read in your Bible frequently, more especially on Sundays.

3. Avoid swearing and even an irreverent use of your Creator's name. *Flee* youthful lusts.

4. Be courteous and gentle in your behavior to your fellow passengers, and respectful and obedient to the captain of the vessel.

5. Attend public worship regularly every Sunday when you arrive at Calcutta.

II. KNOWLEDGE

1. Begin by studying Guthrie's *Geography.*[2]

2. Read your other books *through* carefully, and converse daily upon the subjects of your reading.

3. Keep a diary of every day's studies, conversations, and transactions at sea and on shore. Let it be composed in a fair, legible hand. Insert in it an account of the population, manners, climate, diseases, &c., of the places you visit.

4. Preserve an account of every person's name and disease whom you attend.

III. HEALTH

1. Be temperate in eating, more especially of animal food. Never *taste* distilled spirits of any kind, and drink fermented liquors very sparingly.

2. Avoid the night air in sickly situations. Let your dress be rather warmer than the weather would seem to require. Carefully avoid fatigue from all causes both of body and mind.

IV. BUSINESS

1. Take no step in laying out your money without the advice and consent of the captain or supercargo. Let no solicitations prevail

with you to leave the captain and supercargo during your residence in Calcutta.[3]

2. Keep an exact account of all your expenditures. Preserve as vouchers of them all your bills.

3. Take care of all your instruments, books, clothes, &c.

Be sober and vigilant. Remember at all times that while you are seeing the world, the world will see you. Recollect further that you are always under the eye of the Supreme Being. One more consideration shall close this parting testimony of our affection. Whenever you are tempted to do an improper thing, fancy that you see your father and mother kneeling before you and imploring you with tears in their eyes to refrain from yielding to the temptation, and assuring you at the same time that your yielding to it will be the means of hurrying them to a premature grave.

BENJN RUSH
JULIA RUSH

MS (draft, with both signatures in BR's hand): Library Company of Philadelphia, Rush MSS. BR docketed the paper with this note: "Copy of a letter to Jno. Rush—written the night before he sailed for Calcutta—and subscribed by his father and mother, to be delivered to him by Captain M:Callister a week after he leaves the city."

[1] John had been enrolled as an apprentice to his father in September 1794; he was now sailing as "surgeon of an Indiaman" (BR's MS List of Apprentices; BR to J. R. Coxe, 25 May 1796). I have not identified the vessel.

[2] This was doubtless William Guthrie's *New System of Modern Geography*, London, 1770, a popular work frequently reprinted (Allibone, *Dict. of Authors*).

[3] This sentence was added in Mrs. Rush's hand.

To John Redman Coxe

My dear Friend,   Philadelphia, May 25, 1796

I send you herewith a few theses. Dr. Caldwell's you will perceive is stolen from my publications and lectures.[1] I convicted him of plagiarism at the public examination of his thesis. He was so much hurt at being thus detected and exposed that he is preparing to defend himself by an appeal to the public. In answer to him Dr. Mease has undertaken to publish half a dozen certificates from my former pupils which will establish the charges I brought against him. Some of them are so severe that if he possessed the feelings of a candid man he would never show his face in our city after they are published.

My 2nd volume on the yellow fever will I hope be committed to the press next month. It has been delayed by an unusual hurry of business occasioned by the prevalence of the measles and by the confusion in the situation of my books and papers from being obliged to remove from Mr. Shippen's house to the one formerly occupied by Mr. Ketland at the southeast corner of 4th and Walnut Streets.[2] Mr. Shippen has taken possession of the house I left. I have purchased the one I now occupy.

Dr. Alexander is about settling in Baltimore with fair prospects. Dr. Fisher is settled near Petersburgh in Virginia. Dr. Otto and Dr. Potter are about to settle in Philadelphia.

My son John sailed a few days ago for Calcutta as surgeon of an Indiaman. An obstinate slow intermittent which threatened a consumption rendered this premature voyage necessary for him.

My dear Mrs. Rush and all my young folks who are at home join in love to you and your dear parents and family with, my dear friend, yours sincerely,

BENJN: RUSH

P.S. Do try to pick up Dr. Primrose's *Vulgar Errors in Medicine*[3] for me at some of the second-hand book stores. I have read Smith on Old Age[4] (a book you obtained in that way) with great pleasure.

Addressed: Dr John Redman Coxe at Paris.
MS: Historical Society of Pennsylvania, Dreer Collection.

[1] Charles Caldwell (1772-1853), of North Carolina, M.D., University of Pennsylvania, 1796, was one of the most energetic, ubiquitous, and stormy figures in early American medical history. He is especially remembered as a founder of medical colleges in Kentucky and Tennessee and as the author of an *Autobiography* (Phila., 1855) which is remarkably candid and caustic in its treatment of the writer's professional colleagues. The present letter alludes to the first of Caldwell's quarrels with his teacher. The thesis of which BR complains was entitled *An Attempt to Establish the Original Sameness of Three Phenomena of Fever*, &c., concerning which more can be learned from a letter written by BR to Ashton Alexander, 21 May 1796 (N.Y. Academy of Medicine); BR therein requested Alexander to send him an affidavit stating that certain therapeutic measures and the doc-

trine of the unity of disease had been expounded by BR before the appearance of Caldwell's thesis. Caldwell presented his side of the quarrel in his *Autobiography*, p. 230ff., reporting, among other things, that BR refused his signature on Caldwell's diploma. In the following year a reconciliation occurred, and Caldwell joined the Academy of Medicine group that supported BR's doctrine of the local origin of yellow fever. In 1809-1810 another dispute arose between the two men; see BR to James Rush, 22 Dec. 1809. More interesting and important than these contentions are Caldwell's sharply etched delineations of BR in his *Autobiography* (see especially p. 116ff., 143ff., 153ff.) and in *Delaplaine's Repository of the Lives and Portraits of Distinguished American Characters*, Phila., 1815-1816, I, 27-44.

[2] BR remained in the house he pur-

chased of Thomas Ketland until 1806, when he purchased the Shippen house and moved back into it; see note on letter to Mrs. Rush, 27-28 Oct. 1793.

³ This was a treatise by James Primrose, or Primerose, M.D. (d. 1659), of Hull, first published in Latin, London, 1638, and in English as *Popular Errours, or the Errours of the People in Physick,* London, 1651 (DNB; Surg. Gen. Off., *Index-Cat.,* 1st ser., XI, 650-1).

⁴ Ιηροχομια Βασιλικη: *King Solomon's Portraiture of Old Age,* &c., by John Smith, M.D. (1630-1679), London, 1666. The author of this curious work demonstrated, to his own satisfaction at least, that Solomon knew and described "the circular motion of the blood." (DNB; Surg. Gen. Off., *Index-Cat.,* 1st ser., XIII, 214; Allibone, *Dict. of Authors.*)

To James Currie

Dear Sir,   Philadelphia, July 26, 1796

Accept of my thanks for your friendly letter¹ and the papers which accompanied it, which I received by Mr. Evans.

For some years past I have been so abstracted from politics that I hardly dare to give an opinion upon that part of your letter which relates to the principles and conduct of our government. Many of the patriots of 1796² I perceive to be dissatisfied. They complain of British influence in all our cities, which extends through the medium of commerce to our country and is reflected back again from thence to the councils of the United States. Many people now speak, and a few write openly in favor of the British form of government. The conduct of the French Convention under the Jacobin administration has favored this departure from republicanism in our country. It is expected that Mr. Washington will retire next fall. If so, the contest for his successor will be between Mr. Adams and Mr. Jefferson. The former is devoted to monarchy in all its forms and consequences. The latter is a pure republican, enlightened at the same time in chemistry, natural history, and medicine. He is, in a word, a Citizen of the World and the friend of universal peace and happiness. How the contest will end I know not. Mr. Washington's friends will support Mr. Adams. His enemies (for enemies he has) will support Mr. Jefferson. Our country will flourish I hope under any issue of the election, for Mr. Adams, with monarchical principles, is a republican in his manners and a most upright, worthy man. He will govern without a council, for he possesses great knowledge and the most vigorous internal resources of mind.

I was once a republican, but residence in a large city and a wife and eight children have degraded me into a mere physician. I once vented good wishes in favor of France, but I now hear her called by a thousand hard names without daring to say a word in favor of her[3] cause. She does not require the feeble aid of foreign advocates. Her arms will soon settle the fate of the world. I believe in a general and particular providence, having long been a disciple of Dr. Hartley.[4] *All will end well.*

I expect to publish a 4th volume of *Medical Inquiries and Observations* in a few days. It will contain an account of the yellow fever in 1794, an inquiry into the proximate cause of fever, and a defense of bloodletting. I have simplified diseases in every part of it much more than in my volume on the yellow fever of 1793. It will therefore of course offend one of your principles in medicine.

I subscribe to all you have said of Dr. Darwin. He is an Electron Per Se.

Adieu, my dear sir, and be assured that I am most cordially your friend and brother,

BENJN: RUSH

Addressed: Dr: James Currie Physician in Liverpoole. Per the Hebe.
MS: Henry E. Huntington Library.

[1] Dated from Liverpool, 16 May 1796; Rush MSS, III.
[2] Doubtless an error for 1776.
[3] BR inadvertently (but significantly) wrote "our."
[4] David Hartley (1705-1757), the elder, a physician and the author of *Observations on Man, His Frame, His Duty, and His Expectations*, London, 1749; several times reissued (DNB). This was BR's favorite philosophical work and is mentioned and quoted frequently throughout his writings. In a letter to John Adams, 31 Oct. 1807, BR speaks of "the great and good, I had almost said the inspired, Dr. Hartley."

To Samuel Bayard[1]

Dear Sir,   Philadelphia, September 22, 1796

We have found Mr. Rigal[2] a sensible and agreeable man. His lady is a charming woman. They are both in circulation in our city.

Accept of my thanks for your attention to my request respecting my essay on the gout.[3] I have concluded to print it in Philadelphia next spring.

Mr. Dobson has lately sent 200 copies of my last work to Mr. Dilly for sale in London. It has had a quick sale in our country.

Our city has been uncommonly healthy for two months past. But the yellow fever is now desolating Charleston and has carried off near 30 persons in Newbury port in Massachusets. The opinion of its domestic origin has become universal in the United States.

Benjamin Rush
Medallic Portrait by Moritz Furst, 1808

Penn's Tree, with the City & Port of Philadelphia, on the River Delaware near Kensington

I refer you to your brother[4] and to your other correspondents for political news. All is calm at present in our country. Mr. Adams and Mr. Jefferson are talked of as successors to General Washington at the approaching election. The former it is said will be the successful candidate.

The late speculations in land in the United States have proved ruinous to several and hurtful to many of our citizens. Your father's and my old friend Dr. Ruston is now expiating his avarice and rapacity in the new jail. His debts it is said amount to 200,000 dollars. He settled the principal part of his productive estate upon his wife and children before he contracted those debts.

Are you acquainted with the Reverend Henry Hunter?[5] His sacred biographical lectures are admirable performances. The public owe him great obligations likewise for his translation of St. Peire's *Studies of Nature*. It is a charming work. He has made our globe to be the echo of the song of the angels at the birth of our Saviour. Everything in nature according to his system breathes kindness and good will to man.

Adieu. With love to Mrs. Bayard, in which my dear Julia and all the young folks join, I am yours affectionately,

BENJN RUSH

Addressed: Samuel Bayard Esqr: American Agent London.
MS: Princeton University Library.

[1] Samuel Bayard (1767-1840), son of BR's friend Col. John Bayard, was a graduate of the College of New Jersey, 1784; studied law with William Bradford and became his partner; served with notable success for several years as special U.S. prosecutor in England for claims under the Jay Treaty; settling in Princeton, 1806, he was appointed judge of the Somerset court of common pleas and was long active in academic and religious affairs (DAB; S. B. Dod, ed., *Journal of Martha Pintard Bayard, London, 1794-1797*, N.Y., 1894).

[2] Henry Rigal, gentleman, is located at 180 South Fourth St. in the 1797 *Directory*, but not in later ones.

[3] "Observations upon the Nature and Cure of the Gout" first appeared in BR's *Med. Inq. & Obs.*, v, Phila., 1798.

[4] Bayard had three brothers living at this time—Andrew, John, and Nicholas (James G. Wilson, "Colonel John Bayard," p. 71).

[5] Henry Hunter, D.D. (1741-1802), pastor of the Scotch Church, London Wall, 1771-1802, "the author and translator of several valuable works," including *Sacred Biography*, 6 vols., 1783-1792, and J.-H.-B. de Saint-Pierre's *Studies of Nature*, 5 vols., 1796-1797 (DNB; Allibone, *Dict. of Authors*).

To Samuel Bayard

My dear Sir,   Philadelphia, November 25, 1796

Your epitaph upon our much beloved friend[1] is too good. It contains too many ideas—all just, and forcibly expressed. I have not yet seen Mr. Boudinot, who must alone determine whether it requires or will bear an abridgment. I have always preferred brevity in such compositions. My venerable mother's eulogium consists of but one line. After mentioning her name and age, I have simply added: "Best of Mothers!—Benjn Rush." My dear sister's is somewhat longer. It is as follows:

"An affectionate and grateful brother hath caused this stone to be erected in memory of Rebecca Wallace, who died October 1st, 1793, while she was performing the highest acts of kindness to him, and of humanity to the distressed citizens of Philadelphia."

I refer you to your other correspondents for the news of our country. A few weeks will determine who is to be the successor of General Washington as President of the United States. A bad choice cannot be made, for all the candidates possess talents and virtue equal to the station. Under the influence of this opinion, I did not vote at the late general suffrage for electors. From present appearances it would seem as if Mr. Adams would be the successful candidate. A plurality of votes for Mr. Pinckney as Vice-President may possibly defeat the expectations of his friends.

The French minister, Mr. Adet,[2] complains loudly of our government, whether justly or not I cannot say, for I have not read any of his publications. The candle of my life begins to burn low. My patients, books, and family now engross all my time and affections. Heaven will I hope continue to take care of our country.

The eulogium upon Mr. Rittenhouse[3] will be delivered (health and life permitting) next month.

My dear Mrs. Rush joins in love to Patty and Lewis with, my dear sir, your sincere friend,

BENJN RUSH

P.S. Are you acquainted with Mr. Ross Cuthbert[4] at the Temple? How does he employ his time? We take an interest in his character and happiness.

Addressed: Samuel Bayard Esqr: American Agent London. ℔ the Ceres.
MS: Historical Society of Pennsylvania, Sprague Collection.

¹ William Bradford, late attorney general of the U.S., and Bayard's former partner.

² Pierre-August Adet was technically no longer minister, having been recalled, but he took an active part in the presidential election of 1796, writing open letters to the Secretary of State that were published in the *Aurora* (McMaster, *Hist.*, II, 300-2).

³ *An Eulogium, Intended to Perpetuate the Memory of David Rittenhouse*, Phila.: Ormrod, n.d., delivered by BR before the Philosophical Society on 17 Dec. 1796.

⁴ Ross Cuthbert (1776-1861) was evidently already engaged to the Rushes' daughter Emily, whom he married in Mch. 1799. The son of a Scottish soldier who had purchased the seigniory of Lanoraie, near Berthier, Province of Quebec, Cuthbert was educated at the College of Douai, France, practised law, and became a prominent political figure in the province, being for many years a member of the Assembly of Lower Canada; he also published several literary works. (W. Stewart Wallace, comp., *Dictionary of Canadian Biography*, Toronto, 1926; Biddle, *Memorial*, p. 242-3; Régis Roy, "Cuthbert," a communication in *Bulletin des recherches historiques* [Quebec], XL [1934], 627-9.) There are letters from Cuthbert to BR in Rush MSS, XXXIII.

To John Seward¹

Dear Sir, Philadelphia, December 28th, 1796

I have been much gratified by your friendly letter. Similar acknowledgments with those you have made with so much politeness, from many of my pupils who are now in practice in different parts of the United States, satisfy me that my principles are true and encourage me to persevere in propagating them at the expense of friends, business, and sometimes personal happiness.

I have lately published a 4th volume of *Medical Inquiries and Observations*. It contains an account of the yellow fever as it appeared in Philadelphia in 1794, together with observations on the proximate cause of fever and a defense of bloodletting.

I lament the change in the principles of my old and much beloved friend Dr. Jones. Godwin² has some great and original ideas upon morals and government, but upon the subject of religion he writes like a madman. "Christianity," says Montesquieu, "is full of good sense." Yes, it is more than this. It contains the greatest scope for genius of any science in the world, nor is philosophy opposed to any of its principles or precepts when they are properly understood and explained. To vanquish infidelity, the clergy must take new ground. The Deity must be represented as the impartial Father of the *whole* human race, the Atonement must be extended and made effectual to the happiness of all, and evil of course be ultimately annihilated. The works of Dr. Hartley, of Mr. Winchester, and of

Dr. Stonehouse[3] are worth consulting upon each of those subjects. A clergyman's library is not complete without them.

Dr. Darwin's *Zoonomia* and a 2nd volume upon the practice of physic are works of great ingenuity. You will do well in reading them. Some of his opinions are grossly erroneous. But your principles in medicine will readily enable you to correct them.

I have lately found *copious* bleeding, purging, a salivation, and afterwards the cold bath (if necessary) to be very effectual in the [cure][4] of recent and acute mania in our Hospital. I consider it as a *state of fever*. No wonder that it yields to the common remedies for fever.

From, dear sir, your sincere friend,

BENJN: RUSH

Addressed: The Revd: Dr: John Seward Physician Northumbd: County Virginia.

MS: Welch Library, Johns Hopkins Medical School.

[1] John Seward, clergyman and physician of Northumberland co., Va., had attended BR's lectures in 1794; his card of admission for that year is in the Welch Library, Johns Hopkins University. BR is replying to a letter from Seward dated 24 Nov. 1796 (Rush MSS, xv).

[2] In subsequent allusions to the perfectibilitarian doctrines of William Godwin (1756-1836), as set forth in the celebrated *Enquiry concerning Political Justice*, London, 1793, BR has nothing good to say of them or their author; see especially a letter to Ashbel Green, 31 Dec. 1812. On Godwin, see DNB.

[3] Sir James Stonhouse (1716-1795), 11th baronet, was both a physician and a clergyman; he published several devotional tracts (same; also Allibone, *Dict. of Authors*).

[4] MS torn by seal.

To Thomas Jefferson

My dear Friend,   Philadelphia, January 4th, 1797

I enclose you a humble tribute to the memory of our great republican and philosophical friend Mr. Rittenhouse. It is a feeble expression of respect for his character compared with yours in your defense of the genius of the Americans.[1] Few such men have ever lived or died in any country.

Accept of my congratulations upon your election to the Vice-President's chair of the United States and upon your *escape* of the office of President. In the present situation of our country, it would have been impossible for you to have preserved the credit of republican principles or your own character for integrity had you succeeded to the *New York* administration[2] of our government. The seeds of British systems in everything have at last ripened. What a harvest of political evils is before us!

It has given me great pleasure to hear of Mr. Adams' speaking with pleasure of the prospect of administering the government in a connection with you. He does you justice upon all occasions, and, it is currently said, views the attempt which originated in New York to prefer Mr. Pinckney[3] to him in its proper light.

The Philosophical Society purpose to place you in the chair vacated by the death of Mr. Rittenhouse.[4] This will be done in consequence of your declaration in your letter to Mr. Madison that you will not refuse the office of Vice-President of the United States if elected to it. We shall expect you to preside in our winter meetings.

From, dear sir, your sincere old friend,

BENJN RUSH

MS: Library of Congress, Jefferson Papers.

[1] In Jefferson's *Notes on the State of Virginia* (*Writings*, ed. Ford, III, 166-70).

[2] Alexander Hamilton, though out of office, continued to dominate Federalist policy.

[3] Thomas Pinckney, Federalist candidate for the vice-presidency, whom Hamilton endeavored to maneuver into the presidency in order to defeat Adams (Edward Stanwood, *History of the Presidency*, Boston and N.Y., 1912, p. 49-51).

[4] Jefferson was elected president of the Society two days later and served until 1815 (Amer. Philos. Soc., *Early Procs.*, p. 250, 449).

To Thomas Jefferson

Dear Sir,   Philadelphia, 4th February 1797

Your communication upon the subject of the large claws and bones of the lion-kind animal will arrive time enough to have a place in the volume of the *Transactions* of the Philosophical Society which is now in the press.[1]——I have often been struck with the analogy of things in the natural, moral, and political world. The animals whose stupendous remains we now and then pick up in our country were once probably the tyrants of our forests and have perhaps been extirpated by a confederacy and insurrection of beasts of less force individually than themselves. In like manner, may we not hope that kings will be extirpated from the face of the earth by a general insurrection of the reason and virtue of man, and that the exhibition of crowns, scepters, and maces, like the claws and bones of extinct animals, shall be necessary to prove to posterity that such cannibals ever existed upon our globe?

Your Philadelphia friends will rejoice in taking you by the hand after the 3rd of March. Dr. Priestley, who will be in town at that time, longs for the pleasure of your acquaintance. You will be charmed with his extensive information and amiable simplicity of manners. I will give you a specimen of his republicanism. "The time," said he to me, "will I hope one day come when *laws* shall govern so completely that a man shall be a month in America without knowing who is President of the United States."

I am now preparing a paper for our Society in which I have attempted to prove that the black color (as it is called) of the Negroes is the effect of a disease in the skin of the leprous kind.[2] The inferences from it will be in favor of treating them with humanity and justice and of keeping up the existing prejudices against matrimonial connections with them.

Adieu. From, dear sir, your sincere and affectionate friend,

BENJN: RUSH

Addressed: Thomas Jefferson Esqr: Montecelli, Virginia.
MS: Library of Congress, Jefferson Papers.

[1] "A Memoir on the Discovery of Certain Bones of a Quadruped of the Clawed Kind in the Western Parts of Virginia," read to the American Philosophical Society 10 Mch. 1797, and printed in the Society's *Transactions*, old ser., IV (1799), 246-60. See also BR to Jefferson, 1 Feb. 1811.

[2] This astonishing performance, "Observations Intended to Favour a Supposition That the Black Color (as It Is Called) of the Negroes Is Derived from the Leprosy," was read to the Society 14 July 1797, and printed in its *Transactions*, old ser., IV (1799), 289-97.

To John Dickinson

My dear Sir,   Philadelphia, May 2nd, 1793 [*i.e., 1797*][1]

I answered your letter in which you consent to be known as the author of "Fabius" by Saturday's post.[2] I have in one instance only yielded to a suspicion that the letters alluded to came from your pen. Hereafter *I* shall be silent upon that head—but in spite of every effort to the contrary, I foresee from the impression your opinions are making upon the public mind that your name cannot long be concealed from the world.

The friends of monarchy and Great Britain are making great efforts through the medium of their papers to excite a spirit of revenge and war against France. Your letters I hope will eventually counteract it. It is said a majority of the House of Representatives will be in favor of negotiation and peace.

Adieu. Yours—yours—yours, my dear friend, and friend of peace and mankind,

BENJN RUSH

Addressed: John Dickinson Esqr: at Dover State of Delaware.
MS: Historical Society of Pennsylvania, Logan Papers.

¹ BR's error in the year is apparent from the facts known about Dickinson's second series of "Fabius" letters; see the next note.

² On 27 Apr. 1797 Dickinson informed BR that he had written within a month fifteen public letters attacking the Federalists' plans for a war against France (MS letter in Historical Society of Delaware). This second series of "Fabius" letters, which appeared in the Philadelphia *New World*, was published collectively later this year; see BR to Dickinson, 11 Oct. 1797. By the first sentence in this letter BR means that Dickinson has consented to be known to BR (but not to the public) as the author. The acknowledgment "by Saturday's post" (29 Apr.) is missing.

To John Montgomery

My dear old Friend,   Philadelphia, June 16, 1797

I am indebted to you for two letters, for both of which I sincerely thank you. The review of the toils and calumnies we suffered together to promote the reputation and interest of our College and of its principal has united me so closely to you that no time I hope will ever separate us. We both aimed well. Heaven will forgive and reward us.

A war with France seems to be inevitable. "Ah! why will men forget that they are brethren." Honor! Dignity! Glory!—how I hate the words when applied to kings or governments. To engage in a war in defense of either of them is nothing but duelling upon a national scale. Even the property we have lost by French spoliations is not a sufficient or just cause for war. A single life outweighs in value all the ships in the world, and yet thousands of these must be sacrificed to indemnify us for the loss of a few cargoes of sugar and rum. By a suspension of our trade for one year a war might be avoided, and the proudest nations in Europe might thereby be forced to do us justice.

Adieu, my dear friend. From yours sincerely,

BENJN RUSH

MS: Library Company of Philadelphia, Rush MSS.

To Horatio Gates

My dear Friend,   Philadelphia, 25th of August 1797

My second son[1] has just passed his examination at the Jersey College and is now gone to spend a few days in New York previous to his graduating. I have directed him to pay his respects to you. He is a boy of promising talents and temper. I have excited strong prejudices in his mind in your favor. He is a genuine republican and as sincere an unbeliever in kings and conjurors as yourself or his father.

Our old Revolutionary friend General Kusiasco[2] is now in our city. I relieve myself from the toils of the day by passing an hour with him every evening. His conversation is a repast of noble republican sentiments. There has been such a defection from the principles of the year 1776 in our country that I fear he will not be as happy among us as he expected. He speaks of some of the customs introduced by the late administration of our government with surprise and horror. Do come and see him. The part of the town where he lodges is perfectly safe. The fever, which has unreasonably alarmed our citizens, is confined chiefly to one part of the city, and from appearances this day is evidently upon the decline.[3]

From, dear sir, your sincere old friend,

BENJN RUSH

Addressed: Horatio Gates Esqr: near New York.
MS: New-York Historical Society, Gates Papers.

[1] Richard.
[2] Tadeusz Kościuszko (1746-1817), Polish patriot and brigadier general in the Continental Army. During 1797-1798, in an interval between his efforts to achieve the independence of Poland, he was in the United States for about ten months. (DAB.)

[3] This was a bad prophecy; the yellow fever shortly attained near-epidemic proportions. See *Short History of the Yellow Fever, That Broke Out in the City of Philadelphia, in July, 1797: with a List of the Dead*, Phila.: Richard Folwell, 1797.

To Horatio Gates

My dear Friend,   Philadelphia, September 3rd, 1797

Our illustrious friend Kusiosco left this city a few days ago and is now pleasantly and hospitably accommodated at General White's at Brunswick.[1] His wounds are all healed. One of them on his hip has left his thigh and leg in a paralytic state. Time has done a little towards restoring it. I do not despair of his being yet able to walk. He will always limp, but what then? To use an ancient play upon words, "Every step he takes will remind him of his patriotism and bravery."

I take it for granted you will pay your respects to him at Brunswick. How gladly would I witness your first interview! His soul is tremblingly alive to friendship. He loves your very name.

The malignant fever increases, but with much less rapidity and mortality than in 1793. I this day followed to the grave one of my most intimate and worthy friends, Dr. Way.[2] Our connection with each other began when we were boys, and we have ever since lived together as brothers. Under such painful and frequent bereavements, I find no consolation but in a firm belief in a future state of existence, where the evil and misery introduced into our world by the fall of man will be done away, where virtuous friendships will be renewed and rendered perpetual, and where just principles of every kind will produce their full harvest of moral happiness.

From, dear sir, your sincere old friend,

BENJN RUSH

Addressed: Horatio Gates Esqr near New York.
MS: New-York Historical Society, Gates Papers.

[1] Anthony Walton White (1750-1803), of New Brunswick, N.J.; colonel in the Continental cavalry and later a brigadier general (Heitman, *Register*; Anna M. W. Woodhull, "Memoir of . . . White," N.J. Hist. Soc., *Procs.*, 2d ser., VII [1882-1883], 105-15).
[2] Nicholas Way (ca. 1747-1797), M.D., College of Philadelphia, 1771, had been a leading practitioner in Wilmington, Del.; treasurer of the U.S. Mint in Philadelphia, 1794-1797 (Univ. of Penna. *Gen. Alumni Cat.*; Ruschenberger, p. 287; Frank Stewart, *History of the First United States Mint*, Camden, N.J., 1924, p. 80). On Way's death, which precipitated an ugly controversy, see further, BR's *Med. Inq. & Obs.*, 2d edn., 1805, IV, 30-2, and the letter to Ashbel Green, 10 Sep., which follows.

To Ashbel Green[1]

Dear Sir,   September 10, 1797

In addition to the account I have given you of Dr. Way's case, I beg you would communicate to your friends that Dr. Way lost at six bleedings but between 40 and 45 ounces of blood, a quantity by far too little to kill any person (as Dr. Hodge informed you) of Dr. Way's habit of body* and force of disease. As Dr. Hodge saw him only in the remission of his fever, and on the second day of his disease only, the opinion he gave of the cause of his death was rash and cruel in the highest degree.

From, dear sir, your sincere friend,

BENJN RUSH

* From the Doctor's size, he could not have had less than 400 ounces of blood in his body in his ordinary health. In the beginning of disease, this quantity is often increased by the sudden stoppage of all the excretions.

$\mathcal{M}S$: New York Public Library, Emmet Collection.

[1] This was BR's second letter of this date to Green. The earlier one, extant as a draft in the Rush MSS, XXIX, gives a circumstantial account of Dr. Way's death intended to refute a report, attributed to Drs. Hugh Hodge and Caspar Wistar, that BR had bled Way to death after Hodge and Wistar had found Way free of fever. Green's replies, with other documents relative to the quarrel, are in Rush MSS, XXIX.

To John R. B. Rodgers[1]

Dear Sir,   Philadelphia, September 25th, 1797

Accept of my thanks as well as those of my dear Mrs. Rush for your polite attentions to my son Richard. He speaks with gratitude and affection of every branch of your amiable family.

Our fever, which still continues to prevail, is attended with a malignity which was less common in the fevers in 1793 and 1794. Nearly every case of it requires the exertions of a single combat in a battle to overcome it. Such is the force with which it affects the system in many cases on its first attack, and so completely are the parts essential to life disorganized in a short time, that remedies whether depleting or stimulating make no impression upon it. In some of these cases the force of the remote cause is so great as to destroy all sensations, and hence the deluded patients walk about and consider themselves[2] as in no danger till a day or two before they die. The modes of practice are different amongst our physicians. *All* of them prescribe mercury, and *most* of them bleed more or less in every case where symptoms of great morbid action or oppression take place. It is impossible at present to determine the comparative success of the plentiful or scanty use of depleting remedies, for none who recover who are plentifully bled and purged are admitted to have had the disease, while most of those who are lost under a contrary treatment are said to die of worms, falls, colds, and twenty other diseases. I have seen a letter from a physician in Baltimore in which he says the fever in that town is more malignant than it was in 1794. In Norfolk I am assured that it is much less under the power of medicine than it was in 1795. These changes in the force of diseases have long been noticed by writers upon epidemics. Time will I have no doubt discover the causes of them.

I have as yet not lost a single patient in whom I have been able to excite a salivation. For this purpose I apply mercurial ointment to the body as well as give calomel internally in frequent doses from the first hour I am called to a patient. The success of this valuable medicine as well as of bloodletting have been limited in many cases by a revival of the old clamors and prejudices against them. Testimonies will I hope be produced hereafter in their favor which will amply refute the calumnies against them, and show that when judiciously used they are by far the most successful remedies that have ever been employed in malignant fevers.

It will appear further that the advocates for venesection are falsely accused of using it indiscriminately in all cases.[3] We cure many with but one or two venesections, and some by purges only or a salivation. In all our prescriptions we are governed by the pulse, which, when understood in all its states and changes, affords more knowledge of the state of the disease than any other symptom. We consider fever as an unit and are governed in our prescriptions by its *force*, by the predisposition and habits of our patients, and lastly by the pulse.

My son John, who is now my principal assistant in my business, joins in much love to you, with, dear sir, your sincere old friend,

BENJN RUSH

P.S. I have no objection to your publishing with my name what relates to the fever. It may be useful elsewhere. *Here*, where I am scarcely tolerated, it can do no good. This—inter nos.

MS (draft): Library Company of Philadelphia, Rush MSS.

[1] This draft was written under difficulties. Portions of the text are abbreviated to the point of incomprehensibility, and several afterthoughts are subjoined without clear indications of where they should be inserted. I am not confident that all the pieces have been fitted together in the order BR intended.

[2] MS: "them."

[3] A good example of some of BR's fellow-townsmen's view of his conduct is furnished in a letter from Samuel Hodgdon to Timothy Pickering, 17 Aug. 1797:

"Rush behaves like a Man escaped from Bedlam, he has told two Gentle-men of my acquaintance within two days past, to *fly*, for Contagion was every where, and that respiration could not be performed without the utmost hazard. One of the persons laughed at him, the other whose nerves were not so strong was very much affected. If I should hear such language from him I shall advise him to have his head shaved and take his seat in the Hospital. I am not disposed to be severe upon him, but such speeches coming from *him* will do our City more injury than a thousand such Men and such talents as he has credit for could ever with the best disposition do it good. . . . Good God can the people be any longer deceived by a Mountebank and resign all their comforts into the bloody hand of experiments and

inconsistency" (Mass. Hist. Soc., Pickering Papers).

To Andrew Brown, Jr.[1]

Mr. Brown,   *[Philadelphia, 2 October 1797]*

Having brought actions against John Fenno, junior,[2] and William Cobbett, for their publications against me in their papers, I request you not to insert anything in your paper which may be offered in answer to those publications, or in defense of my character.

BENJ. RUSH[3]

Printed: Philadelphia Gazette, 2 October 1797.

[1] Andrew Brown, Jr. (1774-1847), son of the former proprietor of the *Federal Gazette* and *Philadelphia Gazette*, who had died earlier this year; the son returned to England about 1801 (BR to Andrew Brown, 1 Oct. 1788; Brigham, *Hist. and Bibliog. of Amer. Newspapers*, II, 911; *Hist. Cat. St. Andrew's Soc. Phila.* [1], 127-8; Brown & Brown, "Directory of Book-Arts"). For the background and consequences of this communication, see below, Appendix III: The Cobbett-Rush Feud.

[2] John Ward Fenno (d. 1802), son of the John Fenno who had founded the arch-Federalist *Gazette of the United States*, conducted the *Gazette* at times for his father and took it over for a brief period after his father's death from yellow fever in 1798 (DAB, under John

Fenno; Drinker, *Journal*, p. 371; Brown & Brown, "Directory of Book-Arts").

[3] Cobbett reprinted this announcement in *Porcupine's Gazette*, 5 Oct. 1797, and subjoined this comment:

"Now, the view of this publication is easily seen into. The Doctor finds his little reputation, as a physician, in as dangerous a way as ever a poor yellow fever man was in, half an hour after he [BR] was called to his aid; and he vainly imagines that this notification, requesting Brown not to publish any thing on the subject, will be a hint to Fenno and me to forebear. We wanted no hints from Dr. Rush. We know very well what we ought to do; and, if God grants us life, we shall do it completely" (*Porcupine's Works*, London, 1801, VII, 229).

To John Dickinson

My dear Friend,   Philadelphia, October 11, 1797

Your pamphlet and letter came safe to hand.[1] Never till now did I know you were the author of the letters under the signature of Fabius in defense of the general government. I read them with pleasure at the time and have often since spoken of them as the most practical and useful things published upon the controversy which then agitated the public mind.

I will cheerfully undertake to forward three or four copies of the work to France and accompany it with a short preface in which I shall give an account of the author. Your name was well known in France in 1769. Your letters added to the seeds of liberty planted in that country by Montesquieu, Ruisseau,[2] and Voltaire.

Our fever is evidently upon the decline. Such seasons as we have just witnessed are called "the doctors' harvests." To me it has been a harvest, but it has been of unprofitable labor, anxious days, sleepless nights, and a full and overflowing measure of the most merciless persecution. I have not merited the indifference with which the citizens of Philadelphia have witnessed the butchery of my character. When the fever first appeared in our city, my dear and excellent wife spent many hours in urging me to leave it. My second daughter, a girl of 13 years of age, added tears to the entreaties of her mother to prevail upon me not to expose myself a second time to the dangers and distresses of the year 1793. To their entreaties and tears I made the following reply: "If I thought by remaining in the city, I should *certainly die*, I should think it my duty to stay. I will not quit my post."

The religion in which you and I believe has been my only support under the malice of enemies and the ingratitude of friends. The persecutions of our Saviour were most aggravated at the time he was performing the highest acts of mercy to his creatures. It is only by experiencing the malice and rage of man that we can comprehend what is meant by having fellowship with the sufferings of the Son of God.

Adieu, my dear friend. With love as usual to Mrs. Dickinson and the young ladies, I am ever yours,

BENJN RUSH

P.S. My remedies for the yellow fever would have met with no opposition this year had I not signed the Declaration of Independence and latterly declared myself a Republican in the *Eulogium* upon Mr. Rittenhouse. I consider Federalism and Republicanism as synonymous, but many people mean by Federalism the monarchy of Great Britain.

MS: Historical Society of Pennsylvania, Logan Papers.

[1] Dickinson's letter, dated 30 Sep. 1797, is now in the Dickinson College Library. The pamphlet accompanying it was *The Letters of Fabius, in 1788, on the Federal Constitution; and in 1797,* *on the Present Situation of Public Affairs*, Wilmington, 1797. See BR to Dickinson, 2 May 1797.

[2] BR's usual spelling for Rousseau.

To John R. B. Rodgers

My dear Friend,   [*Philadelphia, 16? October 1797*][1]

The persecutions of that memorable year 1793[2] have lately revived against me and with accumulated asperity. [My political conduct during the war and my present political principles (being
republican) have been the procuring causes of these persecutions.][3]
Ever since the year 1793 I have lived in Philadelphia as in a foreign
country. This situation is far from being agreeable to me, but it is
much less so to my family. My business for several years past has
been upon the decline, and were I not employed by strangers I
could not maintain my family by my Philadelphia patients. Under
the influence of these events, I have contemplated leaving this city
and settling in New York. One thing only is necessary to determine
my conduct, and that is a certainty of getting a professor's chair in
your University in which I can disseminate my medical principles.
As I would practise only in consultations, and prescribe only to such
chronic patients as could visit me, I would prefer a residence out of
town and near the University. The income of a professorship with
that of my estate in Pennsylvania would be sufficient, with a garden
and pasture lot, to maintain my family. If you think there is any
chance of the above proposition succeeding, you are at liberty to
commend it in confidence to some of the regents of the University.
If not, you will please to burn this letter.[4]

Our fever is attended with a malignity and obstinacy which were[5]

MS (draft): Library Company of Philadelphia, Rush MSS.

[1] The date is conjecturable from Rodgers' answer, which, though dated from
New York on 17 Oct., contains the
statement that it was not sent until the
receipt of BR's letter of the 16th. There
is of course a possibility that the present
letter was sent earlier and that the
letter of the 16th is missing. Rodgers'
reply, with others of this period, is in
Rush MSS, xxv.

[2] The year is inadvertently crossed
out in MS.

[3] Brackets in MS; this passage was
probably omitted in the letter as sent.

[4] The upshot was curious. Rodgers
and his colleagues on the Columbia
medical faculty were enthusiastic over
the prospect of BR's joining them, and
unanimously resolved that he be recommended for the chair of the practice
of medicine (Rodgers to Rush, 20 Oct.).
However, in a meeting of the Columbia
board of trustees on 3 Nov., Alexander
Hamilton effectively blocked the nomination. Rodgers reported this to BR on
the following day, adding that BR's
friends intended to try again to discover
"whether the old leaven of Bigotry &
political resentment shall triumph or
not." But a change in BR's circumstances
caused him to request Rodgers to go no
further; see the following letter.

[5] The text of the draft here breaks
off without explanation.

To John R. B. Rodgers

My dear Friend,   November 6, 1797

When I proposed removing from Philadelphia to New York, I contemplated a situation in which I could follow the wishes of my heart to live in peace with everybody, and where, from the universal prevalence of the same opinion which I have held of the domestic origin of the yellow fever, I expected to avoid the principal source of hostility to me. In this wish and expectation, I perceive by your letter, I have been disappointed.[1] I therefore request that you would stop the business in its present stage, and assure the trustees of the University that I shall not accept of the appointment should it be offered to me after the obstacles that have been thrown in the way of it by Mr. Hamilton.

It is peculiarly gratifying to me to learn that the opposition to my appointment has come from that gentleman.

I beg my most grateful and affectionate acknowledgments may be made the medical faculty of the University for the liberal and disinterested friendship they have manifested to me upon this occasion.

My determination to retire from my present scene of strife is *unshaken*, and I am happy in being able to inform you that prospects of independence and usefulness have lately been opened to me in my native state far more respectable, though much less agreeable, than the one I wished for in your University.[2] My wish is to escape from the eye of the public and in a retired situation to devote the few remaining years of my life to the completion of my system of medicine. My estate, though insufficient to support me without business in a city, would afford me an affluent maintenance upon a farm.

For your friendship, zeal, and goodness[3] in the whole of this affair, accept of my sincere thanks. With love as usual, I am &c.,

BENJN RUSH

MS (draft): Library Company of Philadelphia, Rush MSS.

[1] See note 4 on preceding letter.
[2] BR refers to his appointment as treasurer of the U.S. Mint, on which see below, Appendix II.
[3] Preceding two words struck out, but apparently by accident in revision of the preceding sentence.

To Horatio Gates

My dear Friend,   Philadelphia, November 30th, 1797

Mr. Garnet[1] shall command my best services.

The opposition that was made to my appointment to a medical chair in your University determined me *not* to remove to your city. The confederacies against me in Philadelphia have rendered the further exercise of my profession here impracticable consistent with my judgment and conscience. I have taken one step towards an escape from it by accepting of an office in the Mint. In a short time, I hope to be retired altogether from the city and to devote the evening of my life to books and my family. I shall not carry into retirement with me the least hostility to any man. My fate is not a singular one. It originates in the weakness of human nature.

My dear Mrs. Rush joins in respectful compliments to Mrs. Gates with your sincere old republican friend,

BENJN: RUSH

P.S. The affairs of nations as well as of individuals are under the direction of a wise and just Providence. If the time be come for the extinction of ignorance and error, whether they relate to *witchcraft* or *kingly power*, no machinations of weak or wicked men can prevent the fulfilment of the benevolent decrees of heaven.

Addressed: Horatio Gates Esqr near New York.
MS: New-York Historical Society, Gates Papers.

[1] An emigrant from England who was related to Gates (Gates to BR, 23 Nov. 1797; *Biddle Papers*, pt. iii, No. 130).

To Ashton Alexander

Philadelphia, February 20, 1798

I find my pupils grateful in proportion to the *smallness* of their obligations to me. The greatest injuries that I have suffered in the course of my life have been from persons whom I have obliged *most*. This has been the case in so many instances that I have sometimes said jokingly "that when a man called upon me for a favor, before I granted it I would demand a security from him that he would not at some future day *cut my throat*."

I have passed thus far a busy and laborious winter. My business has consisted in making additions to my lectures, in attending the Hospital and many private patients, and in assisting in the forming a new medical society, called the "Academy of Medicine."[1] This institution will flourish. Dr. Physick is our president. Dr. Caldwell is senior vice-president. Our first publication will appear in a few weeks. It will contain the proofs of the domestic origin of the yellow fever lately presented to the government of Pennsylvania, together with some remarks upon the report of the College of Physicians upon the same subject.

The Mint employs a few minutes only of my time 3 or 4 times a week.[2] Once a quarter it will employ a few hours to prepare my accounts for the inspection of those persons appointed to examine them. . . .[3] I dare say you deplore with all good men the politico-mania of the two great parties which now divide our country. I still preserve my neutrality upon all public questions by the most studied ignorance of them. Happy should I be could I escape to the foot of some western mountain where I should never hear the names of liberty and government. . . . Soon after I received my commission as treasurer of the Mint, I told the President of the United States that I must act towards him as Dr. Ambrose did to Henry the 4th of France when he sent for him to be his family physician. He stipulated with the King "never to see a battle nor to change his religion." I begged in like manner to be forever excused from taking a part in any political controversy. The President smiled and did not appear offended at the application of the anecdote to the case in point.

Printed (in part): Stan V. Henkels, Sale Catalogue No. 1223 (5 December 1918), lot 184.

[1] This was a short-lived organization formed principally to promote the view, in opposition to that of the College of Physicians, that the yellow fever was local in origin. Members other than those mentioned in the letter were William Dewees, John Redman Coxe, James Reynolds, Francis B. Sayre, John C. Otto, William Boys, Samuel Cooper, James Stuart, Felix Pascalis, and Joseph Strong. Their "first publication" (from which the information above is derived) was a tract of forty-nine pages sufficiently described by its title: *Proofs of the Origin of the Yellow Fever, in Philadelphia & Kensington, in the year 1797, from Domestic Exhalation; and from the Foul Air of the Snow Navigation, from Marseilles: and from That of the Ship Huldah, from Hamburgh, in Two Letters, Addressed to the Governor of the Commonwealth of Pennsylvania,* Philadelphia, 1798. For their further activities during the epidemic of 1798, see Condie & Folwell, *Hist. of the Pestilence, passim.*

[2] The duties of the treasurer are described in a paper in the Rush MSS, XXIX, printed in Goodman's *Rush,* p. 214. The treasurer was little more than a bookkeeper, and from the early records of the Mint now in the National Archives, Fiscal Records, it appears that an assistant named George Ehrenzoller eventually signed for BR most of the receipts for bullion and coin.

[3] This and the following omission are in the printed text.

To Mathew Carey

Dear Sir,   April 5, [17]98

The late events, public and private, which have taken place in our city, have so far lessened my receipts of money that I have lately been obliged to borrow for the exigencies of my family.——Yours sincerely,

B R.[1]

MS: Welch Library, Johns Hopkins Medical School.

[1] The precise circumstances prompting this note are not known. Carey was BR's close ally and sympathizer in the Cobbett affair and carried on his own inky war with the redoubtable English journalist. See the preface to Carey's *Porcupiniad: A Hudibrastic Poem . . . Addressed to William Cobbett*, Phila., 1799.

To Noah Webster

Philadelphia, April 27, 1798

The Academy of Medicine have published their proofs of the domestic origin of our late epidemic.[1] It cannot be refuted, but it will not produce in our city such an effect as to clear a single gutter of its filth. I fear nothing but another visitation by the yellow fever will cure us of our infidelity upon this interesting subject. Go on—go on with your inquiries.[2] Cause physicians to blush, and instruct mankind to throw off their allegiance to them. Posterity will do you justice. The man who produces truth upon the origin of pestilential fevers, and persuades the world to conform to it, will deserve more of the human race than all the heroes or statesmen that ever lived.

Adieu. Yours sincerely.

Printed (in part): Ford and Skeel, *Notes on the Life of Noah Webster*, I, 461.

[1] See letter to Ashton Alexander, 20 Feb. 1798.
[2] Webster had undertaken a work that appeared in two volumes as *A Brief History of Epidemic and Pestilential Diseases*, Hartford, 1799; there are numerous inquiries for medical and bibliographical information among Webster's letters to BR at this period (Rush MSS, XXX).

To Samuel Coates

April 30th, 1798

Mr. Coates will please to recollect the following propositions to be laid before the Managers for the benefit of the asylum for mad people, viz.: 1st. Two warm and two cold bathrooms in the lowest floor—all to be connected; also a pump in the area to supply the baths with water.

2nd. Certain employments to be devised for such of the deranged people as are capable of working. Spinning, sewing, churning, &c., might be contrived for the women. Turning a wheel, particularly grinding Indian corn in a hand mill for food for the horse or cows of the Hospital, cutting straw, weaving, digging in the garden, sawing or planing boards, &c., &c., would be useful for the men.

BENJ. RUSH

Printed: Morton, *History of the Pennsylvania Hospital*, p. 145-6.

To Noah Webster

July 20th, 1798

I perceive you are aiming still to make men *politically* as well as *physically* happy. I have read your *Oration*[1] with great pleasure. But alas! my friend, I fear all our attempts to produce political happiness by the solitary influence of human reason will be as fruitless as the search for the philosopher's stone. It seems to be reserved to Christianity alone to produce universal, moral, political, and physical happiness. Reason produces, it is true, great and popular truths, but it affords *motives* too feeble to induce mankind to act agreeably to them. Christianity unfolds the same truths and accompanies them with *motives*, agreeable, powerful, and irresistible. I anticipate nothing but suffering to the human race while the present systems of paganism, deism, and atheism prevail in the world. New England may escape the storm which impends our globe, but if she does, it will only be by adhering to the religious principles and moral habits of the first settlers of that country.

Printed (postscript only): Ford and Skeel, *Notes on the Life of Noah Webster*, I, 466.

[1] *An Oration Pronounced before the Citizens of New-Haven . . . , July 4th, 1798*, New Haven, 1798. This performance, being strongly Federalist in tone, was not likely to elicit BR's wholehearted praise.

To James Craik

Dear Sir,   Philadelphia, July 26, 1798

Permit me to congratulate you upon your late appointment of Physician General of the Army of the United States. I cannot help admiring that patriotism which has led you at an advanced period of life to engage a third time in the service of your country.[1]

Under a feeble influence (compared with yours) of the same principle, I have sat down to suggest a few things to you (without any regard to language or order) which are intended to prevent in some degree the terrible calamities we both witnessed, from ignorance, negligence, and peculation, in the military hospitals of the United States during the late war.

In the enclosed copy of a letter[2] to General Knox upon the use of the rifle shirt, you will perceive several ideas which I conceive to be of great consequence in the preserving the health of soldiers.

I admit with General Washington in a late letter[3] to Mr. Adams that the physician general of an army "should be one of the limbs of a commander in chief." He should reside in his family. No order for marching, encamping, eating, drinking, or even fighting (as far as it relates to the *time* of a battle) should be issued without his knowledge or concurrence.

This will prevent much sickness and mortality. In an ingenious work published last year by Dr. Hector McClean [*Maclean*], entitled *An Inquiry into the Nature and Causes of the Great Mortality among the British Troops at St. Domingo*,[4] I observe he ascribes much of it to the feeble influence of the physicians of the army in regulating the diet, encampments, and exercise of the soldiers.

The extent of this mortality may be easily conceived from a single fact. The 82nd Regiment arrived at St. Domingo with 950 men, including officers and privates. In less than *one year* 800 privates and 20 officers of this regiment perished with the fever of the country.

To prevent the evils which existed last war in our army from ignorant regimental and naval surgeons and mates being appointed by the executive of the United States, I have proposed to Mr. McHenry[5] and Mr. Stoddart[6] that[7] of 3 medical gentlemen in the great cities of the United States, whose business it should be to examine all candidates for medical appointments (who have not graduated at some college of medicine) in surgery and the practice of physic, and to testify their qualifications before they receive their commissions. Both those gentlemen approved of the proposition. It has not yet been adopted. A few lines from you or from the commander in chief may accelerate the measure.

It cannot take place too soon. If published in the newspapers, it will prevent improper applications.

In the law for raising 12 regiments, I am sorry to observe the quantity of their ration of animal food increased ¼ of a pound. I wish the sum appropriated for that extra quantity of meat had been applied to the purchase of bread or a few potatoes. Many of the bowel complaints of our soldiers during the late war arose from their eating too much *fresh* meat. They were less frequent as soon as they were fed upon *salt* meat, to which they had been accustomed before they became soldiers. They appeared moreover to derive more strength and spirits from salted than from fresh meat.

Potatoes have become a universal and cheap article of cultivation and diet in our country. I wish they could form a constant part of the diet of our army and of the ration of a soldier.

Caesar fed his troops frequently with boiled wheat. It is a pleasant aliment, and might be used at those times when it was difficult or impossible to bake bread. Indian corn affords a great deal more nourishment and strength than any other grain. Could no means be contrived to have it introduced into the army? The eastern and southern troops could not fail of being pleased with it. What do you think of lessening the quantity of rum in a ration and substituting molasses in its place? Dr. McClean recommends, in the work before alluded to, the formation of a medical board in the army to consist of 3 or 5 physicians whose business shall be to appoint and dismiss regimental surgeons and mates as well as the mates of the hospitals. Perhaps at a future day the examination of candidates for medical appointments might be committed to them.

There are several ingenious physicians in this city of extensive educations who are willing to accept of appointments in the hospitals. They are Drs. Mease, Coxe, Caldwell, and Otto. Dr. Miller[8] of New York has expressed a desire of a place in the medical staff. He is a man of first-rate abilities and of great worth. He would be to you what Achates was to Aeneas. Dr. Physick, who is at the head of the surgery in this city, has offered his services to the United States. With such a phalanx of respectable men under your direction, your success and reputation in your present station would be certain.

The present establishment of your rank and pay, I have been told, will undergo an alteration next winter. Your title should have been "Director General," and your pay equal to a major general's.

My late labors have worn me to the stump. I can at present do but little more than pray for the welfare of our common country. The remains of my strength are still at her service, but they can *only* be exerted in suggesting to my friends who are, like you, *young* or *active* such hints as may prevent evil.

I neglected to mention in its proper place the use of onions as part of the ration of a soldier. They are a kind of solid dram and are remarkable for imparting vigor to the body when debilitated by heat, cold, or great labor. The old Romans used them to lessen their fatigue of their harvest fields. The French soldiers use them as an ingredient in all their made dishes. The New England troops I have no doubt would prefer them to any other vegetable. Dr. McClen advises bathing frequently in cool water to promote cleanliness and to strengthen and refresh the body in warm weather, but he urges in strong terms the necessity of the soldiers' being attended, when they use this wholesome exercise, by a surgeon and an officer.

Excuse the liberty I have taken in writing this letter. It is dictated not only by a love to our country, but by a sincere regard for that gentleman to whom she has committed the health and lives of her most patriotic citizens.

From your affectionate friend,

BENJN RUSH

MS (copy, not in BR's hand): Library Company of Philadelphia, Rush MSS, Notebooks, vol. 2.

[1] On Craik, see BR to William Duer, 13 Dec. 1777. It is said that Washington, in accepting the command of the troops being raised for the expected war with France, stipulated that Craik be placed at the head of the medical service (DAB, under Craik).

[2] Dated 28 Mch. 1792, and printed above.

[3] Dated 4 July 1798; Washington, *Writings*, ed. Fitzpatrick, XXXVI, 315. Washington said, however, that the principal staff officers should be the "limbs" of the commander, and that the physician general was "important."

[4] Published in London, 1797; BR has inserted the word "British" in the title; see Surg. Gen. Off., *Index-Cat.*, 1st ser., VIII, 489.

[5] James McHenry, at this time secretary of war.

[6] Benjamin Stoddert (1751-1813), a Maryland merchant who had been appointed first secretary of the navy in the preceding May (DAB).

[7] BR means "the appointment of."

[8] Edward Miller (1760-1812), brother of BR's friend Rev. Samuel Miller; M.D., University of the State of Pennsylvania, 1789; a founder and editor of *The Medical Repository*, 1797; first professor of the theory and practice of physic, College of Physicians and Surgeons, N.Y., 1807. He was long a close friend and correspondent of BR, who undertook to write a memoir of Miller's life in 1812 but died before doing so. (DAB; Samuel Miller's Introduction to Edward Miller's *Medical Works*, N.Y., 1814; letters from Edward Miller in Rush MSS, XXVII.) BR's letters to Miller have not been found.

To Mrs. Rush[1]

My dearest Julia,   August 26, 1798

I write to you for the first time from our little *hut* on Timberlane.[2] I lodged here last night and was well accommodated. The noise of rural insects,[3] the sight of domestic animals coming to the well to drink before they retired to rest, the purity and coolness of the air, a pleasant and frugal supper of fruit and milk, and the greatest kindness and attention from Betsey, Charlotte,[4] Billy, and both our sons, created for a few hours a flow of peaceful and happy feelings such as I have seldom experienced since I left the country school in which I received the first elements of my education. I forgot for a while the disputes and convulsions which now agitate our country and the globe. The principles and claims of monarchists and democrats appeared to me to partake of equal absurdity and madness. I forgot the persecutions of my enemies and felt as if I could welcome the most inveterate of them to partake of the simple fare of our little cottage. One thing I could not forget—the sufferings of the sick, the afflicted, and the dying in the city of Philadelphia. My heart was torn with anguish in looking towards it. The deaths yesterday were 40. Three more persons were admitted into the hospital[5] yesterday than on any one day in 1793. Poor Henry,[6] my English friend, died there last night. Miss Conyngham[7] died this morning. The grief occasioned by her death will last till time with respect to her mother shall be no more. This day my carriage was stopped as in 1793 by several people praying for a visit to their friends or families. My pupils continue ill, but I do not despair of them. Mr. Hickman,[8] whom I saw this morning, is out of danger. An emetic armed with the force of an 18-pounder saved him. My business *in the country* increases. I dined yesterday at Dr. Edwards' and this day at Mr. Boudinot's. My indisposition, which gave me some uneasiness, left me the night before last. All the family in hut[9] join in love to you and all our dear children and friends with yours affectionately,

BENJN RUSH

Addressed: Mrs Julia Rush at Richd Stockton Esqr: Princeton.
MS: Josiah C. Trent, M.D., Durham, North Carolina.

[1] With the outbreak of the yellow fever in midsummer, Mrs. Rush, with most of the family, left Philadelphia for Princeton. BR began writing her on 6 Aug. and continued for a time almost as regularly as in 1793. Some of the letters in this sequence appear to be lost; others that are known are not available for publication at this time.

[2] This is BR's first mention of the

villa that he gave the name "Sydenham." There is no doubt that he acquired it with the idea that he might be obliged to give up practice in Philadelphia; as things turned out, he used Sydenham as a summer retreat and continued active practice from there. The retreat is well described by BR himself in subsequent letters, particularly in that of 28 Sep. 1798. It was situated two and a half miles directly north of the then center of town, at the junction of Timber and Slumb Lanes; see the Varlé-Scott "Plan of Philadelphia and Environs," ca. 1802, the earliest that locates "Dr. Rush's" seat. Nothing marks its site at Fifteenth and Columbia Streets in the modern city. Sydenham Street, cut through between Fifteenth and Sixteenth about 1860, doubtless derives its name from the Rush country seat, which was occupied successively by BR's widow and his son Richard, whose sons sold it in 1860 (deed of sale in Rush Family Papers, deposited in Princeton Univ. Libr.).

³ MS: "insents."
⁴ Probably a servant.
⁵ This was the "City Hospital," established by the Board of Health, probably in 1797, in the Wigwam Hotel at the foot of Sassafras (now Race) Street on

the Schuylkill, for yellow-fever patients. BR was one of the physicians in attendance there in 1798 and 1799. This temporary institution, the forebear of the Municipal Hospital for Contagious and Infectious Diseases, is not to be confused with the Philadelphia Almshouse and House of Employment, which early functioned as a hospital and on whose staff BR served as early as 1773; it ultimately became the Philadelphia General Hospital; see Robert J. Hunter, "The Origin of the Philadelphia General Hospital," PMHB, LVII (1933), 32-57. There is a full and graphic account of the City Hospital in 1798 in Condie & Folwell's *History of the Pestilence*, p. 51-3, 83-5. See also William H. Welch, in F. P. Henry, ed., *Founders Week Memorial Volume*, Phila., 1909, p. 521; BR, *Med. Inq. & Obs.*, 2d edn., 1805, IV, 11; BR to Rachel Bradford Boudinot, 18 July 1799.
⁶ John Henry, on whom I have no further information (Condie & Folwell, *Hist. of the Pestilence*, Appendix).
⁷ Ann Cunningham, buried in the Second Presbyterian churchyard (same).
⁸ Selby Hickman, tailor, 35 and 37 Spruce St. (1798 *Directory*).
⁹ Thus in MS.

To Mrs. Rush

My dear Julia,   Sydenham Hut, August 29th, 1798

My poor heart is sore. Even the retirement and silence of our little hut will not compose it. This day my worthy pupil Mr. Smyth¹ breathed his last. Mr. Cocke² is still in danger and I fear will sink this night under deep depression of spirits. Dr. Otto is ill at Woodberry [*Woodbury, N.J.*]. He sent for me yesterday to visit him. My present distressing engagements forbade it. I sent him a good nurse, for his physician, Dr. Campbell,³ informed me that he was deserted and shunned by the whole village, and that not a creature but himself would hand him even a drink of water. Dr. Sayre,⁴ Dr. Cooper,⁵ and Dr. Proudfit are all confined in Philadelphia. It seems as if no part of the city would escape our terrible visitation. The two hot days last week have added much to the malignity and mortality of the fever. The cool weather will probably increase the number of sick, but it will probably render the disease more manageable. This was the case in 1793.

I called this day for the last time to see Mrs. Barry, the wife of one of the men to whom under God we owe your life.[6] I found her returning from market with a basket of meat and vegetables in her hand. Her recovery has soothed my distress a little for the loss of other patients. She is a decent woman and seems to be happy in her husband. She inquired every time I saw her "how *Miss* Rush did."

Don't be uneasy about your best friend. I have escaped a Lion and a Bear in 1793 and 1797. Why should I fear to meet our present Goliah? "He that would save his life shall lose it, and he that will lose his life for my sake shall save it."[7] It is but seldom God furnishes any of his creatures with an opportunity of manifesting their love to their fellow men by risking their lives for their benefit. I am honored by him in being placed in that situation. The way is now open and smooth for my usefulness. Public confidence is again placed in me, and my opinions and advice have at last some weight. Under these circumstances I cannot think of retiring altogether. My business is confined chiefly to my old patients, to strangers, and the poor. I refuse applications daily to wealthy and respectable people. I go to town about 9 o'clock in the morning and return to our hut always before sunset. I am seldom fatigued and have as yet felt (one day excepted) none of the aches and pains of 1797. ——Adieu.——All here join in love to you. Richd. is useful to me in putting up medicines for my patients. Love as usual.

BENJN RUSH

Addressed: Mrs: Julia Rush at Richard Stockton Esqr: Princeton.
MS: Princeton University Library.

[1] BR inadvertently wrote "Symth." This was Leopold Smyth, of Georgia, apprenticed to BR in the preceding month (MS List of Apprentices).

[2] Samuel Cocke, of Virginia, apprenticed to BR in 1797 (same).

[3] Not further identified.

[4] Francis Bowes Sayre, a former apprentice of BR's, 1787, and M.D., College of Philadelphia, 1790; he died on 2 Sep. (MS List of Apprentices; Sayre's inaugural thesis [copy in Coll. Phys. Phila.]; Condie & Folwell, *Hist. of the Pestilence*, Appendix).

[5] Samuel Cooper, resident apprentice and apothecary at the Pennsylvania Hospital, 1792-1797; in charge, with Physick, at the City Hospital, 1798; he died during the epidemic and bequeathed his estate to the Pennsylvania Hospital (Morton, *Hist. of the Penna. Hospital*, p. 534; Condie & Folwell, *Hist. of the Pestilence, passim*).

[6] There is a graphic account of the accident to which BR alludes, in a letter from Elias Boudinot to his wife dated 17 June 1798:

"Mr. & Mrs. Leston [i.e., Robert Liston, the British minister], Dr. Rush, Mrs. Rush & children with Lord Henry Stewart [i.e., Stuart, secretary to the British legation] all took a ride yesterday to see Mr. & Mrs Peters—On their return Mrs Rush knowing Dr. Rush to be complaining got into the chair with Lord Henry & gave the Dr. her seat in the coach it was near night and when they came to the Bridge the Dr. in the Coach with Mr. & Mrs Leston stopped to pay the fare & Lord Henry drove over the Bridge—There happened to be a large Lancaster wagon on the Bridge before them the driver of which was not very accomodating. Lord Henry attempted to pass the waggon, when the Horse took a fright ran back, broke the arms of the Bridge, and plunged Chair Riders & all into the River—Lord Henry (being a good swimmer) exerted himself to the utmost to save Mrs. Rush. He clasped her in his arms—then took her by the Head —then by the middle—but it would not do, he finally lost hold of her—her presence of Mind did not forsake her but she struggled to keep herself up as much as she could—Just as she was going down the last time, two men appeared on the Bridge & attempted to reach her but could not—Lord Henry still in the water called on them to save her for God's sake. The men begged her to extend her arms—Lord Henry finding she must drown made a desperate attempt to reach her and pushed her so that in the last struggle she threw out her arms when one of the men secured her hand and dragged her on the Bridge—She was between the Horse and the Bridge by which her head and face were much bruised—In this situation Dr. Rush heard a cry that the Chair was gone—He burst open the door

of the coach & ran like a distracted man, and just found her raised by the two men & supported between them— After getting Lord Henry out of the water and getting dry clothes they reached home—the Horse was drowned but the chair saved—I have just been to see her, not hearing of it till after Church was out—She spent a very restless night—but slept well in the morning—She is no ways hurt but in the Head, Eyes & Temples, These, are more [mere?] external bruises, and there is no doubt but that a few days will restore her, a blessing to her Family—" (Boudinot, *Boudinot*, II, 137-9).

The bridge on which the accident occurred was one of the three "floating bridges" over the Schuylkill; for an account of their construction, see Isaac Weld, *Travels through the United States*, 4th edn., London, 1807, I, 33-4. Mrs. Drinker always walked rather than rode over these bridges, for fear of accidents; see her *Journal*, p. 376. From the evidence available, it is not possible to say with certainty whether the bridge over which the party traveled was the "upper" one at present Spring Garden Street or the "middle" one at present Market Street. In one of his pocket notebooks, under the date of the accident, BR set down the names of Mrs. Rush's rescuers thus: "Richard Perry—Alexr. Austin—the names of the men who took my wife out of Skuilkill" ("Notes on Continental Congress &c.," vol. 3). See also BR to Mrs. Rush, 28 Sep. 1798.

[7] Compare Matthew 10:39; Luke 9:24.

To William Marshall[1]

My dear old Friend,   Philadelphia, September 15th, 1798

As cold water to a thirsty soul and good news from a far country, so is the kind remembrance of an old friend.

Our globe exhibits indeed a melancholy spectacle of human misery: Asia and Africa prostrated by universal and the most unqualified slavery; a war of extermination carrying on in every part of Europe; and pestilence pervading all the cities and many of the villages of the United States. "Seekest thou great things? Seek them not, for behold I bring evil upon all flesh."[2] It is some mitigation to the sorrows which for some time past have torn my heart that the probability lessens of the calamities of war being added to those of disease in our country. I hope the account you have given me of the pacific disposition of France towards the United States may prove true. If it should, Mr. Gerry will deserve more from his country than ever she can pay him.[3]

I agree with you in deriving our physical calamities from moral causes. Antifederal infidelity and Federal hypocrisy, with all the vices that flow from both, pervade every part of the United States. A bitter and unchristian spirit has likewise divided our citizens. We have not, it is true, erected a guillotine in our country, but we enjoy similar spectacles of cruelty in the destruction of public and private characters in our newspapers. We have not instituted divine honors to certain virtues in imitation of the inhabitants of Paris, but we ascribe all the attributes of the Deity to the name of General Washington. It is considered by our citizens as the bulwark of our nation. God would cease to be what HE is, if he did not visit us[4] for these things.

Our fever increases. It is much more malignant than in 1793 and 1797, and requires in many instances a different treatment from the fever of those years. In many cases it will bear but small bleedings, and in some none at all. Those cases which bear plentiful bleeding generally end favorably. I sleep two miles from the city, but visit from 12 to 20 patients daily in the city and spend some time afterwards with Dr. Physick at the city hospital, where I witness more suffering in one hour than I have been accustomed to see in common times in a year. Ah! my friend, what different scenes are now familiar to us compared with those which our world and our country exhibited in the first happy years of our acquaintance! Through divine goodness I still enjoy good health and great composure of mind. Adieu. "Brethren, pray for us!"[5] Yours affectionately,

BENJN RUSH

P.S. No part of this letter must be made public. Persecution at present *sleeps* against me.

Addressed: The Revd: Mr William Marshall at Mr G: Gorman's Corner of Liberty & Greenwich Streets New York.
MS: Library Company of Philadelphia, Rush MSS.

[1] Rev. William Marshall (ca. 1740-1802), born in Scotland, minister of the Associate or Scots' Presbyterian Church, 1768-1786, and afterwards of a seceding

portion of that congregation which organized the Associate Reformed Church. BR attended Marshall in his last illness and was devoted to his memory. (Scharf & Westcott, II, 1269, 1274-6; BR, *Autobiography*, p. 312-13; BR to John Adams, 20 July 1811.)
² Jeremiah 45:5.

³ Believing he could prevent war, Elbridge Gerry had stayed on in France after his colleagues on the famous "X.Y.Z." mission returned home (DAB).
⁴ This word omitted in MS.
⁵ I Thessalonians 5:25; II Thessalonians 3:1.

To Mrs. Rush

My dearest Julia,   Philadelphia, September 28, 1798

I have hitherto concealed the extent of my improvements from you on purpose to surprise as well as please you when you visit *your* little farm. You shall now have a short detail of them. I have built a neat *brick* kitchen, 16 by 12, with a convenient garret room over it, between the old brick house and the well. I have added a story and an half to the old brick house, by which means we shall have two comfortable lodging rooms instead of one uncomfortable one over the common first floor of the said old house. The three cellars which were separated by stone walls are made into one, which, from my having lessened the number of windows in them, is now large, dry, and very commodious. It remains now only to pull down the old frame kitchen and to replace it with a brick building which will be connected with the old brick house at the beginning of the roof. The division of this part I leave *wholly* to you. It shall be divided as formerly into a small room and a pleasant cool entry, or the whole shall be thrown into one room, 24 by 12, just as you please. Above it will be two neat bedrooms, communicating by a door with the bedroom on the 2nd story of the old brick house. Ample space has been left everywhere for closets. The building when finished will be convenient, cool, tight, and large enough to accommodate all such of our family as it will be proper to leave the city in warm weather.¹ The many cases of fever which have occurred in persons who left our city in *July* have determined me to imitate the examples of Mr. Peters, Mr. Conyngham,² and Mr. Ross³ by sending my family out of town in *May* or *June*. The farm will be pleasant and healthy till August, at which time you and the girls may retire to Jersey and spend the sickly months with your friends. The garden *under your eye* and a better gardener than Billy may be greatly productive. Richard has enlarged the strawberry bed to nearly half an acre. The garden is to be made square and brought forward towards the road so as to take in one half the house. A wagon house is to be made behind and contiguous to the barn out of the materials of the two old houses. Should my life be spared, I hope not only to visit you but to spend many evenings and nights with you in this charming spot. The neighborhood is a pleasant one. Old Mr. Willing is to build on his son's lot next spring. He has bought his son and son-in-law out, and now owns 36 acres adjoining us.

I have one thing more to add upon the subject of our improvements that I am sure will give you pleasure. They have been carried on under the direction of Richard Perry,[4] one of the men who dragged you from the water on the 16th of last June. I undertook them at *this time* for two reasons: 1. to give bread to a man to whom I owe an immense debt of gratitude, whom the fever had thrown out of business, and 2ly, to save the expenses which attend men working when the owner of the work is absent from them. Dr. Edwards calculates the savings in this way at 7/6 an hour. From the economy hitherto used in materials, from the reduced price of labor, and from the simplicity of the work, the expenses have as yet been moderate compared with the same mass of work two years ago.

We shall do nothing to the old frame house till the old brick building is so far completed as to accommodate us. This will be the case, we expect, next week, after which time I shall be happy, very happy, to receive my pair of Julias.

The deaths, alas! this day have been 106. The mortality in our city hospital lessens, owing to the increase of room for our sick. Dr. Mease and Dr. Stewart[5] rode out this day. Dr. Leib is still in great danger. I took leave this day of Mr. Liston's Stewart.[6] He has been roughly handled both by his disease and his doctor.

My most affectionate love awaits our dear children. May the blessings your dear and excellent mother implores for me descend likewise into her own bosom! With love to all your brother's family, I am ever yours,

BENJN RUSH

P.S. Betsey, Charlotte, and the boys send love to you. Peter is a treasure to us. He is market man, gardener, farmer, hostler, and occasionally coachman. Yesterday he and Richd. gathered the remains of our apples. They amounted to 10 bushels, some of which are equal to any we have ever seen in our market. Richd. intends to barrel up six bushels for your winter store.

Addressed: Mrs: Julia Rush at Richd: Stockton Esqr Princeton.
MS: Josiah C. Trent, M.D., North Carolina.

[1] This is ungrammatical, but BR's thought is clear from a phrase he crossed out: "all such of our family *as prefer the country to the city* in warm weather."

[2] David Hayfield Conyngham (1750-1834), educated at the Philadelphia Academy and Trinity College, Dublin, was a partner for many years in Conyngham & Nesbitt, the firm of shipping merchants founded by his father, Redmond Conyngham. David H. served during the Revolution as a commercial agent in France for the Continental Congress, and also with the First City Troop of Light Horse. His shipping office and town house were on Front Street, and his country place was "Woodford," on the Ridge Road in the present Fairmount Park; he acquired a home in Germantown about this time. (Conyngham's "Reminiscences," *passim*.)

[3] There are a dozen Ross's in the 1798 *Directory*.

[4] The initial letter has been written over and may have been meant, finally, for either *B* or *P*. BR had trouble remembering this man's name, for he spelled it in two, perhaps three, different ways.

[5] James Stuart (ca. 1772-1809), M.D., University of Pennsylvania, 1798; BR gives an account of his death and character in his Commonplace Book (Univ. of Penna., *Gen. Alumni Cat.*; BR, *Autobiography*, p. 317).

[6] Robert, afterwards Sir Robert, Liston (1742-1836), a diplomat of long experience, was British minister to the United States, 1796-1802 (DNB). He was with the Rushes when Mrs. Rush was nearly drowned in the preceding June. I have not identified his "Stewart" (Lord Henry Stuart, secretary of legation, would not be thus referred to by BR); perhaps this is a slip of the pen for "servant."

To Richard Bushe, Jr.[1]

Sir,   Philadelphia, December 29, 1798

So much of my time has lately been taken up in answering letters for advice for which I have received no compensation, and for which I am obliged to pay the postage, that I have been compelled to resolve to reply to no letter for advice which is not accompanied with a fee, unless it comes from persons who acknowledge themselves to be poor. You will not I hope complain of this conduct when I add *(that I am not rich, that my business in Philadelphia has been nearly ruined by the public and private persecutions to which my principles and practice in medicine have exposed me, that I have a large family, and that I do not think it just to work for nothing for those who are able to pay for my services. While I mention my obligations to my family, I must add that I do not suffer them to interfere with my duties to the poor. They share a part of all my earnings.)* that should you think it worth while to write to me a second time upon the subject of your health and enclose ten dollars in your letter, it shall be given in charity to the Pennsylvania Hospital, and the history of your case shall be faithfully and minutely attended to by, sir, your most obedient servant,

BENJN RUSH[2]

MS (draft): Library Company of Philadelphia, Rush MSS.

[1] Not further identified. BR's draft is as interesting for what he struck out from it as for what he finally wrote to Bushe.

[2] A memorandum by BR on the back of the letter states: "This money was received and given to the Hospital."

To Noah Webster

Sir,   Philadelphia, June 20th, 1799

I have made a second unsuccessful attempt to dispose of your book.[1] Our printers and booksellers (one excepted) are among the believers in the importation of the yellow fever, and hence they cannot easily be persuaded duly to appreciate your opinions, which are universally known to be on the other side of the question. The prejudices against the truth upon this subject are as strong as ever. Currie in a late publication has attempted to prove the assertion of the domestic origin of the yellow fever to be equal to treason, and has advised that the authors of it should "no longer be tolerated." Cobbet, after accusing our climate for two years for[2] generating the yellow fever, now conforms so far to the current opinion of its foreign origin as to abuse me publicly for denying it. In short, some demon seems to have blinded our citizens as if to prepare the way for their future and greater sufferings from that disease.

After this information, I hope you will not hesitate in sending your book to London to be printed. I will give you an introduction to Dr. Lettsom and will aid its sale by letters to all my medical friends. Your name is well known in England. All your publications I perceive are highly commended by the Analytical Reviewers.[3]

The inflammatory constitution of our atmosphere has not yet passed away. The diseases of the late spring were all tinged with bile and yielded only to powerful remedies. An influenza has lately prevailed partially in our city. Our merchants begin to complain of their long and expensive quarantines. Time may cure them of their folly. I feel the same pity and contempt for men in company who defend the importation of the yellow fever that I do for the first settlers in New England who believed in witchcraft. Mr. Hare, the Speaker of the Senate of Pennsylvania, in a conversation upon our health law insisted upon sugars being taken out of vessels and brought up in lighters for, said he, "the yellow fevers may be imported in a hogshead of sugar."

You may rely upon each of my pupils (generally from 80 to 100 yearly) purchasing a copy of your work. I long very much to see it.——Adieu.

BENJN: RUSH

Addressed: Noah Webster Esqr: New Haven Connecticut.
MS: New York Public Library, Webster Papers.

[1] *A Brief History of Epidemic and Pestilential Diseases*, published at Hartford later this year.
[2] Thus in MS.

[3] *The Analytical Review; or, History of Literature, Domestic and Foreign*, was a London periodical.

To John Montgomery

My dear Friend,   Philadelphia, June 21, 1799

It would have given me very great pleasure to have witnessed the laying of the cornerstone of our College.[1] I would have blended a tear for the sufferings it has cost me with my prayers to heaven for its usefulness to the civil and religious interests of mankind. May it become in a more especial manner the nursery of the Church of Christ, and may many precious streams issue from it to make glad the cities of our God! I lament Dr. Nesbitt's coldness and indifference to the undertaking. His eyes and his heart should never be idle until the building is completed. How great the difference, my friend, between a speculative and a practical Christian! Dr. N.'s politics, I fear, hurt our College.[2] It should be of no party. Democratic money weighs as heavily in our treasury as the money of the Federalists. The western counties of the middle states on which we depended chiefly for scholars are in general Democrats. They should not be offended; on the contrary, they should be allured to the College by the silence of our professors upon subjects which do not belong to the essence of good government. Let Belzibub go on in making war upon *himself*. Let Democratic tyranny and wickedness punish the overgrown crimes of monarchical tyranny in Europe. Schoolboys should have nothing to do with their squabbles, any more than with the battles of the tigers and wolves of our wilderness. It is enough if they are taught to love and admire our present excellent Constitution, and to believe with its destruction will perish the remains of all the liberty in the world.

I have no objection to receiving the interest at the treasury upon our certificates. Perhaps General Gurney[3] may be pleased with this mark of confidence. He deserves well of our College. In our late begging excursion through our city he outdid all my former doings in pleading the cause of learning, liberty, religion, and good government, all of which he said would be advanced by promoting the interest of our institution. Consider further, he is a member of our legislature, and that we shall require his aid next year in our application for money to the state.

A son of our old friend Mr. Linn is settled in Market Street Church.[4] He is a promising youth. He speaks well and seems to be in earnest in his attempts to do good. The young and the gay of all denominations flock to hear him. John Smith is again settled in Pine Street. He is as apostolic as ever in his preaching and living. Such men are a blessing to a city. God grant they may, by the efficacy of their prayers and sermons, keep war and yellow fever from our doors!

My family join in love to you. My children have begun to scatter. My eldest son has quitted physic and is now a lieutenant in the navy.[5] My eldest daughter is happily married to a young lawyer of the name of Cuthbert, of excellent character, and is soon to go with him to Canada.

Adieu, my dear friend. From yours very affectionately,

BENJN: RUSH

P.S. Since writing the above, I have seen General Gurney. He will act as attorney for our College in receiving our interest. He advises to lay out all the payments by the treasury on our 6 percents, in 8 percents. They may now be had at 5 percent below par. We have agreed to make a second attempt to collect for the College in the fall. Perhaps we may add 200 dollars to our late subscription.

Addressed: John Montgomery Esqr Carlisle Pennsylvania.
MS: Library Company of Philadelphia, Rush MSS.

[1] This was the first building erected for the use of Dickinson College; John Montgomery laid the cornerstone on 20 June 1799. After a long struggle to complete the edifice, it burned just at the time of completion, Feb. 1803. Principal Nisbet had never approved of the building, believing that the Public Works should have been purchased (Morgan, *Dickinson College*, p. 80-9).

[2] Nisbet had become an arch-Federalist in his politics, and he propagated his "decidedly anti-Republican" views in his classes; see Roger B. Taney's reminiscences of his student days at Dickinson College, quoted in Morgan, *Dickinson College*, p. 113.

[3] Francis Gurney (1738-1815), Philadelphia merchant, had served in the French and Indian War and as lieutenant colonel of the 11th Penna. Line in the Revolution; member of Pennsylvania Assembly and Senate at various times; brigadier general, 1799; trustee of Dickinson College, 1798-1815 (Simpson, *Eminent Philadelphians*; Dickinson College, *Alumni Record*, p. 12).

[4] John Blair Linn (1777-1804), son of Rev. William Linn, a graduate of Columbia College, 1795; published plays

and other literary compositions; studied law but abandoned it for theology; called in 1799 to the First Presbyterian Church, Philadelphia, as Ewing's colleague (DAB; Simpson, *Eminent Phila-*

delphians).
[5] John Rush's commission as lieutenant is dated 5 Mch. 1799; see Dr. Corner's account of John's naval career, in BR's *Autobiography*, p. 370-1.

To Rachel Bradford Boudinot

My dear Madam,   Philadelphia, July 18th, 1799

The swellings in Mr. Boudinot's[1] feet are occasioned by what is called the *dumb* gout. I have often seen them and seldom with any danger to health or life. Continue the frictions in the manner I directed. If they fail of removing the swellings, let three or four small punctures be made in each foot with a lancet to drain off the water. I lately cured swellings from the gout in the feet and legs which had existed several months, in ten days, by means of the last-named remedy. Too long sitting with depending feet should be avoided. I have known a tight roller of fine flannel worn on the ankles under the stockings do great service. Let it be tried.

Mrs. Rush and three of our children are comfortably settled in our farmhouse at Sydenham two miles and ½ from town. I visit them two or three times a week. If the fever should become general, I shall take lodgings with them. The situation is conveniently situated to the city hospital, of which I have taken charge with Dr. Physick and which will be the principal object of my labors and care. We have had eight patients already. The disease at present is stationary. I have not now a single case of it out of the hospital. Perhaps there are not more than five cases of it now in the whole city. Still, it may be epidemic. It began in the same creeping and fluctuating way in former years. It is alas! as yet but the 18th of July.——The origin of our fever cannot be traced even to the timbers of a West India ship. Our citizens are puzzled. The College of Physicians are silent. In this favorable situation of the public mind to receive truth, I have made one more effort to prove the domestic origin of the fever, in a pamphlet of 20 or 30 pages which is now in the press.[2] It will be published in a few days.——Adieu. With love to Mr. Boudinot and the children, I am ever yours,

BENJN: RUSH

MS: Historical Society of Pennsylvania, Dreer Collection.

[1] Elisha Boudinot.
[2] *Observations upon the Origin of the Malignant Bilious, or Yellow Fever in* *Philadelphia, and upon the Means of Preventing It: Addressed to the Citizens of Philadelphia,* Phila.: Dobson, 1799.

To Timothy Pickering

Dear Sir,   Near Philadelphia, September 24, 1799

The board of health early sent Dr. Bolke's medicine[1] to the city hospital, but as Dr. Physick and myself were ignorant of its composition, we did not think it prudent to use it. The great variety in the *force, seat,* and *symptoms* of our prevailing fever forbids its being attacked by any one medicine, particularly by one which is to act *specifically* upon it. We have yielded to public prejudice and importunity by prescribing yeast, limewater and milk, and several other simples, but all to no other purpose than now and then easing a troublesome symptom. From the experience of six years, I am satisfied the disease can be cured when in its malignant form *only* by *depleting* remedies. These may admit of some variety in different seasons and constitutions, but the operation of them all, whether they act immediately upon the stomach, bowels, pores, salivary glands, or blood vessels, is—to *evacuate,* and thereby to weaken and reduce the system preternaturally excited or convulsed by the stimulus of a poison acting upon it. The success of my private practice by the use of the above remedies has been such as to increase my attachment to them, having lost out of about 50 patients but two, and these I did not see till the 3rd day of the disease. They both moreover refused to submit to several of my prescriptions.

The cool weather of Sunday and yesterday has produced a few new cases of the fever. Today appearances are again favorable, and our citizens are in many places preparing to return to the city.

From, dear sir, your sincere friend,

BENJN: RUSH

P.S. I was much pleased to observe by the papers that our sons are to meet as servants of the public in the navy.[2] My boy has become an enthusiast in his *new* profession.

Addressed: Timothy Pickering Esqr: Secretary of State Trenton.
MS: Massachusetts Historical Society, Pickering Papers.

[1] In a letter to BR of the day before, Pickering reported that in August he had sent the Philadelphia board of health sixteen bottles of yellow-fever medicine transmitted by the American consul in Hamburg from a Dr. Bölke of that city; Pickering supposed that Bölke hoped for an invitation to come to the United States at government expense (Mass. Hist. Soc., Pickering Papers).

[2] Timothy Pickering, Jr. (1779-1807), a graduate of Harvard, 1799, served as a midshipman in the navy, 1799-1801; he suffered from a throat infection that baffled the skill of BR and other physicians, and died young (E. W. Callahan, *List of Officers of the Navy of the United States*, N.Y., 1901; Pickering and Upham, *Pickering*, III, 325; IV, 113, 119, 396).

To Timothy Pickering

Dear Sir,   Near Philadelphia, September 30, [17]99

Mr. Webster will endeavor to account for our present malignant fevers *chiefly* by proving that our atmosphere has undergone a change, perhaps from some late planetary influence, and that a new stimulus has thereby been infused into it.[1] I agree with him in this opinion, but I cannot believe it would produce a yellow fever without the cooperation of noxious air or putrid exhalations. It acts by rendering exhalations hurtful which were formerly harmless; or by rendering diseases formerly mild, malignant and mortal. I enclose you a small pamphlet which contains my opinions more fully upon this subject.[2]

The election will be held at the Center house.[3] It would have been equally safe at the State house. The number of cases of fever in the city has diminished *one half* since last week, and the admissions into the city hospital have for several days past been but *three* a day.

The board of health are unanimous in their opinion that our present fever is of domestic origin. This opinion they intend to communicate to the corporation of the city and to the legislature of the state.——Yours sincerely,

BENJN: RUSH

MS: Massachusetts Historical Society, Pickering Papers.

[1] For an exposition of Webster's contribution to epidemiology, see C.-E. A. Winslow, *The Conquest of Epidemic Disease*, Princeton, 1943, p. 207-34.

[2] The *Observations* cited in BR's letter to Rachel Boudinot Bradford, 18 July.

[3] This was the engine house in Center Square (on the site of the present City Hall), erected this year as a means of distributing water to the city (Jackson, *Encyclo. of Phila.*, under Centre House and Water Supply).

To Brockholst Livingston[1]

Dear Sir,   March 5, 1800

The late publications of Wm. Cobbet have renewed in my family part of the scenes of anxiety and distress which were produced in it by him in 1797.[2]

This morning my second son ⟨*assaulted*⟩[3] insulted Dr. Glentworth for the lie which Cobbet has published upon his authority in his last pamphlet.[4] For this offense he is bound over by a suit in the mayor's court. This I fear is but the beginning of my family troubles from the ⟨intemperate⟩ feelings of my sons. This day my eldest son, John Rush, set off in the mail stage for New York to ⟨attack⟩ obtain satisfaction of Cobbet for the falsehoods he has published against him.[5] His spirit is uncommonly firm and determined, and his resentments are keen upon the present occasion. I tremble therefore for the consequences of a meeting between them. The design of this letter is to call upon you as a *friend* to find him out and by persuasion or the force of law to arrest him in his present undertaking. He will probably be met with in a sailor's *undress* near Cobbet's door, where his purpose was to wait for an interview with him.

To prevent the repetition and continuance of his abuse, Mr. and Mr.[6]   advise a suit (criminal or civil as you may think proper) immediately to be instituted against him for his late publications, and if he publishes after the suit is commenced, to have him confined and fined for a contempt of court.[7] Surely your judges and citizens will not be tame or indifferent spectators of the outrages offered by ⟨him⟩ an alien to the laws and courts of a sister state—much less can they hear without sympathy and honor of the risk ⟨I run every hour⟩ a grayheaded and inoffensive citizen runs every hour of his life of hearing of murder being connected in one way or other with the names of his sons.

I leave this business wholly to your judgment and friendship. Let nothing be done in it unless you are sure the force of law can be effectively employed to silence him, and thereby to restore my sons to calmness and safety. You are a father. *Feel* and *act* as you would wish me to do for your children in a similar situation. If assistance be necessary in conducting this business, call upon Colonel Burr or any other of your eminent lawyers. Your services shall be liberally compensated. ⟨*I enclose you 10 dollars to defray the expenses of serving the writ.*⟩

I have one more favor to beg of you, and that is that my son should not know that I have written you this letter, and that your advice to him should be such as shall comport with his feelings and character of an officer, as well as with the laws of his country.

With great regard, I am, dear sir, your distressed friend and humble servant,

BENJN RUSH

P.S. An answer to this letter as speedily as possible will be highly acceptable.

MS (draft): Library Company of Philadelphia, Rush MSS.

[1] Henry Brockholst Livingston (1757-1823), who after 1783 dropped his first name, was the son of William, the former governor of New Jersey; a graduate of the College of New Jersey, 1774, he served in the Revolution and afterwards prospered as a lawyer in New York; he was appointed to the U.S. Supreme Court in 1806 (DAB). His letters to BR relating to the Cobbett affair are in the Rush MSS, XXIX. See further, Appendix III: The Cobbett-Rush Feud.

[2] The late publications were the farewell number of *Porcupine's Gazette* and *Rush-Light*, No. 1, the first issue of a periodical devoted almost exclusively to vituperation of BR and his supporters.

[3] Only the more significant expressions lined out by BR in the draft have been restored in the present text.

[4] In the *Rush-Light*, No. 1, Cobbett had quoted testimony from Dr. Plunket F. Glentworth on BR's hysterical behavior when Glentworth refused to be further bled during the epidemic of 1793.

[5] John had an old score to settle with Cobbett. During the quarrel between BR and Dr. Andrew Ross (whom BR had supposed the author of an offensive communication in Fenno's *Gazette* in Oct. 1797), Cobbett declared in *Porcupine's Gazette*: "I affirm this John Rush to be an *impertinent puppy*, a *waylaying coward*, a *liar*, and a *rascal*." This affirmation was repeated in *Rush-Light*, No. 1. Thus Lt. Rush's mission to New York. From Livingston's reply (dated 8 Mch. 1800, Rush MSS, XXIX) to BR's appeal,

we learn that after inquiring at the mail-stage office and reconnoitering near Cobbett's shop, Livingston had at length found John at a playhouse. John promised Livingston he would not seek Cobbett out, but, according to *Rush-Light*, No. II, John sent a military friend on the same mission. This was a Capt. Still, or Stille, of Fort Jay, who, says Cobbett, "came to my house, to call me to account, on the part of Lieut. Rush, about a passage in the first number of the Rush-Light. He was armed '*à la mode de Rush*,' to wit: with a *bludgeon cane*, which, as it had an *iron poker* to encounter, remained quiet in his hand; and so the noble Captain marched off without beat of drum." All this appeared in a public letter Cobbett addressed to Secretary of War McHenry on Capt. Stille's conduct. Lt. Rush was obliged to be satisfied with a long self-justification in the New York *Commercial Advertiser* for 11 Mch. (Mary E. Clark, *Peter Porcupine in America*, Phila., 1939, p. 164-5).

[6] Blanks in MS.

[7] Cobbett got wind of the possibility of another suit and went promptly to Alexander Hamilton, who, he wrote privately, "refused any fee, and who told me, that he should think himself honoured in defending me. . . . He behaved with great kindness to me, and assured me that I had nothing to fear from *injustice* in New York" (To Edward Thornton, 14 Mch. 1800; *Letters from William Cobbett to Edward Thornton.* . . . *1797-1800*, ed. G. D. H. Cole, London, &c., 1937, p. 72).

To James McHenry

Dear Sir,   Philadelphia, August 12, 1800

The bearer[1] has been unfortunate in business in our city, owing chiefly to his connection with a man from whom he expected better things. He wishes to try his fortune in Baltimore and has therefore applied to me for a letter to you to *advise* him what to do. A subordinate place in your customs or the oversight of a farm would suit him. He has physical energy and mind enough for either of the above situations.

Permit me to congratulate you upon your recovering your freedom and independence by retiring to private life.[2] Public measures and public men appear very differently to persons who see them at a distance from what they appear to persons who are actors in or under them. If your feelings are like mine in their relation to politics, you would not give up your present abstraction from them to be President of the United States. While children dispute and fight about their gingerbread and nuts, and party men about posts of honor, the pleasure of one evening's successful investigation of a moral or physical truth, or an hour spent in literary or philosophical society, will more than outweigh all that Ambition ever conferred upon her votaries.

You carry into retirement the love and esteem of all good men. To me you have ever been very dear, and never more so than at the moment I subscribe myself your ever affectionate friend,

BENJN: RUSH

Printed: Bernard C. Steiner, *Life and Correspondence of James McHenry*, Cleveland, 1907, p. 464-5; photostat in Library of Congress, McHenry Papers; original not located.

[1] Unidentified.
[2] At President Adams' request, McHenry had retired from his office as secretary of war in the preceding May (DAB).

To Thomas Jefferson

Dear Sir,   Philadelphia, August 22nd, 1800

The following thoughts have lately occurred to me. To whom can they be communicated with so much propriety as to that man who has so uniformly distinguished himself by an attachment to republican forms of government?

In the Constitution of the United States, titles are wisely forbidden, and pensions for public services are considered as equally improper by many of our citizens. There is a mode of honoring distinguished worth which is cheap and which, if directed properly, would stimulate to greater exploits of patriotism than all the high-sounding titles of a German, or the expensive pensions of a British, court. It consists in calling *states, counties, towns, forts*, and *ships of war* by the names of men who have deserved well of their country. To prevent an improper application of those names, the power of conferring them should be exercised only by our governments. No man should have a town, county, fort, or ship called by his name till after his death; and to prevent any ambiguity in the names thus given, the act of government which confers them should mention the persons' families, places of former abode, and the services, civil, military, philosophical, or humane, which they rendered to their country. From the connection between *words* and *ideas* much good might be done. A map of a state and the history of travels through the United States would fill the mind with respect for departed worth and inspire exertions to imitate it. Some advantage likewise would arise to the public by preventing the confusion in business which arises from the multiplication of the same names in different states, and sometimes in the same state, and which is the unavoidable consequence of those names being given by individuals. An end would likewise be put, by the practice which is here recommended, to those indications of vanity which appear in the numerous names of towns given by their founders after themselves and which too frequently suggest other ideas than those of public or even private virtue.[1]

The citizens of Boston in the republican years of 1776 and 1777 rejected the royal names of several streets and substituted in the room of them names that comported with the new and republican state of their town. Why has not Virginia imitated her example? If I mistake not, most of your old counties bear the names or titles of several successive British royal families. They are the disgraceful remains of your former degraded state as men, and should by all means be changed for the names of those worthies on whose characters death has placed his seal and thereby removed beyond the power of forfeiting their well-earned fame.

A spirit of moderation and mutual forbearance begins to revive among our citizens. What the issue of the present single and double elective attractions in our parties will be is difficult to determine. As yet appearances are turbid. Much remains to be precipitated before the public mind can become clear. As a proof of the growing moderation of our citizens, I shall mention two facts. Mr. Bingham lamented your supposed death in the most liberal and pathetic terms, and Judge Peters spoke of you yesterday at his table in my hearing in the most respectful and even affectionate manner. This is between ourselves.

You promised me, when we parted, to read Paley's last work[2] and to send me your religious creed.[3] [. . . .][4] I have always considered Christianity as the *strong ground* of republicanism. The spirit is opposed, not only to the splendor, but even to the very forms of monarchy, and many of its precepts have for their objects republican liberty and equality as well as simplicity, integrity, and economy in government. It is only necessary for republicanism to ally itself to the Christian religion to overturn all the corrupted political and religious institutions in the world.

I have lately heard that Lord Kaims[5] became so firm a believer in Christianity some years before he died as to dispute with his former disciples in its favor. Such a mind as Kaims' could only yield to the strongest evidence, especially as his prejudices were on the other side of the question.

Sir John Pringle had lived near 60 years in a state of indifference to the truth of the Christian religion. He devoted himself to the study of the Scriptures in the evening of his life and became a Christian. It was remarkable that he became a decided republican [...][6] at the same time. It is said this change in his political principles exposed him to the neglect of the royal family, to whom he was physician, and drove him from London to end his days in his native country.

Our city continues to be healthy, and business is carried on with its usual spirit. It is yet uncertain whether we shall enjoy an exemption from the yellow fever. It is in favor of this hope that vegetation has assumed its ancient and natural appearance, that all our fruits (the peach excepted) are perfect, that we have much fewer insects than in our sickly years, and that the few diseases we have had in general put on a milder type than they have done since the year 1793.

An ingenious work has lately arrived here by Dr. Darwin,[7] full of original matter upon botany and agriculture. Dr. Barton speaks of it in high terms. A translation of Sonnoni's travels into Egypt[8] is likewise for sale in our city. They will be memorable from the information they gave to Buonaparte in that country. They contain a good deal of physical matter, particularly upon the diet, diseases, and medicine of the inhabitants.

Adieu! From, dear sir, your sincere old friend of 1775,

BENJN: RUSH

MS: Library of Congress, Jefferson Papers.

[1] BR had already put into practice the idea he proposes here. He had named the settlements on his land along the upper Susquehanna for Lettsom and Fothergill (see section of map reproduced in Abraham's *Lettsom*, p. 374), and his proposed Negro farm colony in Bedford co. was to be named Benezet (letter to the President of the Abolition Society, 1794?).

[2] William Paley, *A View of the Evidences of Christianity*, London, 1794; reissued in Philadelphia, 1795. This book remained for generations a widely read work, being, according to the DNB, "a compendium of a whole library of

argument produced by the orthodox opponents of the deists during the eighteenth century."

³ Jefferson eventually sent BR a remarkable statement of his creed, under the title of "Syllabus of an Estimate of the Merit of the Doctrines of Jesus, compared with those of others." The views there set forth, Jefferson said in his covering letter, "are the result of a life of inquiry and reflection, and very different from that anti-Christian system imputed to me by those who know nothing of my opinions" (letter of 21 Apr. 1803; *Writings*, ed. Lipscomb and Bergh, X, 379-85). See BR's answer, 5

May 1803.

⁴ Three lines heavily scored out.

⁵ Henry Home, Lord Kames (1696-1782), a Scottish writer on philosophical and other subjects, was tremendously influential in his day (DNB).

⁶ Five or six words scored out.

⁷ *Phytologia; or, the Philosophy of Agriculture and Gardening*, London, 1800 (*L.C. Cat.*).

⁸ C. N. S. Sonnini de Manoncourt, *Travels in Upper and Lower Egypt. Undertaken by Order of the Old Government of France*, London, 1799, 3 vol.; originally published at Paris, 1799 (same).

To John K. Read¹

Dear Sir,   Philadelphia, September 15th, 1800

The words *debility* and *putrefaction* have destroyed perhaps nearly an equal number of lives with the sword within the last seven years in different parts of the world. The gentlemen who use them with an application so destructive to human life do not recollect that *debility* is the *predisposing* cause and *symptom* only of disease, and that disease consists in preternatural strength or motion, or a prostration of both from an excess of stimulus. They forget likewise that putrefaction cannot take place for a moment in the blood vessels consistent with life, and that what are considered signs of putrefaction are nothing but the effects of a violent, rapid, and high grade of morbid or inflammatory action in the system which in its first stage calls for copious depleting remedies. These opinions have been ascribed to me as their author, and I have suffered no small obloquy upon their account; but they have a much higher original. They are derived wholly from the writings of the venerable and excellent Dr. Sydenham, who taught them above an hundred years ago.

The *natural* pulse you mention in your letter is a common symptom in our malignant bilious or yellow fever, and generally portends death to be at hand. I have seen but few recoveries after it has taken place. The *cool* skin and the *natural* tongue are equally alarming when they occur with symptoms of danger in other parts of the body. They all indicate the force of the disease to be concentrated in some vital part. A facility in the operations and uncommon tranquillity of the mind appear to arise from the same cause, and are generally followed by a fatal issue of the disease. But to what purpose do we observe and record facts or reason in our treatment of epidemics? [While physicians are traders in medicine, and consider the lives of their patients and the improvement of their profession as subordinate objects to acquiring fortunes, we cannot expect they will listen to our observations or reasonings upon the diseases of our country.][2] As far as I can judge, we are becoming retrograde upon the subject of the yellow fever in many parts of the United States. The lenient mode of treating it with gentle purges, diluting drinks, and the warm bath is generally preferred in Philadelphia. Death in severe cases is the usual consequence of this practice. The depleting practice is generally successful when physicians who use it are called on the first day of the disease and use it to an extent regulated by the state of the system. It abates pain and prevents yellowness, hiccup, and the black vomiting, and thus renders the cure short and safe to the constitution. These circumstances have unfortunately operated against it, for it has led the persons who have seen it, and some who have experienced its rapid and effectual benefits, to deny that they were cured of the yellow fever.

Let us not complain of the folly or ignorance of our fellow citizens. If Dr. Sydenham wrote in vain, how can we expect to succeed in our attempts to introduce his principles or practice into our country?

We have had a healthy and pleasant summer in Philadelphia. What few diseases we have had (compared with our late epidemic) have been like second mourning compared with a dress uniformly black. The dysentery has borrowed a *vomiting* and *active pulse* from the yellow fever. Our long absent chronic autumnal fever of [. . .][3] has returned, has been protracted to 15, 20, and 30 days, but showed its unity with the yellow fever by an irritable stomach and dark-colored intestinal evacuations. Both forms of disease required from one third to two-thirds of the force of remedies to subdue them which are necessary to overcome a malignant yellow fever. It is thus diseases appear to taper off from malignant fevers before and after they have prevailed in all countries. The fevers which preceded [*and followed*][4] the plague in 1664 were accompanied with uncommonly inflammatory symptoms. The latter was so violent as to be called by Dr. Sydenham a pestilential fever. The diseases of 1791 and 1792 in Philadelphia rose several grades before the year 1793. They are now descending from their first grade, but whether in a tendency to leave us for years or not, I am not able to determine.

[With respectful compliments to Mrs. Read and the rest of your amiable family I am, dear sir, your sincere old friend,][5]

BENJN RUSH

MS (draft): Library Company of Philadelphia, Rush MSS.

[1] Included because it contains a valuable statement of BR's medical theory, this letter is unusually erratic in its text, even for a draft. The bracketed passages probably indicate that a copy of this letter was prepared for publication in a newspaper or medical journal. The MS is docketed: "Rough copy of a letter to Dr. J. Read, Norfolk." John K. Read (1746-1805) was a nephew of Deborah Read (Mrs. Benjamin Franklin) and a close friend of John Paul Jones. It is not known where he received his medical training. He early moved to Virginia, served in the military hospitals during the Revolution, and afterwards kept an apothecary's shop and practised medicine in Richmond and Norfolk. Between 1796 and 1805 he was at various times port physician (or health officer), alderman, and mayor of Norfolk (Blanton, *Medicine in Va. in the Eighteenth Century*, p. 37, 39, 344-6).

[2] Brackets in MS.

[3] There is a brief, illegible interlineation here.

[4] Supplied because this is quite certainly what BR meant. What he wrote does not make sense: "The fevers which preceded the plague follow [or following?] in 1664 were accompanied," &c.

[5] Brackets in MS.

To Thomas Jefferson

Dear Sir,   Philadelphia, October 6th, 1800

I agree with you in your opinion of cities.[1] Cowper the poet very happily expresses our ideas of them compared with the country. "God made the country—man made cities."[2] I consider them in the same light that I do abscesses on the human body, viz., as reservoirs of all the impurities of a community.

I agree with you likewise in your wishes to keep religion and government independent of each other.[3] Were it possible for St. Paul to rise from his grave at the present juncture, he would say to the clergy who are now so active in settling the political affairs of the world: "Cease from your political labors—your kingdom is not of *this* world. Read my Epistles. In no part of them will you perceive me aiming to depose a pagan emperor or to place a Christian upon a throne. Christianity disdains to receive support from human governments. From this it derives its preeminence over all the religions that ever have or ever shall exist in the world. Human governments may receive support from Christianity, but it must be only from the love of justice and peace which it is calculated to produce in the minds of men. By promoting these and all the other Christian virtues by your precepts and example, you will much sooner overthrow errors of all kinds and establish our pure and holy religion in the world than by aiming to produce by your preaching or pamphlets any change in the political state of mankind."

A certain Dr. Owen,⁴ an eminent minister of the Gospel among the dissenters in England, and a sincere friend of liberty, was once complained of by one of Cromwell's time-serving priests, "that he did not preach to the *times*." "My business and duty," said the disciple of St. Paul, "is to preach to *Eternity*, not to the times." He has left many volumes of sermons behind him that are so wholly religious that no one from reading them could tell in what country or age they were preached.

I have sometimes amused myself in forming a scale of the different kinds of hatreds. They appear to me to rise in the following order: *odium juris-consultum, odium medicum, odium philologicum, odium politicum*, and *odium theologicum*. You are now the subject of the two last. I have felt the full force of the 2nd and 4th degrees of hostility from my fellow creatures. But I do not think we shall ultimately suffer from either of them. My persecutions have arrested or delayed the usual languor of 55 in my mind. I read, write, and think with the same vigor and pleasure that I did fifteen years ago. As natural stimuli are sometimes supplied by such as are artificial in the production of human life, so slander seems to act upon the human mind. It not only supplies the place of fame, but it is much more powerful in exciting our faculties into vigorous and successful exercises.

To persevere in benevolent exertions after ungrateful returns for former services, it is only necessary to consider mankind as Solomon considered them several thousand years ago, viz., as laboring under madness. A few cures, or even a few lucid intervals produced in a state or nation, will repay the unsuccessful labors of many years. "No good effort is lost" was a favorite saying of the late Dr. Jebb.⁵ A truth cannot perish, although it may sleep for centuries. The Republics of America are the fruits of the precious truths that were disseminated in the speeches and publications of the republican patriots in the British Parliament one hundred and sixty years ago. My first American ancestor, Jno. Rush, commanded a troop of horse in Cromwell's army. He afterwards became a Quaker and followed Wm. Penn in 1683 to Pennsylvania. My brother possesses his horseman's sword. General Darke,[6] of your state, who is descended from his youngest daughter, owns his watch. To the sight of his sword I owe much of the spirit which animated me in 1774, and to the respect and admiration which I was early taught to cherish for his virtues and exploits I owe a large portion of my republican temper and principles. Similar circumstances I believe produced a great deal of the spirit and exertions of all those Americans who are descended from ancestors that emigrated from England between the years 1645 and 1700.

I send you herewith some muskmelon seeds of a quality as much above the common melons of our country as a pineapple is superior to a potato. They were brought originally from Minorca. The ground must be prepared for them at the usual time by having some brush burnt upon it. The fire destroys the eggs of insects in the ground, and the ashes left by it manure the ground so as to prepare it for the seeds. No vine of any kind should grow near them. They are, when ripe, a little larger than a child's head, round, and have a green rind. They are never mealy, but juicy, and cannot be improved by sugar, pepper, salt, or any other addition that can be made to them.

We have had a few cases of yellow fever in our city, enough to satisfy unprejudiced persons that we have not been defended from it by our quarantine law. They were all evidently of domestic origin.

I reciprocate your kind expressions upon the probability of our not meeting again, and feel sincere distress upon the account of it. I shall always recollect with pleasure the many delightful hours we have spent together, from the day we first met on the banks of Skuilkill in the year 1775 to the day in which we parted. If the innocent and interesting subjects of our occasional conversations should be a delusive one,[7] the delusion is enchanting. But I will not admit that we have been deceived in our early and long affection for republican forms of government. They are, I believe, not only rational but practicable. As well might we reject the pure and simple doctrines and precepts of Christianity because they have been dishonored by being mixed with human follies and crimes by the corrupted churches of Europe, as renounce our republics because their name has been dishonored by the follies and crimes of the French nation. The preference which men depraved by false government have given to monarchy is no more a proof of its excellence than the preference which men whose appetites have been depraved by drinking whiskey is a proof that it is more wholesome than water. Thousands have derived health and long life from that wholesome beverage of nature, while tens of thousands have perished from the use of the former liquor.

Representative and elective government appears to be a discovery of modern times. It has met with the fate of many other discoveries which have had for their objects the melioration of the condition of man. It has been opposed, traduced, and nearly scouted from the face of the earth. The science of medicine abounds with instances of new truths being treated in the same manner. The cool regimen which Dr. Sydenham applied with general success to the smallpox was exploded before he died by his contemporary physicians. In the year 1767 it was revived in London by Dr. Sutton and now prevails all over the world.

Excuse the length of this letter. My pen has run away with me. Pray throw it in the fire as soon as you have read it. Not a line of it must be communicated to a human creature with my name.

When you see Mr. Madison, please to tell him he is still very dear to *his* and *your* sincere and affectionate friend,

BENJN: RUSH

P.S. From the difficulty of packing up the melon seed so as to send them by the post, I have concluded to send them to you in the winter at the federal city by a private hand.

MS: Library of Congress, Jefferson Papers.

[1] Jefferson had expressed the idea that one possible good effect of the yellow-fever epidemics would be curbing the growth of cities, which are "pestilential to the morals, the health and the liberties of man" (to Rush, 23 Sep. 1800; *Writings*, ed. Lipscomb and Bergh, x, 173).

[2] BR has misquoted the now familiar line: "God made the country, and man made the town" (*The Task*, 1785, I, 749).

[3] Jefferson had referred in his letter to the concerted opposition of the clergy to his election to the presidency. This letter contains Jefferson's statement that he had "sworn upon the altar of God, eternal hostility against every form of tyranny over the mind of man" (*Writings*, ed. Lipscomb and Bergh, x, 175).

[4] John Owen, D.D. (1616-1683), a staunch defender of religious freedom throughout a long and distinguished career (DNB).

[5] Probably John Jebb (1736-1786), clergyman, physician, and miscellaneous writer, of Cambridge and London; his *Works* were published in three volumes, London, 1787 (DNB). This saying became one of BR's favorites.

[6] William Darke (1736-1801), Virginia frontiersman and Continental officer; member of the Virginia ratifying convention, 1788; brigadier general; 1791; his home was near Charleston, W. Va. Like BR, he was a great-great-grandson of Cromwell's captain, John Rush. (DAB; Biddle, *Memorial*, p. 235.)

[7] Thus in MS; BR perhaps supposed he had written "pleasure" instead of "subjects."

To Noah Webster

Dear Sir,   Philadelphia, December 9th, 1800

In the *British Critic* for August of the present year there is a high character given of your account of pestilential diseases, together with copious extracts from it.

In a lecture I gave a few days ago I took pains to promote its credit and sale in our country.

The late shocks of earthquakes in our state and in the states of Delaware and Maryland afford a new evidence of the truth of your principles.[1] But how melancholy the consideration! that while derangements in the whole animal and vegetable creation, *in* the *sky*, *on* the earth, and *under* the earth, all combine to prove the domestic origin of epidemic diseases, that we continue to derive them from foreign countries. Thus we are forced to submit to Dean Swift's definition of our species. We are "capax rationis," not reasoning animals.[2] Our exemption from the yellow fever last fall has confirmed the prejudices of our citizens in the efficacy of their quarantine law. Our opinions are now more odious than ever.

Adieu. Your fellow laborer and friend,

BENJN: RUSH

P.S. There were about 50 sporadic cases of yellow fever in our city during the last summer and autumn. Most of them were in Spruce and Dock Streets, near the exhalations of the old Drawbridge. They were derived by our citizens from Baltimore, or ascribed to the beds that were infected by the fever in 1799. Upon close inquiry, they all appeared to be decidedly the offspring of domestic and recent causes.

Addressed: Noah Webster Esqr: New Haven Connecticut.
MS: Pierpont Morgan Library.

[1] Webster had endeavored to prove that earthquakes were associated with an "epidemic constitution of the atmosphere," which favored, if it did not cause, epidemics.

[2] "I have got materials toward a treatise, proving the falsity of that definition *animal rationale*, and to show it would be only *rationis capax*" (Swift to Pope, 29 Sep. 1725; Swift's *Correspondence*, ed. F. E. Ball, London, 1910-1914, III, 277). Swift's "treatise" was of course *Gulliver's Travels*.

V.

Literary Fame

&

Domestic Tranquillity

1801-1808

1801-1805. James Rush at the College of New Jersey.

1805. Correspondence with John Adams resumed.

1805. *Medical Inquiries and Observations*, second edition (first collective edition), published in four volumes simultaneously at Philadelphia, Baltimore, Washington, Petersburg, and Norfolk.

1807 Oct. 1. John Rush's duel at New Orleans.

1807 Nov. 2. Delivers lecture on "The Duty and Advantages of Studying the Diseases of Domestic Animals."

1808 December. Acts as one of the founders of the Philadelphia Bible Society.

Part V. *Literary Fame &* *Domestic Tranquillity*

1801-1808

To Thomas Jefferson

Dear Sir,   Philadelphia, March 12th, 1801

Your character as a philosopher and friend of mankind predominates so much more in my mind over that of your new station, that I cannot resist the habit of addressing you as I have done in any former letters. Your new official title has added nothing to my respect for your person. It could not add to my friendship for you.

You have opened a new era by your speech on the 4th of March in the history of the United States.[1] Never have I seen the public mind more generally or more agreeably affected by any publication. Old friends who had been separated by party names and a *supposed* difference of *principle* in politics for many years shook hands with each other immediately after reading it, and discovered, for the first time, that they had differed in *opinion* only, about the best means of promoting the interests of their common country. It would require a page to contain the names of all the citizens (formerly called Federalists) who have spoken in the highest terms of your speech. George Clymer (one of our colleagues in July 1776) and Judge Peters have taken the lead in their encomiums upon it. A Mr. Joseph Wharton[2] (an active but republican Federalist) has read it (he says) *seven* times, and with increasing pleasure. I need hardly tell you how much every sentiment and even word in it accord with my feelings and principles. I consider it as a solemn and affecting address to your fellow citizens, to the nations of Europe, to all the inhabitants of the globe, and to posterity to the latest generations, upon the great subject of political order and happiness. You have concentrated whole chapters into a few aphorisms in defense of the principles and *form* of our government. It is owing to the long sleep of such sentiments in diplomatic performances that the young men of our country have been seduced from it to admire and prefer the British constitution. It never occurred to them till last week that a republic was a government of *more* energy

[831]

than a monarchy. It is equally true, though constantly denied by the monarchists of our country, that national *stability* of opinion and conduct with respect to public men, as well as national *integrity* and *humanity*, are more common virtues in a republic than in royal governments. The *first* is proved by the conduct of the Americans to their first magistrates in all the states, not one of them having been dismissed by a general suffrage from office since the formation of our state governments in 1775. The *second* is proved by the general fidelity with which the duties upon imports are paid in every part of the Union. Mr. Latimer[3] assured me a few days ago that in the course of three years he had not detected a single American in an attempt to elude the duty upon imported goods. The few smugglers whom he had detected and punished were Europeans. In the United States every citizen feels the injury committed by public fraud as done to *himself*. In a monarchy the mischief of fraud is said to extend only to the king, who in the common sense of his subjects is considered to possess millions of property not his own, and of course that it is not criminal to rob him. Both *national* humanity and integrity are proved by the manner in which the late election for the first magistrate of the United States was conducted by four millions of people. Not a dollar I believe was expended in a bribe, nor was a black eye created by it in any part of the Union. Our newspapers, like chimneys, peaceably carried off the smoke of party rage without doing any harm.[4] This fact did not escape the notice of the late British minister, Mr. Liston, and led him to remark in his farewell visit to my family that it promised a continuance of our republican form of government "for many ages to come."

In contemplating the change you have produced in the public mind, I have been carried back to an interesting conversation with you about two years ago in which you *predicted* it. I did not concur with you, for our country was then so much under the influence of the *name* of ———, the plans of ———,[5] and the press of Peter Porcupine, that I despaired of a resuscitation of its republican spirit. You said the death of two men (whom you named) would render your prediction *speedy* as well as *certain*. They both died in 1799.[6] In the third month of the year 1801 we have become "all Republicans, all Federalists."

I fear I have trespassed upon time now more precious than ever by this long letter. I have only to add that the pleasure created by your speech has been increased by your late appointments and by your declaration to several of your friends that you did not intend to consider political opinion or conduct as crimes in the present officers of the government.

Declining as I am in years, and languishing for retirement in order more exclusively to pursue my medical researches, I can do nothing to render your administration easy and prosperous but unite with thousands in imploring the direction and blessings of that Being upon it to whom you have publicly and solemnly committed the "destiny" of our nation.

From, dear sir, with increasing regard, your sincere and faithful friend,

BENJN: RUSH

MS: Library of Congress, Jefferson Papers.

¹ That is, Jefferson's First Inaugural, which BR echoes at several points in the present letter and which is most admirably characterized by BR's statement: "You have concentrated whole chapters into a few aphorisms in defense of the principles and *form* of our government."

² Joseph Wharton, Jr. (1733/4-1816), of the great Philadelphia mercantile family, retired from business after the Revolution because of a series of reverses, and lived in Germantown. He is said to have had unusual attainments in classical learning. His letters to BR show him to have been a warmhearted friend and supporter of BR in his professional trials. (PMHB, I [1877], 457-8; obituary in *Poulson's Amer. Daily Advertiser*, 30 Dec. 1816; Wharton's letters in Rush MSS, XXV.)

³ George Latimer (1750-1825), Philadelphia merchant and civil servant; member of the ratifying convention of 1787; member of Assembly, 1792-1799, and speaker, 1794-1799; collector of customs at the Port of Philadelphia, 1798-1804 (McMaster and Stone, *Penna. and the Federal Constitution*, p. 737).

⁴ BR used this effective image again in his *Diseases of the Mind*, p. 68-9.

⁵ BR left these two blanks in the MS, but Jefferson, remarkably enough, supplied the names "Washington" and "Hamilton" above the first and second blanks, respectively.

⁶ The two men were unquestionably George Washington and Patrick Henry. It is well known that Jefferson was more than irritated by Washington's lending support to Federalist policies that Jefferson considered reactionary. As for Patrick Henry, Jefferson had regarded him as a dangerous man for many years. Henry was a particular thorn in Jefferson's flesh throughout the party struggles of 1795-1799: successfully wooed by the Federalists, he had intervened to help elect John Marshall to Congress in 1798, and in the following spring, just before his death, he had himself returned to the Virginia Assembly in order to frustrate Jefferson and Madison's Virginia Resolutions against the Alien and Sedition Acts. Jefferson always considered Henry a demagogue and apostate. (Professor Douglass Adair, of the College of William and Mary, suggested Henry as the second of the "two men," and supplied a commentary that I have drawn on in this note. See also Irving Brant, *James Madison, the Nationalist*, Indianapolis and N.Y., 1948, p. 345; and Jefferson's letters to William Wirt on Patrick Henry, PMHB, XXXIV [1910], 385-418.)

To John Montgomery

Dear Sir,   Philadelphia, June 6, 1801

Your acceptable letter containing an account of your recovery from your late dangerous illness came safe to hand.[1] I rejoiced in hearing that you had retired to your farm to acquire strength. Country air to invalids and old men is the best cordial in nature. How gladly would I sit down to review with you the toils and vicissitudes of our lives! But this pleasure is denied me. An addition of a 9th living child[2] to my family a few weeks ago will protract my labors in Philadelphia for many years to come. Let us bear with patience the dispensations of providence. We shall meet, I hope never to be parted, in a world where pain, sickness, and slander shall never be known.

The vacancy in the College of New York can only be filled according to its constitution by an Episcopalian. Dr. Wharton, a learned and respectable clergyman of Burlington, it is said will be the man.[3]

I lament, deeply lament, the declining state of *our* College. The cause of it need not be mentioned. Nothing can be done to retrieve its character while *high-toned* Federal politics are taught in it. They are as contrary to truth and order as the Jacobinical politics which prevailed in our state during our Revolutionary War were to the peace and happiness of Pennsylvania.

The affairs of the Old World are still in a state of great disorder. Many pious people expect we are upon the eve of the millennium. I am not of that opinion. There is a great deal of preparatory work to be done before that event can take place, and which will probably be brought about by natural means. Civilization, human knowledge, and liberty must first pervade the globe. They are the heralds of religion. They do not confer happiness, but they prepare the minds of mankind for it. From the present general prevalence of barbarism, ignorance, and slavery in the world, it would seem that a century or more would be necessary to remove them. In the meanwhile, Christians should endeavor to cultivate the peaceful dispositions which the millennium is to introduce into the mind, and daily repeat in their prayers, "Thy kingdom come."

Adieu! my dear friend, and believe me to be yours very affectionately,

BENJN: RUSH

P.S. You will oblige me by sending to me, or *burning*, all my letters which contained any remarks upon the conduct of Dr. Nisbet or any other person since the commencement of our correspondence.[4]

Addressed: John Montgomery Esqr: Carlisle Pennsylvania.
MS: Library Company of Philadelphia, Rush MSS.

[1] BR is answering two of Montgomery's letters, dated 2 and 4 May 1801, both in Rush MSS, XLII.

[2] William, the Rushes' last child, was born 11 May 1801; A.B., 1819, and M.D., 1823, University of Pennsylvania; on the staff of the Pennsylvania Hospital, 1834-1837; he married Elizabeth Fox, daughter of Hugh Roberts, 1827, but no children of this marriage survived (Biddle, *Memorial*, p. 261-2; Morton, *Hist. of the Penna. Hospital*, p. 506; Univ. of Penna., *Biog. Cat. of Matriculates*). There are delightful glimpses of William's childhood in BR's later letters.

[3] Montgomery had reported the pos-

sibility of Nisbet's being invited to succeed William Samuel Johnson as president of Columbia College. The successor, already chosen, was Charles Henry Wharton (1748-1833), rector of St. Mary's Church, Burlington, N.J., since 1798, who, as it happened, resigned at the end of the year to return to Burlington (DAB; Thomas, *Columbia Univ. Officers and Alumni*, p. 3). -

[4] All BR's letters to Montgomery were returned after Montgomery's death; see BR to an unidentified correspondent (probably Robert Davidson, Montgomery's son-in-law), 7 Jan. 1809, Haverford College Library.

To James Madison[1]

Dear Sir,   Philadelphia, June 23rd, 1801

Permit me to revive a friendship, once very dear to me, by addressing you upon a subject highly interesting to the United States.

The commerce of our country has suffered greatly by our absurd quarantine laws in the different states. These laws, which admit the contagious nature of our American yellow fever, have produced a reaction in the governments of Europe which has rendered our commerce with the cities of Europe extremely expensive and oppressive.

The evils complained of abroad can only be remedied by removing them at home, and this can only be done by convincing our citizens that our fever is not contagious and that it is always of domestic origin. The arguments in favor of these opinions you will find in the enclosed pamphlets.[2]

The benefits to commerce and to national population and prosperity which the abolition of quarantine laws and a regard to cleanliness in our cities would produce, are beyond calculation.

Posterity will be grateful to that government which shall take the lead in this important business. Hitherto science has been scouted from the cabinets of the rulers of the world. It bears the hateful name of philosophy. But we look for more correct associations of things under the present administration.

I enclose you a letter from Mr. Webster upon the subject of mine. He deserves well of humanity and of his country for his labors in exposing the disgraceful ideas to human reason which have prevailed, time immemorial, upon pestilential diseases.

Accept of my best wishes for your health, and believe me to be with great regard your sincere old friend,

BENJN: RUSH

MS: Mr. Lloyd W. Smith, Madison, New Jersey.

[1] Madison had just become secretary of state. For BR's views on international quarantine practices, see also his letters to Lettsom, 13 May 1804, and to Jefferson, 15 June, 6 Dec. 1805.

[2] BR himself had not published anything on this subject since his *Observations upon the Origin of the Malignant Bilious, or Yellow Fever in Philadelphia*, 1799.

To John Montgomery

My dear Friend,   Philadelphia, August 5th, 1801

I was made happy by your letter of July the 28th.[1] I rejoice in the account you have given of your health and of the product of your farm. How delightful must it be to review in retirement the labors of a useful life! This pleasure is yours. I now cultivate about twelve acres of ground two miles from our city, to which I retire two or three times a week in an afternoon to take tea with my family, and where I forget for a few hours the bustle, the sickness, the selfishness, and scandal of Philadelphia. I enjoy the songs of the little feathered tribes who jump from twig to twig over my head and sometimes peck their food at my feet. I consider them as my charge and feel the affection of a master for them. This affection will not be repaid with ingratitude, for they are unskilled in the arts of deceit and treachery. I enjoy likewise the luxuriant foliage, the fragrant flowers, and the pleasant fruit of trees planted and cultivated by my own hand. My care of them will not be repaid with persecution, for they have *never grown in the city of Philadelphia*. Ah! when shall I enjoy these delightful scenes without the alloy of a laborious, a distressing, and a vexatious profession?— But I retract the wish. I will endeavor to reconcile myself to my present situation and to fulfil my present duties until it shall please God to call me from them. "I was ashamed to take rest here," said good Dr. Finley on his deathbed. "Eternity will be long enough to rest in." The prayer of my heart is that I may be actuated by the same spirit which dictated those noble and Christian sentiments.

In looking in the history of the Church, I find that pious men have in all ages constantly expected the second coming of the Messiah to be near at hand in times of general distress from wars, pestilence, and other national evils. It is probable the good men of the present day are committing the same mistake. Much yet remains to be done before that great event can take place. Infidelity must increase and prevail much more than it now does, so that when he comes, "shall he find faith on the earth?"[2] *Knowledge* likewise must become *universal*. The effects of this knowledge will be to produce revolutions, liberty, a general intercourse of all nations by means of commerce, and—be not surprised when I add—*universal misery*. The more nations and individuals know, till they know God, the more unhappy will they be. The effects of this unhappiness in nations and individuals will appear in a general dissatisfaction with their governments (though the work of their own hands), with *each other*, and with *themselves*. Injustice, vice, and tyranny will prevail everywhere. Then and not till then will all nations, worn down by their sufferings, unite in wishing for a Deliverer, and then and not till then will "the DESIRE of *all* nations come."[3] Millions, nay all the inhabitants of our world, will hail his descent to our globe and unanimously commit its government wholly to him. But should he come now, in the present temper of mankind, he would not be welcome. Britain would prefer her present king and constitution to him. France would not exchange her warlike and popular usurper for him. The Germans and northern nations of Europe would adhere to the standard of their princes. Asia and Africa would not be awakened from their long repose in ignorance and slavery by the harps of all the angelic hosts which are to accompany him to our earth, and even the citizens of the United States of America would probably concur with all the nations that have been mentioned in declaring with the ancient Jews, "We will not have this man to reign over us."[4]

"He that believeth shall not *make haste*."[5] Let us wait with patience for the fulfilment of all God's promises. "Overturn—overturn—overturn" is the order of Eternity.[6] Thrones and kings and secular priests and usurpers must fall and perish. Their doom is fixed in the Scriptures of truth. The Messiah alone shall reign as King of Saints and Lord of the whole earth. *All will end*, not only *well*, but gloriously for those who believe and trust in his name.

The people of Europe and of our country are divided into two great classes: the one is contending for *ancient disorder*, that is, for the carcasses of putrefying civil and ecclesiastical institutions; while too many of the other class are contending for a *new disorder* of things, that is, for governments that shall exclude religion and for the empire of intoxicated human reason in the affairs of the world. Let us avoid belonging to either of them. Both parties are in an error—and both will be disappointed. I have only room to bid you adieu! and to add a prayer for the prosperity of our bantling, the College of Carlisle.——Yours affectionately,

BENJN RUSH

Addressed: John Montgomery Esqr: Carlisle Pennsylvania.
MS: Library Company of Philadelphia, Rush MSS.

[1] In Rush MSS, XLII. Montgomery had indulged in speculation on the realization of the Scriptural prophecies, and BR in his reply reveals how far he has retreated from politics into religion.

[2] Luke 18:8.
[3] Haggai 2:7.
[4] Luke 19:14.
[5] Isaiah 28:16.
[6] See Ezekiel 21:27.

To the Earl of Buchan

My Lord,   Philadelphia, October 6th, 1801

Permit me to introduce to your lordship Dr. Nathl. Chapman,[1] a former pupil of mine and a graduate of the University of Pennsylvania. He is a native of Virginia and has been from his childhood a near neighbor of the late General Washington. His talents have commanded the respect of all his teachers, and his manners have procured him as many friends as he has acquaintances. He is well acquainted with the details of the public affairs of our country, and can answer all such questions relative to public men and measures as are usually asked by strangers and persons interested in the welfare of the only representative and elective government (in all its parts) upon the face of the earth.

I have the honor to subscribe myself your lordship's most obedient servant,

BENJN RUSH

Addressed: The Right Honble: The Earl of Buchan Dryburgh Abbey or Edinburgh Dr Chapman.
MS: New York Public Library, Emmet Collection.

[1] Nathaniel Chapman (1780-1853), of Fairfax co., Va., after private study with BR took his M.D. at the University of Pennsylvania, 1801; after further

study abroad he began in 1804 a long and distinguished career as a practitioner in Philadelphia; he held successive chairs in the medical school from 1810 to 1850, wrote numerous medical treatises, and was first president of the American Medical Association, 1848 (DAB; Gross, *Lives of Physicians and Surgeons*). Chapman brought back to BR an interesting gift from Buchan, but the later relations between BR and his former pupil were not always harmonious; see BR to Buchan, 22 Oct. 1806; to James Rush, 19 Mch. 1810; and to John Adams, 8 Sep. 1810.

To James Currie

Philadelphia, November 20, 1801

Dr. Rush requests Dr. Currie's acceptance of a small publication.[1]

Dr. Rush is happy in being able to inform his friend Dr. Currie that liberty, peace, order, and plenty continue to pervade every part of the United States. Out of nearly five millions of people in our country, not more probably than twenty persons with healthy appetites have passed this day without two or [more?][2] comfortable meals. Of what country upon the face of the earth can the same thing be said on *any one* day of the year?

MS: Captain F. L. Pleadwell, Honolulu.

[1] In all likelihood this was BR's *Six Introductory Lectures, to Courses of Lectures, upon the Institutes and Practice of Medicine*, Phila.: Conrad, 1801. [2] MS torn.

To James Rush

My dear Son, Philadelphia, November 23rd, 1801

Your letter diffused pleasure through all our family.[1] It is correctly written. I hope all your letters will be composed with the same regard to spelling, punctuation, and grammar. In the use of capitals remember to use them only in the beginning of sentences and for the names of persons, cities, countries, and important words such as Religion, Revolution, Reformation, and the like.

We are much pleased with your roommates. I hope you will imitate them in diligence and regular conduct.

Your Mama is so much dissatisfied with your brown coat that she has concluded not to send it to you. She will send you the cloth for another as soon as you will inform her what color will be agreeable to you. It can be made at Princeton.

Keep your receipts carefully in your trunk, and bring them home with you in the spring.

Remember, my dear son, my parting advice to you. You are very dear to me, and be assured no exertions on my part shall be wanting to promote your interest and happiness.

Your Mama and all the family join in love to you with your affectionate father,

BENJN RUSH

Addressed: Mr James Rush Student at the College of Princeton New Jersey. *MS*: Library Company of Philadelphia, Rush MSS.

[1] James had just entered the College at Princeton. Though the letters of all the members of the Rush family *to* James while at Princeton have been gathered together in the Rush MSS, Box No. 10, James' letters from college have most disappointingly not been found; evidently James destroyed them.

To Thomas Jefferson

Philadelphia, November 27th, 1801

Accept, much honored and dear sir, of a copy of the enclosed publication.[1]

How joyful the sound of PEACE![2] It brings a thousand blessings in its train, among which the revival and diffusion of knowledge will not I hope be the least.

Receive again and again assurances of the friendship of, dear sir, your affectionate humble servant,

BENJN: RUSH

P.S. *Vaccination*, as you have happily called it, has taken root in our city and will shortly supersede the old mode of inoculation.[3] I consider it as a complete antidote to the ravages of war in its influence upon population. It is computed 210,000 lives will annually be saved by it in Europe. It is only necessary to believe the plague *everywhere* is the offspring of *domestic* causes, and not propagated by contagion, to extirpate it in like manner from the list of human evils.

MS: Library of Congress, Jefferson Papers.

[1] BR's *Six Introductory Lectures.*

[2] A preliminary peace had been signed, 1 Oct. 1801, by France and Britain; the formal Peace of Amiens was not negotiated until 1802 (J. H. Rose, *The Revolutionary and Napoleonic Era*, 6th edn., Cambridge [England], 1907, p. 130).

[3] A pioneer in the technique of variolous inoculation (see letter to John Morgan, 21 Oct. 1768), BR was also an early and staunch supporter of the discovery of vaccination, which infected the subject, not with a mild case of smallpox, but with a much milder disease, cowpox. The discovery was announced by Edward Jenner in England

in 1798 and introduced into this country by Benjamin Waterhouse, of Boston, with the active collaboration of President Jefferson. It was Jefferson who, after superintending successful vaccinating operations in Virginia, furnished the first vaccine to be used in Philadelphia. (BR to Waterhouse, 9 Feb. 1802; Drinker, *Not So Long Ago*, ch. v; Robert H. Halsey, *How the President, Thomas Jefferson, and Dr. Benjamin Waterhouse Established Vaccination as a Public Health Procedure*, N.Y., 1936.)

To James Madison

Dear Sir,   Philadelphia, December 5, 1801

My second son, Richard Rush, has long felt a strong desire to visit Europe in the capacity of a private secretary to a foreign minister. He has been regularly educated to the profession of the law and has begun to do business in our city. His master, Mr. Lewis, and all his professional brethren speak in high terms of his knowledge and talents. His application to study has been unwearied. In addition to his attainments in the law, he has laid in a large stock of information in history and politics, nor has he neglected those branches of polite literature which are necessary to enable him to communicate his ideas with facility and elegance upon paper. His principles and temper are alike republican and have been so in times when it was not popular to avow or defend them. His morals are pure and his manners amiable. In a word, it is not possible for a son to be more dear to his parents. We do not wish to part with him, even for a year, and we have yielded with reluctance to his importunities in communicating his wishes to you through the medium of this letter.

Should an opportunity offer of gratifying my son's request, you will much oblige me by mentioning his name to Mr. Jefferson. He will probably recollect my presenting him to him in Philadelphia when he was but 17 or 18 years of age.

The subject of this letter I hope will be *private* in any issue of the design of it. Although it is written by a father, it contains no more in favor of his son than has been said an hundred times by his friends.[1]

With great regard I am, dear sir, your sincere and unaltered friend,

BENJN: RUSH

MS: Rush Family Papers, deposited in Princeton University Library.

[1] This letter ultimately came back to Richard himself, who in 1855 wrote a long note on a blank sheet at the back: "This letter from my father to

Mr Madison, then secretary of State, writtten when I was 21, turned up to be among a file of ancient letters I laid my hands upon." Richard went on to explain that his father must have intended to pay Richard an allowance during the proposed year of foreign service, since at that time "no such thing was known as the appointment or office of secretarys of Legation by the government. . . . Doubtless I wanted to see something of the world under good auspices before settling down to the hard work of my profession; and my own family at least may find some curiosity after my decease in opening an ancient letter like this, . . . however overdrawn may be the too partial account of the subject of it." Though Madison replied to BR on 23 Dec. 1801 that he would lay the matter before President Jefferson (*Biddle Papers*, pt. ii, No. 200), nothing came of the proposal.

To James Rush

My dear Son,   Philadelphia, January 25, 1802

I have no doubt of your having faithfully applied all the money you took with you to the purposes for which it was intended. But it would have been satisfactory to both your parents to have had an accurate statement of the sums paid to different people, from under your own hand.

I enclose you herewith five dollars. I hope it will last much longer than the ten dollars you retained. Avoid *borrowing* and *running* in debt for cash articles, as you value your independence and a good character. I will always supply your reasonable wants. But remember, always remember, the size of your father's family.

We are all, thank God, in good health. John is with us, but leaves us tomorrow for Washington, where he will either resign or sail immediately upon a cruise against the Tripolitans.[1]

I was glad to hear you were not concerned in the late insurrection in the College.[2] You say nothing to me of your studies nor of your standing in your class. Let us hear from you every two weeks.

All the family join in love to you with your affectionate father,

BENJN: RUSH

Addressed: Mr James Rush Student at the College at *Princeton* New Jersey.
MS: Library Company of Philadelphia, Rush MSS.

[1] On this date BR wrote to Robert Smith, secretary of the navy, asking permission for John to resign in order to take a berth on an Indiaman (Rush MSS, XXXIX). John resigned on 29 Jan. (E. W. Callahan, *List of Officers of the Navy of the U.S.*, N.Y., 1900, p. 477).

See also BR to Jefferson, 12 Mch. 1802.
[2] Probably the disturbance recorded in the Princeton Faculty Minutes of 31 Dec. 1801, and mentioned by Professor Wertenbaker (*Princeton, 1746-1896*, p. 136) as typical of the time.

To Lyman Spalding[1]

Dear Sir,   Philadelphia, February 9, 1802

Accept of my thanks for the copy of a bill of mortality of the town of Portsmouth. It is an ingenious improvement of that species of publication and calculated to add to the certainty of our knowledge upon several medical subjects. I wish a similar mode of ascertaining the ages and diseases of persons who die, and the months in which their deaths occur, could be instituted in all the towns and cities in America. Its advantages to our science would be incalculable.

Several things struck me in reading your publication:

1. The small number of deaths, compared with your population.

2. The great number of persons above fifty out of the hundred, who died in your town in the course of the last year.[2]

3. The great proportion who died of the pulmonary consumption, being 1/5 of the whole number, also their *ages*, most of them being above 50 years of age.

4. The connection of palsy with a tendency to old age. Eight out of twelve who died with that disease being above fifty.

A Dr. Daignan of France has published two very interesting volumes upon the subject to which you have devoted a part of your time.[3] They are well worth your reading. I have derived many important facts from them which I have occasionally introduced into my lectures. They were put into my hands many years ago by Mr. Jefferson.

With great respect I am, dear sir, your friend and brother in the Republic of Medicine,

BENJN. RUSH

Addressed: Dr Lyman Spalding Physician Portsmouth. New Hamshire.
MS: Welch Library, Johns Hopkins Medical School.

[1] Lyman Spalding (1775-1821), of Portsmouth, N.H., and later of New York City; student and friend of Dr. Nathan Smith; M.B., 1797, and M.D., 1811, Harvard; served for some years on the Dartmouth medical faculty. "He originated and distributed 'bills of mortality' which gave the causes of death of all persons in Portsmouth from 1800 to 1813"; and among other contributions to American life, he invented a soda fountain. (DAB; Harvard University, *Quinquennial Catalogue of the Officers and Graduates*, Cambridge, 1925.)

[2] BR's ambiguous punctuation has not been disturbed. What he meant, doubtless, is: "The great number of persons over fifty years of age among the hundred who died," &c.

[3] Guillaume Daignan (1732-1812), *Tableau des variétés de la vie humaine*, Paris, 1786, 2 vol. (Surg. Gen. Off., *Index-Cat.*, 1st ser., III, 582).

To Benjamin Waterhouse[1]

Dear Sir,   Philadelphia, February 9, 1801 [*i.e., 1802*][2]

Accept my thanks for your friendly and instructing letter. Our whole city will, I hope, be benefited by it, as well as myself; for I have put the most important facts into the hands of a printer, and they will appear in a day or two in one of our daily papers.

In answer to your letter, I shall send you a copy of part of a lecture I delivered to my class a few weeks ago, upon the new mode of inoculation from vaccine matter, from which you will perceive that I have adopted the discovery with as much zeal and confidence as you have done, and that I look forward to the complete extinction of the smallpox by it.

"There was a time when the very name of the smallpox inspired more terror than war, famine, earthquakes, and pestilence; and with reason, for more of the human race have been destroyed by it than by any one of them, or perhaps by all of them, in a given time, put together. War has its intervals of peace; famine is often preceded and followed by years of plenty; earthquakes are extremely limited in their destructive effects upon human life; and even the plague itself is a less evil than the smallpox. The truth of this last assertion will appear when we consider that the plague is confined to filthy cities and marshy countries, whereas the smallpox prevails in all situations. Cleanliness and the cultivation of the earth are no securities against it. The plague prevails only in certain years and seasons, and requires the concurrence of a malignant constitution of the atmosphere, whereas the smallpox prevails in all seasons and states of the air. The plague now and then ceases, like war, from the face of the earth; but the smallpox has never ceased for a single year to spread death over some parts of our globe since it made its first appearance in the year 572. It has been computed that forty millions of people have died of it in different parts of the world in the course of the last century, during part of which time its mortality was much lessened, compared with former centuries, by means of inoculation. Allowing for its being confined for many centuries in its ravages upon human life to its birthplace in Africa, it is still probable several hundred millions of people have perished by it since its first introduction into the world. In contemplating this immense destruction of our species by a single disease, together with the ravages it has occasionally committed upon the senses, upon beauty, and upon health in persons who have survived it, we are struck with horror at the retrospect, and are led to mourn over the wide-extended scene which it exhibits of human misery. But happily for mankind, this general mortality and misery will be felt and seen no more. A new era is begun in the medical history of man, and the most mortal of all diseases is about to be struck out of the list of human evils. Its destiny is fixed, and the day is not very remote when the very name of the smallpox shall be found only in books of medicine. I need hardly add that this great revolution in favor of the population and happiness of our species has been effected by the substitution of a harmless disease, taken from a domestic animal, to the smallpox. Thick and lasting be the honors of that highly favored physician who first discovered and established this safe and delicate antidote to a mortal and loathsome disease. Unknown, till lately, beyond the limits of the district in which he practised, the name of Dr. JENNER has extended to every part of the globe and will be coeval with time itself. His extensive and durable fame will be merited, for he has introduced into the world the means of saving millions and millions of lives.

"For a full account of the advantages of vaccine inoculation above inoculation for the smallpox, I refer you to Dr. Aikin's epitome of nearly all that has been published upon this subject.[3] I shall briefly enumerate them.

"1. It requires no preparation in diet and medicine.

"2. It may be performed with equal safety at all seasons.

"3. It is a mild disease, seldom confining a patient to his house or interrupting his business.

"4. It risks no sense and does no injury to beauty.

"5. It is not contagious.

"6. It sometimes carries off chronic diseases.

"7. It is never mortal, except when it is accidentally combined with other diseases.

"Let us not be discouraged by the new instances which have occurred of the vaccine matter having failed to produce the disease. Time and experience will soon correct our errors and perfect our knowledge in this branch of medicine. I well recollect the time when inoculation for the smallpox was attended with much less certainty and success than it is at present, and when the deaths and sore arms from it had nearly banished it from our country. So unpopular was it, from those and other less reasonable causes, that Dr. Boylston had the windows of his house broken for attempting to introduce it into the then province of Massachusetts.[4]

"In expressing our triumph in the conquest which reason and humanity have lately obtained over the most mortal of all diseases, we are led to anticipate the time when they shall both obtain a similar conquest, by applying the means which *have been discovered*, to the prevention and annihilation of the plague. How long the blindness which has perpetuated this disease for so many ages may continue, I know not; but I believe it is as much out of the power of prejudice, error, and interest to prevent its final and total extinction as it is to prevent the change of the seasons or the annual revolutions of our globe around the sun."

[....][5] Continue to diffuse the results of your inquiries and observations through our country. Dr Mead's[6] *"non sibi, sed toti"* should be the motto of every physician.

From, dear sir, your friend and brother in the Republic of Medicine,

BENJAMIN RUSH

P.S. I have presented the curious and elegant engraving you sent me of the vaccine and variolous pustules to Dr. Coxe, who proposes to frame it and give it a place upon the wall of his parlor.

Printed: Waterhouse, *A Prospect of Exterminating the Small Pox . . .* , Part *II*, Cambridge, 1802, p. 71-4.

[1] Benjamin Waterhouse (1754-1846), Boston physician, inaugurator of vaccination in the United States, and miscellaneous writer, was a figure whose career presents striking parallels with that of BR. Born in Rhode Island, he studied in Scotland, England, and Holland, returned home in 1782, and joined the first faculty of the Harvard Medical School, where he taught from 1783 to 1812. Waterhouse's pioneering work in vaccination engaged him during the years 1799-1802. (DAB; J. C. Trent, "Benjamin Waterhouse," *Jour. Hist. Med.*, 1 [1946], 357-64; see also BR to Jefferson, 28 Nov. 1807, and to Adams, 8 Jan. 1813.)

[2] BR was replying to a letter from Waterhouse dated 2 Feb. 1802 (Rush MSS, XXX, q.v. also for other letters from Waterhouse to BR). Whether the error of 1801 for 1802 was BR's, Waterhouse's, or the printer's is now impossible to determine.

[3] This was a pamphlet by Dr. Charles Rochemont Aikin (1775-1847), entitled *A Concise View of All the Most Important Facts Which Have Hitherto Appeared concerning the Cow-Pox*, London, 1801, reprinted in Charlestown, Mass., and in Philadelphia in the course of the same year (DNB; *L.C. Cat.*).

[4] Zabdiel Boylston (1679-1766), physician of Boston, who, in collaboration with Cotton Mather, introduced inoculation for smallpox into America, 1721; both Boylston's and Mather's houses were attacked by enraged mobs (DAB).

[5] In the text a line and a half of asterisks appear, with a note by Waterhouse: "A considerable part of this paragraph being complimentary is for that reason omitted."

[6] Richard Mead, M.D. (1673-1754), one of the most eminent physicians and men of science in eighteenth-century England (DNB).

To Thomas Jefferson

Dear Sir,   Philadelphia, March 12, 1802

Having just finished the labors of the winter in the University and Hospital, I sit down with great pleasure to acknowledge your favor of December last.[1] One part of it commands my first attention, and that is your communication of a discovery of a *flaw* in your constitution from which you anticipate a certain but easy passage out of life. Permit me, my dear and long respected friend, to request you to inform me of the seat and nature of that flaw. Perhaps it is in the power of medicine to heal it or to protract its fatal effects to a very distant day. Should my reading or experience be insufficient for that purpose, I will lay the history of your case before the most intelligent members of our profession in Philadelphia (without mentioning your name) and transmit to you our united opinions and advice. The result of all that has passed or shall pass between us upon this subject shall descend with me to the grave.

Accept of my thanks for your friendly hint to Mr. Smith[2] to attend to the interests of my son while he was an officer in the navy. He feels with myself his obligations to your goodness, and regrets that the limited prospects of providing for sickness and age while in that situation rendered it necessary for him to quit the service of his country. He is still attached to the sea and expects to sail shortly probably to an East India port.

I am happy in being able to inform you that the vaccine inoculation is generally adopted in our city and that its success has hitherto equaled the best wishes of its most sanguine and zealous friends.

For several years past I have been engaged in investigating the causes, seats, and remedies of madness and other diseases of the mind. Before I commit the results of my inquiries and observations to the press, I wish to read everything that has been published upon those subjects. Le Tude's history of the Bastile and of a lunatic hospital in which he was confined under pretense of madness, I have heard, contains many curious facts upon that disease.[3] In my inquiries for this curious book I was informed that you had a copy of it. Could you favor me with the reading of it, you would add greatly to my obligations to you. It shall be returned in a week or ten days after I receive it.

What means, alas! the renewal of the horrors of war in the West Indies?[4] Does our globe, like a diseased body, stand in need of a perpetual issue of blood? I tremble for its consequences everywhere and particularly in our country. Can nothing be done by concession and partial emancipation to avert the storm from the southern states? But I must quit a subject upon which I am unable to suggest anything new or useful and which I am sure has long commanded all the resources of your understanding and feelings of your heart.

With great respect and affection, believe me to be your sincere old friend,

BENJN: RUSH

MS: Library of Congress, Jefferson Papers.

[1] Jefferson's letter, dated 20 Dec. 1801, is printed in his *Writings*, ed. Lipscomb and Bergh, x, 303-4.

[2] Robert Smith (1757-1842), a graduate of the College of New Jersey, 1781, and lawyer in Baltimore, was secretary of the navy, 1801-1809 (DAB).

[3] Henri Masers de Latude (1725-1805), a French state prisoner for many years, was for a time, though sane, committed to the Bicêtre hospital for lunatics in Paris; he also perpetrated a remarkable escape from the Bastille; his *Mémoires* were published at Paris, 1791-1792, in three volumes (*Biog. Univ.*).

[4] This alludes to the sanguinary French invasion of San Domingo (Haiti), Jan. 1802, in order to overthrow Toussaint Louverture (Winsor, *Narr. & Crit. Hist.*, VIII, 285).

To Joseph Saunders Coates[1]

My dear young Friend,　　　　　Philadelphia, May 3rd, 1802

We plant trees, says Stern, and we water them because we have planted them.[2] Having once been the instrument in the hands of heaven of saving your life, I feel a solicitude for the preservation of it. I have therefore sat down to suggest to you such directions as I hope will be effective for the purpose in the sickly countries to which you are about to sail in a few days.

1. Live temperately, but not abstemiously. The less fresh meat you eat, the better. Salted meat with vegetables are the most healthy diet in warm seasons and climates.

2. Keep your bowels gently open. The fevers of warm climates generally come on with costiveness, which should always be obviated by a gentle dose of purging physic. I herewith send you some pills, two of which or more may be taken for that purpose.

3. Never go abroad before breakfast. Avoid long intervals between your meals.

4. Avoid the night air, and when necessarily exposed to it, increase the quantity of your clothing.

5. Wear thin flannel constantly near to your skin.

6. Never stand in the sun.

7. Avoid fatigue from all its causes, both of body and mind.

8. Wash your body occasionally with salt water.

9. Avoid late hours.

To these directions for the preservation of your health and life, I shall add one which relates to the improvement of your mind, recommended to me by the late Israel Pemberton[3] when I called to take leave of him just before I sailed for England in the year 1766: "Keep older and wiser company than thyself."

From your sincere friend,

B R

MS (draft): Library Company of Philadelphia, Rush MSS.

[1] Joseph Saunders Coates was the third child of BR's close friend Samuel Coates (Mary Coates, *Family Memorials and Recollections; or Aunt Mary's Patchwork*, Phila., 1885, p. 35).

[2] I have not found this observation in Sterne.

[3] Israel Pemberton (1715-1779), one of the most substantial Quaker merchants of his time; a manager of the Pennsylvania Hospital from 1751 to his death, and active in other philanthropic causes; died as a result of his exile to Virginia for opposition to the Revolutionary War (DAB).

To James Rush

My dear Son,   Philadelphia, May 25, 1802

Your letter which we received on Wednesday morning last gave great pleasure to all the family. I examined it critically and do not recollect to have met with but one word improperly spelled—and none improperly written. Continue to cultivate a taste for correctness in everything that comes from your pen. A man's fortune has sometimes been made by his letters' being seen by persons of judgment, and on the contrary many men have lost their characters for good sense and education from the same cause. Never write in a hurry. Even a common note upon the most common business should be written as if it were one day to be read in a court or published in a newspaper.

I was much pleased to find that you begin to appreciate *time*. Recollect, my dear boy, your age and the years you have lost. Improve every moment you can spare from your recitations in reading useful books. Your uncle's[1] library I presume will always be open to you, where you will find[2] history, poetry, and probably other books suited to your age. The last King of Prussia but one used to say, "A soldier should have no idle time." The same thing may be said of all schoolboys. Their common plays and amusements I believe, instead of relaxing, often enervate their minds and give them a distaste to study.[3] I do not advise you against such exercises as are necessary to health, but simply to avoid sharing in what are commonly called "plays." The celebrated Mr. Madison when a student at the Jersey College never took any part in them. His only relaxation from study consisted in walking and conversation. Such was the character he acquired while at college, that Dr. Wetherspoon said of him to Mr. Jefferson (from whom I received the anecdote) that during the whole time he was under his tuition he never knew him to do nor to say an improper thing.

Remember the profession for which you are destined. Without an extensive and correct education you cannot expect to succeed in it. Do not, my dear son, disappoint my expectations and wishes of bequeathing my patients to an enlightened and philosophical physician. If you discover a relish for knowledge, your wishes shall be gratified to the utmost of my power in your education after you leave college. You shall visit Europe, if my life be spared, and draw from foreign universities all that you require to enable you to settle with advantage in Philadelphia. Think of these things and act up to them. But above all, preserve a conscience void of offense towards God and man. All true wisdom begins in true religion. Adieu! All the family join in love to you with, my dear son, your affectionate father,

BENJN: RUSH

P.S. We shall expect to receive a letter from you next Wednesday morning. Compliments to Mrs. Still.[4]

Addressed: Mr James Rush Student at the College at Princeton New Jersey.
MS: Library Company of Philadelphia, Rush MSS.

[1] Richard Stockton the younger, of Morven.
[2] This word inadvertently omitted in MS.
[3] For BR's views on this subject, see his "Thoughts upon the Amusements and Punishments Which Are Proper for Schools," in his *Essays* (1798), p. 57-74; also his letter to James of 31 May 1804.
[4] Not identified. The name is perhaps "Stall."

To John Warren

Dear Sir,   Philadelphia, August 6, 1802

The bearer, Dr. Otto,[1] formerly a pupil of mine and now a respectable physician of Philadelphia, purposes to spend a few days in Boston. Permit me to solicit your civilities to him. Mankind are often said to be members of one family. This should be true in a more especial manner of the members of our profession. The bond of our union should be common studies, common labors, common acts of self-denial,[2] and, when they dare to charge their native cities with generating pestilential diseases, common persecutions.

From, dear sir, your sincere old friend and brother in the science of medicine,

BENJN: RUSH

Addressed: Dr John Warren Physician Boston favoured by Dr Otto.
MS: Massachusetts Historical Society, John Warren Papers.

[1] John C. Otto, on whom see BR's letter to John Redman Coxe, 28 Apr. 1796.
[2] MS: "self-dial."

To William Smith

Dear Sir, Philadelphia, 10th August 1802

All the effusions of your pen, whether upon light or serious subjects, bear the marks of the fire and originality of genius which characterized all your performances in the early and middle parts of your life. If in anything they discover the marks of old age, it is the old age of Dr. Smith.

I do not know that ever I wrote a line of poetry in my life, but I have sometimes amused myself when a schoolboy in making rhymes. The success of your little flight contained in your friendly letter,[1] with wings completely silvered by time, has encouraged me to attempt to flap mine upon the same subject. They are, it is true, less white than yours, but they are tipped with gray and have nearly grown to my sides by the long and dull labors of the pestle and mortar.

You have misapprehended me in supposing I was present at the entertainment given by Governor Mifflin to the faculty of the College. The anecdote which has given birth to our epigrams was communicated to me by Dr. Andrews,[2] who was one of the company. Some person having noticed that the lightning and thunder were unusually terrible, you replied to the remarks nearly in the words stated in the following lines:

"What means that flash! The thunder's awful roar!
The blazing sky! unseen, unheard before?
Sage Smith replies 'Our Franklin is no more;

[851]

The clouds, long subject to his magic chain,
Exulting now, their liberty regain.' "³

Dr. Franklin had died a day or two before this thunderstorm.

Your villa will hereafter have an additional hold upon my memory by being the place where I first met a man whose talents for conversation have commanded nearly as much admiration as his pencil, I mean the celebrated Mr. Stewart.⁴ Thirty years ago I communicated to Mr. Peale a wish to see a gallery of portraits of sick people laboring under such diseases as show themselves in the features and countenance. These are chiefly madness, melancholy, fatuity, consumption, dropsy, jaundice, leprosy, gutta rosea,⁵ stone, cancer, colic, dysentery, smallpox, measles, scarlet fever, and plagues of all kinds. In the Church of Notre Dame in Paris I once saw a picture of a woman with the plague, raised up in her bed and receiving the Sacrament from the hand of a priest. Pain, sickness, sallowness, and despair appeared in every feature and expression of her face. The sight of this picture, like Virgil's description of a storm (according to Mr. Addison),⁶ seemed for a moment to disorder the stomach. A lively recollection of it was excited in my imagination a few days ago in visiting a young man in the last stage of the yellow fever. He felt no pain, and his mind was tranquil, but his countenance exhibited a certain lugubrious appearance, a vacant sadness, and an unconscious distress such as the pen cannot describe and which, if it could, a reader could not receive just impressions of them from books. A pencil only could perpetuate them so as to produce just ideas of them in the mind. By means of a gallery of portraits such as I have hinted at, the study of medicine might be much aided, and benevolent sympathies be excited in persons who from education, situation, or too much sensibility are precluded from seeing the originals in sick rooms or hospitals.

Suppose you suggest the idea of such an undertaking to Mr. Stewart. If in revolving it in his mind he should feel any fear of being infected with the last-named disease, you may assure him from much higher authority than mine that the yellow fever is *not* contagious, and spreads only through the medium of an atmosphere rendered impure by putrid exhalations. A patient in the country therefore, who had carried the disease from our city, might be approached, viewed, and painted with as much safety as a person in the gout or toothache. These opinions, though strictly true, I know to be more unpopular than ever in Philadelphia, from which I am forced unwillingly to believe that mankind are as much destined by the present obliquity of their understandings to be destroyed by plagues as they are by the present disorder of their passions to be destroyed by war, for——perhaps many centuries to come.

From, dear sir, your sincere friend,

BENJN: RUSH

MS: Historical Society of Pennsylvania, William Smith Papers, deposited by Jasper Yates Brinton.

¹ Dated 5 Aug. 1802; Rush MSS, XXII. For Smith's verses, see note 3, below.

² John Andrews (1746-1813), Episcopal clergyman and classical scholar; A.B., College of Philadelphia, 1764; principal of the Episcopal Academy, Philadelphia, 1785-1791; professor of moral philosophy and the classics, 1791-1812, and provost, 1810-1812, University of Pennsylvania (DAB).

³ These lines are BR's rhyming version of a quip that Smith was said to have made at Gov. Mifflin's dinner party in Apr. 1790. Franklin having recently died, and a thunderstorm having come up, Smith was reported as saying: "The clouds . . . seem to show by their unusual noise that their master is dead, and that no earthly power can now control them" (thus reported in a fragmentary draft of the present letter in Rush MSS, XXII). BR had reminded Smith of this anecdote at their meeting a week or so before this letter was written. On 5 Aug. Smith wrote BR saying he did not remember making the remark BR attributed to him, but he *wished* that he had spoken the following lines, since Rittenhouse had also been a guest at Gov. Mifflin's:

"Cease, cease, Ye Clouds, your elemental Strife;
Oh! rage not thus, as if to threaten Life!
Seek, seek no more to shake our Souls with Dread!
What busy Mortal told You—FRANKLIN'S DEAD?
What though he Yields to JOVE's imperious *Nodd?*
With RITTENHOUSE, he left his MAGIC ROD!"

These facts are badly garbled by Horace Smith in his biography of Provost Smith. He says (II, 324-5) that the Mifflin dinner party was actually interrupted by news of Franklin's death, that Provost Smith composed the verse epigram immediately above "without leaving the table," and that thereupon another guest, Thomas Willing, countered with another impromptu—the lines by BR in the letter above.

⁴ Gilbert Stuart (1755-1828), the celebrated portrait painter (DAB).

⁵ Literally "rose drop"; described in *Quincy's Lexicon* (N.Y., 1802) as "Little fiery tubercles dispersed about the face and nose."

⁶ I have not located this observation attributed to Addison.

To Ashbel Green

Dear Sir,   December 9, 1802

The young man[1] recommended to your notice and my care is not yet come to town. When he arrives and it is proper for you to visit him, you shall know it.

I cannot omit this opportunity of expressing to you the great pleasure I have derived by learning from my son James that instruction in the evidences of the Christian religion has at length become a part of the education of a young man at the Jersey College.[2] I have often publicly as well as privately advised it. Three-fourths of all the infidelity of the gentlemen of our country I believe have arisen from the neglect of it. To perfect the plan now happily introduced into the College, it only remains to pass a law to oblige candidates for degrees to undergo an examination in theological science as well as in the sciences which relate only to our existence in this world. The lyceums and other schools among the pagans were founded chiefly for instructing youth in their mythology, and the schools of the prophets among the Jews were devoted I believe only to teach the meaning of their types and ceremonies and their reference to the events accomplished in the New Testament. Should the new branch of education introduced into the College be attended with the success and benefits which are contemplated, it will soon appear that the late attacks upon our religion by Paine, Godwin, and others have been permitted for wise and good purposes. In addition to Paley and Campbell's defenses of Christianity,[3] would not a few lectures upon Jewish antiquities, as far as they relate to the connection between the Old and New Testaments, be useful? Infidelity generally makes its first approaches by attacking the supposed absurdities and cruelties of the Jewish worship. By explaining them properly and showing the relation of every part of it to the New Testament institutions, much evil might be prevented in the minds of young men. The antidote would be administered before the poison would have time to produce its effect.

I have taken the liberty of expressing these thoughts, and the pleasure my son's letter gave me, to you, because I have reason to believe the excellent additions to a college education above-mentioned have been chiefly introduced by your influence.

I cannot omit this opportunity of further testifying the pleasure with which I read for the *first time in my life*, in your charge to the students at the College,[4] a denial of the existence of a "Religion of Nature." It is high time to chase the Deists from that ground. It belongs exclusively to the Christians, for everything good in man, and all his knowledge of God and a future state, are derived wholly from scattered and traditional rays of the successive revelations recorded in the Bible. Without them, men would have been elevated above beasts of prey only in wickedness and misery.

From, dear sir, yours very sincerely and affectionately,

BENJN: RUSH

MS: John Carter Brown Library.

¹ Not identified.

² Ashbel Green was at this time the acting president of the College, President Samuel Stanhope Smith being absent on a prolonged tour to raise funds following the burning of Nassau Hall in the preceding March. To Green (as BR opined) may be attributed the institution of required religious studies at Princeton; they were part of a general reform program inspired by fears that Godwinian free-thinking was sweeping the student body. (Godwin was by some held virtually responsible for the Nassau Hall fire.) The favorite of those trustees who hoped to revive the primitive piety of the early College, Green eventually displaced Smith as president. In perspective it is clear that Princeton, like other colleges in the early years of the century, was undergoing gradual but steady secularization. This was recognized by leaders in the Presbyterian

organization, and the founding, in 1811, of a separate seminary for training ministers was a result. BR anticipated the plan of a seminary in a remarkable letter, probably to Green, of 22 May 1807, q.v. See also BR to Green, 31 Dec. 1812; Wertenbaker, *Princeton, 1746-1896*, ch. IV; Maclean, *Hist. Coll. N.J.*, II, 50-1.

³ BR probably refers to William Paley's *View of the Evidences of Christianity*, London, 1794, and to George Campbell's *Dissertation on Miracles: containing an Examination of the Principles Advanced by David Hume*, Edinburgh, 1762, a frequently reprinted work (*Brit. Mus. Cat.*).

⁴ *Address to the Students and Faculty of the College of New Jersey, Delivered May 6th, 1802, the Day on Which the Students Commenced Their Studies after the Burning of the College Edifice*, Trenton, 1802.

To John Montgomery

Philadelphia, February 11th, 1802 [*i.e.*, *1803*]¹

My dear Friend,

I have not ceased to mingle my tears with yours ever since I received your letter containing the distressing intelligence of the destruction of our College by fire.² It has added a fresh instance to the number of the unsuccessful and abortive issue of the labors of my life. My feelings upon the occasion would be insupportable, did I not recollect a conversation I had with the late Reverend Mr. Marshall of our city a few days before he died. Upon his telling me that my life had been a useful one, I interrupted him by saying that all the public enterprises I had devoted myself to had ended in disappointment and mortification, and that I did not know that I had ever done any good in the course of my life. "Well, Doctor," said he, "admit this to be the case—you have *aimed* to do good and to promote the best interests of your fellow creatures; and remember, our Saviour at the day of Judgment will say to his followers, 'Well done'—not 'thou good and *successful*'—but 'thou good and *faithful* servant—enter thou into the joy of thy Lord.'"

What is to be done? Shall we sit down in despair and give up our College for lost? By no means! To what quarter shall we fly for

[855]

relief? Not to our citizens; they have been exhausted by contributions to the Jersey College, to the sufferers by the fire at Portsmouth,[3] and to the persons who have been distressed and ruined by our yellow fever. Our principal and first resource should be in the patriotism and humanity of our state legislature. Let a petition be composed and addressed to them immediately, and let the Governor be requested to accompany it with a recommendation. There is not an hour to be lost in this business. If our rulers cannot think, they can feel. By delay, their sympathy may cool. Let us strike while the iron is hot, and may Heaven kindly bless and prosper our efforts to revive the object of our labors and affections.

Adieu! my dear friend. From yours very affectionately,

BENJN RUSH

MS: Library Company of Philadelphia, Rush MSS.

[1] For the correction of BR's date, see the following note.

[2] The newly erected first college building at Carlisle was destroyed by fire on 3 Feb. 1803, which determines the true date of this letter. See Morgan's *Dickinson College*, p. 87-9, for newspaper accounts of this event.

[3] A fire that broke out early on 26 Dec. 1802 in Portsmouth, N.H., destroyed buildings and property estimated at $200,000 in value (Nathaniel Adams, *Annals of Portsmouth*, Portsmouth, 1825, p. 324-5).

To Thomas Jefferson

Dear Sir,   Philadelphia, March 12th, 1803

The solicitude I felt upon the account of your health, excited by your letter of last summer, is in a great measure removed by the history you have given me of your disease in your favor of the 28th of February.[1] Chronic diseases even in persons in the decline of life are far from being incurable, and I have great pleasure in assuring you that complaints of the bowels, such as you have described yours to be, have very generally yielded to medicine under my care, and that too in some instances in old people. The remedies which appear to me proper in your case are:

1. A diet consisting chiefly of *solid* aliment, taken at *short* intervals. The stomach should never be full nor empty. Like a schoolboy when idle, it does mischief to itself or to parts connected with it. Fish and every other article of food that disagrees with your bowels should be avoided. The most inoffensive vegetable that you can take with animal food is the potato. Biscuit or toasted bread or boiled rice should be taken, when convenient, with all your meals.

Sherry wine or madeira, when pure and old, may be taken in moderation, alone or with water, daily. Port wine may be taken occasionally, but it is too gouty for habitual use.

2. The utmost care should be taken to promote a constant determination of the powers of the system externally, and of the discharges through the skin which are natural to it. Perspiration is an excretion of the first necessity to health and life. The means of promoting and increasing it in your case should be the warm bath in cool weather and the cold bath in summer. The best time of using them is about 12 or 1 o'clock. The system bears them best at those hours. With the warm and cold baths, flannel should be worn next to your skin, and uncommon pains should be taken to keep your feet constantly *warm*. They are the avenues of half the paroxysms of all chronic diseases when cold. It will be the more necessary to promote warmth and vigor in your feet, as the disease in your bowels is probably the effect of a feeble, misplaced gout.

3. Gentle exercise should be used at those times when you feel *least* of your disease. When your bowels are much excited, rest should be indulged. Riding on horseback should be preferred to walking or riding in a carriage. Avoid exercise of every kind before breakfast, in damp weather, and after sunset. Your custom I recollect formerly was to breakfast as soon as you left your bed. That custom is now more necessary than ever to your health. Carefully avoid fatigue of body and mind from all its causes. Late hours and midnight studies and business should likewise be avoided. It will be unsafe for you to sit up later than 10 o'clock.

4. To relieve the diarrhoea when troublesome, laudanum should be taken in small doses during the day, and in larger doses at bedtime so as to prevent your being obliged to rise in the night. I have seen the happiest effects from a syrup prepared in the following manner: Take of the powder of oak galls six drachms and cinnamon two drachms. Boil them in a pint of water to half a pint, then strain them and add to the liquor half a pint of brandy and as much loaf sugar as will make them over a slow fire into a syrup, of which take a tablespoonful or more three times a day. Peppermint tea may be taken occasionally with both the above remedies for paroxysms of your disease. In cases of severe pain, an injection composed of forty drops of laudanum mixed with a tablespoonful of starch and half a pint of water will give ease. The laudanum when thus received into the system seldom affects the stomach with sickness or the head with pain afterwards.

5. If the above remedies do not relieve you, blisters should be

applied occasionally and alternately to your wrists and ankles. Such is the sympathy between the skin and bowels, that the irritation of the blisters on the skin suspends all morbid action in the bowels. In the meanwhile astringent medicines act with double or perhaps quadruple force upon them.

6. If the blisters in addition to the other remedies that have been mentioned do not cure you, recourse must be had to as much mercury, either used internally combined with opium, or externally in an ointment, as will excite a gentle salivation. This remedy is a radical one. I have not often been obliged to resort to it in obstinate diarrhoeas; but when I have, it has seldom failed of performing an effectual and permanent cure.

To encourage you to expect relief from your present disease, I could furnish you with many histories of the efficacy of *each* of the above remedies. I shall mention the effects of but one of them. The Reverend Dr. Ewing, late provost of our University, was cured of a diarrhoea of several years' continuance in the 66th year of his age by the use of the cold bath.

I have been much struck in observing how seldom a diarrhoea (where the stomach is unimpaired) shortens the duration of human life. The late Wm. Smith of New York, afterwards chief justice of Canada,[2] was affected with it for fifteen years in the middle stage of his life, and General Gates (now between 70 and 80 years of age) was seldom free from it during our Revolutionary War and I believe for some years afterwards.

I beg you would continue to command my advice in your case. All your communications upon it shall be confined to myself.

I shall expect to see Mr. Lewis in Philadelphia, and shall not fail of furnishing him with a number of questions calculated to increase our knowledge of subjects connected with medicine.[3]

The venerable Dr. Priestley is now, we fear, upon his last visit to our city. His health and strength have declined sensibly within the two last years, but his spirits are unimpaired or rather improved, and his conversation is as instructive and delightful as ever. The Philosophical Society did homage to his genius and character a few days ago by giving him a public dinner. The toasts will be published shortly. They were confined wholly to philosophical characters and institutions.

Have you seen Acerbi's *Travels into Sweden, Finland, and Lapland*?[4] They are more interesting than any work of that kind yet published, inasmuch as they embrace both science and literature. The author is an Italian, but he writes in an elegant English style.

I return Latude[5] with many thanks. It is, I find, an abridgement only of a large work in which is contained an account of a hospital of deranged people with whom he lived for some time after he left the Bastile.

I have only to add a single thought foreign to the subjects of this letter, and that is, fatal as has been the issue of the struggle for republicanism in Europe, and precarious as the tenure may be by which we hold our excellent republican form of government, I still continue in my abstracted situation and private pursuits in life to admire and prefer it to all others as most consistent with the rational nature and the moral and religious obligations of man.

With the most cordial wishes for your health and every blessing that can be connected with it in public and private life, I am, dear sir, your sincere old friend,

BENJN: RUSH

P.S. I recollect you were in the practice formerly of washing your feet every morning in cold water *in cold weather*. It is possible that practice, so salutary in early and middle life, may not accord with your present age. The bowels sympathize with the feet above any other external part of the body, and suffer in a peculiar manner from the effects of cold upon them. As warm and cold water produce the same ultimate effects upon the feet, suppose you substitute the former to the latter hereafter in the winter months. The warm water acts as a direct stimulant, while the cold water produces action and warmth indirectly only, after first inducing weakness and cold in the parts to which it is applied. The *action* and *warmth* are induced only by reaction, and when the energy of the feet is not sufficient for that purpose (as is sometime the case in the decline of life), the cold water may do harm. The whole system will often react against cold when a part of it, especially a part remote from the heart and brain, will not. Hence a general cold bath will sometimes be inoffensive and even useful when a partial one will be hurtful.

Should you conclude to use the cold bath in summer, begin with water at 90° or 85°, and let its heat descend gradually to 55° or 60°.

MS: Massachusetts Historical Society, Jefferson Papers.

[1] In Jefferson's *Writings*, ed. Ford, VIII, 219-21. The President therein introduced Meriwether Lewis to BR (see further on in the present letter), and described in some detail his own recur- rent diarrhoea. In replying, BR pays due regard to Jefferson's well-known skepticism respecting medical theories of all kinds and sticks to empirical remedies. It is noteworthy that thirteen years

later, in returning BR's letters at the request of Richard Rush, Jefferson retained this letter and that of 5 May 1803, "because a return of the complaint might happen and again render them useful" (to Richard Rush, 16 Dec. 1816, Rush Family Papers, deposited in Princeton University Library).

[2] William Smith (1728-1793), the eminent jurist and tory (DAB).

[3] Meriwether Lewis (1774-1809), captain, U.S. Army, formerly Jefferson's private secretary, and now about to undertake his exploratory mission with William Clark in the Northwest (DAB). He was being sent to Philadelphia for what would now be called "briefing" in certain scientific skills. See further, BR to Jefferson, 11 June 1803.

[4] Giuseppi Acerbi, *Travels through Sweden, Finland, and Lapland, to the North Cape, in the Years 1798 and 1799*, London, 1802, 2 vol. (*L.C. Cat.*).

[5] See BR to Jefferson, 12 Mch. 1802.

To James Rush

My dear Son, Philadelphia, March 29th, 1803

We considered your letter to your sister Julia as addressed to the whole family; of course your parents are not offended at you. My neglecting to write to you was occasioned by an unusual hurry of business, for our city has been sickly with colds and pleurisies. I have besides been employed two hours of every day for two weeks since the 10th of the month in examining candidates for degrees in medicine, 16 of whom we expect will graduate in June.

The family continue to enjoy good health. Your brother John has become as close a student as Richard.[1] "Study" I hope will be the motto of all my sons. Remember that *labor* is the lot and destiny of man, and that it must be submitted to by all young men who are not born to inherit large estates. It is not necessary, to fulfil this destiny, that a man should work with his hands. He may fulfil it by the labor of his brains. But he will be singular in going through life if he be not compelled to work not only with his brains, but with his hands and heels at the same time. In this threefold kind of labor your father has been employed (with the exceptions of three years) ever since he was 16 years old. He does not complain notwithstanding of his lot. On the contrary, his life has been upon the whole a happy one. He would not even at this period of it exchange his labors for the independent situation of any idle, sauntering, purse-proud citizen of Philadelphia.

Let me know how much cash you will require to pay your debts at Princeton and bring you home. We expect your friend Mr. Monk[2] will accompany you.

Your Mama has begun her labors in her garden at Sydenham. Ben goes out with her tomorrow to engraft some fruit trees.

All the family join in love to you with your affectionate father,

BENJN: RUSH

[860]

P.S. In composing letters or other things, always make choice of those words which are *appropriate* to the idea you wish to convey. In your letter to me, you say you have "wronged" your parents by not writing to them. The appropriate word in that case should have been *offended*. You have used the adjective[3] *scarce* instead of the adverb *scarcely*.

Recollect Dean Swift's definition of style. It is "proper words in their proper places."[4]

Addressed: Mr James Rush Princeton College New Jersey.
MS: Library Company of Philadelphia, Rush MSS.

[1] John was studying medicine at the University; Richard had been admitted to the bar in Dec. 1800.

[2] Charles William Monk (b. 1788), of Halifax, son of James Monk, chief justice of Nova Scotia; he evidently died as a young man (Alumni Records, Secretary's Office, Princeton Univ.).

[3] Ironically enough, BR wrote this word as "advective."

[4] From Swift's *Letter to a Young Gentleman Lately Entered into Holy Orders*, 1721.

To Mary Rush

My beloved Daughter,   Philadelphia, April 1st, 1803

I have received and read with uncommon emotions your sister's letter of the 11th of last month, and have seldom been more at a loss in deciding upon any subject than I am to write an answer to it. In addition to what your Mama has said in her two last letters upon the subject now under consideration, I have only to add that we are highly gratified with the excellent character of the gentleman who has done you the honor to prefer you to all your sex, and are much pleased with the candor he has discovered in his account of his situation and prospects in life.[1] Mr. McIlvery[2] of Montreal, who is now my patient, in speaking of the officers of the 49th Regiment, has more than once accidentally introduced Mr. Manners' name and spoken of him as a gentleman of great worth and of "highly polished and attracting manners." Under all these prepossessing circumstances, your parents unite in declaring our willingness to adopt him as a son from his character as a man. The objection which would have arisen to his unsettled mode of life is obviated by your sister's saying he purposes to leave the army after the expiration of a year. We are further reconciled to your separation from us (although the surrender of your society so necessary to our comfort in the approaching evening of our lives would be extremely painful to us), provided his and your interest

[861]

and happiness can be best promoted by it. Our only fears arise from the scanty resources upon which you must depend for several years for the support of a family should you come together. As most of your father's children are still young and uneducated, and a great part of his estate locked up in unproductive property, it will not be in his power to give you more than six or seven hundred pounds at your marriage, and perhaps no more afterwards before his death. Recollect, my dear girl, how much a gentleman brought up as Mr. M. has been may be disposed from his habits and compelled by the rank of his connections to live beyond his income. Consider further, however much Mr. M. may esteem and love you, he has offered you his hand *without* the consent or knowledge of his father, that it is possible he may have destined him to a more wealthy and advantageous alliance, and that his whole family may complain of your having interfered in their plans of domestic establishments. Think seriously and coolly, my dearest Mary, of these suggestions of parental love, and do not fail at the same time to look up to Heaven for direction in the present difficult crisis of your life. Our prayers shall be joined with yours that you may be disposed to act wisely and prudently, and that your happiness here and hereafter may be the result of your deliberations. We earnestly request the assistance of Mr. Cuthbert and your sister's advice in determining your conduct. One thing we think we have a right to insist upon, and that is that you form no engagement with Mr. M. until his father's approbation be obtained to the proposed connection of our respective families. Mr. M.'s dependence upon him for a settlement, and your proper and kind reception by his family render this step indispensably necessary.

Adieu! my ever dear and beloved child. All the family join in love to you, Mr. Cuthbert, your sister Maria, and Master James,[3] with your affectionate father,

BENJN: RUSH

Addressed: Miss Mary Rush at Ross Cuthbert's Esqr: Montreal Lower Canada.

MS: Joseph E. Fields, M.D., Joliet, Illinois.

[1] "The gentleman" was Thomas Manners (d. 1834), captain in the 49th British Regt. and a connection of the ducal house of Rutland; he served in Canada at several periods, including that of the War of 1812. He was married to Mary Rush in Philadelphia, 29 Dec. 1803; they had two children, who both lived in England. (Biddle, *Memorial*, p. 256; Manners' letters to BR, Rush MSS, XXXIV; BR's references to the Manners family in later letters, especially p. 883). Mary (Rush) Manners lived until 1849 and died near Rochester, England (Biddle, *Memorial*, p. 256).

2 Not further identified.

3 James was BR's first grandchild, son of Ross and Emily (Rush) Cuthbert, born 1800, died 1842 (Biddle, *Memorial*, p. 243). Maria was doubtless a sister of Ross Cuthbert.

To Ashbel Green

Dear Sir,   April 26, 1803

As it is not my time of attendance in the Hospital, I cannot tell whether there is a vacancy for a poor patient in it. Tomorrow is the public admission day. Please to send your poor neighbor to the Hospital about 11 o'clock or a little before that hour. I will attend there and plead his cause (with your note in my hand) with the managers. If he should be admitted without pay, it will only be necessary for a friend to give an obligation for five dollars to defray the expenses of his interment in case of his death. From the report of one of my pupils of the Hospital being less filled than usual with patients, I think it highly probable there will be little or no difficulty in getting your neighbor admitted.

Yours very affectionately,

BENJN RUSH

MS: Captain F. L. Pleadwell, Honolulu.

To Thomas Jefferson

Dear Sir,   Philadelphia, May 5th, 1803

I was made very happy by learning from your letter of the 23rd of April[1] that your disease is less troublesome than formerly. As I know you have no faith in the *principles* of our science,[2] I shall from time to time combat your prejudices and your disease (should it continue) by means of *facts*. Ever since I began the practice of medicine, I have kept commonplace books in which I have recorded the results of the observations of my patients and friends upon the causes, symptoms, and cure of diseases. From these sources I think I have derived much useful knowledge. In the course of the last month I have added to my stock of facts upon the diarrhoea the history of the following cases:

1. A gentleman of great worth, Mr. George Clymer, informed me a few days ago that he had been afflicted occasionally for fifteen years with a bowel complaint, and that it had yielded to his wearing muslin shirts only, for the last two years of his life.

[863]

2. An old nurse whom I met a few weeks ago in a sickroom told me she had been cured of a diarrhoea of three years' continuance by drawing the breasts of a woman (who had lost her child) and swallowing her milk. The cure in this case was accidental, for she did not expect it. It was effected in a single month. Cows' milk may be made to partake of the qualities of women's milk by adding a little sugar to it.

I have read your creed[3] with great attention and was much pleased to find you are by no means so heterodox as you have been supposed to be by your enemies. I do not think with you in your account of the character and mission of the Author of our Religion, and my opinions are the result of a long and patient investigation of that subject. You shall receive my creed shortly. In the meanwhile we will agree to disagree. From the slender influence which opinions in religion have upon morals, and from the bad practices of many people who have graduated themselves at the highest point in the scale of orthodoxy, I have long ceased to consider principles of any kind as the criterion of disposition and conduct, and much less of our future acceptance at the bar of the Supreme Judge of the World.[4]

The prevalence of a narrow spirit in our country with respect to principles, to which you allude, shall induce me faithfully to comply with your request by not communicating the contents of your creed even to your friends.

Adieu! my dear sir. May the Ruler of Nations direct and prosper you in all your duties and enterprises in the present difficult and awful posture of human affairs!

From your sincere *old* friend,

BENJN: RUSH

P.S. I am sorry to inform you that your friend Mr. Mason[5] is in the lowest stage of a general dropsy under Dr. Reynolds'[6] and my care. He has precipitated the danger by his long, rapid, and debilitating ride to our city.

MS: Library of Congress, Jefferson Papers.

[1] Printed in Jefferson's *Writings*, ed. Lipscomb and Bergh, XIX, 133.

[2] Of many statements by Jefferson on the folly of medical theorizing and his preference for letting nature take its course when reliable clinical data on a disease were lacking, one of the best is his letter to Dr. Caspar Wistar, 21 June 1807 (same, XI, 242-8). The subject of Jefferson and medical science has been suggestively treated by Karl Lehmann in *Thomas Jefferson, American Humanist*, N.Y., 1947, ch. v, but it deserves a monograph.

[3] "Syllabus of an Estimate of the Merit of the Doctrines of Jesus, com-

pared with those of others," sent to BR with Jefferson's letter of 21 Apr. 1803 (printed in *Writings*, ed. Lipscomb and Bergh, x, 379-85). At Jefferson's request, his letter and "Syllabus" were returned to him after BR's death (Jefferson to Richard Rush, 31 May 1813, Rush Family Papers, deposited in Princeton University Library).

[4] BR apparently never sent his own "creed" to Jefferson. In his comment on Jefferson's, BR reveals how tolerant he remained of others' religious views while growing more conservative in his own.

[5] Stevens Thomson Mason (1760-1803), a graduate of the College of William and Mary and a leading Virginia lawyer and politician, had been a U.S. senator from 1794 and a staunch supporter of Jefferson; he died on 10 May (DAB).

[6] James Reynolds (d. 1808), Irish patriot and exile, had practised in Philadelphia since 1796, and is reported by BR to have died of alcoholism. BR nevertheless esteemed Reynolds' "talents and knowledge"—an esteem perhaps enhanced by the fact that Cobbett had attacked Reynolds along with BR. (BR, *Autobiography*, p. 322 and note; William Cobbett, *Rush-Light*, No. II, p. 62.)

To James Rush

My dear Son,   Philadelphia, May 24, 1803

At the request of your mother I sit down to answer your letter of the 17th of this month. I shall begin by taking notice of several things in your letter which are faulty in point of spelling and composition. You have spelled *regions—reigions, sure—shure, bad—bade, everbody—everybody,*[1] and the words *again* and *draw* occur too often in a near connection with each other. Avoid these inaccuracies in future. Always suppose when you are writing, even a note upon the most trivial subject, that your performance may fall into the hands of an enemy and be conveyed by him into a newspaper, and if it should be incorrectly written that it may ruin your reputation as a scholar and a gentleman for life. Attend to punctuation in writing. Your last letter is deficient in it. The best writers use the greatest number of points.[2] They add very much to the perspicuity of all compositions.

We were all much pleased with your generosity to your aunt in giving her your portion of oranges. We regret that you forgot to carry the little book I gave you to be presented to her. It shall be sent by the first private opportunity that offers.

We have heard such satisfactory accounts from your sister Emely (since you left us) of the character, prospects, and family of Mr. M. [*Manners*], that your parents have consented to his wishes without requiring him to relinquish his profession. He is the eldest son of a man of fortune who is now very old. He expects to be provided for when his father dies, at which time he will return to private life in his native country. Nothing must be said upon this subject to anybody till you hear further from us.

Adieu! All the family join in love to you. We were pleased to hear of Mr. Howard[3] being your roommate. Cherish a friendship for him. All his connections in Philadelphia have always treated your Mama and sisters with kindness and respect.

From your affectionate father,

BENJN: RUSH

P.S. Read—read—read. Remember the most precious drop time distills from its alembic is the present NOW.

Addressed: Mr James Rush at the College at Princeton New Jersey.
MS: Library Company of Philadelphia, Rush MSS.

[1] BR has confusingly reversed the order in the last pair of words, and *may* have done so in the next-to-last pair.
[2] Happily BR did not usually follow this bad principle.
[3] John Eager Howard, Jr. (1788-1822), who graduated at Princeton in 1806, was the son of a well-known governor of Maryland (see DAB); his mother was Margaret Chew of Germantown; he later served as an officer in the volunteer forces gathered to resist the British invasion of Maryland, 1814, and in the Maryland Senate, 1816-1817 (Alumni Records, Secretary's Office, Princeton Univ.).

To John Montgomery

My dear Friend,   Philadelphia, May 30th, 1803

You will perceive by a letter addressed to you as president of the board of trustees that we have been obliged to decline an application to our citizens for subscriptions for the College. At the present time distress from numerous failures is nearly universal, especially among that class of people who are most disposed to give to public institutions. In addition to this cause of declining to solicit benefactions, the stock of charity and public spirit has been nearly exhausted by our late liberal contributions to the College of Princeton—and to the sufferers by the fire at Portsmouth and by the yellow fever in our own city as well as in other cities of the United States.

I *am not* pleased with your proposed plan for extending and enlarging your building so as to accommodate the students under one roof.[1] It will require more money to finish than you will collect in half a century in our country and will moreover prevent your paying your just debts, particularly the large debt due to Dr. Nesbit. After all your labor should you succeed in it, you will not thereby advance the true interests of the College. Crowding boys under one roof has always been found unfriendly to order and hurtful to morals. The boys at Princeton were never so orderly as they were while they were boarded in private houses during the rebuilding of the College. This was so remarkable that I yesterday heard a gentleman from that village say it would be an advantage to the students if the College were again to be burned down. Think, my friend, of these things before you get swamped in mortar in attempting to carry your new plan of building into execution. The sum at present collected will, I have been told, replace the old house with some improvements. Let the next generation extend and enlarge it, if it should be necessary.

We have had a large and truly respectable meeting of the ministers of the Presbyterian Church in Philadelphia. Great harmony and brotherly love has appeared among them, and great zeal and industry in promoting the objects of their meeting. Several of their popular preachers have excited the attention of citizens and drawn crowds of hearers after them, particularly Dr. Dwight,[2] President of the College at New Haven, Mr. Kollock[3] of Elizabeth town, and Mr. Miller[4] of New York. Dr. Dwight pleases and instructs in conversation not less than in the pulpit. He is animated, polite, and full of matter in all companies. Mr. Kollack is zealous, eloquent, and impressive in his manner, while his sermons are rich with pious sentiments. Mr. Miller is sensible, elegant, and correct, and never permits attention to flag for a moment. Besides those three excellent preachers, we have had a number of fervent discourses from young men who have witnessed the late revivals of religion in the western parts of our country.

Adieu! from, my dear friend, yours sincerely,

BENJN: RUSH

Addressed: John Montgomery Esqr: at Carlisle Pennsylvania.
MS: Library Company of Philadelphia, Rush MSS.

[1] The board nevertheless proceeded to erect the handsome and commodious building, still standing, known as West College, from plans to which Benjamin H. Latrobe contributed (Morgan, *Dickinson College*, p. 90ff.; Latrobe to H. H. Brackenridge, 18 May 1803, *Dickinson Alumnus*, Dec. 1948, p. 21-3). BR contributed generously to the new building, but he emphatically declined to have his name publicly inscribed as a donor; see his letter to

James Hamilton, 27 June 1810.

[2] Timothy Dwight (1752-1817), Congregational clergyman, poet, traveler, and president of Yale, 1795-1817 (DAB).

[3] Henry Kollock (1778-1819), a graduate of the College of New Jersey, 1794; minister of the Presbyterian church at Elizabeth, 1800-1803; professor of theology at Princeton, 1803-1806; afterwards minister of a church

in Savannah; a noted preacher (Sprague, *Annals*, IV, 263-74).

[4] Samuel Miller (1769-1850), brother of BR's friend Dr. Edward Miller and a graduate of the University of Pennsylvania, 1789, studied theology under Nisbet at Carlisle; D.D., College of New Jersey, 1792; one of the pastors of the associated Presbyterian churches, N.Y., 1793-1809, and pastor of the Wall St. Church, 1809-1813; thereafter professor of church history and government in Princeton Theological Seminary, of which he was one of the founders. Miller was a prolific writer of books and pamphlets on a great variety of sub-

jects, but his most remarkable performance was *A Brief Retrospect of the Eighteenth Century*, N.Y., 1803, 2 vol. —a review of all cultural fields that is still well worth consulting. BR, as some letters below indicate, occasionally helped Miller with his biographical works and was an admirer of his talents. In 1808 BR did his best to induce Miller to accept the presidency of Dickinson College, but Miller knew Nisbet's difficulties too well to accept. (DAB; Princeton Univ., *Gen. Cat.*, 1908; BR's letters to Miller, especially in 1808, below; Miller's letters to BR, in Rush MSS, XXVII.)

To Thomas Jefferson

Dear Sir,   Philadelphia, June 11th, 1803

I have endeavored to fulfil your wishes by furnishing Mr. Lewis with some inquiries relative to the natural history of the Indians.[1] The enclosed letter contains a few short directions for the preservation of his health, as well as the health of the persons under his command.[2]

His mission is truly interesting. I shall wait with great solicitude for its issue. Mr. Lewis appears admirably qualified for it. May its advantages prove no less honorable to your administration than to the interests of science!

The enclosed letter from Mr. Sumpter[3] contains some new views of the present military arrangements of France and Great Britain. You need not return it.

From, dear sir, yours very respectfully and sincerely,

BENJN: RUSH

MS: Rush Family Papers, deposited in Princeton University Library.

[1] BR's "Questions [concerning the western Indians] to Merryweather Lewis before he went up the Missouri" are printed in BR's *Autobiography*, p. 265-6, from a copy in his Commonplace Book.

[2] These "Directions," not now with the letter (which was returned by Jefferson with some other BR letters to Richard Rush in 1816), are also printed in the *Autobiography*, p. 267, from the

Commonplace Book. It is worth noting that Jefferson took a copy of them for his own files, which is in L.C., Jefferson Papers, under the present date. There are several mentions of the remarkable effectiveness, on whites and Indians alike, of Dr. Rush's "opening" pills (no doubt the old and powerful compound of calomel and jalap) in R. G. Thwaites' edition of the *Original Journals of the Lewis and Clark Ex-*

pedition, N.Y., 1904-1905, I, 269; II, 278-81.

[3] Thomas Sumter, Jr. (1768-1840), of South Carolina, was secretary of lega-

tion in Paris, 1801-1803, and minister to Brazil, 1810-1821 (A. K. Gregoire, *Thomas Sumter*, Columbia, S.C., 1931, p. 30, 247-8, 254, 262, 267).

To James Rush

My dear Son,   Philadelphia, June 22, 1803

Your letter dated 21st of June is just now received. We had not forgotten you, but having nothing new to communicate, we deferred writing till something should seem worthy of your notice.

We have had several letters from Canada within these few weeks. Your sisters are both well. As no opportunity will probably offer of Mary returning in the manner she expected, we have concluded to send your brother Richard for her. He will pass through Princeton about the middle of July, and if no evil befalls them they will return in August or about the beginning of September. All matters are now settled between Mary and Mr. ——— [*Manners*] to the satisfaction of both parties. They wait only to hear from Mr. M.'s father to know whether the business will end in a connection for life.

We are all, thank God! in good health. Little William terrified the whole family a few days ago by a fall which has cut through his eyebrow and a portion of his forehead. He behaved like an old man while it was dressed. It is now healing kindly, and he is again as playful and talkative as ever.

I observe in your letter of this morning you have divided the word *remembrance* in the middle of a syllable. This should never be done in writing. I observe likewise you subscribe your name in a different hand from that in which your letter is written. Avoid this in future. It looks like affectation. Dr. Franklin avoided it in all his letters. "Ex simplicitate decus"[1] should govern our most trifling compositions. Dr. Franklin when a young man was in the habit of writing his name with a flourish. An old man who saw it by accident cried out, "What fool's name is this?" Ever afterwards the Doctor wrote his name in a plain and simple manner. Take care of your teeth. Take care likewise of your health. Use gentle but general exercise of your body. Avoid sleeping with your windows open or sitting near a current of air when you are warm. A cold taken at your time of life, or weakness of body contracted from the want of exercise, might end in disease in your breast that would terminate your studies or even your life.

Adieu! We all love you—nay more, we respect you, for we hear of your sober and amiable conduct by every person that knows you at Princeton.

Continue to visit in your uncle's family and to treat every branch of it with respect and affection.

From, my dear son, your affectionate father,

BENJN: RUSH

P.S. Do not, my dear son, forget the design of [. . .]ing² studies in your rooms which I mentioned to you the morning you left Philadelphia.

𝑀𝑆: Library Company of Philadelphia, Rush MSS.

¹ "Dignity derives from simplicity." I have not identified the source.
² Illegible. BR may have intended "evening studies," but he has not written it.

To Horatio Gates

My dear and venerable Friend,   Philadelphia, July 27th, 1803

Old age has no cure, but its aches and pains may be alleviated by medicine, and life may thereby be protracted. Happy shall I think myself if I can suggest any remedies that shall have that effect upon yours. If my skill were equal to my respect and affection for you, you should not only enjoy your wishes to see the close of the present war between Great Britain and France in their utmost extent, but you should live to see all the fond hopes we entertained during our Revolution completely realized, of the extinction of wars and of universal liberty and happiness pervading every part of our globe, for these events are predicted in holy writ and must come to pass as certainly as the rising of tomorrow's sun.

The remedies which appear to be proper in your case are:

1. The warm bath. It was this which smoothed the descent of Dr. Franklin down the hill of life and helped to prolong it beyond 84 years. Begin with water about the heat of your body, and gradually increase it two, three, or four degrees. It may be used three times a week or daily, according to its effects upon you. The best time of using it is between twelve and one o'clock. The body should be well dried and gently rubbed afterwards, and rest should be taken until 2 o'clock or the usual hour of dining.

2. We had a physician in our city many years ago who lived to be between 80 and 90, who took, after he began to feel the pains and weaknesses of age, a clove of garlic every morning and evening. It is cordial, and alike invigorating to the body and mind.

3. Port wine, also old brandy with loaf sugar dissolved in it, have often restrained discharges from the bowels from all their causes. There are likewise many astringent medicines, such as every doctor or apothecary can mention to you, that are useful for the same purpose. In addition to those remedies, try injections into your bowels composed of a gill of flaxseed tea, or mutton broth, or milk, with from 20 to 50 drops of laudanum in each of them every day. They will be most useful at bedtime but will be proper likewise in the morning.

4. Your food should be of a cordial nature. Small and frequent meals should be preferred to but one or two in the day. Eat as soon as you wake in the morning, and if you are sleepless or restless, eat even without appetite in the middle of the night.

5. Go to bed early. Also, 6ly. Lie down occasionally during the day. Sleep upon the first floor of your house. Few things are more fatiguing and disagreeable to old people than climbing a pair of stairs.

7. Sit, also sleep in a stove room well ventilated in cool and cold weather. Let the heat of this room be the same in the night that it is in the day. An old German physician of the name of Dr. Wit[1] died at Germantown about 40 years ago who owed a life of nearly an 100 years chiefly to his living after he was 70 in an artificial warm climate, rendered so by means of stoves kept always in an uniform temperature.

Accept of my dear Mrs. Rush's and my thanks for your kind invitation to visit you and your good lady at Rose hill. Gladly, very gladly, would we accept of it, but a large and expensive family chain me to the pestle and mortar. Be assured you have no friend in the United States who more highly appreciates your worth than I do, or who thinks and talks of you with more affection. The pleasant day we passed together in the month of July 1777, on your way to take the command of the army which captured General Burgoyne, can never pass from my mind. We feasted upon schemes and plans of national happiness, for the words "national glory" had no place then in the political vocabulary of the United States. They should be written or printed with red ink whenever they are used, to denote that they have issued in all ages and countries from rivers of human blood.

Adieu. Mrs. Rush joins in affectionate regards to Mrs. Gates with your sincere old friend,

BENJN: RUSH

P.S. In my 59th year I am blessed by a kind providence with uncommon good health. My labors and studies are now directed exclusively to the benefit of my patients and the happiness of my family. Thus limited in my pursuits, and patiently suffering ignorance and error to enjoy their repose upon subjects on which I once disturbed them, I am kindly *tolerated* by my fellow citizens and at last live peaceably with all men.

Addressed: General Horatio Gates Rose Hill near New York.
MS: New York Public Library, Emmet Collection.

[1] Christopher Witt (1675-1765), last survivor of Kelpius' "Mystic Community" on the Wissahickon, practised for many years in Germantown; a botanist, clockmaker, musician, and astronomer, he was regarded by the superstitious as a "hexen-meister" or magus (J. F. Sachse, *The German Pietists of Provincial Pennsylvania*, Phila., 1895, p. 402-18).

To Thomas Jefferson[1]

Dear Sir,   Philadelphia, August 5th, 1803

I return you herewith Sir John Sinclair's pamphlet upon Old Age with many thanks.[2] I have read it with pleasure and subscribe to the truth of most of his opinions. They accord with opinions which I published many years ago in the 2nd volume of my *Medical Inquiries and Observations*.[3]

I have just finished reading Colonel now Sir Robt. Wilson's account of the British campaign in Egypt.[4] It is well written and is a very popular work in our city, chiefly from its containing the history of the cruelties exercised by Bonaparte's army[5] in that country. Its merit to me consists much more in the facts he has related respecting the plague. The annexed extract from one of our newspapers contains the substance of them. They will be followed, Sir Robert says, by several valuable publications by medical men in which the nonimportation, noncontagion, and domestic origin of the plague will be fully and clearly proved. I wish this subject occupied more of the attention of the legislators of all countries. The laws which are now in force in every part of the world to prevent the importation of malignant fevers are absurd, expensive, vexatious, and oppressive to a great degree. Posterity will view them in the same light that we now view horseshoes at the doors of farmers' houses to defend them from witches. We originally imported our opinions of the contagious nature of the plague from the ignorant and degraded inhabitants of Egypt. It is high time to reject them from countries where free inquiry is tolerated upon all subjects connected with the interests and happiness of nations. There is more hope upon this subject from *laws* than upon many others. A thousand considerations oppose the extinction of wars which cannot operate upon the extermination of pestilential diseases. There is no moral evil in them, and of course no obstacles to their destruction but what arise from ignorance and prejudice. It would seem as if a certain portion of superstition belonged necessarily to the human mind, and that that part of it which had been banished from religion had taken sanctuary in medicine; hence thousands of the citizens of the United States who would be ashamed to exclaim, "Great is Diana of Ephesus,"[6] now openly and zealously cry out, "Great are the quarantines of all our states."

From, dear sir, with great respect, your sincere old friend of 1775,

BENJN RUSH

P.S. Had not Bonaparte been a believer in the contagion of the plague, he would not have added to his other crimes the destruction of 580 of his soldiers who were confined with the plague, lest they should infect his whole army. There is no calculating the amount of the cruelty and misery which have issued from a belief in that most absurd doctrine. It is just now beginning to produce distress of every kind in the city of New York. Our citizens instead of offering its inhabitants an asylum have this day interdicted all intercourse with them by land and water.

MS: Not located; typewritten transcript in University of Pennsylvania Library.

¹ Though the MS of this letter has not been located, its authenticity is attested by an entry for it in Jefferson's Epistolary Record (L.C.). Undoubtedly the original was one of the several returned by Jefferson to Richard Rush, at the request of the latter, after BR's death (Jefferson to Richard Rush, 16 Dec. 1816, Rush Family Papers, deposited in Princeton University Library), for the transcript bears a copy of an endorsement reading: "My father to Mr. Jefferson," &c.
² *An Essay on Longevity*, London,

1802.
³ "An Account of the State of the Body and Mind in Old Age," *Med. Inq. & Obs.*, II (1793), 293-321. BR's "Account" was later reprinted in Sir John Sinclair's compendium called *The Code of Health and Longevity*, Edinburgh, 1807, IV, 514-31.
⁴ Sir Robert Thomas Wilson, *History of the British Expedition to Egypt*, London, 1802; frequently reissued (Allibone, *Dict. of Authors*).
⁵ This word omitted in transcript.
⁶ Acts 19:34.

To John Dickinson

Philadelphia, August 6th, 1803

Permit an old and sincere friend to express his sympathy with you in the late afflicting dispensation which has occurred in your family.[1] To a mind stored as yours is, with that kind of knowledge which alone can afford comfort when our friends die, or when we are to die ourselves, nothing new can be suggested. I am sure (to use the words I once saw upon a ring) you believe the beloved friend and companion of your life is "not lost but gone before."

Often have I lamented my inability from increasing labors and duties in Philadelphia to accomplish my long wished-for visit to Wilmington. We once proposed meeting and spending a long evening at Chester. How many subjects would open upon us! A week would not be sufficient to talk over all that *has been* since we parted and all that is *now* passing before us in different parts of the world. Of what is to be hereafter, it would become us to be silent or only to say, "Thy kingdom come, thy will be done."

Please to communicate my respectful compliments to the young ladies of your family, and accept of assurances of esteem and affection of your sincere friend,

BENJN: RUSH

MS: Historical Society of Pennsylvania, Logan Papers.

[1] Dickinson's wife had died on 23 July (Keith, *Provincial Councillors*, p. 53).

To Thomas Eddy[1]

Dear Sir, Philadelphia, October 19, 1803

Tired out, and distressed with the unsuccessful issue of all my public labors for the benefit of my fellow citizens, I have for some years past limited my studies and duties wholly to my profession. Of course I must be excused from undertaking the work you have suggested to me. I shall mention it to Charles Brown.[2] He possesses talents more than equal to it. The subject would glow under the eloquent strokes of his masterly pen. I wish the history of our prison may not some years hence end with an account of the restoration of our old laws for whipping, cropping, burning in the hand, and taking away life. Many of our citizens wish for it, and I am sorry to say the manner in which our mild penal code has of late years been executed has furnished too much reason for retrograde opinions upon this important subject.

I have read your publication[3] with great satisfaction. It is well composed and is calculated to silence all controversy upon the practicability of our system of conforming punishments to Christian principles. I concur with you in all the amendments you have proposed to the arrangements of your prison. Solitary beds and rooms are a great desideratum for the convicts. They are calculated to awaken delicacy, which is one of the outposts of virtue, and to favor reflection, repentance, and silent or oral devotion. The salt meat or salt fish in the diet of the prisoners in the summer and autumnal months I conceive to be judicious. It has been known in many instances to prevent fevers and bowel complaints, both of which I observe are common diseases in your jail. In addition to the common diet mentioned in your publication, what do you think of allowing them from private contributions a more plentiful meal of less cheap or common aliment once or twice a year on some public day? Would it not tend to show them that the ties which once connected them with their fellow men are not totally dissolved, and that a fund of kindness still existed in their breasts towards them even while they were suffering for the injuries they had done to them? In this way the kind parent of the human race often visits his most refractory children, and sometimes by that means brings them back again to himself. The practice would tend further to convey to the criminals an idea of the mixture of divine mercy with divine justice, so as to extinguish all resentments against their fellow creatures as far as they were excited by their conviction and punishments, and to work upon the *fragments* of *good* which are left in them, for I believe there never was a soul so completely shipwrecked by vice that something divine was not saved from its wreck.

I shall never think our penal code perfect till we deprive our laws of the power of taking away life for *any* crime. It is in my opinion murder to punish murder by death. It is an act of legal revenge, for it does justice to neither the injured friends of the deceased nor to the state. Noah's command[4] is no more an authority for it than his excess in drinking is a precedent for drunkenness. We should found our laws wholly upon the mild religion and just precepts of Jesus Christ.

With great respect for your zeal and industry in advancing the interests of humanity and justice, I am, dear sir, your sincere friend,

BENJN: RUSH

[875]

Addressed: Mr. Thomas Eddy New York.
MS: New York Public Library, Miscellaneous Papers.

[1] Thomas Eddy (1758-1827), of Philadelphia Quaker origins, made a fortune in trade in New York, devoted himself to philanthropic causes, and earned the name of "the Howard of America." Inspired by the reformed regime at the Walnut Street jail in Philadelphia, he supervised the construction of a penitentiary in New York. (DAB.) In a letter of 6 Oct. 1803 (Rush MSS, IV), to which BR is replying, Eddy had urged BR to prepare a history of the penal laws of Pennsylvania.

[2] Doubtless the novelist Charles Brockden Brown (1771-1810), who was then in Philadelphia (DAB).

[3] Probably *An Account of the State Prison or Penitentiary House in the City of New York*, 1801, which is an important contribution to prison reform.

[4] I.e., God's command to Noah; see Genesis 9:6.

To James Rush

My dear Son,   Philadelphia, November 18, 1803

Herewith you will receive your boots. They will serve I hope two purposes: 1st, to keep your feet and legs warm during the winter, and 2ly, to remind you that you have a father and mother in Philadelphia who have never forgotten you for a *whole week* since you came into the world. O fie—O fie, James!

I never knew an instance of a man becoming eminent, respectable, or even wealthy in the profession of medicine who was deficient in punctuality in letter writing.

Adieu! From your affectionate though neglected parents,

BENJN and JULIA RUSH[1]

Addressed: Mr James Rush at the College at Princeton New Jersey. By Mr Riddle.
MS: Library Company of Philadelphia, Rush MSS.

[1] Both signatures are in BR's hand.

To James Rush

My dear Son,   Philadelphia, November 25th, 1803

Your parents were so much pleased with your letter that they have agreed to absolve you for your neglect of them after your return to college. We suppose the poetry contained in it to be yours. It has merit, and though not perfectly correct is a fair and promising specimen of future excellencies in that species of composition. A talent for poetry is often connected with that talent for extensive observation which has been found eminently useful in the science of medicine. Some of our best physicians have been poets, and some of the best descriptions of diseases that are extant have been written by poets who were not physicians. There is no history of madness in a medical book equal to Shakespeare's descriptions of it in the characters of Lear and Edgar.[1] Take care only that an attachment to poetry does not seduce you from the more solid and useful studies in which you are engaged.

I am sorry to hear that your eyes are diseased. Take a little physic, and abstain from eating meat and butter for a few days. Wash them at the same time frequently with *cold* water. When the inflammation is a little reduced, wash them in a solution of a scruple of sugar of lead in a common-sized teacupful of water or green tea.

Sitting one day or two in a dark room will be useful if the above remedies do not relieve you. Consult Dr. McClen[2] or Dr. Stockton[3] in your case. My respectful compliments to them!

All the family except John are well. He is a good deal afflicted with the jaundice. Should you see your Aunt Stockton soon, give my love to her, and tell her her new neighbor Mrs. Scudder[4] is a relation of mine and is an amiable and well-educated woman, worthy of her acquaintance and patronage. Your Mama thinks highly of her. I beg *you* would, when an opportunity offers, introduce yourself to her, and when convenient, visit her. She is the daughter of a much beloved first cousin of your father's.

Adieu! All the family join in love to you with yours affectionately,

BENJN: RUSH

Addressed: Mr James Rush Student at the College at Princeton New-Jersey.
MS: Library Company of Philadelphia, Rush MSS.

[1] In *Diseases of the Mind*, BR speaks of *King Lear* as an "inimitable history of all the forms of derangement" (p. 94), and quotes from it some eight or ten times in the course of his treatise.

[2] John Maclean, M.D. (1771-1814), a Scot who had been trained at Glasgow and other European scientific centers, came to Philadelphia in 1795 and was advised by BR to settle at Princeton. Beginning his practice in partnership with Ebenezer Stockton (see next note), he was shortly appointed to the chair of chemistry and natural history in the College, and in 1797 to that of mathematics and natural philosophy. He made pioneer contributions to chemical knowledge, and his son John became tenth president of Princeton. (DAB; John Maclean, *A Memoir of John Maclean, M.D.*, Princeton, 1876.)

[3] Ebenezer Stockton (1760-1837), son of Maj. Robert Stockton of Princeton and hence a relative of Mrs. Rush's, graduated from the College of New Jersey, 1780; surgeon in the Continental army both before and after his graduation. It is not known where he was formally trained, but he practised successfully in Princeton for many years. (Hageman, *Hist. of Princeton*, I, 223-4; Alumni Records, Secretary's Office, Princeton Univ.)

[4] Not further identified.

To John Montgomery

My dear Friend,   Philadelphia, February 9th, 1804[1]

I sincerely condole with you in your grief for the death of your son and my former pupil.[2] He had uncommon talents and great integrity. I hope his conduct was in all respects such that you and his other connections will be able to say of him, "not lost, but gone before."

The death of Dr. Nesbit was expected in our city before your letter came to hand. He has carried out of our world an uncommon stock of every kind of knowledge. Few such men have lived and died in any country. I shall long, very long, remember with pleasure his last visit to Philadelphia, at which time he dined with me in company with Dr. Dwight of New Haven and Dr. Cooper of our state. His conversation was unusually instructing and brilliant, and his anecdotes full of original humor and satire. I hope the trustees have done honor to his memory by a funeral sermon and by defraying the expenses of his interment.[3]

Who is to be his successor?

The College at Princeton has revived and flourishes more than ever in consequence of the uncommon pains that are taken to instruct the young men in the principles of the Christian religion. They recite lessons constantly out of the Bible and Campbell's and Paley's evidences of the truth of Christianity, and they are to be examined from each of those books previously to their being admitted to the honors of the College. In this way only they will be prepared in future life to resist the flimsy declamations of infidel writers, as well as to regulate their conduct by a system of morals which they never can cease to believe are of divine original.

I hope a similar mode of instructing young men in the evidences of the truth of our religion and in Scriptural knowledge will be introduced into the College of Carlisle.

Adieu! my dear old friend, from your very affectionate friend,

BENJN: RUSH

Addressed: John Montgomery Esqr Carlisle Pennsylvania.
MS: Library Company of Philadelphia, Rush MSS.

[1] After the return of this letter BR added a note on the date saying, "It should be later." But it is certainly correct, for Nisbet had died on 18 Jan. 1804 (Morgan, *Dickinson College*, p. 154).

[2] William Montgomery; he had been apprenticed to BR in 1779 (MS List of Apprentices).

[3] Whether or not these suggestions were followed, the trustees made a settlement of nearly $7,000 with Nisbet's heirs for the salary arrears due to the late Principal (Morgan, *Dickinson College*, p. 154).

To James Rush

My dear Son,   Philadelphia, March 27, 1804

The delay of your parents to answer your last letter was occasioned by the treatment they have received from you ever since your last return to Princeton, *manifested* in the careless manner in which your letters to them have been written. Your last was scarcely[1] legible, and in point of composition such as we thought very improper for a junior student in the College at Princeton and a young man of 18 years of age. From a sense of duty I shall continue my usual kindness to you. I have therefore enclosed you the money you have requested (25 dollars) from your distressed and offended father,

BENJN: RUSH

P.S. [*in Mrs. Rush's hand*] Bring home all your old clothes. We have a boy to whom they will be useful.

J R

Addressed: Mr James Rush Student of the College of New Jersey Princeton. *MS*: Library Company of Philadelphia, Rush MSS.

[1] MS: "scarely"!

To David Howell

Dear Sir,   Philadelphia, April 27, 1804

Scabs such as you have described on your face often occur between the ages of 60 and 70.[1] They rarely end in cancer, and never except when they are neglected or treated with improper remedies.

A plaster made of equal parts of tar and beeswax should be spread on a piece of black silk or leather and worn constantly upon the affected parts. It will do most service when applied immediately after the falling of the scab.

If this application do not cure the sores in five or six weeks, apply to them a little white arsenic wetted with water, and cover them afterwards with a soft plaster made of beeswax and sweet oil. Repeat the application of arsenic three or four times at intervals of three or four days, still covering it with the plaster of wax and oil. This remedy is generally so effectual in removing the disease for which I have prescribed it, that it will be unnecessary to mention any others.

Your diet should by no means be abstemious. You may eat eggs, oysters, fish, and a little animal food daily with safety and advantage. The sores on your face are of a local nature. Your blood is not in the least tainted with any humor connected with them. A little wine may be taken with the above food.

I shall not name a cancer doctor to you, for you are in no more danger of that disease from your present trifling and superficial complaint than you are of a dropsy or pulmonary consumption.

Dr. Physick concurs with me in the above advice.

No internal medicines of any kind are indicated in your case.

From, dear sir, yours very respectfully,

BENJN: RUSH

Fee 5 Dollars.

Addressed: David Howell Esqr: Providence Rhode Island.
MS: Mr. Lloyd W. Smith, Madison, New Jersey.

[1] BR is replying to a letter from Howell dated from Providence, R.I., 22 Apr. 1804; in Rush MSS, VII.

To John Coakley Lettsom

Dear Sir, Philadelphia, May 13, 1804

I am sorry to perceive by your letter[1] that we still differ in our opinions respecting the origin and means of preventing the yellow fever. It is always the offspring of putrid exhalations from *dead* animal and vegetable matters. Beyond and out of the reach of such exhalations, a yellow fever never did exist, as an epidemic, in any age or country. It is *not* contagious, and never spreads beyond the influence of the atmosphere in which it is generated. It dies when carried into the country, even in crowded rooms where the attendants upon the sick receive their breath for days and weeks. It even dies in our yellow-fever hospitals in the vicinity of our cities. It is true it sometimes puts on the symptoms of your typhus fever. This, however, is rarely the case; but it differs materially from your typhus, which is the offspring of exhalations from sickly or filthy or half-famished human bodies, and which spreads by what is called the contagion of excretion within the circle of the persons who attend or visit the sick. This fever spreads alike in country places and cities, under equal circumstances of filth, famine, and confinement. I lament very much that two forms of fever, so different in their causes and characters, have been confounded, inasmuch as error is calculated to increase and perpetuate the evils produced by the yellow fever, by unnecessary and nugatory quarantines and the total neglect of cleanliness.[2]

From the sameness of the stories with respect to the contagious nature of the yellow fever, published by two or three weak and illiterate practitioners of medicine in our city (all of which are not only erroneous but highly ridiculous), with those that are intended to establish the contagious nature of the plague, I am still disposed to believe the latter disease can originate and spread *only* in an atmosphere contaminated by exhalations from putrid animal and vegetable matters.

The separation of the sick from the healthy has been repeatedly tried to no purpose to check the progress of our yellow fever. It originates frequently in half a dozen places in our city remote from each other and at the *same* time.

Be assured, my friend, our yellow fever is no other disease than a higher grade of the common bilious fever of warm climates and seasons. From causes unknown, but probably existing in a change in the atmosphere, it has appeared of late in many parts of the world that have for centuries been strangers to it. A less malignant grade of it than that which prevails in our country has lately visited yours. Dr. Simson[3] has described one at Birmingham, and Mr. White[4] one at Bath. The latter calls it, very happily, "a diminutive yellow fever."

Our epidemic of last year yielded to sudorific medicines only when they were preceded or aided by bleeding and purges.

The extremes of heat and cold, by producing greater extremes of violence in our fevers than in yours, call for more depletion, and from more outlets, than the fevers of Great Britain.[5] Your citizens in the first ranks are debilitated by luxury, while those of the lower ranks are debilitated by scanty food and excess of labor. Hence the low and chronic forms of your fevers, and hence also the propriety of the cordial and tonic remedies employed in curing them. Our citizens of the first rank live plentifully, but upon simple food, and spend the intervals between their meals in active business instead of enervating pleasures. Our lower classes of citizens likewise live plentifully and enjoy frequent relaxations from labor; hence the inflammatory type of our fevers, and hence also the propriety and success of the depleting remedies so generally employed among them.

I remain, &c.,

BENJ. RUSH

Printed: Pettigrew, *Lettsom*, III, 196-9.

¹ Of 22 Feb. 1804; in Rush MSS, XXVIII.

² Since BR believed that yellow fever originated locally, he held that the only method of prevention was by local sanitation; those who believed the fever was imported urged quarantine measures. Both sides were right, for both sanitation and quarantine were essential to prevention. See Dr. Corner's note in BR's *Autobiography*, p. 98.

³ Not identified.

⁴ Perhaps Charles White (1728-

1813), eminent surgeon and obstetrician of Manchester and a founder of the Literary and Philosophical Society of Manchester, who wrote on a variety of medical and scientific subjects (DNB).

⁵ This was a favorite dogma of BR's, accounting in part for his "heroic" therapy. See Ramsay's approving comment on this dogma in his *Eulogium*, p. 22, 27, and Oliver Wendell Holmes' trenchant disapproval in *Currents and Counter-Currents in Medical Science*, Boston, 1861, p. 11, 27.

To John Syng Dorsey¹

My dear young Friend,   Philadelphia, May 23rd, 1804

Your agreeable and unexpected letter gave me great pleasure. I am glad to find you are so well employed. I hope you will bring home with you all the new opinions and modes of practice in medicine and surgery of the London physicians. Their practice in fevers is probably perfectly correct, notwithstanding they do not use the lancet as liberally as your fathers in medicine. The luxurious or scanty diet, and the great excess which prevails among the citizens of London in labor and pleasure, all alike concur to prevent that reaction in the system which renders bleeding necessary, and bark and other stimulating remedies hurtful, in the fevers of your native country.

A wide field opens for medical investigations in the United States. The walls of the "Old School" are daily falling about the ears of its masters and scholars. Come and assist your uncle and his friends in erecting a new fabric upon its ruins. We expect industry, ingenuity, and independence from you, and that under your hands the building will receive some of its neatest and most useful touches. One thing we are confident of—you will never conceal nor deny your opinions when the safety and lives of² a whole city require their being made public.

We expect to confer the first medical honor of our University upon fifteen young men on the 6th of next June. Four of them are my pupils, all of whom are known to you. My son writes upon "the causes of sudden death and the means of preventing it."³ Mr. Pugh against "the healing powers of nature."⁴ Mr. Cocke against Jno. Hunter's doctrine of "air inflaming cavities by its specific qualities, and in favor of its doing so by its inferior grade of heat inducing debility and *that* inviting morbid action."[5] Mr. Jenks writes upon the "sameness of the plague and yellow fever in its causes and modes of prevention."[6] The subjects of the theses of the young gentlemen who do not belong to my shop are chiefly upon pathological or practical subjects. One of them, by Mr. Darlington, will have great merit. It is "upon the influence of habit in curing diseases, and of diseases in curing habits."[7]

Your account of my friend Dr. Pinkard's[8] attentions to you gave me great pleasure. He has knowledge from observation and reflection as well as books. Of how few physicians can the same thing be said!

The marriage of my daughter to the brother of the gentleman[9] whom you met at Dr. Pinkard's table took place in December last. She is now with her husband in Upper Canada. We hear from them weekly. They say they are happy. I am sure they deserve to be so. But the pang which attended the separation of our daughter from her parents is still felt; time we hope will reconcile us to it.

When you see Dr. Pinkard, Dr. Jackson,[10] and Dr. Lettsom, pray make my respectful compliments to them. I have written to Dr. Lettsom lately and suggested some facts in my letter which are intended to shake his belief in the specific contagion of the yellow fever. Does he know the *two pillars* on which he has rested his opinions and reputation on that subject? One of them, Dr. C. [*Currie*], is now a member of our board of health. From the moderation he exercises towards vessels from W. India ports, a suspicion might be inferred that he has changed his opinion. A great relaxation upon the subject of importation has [. . .][11] taken place in the opinions of our merchants. The lapse of a few years I hope will produce universal conviction among them.

Adieu! my dear young friend, and be assured of the continuance of the regard of your sincere friend,

BENJN: RUSH

P.S. Mrs. Rush and all my family join in best wishes for your health and happiness.

My respects to Dr. Carter.[12] I have received his friendly and elegant letter.

I hope you will bring over with you a copy of Dr. Haighton's physiological lectures.[13] Dr. Carter commends it highly.

Addressed: Dr: John S: Dorsey To the Care of Messrs: Bainbridge, Ansley & Co: Merchents London. By the Active Capt L: Jones.

MS: University of Pennsylvania Medical School Library.

[1] John Syng Dorsey (1783-1818), nephew and student of Philip Syng Physick, obtained his M.D. at the University of Pennsylvania, 1802, and studied for two years in London and Paris, returning with a brilliant reputation; adjunct-professor of surgery at the University, 1807, and professor of materia medica, 1816; wrote treatises on surgery (DAB). Some of his letters written while abroad are in the sketch of Dorsey in Gross' *Lives of Physicians and Surgeons*; that to which BR is replying, dated from London, 30 Mch. 1804, is in Rush MSS, XXI.

[2] MS: "and."

[3] John Rush, *An Inaugural Essay on the Causes of Sudden Death and the Means of Preventing It*, Phila., 1804.

[4] Whitmell Hill Pugh, of Virginia, apprenticed to BR in 1802; M.D., 1804; afterwards settled in Windsor, N.C. His thesis was entitled *An Inaugural Essay on the Supposed Powers of Nature in the Cure of Disease*, Phila., 1804. (BR's MS List of Apprentices; Pugh to BR, 3 May 1805, Rush MSS, XIII; Univ. of Penna., *Gen. Alumni Cat.*; *L.C. Cat.*) For BR's own opinions on this point, see his lecture in 1806 on Hippocrates, in which he remarks: "It is impossible to calculate the mischief which Hippocrates has done by first marking nature with his name, and afterwards letting her loose upon sick people" (*Sixteen Introductory Lectures*, p. 286).

[5] James Cocke (ca. 1780-1813), of Virginia, M.D., 1804; he had earlier studied under Astley Cooper in London, and in 1807 became first professor of anatomy in the Medical College of Maryland. His thesis was entitled *An Attempt to Ascertain the Cause of the Extensive Inflammation Which Attacks Wounded Cavities and Their Contents*, Phila., 1804. (E. F. Cordell, *University of Maryland, 1807-1907*, N.Y. and Chicago, 1907, I, 134; Surg. Gen. Off., *Index-Cat.*, 1st ser., III, 241.)

[6] Phineas Jenks, of Pennsylvania, apprenticed to BR, 1801, and M.D., 1804; his thesis was entitled *Essay on the Analogy of the Asiatic and African Plague and the American Yellow Fever, with a View to Prove That They Are the Same Disease Varied by Climate and Other Circumstances*, Phila., 1804 (Univ. of Penna., *Gen. Alumni Cat.*; Surg. Gen. Off., *Index-Cat.*, 1st ser., VII, 236).

[7] William Darlington (1782-1863), of Chester co., Penna., who was to live to earn the name of "the Nestor of American botany" bestowed by Asa Gray. Concerning his extremely interesting thesis, entitled *A Dissertation on the Mutual Influence of Habits and Disease*, Phila., 1804, there is an entertaining anecdote recorded by Darlington in his own copy of the work (now in the possession of Mr. Lucius Wilmerding of Princeton, and quoted with his kind permission):

"When, on the day previous to the *Commencement*, Professor *Rush* called up this *Thesis*, and its *Author*, for examination on its merits, he made the following remarks to the *Faculty* and *Trustees* present. 'This Dissertation, Gentlemen, is a successful application of Metaphysics to the Practice of Physic: I have read it twice through with attention, and have no objection to make to it.' A fellow-graduate, who had just been critically examined, turned to the Author, and laughingly inquired,—'Darlington, is that what you call *defending* your Thesis?' "

[8] George Pinckard, M.D. (1768-1835), had served as a British army physician in the West Indies and had visited Philadelphia in 1797-1798, upon which occasion BR introduced him to Jefferson; he was afterwards physician to the Bloomsbury Dispensary in London (DNB; BR, *Autobiography*, p. 241, 308; see also BR to James Rush, 7 Feb. 1810).

[9] I.e., a brother (not further identified) of Capt. Thomas Manners, whom Mary Rush had married in Canada; see BR to Mary Rush, 1 Apr. 1803, note 1.

[10] Doubtless Robert Jackson, M.D. (1750-1827), who had served in the British military hospitals during the Revolution; he later became inspector general of army hospitals and wrote important works on febrile diseases and military medicine (DNB).

[11] Text torn by seal; one word missing.

[12] Robert Carter (d. 1805), of Shirley on the James, Va.; M.D., Univ. of Penna., 1803; he died, aged 31, soon after his return from his studies in London and Paris (Univ. of Penna., *Gen. Alumni Cat.*; obituary in the Richmond *Virginia Gazette*, 27 Nov. 1805; B. M. Carter to BR, concerning his brother's illness, 5 Sep. 1805, Rush MSS, III). Carter's letter mentioned by BR was dated from London, 25 Feb. 1804, and is in Rush MSS, XXVI.

[13] John Haighton, M.D. (1755-1823), lectured from ca. 1788 on physiology for the united hospitals of St. Thomas' and Guy's; published syllabuses of his lectures at various dates (DNB).

To James Rush

My dear James,   Philadelphia, May 31th[1] 1804

I am very anxious that you should invigorate your system from the relaxation contracted by study and sitting long in one posture, but there are other modes of doing it than by learning to fence, which is an art that can never be used by you in future life, for the small sword has ceased to be the instrument of death in battle and is now laid aside even in private murders, commonly called duelling. Walking, not running, will exercise your *lower* limbs; riding a mile or two on horseback once a week will exercise and strengthen the *trunk* of your body; and playing at shuttlecock or at ball or ninepins, or even carrying stones from one spot to another and carrying them back again the next day, will remove the languor and weakness contracted by a studious and sedentary life from your *arms* and *breast*.

In studying, avoid bending your neck. This may be done by placing your book in a diagonal line from your eyes and body. Great advantage to health will arise from elevating your table and reading and writing upon your feet two or three hours every day.

To *preserve* your *eyes*, always receive the light upon your book or upon your paper *over* your shoulders or in a *side* direction. Place your book in such a manner as neither to look upwards nor downwards in a right line upon it. The eye should rest, in reading, upon the bottom of the socket which contains it, and that position of a book which favors that easy state of the eye will seldom give it any pain or injure vision.

All the family join in love to you. We have lately heard from both your sisters. They are in good health.

Continue to deserve the esteem and praise of your teachers, and by all means study to please and gratify your parents by writing a *fair and legible hand.*

From your affectionate father,

BENJN: RUSH

Addressed: Mr James Rush Student at the College at Princeton. favd by Mr Pintard.

MS: Library Company of Philadelphia, Rush MSS.

¹ Thus written by BR.

To Thomas Jefferson

Dear Sir,   Philadelphia, August 29, 1804

Your letter from Monticello of the 8th of August¹ was perfectly satisfactory to me. I applied for the private secretaryship to a supposed English embassy for my son only to gratify his repeated solicitations to me for that purpose. He is daily acquiring business, and his prospects in his profession (which a voyage to Europe would have interrupted) are very flattering. He possesses talents and a wish for public life. To the latter I am constantly opposing my experience and advice. The time, I fear, is past in our country in which happiness or even usefulness is to be expected from public stations. How different were our feelings in the years 1774, 1775, and 1776, and how much did the words *country* and *liberty* import in those memorable years!

I shall receive with pleasure the publication you have promised me upon the character of the Messiah,² but unless it advances it to divinity and renders his *death* as well as his *life* necessary for the restoration of mankind, I shall not accord with its author. There is a writer of the name of Abbadie³ whose opinions are mine upon this subject. He is learned, ingenious, and logical, and perfectly free from enthusiasm. You will probably find it in the library of your parish minister or of some of the clergy in your neighborhood.

I am now devoting all my leisure hours to preparing a new edition of my medical works for the press. They will contain some corrections, particularly a retraction of my former belief in the contagion of the yellow fever, and many additions suggested by the experience and observations of the last years of my life. They will be comprised in four large octavo volumes.⁴

Our city is more healthy than usual at this season of the year, owing to the frequent rains which have washed the miasmata from our atmosphere and conveyed a large portion of the filth of our streets which exhale from them, into the Delaware.

With sincere wishes for your health and happiness, I am, dear sir, very respectfully,

BENJN: RUSH

MS: Library of Congress, Jefferson Papers.

[1] Printed in *Old Family Letters, A*, p. 471-2. Jefferson there apprised BR (in answer to a missing letter from BR of 1 Aug. 1804) that the secretaryship of the London legation was not open, as BR had supposed.

[2] In his letter of 8 Aug. Jefferson said he had in preparation "a little volume" intended to exemplify "what I advanced in a former letter as to the excellence of 'the philosophy of Jesus of Nazareth.'" This was the preliminary form of the so-called "Jefferson Bible," which was finished years later on a plan not intended for publication. See Henry S. Randall, *Life of Thomas Jefferson*, N.Y., 1858, III, 654-5, and Cyrus Adler's introduction to the facsimile edition of Jefferson's *Life and Morals of Jesus of Nazareth*, issued by order of Congress, Washington, 1904.

[3] Jacques Abbadie (1654?-1727), Protestant theological writer, born in France but afterwards Dean of Killaloe in Ireland; author of *Traité de la divinité de notre-seigneur Jésus-Christ*, Rotterdam, 1689, a work immensely popular in England and America for more than a century; BR perhaps used the edition published at Burlington, N.J., in 1802 under the title of *The Deity of Jesus Christ Essential to the Christian Religion* (DNB; L.C. Cat.; Cat. Bibl. Nat.).

[4] The second edition of BR's *Medical Inquiries and Observations* was issued in four volumes in 1805 by a syndicate of publishers in Philadelphia, Baltimore, Washington, Petersburg, and Norfolk—an arrangement indicative of BR's repute in the South.

To John Marshall[1]

Sir,   Philadelphia, September 5, 1804

I wrote to you a few days ago upon an interesting subject, but as the letter was addressed to you at Washington (supposing you were now there), I fear it will not reach you in time to produce the effect intended by it.[2] I shall therefore briefly mention its object.

On the 27th of August last I heard that a letter written by me on the 12 of January 1778 to Governor Henry, which was sent by him to General Washington, was to be printed in the 3rd volume of his *Life*, with a letter to the Governor from the General in which he says, April 27,[3] 1778, *long since* the writing of the letter to Mr. Henry I had "used the most elaborate and studious professions of regard for him." This, sir, is certainly a mistake. I wrote two letters to General Washington from Princeton in December 1777, the one stating the abuses and distresses which prevailed in the military hospitals under my care, the other containing complaints against the conduct of the Director General of the hospitals. These letters were concluded with the common expressions of respect to persons in high stations. They were sent to Congress, where I was summoned to meet the Director General immediately afterwards. For reasons not necessary to be mentioned, I resigned my commission in disgust on the 30 of January, 18 days after the date of my letter to Mr. Henry, from which time no intercourse took place between General Washington and me.[4] I retired to a place distant from the army and spent the remainder of the winter and part of the spring at my father-in-law Mr. Stockton's. Nor did I even see him until 14 months[5] afterwards at Morristown, when before I had waited upon him he asked me to dine with him and treated me with a degree of attention which led me to believe he had magnanimously forgotten my letter to Governor Henry. In consequence of this friendly conduct, I visited him every time he came to Philadelphia and was uniformly treated by him as I had been at Morristown.

⟨*It is no secret that a different opinion was entertained by many people of the military talents and conduct of General Washington towards the close of the year 1777 from that which a sudden change in the affairs of the country produced afterwards. I had but a slender personal knowledge of him. I saw and felt the effects of great military disorder and distress in the department in which I acted.*⟩ I declare I neither conversed with nor corresponded with the gentlemen who were publicly said to be hostile to General Washington. The fears and apprehensions I expressed in my letter to Governor Henry were founded upon the fatal tendency of the disorders I saw in the department of the army in which I acted, and upon some private anecdotes that had been communicated directly or indirectly to me by officers and citizens of high rank and respectability. Some of them died in friendship with General Washington. The survivors venerate his memory. They all I believe altered their opinions immediately after the sudden and happy change which took place in the affairs of the army and our country in the summer of 1778. ⟨*Such changes in the opinions and feelings of men towards each other belong to the character of man.*⟩ The private anecdotes alluded to, with the names of the persons who related them, I have always intended should descend to the grave with me. They were not suspected of entertaining them. You will be surprised when I add that *Governor Henry was one of them.*

I assure you, sir, no expressions or conduct of mine, between the 12th of January and the 27th of April 1778 (the day on which

General Washington's letter is dated) could warrant the injurious reflections upon me that are contained in it.

After this statement of facts, permit me to request, as an act of justice as well as a favor to me, that you would erase the passages objected to from the General's letter.[6] I repeat again—they are certainly founded in a mistake.

Your speedy attention to my request will much oblige, sir (with great respect), your most obedient servant,

BENJN RUSH

MS (draft): Library Company of Philadelphia, Rush MSS.

[1] Chief Justice Marshall was at this time in the midst of that "least satisfactory of all the labors of [his] life" (as Albert Beveridge characterized it)— *The Life of George Washington*, Phila., 1804-1807. The work was being printed and published in Philadelphia by Caleb P. Wayne. Two volumes had been published, and members of BR's family were reading the biography, when BR heard late in August, from his friend Samuel Bradford, that the fatal unsigned letter which BR had written to Patrick Henry on 12 Jan. 1778 (printed above), together with Washington's animadversions thereon, was to be printed in Marshall's third volume, then in the press. BR promptly addressed a series of urgent pleas to Judge Bushrod Washington, nephew of the first President and Marshall's middleman with Caleb Wayne, requesting that at least General Washington's condemnation of BR's hypocrisy be suppressed, since it was founded on an apparent mistake. The four letters to Judge Washington, dated 29 Aug., 13, 21, and 24 Sep. 1804, have been printed from the Rush MSS, XXIX, by Good (*BR and His Services to Education*, p. 62-9) and again by Goodman (*Rush*, p. 118-22). BR also wrote twice to Marshall directly. The first of these letters is missing; the present letter is the second of them, and sums up BR's whole case, such as it was. In the course of stating his case, BR made at least three errors in fact, which are pointed out in the notes below. He made all of them innocently, I believe, but he unfortunately rested the validity of his whole argu-

ment on one of them. The MS of the present draft reveals the agitation under which he wrote. The scoring-out and interlineations are so heavy that it would be impossible to represent them except in a facsimile. Two especially significant scored-out passages have, however, been restored in angle brackets. On this affair at large, see below, Appendix I.

[2] A note by BR on the MS states that the present letter was sent to Marshall at Front Royal, Frederick County, Virginia.

[3] An error; Washington's letter quoted by BR was dated *March 28*, 1778. BR may of course have been misinformed of the date by Bradford. (The full text of Washington's remarks on BR was printed for the first time in Washington's *Writings*, ed. Sparks, V, 515.)

[4] An error, and a much more material one. BR has here overlooked his letter to General Washington of 25 Feb. 1778 (printed above), which concludes with "the warmest sentiments of regard and attachment"; or, more probably, *he has supposed that letter to have been written in December 1777.* (Only one of the "two letters" to Washington in December, mentioned above, can be accounted for.) Since BR had in 1800 given the correct date of the second letter in his *Autobiography* (p. 136), one may well be startled by his error. Yet he could not have knowingly made a denial of a matter of record. We can only conclude that, upon hearing the news from Bradford, BR seized his pen and wrote to both Bushrod Washington

and John Marshall without consulting his own papers. He probably never discovered that he himself rather than George Washington had distorted the facts in this case. The incident concerning Marshall's *Washington* certainly deepened BR's sense of injury.

[5] This is BR's third error; it should be twenty-six months, since it refers to BR's stay in Morristown for the trial of Shippen in Mch. 1780.

[6] The ironical fact is that Marshall had already instructed the printer to omit the matter objected to by BR. In a letter of 27 June 1804 he told Caleb Wayne: "I am unwilling that any allusion should be made to the author [of the unsigned letter to Henry], and if the second letter of Mr. Henry [dated 5 Mch. 1778] should be inserted, I wish a blank substituted for 'General Mifflin'" (Hist. Soc. Penna., Dreer Coll., Washington-Henry Correspondence). Though he suppressed BR's name, the printer did not carry out Marshall's instructions in all details; see the *Life of Washington*, III, Appendix, p. 12-18.

To John Adams

Philadelphia, February 19, 1805

My much respected and dear Friend,

Your letter of the 6th instant revived a great many pleasant ideas in my mind.[1] I have not forgotten—I cannot forget you. You and your excellent Mrs. Adams often compose a subject of conversation by my fireside. We now and then meet with a traveler who has been at Quincy, from whom we hear with great pleasure not only that you enjoy good health, but that you retain your usual good spirits, and that upon some subjects you are still facetious.

I have waited for some time for the publication of a new edition of my medical works (which has been unexpectedly delayed) to accompany them with a letter to request from you a more minute account of your health and happiness.

Many thanks to you for your kind inquiries after my family. My eldest daughter is still happy with an excellent husband at Montreal. My second daughter visited her in 1803, where she was addressed by a captain in the British army. Both her parents objected to a connection with him. Her sister and brother-in-law became intercessors for him, and we reluctantly submitted to his taking her from us in February 1804. He appeared to be a man of uncommon worth. We were sometimes disposed to wish he were not so, that we might have had a good excuse for refusing him our daughter. She is now with him at a remote post in Upper Canada. They both say they are contented and happy. We deplore her as lost to us—for life. They will soon sail for England.

My son John, whom you honored with two commissions, left the navy after its reduction in 1802 and resumed the study of medicine.

He graduated in June last but soon afterwards lost his health, to recover which he went to South Carolina in October, where he will probably settle, and he says with far better prospects than he left in Philadelphia.[2]

My second son, Richard, is still studious. The hostility of our legislature to the bar has rendered the progress of young lawyers slow in business, but he expects soon to rise superior to the obstacles that have been thrown in their way.

By the second part of your letter I am reminded of the answer of Sancho in *Don Quixote* when he was asked how he liked his government. "Give me," said he, "my shoes and stockings."[3] In like manner I feel disposed to reply to your questions relative to the present state of the United States, "Give me my lancet and galli-pots." My children are often the witnesses of my contrition for my sacrifices and of my shame for my zeal in the cause of our country. Among the fatherly cautions I deliver to them, none are repeated oftener than the dangers of public and the sin of party spirit.

I live like a stranger in my native state. My patients are my only acquaintances, my books my only companions, and the members of my family nearly my only friends. The odious opinions I have propagated respecting the domestic origin of our American pesti-lence have placed me *permanently* in the same situation in Phila-delphia that your political opinions placed you for *a while* in the year 1775. Linnaeus in conversing one day with a brother natu-ralist at Upsal pointed suddenly to some little boys whom he saw playing before his door and said, "These are our judges." How consoling these reflections to those who have been the subjects of the injustice and cruelty of their contemporaries in their journey through life!

My dear Mrs. Rush and my son Richd. unite in cordial and affectionate regards to you, Mrs. Adams, and your son Thomas[4] with, my dear and much esteemed friend, your grateful and affec-tionate friend,

BENJN: RUSH

MS: Adams Manuscript Trust, Boston.

[1] Adams' letter, the first exchanged between the two old friends in twelve years, begins, characteristically: "It seemeth unto me, that you and I ought not to die without saying Goodby or bidding each other Adieu. Pray how do you do? How does that excellent Lady Mrs. R.? How are the young Ladies? Where is my Surgeon and Lt.? How fares the Lawyer?" (*Old Family Letters, A*, p. 61-2). The resumption of this correspondence was to provide one of the principal occupations and comforts of BR's old age.

[2] John Rush had gone to South Carolina in Oct. 1804 with his father's friend Pierce Butler. Little is known of this venture, which lasted less than a year, for John reentered the navy as a sailing-master in Sep. 1805 (BR, *Autobiography*, p. 269, 370).

[3] I have not located Sancho's remark, which BR quoted more than once.

[4] Thomas Boylston Adams (1772-1832), the Adams' youngest child; A.B., Harvard, 1790; practised law in Philadelphia, 1792-1794, 1799-1804, having in the interval served as his brother John Quincy's secretary abroad; practised later in Quincy and was a member of the state legislature, 1805-1806, and a justice of common pleas, 1809-1811 (information kindly furnished by Mr. Henry Adams, 2d, Boston).

To John Adams

Philadelphia, March 23rd, 1805

My much respected and dear Friend,

I was much gratified by your early answer[1] to my letter and by your kind inquiries after several branches of my family.

My second daughter's husband's name is Thomas Manners. He is a branch of the Rutland family. His father is wealthy, but as his estate will be divided among nine children, my son-in-law will probably be dependent upon a military commission for the support of his family as long as he lives. The only hope we have of its being otherwise arises from his being a favorite with two rich maiden aunts. He is a most amiable and worthy man, well educated, and alike correct and agreeable in his morals and manners.

My third and only girl that has escaped British spoliations is called Julia, after her mother. She is now between 12 and 13 years of age and is everything that the fondest parents could wish an only child to be. In point of interest she is the first of all my children. My third and fourth sons are at the Jersey College. The 3rd, James, who will graduate I hope next fall, has destined himself for the profession of medicine. His talents encourage hopes that he will succeed in it. My 4th boy, Ben, is a freshman.[2] He is sprightly and good-tempered but as yet without habits or a formed character. My 5th son, Sam,[3] is learning to read, write, and cipher in Philadelphia, and my youngest, William, began his A.B.C. a few days ago at a mistress' school. I have thus given you in this and in my former letter a short history of all the branches of my family.

In the conclusion of your letter you say it is the duty of every man who loves his country to step forth in defense of its institutions. To this paragraph, as far as it was intended to awaken me to exertion, I shall reply by giving you an account of a singular dream.

About the year 1790 I imagined I was going up Second Street in our city and was much struck by observing a great number of people assembled near Christ Church gazing at a man who was seated on the ball just below the vane of the steeple of the Church. I asked what was the matter. One of my fellow citizens came up to me and said, the man whom you see yonder has discovered a method of regulating the weather, and that he could produce rain and sunshine and cause the wind to blow from any quarter he pleased. I now joined the crowd in gazing at him. He had a trident in his hand which he waved in the air, and called at the same time to the wind, which then blew from the northeast, to blow from the northwest. I observed the vane of the steeple while he was speaking, but perceived no motion in it. He then called for rain, but the clouds passed over the city without dropping a particle of water. He now became agitated and dejected, and complained of the refractory elements in the most affecting terms. Struck with the issue of his conduct, I said to my friend who stood near to me, "The man is certainly mad." Instantly a figure dressed like a flying Mercury descended rapidly from him, with a streamer in his hand, and holding it before my eyes bid me read the inscription on it. It was: "De te fabula narratur."[4] The impression of these words was so forcible upon my mind that I instantly awoke, and from that time I determined never again to attempt to influence the opinions and passions of my fellow citizens upon political subjects.

Your friend and my brother-in-law, L. H. Stockton,[5] is still at Trenton devoted wholly to the duties of his profession, in which he is daily acquiring reputation and property. He has I believe ceased to be active in the politics of his state.

My dear Mrs. Rush joins in affectionate regard to Mrs. Adams and great respect for yourself with, dear sir, your sincere and grateful old friend,

BENJN: RUSH

P.S. Since writing the above, we have been favored with a visit from your son and his lady and Miss Johnson.[6] They propose to set off for Massachussets on Monday. Your son will deliver you a small pamphlet which I have lately published upon the pernicious effects of ardent spirits upon the bodies and minds of men.[7]

MS: Adams Manuscript Trust, Boston.

[1] Dated 27 Feb. 1805; in *Old Family Letters*, *A*, p. 63-5.
[2] Benjamin Rush, Jr., matriculated at Princeton in Nov. 1804, was advanced to the sophomore class a year later, but dropped to the freshman class in Jan. 1806, and at some time during that year was withdrawn (Faculty Minutes, Secretary's Office, Princeton Univ.).
[3] Samuel Rush (1795-1859), the

Rushes' twelfth child; A.B., University of Pennsylvania, 1812; trained for the law in the office of Moses Levy and admitted to the bar, 1817; held a succession of municipal and county posts from 1819, including that of Philadelphia city recorder, 1838-1841 (Univ. of Penna., *Biog. Cat. of Matriculates*; Biddle, *Memorial*, p. 259; Martin, *Bench and Bar*, p. 97, 308; Moses Levy to BR, 6 Feb. 1812, Rush MSS, IX). For Samuel's role in connection with BR's papers, see Dr. Corner's Introduction to BR's *Autobiography*, p. 5-8.

4 "The story is told of you yourself." Horace, *Satires*, I, i, 69-70.

5 Lucius Horatio Stockton (d. 1835), a younger brother of Mrs. Rush, graduated from Princeton, 1787; U.S. district attorney for New Jersey, 1798-1802; appointed secretary of war by Adams in 1801, but never served (Princeton Univ., *Gen. Cat.*, 1908; Hageman, *Hist. of Princeton*, I, 88).

6 BR probably first met John Quincy Adams in Sep. 1801, when the latter returned from his ministry in Berlin and BR "waited on" him and his lady to glean some information on Germany (BR, *Autobiography*, p. 255-6). They remained on the most cordial terms, as a number of later references in these letters indicate, and the Rush-Adams friendship was carried over into another generation by the close political association of J. Q. Adams and Richard Rush. Adams records the present visit, made on his return from the U.S. Senate, in his *Memoirs*, ed. C. F. Adams, Phila., 1874-1877, I, 147. Mrs. Adams was the former Louisa Johnson of Maryland; Miss Catherine Johnson was her sister (DAB; Adams' *Memoirs*, II, 3).

7 This was a revised and enlarged version of BR's tract against spirituous liquors, issued under the new title of *An Inquiry into the Effects of Ardent Spirits upon the Human Body and Mind*, Phila.: Dobson [1804 or 1805]. It proved to be even more popular than the earlier work.

To Thomas Jefferson

Dear Sir,   Philadelphia, April 29th, 1805

Mr. Boudinot having lately built a house at Burlington in the State of New Jersey, and purposing to remove there with his family in the course of two months, it is presumed he intends to resign the directorship of the Mint of the United States. Should this be the case, I have been induced by the wishes of all the other officers of the Mint, as well as by other considerations, to solicit the favor of being his successor. Large sacrifices made during our Revolution, more recent losses incurred by the clamors and calumnies which have followed my new and (once) unpopular opinions in medicine, a numerous family, and the near approach of that period of life in which the labors of my profession must be performed with difficulty, will render the appointment peculiarly acceptable to, dear sir, your sincere old friend,

BENJN: RUSH

P.S. I beg the contents of this letter for the present may be private.[1]

[894]

MS: The National Archives, Record Group 59 (General Records of the Department of State), Applications and Recommendations for Office.

[1] For the upshot of this request, see BR's letter to Jefferson, 15 June 1805, and note 1 there.

To James Rush

My dear Son,   Philadelphia, June 4th, 1805

I was much affected in reading your letter. Dr. Vancleif's[1] prescription for the pain in your breast was a proper one and should be repeated if the pain and oppression should return. The ride to Whitehill[2] I hope has proved useful to you. It is possible you walk *too much*. Hereafter it will be better for you to *ride* three or four miles every evening. Return before sundown, and never push your horse beyond a quick walk or a very gentle gait beyond it. Eat meat sparingly while you feel the pain and fullness in your breast. Such studies as require great attention or induce fatigue should be intermitted for a few days, or *weeks*, if necessary. Carefully avoid the night air.

My duties as dean of the faculty this year have so fully occupied me that I have not had time to compose your oration. As I shall be relieved from those duties tomorrow by a medical commencement, after which I will comply with your request.[3] I have chosen for the subject of your oration "the influence of female education and the elevation of the female character upon the prosperity of our country." Will this subject be acceptable and popular? If not, let me hear from you by the next post.[4]

Adieu! Richard and Sam send their love to you and Ben, accompanied with that of your affectionate father,

BENJN: RUSH

P.S. Show the part of this letter to Dr. Smith which recommends riding and the intermission of a part of your studies. Suppose you hire your horse by the week. He may be obtained in this way probably at a less price than by the day or the afternoon.

Addressed: Mr James Rush Student at the College of Princeton New-Jersey.

MS: Library Company of Philadelphia, Rush MSS.

[1] John Vancleve, or Van Cleve (1778-1826), a graduate, 1797, and later a trustee of the College of New Jersey; practised medicine for many years in Princeton (Alumni Records, Secretary's Office, Princeton Univ.; Hageman, *Hist. of Princeton*, I, 243).

[2] Residence of James' uncle, Robert

Field (1775-1810), on the Delaware, Burlington co., N.J.; Mrs. Field was the former Abigail Stockton (Hageman, *Hist. of Princeton*, I, 344-5; Stockton, *Stockton Family*, p. 81).

³ BR's sentence structure here leaves something to be desired.

⁴ Evidently (though surprisingly) the subject proved not to be acceptable. In the notice of the commencement at Princeton on 25 Sep. 1805, the Trenton *Federalist* (30 Sep.) records that James Rush delivered an oration "on the prospects of America." BR in a letter to Adams, 21 Sep. 1805, paraphrases the conclusion of the oration and states that James' brother Richard had composed it.

To Thomas Jefferson

Dear Sir,   June 15, 1805

I have just now received your friendly letter and take the earliest opportunity to express my entire satisfaction with the contents of it.¹ No man could have been nominated as Mr. B[*oudinot's*] successor that would be more agreeable to me than Mr. Patter[*son*],² and had I known before that he was a candidate for the appointment I should not have requested it. He will likewise I have no doubt be equally agreeable to all the officers of the Mint, all of whom are worthy men and very much your friends.

I have only to beg that my application to you may remain a secret in your own bosom.

The yellow fever, the scourge of our country, begins to engage the attention of the courts in Europe. I have lately received a number of queries upon the subject of its nature and origin from the governments of Etrutria³ and Prussia—the one through the hands of a Dr. Palloni,⁴ the other from the Prussian minister at the Court of London.⁵ My answers to those queries were calculated to impress in the strongest terms the domestic origin of the disease and that it never did and never can spread from importation or contagion. I mention these facts in order to submit to your judgment whether measures similar to those taken by the above courts might not be taken by our national government. Would a recommendation of such an inquiry be foreign to a message to Congress?⁶ Our state legislatures have erred equally and chiefly through ignorance in their laws for preventing the importation of the fever, and thereby embarrassed and injured our commerce both at home and abroad.

Excuse the liberty I have taken in communicating this hint, and believe me to be as usual your sincere old friend of 1775,

B RUSH

MS (draft): Josiah C. Trent, M.D., Durham, North Carolina.

¹ Jefferson had written two days earlier in answer to BR's application (dated 29 Apr. 1805, q.v.) for the directorship of the Mint. The President stated that he had designated Robert Patterson as Boudinot's successor before receiving BR's application. (Jefferson's letter to Patterson was dated 27 Apr. 1805; Frank H. Stewart, *History of the First United States Mint*, Woodbury, N.J., 1924, p. 69.) Interestingly, Jefferson does not offer this previous commitment as his principal reason for refusing BR's request. He cites the need for mathematical talents in directing Mint business, instancing the appointment of Isaac Newton in England and of Rittenhouse in the United States. Explanations of this sort, Jefferson went on, "are the most painful part of my duty, under which nothing could support me but the consideration that I am but a machine erected by the constitution for the performance of certain acts according to laws of action laid down for me, one of which is that I must anatomize the living man as the Surgeon does his dead subject, view him also as a machine and employ him for what he is fit for, unblinded by the mist of friendship" (L.C., Jefferson Papers).

² Robert Patterson (1743-1824), Irish-born mathematician and astronomer, served as brigade major in the Revolution and was appointed professor of mathematics in the University of the State of Pennsylvania, 1779; he held this post until 1814 and discharged its duties with distinction; author of numerous papers and books in his field; director of the Mint from 1805; president of the American Philosophical Society from 1819 (DAB).

³ Thus in MS; elsewhere BR spells the name "Itruria."

⁴ Drafts of BR's answers to Palloni, one dated 14 May 1805 and the other undated, are in Rush MSS, XXXVIII. Gaetano Palloni (1766-1830), physician of Leghorn, was the author of several works, on yellow fever and other diseases, that had wide circulation in Europe (Surg. Gen. Off., *Index-Cat.*, 1st ser., X, 376-7); his letters to BR are in Rush MSS, XIII, XXXVIII. In 1806 Marie Louise, Queen of the short-lived Kingdom of Etruria, bestowed on BR a gold medal for his communications to her court on the yellow fever (Thomas Hall to BR, 20 Nov. 1806, and BR to Luigi Lustrini, 2 May 1807, both in Rush MSS, XXXIX; see also BR to John Adams, 12 May 1807).

⁵ I.e., Constans Phillipp Wilhelm, Baron von Jacobi-Kloest (1745-1817), a well-known diplomat of the Napoleonic era (*Allgem. deutsche Biog.*). His inquiry had been transmitted to BR in a letter from George W. Erving, London, 1 Mch. 1805, which, with an undated draft reply to Erving, will be found in Rush MSS, XXXIX. Kloest's acknowledgment, stating that he is transmitting to BR through James Monroe (American minister in London) a "gold medal of coronation" from the King of Prussia, is in Rush MSS, Box 10.

⁶ Jefferson complied with this suggestion; see note on BR to Jefferson, 6 Dec. 1805.

To John Adams

My dear old Friend,   Philadelphia, June 29, 1805

Having been called upon lately to bear a part in the examination and exercises of twenty-four candidates for degrees in medicine, I have been prevented from attending to my duties to my correspondents for several weeks. I now sit down to resume the exercise of that duty by thanking you for your friendly letter of the first of last month.¹

I shall first reply to your question relative to the persons who accompanied us in the boat in our return from Point no Point in the spring of the year 1776.[2] They were I think David Humphries, then a member of Congress from Pennsylvania, Michl. Hellegas, then treasurer of Congress, and if my memory does not deceive me, Owen Biddle, then an active and enlightened member of the Council of Safety of Pennsylvania. I recollect no part of the conversation that took place in that company except a jocular proposal to write a letter to Lord North with a supposed discovery of some state secrets, with which I well remember Mr. Hellegas was so much pleased as to urge its being carried into effect.

I seldom see any of the persons who now ride in the whirlwind and direct the storm of politics in Pennsylvania, but my son Richard, who mixes with the parties, says it is impossible from all he can collect of their relative strength and intentions to tell who will be the successful candidate for the chair of our state next October.[3] The friends of Mr. McKean and Mr. Snyder[4] are alike sanguine, but the latter are far the most industrious. The leading Federalists will be passive in the controversy. T. Payne has said in one of his publications that it is "impossible to unknow a truth that has been once believed."[5] Sad experience has refuted this assertion in Pennsylvania, for alas! all the errors upon the subjects of government, [. . .][6] and lawyers that were written down in the year 1789 have revived and are now in full operation in every part of our state. Do you remember a speech you made to me at Mrs. Yard's[7] door in September 1776, the evening after Congress passed a resolve to hold an intercourse by means of commissioners on Staten Island with Lord Howe? It was: "It would seem as if mankind were made to be slaves, and the sooner they fulfill their destiny the better." I will hope that if the liberties of Pennsylvania should expire in the present struggle, our sister states will not follow our example. Many things will contribute to our ruin that cannot operate in other states. We are divided by local, national, and religious prejudices, each of which by a constant repulsive agency prevents union in public and general enterprises. A large portion of our citizens are ignorant, and an equal portion are idle and intemperate. We have at present no *native* Pennsylvanians preeminent for genius or patriotism among us, and if we had, they would have no natural or American allies, for a majority of the old and wealthy *native* citizens of our state are still Englishmen in their hearts and would afford them no support. This was exemplified in Peters, Clymer, Hopkinson, and some others who were deserted by that class of people as soon as the repeal of the test law restored them to the right of suffrage and a participation in the power of the state. It was in part from this view of things in 1790 that I ceased to labor for the several interests of my country, nor do I repent of it. My family and my profession afford me pleasures and pursuits so adequate to my wishes that I often look back upon the hours I spent in serving my country (so unproductive of the objects to which they were devoted) with deep regret. A chair in my study is now to me what Dr. Johnson used to say a chair in a tavern was to him, "the throne of human felicity."[8]

Do you ever see our Philadelphia papers which contain the publications of the two contending parties in our state? If you wish to look over them, my son shall send such of them to you as are interesting. He reads them all and occasionally at our meals gives me an epitome of them, for I seldom read one of them. I have not even read the three much talked-of addresses to our citizens from the Assemblymen, the Constitutional Society, and the Friends of the People.[9]

A new edition of my medical works is in the press. I have allotted a copy for you. It will contain a retraction of some errors, and many new facts upon the subject of our American pestilence.

Adieu! my much esteemed friend. All my family join in love to you and your excellent lady. Often, very often, do we review and endeavor to enjoy over again the happy hours we passed at your house in Philadelphia. Continue, my dear sir, to favor me with your correspondence. You will find me hereafter more punctual and prompt in cherishing it. Again adieu!

From your ever affectionate and grateful friend,

BENJN: RUSH

P.S. I need hardly suggest that certain parts of this letter must not be read out of your own family.

MS: Adams Manuscript Trust, Boston.

[1] This letter is missing.

[2] See BR's letter to Adams of 13 Apr. 1790 for an account of this episode. In the present version there are two errors: the date should be Sep. 1775, and "David Humphries" should be corrected to Charles Humphreys.

[3] What was occurring at this time in Pennsylvania politics was an intra-party feud of peculiar, perhaps unsurpassed, bitterness. Despite his disclaimers, BR

followed this struggle with interest, and he alludes to political personalities and issues so frequently in the following letters to Adams that a short exposition of current state politics is essential to grasp much that he reports. The following statement is a summary of James H. Peeling's valuable article, "Governor McKean and the Pennsylvania Jacobins (1799-1808)," PMHB, LIV (1930), 320-54. The Federalist party was overthrown earlier in Pennsylvania than elsewhere by the election of Thomas McKean as governor in 1799. A conservative by instinct, McKean was somewhat accidentally a Democratic-Republican leader, and his alliance with the Jeffersonian radicals in the state was an uneasy one. The principal leaders of the Philadelphia wing of the Jeffersonian party—William Duane, publisher of the *Aurora*, and Dr. Michael Leib, BR's former pupil and now a congressman—were lukewarm in support of McKean in the gubernatorial election of 1802, and by 1805 they came out openly against him. They were now allied with the back-country democracy, which had long been clamoring for judicial innovations that McKean had consistently vetoed, and which was now agitating for a new constitution. (The situation was strikingly parallel to that which had resulted in the radical Constitution of 1776.) Dominating the party machinery, McKean's opponents selected as their candidate Simon Snyder, a homespun "Northumberland farmer . . . distinguished for his tirades against lawyers, learning, and the Philadelphia aristocracy" (Peeling, p. 353). Thanks to the efforts of Alexander J. Dallas, McKean retained enough moderate ("Quid") support from his old party and enough grudging Federalist votes in addition to be reelected in 1805 for his third (and constitutionally his last) three-year term. A good share of this term was devoted to the attempted impeachment of the governor by his defeated rivals. Their charges were for the most part implausible, and McKean was vindicated, though not until after a desperate and rancorous struggle. Upon McKean's retirement in 1808, the radicals won a sweeping victory with Snyder as their candidate.

[4] Simon Snyder (1759-1819), characterized in the preceding note, was the son of a German immigrant; member of the state constitutional convention of 1789; member of Assembly, 1797-1807; governor, 1808-1817 (DAB).

[5] I have not found this observation attributed to Paine.

[6] Illegible word, partly lost in margin.

[7] Mrs. Yard, in Second Street, was John and Samuel Adams' landlady when they attended Congress in Philadelphia; see BR to John Adams, 12 May 1807.

[8] Quoted in Boswell's *Life of Johnson* (ed. Birkbeck Hill, Oxford, 1887, II, 452) on the authority of Sir John Hawkins.

[9] Documents in the fight over the Constitution of 1790: the Assemblymen's address, denouncing McKean, emanated from a caucus of radical legislators; the Constitutional Society was a group organized by A. J. Dallas in support of McKean and the Constitution; the Friends of the People, led by Duane and Leib, advocated a constitutional convention (Peeling, "Governor McKean," p. 334-41; Scharf & Westcott, I, 520; McMaster, *Hist.*, III, 160-2; Raymond Walters, *Alexander James Dallas*, Phila., 1943, p. 136-8).

To John Adams

My dear old Friend,   Philadelphia, August 14th, 1805

Your letters are full of aphorisms. Every paragraph in them suggests new ideas or revives old ones. You have given a true picture of parties in our country.[1] We have indeed no national character, and however much we boast of it there are very few true Americans in the United States.

We have four distinct parties in Pennsylvania: 1. old tories, 2. honest Federalists, 3. violent Democrats, 4. moderate Republicans. The 1st united with the 2nd in the struggle for the establishment of the general government. They were patronized by General Washington and Colonel Hamilton, probably from pure motives, and soon acquired a complete ascendancy over the party that had taken them by the hand. They discovered this in all their nominations for public appointments. It was their preference for one of themselves that threw Swanwick[2] into Congress. Their English antigallican prejudices against the peace you made with France first led the Federalists to see they were not an homogeneous party, for they[3] were pleased with it. Ever since that time the Federalists ascribe their downfall to their union with the tories. I predicted it when I saw those people flattering and almost worshiping Cobbet as the apostle of their restoration to Great Britain or to a kingly government in America. I now and then mention that prediction to persons who unjustly accused me at that time of a partiality for the detestable principles and conduct of France. The 3rd and 4th parties united in the choice of Mr. McKean and Mr. Jefferson, but the late attack upon the Constitution of our state has divided them. The moderate Republicans are few in number compared with the violent Democrats, and unless most of the honest Federalists join them at the next election, Mr. Snyder will be our governor, and Dr. Franklin's Constitution will again be the Constitution of Pennsylvania.

Ever since the Revolution, our state has been like a large inn. It has accommodated strangers at the expense of the landlord and his children, who have been driven by them from the bar and their bedrooms, and compelled at times to seek a retreat in their garret and cellar. In consequence of this state of things, everything not connected with individual exertions languishes in our state, particularly our commerce, which is tending fast to annihilation from the operation of a most absurd quarantine law, the result of Boeotian ignorance and disbelief. I am kept from feeling the anger and contempt which such conduct is calculated to create by considering our citizens as *deranged* upon the subject of their political and physical happiness.

I well remember your early cautions to your country upon the subject of treaties. In Baltimore you advised Congress to be careful how they threw themselves into the arms and power of France when they applied to her for aid, for "the time might come," you said, "when we should be obliged to call upon Britain to defend us against France." In being deprived of the credit of that just opinion as well as the honor of your accumulated services to your country, you share the fate of most of the patriots and benefactors to mankind that ever lived. I have lately seen a copy of an original letter from Columbus to the King of Spain written from Jamaica on his 4th and last voyage to the countries he had discovered. After describing his numerous sufferings of body and mind, he adds, "So that he who gave Spain another world has neither in *that* nor in the *old* world a cottage for himself or his wretched family."[4] The French and American Revolutions differed from each other in many things, but they were alike in one particular—the former gave all its *power* to a single man, the latter all its *fame*. The only credit which the other servants of the public in the successful contest for American independence possess with the world and will possess with posterity is and will be wholly derived from their imitating the example and carrying into effect the counsels of General Washington in the cabinet and the field. In reviewing the numerous instances of ingratitude of governments and nations to their benefactors, I am often struck with the perfection of that divine government in which "a cup of cold water" (the cheapest thing in the world), given under the influence of proper principles, "shall not lose its reward."[5]

I once intended to have published a work to be entitled "Memoirs of the American Revolution," and for that purpose collected many documents and pamphlets.[6] But perceiving how widely I should differ from the historians of that event, and how much I should offend by telling the truth, I threw my documents into the fire and gave my pamphlets to my son Richard. Of the former I have preserved only a short account of the members of Congress who subscribed the Declaration of Independence, part of which I once read to you while you were President of the United States. From the immense difference between what I saw and heard of men and things during our Revolution and the histories that have been given of them, I am disposed to believe with Sir R. Walpole that all history (that which is contained in the Bible excepted) is a romance, and romance the only true history.

You remark in your last letter that the tories have hunted down all the Revolutionary characters of our country. To this General Washington and Colonel Hamilton are exceptions. They are both idolized by them, and to their influence is owing the almost exclusive honor those gentlemen possess of having begun, carried on, and completed the American Revolution. Colonel Hamilton is indebted for much of his fame to his funding system, the emoluments of which centered chiefly in the hands of the tories. They may say of him what Leo the X impiously said of the Christian religion, mutatis mutandis: "Quantas divitias peperit nobis hoc nomen Hamiltoni."[7]

None of your letters are read out of my family. They deeply interest my son Richard. I have not seen T. Paine since his return to America. I do not know even the person of Wm. Duane,[8] nor have I had the least intercourse with T. Coxe since the year 1800. He is at present out of the eye of the public and alike neglected and avoided by all the parties of the state.

Mr. Madison and his lady[9] are now in our city. It gave me great pleasure to hear him mention your name in the most respectful terms a few days ago. He dwelt largely upon your "genius and integrity," and acquitted you of ever having had the least unfriendly designs in your administration upon the present forms of our American governments. He gave you credit likewise for your correct opinion of banks and standing armies in our country. Colonel Burr also in his visit to my family last spring spoke of your character to me with respect and affection. Your integrity was mentioned by him in the highest terms of commendation. For what virtue above all others would a good man wish to be generally known by the world and by posterity? I should suppose integrity.

This long letter has been written at three different sittings. I mention this fact as an excuse for its length and its want of correctness and method.

Adieu! my venerable and dear friend. My dear Mrs. Rush and son join me in affectionate remembrance of your excellent Mrs. Adams and all the branches of your family. From your sincere and obliged friend,

BENJN: RUSH

P.S. You see I think *aloud* in my letters to you as I did in those written near 30 years ago, and as I have often done in your company. I beg again they may be read only in your own family. I live in an enemy's country.

MS: Adams Manuscript Trust, Boston.

[1] BR is answering Adams' letter of 7 July 1805 (*Old Family Letters, A,* p. 69-73).

[2] John Swanwick (1740-1798), Philadelphia merchant; partner in Willing, Morris, & Swanwick, 1783; member of Congress, 1795-1798; he had some literary pretensions and published a volume of *Poems,* 1797 (*Biog. Dir.* *Cong.*; Abraham Ritter, *Philadelphia and Her Merchants,* Phila., 1860, p. 48; Allibone, *Dict. of Authors*).

[3] I.e., the "honest Federalists" as distinct from "old tories."

[4] This famous letter, dated from Jamaica, 7 July 1503, is commonly known as the *Lettera Rarissima.* The passage quoted by BR may be found, in

English translation, in *The Northmen, Columbus, and Cabot,* ed. J. E. Olson and E. G. Bourne, N.Y., 1906, p. 393. One may only conjecture as to what sort of copy of this letter BR saw.

[5] Matthew 10:42.

[6] On this project and its fate, see BR to Adams, 22 Jan. 1789.

[7] "What riches the name of Hamilton has brought us!" Source not traced.

[8] William Duane (1760-1835), a printer of colorful international background, in 1798 succeeded B. F. Bache as proprietor of the Philadelphia *Aurora,* which was for some years the most powerful Jeffersonian newspaper in the country under Duane's spirited management; during those years he was the Democratic-Republican "boss" of Philadelphia, but his later career was anticlimactic (DAB).

[9] Dolly (Payne) Todd Madison (1768-1849), famous in the social annals of the United States, had lost her first husband, John Todd, in the epidemic of 1793 and had married Congressman James Madison a year later (DAB; BR to Mrs. Rush, 24-25 Oct. 1793).

To John Adams

Philadelphia, September 21st, 1805

My venerable and dear Friend,

The hurry always connected with the prevalence of a yellow fever in our city has prevented my answering your letter of August 25th[1] at an earlier day.

The opinion relative to too close an alliance with France in the year 1776 was communicated to me by you, I think for the first time, in Baltimore. I was led from this circumstance to believe you had delivered it on the floor of Congress in *that* place. I well recollect to have heard you repeat it during our intercourse in Philadelphia and have often since been struck with the propriety of it. Many other of your opinions respecting that country and its late unfortunate Revolution have been revived in my mind by the events that have been produced by it. At Bush hill[2] I well remember your once saying, "The conduct of France would determine the fate of the world, for that she was at the head of human affairs." One day, sitting with you and Mrs. Adams in your garden while you were President of the United States, you said to me, "Expect, Doctor, no changes in the condition of the human race for the better from the present convulsions in Europe. Things will wind up as they began, and the affairs of the world will go on for two or three centuries to come as they have done for centuries past." Upon the same subject you said to me in your front room upstairs, "Don't deceive yourself, Doctor, in a belief that a republic can exist in France. The present Revolution will certainly end in the restoration of the Bourbon family or in a military despotism." I have mentioned these predictions to some of my philosophical friends, who have given you full credit for them.

There is quackery in everything as well as in medicine, and it is because politicians neglect to form principles from facts that so many mistakes are committed in calculations upon the issue of commotions in human affairs. Lewis the 14th lamented that we were only fit to live in the world when we were called to leave it. I feel the truth of this remark daily in myself as well as see it in others. *Learned* men I now find know what *was; weak* men know what *is*; but men made *wise* by reflection only know *what is to come*.

The time will soon be at hand which will settle the present controversy between the Democrats of Pennsylvania. Some of the most thinking men who speak of it suppose we shall return sooner to order if the friends of Duane succeed than if Governor McKean is reelected and the Constitution preserved. We seldom, they say, do right until we have reached the extremity of error. I am encouraged by their opinions not to despair of the once beloved asylum of my ancestors and my native state. The late Dr. Edwards[3] told me on his deathbed that Sir John Sinclair[4] had informed him he once said to Adam Smith (the author of *The Wealth of Nations*) "that the British nation was on the brink of ruin." "Hold, young man," said Mr. Smith. "You are mistaken. There is a great deal of ruin in a nation. We are far from the brink of it." In like manner I hope there is yet a large mass of ruin left for poor Pennsylvania.

Although I have not paid my respects to a public man for many years, sympathy with his sufferings led me to visit General Moreau[5] upon his arrival in our city. I was charmed with him. There is a rare mixture of simplicity and dignity in his manners. Such is his modesty that I was obliged frequently to revive in my mind the idea that I was in company with the first hero and general of the age. I asked him if Bonaparte's military talents were as great as fame had reported them to be. He said yes, he had consummate military abilities; that he was however not without faults, but such was the activity of his genius that he always corrected them before his enemies had time to take the advantage of them. Of this he mentioned a striking proof at the battle of Maringo. Upon his return from Italy after that battle, General Moreau asked him why he chose to descend with his army the frozen mountain of St. Bernard when he might have passed a nearer or less hazardous way. He replied "It was the scenery of the business. I thought its boldness would have a good effect." The General said further that "the order and repose of France depended upon Bonaparte, for that at present no one of his genius was qualified to succeed him." I was much struck in hearing him speak in such respectful and dispassionate terms of a man who had attempted to take his life, who had afterwards robbed him of a large portion of his fortune, and finally made him an exile from a country over which his victories more than Bonaparte's had made him an emperor and a king.

A new era has begun in the science of medicine in our city since the appearance of the yellow fever among us. No channel has as yet been discovered through which it could have been conveyed to us from a foreign country; and what is more against its importation, no one of the persons who have been infected by the foul air emitted by a large bed of putrid oysters in Southwark and who has sickened or died in the city, has propagated the disease. Many of our citizens of the second class have been led by these facts to believe it to be generated in Southwark and that it is not contagious. But our merchants and house-owners scout the opinion and are more indignant than ever against the man who first broached it in our city. When Fort Washington was taken, General Lee in the first transports of his rage and grief cried out, "Had it been called Fort Lee, it would have been evacuated long ago." Had a tory physician first promulgated the doctrine of the domestic origin of the yellow fever in Philadelphia, it would have been universally believed long ago. Did you ever know any of that class of people forgive or alter their minds upon a political subject? The folly of our citizens in attempting to preserve our city from the yellow fever by a quarantine law has nearly ruined its commerce. Its inefficacy is acknowledged by the experience of 12 years, and yet it is dangerous to speak against it. Do you not admire Governor McKean's patience and command of temper in giving such mild epithets to the people of Pennsylvania?[6] Our merchants are not fools nor geese—they are deranged and are daily committing suicide upon their commerce and property.

Your political anecdotes are very interesting, particularly to my son Richard. Did you ever hear who wrote General W's farewell address to the citizens of the United States? Major Butler[7] says it was Mr. Jay.[8] It is a masterly performance. I think however I have seen many of the General's letters (certainly written by himself) not much inferior to it. He possessed a talent for letter writing, and so anxious was he to appear neat and correct in his letters that General Mifflin informed me he had known him when at Boston copy a letter of 2 or [3?][9] sheets of paper because there were a few erasures in it.

Adieu! my dear friend. My pen has run away with me. With respects and love as usual, in which my dear Mrs. Rush would join were she at home, I am, my dear sir, your affectionate and obliged friend,

BENJN: RUSH

P.S. My wife and daughter are gone to Princeton to attend a commencement at which my third son is to graduate. The subject of his oration is on the future prospects of America.[10] It was composed by his brother Richard. In the close of it he describes the great council of our country legislating in great pomp on the banks of one of our western rivers a hundred years hence. In that council he hears peals of eloquence from the descendants of the Washingtons, Adams, &c., of the Revolution. Among them he hears one of the posterity of Moreau rejoicing in his father's exile and in his own birth in a land of liberty. Above them he sees Columbus and hears him exulting in his toils and sufferings, and declaring that the everflowing stream of time never fails of doing justice to the benefactors of mankind.

MS: Adams Manuscript Trust, Boston.

[1] Adams' letter of 23, not 25, Aug. 1805 is in *Old Family Letters, A*, p. 73-7.

[2] Adams lived at Bush Hill during a part of his vice-presidency.

[3] Doubtless Enoch Edwards; see BR to Mrs. Rush, 8 Nov. 1793.

[4] Sir John Sinclair, bart. (1754-1835), M.P., the well-known Scottish agricultural and economic writer; he corresponded with Washington and other Americans (DNB).

[5] Jean-Victor-Marie Moreau (1763-1813), victor of Hohenlinden, one of Napoleon's ablest commanders and eventually the center of royalist intrigue against Napoleon; arrested and banished, 1804, he lived on a large estate he acquired at Morrisville, Penna., 1805-1813; took service with the Russian army and was killed at Dresden (*La Grande Encyclopédie*; D. K. Turner, "General Jean Victor Maria Moreau," Bucks Co. Hist. Soc., *A Collection of Papers*, III [1909], 632-44).

[6] McKean outraged his own party by allegedly declaring, in an interview with certain radical Republican leaders in Mch. 1805, that the mass of the people in Pennsylvania were "clodhoppers, ignoramuses, geese, and fools" (Peeling, "Governor McKean," p. 338-9).

[7] Pierce Butler (1744-1822), South Carolina planter, had been a major in the British army before the Revolution; he had a long and varied political career and was currently U.S. senator from South Carolina, though shortly afterwards he resigned. Butler maintained a residence in or near Philadelphia and was on terms of closest intimacy with BR. (DAB; John T. Faris, *Old Roads Out of Philadelphia*, Phila., 1917, p. 263; BR's letters of 19 Sep. 1806 and 1 Apr. 1809; Butler's letters to BR in Rush MSS, XXI.)

[8] On the complicated question of the authorship of the Farewell Address, see V. H. Paltsits, *Washington's Farewell Address*, N.Y., 1935. Madison, Hamilton, and Jay all contributed.

[9] Omitted in MS.

[10] See BR to James Rush, 4 June 1805.

To John Adams

My very dear Friend,   Philadelphia, November 21, 1805

I am pleased in reflecting that I destroyed all the documents and anecdotes I had collected for private Memoirs of the American Revolution. I discover from your letter[1] that I have now nothing but the "scenery of the business," and know but little more than what servants who wait upon table know of the secrets of their masters' families, of the springs of the events of the war and of the administration of the general government since the year 1791. I am however satisfied that the whole business was a drama and that some persons who acted a conspicuous part in it never composed a single act nor scene in the play. There is as the logicians say a "non causa, pro causa" in everything. Our citizens ascribe the late partial or limited prevalence of the yellow fever in Philadelphia to the quarantine law. Governments, armies, colleges have all their quarantine laws, that is, an exemption from evils from causes that either have had no operation or that have had a contrary effect.

In your account of the consequences of not giving commissions to Colonel Burr and General Muhlenberg, you were I am sure perfectly correct. I well remember when I presented a letter from the latter gentleman to you in which he offered his services to the United States. You said, "Is he not a Democrat?" I said, "Yes, but a worthy man and a good officer." You replied that you believed he was, and expressed a good deal of satisfaction with the offer he had made. When the list of appointments for the army was published, I lamented that General M's name was not among them and predicted the consequences at the next election in Pennsylvania. That his influence produced the change in the legislature of our state I infer from its having turned the scale in favor of Mr. McKean and the Constitution at the last election. While he was passive and apparently neutral, wagers were in favor of Snyder. The best-informed men believed his election to be certain. A single letter of General Muhlenberg to one of his friends in Berks County, which was printed in German and English and circulated through every part of the state, created contrary expectations and a contrary issue to the contest. Fred. Augt. Muhlenberg[2] was likewise opposed to your reelection, but his influence was very limited compared with his brother's, who has long been and still is the most popular and powerful German in Pennsylvania.

I always believed that General W. relied chiefly upon the understanding and knowledge of General H., but I did not know that his influence extended over his very passions until I read your last letter. That he governed his judgment after he left the Treasury, I believe from several circumstances that came to my knowledge. I shall mention one of them. In the interval between the application to General W. by Congress for the documents of the British treaty, two letters were put into the post office, one to A.H———— and another to J. Jay franked G.W., and *two* were sent to him from New York a few days afterwards and the day before his answer and refusal were sent to Congress.

I shall always retain a grateful sense of the *honor* as well as the favor conferred upon me by you in the appointment I now hold in the Mint. It was given at a time when the calumnies published against my medical character had reduced my business to nearly 2/3rds below what it had been in former years. The expenses of my family had increased, and the losses incurred by paper money and public services during the Revolution had left me but scanty private resources for their maintenance or for retirement from the city. In this situation, the addition you made to my income enabled me to keep my ground.————It has pleased God to produce a reaction of the public mind towards me since the year 1802. Some of my old patients have returned to me, and many new ones have been added. The emoluments of my profession are moreover considerably increased, so that I am enabled not only to live comfortably with a large family and in an expensive city, but to save something every year for the branches of my family that are to survive me. Even my pen has lately added to my resources. I am to receive 1000 dollars for the copyright of the new edition of my medical works which will be published in a week or ten days.

Adieu! my dear friend. Your son and his lady are now in our city.[3] They are to do us the favor of spending a day with us before they set off for Washington. My dear Mrs. Rush and son Richard join in respects and love to your excellent Mrs. Adams with your ever affectionate and obliged friend,

BENJN: RUSH

P.S. What do you allude to in the hint of what passed between G. W. and General H. at York town?

MS: Adams Manuscript Trust, Boston.

[1] Of 30 Sep. 1805 (*Old Family Letters*, *A*, p. 78-86).

[2] Frederick Augustus Conrad Muhlenberg (1750-1801), second of the three eminent brothers with whom BR was friendly, gave up his Lutheran pastorate to enter politics; chairman of the Pennsylvania ratifying convention of 1789; member of Congress, 1789-1795; while speaker of the First Congress, he ad-

dressed frequent letters to BR on political affairs, but BR's letters to Muhlenberg have not been found (DAB; *Biddle
Papers*, *passim*).

Adams noted in his diary that BR had
conveyed to him from Madison and
Jefferson the provisional offer of a
diplomatic post (*Memoirs*, ed. C. F.

[3] Under 25 Nov. 1805 John Quincy

Adams, Phila., 1874-1877, I, 374-5).

To James Madison

My dear Friend,   Philadelphia, December 3, 1805

To a person acquainted with the great events which characterized the first years of the French Revolution, it might be sufficient barely to say—the bearer of this letter is General Miranda.[1] But much more may be said of him. He is still the friend of liberty and a believer in the practicability of governments that shall have for their objects the happiness of nations instead of the greatness of individuals. He knows your character and longs to do homage to your principles. He will repay you for your civilities to him by streams of knowledge and information upon all subjects. From, dear sir, yours affectionately,

BENJN: RUSH

MS: Library of Congress, Madison Papers.

[1] Francisco de Miranda (1750-1816), a native of Venezuela, soldier of fortune, and martyr to the cause of South American independence. BR had first met Miranda in 1783. Their acquaintance was renewed when Miranda returned to the United States to obtain men and supplies for an uprising against Spanish authority in his native country. Undertaken with one ship and 200 men, Miranda's expedition of 1806 was a flat failure and had to be discountenanced by President Jefferson. Miranda spent the next years in England and almost succeeded in obtaining a British force under Arthur Wellesley as a liberating army. In 1810 he tried again on his own, but, after temporary success,

failed once more and was captured. In another and equally glowing letter of the present date, BR introduced Miranda to Jefferson. These letters show that BR, who, like others, was captivated by the handsome adventurer, gained access for Miranda to the highest government circles in the United States. (Miranda, *Diary: Tour of the United States, 1783-1784*, ed. William S. Robertson, N.Y., 1928, p. 30, 39; William S. Robertson, *The Life of Miranda*, Chapel Hill, 1929, *passim*; BR to Jefferson, 3 Dec. 1805, Rush Family Papers, deposited in Princeton University Library; and, below, to John Adams, 6 Jan. 1806, and to Miranda, 27 Mch. 1811.)

To Thomas Jefferson

Dear Sir,   Philadelphia, December 6, 1805

I have the honor to enclose you with this letter two pamphlets upon the yellow fever[1]—one of them for yourself and the other

to be sent to the chairman or any other active member of the committee appointed to consider of that part of your message which
relates to the quarantine laws of the United States.[2] I wish the
pamphlet to be sent in *your* name and that *mine* may not be mentioned in the business.

The progress of truth upon the subject of our American pestilence
has been slow. Your public declaration of a belief in its being an
endemic of our country will promote investigation everywhere,
and nothing but investigation and reflection are necessary to produce
a conviction that it is the offspring of putrid exhalations and that
it may be exterminated with as much certainty as its kindred native
diseases, the mild remittents and intermittents of our country. The
boards of health and quarantine laws of the states have been found
to be ineffectual for that purpose. Indeed their operation upon our
commerce have been more injurious than the yellow fever itself.

From, dear sir, with great respect, your sincere old friend,

BENJN: RUSH

MS: Library of Congress, Jefferson Papers.

[1] Doubtless BR's *Inquiry into the
Various Sources of the Usual Forms of
Summer and Autumnal Diseases in the
United States, and the Means of Prevent-
ing Them. To Which are Added, Facts
Intended to Prove the Yellow Fever
Not to Be Contagious*, Phila., Balti-
more, &c., 1805; this was a separate
issue of two long articles in *Med. Inq.
& Obs.*, 2d edn., 1805, IV.

[2] In his Fifth Annual Message, 3
Dec. 1805, Jefferson took note of the
ravages of yellow fever in American
seaports, reported the steps taken to
prevent unreasonable quarantines on our
ships in foreign ports, and suggested an
inquiry into the state quarantine laws,
whose "efficacy merits examination"
(*Writings*, ed. Lipscomb and Bergh,
III, 384-6).

To John Adams

Philadelphia, January 6th, 1806

My venerable and dear Friend,

I committed to Mr. Vauhan[1] a few days ago a copy of the new
edition of my *Medical Inquiries and Observations*, who kindly
promised to convey them to you in a small box consigned to Mr.
Gideon Snow, merchant in Boston. Some of the essays contained
in them will I hope interest you, particularly those upon animal life,
the influence of physical causes upon morals, and the thoughts upon
old age. Perhaps you may be induced to glance your eyes over the
histories of all our yellow fevers since the year 1793, and upon the
facts which are intended to prove their origin in the filth of our

city. If that part of the work and others more simply medical should not arrest your attention, put it into the hands of your family physician. Should he meet with anything in it that should suggest a new remedy for the aches and pains which await your or your dear Mrs. Adams' descent into the vale of life, it will give[2] to me a gratification sweeter than the common rewards for the toils of authorship.

General Miranda, whose name you have mentioned in your last letter, called upon me on his way to and from Washington. He appeared to be as animated as he was two and twenty years ago, but much better informed. He reminded me, in his anecdotes of the great characters that have moved the European world for the last twenty or thirty years, of *The Adventures of a Guinea*,[3] but with this difference—he has passed through, not the purses, but the heads and hearts of all the persons whom he described. Of Catharine of Russia he spoke with admiration; of Frederick the IInd with some respect; of the late King of Poland with contempt; and of Napoleon with horror. He confirmed all that Sir Robt. Wilson has said of his cruelty in Egypt. His court he says is the focus of crimes. Tallerand[4] is the least vicious character in it. He said further that we had everything to fear and nothing to hope for from the Courts of Britain and France. They both hated the spirit of liberty which existed in our country. Mr. Pitt he thinks is restrained from destroying the remains of liberty in Britain only by the asylum which the United States offer to the people of that country. He was treated with politeness at Washington, but says as the result of his conversations with many of the members of the government that there will be no war. In one of the long evenings he spent with me he mentioned his intimacy with General Hamilton in his former visit to this country, and surprised me very much by informing me that the General spoke with great contempt of the person[5] whom he threatened with a pamphlet at York town. Miranda told him his fame in Europe with posterity was placed beyond the reach of his hostility to him. "No, it is not," said H. "I have written a history of his battles, campaigns, &c., and I will undeceive them." This history I presume was destroyed after he became secretary of the treasury.

What an excellent sermon might be preached upon the text "Men of high degree are a lie, and men of low degree are vanity."[6]

> "non Rabillans solus, sed aula,
> Eclesia, exercitus, imo, totus mundus
> *histrionem* agunt."[7]

In return for your anecdote of the redoubt at Yorktown, I will give one which would have made a part of my memoirs of the Revolution. Thirteen members of Congress voted against the funding system. One of these members assured me that while that business was depending, a gentleman came to him and offered him 200,000 dollars at 4/6 in the pound for his note payable a year afterwards. The offer was promptly and decidedly refused. Within the year the funded debt sold for 23/ in the pound.

Ah! Why did I ever suffer myself to be withdrawn a moment from the noise of pestle and mortar to be thus distressed and disgusted with the impostures and frauds of public life?

Our citizens are showing their respects to General Moreau, General Eaton,[8] and Captain Decater[9] by public entertainments. They have all deserved I believe the honors they have received from the world. Captain Decater charms his fellow citizens as much by his modesty as he once delighted and astonished them by his exploits in the Mediteranean.

With the most cordial respects and compliments to Mrs. Adams, in which my dear Mrs. Rush and son Richard join, I am, my dear sir, ever your obliged friend,

BENJN RUSH

MS: Adams Manuscript Trust, Boston.

[1] This might be either Benjamin Vaughan (1751-1835), of Hallowell, Me., physician, political economist, scientist, and intimate correspondent of BR, or his brother John (1756-1841), of Philadelphia, secretary of the American Philosophical Society and friend of the great (J. H. Sheppard, "Reminiscences and Genealogy of the Vaughan Family," *New Engl. Hist. & Geneal. Reg.*, XIX [1865], 343-56). Letters to BR from Benjamin, John, and other members of this distinguished Anglo-American family are in Rush MSS, XVIII; and some of BR's letters to the Vaughans are in Amer. Philos. Soc.

[2] This word omitted in MS.

[3] *Chrysal, or The Adventures of a Guinea*, a popular novel by Charles Johnstone published in London, 1760-1765.

[4] Talleyrand was at this time Napoleon's minister of foreign affairs.

[5] George Washington; see *Old Family Letters, A*, p. 88.

[6] Psalms 62:9.

[7] "Not Rabillans [perhaps Rabillaris] only, but courts, the church, the army, nay the whole world, control the actor." "Eclesia" should be "ecclesia," and "imo" should be "immo." I have not found the source of this quotation, which BR uses again in a letter to Adams of 22 Sep. 1808.

[8] William Eaton (1764-1811), who had recently returned from his remarkable mission in North Africa as "Navy Agent to the Barbary States," the objective of which had been the restoration of the exiled Pasha Hamet Karamanli to the throne of Tripoli. The dinner tendered to him took place on 2 Jan. (DAB; Scharf & Westcott, I, 523.)

[9] Stephen Decatur (1779-1820), naval hero of the Tripolitan War; promoted to captain, 1804, for his exploit in boarding and burning the U.S. frigate *Philadelphia*, which was grounded and in the hands of the enemy. His testimonial dinner occurred on 9 Jan. (DAB; Scharf & Westcott, I, 523.)

To James Madison

Dear Sir,   Philadelphia, January 30th, 1806

Many years have passed away since I have read a political pamphlet. The subject and name of the author of the one which you have done me the honor to send me will force me from my habits of neglect of such publications. My son is now devouring it. It is spoken of in all the circles in our city with the highest praise and admiration.[1]

Connected with our present controversy with Great Britain, permit me to relate the following fact. In the spring of 1777 I called to see Mr. John Adams at his lodgings in Philadelphia soon after his return with Congress from Baltimore. He informed me in the course of our conversation that he had been much gratified by a communication recently made to him by Colonel Henry Laurence [*Laurens*], who had lately returned from a long residence in England and who had at that time just taken his seat in Congress. Previously to his sailing for America, he waited upon George Greenville [*Grenville*] and entered into a discussion with him of the American claims to an exemption from taxation by the British Parliament, and urged the impropriety of risking the loss of the colonies for the sake of the trifling revenue which was the object of the controversy. "Hold," said Mr. Greenville. "Mr. Laurence, you mistake the designs of this country. We do not expect much revenue from you. The present contest with America is for the empire of the ocean. *You spread too much canvas upon our seas, and we are determined to clip it.*"[2]

The late conduct of the Court of Britain shows that the declaration of Mr. Greenville has been hereditary in it.

You may make any use you please of the above anecdote—only keep my name from the public eye.

From, dear sir, your sincere and affectionate old friend,

BENJN: RUSH

Addressed: James Madison Esqr: Secretary of State of the United States. City of Washington.

MS: Historical Society of Pennsylvania, Dreer Collection.

[1] Madison's long pamphlet, published anonymously without place or date, was entitled *An Examination of the British Doctrine, Which Subjects to Capture a Neutral Trade, Not Open in Time of Peace*; in Madison's *Writings*, ed. Gaillard Hunt, N.Y., 1900-1910, VII, 204-375. Though an able presentation of the American position, it was not inaptly characterized by John Randolph of Roanoke as "a shilling pamphlet hurled against eight hundred ships of war" (DAB, under Madison).

[2] See BR's letter to the Editor of the *Pennsylvania Journal*, 4 July 1782.

To John Adams

My dear and excellent Friend,   Philadelphia, March 15th, 1806

I avail myself of the first leisure hour I have had since the conclusion of my lectures to acknowledge your last favor.[1] I shall
begin my answer to it by answering the question with which you
concluded it. The barilla[2] is a native of the seacoast of the United
States. It is to be found on the shores of Massachussets and of the
Delaware State.

From the interest you have kindly taken in my principles and
fate in medicine, I shall take the liberty of transcribing a part of the
farewell lecture with which I concluded my labors in our University
a few days ago.

"I am aware, gentlemen," said your friend, "of the import of the
declaration that I have taught a new system of medicine. The declaration has been forced upon me by its enemies, from whom it first
received that odious and unpopular name. It has since been given
to it by its friends in different and remote parts of the world. The
fate of this system of medicine has been a singular one. Upon its
first appearance, it was considered as a sickly brat that would perish
as soon as it was exposed to the inclemency of a cold or rainy day.
Contrary to calculation, it lived through stormy seasons, but in
great weakness and penury. For many years it rambled up and
down the streets of Philadelphia like a little beggar boy, without
a friend and without any other shelter than the scanty one afforded
by its father. A few gentlemen of the faculty[3] (whose names will
ever be dear to me) admitted him into their homes and assisted
me in feeding and clothing him. But a great majority of the physicians of the city scouted him from their doors. Some of them did
more. They either hired the vagabonds of the city to pelt him with
stones, or they rewarded them liberally for doing so by their
friendship and patronage. In spite of this unkind and cruel treatment, the boy has lived to be a man and has acquired such marks
of strength and vigor that he is now admired and cherished in the
families of his former enemies. It is true they have changed his
name and endeavored to disguise his person by a new dress, but his
voice, his features, and his manners discover his descent from his
lawful father.

"Among the many painful circumstances that have attended the
propagation of the new system of medicine I have taught you, my
being obliged to oppose the system of Dr. Cullen was not the least.
He was very dear to me as a master, and I shared largely in his

friendship. I am reconciled to my conduct *only* by reflecting that our objects were the same, and were it possible for his departed spirit to meet me in my study or in an evening walk, he would say to me, '*Go on, my son. Continue to exercise the freedom of inquiry with which it was my pride and pleasure to inspire my pupils. If the empire of death has been lessened in a single instance by your rejection of any part of my principles of medicine, I shall rejoice in the successful issue of your labors.*' Yes! venerable Shade! I am sure you do, for your whole life was animated not less by the love of our science than by the most sublime and disinterested benevolence to your fellow creatures.

"The dead sometimes call upon us from the tombstones and say, '*As you are* NOW, *so once was I. As I am* NOW, *so shortly you shall be.*' I fancy I hear the same awful voice issuing from the tomb of my beloved master. It seems to say to me, '*In the progress of our Science towards perfection, your system of medicine must fully share the fate of mine. Future discoveries in anatomy, physiology, natural history, and chemistry will consign a part of it to the oblivion of the grave and render alterations necessary in every other part of it.*' Delightful intelligence! I anticipate its accomplishment with pleasure. Perhaps I am now addressing the gentleman who shall, from the chair I now occupy, or from the press, expose the errors of my system of medicine. Did I know who was to be that person, I would take him by the hand and cordially wish him success in his noble undertaking. Perish my name and the memory of my labors from the records of time, provided that the science I have loved and cherished be advanced and perfected in the world."

The length of this extract from my lecture has I am afraid so far tired you that you will hardly have patience with me when I add that our governor has lately promoted my brother to be judge of the first district in the state, by which means he will be restored to his official rank and situation in Philadelphia from which Governor Mifflin had removed him.[4] This appointment was unsolicited and unexpected. It has added much to my happiness.

What is to be the fate of our country, of Europe, of the globe, from the operation of the events which have lately taken place in every part of them? The calculations of the philosopher, the wisdom of the statesman, and the energies of the patriot are all prostrated by the aims and ambition of the new Emperor of France. Our only refuge now seems to be in the prayer of the Church—"Save us, good Lord! for there is no other fighteth for us, but only thou, O Lord!"

With affectionate regard to Mrs. Adams, in which my dear Mrs. Rush and all my young folks join, I am, dear sir, ever your obliged and sincere friend,

BENJN RUSH

MS: Adams Manuscript Trust, Boston.

[1] Dated 25 Jan. 1806 (*Old Family Letters*, *A*, p. 89-95).

[2] Adams had asked whether the barilla was ever found in the United States. Barilla, known by various names, is a species of saltwort yielding soda ash, once used in making soap and glass (Webster).

[3] BR means the medical profession. "Faculty" was frequently used in this sense.

[4] The background for these incidents is supplied in a letter from BR to Jefferson, 4 Jan. 1792 (L.C., Jefferson Papers), in which BR requested the Secretary of State's support for Jacob Rush's appointment to a federal judgeship. (The appointment did not materialize.) BR wrote: "Soon after the accession of Mr. Mifflin to the government of Pennsylvania, he gratified his resentment against me for opposing his election, by removing my brother from a seat on the bench of the Supreme Court of Pennsylvania. The public clamor against this cruel and arbitrary measure, and the numerous testimonies which rose up in favor of my brother's integrity and abilities in the execution of his office, induced Mr. Mifflin to appoint him a district judge for four of the frontier counties of the state." Judge Rush had resided at Reading while holding this post; his appointment by McKean as president judge of the court of common pleas for the city and county of Philadelphia brought him back to Philadelphia.

To John Coakley Lettsom

Dear Sir,   Philadelphia, April 18, 1806

It gave me great pleasure a few days ago to read the public testimony of the Jennerian Society in favor of vaccination. I have the honor of according with their opinions in their fullest extent. In no one instance has a disagreeable eruption of any kind followed the vaccine pustule in my practice; nor has a symptom of the small-pox been produced in any one of the patients whom I have afterwards inoculated with the variolous matter.

I lament that you and I continue to think so differently upon the subject of the contagiousness of the yellow fever. Proofs of its domestic origin and of its spreading exclusively from an impure atmosphere, rendered so by putrid exhalation, multiply yearly in every part of our country. The College of Physicians of Philadelphia stand alone among the physicians of the United States in supporting a contrary opinion. *Do, my friend, give the subject a second investigation.* The evils which flow from a belief in the importation of our American pestilence are incalculable. It has perpetuated the disease in our country. It has demoralized our citizens, as far as humanity constitutes moral character. It fosters national prejudice and hostility, and it consigns thousands every year to the grave who might otherwise have been preserved from it.

I remain, &c.,

BENJ. RUSH

Printed: Pettigrew, *Lettsom*, III, 199-200.

To James Monroe

Dear Sir,   Philadelphia, April 21st, 1806

After requesting you to accept of my thanks for your care of a small packet conveyed to me through the hands of Mr. Madison from the Baron Kleist [*Kloest*], permit me to solicit the favor of you to send the packet which will be delivered to you by Captain McDougall[1] to the same nobleman. It contains a copy of the late edition of my inquiries and observations upon the yellow fever[2]— a subject to which the Prussian court has lately directed its attention with a zeal and solicitude that are worthy of the imitation of all the governments in the world.

Accept of my congratulations upon the continuance of the marks of confidence with which your country has lately honored you, and believe me to be with great regard your sincere and affectionate *old* friend,

BENJN: RUSH

Addressed: James Monroe Esqr: Minister from the United States of America to the Court of London favoured by Capt: McDougall.
MS: New York Public Library, Monroe Papers.

[1] BR had recently introduced Capt. John McDougall to Madison as an old friend whose ship had been lost, apparently by seizure on the part of one of the belligerent powers (to Madison, 7 Apr. 1806; L.C., Madison Papers). McDougall lived at 24 Almond St. (*Phila. Directory* for 1806).
[2] Probably the *Inquiry* sent to Jefferson, 6 Dec. 1805, or possibly the fourth volume of *Med. Inq. & Obs.*, 2d edn., 1805.

To John Adams

Philadelphia, June 10th, 1806

My much respected and dear Friend,

My long delay in answering your last letter[1] has arisen from two causes—an unusual share of business from an unusually sickly spring, and the want of subjects for a letter that would be interesting to you.

I perfectly accord with you in your opinions respecting the tendency and issue of the present state of things in the world. Never perhaps was there a time in which there was more to fear from the wickedness and folly, and less to hope from the virtue and wisdom, of man. A newspaper, once the vehicle of pleasing and useful intelligence, is now the sad record only of misery and crimes. All systems of political order and happiness seem of late years to have disappointed their founders and advocates. Civilization, science, and commerce have long ago failed in their attempts to improve the condition of mankind, and even liberty itself, from which more was expected than from all other human means, has lately appeared to be insufficient for that purpose. If we fly from the lion of despotism, the bear of anarchy meets us, or if we retire from both and lean our hand upon the wall of our domestic sanctuary, the recollection of past or the dread of future evils bites us like a serpent.

> "Oh! for a lodge in some vast wilderness!
> Some boundless contiguity of shade,
> Where rumor of oppression and deceit,
> Of unsuccessful and successful war,
> Might never reach me more."[2]

My only hope for suffering and depressed humanity is derived from a belief in a new and divine order of things which we are told will be introduced into our world by the influence of the gospel upon individuals and nations. It was predicted of the Messiah that he would be "the desire of *all* nations."[3] Should the present system of violence and subjugation of the nations continue, that prophecy must soon be fulfilled, for I believe there is at this time scarcely a nation upon the face of the earth that is satisfied with its government or its rulers and that would not exchange both for others, though probably, in their present state of ignorance, not for the government of the future King of Saints and Nations. A few more years of suffering will probably bring about the fulfillment of the prophecy and render him indeed the "desire of *all* nations."

You complain of my reserve upon political subjects. This you know is not natural to me. My silence upon those subjects arises wholly from ignorance and perhaps a criminal indifference to the affairs of our country. You may easily conceive the extent of both when I add no praises or censures pronounced upon J. Randolph's famous speeches could induce me to read them, and that at a time when little else was spoken of in all the fashionable circles in Philadelphia.[4]

I am not surprised at your anecdote of Governor McKean. Were I to turn clergyman, I think I could preach a whole year upon two short texts. They are "Put not your trust in man" and "Beware of men."[5]

I have lately been favored with a visit from a Polish gentleman[6] who spent six weeks in Paris on his way to America. He described the present miserable state of his native country in the most pathetic terms. He dined with Tallerand while in Paris, who spoke with great contempt at his table of the American character. He saw but one man in the United States (he said) who was unwilling to sell everything he possessed. The property held by that man so very dear was "a favorite dog."

I lament that my letters are such feeble echoes of yours. Continue to honor me with your matured reflections upon men and things. The most careless of them afford instruction and pleasure to my whole family. I cannot conclude without offering my sympathy to you and Mrs. Adams in your late domestic afflictions. I hope the name and blood of your grandson[7] will save his life. Miranda has been the unfortunate cause of distress to more families than yours. Colonel Burr, who spent an hour or two with him at my house, said he would fail in his enterprise, for "he is," said the Colonel, "not a practical man."

With cordial salutations to Mrs. Adams, in which my dear Mrs. Rush joins, I bid you an affectionate adieu. Ever yours,

BENJN: RUSH

𝑀𝑆: Adams Manuscript Trust, Boston.

[1] Dated 26 Mch. 1806 (*Old Family Letters*, *A*, p. 95-9).

[2] Cowper, *The Task* (1785), opening lines of Book II.

[3] Haggai 2:7.

[4] John Randolph of Roanoke (1773-1833), the celebrated orator, parliamentarian, and wit, who was at this time moving rapidly from support of Jefferson to opposition (DAB). A few years later BR said that he had "long considered [Randolph] a mischievous boy with a squirt in his hands" (to Adams, 26 Apr. 1810).

[5] I have not located the first text (though see Psalms 146:3, "Put not your trust in princes"); the second is from Matthew 10:17.

[6] Not identified.

[7] William Steuben Smith (1787-1850), son of William Stephens Smith, Adams' son-in-law. The younger Smith, to his grandfather Adams' extreme indignation, left Columbia College just before graduation to join the Miranda expedition. (Roof, *Colonel William Smith and Lady*, ch. XXXII; Abigail Adams, *New Letters*, p. 268.)

To David R. Patteson[1]

Dear Sir,   Philadelphia, June 19, 1806

From the high idea I entertain of the efficacy of a salivation in a pulmonary disease such as you have described yours to be, I am still anxious to excite it in your case. For this purpose I have procured for you a preparation of mercury, called the *phosphate of mercury*, which has been found to be more speedy and certain in acting upon the salivary glands than any other of its preparations. The dose is half a grain mixed with a little of the powder of cinnamon and gum arabic, but as it is a very active medicine, I would advise you to begin with one sixth of a grain three times a day blended with a little opium and cinnamon, and increase it gradually till a salivation be excited. In the meanwhile continue to use all the common palliative remedies for chronic affections of the lungs.

I cannot yet despair of your recovery, although I am much pleased with the humble and resigned temper you discover in your letter. Continue, my dear friend, to trust in the power and to depend upon the mercy of your God. Disease and death have often been conquered by him, and where they have been permitted to prevail in this world, it is only to furnish a more glorious opportunity for the Saviour of mankind to display his power and mercy in the world to come in vanquishing sin and death. BELIEVE IN HIM —and whatever may be the issue of your disease, you will be safe and happy.

From, my dear sir, your sympathizing friend,

            BENJN: RUSH

Addressed: Dr David R: Patteson Physician Warmister Virginia.
MS: Not located; photostat in Virginia State Library.

[1] David R. Patteson left BR's class in 1797 to become a surgeon's mate in the army; he afterwards settled at Warminster, Amherst (now Nelson) co., Va. (Patteson's letters to BR, Rush MSS, XIII). The present letter, written in answer to Patteson's of 11 June 1806, exemplifies BR's habit of mingling medical and religious instruction when advising patients.

To John Adams

My venerable and dear Friend,   Philadelphia, July 11, 1806

At the request of my wife I called upon a friend of mine a few days ago to borrow *The Secret Memoirs of the Court of St. Cloud*.[1] He said he had not a copy of it, but politely put into my hands

Cumberland's *Memoirs of His Own Life*,[2] which I have since filled up the leisure minutes of the day in reading. It is a pleasant work and contains a good deal of information of men and things which would otherwise have never been known. He met with a common share of disappointments in life and with a few instances of unkindness and broken promises from his friends, but upon the whole his life was prosperous and happy. He moved in subordinate situations and often saw the events and characters he describes through the medium of other people's glasses. How much more interesting would a work of the same kind be, written by a man who was the principal actor in the events which he describes and who lived in those times which laid the foundation for the present convulsions among the nations of the earth! I once suggested in a whisper to Mrs. Adams at Mr. Boudinot's table that the history of your political life drawn up by yourself would be an invaluable legacy to the public, or to your family if you should forbid its publication. I am the more anxious for such a record of opinions and facts from the gross ignorance and errors which we daily hear and read from men who were children or not born in the memorable and eventful years which *preceded* the American Revolution. The *Life of Washington*[3] has not lessened the number of those errors. Two military men of high rank have complained loudly of being overlooked in the details of the battles that are included in that history. One of them assured me that the account of one of those battles was so different from what he observed to take place in it that he did not believe for a while that it was the same event. The historian of that work should not be blamed. He is candid and upright. His documents have deceived him. I know the execution of such a work as I have recommended will be attended with difficulties if it should be written so as to meet the public eye before the present tide in favor of error has spent itself. But it may be withheld some years and resorted to only by your family for faithful statements of facts, till time shall remove the persons or lessen the influence of the families that might be offended by it. I shall only mention a single fact to illustrate the injustice and error that take place with respect to opinions and events. When a proposal for mitigating the severity of our penal laws was first published in Pennsylvania, and solitary labor was recommended as a substitute for whipping, cropping, and hanging, the late worthy Judge Bradford treated that proposal with good-humored ridicule. A few years afterwards he adopted all the ideas he had ridiculed, and defended them in a learned and eloquent pamphlet.[4] He is now revered as one of the authors of our new system of penal laws. Dr. Franklin shares with him in that honor, although he never wrote a line nor uttered a sentiment in favor of it to my knowledge, neither before nor after it had taken place in Pennsylvania.

I once heard a pious minister of the Gospel say that "God *threw away* kingdoms and empires upon the most worthless part of mankind." May not the same thing be said in many instances of fame? There is a disease known among physicians by the name of "error loci." If fame is not thrown away upon the worthless part of mankind, it is certainly often given to those to whom it does not belong, thereby constituting an historical "error loci."

But why this solicitude to establish historical or political truth in our world? In what single instance have mankind been the better for it? We not only repeat the errors of other people though warned by their confessions to avoid them, but we repeat errors in spite of our *own* experience and even of our *own* sufferings from them.

I have read two things in our papers lately with great pleasure. The first is the account of your grandson not being in either of the two schooners captured by the Spaniards in Miranda's expedition, and the other is the great respect paid to your name and character at the late public dinner in Boston on the 4th of July.

My eldest son is now or was lately at Salem. He has, very contrary to my wishes and advice, returned to the navy, in which he commands a gunboat. Had he been in New York when Miranda sailed, I have no doubt he would have been an adventurer in his wild and ill-digested interprise.

I thank you for your friendly notice of the compliment paid to my medical opinions by the Court and Medical College at Berlin.[5] The account of it found its way into our papers very much against my inclinations and without my knowledge, for however gratifying it might be to my friends, I did not wish to give pain to my enemies by making it public. For the same reason I have concealed except from half a dozen persons several other flattering marks of attention to my medical opinions in other parts of the world. Providence often gives men a currency which they neither wished for nor expected among their fellow men. My aim when I began to practise medicine was humbly and closely to tread in the footsteps of my illustrious master. To be the author of a new system of medicine was as foreign to my views and even wishes in my profession as it is now to be Archbishop of Canterbury or President of the United States. Thus babes and sucklings often take the place of the mighty and the wise in the affairs of this world as well as in that which is to come.

To resume the subject of the memoirs of your life. Frederick the 2nd asks in his *Seven Years War*, "What did human reason ever do *great* in human affairs?"[6] Where great events are brought about apparently by human reason, men are often I believe prompted to accomplish them by motives that are contrary to *right* reason. I am led to make this remark by recollecting the absurd and frivolous reasons which were given by many of our patriots in 1776 for concurring in the separation of our country from G. Britain. One of these men said to me, "I am now for independence, since the King of G. Britain has employed Hessian mercenaries to assist in subjugating us." Foolish man! As if there was any difference between being killed by a Hessian and a British bayonet! Hundreds advocated the measure only because the Indians were let loose upon our western settlements, as if the British decrees and attempts to enslave us were rendered more absolute by that single link in the chain that was contrived to bind us. Few, very few, consented to our becoming an independent nation from the influence of causes and motives that rendered our reunion with Great Britain as impracticable after what had passed on both sides in 1774 and 1775 as the reunion of a body dissevered from its head by the stroke of an ax. Still fewer were actuated by a prospect of the future and permanent safety, happiness, and prosperity of our country. Indeed we were conducted with our eyes obliquely directed, and backwards, in spite of ourselves, to the haven of peace and independence. We are the causes of our own misery in most cases, but our happiness came to be forced upon us by the kind and invisible hand of heaven.

With respects and love as usual, I am, my ever dear friend, ever yours,

BENJN: RUSH

[1] *The Secret History of the Court and Cabinet of St. Cloud. In a Series of Letters from a Resident in Paris to a Nobleman in London. Written during . . . 1805*, Phila., 1806. The work has been variously attributed to one Stewarton and to Lewis Goldsmith (*L.C. Cat.*; Samuel Halkett and John Laing, *Dictionary of Anonymous and Pseudonymous English Literature*, Edinburgh and London, 1926-1934). Senator William Plumer notes under the date 6 Jan. 1807 in his *Memoradum of Proceedings in the United States Senate, 1803-1807* (N.Y., 1923, p. 559-60) that it was a collection of scandalous anecdotes about Napoleon and not fit to be on the shelves of the Library of Congress. The Librarian of Congress had told Plumer that "no book in the library was in so much demand—It was constantly out—& in the course of a week was several times read—The number [member?] who took it for the

week, read it, & lent it to others."

² *Memoirs of Richard Cumberland. Written by Himself*, London, 1806. Cumberland (1732-1811) was a civil servant, dramatist, and novelist, his best remembered production being *The West Indian*, acted 1771 (DNB).

³ John Marshall's *Life of George Washington*, Phila., 1804-1807.

⁴ William Bradford, *An Enquiry How Far the Punishment of Death Is Necessary in Pennsylvania*, Phila., 1793. For Franklin's interest in penal reform, see Van Doren, *Franklin*, p. 712. But BR

was the prime mover in penal reform in Pennsylvania; see his letters to Dickinson, 5 Apr. 1787, and to Lettsom, 16 Aug. 1788.

⁵ See BR to Monroe, 21 Apr. 1806.

⁶ BR cites the writings of Frederick the Great with such frequency that it is likely that he owned the *Posthumous Works* of that monarch, a thirteen-volume English edition, London, 1789, containing *The History of My Own Times, The History of the Seven Years' War*, correspondence, &c.

To John Adams

My dear Friend,   Philadelphia, August 22nd, 1806

You ascribe wonders to the influence of silence and secrecy in public men.¹ I agree with you in their effects upon characters and human affairs. Dr. South² says the "world was made for the bold." But they possess only half of it—the other half was made for the "artful," among whom I include nearly all silent men. I say nearly all, for we now and then meet with persons who are silent from modesty or some physical cause, but nine-tenths of them are silent from *pride* (predominating over sense and knowledge), *stupidity*, or *art*. One of the greatest impostors I have known in medicine was silent from the influence of all three of those causes. That his silence was dramatical was evident from his being uncommonly talkative out of sickrooms and where the subjects of conversation were scandal or the best means of getting and securing money. The silence of one of the persons named in your letter has been generally ascribed to modesty. Mr. Liston once remarked to me that he was taciturn beyond any man he had ever known in his life, so much so as not even to give an indirect or evasive reply to questions when it was improper for him to answer. I said, "He had derived great reputation from this line of conduct." "Yes," said Mr. L., "he has, but it has cost him very dear," meaning constant restraint and self-denial, for that this was the case I infer from his frank and open conversation and conduct in making bargains and doing his private business. Of his habits of secrecy Mr. Fitzsimons informed me of the following anecdote. Mr. R. Morris applied to him for the office of inspector of the excise for Pennsylvania for Mr. Geo. Clymer. He heard his application, but said nothing. On his way to Congress

Mr. Morris called upon him a second time to solicit the appointment for his friend. He was still silent. When Mr. Morris came into the Senate Chamber, the first thing he heard from the chair was the nomination of Mr. Clymer (which had been sent 2 hours *before*) for the office that had been asked for, for him. Why all this mystery about nothing? The case did not call for it. Good breeding alone, friendship out of the question, called for a different mode of conduct. But he acted probably involuntary,[3] merely from habit.

I think I have remarked that all minds are alike in becoming more or less plethoric from ideas, whether good or bad, whether useful or trifling. Such persons as do not lessen or remove this plethora by conversation in ordinary society do it by conversing with some one friend who is generally below them in rank, with a wife, with a servant, by constant letter-writing, or by means of a diary. The most natural way is by conversation with equal society. The persons who reject this in favor of the latter modes of mental depletion resemble the Quakers, who reject music in their worship but *sing* more in preaching and praying than any other sect of Christians.

From what models human or divine was taciturnity in company derived? Caesar charmed by his conversation even his enemies as well as his friends. Alexander opened his soul over a convivial glass with his generals. If we turn our eyes from these two men (the greatest probably that have lived) to the Saviour of the world, we shall find him affable, sociable, and instructing by his parables and questions or by his allusions to present circumstances, such as a harvest field, a bed of lilies, or a flight of birds, in all companies. I conclude therefore that taciturnity is neither a pagan or a Christian virtue, and certainly not essential to true greatness. On the contrary, I believe (cases of invincible modesty and absence or depression of mind from a morbid state of the nerves excepted) it is always the effect of pride, ill-breeding, or stupidity, or dictated by unfair designs to obtain wealth, power, or fame. Where it is not a mental or bodily disease, it is of course at all times a downright vice.

What shall it profit a man if he gain the wealth, the power, or the fame of the whole world and lose his character for integrity? Conversations in dactyls and spondees, and actions in stucco work are seldom worth hearing or seeing, for they are both unnatural and of course disagreeable. There is nothing within us that vibrates in unison with either of them. We are best pleased with some carelessness in conversation and imperfection in conduct. Thus while we turn with disgust from the monotonous and monstrous virtues of Sir Charles Grandison, we admire, we love, and we pity poor Clarissa Harlowe. Indeed, so consonant is frailty with everything that belongs to human nature, that it may perhaps be truly said that there is something radically wrong in that man who (to the eye of the world) has never erred.

I am much pleased with your son's inaugural lecture.[4] It is full of good sense, and in many parts of it eloquent. My son Richard speaks of it in the highest terms. How much is it to be lamented that the manner in which (he says) business is done in our republican assemblies will prevent the cultivation or employment of oratory in them!

Dr. Priestley's life, written partly by himself and partly by his son, Thos. Cooper, and a Unitarian clergyman of the name of Christey, has just made its appearance.[5] I have read it with pleasure. It contains a list of all his publications on political, metaphysical, theological, philosophical, and *chemical* subjects. Upon the last he discovers great original genius. Chemistry owes more to him than any other science. In theology, as Gibbon happily remarks, "he was always at war with men for believing too little or too much."[6] In metaphysics he has only defended in a new and popular dress ancient opinions upon the action of the will and the materiality of the mind. In philosophy he was useful by embellishing and methodizing the discoveries of other people and by some additions to them made by himself. In politics Mr. Cooper ascribes to him the original idea of the perfectibility of man commonly ascribed to Dr. Price and the Marquis of Condorcet.[7] The account of the few last days of the Doctor by his son is truly interesting. I never was a believer in his peculiar religious principles, but I am forced to own they produced in him in his last sickness uncommon resignation, peace, and composure of mind. He died in a full belief of a happy immortality.

Adieu! my dear friend. I write for a chimney corner. None of my letters I hope will be preserved or read to anybody but your other self, to whom my dear Mrs. Rush sends much love with ever yours,

BENJN: RUSH

P.S. I regret that the reasons you have given in your letter are so weighty for declining "the history of your life and of your own times." What say you to committing it to your son John?

MS: Adams Manuscript Trust, Boston.

[1] Adams in a letter of 23 July 1806 (*Old Family Letters*, *A*, p. 104-9) had instanced Washington, Franklin, and Jefferson as examples of the effectiveness of silence, rather than eloquence, in public assemblies. BR's remarks below refer of course to Washington.

[2] Robert South, D.D. (1634-1716), an Anglican clergyman whose published sermons were long popular (DNB).

[3] Thus in MS.

[4] J. Q. Adams' *Inaugural Oration, Delivered at the Author's Installation, as Boylston's Professor of Rhetorick and Oratory, at Harvard University*, Boston, 1806 (*L.C. Cat.*).

[5] *Memoirs of Dr. Joseph Priestley, to the Year 1795, Written by Himself. With a Continuation to the Time of His Decease, by His Son, Joseph Priest-*ley: *and Observations on His Writings, by Thomas Cooper . . . and the Rev. William Christie*, Northumberland, Penna., 1806 (*L.C. Cat.*).

[6] Gibbon was briefly a Catholic in his youth. The statement quoted by BR may well have been taken from Gibbon's *Memoirs of My Life and Writings* (first published 1796), a work which BR quotes elsewhere; but I have not located it.

[7] Marie-Jean-Antoine-Nicholas Caritat, Marquis de Condorcet (1743-1794), *philosophe* and Girondist, author of a posthumously published *Esquisse d'un tableau historique des progrès de l'esprit humain*, which upholds the idea of unlimited progress through human reason (*Encyclo. Brit.*, 9th edn.).

To Mrs. Rush

My Other and *Best* HALF,   Philadelphia, September 19, 1806

This letter I hope will find you returned and much improved, by your trip to New Ark, in health and spirits.

The affairs of the family and of my business continue to maintain their uniform tenor. Yesterday I drank tea at Major Butler's with Miss Macpherson,[1] in compliance with a wish expressed by her to see me before she left the city. She had received a letter from our son John since her escape from the bed of death on the ocean with which she was much pleased.[2] She spoke of him in respectful terms. Of her sufferings and affliction on the wreck of the *Rose in bloom* she spoke with great feeling and correctness. She was saved by a large and fine body of hair on the back of her head, by which she was dragged to the side of the vessel by a young man of the name of Perry[3] of Boston. She was not ungrateful to her deliverer. Major Butler wrote to him from New York to draw upon him for 3,000 dollars as a reward for his heroic conduct. He declined accepting of it *for the present*, in consequence of his losses (amounting to 7,000 dollars) on board the wreck having subjected him to the necessity of throwing himself upon the lenity of his creditors. He has for some time past supported a mother and two sisters in Boston.

James will carry to Julia all the articles of dress she wants.

Mrs. Griffitts[4] breakfasted with us yesterday morning. Adieu! Ever yours,

BENJN RUSH

P.S. Love as usual.

A Manual for Julia

1. Hold up your head.
2. Let go your fingers.
3. Look the person you speak to in the face.
4. Speak in a distinct and elevated tone of voice.

Addressed: Mrs Julia Rush Princeton New Jersey.
MS: Boston Public Library.

[1] Evidently a relative of Pierce Butler's, but not further identified.

[2] Thus in MS!

[3] This gallant gentleman remains, after much search and inquiry, unidentified. The *Boston Directory* for 1806 lists among other Perrys a John and a George, both dealing in West Indies goods, also a Nathaniel, mariner, in Fish Street. I have not found a newspaper account of the wreck of the *Rose in Bloom.*

[4] Perhaps Mary (Fishbourne) Griffitts, wife of BR's close friend Dr. Samuel P. Griffitts (Thacher, *Amer. Med. Biog.*, p. 284).

To the Earl of Buchan

My Lord,   Philadelphia, October 22nd, 1806

I have been kept from answering your lordship's polite letter by Dr. Chapman by a most unpleasant event. On his way from New York to Philadelphia his trunk was stolen from the external and back part of a stage wagon, and with it the present of the ancient and very estimable box you intended for me. In hopes that an advertisement or the lapse of a year or two would bring it to light and place it in my hands, I have deferred until this time expressing my regrets to your lordship for my disappointment and loss. The virtues and exploits of the illustrious hero who conferred dignity upon the tree that sheltered him, the antiquity of the box, and the rank and character of the noble donor, all concur to render its loss peculiarly distressing to me. I shall carefully preserve your lordship's letter which accompanied it and transmit it to my children as a mark of the high honor intended for me by your lordship.[1]

The convulsions of the European governments have at last affected the repose of the United States. We hope for a continuance of peace with Great Britain, but a war with Spain is very generally apprehended by our citizens. The success of General Miranda in his attempt to excite an insurrection in New Spain may probably prevent it. The character of this extraordinary man is well known to me. He was domesticated in my family 24 years ago. In passing through Philadelphia last year, he renewed his visits to me. I have met with few such men. Profound in ancient and modern literature, eloquent and impressive in his manner of speaking, ardent in his love of liberty, and full of anecdotes of the first personages, royal, political, and military, that have moved or that now move the governments of Europe, he made several long evenings that he spent with me appear like moments by his delightful and instructing conversation. I am not sure that with his uncommon talents and acquirements he possesses the requisites for the leader of an army and the promoter of a revolution. Many men, like Lord Bacon, are great in speculative that are little in practical life. It has been supposed by those who know General Miranda most intimately that he has lived too long in courts and in his closet to succeed in his present difficult military enterprise.

Permit me to congratulate your lordship upon the elevation of your illustrious and excellent brother to the chancellorship of Great Britain and a seat in the House of Lords.[2] His son will be received as minister from the Court of London to the United States with open arms by all classes of our citizens.[3] The name of Erskine has long been dear to Americans.

I am happy in being able to inform your lordship that the family of Palmers, so affectionately protected and so warmly recommended to me by your lordship, have had great reason to rejoice in your advice and friendship. The two young ladies are well married— one of them to a respectable watchmaker, the other to a worthy clergyman. The young men possess a printing office and are doing a great deal of business with fair characters.[4]

In my professional visits to Major Lenox's family[5] I am often gratified by the respectful and affectionate terms in which they speak of your lordship's friendship and civilities to them. We sometimes revive by a delightful retrospect the social, moral, and intellectual pleasures we enjoyed in successive periods of time in your enlightened and happy country.

With great respect I have the honor to be your lordship's most devoted friend and most obedient humble servant,

BENJN: RUSH

MS: Haverford College Library, Roberts Collection.

[1] Concerning the box made from Wallace's Oak, see also BR to Buchan, 25 Oct. 1785, note 3. Buchan had requested Washington to bequeath the box to the American whose patriotism most merited it. "Deeming the selection too delicate," Washington had directed in his will that it be returned to Buchan, who in 1803 entrusted it to Nathaniel Chapman to convey to BR in recognition of his heroic conduct in the yellow-fever epidemics. Though the box never reached BR, he returned the compliment in 1811 by sending Buchan a souvenir made from Penn's Treaty Elm. (Article on BR in Abraham Rees, *Cyclopaedia*, Phila., 1810-1824, XXXII; J. B. Biddle, "Nathaniel Chapman," in Gross' *Lives of Physicians*, p. 671; Washington, *Writings*, ed. Fitzpatrick, XXXII, 25-6, and XXXVII, 285; anonymous article on "George Washington and the Earl of Buchan," in the *Athenaeum*, CV [1895], 738; BR to Buchan, 8 July 1811.)

[2] Thomas Erskine (1750-1823), the famous advocate, named lord chancellor and raised to the peerage as 1st Baron Erskine, 1806 (DNB).

[3] David Montagu Erskine (1776-1855), 2d Baron Erskine, barrister and diplomat; minister to the United States, 1806-1809 (DNB).

[4] The Palmers were immigrants from Kelso, Scotland. The sons may be identified as Thomas and George Palmer, printers at 116 High (Market) and 37 North Eighth Streets; they printed some of BR's publications. George died at New Orleans in 1817. (BR to Buchan, 8 July 1811; *Phila. Directory* for 1806; *Hist. Cat. St. Andrew's Soc. Phila.*, II, 125.)

[5] David Lenox (d. 1828), of a Scottish family, served in the Revolution and became a merchant and banker (*Hist. Cat. St. Andrew's Soc. Phila.* [I], 222-3).

To Benjamin Vaughan

Dear Sir, Philadelphia, October 22, 1806

I am charmed with your prospectus of a literary and scientific periodical work.[1] It discovers a comprehensive view of all the objects of human knowledge. I can only wish it well, for *alone* I can do nothing to support it, and such is the distance at which my opinions and modes of practice have placed me from most of my medical brethren in Philadelphia that few of them will cooperate with me in anything. You will the more readily believe this when I add that, to avoid *insult*, I have long ago retired from the College of Physicians and the Philosophical Society of our city.[2] Neither concession, nor silence, nor forgiveness, nor even time itself has softened in the smallest degree the ferocity of their malice against me. It has increased with every fresh accession of converts to my system of medicine, and in proportion as they have been compelled by their patients to adopt my practice. It began 20 years ago. It became *public* in 1793. It will probably follow me beyond the grave. The history of the various forms of this malice and its effects would be an interesting work. I am not disposed to perpetuate it, and I thank God it is no longer able to injure me. My business, which was reduced 2/3rds by it, is now nearly equal to what it was in the most prosperous years of my life.

I concur with you in your opinion of Dr. Heberden.[3] He was learned and possessed talents for observation, but he wanted reasoning powers.

In my intended publication upon madness I hope to satisfy you that the disease is *arterial*, and that without morbid action in the blood vessels of the brain no form of the disease can exist.[4] The liver and spleen are affected in it symptomatically, but as the symptoms of diseases often require remedies, those viscera require purges by which the brain is much relieved. How often do we see inflammations and obstructions of the liver and spleen for years, and even during a whole life, without a symptom of alienation of mind!

The effects of chronic morbid action on the blood vessels of the brain in producing those associations of ideas and words we call *wit* and *rhyme* have often occurred under my notice. I have taken notice of them in my lectures. In people who are devoid of wit and who are unable to rhyme in health, that symptom is the effect of a new action. In poets the talent of rhyming is the result of original organization of the brain.

I have read Chreighton's works.[5] You will find an extract from them in one of my lectures upon animal life. He has given us some useful facts, but they are uncombined and lead to nothing new or useful in practice. I possess the report you mention on the madness of George IIIrd. Many thanks to you for your kind offer of them.

My opinions suffer by being detailed in detached sentences in my inquiries. I wish you could hear them in their gradual development and connection in my lectures. I can say nothing in their favor but that they hang together and of course are all true or all erroneous. Time must determine which of the two is the case. Adieu. Ever, ever yours,

BENJN: RUSH

P.S. I have just finished an introductory lecture to my next course, "on the medical opinions and practice of Hippocrates."[6] It is to be delivered on Monday sennight in our newly erected medical appendage to the University.[7]

Addressed: Benjamin Vaughan Esqr: Hollowell [*Hallowell*] District of Maine Massachussets.

MS: American Philosophical Society, Benjamin Vaughan Papers.

[1] See Vaughan's letter of 19 Aug. 1806 (Rush MSS, XVIII).

[2] This is the only overt reference by BR to a breach with the American

Philosophical Society, though in the light of the present reference certain remarks in his letter of 20 June 1812, inviting David Hosack to attend a meeting of the Society as BR's guest, take on added significance. BR was an officer of the Society from 1797 to 1800 and again from 1806 until his death, but there is no record of his attending meetings after 1801.

³ William Heberden, the elder, M.D. (1710-1801), an eminent London practitioner, medical writer, and patron of literature (DNB).

⁴ "Having rejected the abdominal viscera, the nerves, and the mind, as the primary seats of madness, I shall now deliver an opinion, which I have long believed and taught in my lectures, and that is, that the cause of madness is seated primarily in the blood-vessels of the brain, and that it depends upon the same kind of morbid and irregular actions that constitute other arterial diseases" (BR, *Diseases of the Mind*, p.

17).

⁵ Sir Alexander Crichton (1763-1856), physician to Westminster Hospital, wrote on both medical and geological subjects (DNB). BR quotes from an essay by Crichton on mental disease in *Med. Inq. & Obs.*, 2d edn., 1805, II, 422-3.

⁶ Delivered 3 Nov. 1806; No. XII in BR's *Sixteen Introductory Lectures*.

⁷ The University at this time was housed in "the President's House" (built for Washington and acquired by the University in 1802) on the west side of Ninth Street between Market and Chestnut. An extension, or annex, was erected for the medical lectures; it is usually said to have been built in 1807, but BR's statement shows that use of it began before the end of 1806 (Cheyney, *Hist. Univ. Penna.*, p. 214; F. P. Henry, *Founder's Week Memorial Volume*, Phila., 1909, p. 235; Mease, *Picture of Philadelphia*, p. 325). See illustration facing p. 973.

To John Adams

Dear Sir, Philadelphia, October 24th, 1806

Ever since the receipt of your last letter I have passed my days like an arrow shot from a bow. At a time of life when (to use an expression in one of your letters written to me soon after your return from England) "nature sighs for repose," I live in a constant round of business which employs both body and mind. Even my studies (the times for which are taken from family society or sleep) are laborious, for they consist chiefly of difficult and long-controverted subjects in physiology. I mention these things not as matters of complaint but to apologize for my apparent neglect of your invaluable letters. I am resigned, patient, and happy in the situation in which it has pleased God to place me in the evening of my life. Blessed with a prudent and sensible wife, I am relieved from all solicitude about the affairs of my family, and even from much of the trouble of instructing my children, which usually falls to the lot of a father. In all this I wish to learn the apostolic lesson of "giving thanks."

The public papers will inform you of the issue of the election in our state. It is supposed the opponents of Mr. McKean and the friends of a convention will compose a majority of both houses of our legislature. Their triumph has been ascribed to a want of union and concert between the Federalists and the *Tertium Quids*[1] (as Duane calls them) or the third party.

Two pamphlets are now in circulation in our city—one called the *Quid Mirror*, which contains a most virulent attack upon the characters of the leading members of the Quid party.[2] It has produced several challenges and one assault and battery. The other pamphlet is a defense of the conduct of General Armstrong in Paris respecting a ship owned by two respectable merchants in Philadelphia.[3] It is said to be well written. Jno. Randolph is the subject of a good deal of abuse in it. I have seen neither of these publications. By preserving my beloved ignorance of the contents of such performances, I am kept from imbibing their spirit and from giving offense by deciding upon their respective merits. Indeed I now consider the disputes of our parties as Hume considered the wars during the heptarchy in England, as "the battles of kites and crows in the air."[4]

Adieu! my dear and venerable friend. Salute your fireside as usual in the names of all my family. I shall expect a call from your son on his way to Washington. Excuse this short and hasty scrawl from the hand and heart of your affectionate and grateful friend,

BENJN: RUSH

Addressed: John Adams Esqr: Woolaston Quincy near Boston.
MS: Adams Manuscript Trust, Boston.

[1] The "Constitutional Republicans," a conservative section of the Democratic-Republican party in Pennsylvania that opposed the movement for a constitutional convention and supported McKean for governor in 1805; their principal leader was A. J. Dallas (Raymond Walters, Jr., *Alexander James Dallas*, Phila., 1943, p. 136-8).
[2] *The Quid Mirror. The First Part*, published in New York, 1806, and promptly reissued in Philadelphia. An extremely scurrilous satire on the Constitutional Republicans, its authorship has been ascribed to William Dickson, a Lancaster newspaper editor (same, p. 142-3).
[3] I have not identified this pamphlet.
[4] See Hume's *History of England*, 1754-1761, I, ch. I.

To John Adams

Dear Sir,   Philadelphia, November 25, 1806

I have seldom been more highly gratified than by the receipt of your letter of November 11th.[1] The latter part of it accords perfectly with opinions I have long cherished. You may see a short account of these opinions in an oration delivered before our Philosophical Society upon "the influence of physical causes upon the moral faculty," published in the first volume of my *Inquiries*. They shocked for a while the prejudices of our citizens, but they are now more reconciled to them. Your letter was further rendered still more interesting to me by my having picked up the volume of Swift's works last summer which contains his *Tale of the Tub* and read it with a pleasure which I was incapable of relishing and with an application to particular characters to which I was a stranger when a boy. The remedies for a yellow fever would do wonders with the heads of the men who now move our world. Ten and ten (as our doses of calomel and jalap were called in 1793) would be a substitute for a fistula in the bowels of Bonaparte. Bleeding would probably lessen the rage for altering the Constitution of Pennsylvania in the leaders of the party who are now contending for that measure. Tonics might be useful to those persons who behold with timidity the insults and spoliations that are offered to our commerce. The cold bath might cure the peevish irritability of some of the members of our Congress, and blisters and mustard plasters rouse the apathy of others. In short, there is a great field opened for new means of curing moral and political maladies. The common remedies for that purpose, that is, Reason and Ridicule, have been used in vain.

I thank you for your excellent strictures upon the visionary ideas of the perfectionists in morals, physic, and government. It was from hearing and reading their nonsense in 1792 that I first despaired of the happy issue of the French Revolution. Perhaps Lord Bacon laid the foundation in part of their madness by the well-known aphorism that "knowledge is power."[2] One of the zealots of this opinion supposed it would extend over matter as well as mind, that it would suspend and invert the laws of nature, and thus destroy the inductions from miracles. I well remember one of his sayings was "that the time would soon come when a man should thrust his head into the fire without burning it." Where are all the vagaries of that eventful year now? The Conventions, Directories, and Emperor of France have dissipated them all, and the foundations of that religion which can alone make men and nations happy have acquired by their destruction a firmness in our world they never had before. Thus not only the wrath but all the follies and crimes of man have, in the language of Scripture, combined indirectly to praise God.

Our political hemisphere is again calm. But the storm, it is said, is only lulled. It is *reported* that our governor will be impeached in the next session of our legislature. Many things are laid to his charge. The principal one is his appointing his son-in-law (though a citizen of Maryland) to a lucrative office in our state.[3] A majority of the Senate (who are to be his judges) are said to be his friends.[4]

Adieu! my venerable and dear friend. My dear Mrs. Rush and sons join in love and respect to you and yours with your ever grateful and affectionate friend,

BENJN: RUSH

MS: Adams Manuscript Trust, Boston.

[1] *Old Family Letters*, *A*, p. 114-20. Adams there developed the proposition that all great conquests, philosophical discoveries, &c., were effected by persons "whose Brains had been shaken out of their natural position."

[2] "Nam et ipsa scientia potestas est." Bacon, *Religious Meditations* (1597), "Of Heresies."

[3] Dr. George Buchanan, of Baltimore, Governor McKean's son-in-law, was appointed lazaretto physician in Philadelphia, July 1806. Duane's *Aurora* pointed out, in an article headed "The Royal Family," that this put twelve McKeans and McKean connections in state offices (Roberdeau Buchanan, *Genealogy of the McKean Family*, Lancaster, 1876, p. 97).

[4] For the abortive impeachment proceedings, see Peeling, "Governor McKean," p. 346-53.

To John Adams

My dear Friend,   Philadelphia, January 23rd, 1807

I have been waiting like Horace's clown till the stream of my business should so far lessen that I could pass over it,[1] in order to acknowledge the receipt of your interesting letter upon the subject of the perfectibility of human nature, but as that stream, from adventitious currents pouring into it, rather increases than lessens, I have seized a few moments merely to testify my gratitude for that letter and to assure you that I subscribe to every sentiment contained in it.[2] By renouncing the Bible, philosophers swing from their moorings upon all moral subjects. Our Saviour in speaking of it calls it "Truth" in the abstract. It is the only correct map of the human heart that ever has been published. It contains a faithful representation of all its follies, vices, and crimes. All systems of religion, morals, and government not founded upon it must perish, and how consoling the thought—it will not only survive the wreck of these systems but the world itself. "The Gates of Hell shall not prevail against it."[3]

Our citizens are now gazing at the storm that has lately risen in the western states.[4] General Eaton, who lately passed through this city on his way to Washington, has mentioned several details of Colonel Burr's propositions to him not published in any of the newspapers. Among others, he said in a large dining company that he asked Burr what he intended to do after establishing the independence of the western states. "Turn Congress out of doors," replied the Colonel, "and hang Tom Jefferson." This declaration, General Eaton added, was extorted by his having made Burr believe he favored his views and was disposed to take part in his enterprises.

All my family join in love to you and yours with, dear sir, your grateful and affectionate friend,

BENJN: RUSH

Addressed: John Adams Esqr: Woolaston Quincy near Boston.
MS: Adams Manuscript Trust, Boston.

[1] See Horace, *Epistles*, I, ii.
[2] Adams' letter is dated 22 Dec. 1806 (*Old Family Letters*, A, p. 120-6.
[3] Matthew 16:18.

[4] The Burr insurrection; among many accounts, that by Henry Adams in his *History of the United States*, III, ch. X-XIV, is one of the best.

To John Warren

Dear Sir,   Philadelphia, February 10, 1807

Doctor Benjn. Shultz, a respectable physician of Northampton County in Pennsylvania and a graduate in our University,[1] has translated from the German into the English language a work which he says is invaluable, upon the practice of physic, by Dr. Weikard.[2] He wishes to be enabled to publish his translation by subscription and has applied to me to introduce him to you and to solicit your patronage to his undertaking. From the high opinion I have of Dr. Shultz's judgment, I have not hesitated to promote his views by placing my name upon his subscription list, and I shall continue to recommend his work as far as my influence extends in this part of our country. The Germans rank high at present in all the sciences, and in none more than in medicine. Dr. Weikard's book will probably convey to us all the new medical opinions and modes of practice of that learned and enlightened nation.

Health, respect, and friendship from, dear sir, yours sincerely,

BENJN: RUSH

Addressed: Dr: John Warren Physician Boston.
MS: American Philosophical Society.

To John Adams

My venerable and dear Friend,   Philadelphia, April 3, 1807

The difficult and complicated labors of my professorship, consisting of teaching, examining, reviewing theses, &c., &c., being now nearly over, I sit down with great pleasure to pay my epistolary debts. You are my largest and most lenient creditor. The first dividend of my time of course is due to you.

I concur with you in your reflections upon the western insurrection, but not altogether in your opinion of Colonel Burr's objects. "Prudence in enterprises and even common business and a guilty conscience," Sully long ago remarked in his character of Count Byron, "are generally incompatible."¹ Burr's plans have been directed like doctors' prescriptions by *pro re nata* circumstances.² I will give you a specimen of them. He applied indirectly to Governor McKean for the chief-justiceship of Pennsylvania just before he set off for Kentucky last year. Success here was as improbable as revolutionizing the western states. "To be unfortunate," says Richlieu, "is to be imprudent." The history of Colonel Burr's pursuits verifies this remark. He failed 1st, in obtaining a foreign embassy the first year he took his seat in the Senate; 2, in supplanting Mr. Jefferson; 3, in obtaining the government of New York; 4, in his western enterprises; and 5, in being chief justice of Pennsylvania. There is often something said or done by men in their youth that marks their destiny in life. I attended the commencement at Princeton at which Mr. Burr took his degree.³ He was then between 16 and 17 years of age. He spoke an elegant oration and with great spirit upon "Building Castles in the Air," in which he exposed its folly in literary, political, and military pursuits. These anecdotes are between ourselves.

Poor Pennsylvania is still upon her broadside. Our governor, who is now the only anchor of our state, is in bad health and upon the eve of being impeached. If not removed by death from office, he will probably be dismissed by the Senate. The lower house of our legislature is under the influence of his enemies. The Senate, though less unfriendly to him, will not, it is thought, dare to acquit him.

A few weeks ago your grandson *left* a letter at my house from his father in which he recommends his son to my good offices.[4] I have in vain attempted to find him out. If he is still in our city (which from the tenor of his father's letter I am disposed to believe is the case), I wish he may be directed to call upon me. My table and fireside shall be to him like the table and fireside of his grandfather. My wife and children will all unite with me in showing their gratitude and affection to his family by civilities to him.

With respectful regard to Mrs. Adams and all your family, in which my dear Mrs. Rush (who is now at work by my side) joins, I am, dear sir, your obliged friend and humble servant,

BENJN: RUSH

MS: Adams Manuscript Trust, Boston.

[1] This is the first reference in BR's letters to a work he was fond of: Maximilien de Béthune, Duc de Sully (1559-1641), *Mémoires*, first published in 1638 and frequently issued in French and English (*Cat. Bibl. Nat.; Brit. Mus. Cat.*).

[2] I.e., "according to the present appearance of affairs."

[3] In 1772.

[4] This was a case of mistaken identity; see BR's letter of 9 July 1807.

To William Roscoe[1]

Dear Sir,   Philadelphia, April 11th, 1807

Accept of my thanks for your acceptable present of a copy of your history of Leo the X. It shall always occupy a distinguished place in my library after it has afforded the usual pleasure of new books in a parlor. My whole family, in which are several readers, are delighted with it. I do not wonder that you have given offense to some of the London critics. But they cannot lessen the credit of your work while a majority of mankind respect the just principles of patriotism, liberty, and religion which you have so happily blended with events and characters.

Permit me to request you to accept of a copy of essays,[2] the origin of which you will find in a short preface which is prefixed to them. The pamphlets upon Negro slavery (to which the preface refers) were published above thirty years ago, a time when just opinions upon that subject were as unpopular in America as they were seven years ago in Great Britain. Since that time a great and universal change has taken place in the middle states of America. A similar change I perceive with great pleasure has taken place in your country in favor of our African fellow men. I rejoiced in hearing that your elevation to a seat in Parliament was the effect of the triumph of that change in the citizens of Liverpool.[3]

I have only to add my cordial wishes that your public life may be as useful as your private pursuits have been honorable, and that late, very late in life, you may enjoy in a future state the rewards which await the benefactors of mankind.

From, dear sir, your obliged friend,

BENJN: RUSH

MS: Liverpool Public Libraries, Roscoe Collection.

[1] William Roscoe (1753-1831), banker and historian, was M.P. for Liverpool, 1806-1807, and a man of broad scholarly and humanitarian interests (DNB). The work that evoked the present letter was Roscoe's *Life and Pontificate of Leo the Tenth*, Liverpool, 1805, 4 vol. Letters from Roscoe to BR are in Rush MSS, XXIII.

[2] Doubtless the 1806 reprint of BR's *Essays*, first published in 1798.

[3] The bill for the abolition of the slave trade was passed by Parliament about a fortnight before this letter was written; Roscoe was one of its principal supporters (DNB).

To John Adams

Dear Sir,   Philadelphia, April 22nd, 1807

I enclose you the letter I mentioned in my last, from the person whom I supposed to be your son-in-law. The letter from his son has been mislaid. I have neither friend nor correspondent in New York of the name of Wm. Smith except your son-in-law, and having never before seen his handwriting and supposing he had dropt his middle name of Stephens, I had no doubt of the letter coming from him. From this statement of facts, you will perceive the whole affair is as much a mystery to me as it has been to you. I have heard of letters being directed by mistake to persons for whom they were not intended. Perhaps this may explain the case in question.[1]

Your remarks upon the characters of three gentlemen mentioned in your last letter I believe to be just.[2] They were all visionary in their principles and projects. The two Americans attempted to rise in the same kind of vehicle but by different kinds of gas—the one was the result of Federal, the other of Democratic putrefaction. They both looked forward to a civil war to place them in the situation to which they aspired. One of them acknowledged it the evening before he fell—the other certainly attempted it. Of this, two letters from my son John,[3] who now commands a gunboat at New Orleans, have furnished me with the most satisfactory (though not legal) evidence. His object was not Mexico but Louissiana, where my son informs us two-thirds of the inhabitants were in favor of his revolutionary enterprise. You have mentioned in your letter the true cause of his success when he became Vice-President of the U. States.

Governor McKean is better. The Assembly have postponed the vote for impeaching him till the next session of the legislature, which will not take place until after another election. I despair of a change for the better in the legislature. The tories and Federalists in our state object to a union with the Quids, and while this is the case the enemies of our governor will continue to pursue him and probably with success. You have aptly compared our state to a ship in a storm. From every view I have taken of our situation I see no prospect of a change for the better in our affairs. Do you not sometimes imprecate the same evils upon the day on which you became a politician that Job did upon the day of his birth? How many of us have reason to cry out in reviewing our Revolutionary services to our country with Caesar's parrot: "We have lost our labor!"[4] Shakespear makes Lord Westmorland wish for one ten thousand of those brave men that did no work on the day before the battle of Agincourt.[5] In looking back upon the years of our Revolution, I often wish for those ten thousand hours that I wasted in public pursuits and that I now see did no *permanent* work for my family nor my country. Such is the delight I now take in my professional studies that I daily regret that ever I was seduced from them for a moment to assist in an enterprise such as the late Catharine of Russia accomplished at Petersburgh, I mean building "a palace of ice." "Vanity of vanities, all is vanity."[6] "I came into the world crying; I lived complaining; and I died disappointed"[7] should be inscribed upon the tombstone of every politician. Say, departed spirits of Pitt and Fox, is not this true?

We have lately graduated 32 young doctors. I send you herewith one of their inaugural dissertations, in which you will find I hope some entertainment.

With respects and love as usual to all your family, in which all mine unite, I am, dear sir, your grateful and affectionate friend,

BENJN: RUSH

P.S. Since writing the above I have been told at the post office that postage is charged upon all packets sent to you. Is it so? Until I hear from you again, I shall withhold the inaugural dissertation.

MS: Adams Manuscript Trust, Boston.

¹ See BR's letter of 9 July 1807.

² The "three gentlemen," discussed in Adams' letter of 12 Apr. 1807, were Burr, Miranda, and Hamilton (*Old Family Letters*, *A*, p. 130).

³ One of these, dated 28 Feb. 1807, is in Rush MSS, XXXII.

⁴ Source not known.

⁵ See *Henry V*, IV, iii, 16-18.

⁶ Ecclesiastes 1:2, and repeatedly.

⁷ A proverbial saying first found in Thomas Fuller (1654-1734), *Gnomologia* (1732), according to Burton Stevenson, *The Home Book of Proverbs, Maxims and Familiar Phrases*, N.Y., 1948.

To John Adams

My venerated and dear Friend,   Philadelphia, May 12th, 1807

In one of your former letters you say as an excuse for your not assuming the reserve of certain public men, that you never believed yourself to be a "great man" and of course did not expect that anything you said and did and wrote would be the subject of public observation and scrutiny. I consider your not preserving a copy of your letter to your youthful friend Mr. Webb as proof of the truth of that assertion.¹ I rejoice in its fortuitous discovery. It does great honor to your head and heart. Even the style of it did not escape commendation by my son Richard. He remarked that it contained the same *nerve* that characterizes your present compositions. What would not the biographers of Franklin and Washington give for such an early specimen of reflection and foresight? It would have served to elevate them above the rank of prophets. It would have made them little ———, I must not apply the epithet that would have been given to them by mortal men. Your letter shall not perish. I recollect, in dining with Dr. Franklin when he was president of the executive council of Pennsylvania, he said that Lord Camden² first suggested to him the idea of American independence at a gentleman's table in Paris some years before it took place. The Doctor revolted at the proposition, for at that time he never (he said) had once conceived of the glory or happiness of America as unconnected with the glory and happiness of Great Britain. Samuel Adams once told me that the independence of British America had been the *first* wish of his heart *seven* years before the commencement of the American Revolutionary War in 1774. An intimate friend of General Montgomery's told me in 1776 that when he returned from America after the peace of 1763 he spoke in raptures of our country and often said, "What might not that country be, were it independent of Great Britain?" but neither of the two last-named gentlemen can date their wishes or views of that event in the year 1755, nor did they hint at the resources of our country for a navy which would one day deprive G. Britain of her empire upon the ocean.

Colonel Burr has paid a short visit to our city. He confined himself to his room during the few days he spent in town. My son Richd. visited him at his request in order to transact a piece of professional business for him. He spoke upon several ephemeral subjects but did not once glance at his having furnished one of the most interesting of those subjects for conversation that has ever occurred in the United States.

Richard Penn³ and his son William⁴ are now in Philadelphia. The former⁵ is a good deal broken, less it is said by age than by pecuniary distress. The latter is a nondescript in the history of human characters. Overflowing with ancient and modern learning, volatile, talkative, regardless of the *hic* et *tunc* in everything he says and does, good-tempered, and at home everywhere, he has struck our citizens with the emotions which are excited by a meteor. I will give you a specimen of his conversation. Upon being asked whether he intended to visit any other parts of our country besides Philadelphia, "Yes," said he, "I intend to visit the falls of Niagara and Jno. Adams, and afterwards the Rock Bridge and Tom Jefferson." He sparkled for several years in the first companies in London. The Prince of Wales once said of him that "he was a pen everybody *cut* but nobody mended."

I enclose you the letter which accompanied the one I received from the *unknown* Wm. Smith of New York. It cannot be from Wm. Smith of S. Carolina.⁶ His son's first name is Thomas.

I thank you for the flattering notice you have taken of my present from the Queen of Etruria.⁷ I have had reason to regret that an account of it found its way into our newspapers. An indiscreet friend has thereby done me more harm in one day than ten enemies could have done me in a year. I live in Philadelphia (though the country of ancestors who accompanied Wm. Penn in 1683 to his wilderness on the Delaware) in an *enemy's* country. To satisfy you that the knowledge of the presents I have received from two crowned heads became public without my consent and contrary to my wishes, I beg leave to mention to you in confidence (what is known but to 2 or 3 persons in our city) that flattering notices of my publications have not been confined to those two sources. My account of the yellow fever of the year 1793 was translated a few years ago into the Spanish language by order by the King of Spain.⁸ His minister lately called upon me for my subsequent publications on that disease. He sent them to his court, since which he has conveyed to me in a polite letter the thanks of his royal master for them.[9] From several literary and philosophical societies in different parts of Europe I have received diplomas, an account of which I have likewise never mentioned to more than three persons out of my own family. These attentions to my professional labors have consoled me under domestic charges of insanity upon medical subjects, and this has been the principal source of the gratification they have afforded me. If it has pleased God to grant me any degree of favor among men, I can truly say it has originated in his goodness. I have not sought fame; on the contrary, my friends have often told me I must throw sixes (to use an allusion from the dice board) to eclipse the ruin of my reputation from the total repugnance of my opinions to the common sense and general practice of physicians in every part of the world. In reviewing my medical life I can find nothing in it that gives me pain except too much ardor in propagating my principles and too little forbearance of the ignorance, dullness, and malice that opposed them. Would to God that I had always said of my enemies "Father, forgive them, they know not what they do."[10] Their hostility to me was indeed the offspring of ignorance. Had they known that by the publications they dictated to Cobbett and Fenno against my opinions in medicine, they would have stimulated me to further inquiries to defend them, and that they would spread my name far beyond the notice it would have otherwise attracted, they never would have acted towards me as they have done. But where has my pen carried me? I have written to you as I used to converse with you in your chamber at Mrs. Yard's in 2nd Street in the years 1774, 1775, and 1776. Let me beg of you to destroy this letter as soon as you have read it, in order to prevent one of your grandsons sending it *fifty-two* years hence to one of my grandsons (not as a mark of the reflection and foresight) but of the folly and vanity of his grandfather.

Have you seen a pamphlet written in England and republished in Philadelphia entitled *The Dangers of the Country?*[11] It is a masterly performance, eloquent and logical in the highest degree. Never were the character and designs of Bonaparte more ably analyzed and exposed. It contains instructions awfully important not only to Great Britain but to the United States. Do not suppose by my mentioning this pamphlet that I have relapsed into political speculations. It is the 2nd pamphlet only that I have read in sixteen years. In reading it I yielded to the request and even solicitation of a valuable friend. I do not repent it. It abounds in good sense, sound policy, and, what is more rare in such publications, true piety.

Poor Pennsylvania continues her wayward course. "I am not of this vile country," said Dean Swift when he was offended at the conduct of the people of Ireland. But I am a native and citizen of Pennsylvania. Our governor has returned from Lancaster to Philadelphia in tolerable health, but with such a lameness in his hand as still to prevent his using his pen.

All my family join in love to you and yours with, dear sir, your sincere and obliged old friend,

BENJN: RUSH

MS: Adams Manuscript Trust, Boston.

[1] Adams had sent BR a copy of a letter on the future of America that Adams had written in Oct. 1755 to Dr. Nathan Webb (*Old Family Letters, A*, p. 136-7). An extraordinarily prophetic performance, it is printed in Adams' *Works*, I, 23-4.

[2] Charles Pratt, 1st Earl Camden (1714-1794), lord chancellor, 1766-1770, was a staunch friend of America both in and out of office (DNB).

[3] Richard Penn (1736-1811), grandson of William Penn the founder of Pennsylvania, had been lieutenant governor of the province, 1771-1773; sympathetic with American grievances, he carried the "Olive Branch Petition" from Congress to the King in the summer of 1775 and stayed on in England, serving various constituencies in Parliament (DNB, DAB).

[4] William Penn (1776-1845), elder son of the preceding, was a writer of minor note and convivial habits; in 1809 he made a scandalous marriage in Philadelphia and spent much of his later life in debtors' prison (Howard M. Jenkins, *The Family of William Penn*, Phila. and London, 1899, p. 220-3; BR, *Autobiography*, p. 285).

[5] BR by mistake wrote "latter."

[6] Probably William Loughton Smith (ca. 1758-1812), Federalist congressman, political writer, and minister to Portugal (DAB).

[7] See BR to Jefferson, 15 June 1805.

[8] *Relacion de la calentura biliosa remitente amarilla, que se manifestò en Filadelfia, en el año de 1793 . . . ,* Madrid: En la Emprenta Real, 1804, 2 vol. This was an elaborate work of Spanish learning, containing an exhaustive bibliography of works on yellow fever, notes, appended dissertations, &c. In a review in the *Phila. Medical Museum*, III (1807), 163-74, Felix Pascalis stated that the editor of the Spanish edition was Sig. Dr. Don Ignacio Ruiz de Luzuriaga, secretary of the Royal Academy of Medicine, Madrid.

[9] The Spanish minister from 1796 to 1806 was Don Carlos Martinez, Marqués de Casa Yrujo (1763-1824), a well-known figure in Philadelphia, where he had married Sally, daughter of Chief Justice McKean, 1798 (Roberdeau Buchanan, *Genealogy of the McKean Family*, Lancaster, 1890, p. 133-8). Yrujo's letter to BR, 11 Sep. 1806, is in Rush MSS, Box 10; a draft of BR's acknowledgement, 12 Sep., is with it.

[10] Luke 23:34.

[11] [James Stephen,] *The Dangers of the Country*, London, 1807; reprinted Phila., 1807. Stephen (1758-1832), a brother-in-law of Wilberforce, was equally ardent in opposition to slavery and in defense of the British orders in council against neutral shipping (DNB).

To Ashbel Green?[1]

Dear Sir,   Philadelphia, May 22nd, 1807

In favor of the plan for establishing "Schools of the Prophets" exclusively for the education of young men for the Gospel ministry, of which we spoke a few days ago, I beg leave to mention the following reasons which have occurred to me in contemplating this important subject:

1. It will increase the number of ministers by lessening the expenses of their education (which at present amount when conducted at colleges, in some instances, to a thousand pounds), and thus destroy the distressing disproportion between the number of congregations and of ministers in the Presbyterian Church of the U. States.

2. It will prevent candidates for the ministry being infected with the follies and vices of young men educated for secular professions or ridiculed by them for their piety.

3. It will render education more *appropriate* to the subsequent duties and labors of the ministers of the Gospel by confining their preparatory studies to subjects connected with theology, and shortening the time now employed in requiring a knowledge of things not related to that divine science. No more Latin should be learned in these schools than is necessary to translate that language into English, and no more Greek than is necessary to read the Greek Testament. One half or two-thirds of the time now misspent in learning *more* of those two languages should be employed in learning Hebrew and in studying Jewish antiquities, Eastern customs, Eastern geography, ecclesiastical and natural history, and astronomy, all of which are calculated to discover the meaning and establish the truth of many parts of the Scriptures. No one of the Latin nor Greek poets nor historians should be read in these schools, by which means a pious ignorance will be preserved of the crimes of heathen gods and men related not only without censure but often with praise. "Take heed to thyself that thou be not snared by following them after that they be destroyed before thee, and that thou *inquire not after their gods*, saying how did these nations serve their gods?" Deuteronomy xii. 30. All that is necessary to be known of the heathen mythology and of the crimes of men may be learned from the Bible, where they are recorded probably only for the sake of showing their immutable and necessary connection with the righteous vengeance of Heaven. Nor should moral philosophy be

taught in these schools. It is in its present form, according to Mr. Edwards' account of it, "infidelity systematized."[2]

4. The plan we have contemplated will favor the growth of practical and habitual godliness in young men intended for the ministry.

5. In favor of it, it may be added further that some of the brightest ornaments as well as strongest pillars of the Presbyterian Church were in a *certain* degree thus educated, viz., the two Blairs, the three Tennents, Dr. Finley, Mr. Davis [*Davies*], Mr. Math. Wilson,[3] Mr. Robert Smith,[4] and Dr. Rodgers.

Let it not be said ministers educated in this sequestered manner will not be bachelors nor masters of arts. What then? A certificate from a presbytery of competency in human learning will supply the place of a degree. In Scotland few of the clergy now graduate in the arts.

In addition to this plan, I hope you will urge the one you mentioned to me for sending forth catechumens or teachers into the church amply qualified in divine knowledge without much respect to attainments in human learning.

With great regard, I am, dear sir, yours affectionately,

BENJN: RUSH

P.S. I have been informed by a pious man lately from Ireland that the orthodox Presbyterian ministers in that country, having seen the unfavorable influence of an education in the universities of Scotland upon the principles and conduct of candidates for the ministry, have lately undertaken to educate them at home under the direction of their presbyteries.[5]

MS: Rush Family Papers, deposited in Princeton University Library.

[1] There is every reason to believe that this letter was addressed to Green, who was BR's principal correspondent on the subject of religious training and who for some years had interested himself in plans for a Presbyterian seminary. When the Theological Seminary of the Presbyterian Church was established at Princeton in 1811-1812, Green was a prime mover and was elected first president of its board of directors (*Life of Ashbel Green*, p. 332-7; Hageman, *Hist. of Princeton*, II, 324-30).

[2] This account is not certainly identifiable.

[3] Matthew Wilson (1731-1790), minister of several Presbyterian congregations at Lewes and nearby in Delaware, 1756-1790; D.D., University of the State of Pennsylvania, 1786 (Sprague, *Annals*, III, 178-80).

[4] Robert Smith (1723-1793), born in Ireland, Presbyterian minister at Pequea, Lancaster co., Penna., from 1751; D.D., 1760, and trustee of the College of New Jersey from 1772; he kept a school at Pequea that achieved high repute, one of its products being Smith's son and BR's good friend Samuel Stanhope Smith (Sprague, *Annals*, III, 172-5).

[5] In recommending a program of studies that would result in "pious igno-

rance," BR was moving directly counter to the ideals of the Enlightenment he had supported in earlier decades. His thinking here was partly reactionary against that of Paine and Godwin, and partly merely sentimental: his "Schools of the Prophets" are a nostalgic projec- tion of the famous early Presbyterian country schools like that of the Ten- nents at Neshaminy, that of the Blairs at Fagg's Manor, that of Robert Smith mentioned above, and that of Finley at Nottingham (which BR himself had attended).

To John Adams

My dear Friend,   Philadelphia, June 9th, 1807

Permit me to trouble you with the delivery of the enclosed letter to Dr. Tufts.[1] It contains an account of the death of his patient Mr. Land,[2] and a small sum of money to be sent by the Doctor to Mr. Land's parents in New Hamshire.

I sent you Mr. Stevens' [*Stephen's*] pamphlet "on the dangers of the country" a few days ago. I beg your acceptance of it.

Since the date of my last letter I have been made very happy by a visit from my two daughters, with the husband of one of them (Mr. Cuthbert), and their four children, making with a niece of Mr. Cuthbert's and their servants an addition of ten to my family. The scene of joy produced by this event marks an era in the lives of my dear Mrs. Rush and myself. They purpose to remain with us until the latter end of this month. My daughter Manners has refuted by her cheerful deportment all the gloomy fears I had entertained of her destiny in marriage. Her husband is everything the most indulgent parents could wish a husband to be for an only and favorite daughter. She expects to sail for England with him in the course of the present year.

Expect a longer letter from me shortly. In the meanwhile be assured of the respect and affection of your sincere and obliged friend,

BENJN: RUSH

MS: Adams Manuscript Trust, Boston.

[1] Cotton Tufts (1731-1815), a phy- sician of Weymouth, Mass., and uncle by marriage of Mrs. John Adams; A.B., 1749, and honorary M.D., 1785, Har- vard; one of the founders of both the American Academy of Arts and Sciences and the Massachusetts Medical Society (Thacher, *Amer. Med. Biog.*; Walter L. Burrage, *History of the Massachusetts Medical Society* [Norwood, Mass.], 1923, p. 61-3).

[2] Not further identified; the spelling is uncertain.

To John Adams

My dear Friend,   Philadelphia, July 9th, 1807

I once met Alexander Cruden,[1] the author of the *Concordance of the Scriptures*, at Charles Dilly's. He was then about 70 years of age. The only thing he said while I was in his company made an impression upon my mind which the lapse of near 40 years has not worn away. It was this: "God punishes some crimes in this world to teach us there is a Providence, and permits others to escape with impunity to teach us there is a future judgment." Your two last letters[2] contain some very striking proofs of the truth of the former part of Mr. Cruden's proposition. Your case has been somewhat singular and widely different from mine. My enemies have generally been prosperous in the world. The physicians who, by their publications and desertion of our city in the year 1793, laid the foundation of all the controversies which took place at that time upon the treatment and origin of the yellow fever and of the greatest part of its mortality, have ever since been the favorites of the public, and the more so for the injuries they did to me, for no punishment in the loss of reputation and business has been thought too great for the man who has blasted the character and depreciated the property of Philadelphia by asserting it to be the birthplace of the yellow fever. I mention this fact without complaining of it. Retribution may even yet reach them in this world. If it do not, I am sure it will in the world to come.

In one of your former letters you spoke in high terms of *prudence*.[3] I neglected to reply to your encomiums upon it. General Lee used to call it a "rascally virtue." It certainly has more counterfeits than any other virtue, and when *real* it partakes very much of a selfish nature. It was this virtue that protected the property and lives of most of the tories during the American Revolution. It never achieved anything great in human affairs. Luther, Harvey, and many other authors of new opinions and discoveries were devoid of it; so were the Adamses and Hancock, who gave the signals for war in the year 1775. In private life what is commonly called prudence is little else than a system of self-love. A patient of mine once named me (without my knowledge) with two other persons, one of whom was his brother, as executors of his will.[4] Knowing this brother to be a notorious rogue, and wishing not to act as an executor myself, I called upon my third colleague and urged him instantly to take charge in a legal way of all the property of our deceased friend. He said he could not do this without offending our friend's brother. I asked him if he did not believe he would apply all our friend's property to his own use? He said yes, but that he could not act as I advised without a quarrel with him and "that he never had a dispute with any man in his life." Foreseeing the loss of our friend's property, I qualified as an executor and thereby rescued all his estate from the hands of his brother except 300 dollars which he collected and appropriated to his own use. By acting in this manner, I paid my friend's debts and saved a handsome sum for his only child, and that I might not incur even a suspicion of acting from interested motives, I gave all my commissions on the cash I received or expended to my brother executor who refused to concur with me in offending our friend's brother. The result of this conduct was not a quarrel with the fellow (for he was below a resentful reply), but the most intemperate abuse from him and a threat to expose me in the newspapers for an attack upon his honor and character. My colleague in the meanwhile kept up a friendly intercourse with him and thereby retained the character of a *prudent*, peaceable man.

During the Revolutionary War, while I had charge of the military hospitals, most of the surgeons and physicians connected with me complained of the ignorance, negligence, and above all of the gross and extensive speculations in hospital stores (while the sick suffered from the want of them) of the Director General of the hospital establishment. To obviate these evils I became the organ of their complaints to Congress, by whom they were referred to General Washington, who 18 months[5] afterwards ordered him before a court-martial. The officers of that court were changed in several instances. The Director dined occasionally with several of them at the tables of general officers during his trial. None of the young men who had complained of him appeared against him, but some of them appeared in his favor. They all got credit for their prudence. *John Brown Cutting's* evidence overset mine, and the Director was acquitted, nor was this all. General Washington afterwards gave him a certificate for integrity and good conduct during the time he directed the affairs of the hospitals.[6] He admitted that there had been disorders in them, but ascribed them to the deranged and confused state of the army and to difficulties which arose from the nature of the war. By this certificate he *prudently* avoided offending the Director and a *quarrel* with his two brothers-in-law, who then possessed an unbounded influence over the counsels of Congress. The business ended in my being obliged to resign my commission and leaving the army with the character of a factious, ambitious, *imprudent* man who wished only to occupy the place of the director general of the hospitals.

After the above detail, you will not wonder at my coldness and indifference to public affairs.

While I have thus exposed the counterfeits of *prudence*, far be it from me to deny the reality and excellency of that virtue. Its existence is admitted, and its advantages are extolled by St. Paul. My worthy friend Bishop White has proved by his conduct through life that prudence can exist with firmness and integrity in the highest degree. In the cause of truth and humanity, it may be said of him what the good Regent of Scotland, the Earl of Murray, said of John Knox over his grave. "There lies a man who never feared the face of man." I have often known the Bishop say and do offensive but just things and still retain his friends and character. Such men are as rare as great generals and statesmen.

Alas! The events at Norfolk![7] Where, where will they end?

Colonel Burr retains in his confinement his usual good spirits. He is a nondescript in the history of human nature. Should he be acquitted, you say he may yet be President of the United States. It is possible. Some worse men hold high appointments in every part of our country.

My daughters with their suite left us last week and under distressing apprehension of being long, long separated from us, not only by distance, but by a war between our respective countries.

Adieu! with love and respect as usual, in which Mrs. Rush and all my young folks join, I am, dear sir, your affectionate and obliged friend,

BENJN: RUSH

P.S. I have accidentally discovered the Wm. Smith who recommended his son to me from New York. It is a Scotch clergyman who came recommended to me above 20 years ago and who has lately given up a charge in Connecticut and opened a school in New York.[8]

MS: Adams Manuscript Trust, Boston.

[1] Alexander Cruden (1701-1770), the eccentric compiler of *A Complete Concordance to the Holy Scriptures of the Old and New Testaments*, London, 1737, which is inseparably connected with his name (DNB).

[2] Dated 23 and 25 June, respectively (*Old Family Letters, A*, p. 144, 151).

[3] See *Old Family Letters, A*, p. 131.

[4] I have discovered nothing further concerning the episode BR recounts here.

[5] Thirty months would be more accurate. See Appendix 1, below.

[6] See Washington to Shippen, 13 Feb. 1781 (Washington, *Writings*, ed. Fitzpatrick, XXI, 218-19).

[7] The notorious affair of the British cruiser *Leopard*'s attack on the Amer-

ican warship *Chesapeake*, 22 June 1807, which roused war sentiment in the United States to fever pitch (McMaster, *Hist.*, III, 255-70).

[8] See BR to Adams, 3 and 22 Apr. 1807. This must have been William Smith, D.D. (ca. 1754-1821), who came to the United States in 1785 and served as rector of Episcopal churches in Pennsylvania, Maryland, Rhode Island, and Connecticut, and as a schoolmaster in New York City and elsewhere; he wrote on theology and church music (DAB).

To John Adams

Dear Sir,   Philadelphia, October 31st, 1807

I am ashamed of my long silence after the receipt of the two last letters[1] from my kind friend and benefactor. The hurry introduced into my ordinary mass of business by the influenza and its consequences must be my apology for my seeming inattention to your interesting favors.

You have happily distinguished between *prudence* and *art*. I agree with you in your history of disinterestedness. It is indeed a rare virtue. An Englishman died a few years ago near this city who left the interest of £1500 to be appropriated annually to reward acts of disinterestedness. One of our lawyers has declared the design of the testator cannot be fulfilled, and the brother of the deceased as heir at law has claimed the legacy. I do not think the gentleman you alluded to in your letter upon this subject formed himself or his conduct upon the model of the character described in Rollin.[2] He was self-taught in all the arts which gave him his immense elevation above all his fellow citizens. An intimate friend of Colonel Hamilton's informed me that he once told him that he had never read a single military book except Sims' *Guide*.[3] Sir Hanse Sloan[4] used to show among the curiosities of his museum a list of Dr. Ratcliff's[5] library, which consisted only of half a dozen practical books upon medicine. A friend of Ratcliff's told him of this satire upon his medical character and spoke at the same time of the large size of Sir Hans' library. "That is all right," said Dr. Ratcliff. "D—n the fellow, he requires books." The same remark has been applied to many other men who possess learning and reading, and the same preeminence over them by men who never read has often been ascribed to the gentleman mentioned in your letter. While the resources of genius, reading, and reflection have each had their specific advocates for fame, perhaps Dr. Clark's[6] opinion of the means of becoming eminent in a profession deserves the most credit; it consists, he says, in "reading much, thinking much, and writing much." They mutually assist each other in giving the greatest expansion and correctness to the human mind. For this purpose they should bear a due proportion to each other. Dr. Priestley read and wrote a great deal. Had he *thought* more, he would probably have corrected many of the errors which he defended upon several subjects. Dr. Franklin thought a great deal, wrote occasionally, but read during the middle and latter years of his life very little, and hence the errors of several of his opinions upon government.[7] Our great man wrote a great deal, thought constantly, but read (it is said) very little, and hence the disrespect with which his talents and character have been treated by his aide-de-camp. But enough of great men!—especially to one who has ceased to believe in them from knowing so well how much littleness is mixed with human greatness, how much folly with human wisdom, and how much vice with the greatest attainments in human virtue.

While thousands in our city spend their whole time in speculating upon peace or war, I am quietly pursuing all the objects of my profession. On Monday next I expect to begin my annual course of lectures. The subject of my introductory lecture is "The duty and advantages of studying the diseases of domestic animals, and the remedies proper to cure them."[8] I have given the following reasons for urging the subject upon my class: 1, our relation to domestic animals arising from our being formed at the same time and from the same dust, possessing bodies capable like theirs of pain and subject like theirs to death, and from the dominion over them given to man at the creation; 2, our obligations to them generally and particularly; 3, the inability of nature to cure their diseases; 4, their suffering from quacks; 5, the necessity of knowing their diseases in order to prevent our being injured by the flesh of such of them as compose a part of our aliment; 6, the necessity of preserving the character of their flesh as important and profitable articles of commerce; 7, the advantages to be derived from a knowledge of their diseases in aiding our inquiries into the diseases of the human body; 8, the precepts of the Old and New Testament, which inculcate tenderness to and care of them. My 9th reason is as follows: "I proceed in the last place to mention a reason for making the health of domestic animals the subject of our studies and care which I should hesitate in delivering were it not sanctioned by the name of a man whose discoveries in physiological, metaphysical, and theological science mark an era in the achievements of the human mind—I mean the great and good, I had almost said the inspired, Dr. Hartley, and that is, their probable relation to us in a resurrection after death and an existence in a future state. I shall read a short passage from the Doctor's *Works* upon this subject. After expressing a doubt concerning the redemption of the brute creation, he adds, 'However, their fall with Adam, the covenant made with them after the deluge, their serving for sacrifices for the sins of men and as types and emblems in the prophecies, and their being commanded to praise God, seem to intimate that there is mercy in store for them, more than we may expect, to be revealed in due time. The Jews considered the Gentiles as dogs compared with themselves, and the brute creatures appear by the history of association that has been given to differ from us in *degree* rather than in kind.'[9]

"In favor of these remarks of Dr. Hartley, it may be said that as moral evil and death accompanied each other in the human race, they are probably connected in the brute creation, that they possess nearly all our vices and virtues, that the perfection of the divine government requires that their vices should be punished and their virtues rewarded, that reparation should be made to them for their accumulated sufferings in this world, and that the divine bounty discovered in the gift of their pleasures would be rendered abortive unless they were placed in a situation to make returns for them in praise and gratitude in a future state of existence. It is alike foreign to my inclinations and the design of this lecture to enter further into this question. To such of you as wish to see all the arguments from reason and revelation that are used in its favor, I beg leave to recommend the perusal of an essay in the *Works* of Dr. Hildrop, a learned and pious clergyman of the Church of England, entitled 'Free Thoughts upon the Brute Creation.'[10] In whatever way the controversy may be decided, I shall only add that a belief in the opinion that has been suggested by the physician and defended by the divine whose names have been mentioned is calculated in no one instance to do any harm but on the contrary much good, by increasing our obligations to treat our domestic subjects with tenderness and care. If the opinion be erroneous, let the justice and mercy of the Supreme Being in his conduct to his brute creation remain unimpeached. The divine government in this world may be compared to a dreary prospect of an extensive and highly cultivated country on a winter day. The last revolution of our globe will clothe this prospect with all the beauties of the vernal and all the products of the autumnal months. It will then appear that the apparent discord in the *being* and *end* of all intelligent and animated creatures was 'Harmony not understood,' and that all their sufferings were a necessary part of 'universal good.' "[11]

I was much gratified by your approbation of my declining to preside over our town meeting last summer. I was invited to it by the heads of all the three parties in our city, and urged to it by all my family and several of my friends. My feelings revolted against it, and my judgment disapproved of it. My family and friends *now* think I acted properly. My ever-honored preceptor, the Reverend Dr. Finley, I well recollect when a schoolboy, in taking leave of one of his scholars who was coming to live in Philadelphia, laid before him the temptations to vice to which he would be exposed from the solicitations of bad company, and concluded his advice to him by saying in an emphatical tone, "Learn to pronounce that bold word NO." Happy, happy had it been for me had I upon a hundred occasions used that bold monosyllable with the same decision that I did upon the occasion to which I have alluded. The misfortunes of most men in moral, commercial, and political life arise from their inability to pronounce that ark-like word.

What would have been the present state of our country had you used that word half a dozen times at the time the appointments were made in the late American army? One of your letters to me two years ago has answered this question. Adieu, adieu. With love as usual, I am, my dear friend, ever yours,

B: RUSH

P.S. My son Richard has just returned from Norfolk, where he went to take a part in the inquiry into the conduct of Captain Barron.[12] On his way home he stopped at Richmond,[13] where he saw and heard many things which it is not lawful to tell. Federalism! Democracy! law! order! "Libertas et natale solum!" All fine, very fine words. I wonder, in the language of Dean Swift, "where we stole them."[14]

MS: Adams Manuscript Trust, Boston.

[1] Dated 1 September and September without a day, respectively (*Old Family Letters, A*, p. 157, 161).

[2] Adams had pointed out parallels between the career of Washington and that of Dejoces, first king of the Medes, as chronicled in Rollin's *Ancient History*.

[3] Thomas Simes, *The Military Guide for Young Officers*, first published in London, 1772; reissued in Philadelphia in 1775 and 1776 (*Brit. Mus. Cat.; L.C. Cat.*). Washington owned Simes' *Guide*, but he also owned and studied other military works (Washington, *Writings*, ed. Fitzpatrick, III, 293, note; O. L. Spaulding, "The Military Studies of George Washington," *Amer. Hist. Rev.*, XXIX [1923-1924], 675-80).

[4] Sir Hans Sloane, bart. (1660-1753), British physician and botanist; his natural history collections were purchased

by the nation and placed in the British Museum (DNB).

⁵ John Radcliffe (1650-1714), a British physician famous for his skill and also for his candor, even to his royal patient Queen Anne (DNB).

⁶ Unidentified.

⁷ Doubtless alluding to Franklin's support of the Pennsylvania Constitution of 1776.

⁸ A celebrated lecture, delivered 2 Nov. 1807 at the request of the Philadelphia Society for Promoting Agriculture (see Richard Peters to BR, 2 Nov. 1807, Rush MSS, Box 10), and published by the Society in its *Memoirs*, I (1808); also published in the *Phila. Medical Museum*, IV (1808); as Lecture XIII in BR's *Sixteen Introductory Lectures*, 1811; and reissued, in mimeographed form, as recently as 1942, edited by B. W. Bierer [Phila.]. It entitles BR to recognition as a pioneer of veterinary science in the United States. Some of his opinions, however, met with a hostile reception; see letter to Richard Peters, 28 Nov. 1807.

⁹ David Hartley, *Observations on Man* (1749), pt. ii, proposition 95

(4th edn., London, 1801, II, 436).

¹⁰ John Hildrop, D.D. (d. 1756), issued *Miscellaneous Works*, London, 1754; the essay mentioned by BR was long admired (DNB; Allibone, *Dict. of Authors*).

¹¹ See Pope, *Essay on Man* (1733), I, 291-2.

¹² Commodore James Barron (1769-1851), in command of the *Chesapeake* at the time of her disastrous encounter with the *Leopard*; a court-martial subsequently found Barron guilty of negligence and sentenced him severely (DAB).

¹³ Where the Burr trial was in progress.

¹⁴ "Liberty and my native land." The opening lines of Swift's satirical verses entitled "Whitshed's Motto on His Coach" (1724) are:

> "Libertas & natale Solum;
> Fine Words; I wonder where you
>   stole 'um."

William Whitshed was the Irish judge who presided at the trial of Harding, printer of Swift's *Drapier's Letters*. (*The Poems of Jonathan Swift*, ed. Harold Williams, Oxford, 1937, I, 347-9.)

To Thomas Jefferson

Dear Sir,   Philadelphia, November 28th, 1807

I have just now received a letter from Dr. Waterhouse¹ in which he has requested me to address you in favor of his petition to be appointed successor to Dr. Eustis² in the charge of the Marine Hospital at Boston. Dr. Waterhouse stands high with all the scientific members of his profession. The New England states are indebted to him for introducing vaccination into them, and at an expense too of much calumny and injury to his reputation. His whiggism has been conspicuous through his whole life, particularly of late years since it has assumed the name and attributes of republicanism. One more reason remains to be mentioned in behalf of his application. I have heard from himself that, like many men who love their friends, their country, or their books better than themselves, he is poor and relies, to use his own words, upon the benevolence of government to save his children from the accommodations of "an almshouse" should they survive him.

[956]

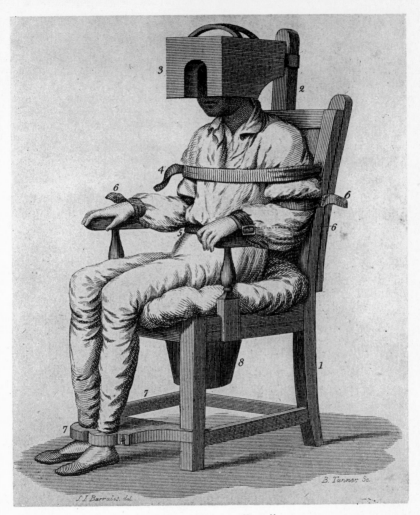

Rush's "Tranquillizer"

Excuse the liberty of this letter, and be assured, dear sir, of the continuance of the friendship of yours very respectfully,

BENJN: RUSH

MS: National Archives, Record Group 59 (General Records of the Department of State), Applications and Recommendations for Office.

[1] Dated 19 Nov. 1807 (Rush MSS, xxx). Despite Waterhouse's contributions to science and learning (see BR to Waterhouse, 9 Feb. 1802, and note), he was unpopular and, like BR, continually involved in controversies. In acknowledging the present letter of recommendation, Jefferson told BR he had nominated Waterhouse for the post desired as "a just tho small return for his merit," but owned at the same time that the appointment had aroused criticism (3 Jan. 1808; MS owned by Dr. Josiah C. Trent, Durham). Waterhouse's irascible temper and his Jeffersonian politics were perhaps equally responsible for the hostility he met with in Boston. BR's sketch of Waterhouse's case of course reflects BR's feelings about his own position in Philadelphia, and gives point to John Adams' observa-

tion in a letter to Waterhouse: "I know not two Characters more alike than Rush's and yours" (W. C. Ford, ed., *Statesman and Friend*, Boston, 1927, p. 91). See also BR to Adams, 8 Jan. 1813.

[2] William Eustis (1753-1825), a Harvard graduate, 1772, studied medicine under Dr. Joseph Warren and served as a surgeon in the Revolution; he was afterwards a congressman, diplomat, governor of Massachusetts, and, 1807-1812, secretary of war (DAB). Eustis never held the post of director of the Marine Hospital at Charlestown, Mass., though he had perhaps declined the appointment at this time; the director from 1804 to 1807 was Dr. Charles Jarvis (John W. Trask, *The United States Marine Hospital, Port of Boston*, Washington, 1940, p. 55-6).

To Richard Peters[1]

Dear Sir,   November 28, 1807

I am so much accustomed to have my *opinions* and *conduct* misrepresented that I have ceased to complain of my medical brethren upon that account. The *tenor* of my lectures and publications have[2] refuted the calumnies upon the *former*, and the *issue* of my life will I hope refute the *latter*. I know from whence the falsehood was derived. The men who propagated it did not believe it.

I believe brutes have souls, but I *never* said nor *never* believed that they were immortal. Wiser and better men than I shall ever be have maintained the latter opinion, among whom I mentioned Dr. Hartley and Dr. Hildrop—the one an eminent philosopher and physician, the other a pious and learned divine of the Church of England.

The lecture which has given occasion to the idle story you mention is now printed. Wherever it is read, it will do us both justice. I have interrogated a number of my pupils upon the subject alluded to. They all understand me perfectly and connected your name *only* with the undertaking or design of the lecture. From, dear sir, yours sincerely,

BENJN: RUSH

December 12th, 1807. P.S. I concluded after writing the above letter to defer sending it till I could accompany it with a copy of the lecture. You will perceive that I have called the authors of the calumny you have mentioned "medical brethren." Were I a governor,[3] I could call them INGRATES, LIARS, APOSTATES, and TRAITORS.

MS: Historical Society of Pennsylvania, Peters Papers.

[1] Peters had communicated to BR some hostile comments on BR's lecture on veterinary science (see BR to Adams, 31 Oct. 1807), but I can throw no further light on this incident.

[2] Thus in MS. BR commonly made this error in this grammatical construction.

[3] Doubtless in allusion to Gov. Mc-Kean's intemperate habit of speaking.

To John Adams

Philadelphia, December 15, 1807

My venerable and dear Friend,

An inflammation in my eyes, which for several days has confined me to my house and rendered writing difficult and painful, must be my apology for the shortness of this letter.

I admire the correctness of your history of the *ten* talents committed to the subject of your letter.[1] Upon the talent of his taciturnity, Mr. Liston gave me the following anecdote: "That he was the only person he had ever known (and he had conversed with several crowned heads and many of the first nobility in Europe) who made *no reply* of any kind to a question that he did not choose to answer."

A clamor has lately broken out in our city against the perpetual residence of Congress at Washington. The dissolution of the Union in case of a war is predicted from it. To which of the generals, aides, secretaries, or major generals must that measure be ascribed?—for the author of it did no wrong.

Torrents of abuse are poured out in all the Virginia papers against J. Marshall and J. Randolph, but the authors of them all qualify their invectives with the most extravagant encomiums upon their "abilities." You have assigned the true reason for this conduct. They both possess the *talent* of being Virginians.

[958]

My whole family were deeply afflicted for a few days with an account of a duel fought by my son John at New Orleans.[2] The history of its cause published in our papers, and several letters from our son and one from a physician formerly my pupil, have greatly alleviated our distress. The latter speaks in high terms of my son's pacific conduct in the business and of his humanity afterwards. He intended to waste his fire, but was led to do otherwise by being assured his antagonist intended "to kill or be killed." The infatuated young man had been called a coward some time before for refusing to accept a challenge, and had become so desperate in consequence of the neglect to which it exposed him that he sought to reestablish his character at the expense of his own or my son's life. He was, my son informs us, a most accomplished young man and an excellent officer. He had distinguished himself at Tripoli under Commodore Prebble.[3] It was remarkable my son was one of a few friends who vindicated his conduct in refusing the challenge and who took pains to reconcile him to himself by assuring him he had acted consistently with his station as an officer and a gentleman.

Adieu! With love as usual, I am yours sincerely,

BENJN: RUSH

P.S. To persons who read newspapers in the years 1774 and 1775 and remember the arguments with which the advocates for Great Britain defended her right to tax us, it is amusing to see how exactly those arguments are repeated in the attempts that are made to defend her right to tyrannize over our ships upon the ocean. Who after this can refrain from crying out with the parrot, "I have lost my labor"? Let us in our retirement pity the bear-leaders who *now* occupy our places in those years.

Addressed: John Adams Esqr: Woolaston Quincy near Boston.
MS: Adams Manuscript Trust, Boston.

[1] In his letter of 11 Nov. 1807, Adams had given a list of the ingredients in Washington's success; one of them was his silence and another his being a Virginian, which alone was "equivalent to five Talents" (*Old Family Letters*, *A*, p. 169).

[2] Since 3 Feb. 1807 John Rush had served as acting lieutenant in the navy (having accepted a demotion upon returning to the service in 1805), and was at this time in command of Gunboat No. 18 on the New Orleans Station. His opponent (and victim) in the duel of 1 Oct. 1807 was Lt. Benjamin Turner, commanding Gunboat No. 15. John was promptly arrested but within a few weeks was ordered to return to duty. In Sep. 1808 he was in difficulty on account of a quarrel and gunplay aboard his vessel. After an investigation he was ordered to Washington, but the next information is in a letter from Captain David Porter to BR, 7 Mch. 1809, announcing that John is insane and has tried to take his own life. A physician friend of BR's in New Orleans (Samuel D. Heap) had hopes of John's

complete recovery; these proved delusive; and John at length was brought home in Feb. 1810. He was shortly committed to the Pennsylvania Hospital and remained there, except for one brief interval, until his death in 1837. (John Rush papers in Rush MSS, XXXII; Records of the Department of the Navy in the National Archives [pertinent references listed by Dr. Corner in BR's *Autobiography*, p. 371]; Benjamin Turner's naval record in U.S. Office of Naval Records and Library, *Register of Officer Personnel* . . . , *1801-1807*, Washington, 1945, p. 56-7; Morton, *Hist. Penna. Hospital*, p. 152; frequent allusions to John Rush in the following letters.)

[3] Edward Preble (1761-1807), who commanded the U.S. squadron that attacked Tripoli in 1804 (DAB).

To John Adams

Philadelphia, February 18th, 1808

My venerable and dear Friend,

I have escaped for ten minutes from the pressure of business, lectures, pupils, and the charge of the Pennsylvania Hospital to drop you a few lines which I beg you will consider as the preface only of a longer letter a few weeks hence when I shall be relieved from three-fourths of my present labors.

Our citizens are making great preparations for celebrating the birthday of the first President of the United States. Is this not a unique in the history of nations *thus* to perpetuate the memories of their benefactors and deliverers? I exclude from this question the homage that has been paid by all nations to the birthday of the Saviour of the World. By such acts we shall gradually be prepared for much higher degrees of devotion to the name of our great man. What do you think of hearing the minister of your church seven years hence begin public worship by saying, "Let us sing to the praise and glory of G. W."?[1]

Great clamors are everywhere excited against the Embargo.[2] How different were the feelings and conduct of our citizens in 1774 upon the subject of the most oppressive nonimportation act of that memorable year! The clamors against the Embargo originate in our cities and chiefly among one class of citizens. "And he causeth all, both small and great, rich and poor, bond and free, to receive a mark in their right hand or in their foreheads, and that *no man might buy or sell* save he had the mark or the name of the beast or the number of his name."[3] It is easy to tell who are the persons alluded to that have received this mark, as also the nature of the impression made by it upon the hand or upon the forehead,[4] but who is the beast that has imposed this mark upon the buyers and

[960]

sellers of our country? Is it Napolion; or is *three* the number of his name—that is, George the third; or is it the Lord and Master of them both, Lucifer the first?

What monuments of ignorance, folly, and pride will Congress leave behind them should they finally escape from the city of Washington!

With affectionate regard to Mrs. Adams, in which my dear Mrs. Rush joins, I am, dear sir, your sincere and obliged friend,

BENJN RUSH

Addressed: John Adams Esqr: Woolaston Quincy near Boston.
MS: Adams Manuscript Trust, Boston.

¹ The celebration of Washington's birthday was long a strictly Federalist function. In 1801 Jefferson told a committee of citizens who waited on him to ascertain *his* birthday that the only birthday he celebrated was that of national independence, the Fourth of July (Margaret Bayard Smith, *First Forty Years of Washington Society*, N.Y., 1906, p. 398). See also Appendix I,

below.
² The Embargo Act, confining our vessels to coastwise trade, had gone into effect 22 Dec. 1807. For the violent and long-continued controversy over this measure, often touched on in BR's letters, see McMaster, *Hist.*, III, ch. XIX.
³ Revelation 13:16-17.
⁴ Note by BR: "An eagle and the figure of liberty."

To Timothy Pickering

Dear Sir,   Philadelphia, March 2nd, 1808

In one of the many agreeable conversations we have had upon philosophical subjects, I recollect that you said you had once met with an old man (I think a sea captain) who told you that from long and close observation he was satisfied the moon had no influence upon the weather. I wish you to repeat to me the particulars of this communication—if I am correct in believing I received it from you. I am at present engaged in an inquiry which I expect will terminate in an exclusion of lunar influence from the human body and perhaps from other parts of our globe.¹

Your son² is now using Dr. Cox's new mode of exercise which I have called a gyrater.³ He submits to it patiently and pleasantly. As yet it has had no effect upon him, but in his stage of derangement it will be well if he discovers signs of amendment after using it six months. He is treated with kindness by all the officers of the Hospital. His name is a protection to him.

From, dear sir, yours affectionately,

BENJN: RUSH

MS: Massachusetts Historical Society, Pickering Papers.

[1] BR believed that light and darkness have substantial influence upon diseases, particularly mental disease, but that the moon *per se* has none. See notes in his Commonplace Book (*Autobiography*, p. 352-3) and also *Diseases of the Mind*, p. 170-3. The terms *moonstruck* and *lunatic* indicate the importance formerly attached to lunar influence. Pickering's reply to BR's query, dated 6 Mch. 1808, was sold in 1943 (*Biddle Papers*, pt. i, No. 185).

[2] William Pickering (1786-1814), whose symptoms of mental derangement had been described by his father in a letter to BR, became a patient in the Pennsylvania Hospital in the preceding fall (Pickering to BR, 5 July 1807, MS owned by Josiah C. Trent, M.D.; same to same, 9 Sep. 1807, *Biddle Papers*, pt. iii, No. 187). He did not recover (Pickering and Upham, *Pickering*, IV, 396-7).

[3] A board to which the victim of "torpid madness" was strapped and which was then revolved around a pivot; the head, being at the outer end, received an accession of blood, which was supposed to be beneficial. The idea appears to have been John Redman Coxe's, but the machine was contrived by BR. See *Diseases of the Mind*, p. 224-5; Deutsch, *The Mentally Ill in America*, p. 79.

To John Adams

My very dear Friend,   Philadelphia, April 5th, 1808

A bad cold added to the pressure of business has delayed my answer much longer than I intended to your last acceptable letter.[1]

You have mistaken the church to which I belong in supposing that prayers will one day be offered up in it to the great man whose birthday has lately been celebrated in our country. During the life of Dr. Ewing, whose influence was very extensive in the Presbyterian Church, I took refuge in the Episcopal Church from his malice and persecutions excited by my opposition to his holding by usurpation the provost's place in the College of Philadelphia. The Episcopal Church at that time had divested itself of many of its absurdities in doctrine and worship. By their restoration by Bishop Seabury,[2] I was thrown out of its pale and have never since visited with any other society, although I constantly worship with them all but chiefly with the society under the care of the Reverend Dr. Green. I have often lamented the squeamishness of my [. . .][3] mind upon the subject of religious creeds and modes of worship. But accustomed to think for myself in my profession, and encouraged to believe that my opinions and modes of practice are just from the success which has attended them even in the hands of their enemies, I have ventured to transfer the same spirit of inquiry to religion, in which, if I have no followers in my opinions (for I hold most of them secretly), I enjoy the satisfaction of living in peace with my own conscience, and, what will surprise you not a little, in peace with all denominations of Christians, for while I refuse to be the slave of any sect, I am the friend of them all. In a future letter I may perhaps give you my creed. It differs materially from Dr. Brown's, as expressed in his *Religio Medici*.[4] It is a compound of the orthodoxy and heterodoxy of most of our Christian churches.

About two weeks ago I was summonsed a second time to give my testimony in favor of the late Wm. Bradford, attorney general of the U. States, having died intestate (after destroying a will in which he had left most of his estate to his wife) and of his having performed, after making this declaration, certain acts in my presence which indicated a sound mind.[5] My testimony was opposed by Mr. Boudinot, Mrs. Bradford's father, and seven other members of Mr. Bradford's family, who deposed that he was deranged at or near the time alluded to and that I had in conversations with them asserted this to be the case. I denied the truth of those conversations and brought two reputable witnesses to refute them. The jury gave a verdict in favor of my single testimony, by which means Mr. Bradford's estate will be divided by the intestate law of our state. In the course of the last seven years I have suffered much from the hostility of Mr. Boudinot's family to me. No intercourse has subsisted between us since the month of July 1800. I have constantly said to my friends that the trial would do me justice and show the world the true character of Mr. Boudinot. It has done both. The latter has been evinced by an act, which became public during the trial, perpetrated by Mr. Boudinot soon after Mr. Bradford's death and while he acted as Mr. Bradford's executor. It consisted in making *upon oath* a return of Mr. Bradford's property to the register's office that did not accord with an inventory from which it was copied and which, by a providential act, fell into the hands of the party that was opposed to Mr. Boudinot's claims. This event is now the subject of general conversation in the city. Poor man! he has added another proof to the truth of the assertion of the Apostle, that "covetousness is the root of all evil." The funding system pampered his canine appetite for wealth and at the same time altered his moral habits. He has ever since been an oppressor of the poor, and tricky in all his bargains. To repel the operation of these acts upon his character, he has every now and then dazzled the public by splendid commutation acts of public and private charity.

I have sometimes classed lies in the following manner. They are *ironical* or *jocular, hyperbolical, exculpative, malicious,* and *fraudulent.* Men who exercise themselves much in the first and second often fall into the subsequent classes. Mr. B. has verified this remark. From a young man he was noted for his jocular and hyperbolical conversation. In Congress at New York, an improbable story (Mr. Clymer informs me) was called a "Boudinot." The transition from telling improbable stories to the remaining grades of a departure from truth has been easy and natural in this fallen man. I never can forget the embarrassment, the confusion, the evasions and contradictions he discovered when interrogated upon the subject of his executorship. What an affecting sight in a man of 69 years of age, worth £60,000, formerly President of Congress, Director of the Mint, an elder in a church, and a literary advocate for Christianity!

From this act of private depravity I pass on to lament that not less than 47 vessels have lately arrived at the Havannah with cargoes of flour, all of which cleared out for American ports and all of which pretend to have been driven from them by bad weather. Can a country stained with such crimes escape the judgments of heaven? And is such a country worthy of the patriotism of honest men?

I enclose you a hasty tribute to the memory of my dear and venerable master, Dr. Redman.[6] I loved him most affectionately. I lived six years in his family, viz., from 1760 to 1766, during which time I was the witness of most of the virtues I have ascribed to him.

"Sic nobis contingat vivere, sicque mori."[7]

Adieu, my dear friend, and believe me to be yours sincerely and affectionately,

BENJN: RUSH

P.S. Mrs. Rush's and my most respectful compliments as usual to your dear Mrs. Adams. Do you not felicitate yourselves in your retirement every time you view the present distracted and perilous state of our country? Were Mr. Jefferson now asked how he liked his present seat at the helm of our government, he would probably answer as Sancho did after having occupied a similar situation, "Give me (not my shoes and stockings, which were the words of Sancho) but give me my telescope and mathematical instruments."

I ought to have mentioned to you, in the history of the trial in which I was called reluctantly to be a witness, that Mr. Bradford had made a will some years before his death in which he had bequeathed the principal part of his estate to his wife. After executing this will, he became suddenly and unexpectedly, from the operation of the funding system, worth £30,000. He learned likewise after this great addition to his estate that his eldest brother was in depressed circumstances. On his deathbed he tore his will and declared to me the law should divide his estate, but in order to give *more* to his sisters than to his brothers and to provide for Miss Read[8] and a charitable institution, he directed me to write promissory notes to each of them, which he executed with calmness and in his perfect senses. An attempt was made in the year 1797 to oppose an *old* will to these notes. This was defeated in court in the same year. Mr. Boudinot attempted to oppose to them in the 2nd trial the will Mr. Bradford had torn and ordered to be burnt, urging that he was delirious when he did so. This effort was equally unsuccessful with the former. Mrs. Bradford succeeds to *half* her husband's personal estate (which half will be £11,000) and to the income of one half his real estate during her life. She will succeed to the whole of her father's estate after his death.

Addressed: John Adams Esqr: Woolaston Quincy near Boston.
MS: Adams Manuscript Trust, Boston.

[1] Dated 25 Feb. 1808 (*Old Family Letters, A*, p. 176-9).

[2] Samuel Seabury (1729-1796), a loyalist in the Revolution, became the first Protestant Episcopal bishop in the U.S., 1784 (DAB). He was unsympathetic with "the prevailing liberalizing ideas of his American brethren," but I have found no evidence on the date of BR's withdrawal from the Episcopalian fold.

[3] MS torn; one word missing.

[4] Sir Thomas Browne's *Religio Medici* (1642) was one of BR's favorite works.

[5] The quarrel between BR and his old friend and relative by marriage, Elias Boudinot, over William Bradford's estate was as protracted as it was unseemly. The principal facts known about it have been concisely set forth by Dr. Corner in an appendix to BR's *Autobiography*, p. 372-6.

[6] "Memoir of the Life and Character of John Redman, M.D.," an anonymous contribution to Poulson's *American Daily Advertiser*, 23 Mch. 1808; reprinted, again anonymously, in the *Phila. Medical Museum*, V (1808), "Medical and Philosophical Register," p. 49-56. This memoir has hitherto been attributed to Redman's grandson, John Redman Coxe.

[7] "So may it be our fortune to live and so to die." Probably an echo of Ovid, *Amores*, I, iii, 17-18: "tecum . . . vivere contingat teque dolente mori."

[8] Not identified.

To John Adams

My venerable and dear Friend,   Philadelphia, June 13th, 1808

Public and private news and anecdotes are now so limited by the present state of our country that I have had nothing worth putting upon paper for your amusement since the receipt of your letter.[1] The principal design of this hasty scrawl is to inform you that you still live in my affections and that few persons occur oftener to my thoughts. Indeed I can scarcely review any of the memorable events of the Revolution or resolve any leading principle of action in man without associating them with your name or with your letters and conversations.

I perceive by the papers that your son is dismissed from the Senate of the United States.[2] I do not regret it. His talents will command the first business in his profession, and the results of that business in the evening of his life will afford him more comfort than the praises of a party or even of his whole country, and perhaps still more than the consciousness of having served a forgetting country with fidelity and success.

O! had I but one ten thousand of those precious days which did no work for my family between the years 1774 and 1780, they should not be again employed in exposing the acts of British tyrants and American demagogues. I feel pain when I am reminded of my exertions in the cause of what we called liberty, and sometimes wish I could erase my name from the Declaration of Independence.[3] In case of a rupture with Britain or France, which shall we fight for? For our Constitution? I cannot meet with a man who loves it. It is considered as too weak by one half of our citizens and too strong by the other half. Shall we rally round the standard of a popular chief? Since the death of Washington there has been no such center of Union. Shall we contend for our paternal acres and dwelling houses? Alas! how few of these are owned by the men who will in case of a war be called to the helm of our government. Their property consists chiefly in bank stock, and that to such an extent that among some of them it is considered as a mark of bad calculation for a man to live in a house of his own. I lately attended an old man who died under my care in the 81st year of his age. Of course he knew America in her youthful and innocent days. In speaking of the change in the principles and morals of our people which has taken place since the Revolution, he said: "They had all become idolaters; they worshipped but one god it is true, but that god was GOD DOLLARS." Were I permitted to coin a word suggested by my patient's remark, I would say we were a "bedollared nation." In walking our streets I have often been struck with the principal subjects of conversation of our citizens. Seldom have I heard a dozen words of which "*Dollar, discount,* and a *good Spec*" did not compose a part. "O! Civitas mox peritura si emptorem invenias."[4] St. Paul places covetousness and uncleanness together as improper subjects of conversation. But not only our streets but our parlors are constantly vocal with the language of a broker's office, and even at our convivial dinners "Dollars" are a standing dish upon which all feed with rapacity and gluttony. But I will quit this loathsome subject and proceed to the conclusion of my letter, but not without mentioning the great pleasure I enjoyed a few weeks ago in hearing your old pupil Mr. Mason[5] of Boston speak of you in terms of the highest veneration. None of your talents or services appear to be lost upon him. My wife and daughter are now at Princeton. Were they at home, they would unite with all my sons in respects to you and your excellent lady with, dear sir, yours sincerely and affectionately,

BENJN: RUSH

P.S. General Moreau compares our country to the trunk and limbs of a giant with the muscles of an infant.

A union has taken place between the Quids and Democrats in favor of Mr. Snyder as our future governor.[6] This union it is said was the effect of the rejection of your son from the Senate of the U. States.

MS: Adams Manuscript Trust, Boston.

[1] Dated 18 Apr. 1808 (*Old Family Letters, A*, p. 179-82).

[2] J. Q. Adams' refusal to follow the Federalist party line in the Senate resulted in a maneuver, devised by Timothy Pickering, to replace him (DAB).

[3] Adams in his reply, 20 June, administered a rebuke for this and similar complaints by BR (*Old Family Letters, A*, p. 184; quoted in the Introduction, p. lxxii-lxxiii, above).

[4] "O! city soon to perish if you find a buyer." Approximately quoted from Jugurtha's speech in Livy, *Epitome*, XLIV; compare Sallust, *Jugurtha*, XXXV. See also BR to Adams, 18 July 1812.

[5] Jonathan Mason (1756-1831), A.B., College of New Jersey, 1774; read law with John Adams; U.S. Senator from Massachusetts, 1800-1803; at this time in private practice (DAB).

[6] In consequence of this, Simon Snyder was elected governor in the fall by a resounding plurality of nearly 30,000 votes (Scharf & Westcott, I, 533).

To Samuel Miller

My dear Friend, Philadelphia, July 5th, 1808

After a good deal of deliberation I have sat down to address you upon a subject highly interesting to yourself and the public.

I have taken the liberty of mentioning your name as the successor to Dr. Nesbitt in the charge of the College at Carlisle. It has been well received by several of the friends of that institution. From the late donations of the legislature (though small) it bids fair to revive from the situation to which it was depressed before Dr. Nesbitt's death. 2,000 dollars are immediately to be laid out in purchasing a philosophical and chemical apparatus, and 2,000 more in purchasing books. The building for the accommodation and instruction of the students is finished, but as yet not occupied for the former purpose. The erection of this house and the payment of a debt contracted to Dr. N. will nearly absorb all the funds of the College, so that the principal resource for the support of the three professors now belonging to the College is derived from the tuition money of about 50 students. From whence then, you will say, is the salary of the principal to be derived? To this question there are two answers given by different members of the board of trustees. One set of them propose to elect a principal, to fix his salary, and to trust to his reputation and exertions to pay it from an increase in the number of students. The other members of the board propose that the principal shall take charge of the new building as if it were his private boardinghouse, appoint a steward to provide for and superintend it, fix a generous price for board, and draw all the profits of it exclusively for your own use. In this way masters of academies have lived comfortably and become wealthy and independent in Great Britain. A Mr. Chapman,[1] an English teacher of some celebrity, now derives from an academy and boardinghouse he has established in the neighborhood in[2] this city an income of £1,000 a year.

I need say nothing to you of the commanding situation of the College of Carlisle for unbounded usefulness to Church and State. But I will suggest what perhaps may be unknown to you, that your talents, your present attainments, your love of knowledge of all kinds, your peculiar and specific manners, and your high character, qualify you in an eminent degree for that eminent station. Education in our country stands in need of a revolution. It should be accommodated to our governments and state of society. I know of no man so fit to lay the foundation of this revolution as Dr. Miller.

I will mention one reason of a private nature for your removal to Carlisle. It will defend your breast from the consumptive air of the seashore and thereby probably be the means of prolonging your life and continuing your labors and your honors in the Church for many, many years to come.

It will not be necessary nor proper to be decisive in your answer to this letter if you incline to give the subject a consideration. I shall be as tender to your honor and feelings in this business as I am anxious for the prosperity of our College. Recollect that I address you only from individual wishes.—From, my dear sir, your sincere friend,

BENJN: RUSH

P.S. Secrecy will be necessary in this business, but this need not prevent your conferring with your brother and family about it.[3]

Addressed: The Revd: Dr: Samuel Miller New York.
MS: Princeton University Library.

[1] Not further identified.
[2] Thus in MS.
[3] In replying, Miller politely but unequivocally declined, pointing out that he was not likely to succeed where the eminent Dr. Nisbet had failed (letter of 16 July 1808; Samuel Miller, *Life*, Phila., 1869, I, 245-7). But for the sequel see BR's letters to Miller, 21 July; to Robert Davidson, 7 Oct.; and to Miller again, 8 Oct. 1808.

To John Montgomery

My dear Friend,   Philadelphia, July 5th, 1808

I have delayed to acknowledge the receipt of the 300 dollars you sent me by Dr. McCrosky until I could hear of something worth communicating to you upon the objects of that money. With the concurrence of Judge Hamilton[1] I have purchased an electrical and a galvanic apparatus for 250 dollars—the former is the most complete and splendid thing of the kind ever imported into our country. Mr. Patterson has seen it and highly commends it. It will add much to the reputation of our College. It will be sent with the galvanic apparatus and a small chemical apparatus for showing the composition of air and water, which I have since purchased, by the first wagon with a careful driver that offers for Carlisle. Mr. Vaughan[2] has written to Boston for an air pump. It will be more complete than those made in Great Britain. I hope the money that will be necessary to pay for it will be sent before it arrives. We shall first hear its price before the contract for it is made.

While we rejoice in the increase of the means of instruction in our College, I cannot help lamenting that we are so negligent in taking steps to obtain a principal for it. I mentioned Dr. Miller's name to you in a former letter as a suitable person for the purpose. He stands high in New York as a scholar, a divine, and a citizen. His letters to his congregation in favor of Presbyterian ordination and in answer to the absurd stuff published by some of the Episcopal clergy in favor of the exclusive validity of Episcopal ordination, have done him great honor and will convey his name and proofs of his talents throughout every part of the Presbyterian Church in the United States.[3] In politics he is a genuine whig but connected with no party. He prefers the name of an American to those of Englishman and Frenchman, and our simple homemade governments to the more splendid governments of royal manufactory in every part of the world.

With such a man as Dr. Miller at the head of our College, I am satisfied many young men would yearly be sent to it from Philadelphia. Princeton has lately lost its popularity among us.

Adieu, my dear old friend. In writing upon the subject of our College I feel now all the ardor I felt at its establishment, nor do I now fear that my zeal will be misrepresented or my labors lost. Let us unite our efforts once more to complete the object of our wishes. Until we secure another principal, remember our College is a widow and our students are orphans—at least they are so in the opinion of the public. Could Dr. Davidson be placed in our principal's chair, I should be highly pleased. He has deserved well of our College, but as this measure is not agreeable to him (under present circumstances), let us as soon as possible turn our eyes to a person equally capable of filling that station.

From, dear sir, your sincere old friend,

BENJN: RUSH

Addressed: John Montgomery Esqr Carlisle Pennsylvania.
MS: Dickinson College Library.

[1] James Hamilton (ca. 1742-1819), of Carlisle, born in Ireland, was a trustee of Dickinson College from 1794; president judge of the 9th district from 1806 (Conway P. Wing, *History of Cumberland County, Pennsylvania*, Phila., 1879, p. 163; Dickinson College, *Alumni Record*, p. 12). There are letters from Hamilton to BR in Rush MSS, VII.

[2] Probably John Vaughan; see BR to John Adams, 6 Jan. 1806.
[3] *Letters on the Christian Ministry*, N.Y., 1807. "This work was answered by John Bowden, D.D., . . . in a Series of Letters to Dr. Samuel Miller, 1808, 2 vols. 8vo. Dr. Miller responded. We believe that the whole controversy was contained in five volumes" (Allibone, *Dict. of Authors*).

To John Adams

My dear old Friend,   Philadelphia, July 13, 1808

The campaign of summer diseases being opened, and my duties calling me at all hours of the day into the field of sickness and distress, I have not had time till now to answer your last letter.[1] I shall abruptly say in reply to the latter part of it that the union of the Democrats and Quids in our state was founded upon the dread of Federal power manifested in the supposed removal of your son from the Senate of the United States. That union, however, was but partial and transient; many of both sects of Republicans will join the Federalists at the next election; and still more of the original Democrats will unite in Clinton[2] and Monroe. The extensive county of Northumberland has lately held a convention in which a vote in favor of those two gentlemen is recommended to the future electors of Pennsylvania. How this great business will end, I know not. The Embargo becomes daily more and more unpopular among both farmers and mechanics. Its influence is in favor of a revolution of the power of our country.

I have lately heard that a life of General Hamilton is preparing for the press.[3] It will consist of many documents which will throw light upon the councils [*counsels?*] of the army and government of the United States during the time Mr. Hamilton acted as aide-de-camp and secretary of the treasury under General Washington. One of Hamilton's friends said in my presence a few days ago, "the intended publication would show General W. to be a *good* man but General Hamilton to be a GREAT man." Let this work end as it will, I shall continue to believe that "great men are a lie, and mean men vanity,"[4] and that there is very little difference in that superstition which leads us to believe in what the world call "great men" and in that which leads us to believe in witches and conjurors.

The papers will inform you of the death of my brother professor and old enemy, Dr. Shippen. He sent for me in his last illness and discovered after he was unable to speak that he carried no hostility out of the world against me. This was a great triumph of truth or of religion in his mind, for he was unfriendly to me ever since my settlement in Philadelphia in 1769. Marriage and death it is said opens everybody's mouth. The Doctor's death has produced a hundred speeches and anecdotes respecting his character. But alas! they all relate chiefly to events that can do him no good in the world to which he is gone. Peace and joy to his departed spirit! He was visited by a pious clergyman on the day of his death, to whom he made signs in answer to questions that were proposed to him, that he had hopes beyond the grave and that these hopes were founded in the mercy of God manifested to the world by the death of his son.[5]

Adieu! my dear friend. Excuse the shortness and haste to[6] this letter, and be assured of the respect, friendship, and affection of yours and your dear Mrs: Adams'

BENJN. RUSH

P.S. You may safely commit your ideas upon the present state of our country to me. No person sees your letters but my son Richard, with whom they are like the voice of an oracle.

Wm. Duane is appointed a colonel in the new army. I send you herewith two pamphlets,[7] the one by my son-in-law, in which you will find marks of a strong and original mind. The other will exhibit a proof of the flourishing state of our medical school.

MS: Adams Manuscript Trust, Boston.

[1] Dated 20 June 1808 (*Old Family Letters, A*, p. 183-7).

[2] George Clinton, currently Vice-President, was the presidential candidate of the anti-Madisonian wing of the Democratic-Republican party, but he was defeated by Madison (DAB).

[3] This contemplated biography probably did not appear. P. L. Ford, *Bibliotheca Hamiltoniana*, N.Y., 1886, lists no biographies between 1804 and 1834.

[4] Psalms 62:9.

[5] Shippen died 11 July 1808. There is another account of his last days in BR's Commonplace Book (*Autobiography*, p. 322-3). Shippen's daughter, Mrs. Livingston, asked BR to "give to the world a few outlines of [Shippen's] excellent character" (letter dated 18 July 1808, Rush MSS, IX), but it does not appear that BR complied.

[6] Thus in MS.

[7] I have been unable to identify either of these.

To Samuel Miller

Dear Sir,   Philadelphia, July 21st, 1808

I have read your letter with regret but dare not urge you to give the subject of it a second consideration.[1]

A few days ago I received a letter from Judge Hamilton, one of the trustees of the College, in which he informs me he had mentioned your name for our principal to a considerable number of the trustees, and that they were all much pleased with it. This day I have received a letter from good old Jno. Montgomery, in which he exults in the prospect of your filling our vacant principal's chair. Dr. Davidson, he says, is much delighted with the same prospect.

Adieu! my dear sir, and believe me to be with unabated regard your sincere friend,

BENJN: RUSH

Addressed: The Revd: Dr: Samuel Miller New York.
MS: Princeton University Library.

[1] See BR to Miller, 5 July; to Robert Davidson, 7 Oct.; and to Miller, 8 Oct. 1808.

The University of Pennsylvania and Its Medical School

Home of John and Abigail Adams at Quincy, Massachusetts

To John Montgomery

Dear Sir,   Philadelphia, August 10, 1808

The seven hundred dollars came safe to hand, in addition to three hundred formerly received. $490 $\frac{50}{100}$ of them have already been paid for a part of our apparatus, which is now well packed up and ready to be put into any wagon that shall offer for Carlisle. I regret that Mr. Little[1] could not take it. We expect the air pump from Salem in Massachussets. It will be a complete one. Perhaps it may arrive time enough to be sent with the apparatus now purchased in Philadelphia.[2]

Since my last, I have thought of a principal for our College, and that is the Reverend Dr. Ashbel Green of our city. You are no stranger to his qualifications and accomplishments for that station. He has genius, scholarship, prudence, dignity, talents for government, and great zeal in his Master's cause. His disposition prompts him more to a studious than to an active life, and hence I believe he would be more useful at the head of a college than at the head of a single congregation, and I believe more happy in the former than in the latter station. I believe further that teaching would be more agreeable to him than preaching, as it would require less exertion of voice and strength, and thus be less hurtful to his health, which is delicate, but not so as to endanger his life or his usefulness as the principal of a college. He has no wife and but three sons, one of whom is a young lawyer—the other two incline to the church. No objection to his removal will of course arise from family considerations. I have not consulted him upon the business, nor do I think it would be prudent to do so. My advice is to convene the trustees immediately and elect him at once without his knowledge. Should he decline the appointment, we shall only be where we were; but I flatter myself this will not be the case. The experiment is worth trying. Offer him a generous salary, and trust to providence and the Doctor's talents and character to pay it. Many, many students of all denominations will follow him to Carlisle from our city, for he is universally esteemed and respected by all classes of our citizens.

Adieu! my dear friend. Keep up your spirits. *All—all will end well.* From your sincere old friend,

BENJN: RUSH

P.S. I wish, if[3] you elect Dr. Green, the business may be finished before he or his friends can hear anything about it. Otherwise pains will be taken to defeat us.[4]

[973]

Addressed: John Montgomery Esqr: Carlisle Pennsylvania.
MS: Dickinson College Library.

[1] Unidentified.
[2] The "philosophical apparatus" was sent on 20 Aug., according to a letter of that date from BR to Professor Davidson (Hist. Soc. Penna., Conarroe Papers). The air pump was obtained and sent on in October (same to same, 7 Oct. 1808).
[3] This word omitted in MS.
[4] Nothing came of BR's proposal of Green as successor to Nisbet.

To John Adams

My venerable and dear Friend,   Philadelphia, August 24, 1808

In contemplating the events that have lately taken place in Spain[1] and their probable consequences, I feel disposed to exclaim in the bold apostrophe of Jeremiah: "O! thou sword of the Lord, how long will it be ere thou be quiet? Put up thyself into thy scabbard, rest, and be still." Chapter 47, verse 6th. Shall we hope that a voice from heaven has arrested the destroyer of nations, or is he to extend his conquest and tyranny by shedding fresh rivers of human blood? I tremble at his name. The levity of a Frenchman, the phlegm of a German, the avarice of a Dutchman, the coldheartedness of a Russian, the solidity of an Englishman, the gravity of a Spaniard, the subtlety of an Italian, and the cruelty of a Turk appear to be united in his character. In no one part of his conduct do we trace the least semblance of any one of the virtues that rescued the name of Alexander and Caesar from total infamy. He is devoid of the occasional magnanimity of the former and the habitual clemency of the latter. What do you think of all the Christian nations in the world uniting in a general fast day to take place six or nine months hence for the sole purpose of supplicating the Father of the human race to deliver them from the fangs of this beast of prey?—But I hasten from the hateful subject with which I have introduced my letter to mention a fact to you which will surprise you not much less than the late events at Bayonne and in Spain.

Accident threw me a few days ago into the company of one of the leaders of the Democratic party in Philadelphia whose name I have more than once heard you mention with an abhorrence of his principles.[2] He addressed me privately in the following words. "Doctor, I have changed my opinion of your old friend Mr. Adams. I once thought him a weak man, but I now think him the wisest man in our country. He foresaw the present state of the parties that now distract our country and pointed out the only remedy to prevent them. I wish to heaven we could *now*, while the people possess all the power of the country, fix upon a *perpetual* and *hereditary* chief magistrate, and limit his powers. If this be not done *soon* and *by the people*, it will take place in *another* way." I submit the anecdote to your reflections. Further your friend and correspondent saith not.

I thank you for the friendly interest you take in the revival of my business.[3] In an examination I have lately made of my books, I find that the diminution, and of course the loss from it, amounted between the years 1797 and 1807 to upwards of 30,000 dollars, calculating from the income of 1796 and adding the defalcations of every subsequent year from that time to the 1st of January 1807. Had it not been for the emoluments of the office you gave me (for which I hope gratitude will descend to future generations in my family), I must have retired from the city and ended my days upon a farm upon the little capital I had saved from the labors of former years. I say *little*, for my sacrifices and losses during the war (which amounted to at least the same sum I have mentioned) had prevented my accumulating more than was sufficient to settle myself comfortably in a country situation. Even with the addition of the income from the Mint which you gave me, I spent for several years from 12 to 15 hundred dollars a year more than the income from my business. In no period of my depression did I regret the conduct that occasioned it. My opinions and practice I was sure were correct, and I believed they would prevail. I acted uprightly and consulted the health of my fellow citizens and the benefit of society more than I did my own interest or fame. Most of my fellow citizens (the physicians excepted) have forgiven me, and *they* dare not openly, as they once did, assail my character. Judge of their hostility to me when I add that Cobbett declared when he left this country that he was not my enemy, that he believed I was ———[4] &c., and that he was instigated to all his publications against me by three of our physicians, whose names he mentioned.[5] They were the tools only of members of the faculty who kept themselves out of sight. My business now through divine goodness is more profitable than ever it was, and if it should please God to continue my life and health a few years longer, I shall, I hope, not burden the poor list with my wife and children when I am taken from them.

Though I dare not mention the attentions I receive from strangers in my native state, I can in confidence mention to you that I some time ago received in a polite letter the thanks of the National Institute of Paris for my publications upon medicine, and that I have lately received a diploma from a new society created (I believe) by Napoleon, entitled the "Italian Society of Arts and Sciences."[6] They meet at Florence.

I am now preparing for the press a small work to be entitled "Rules for the preservation of health and life suited to the climate, manners, and state of society of the inhabitants of the United States."[7] It will contain the application of several of my peculiar opinions in medicine to the science of health and life. This information must not be made public. At present it is known only to my family and my excellent young friend "handsome Bradford,"[8] as you are pleased to style him.

With respects and love to all who surround your daily board, I am, dear sir, ever your grateful and affectionate friend,

BENJN: RUSH

P.S. The strife will be ardent between Ross'[9] and Snyder's friends in October. Both parties are alike sanguine. The Embargo operates in favor of the former. You say it makes cowards of our nation. A physician in this city compared it a few days ago to low diet for the cure of a violent inflammatory fever. Bleeding and other depleting remedies, he said, cure it more promptly and more safely.

MS: Adams Manuscript Trust, Boston.

[1] In April and May 1808 Napoleon forced the abdication of Charles IV and his son Ferdinand at Bayonne, and put his own brother Joseph on the Spanish throne (*Cambridge Modern History*, N.Y. and London, 1902-1912, IX, 430-4).

[2] Unidentified.

[3] See Adams' letter of 25 July 1808 (*Old Family Letters*, *A*, p. 188).

[4] Three words were inked out by BR and a line drawn above them.

[5] The names of the physicians meant by BR can only be guessed at.

[6] These have so far not been found in the Rush MSS.

[7] This work, dealing with a favorite subject, BR continued to plan and labor over for years, but it was never completed. See further, letters to Vine Utley, 25 June 1812, and to Jefferson, 15 Mch. 1813.

[8] William or Samuel Bradford, sons of BR's old friend Thomas Bradford, and both in the family publishing and bookselling business (DAB, under Thomas Bradford).

[9] James Ross (1762-1847), of Pittsburgh; U.S. senator, 1794-1803; repeatedly the Federalist candidate for the Pennsylvania governorship, but never elected (DAB).

To John Adams

My dear Friend,   Philadelphia, September 16, 1808

I shall answer your letter of August 31st[1] by giving you an account of one of my late dreams.

After having recently observed the fatal effects of intemperance in the use of ardent spirits in one of my patients, and reflecting afterwards upon the incalculable evils they are spreading through our country, I went to bed a few evenings ago at my usual hour, and during the night I dreamed that I had been elected President of the United States. At first I objected to accepting of the high and honorable station, but upon recollecting that it would give me an opportunity of exercising my long-cherished hostility to ardent spirits by putting an end to their general use in our country, I consented to accept of the appointment and repaired to the city of Washington, where I entered upon the duties with spirit and zeal. The secretaries brought me a number of letters and reports. I laid them upon a table and told them I would do no business until I got a law passed by Congress to prohibit not only the importation and distilling but the consumption of ardent spirits in the United States. They concurred in my determination, and a law was obtained for those purposes. It set forth the evils of ardent spirits in strong terms, and in the room of them recommended simple water, molasses and water, and small beer. Wise, humane, and patriotic as this law was, it instantly met with great opposition, particularly in those states and counties in which spirits were consumed in the greatest quantities. Petitions flowed in upon me from all quarters to advise Congress to repeal the law, but I refused to comply with them. One day sitting alone in my council chamber, a venerable but plain-looking man was introduced to me by one of my servants. I offered him a chair and delicately asked him what his business was with me. "I have taken the liberty," said he, "Mr. President, to call upon you to remonstrate with you against the law for prohibiting the importation, manufactory, and consumption of ardent spirits. He said the law was well enough for a month or two, during which time all the drunken men in the country had become sober, but, protracted as it was for nearly a year, it did such violence to the physical and commercial habits of our citizens that it had not and could not be carried into general effect; that many of the persons who had conformed to it had been made sick from drinking nothing but cold water; that the plow and the wagon stood still from the want of that strength in the men which they formerly derived from their morning dram; that the stage drivers and coachmen everywhere fell from their seats from the same cause; that the clergy in many places were unable to preach and the lawyers to plead from the want of a little grog to moisten and oil their organs of speech; that the women had everywhere become unusually peevish and quarrelsome from a relaxation of their nerves brought on by the want of a little brandy in their tea; and that all the West India merchants, distillers, and tavern-keepers in the country were in an uproar; and that unless the water and small beer law were instantly repealed, we should soon have our country filled with hospitals and our jails with bankrupts." "Hold, sir," said I. "You don't know the people of the United States as well as I do; they will submit to the empire of Reason, and Reason will soon reconcile them to the restrictions and privations of the law for sobering and moralizing our citizens." "Reason! Reason! Mr. President. Why, you forget that it was Reason in the form of a Goddess that produced all the crimes and calamities of the French Revolution, and that it was by a book entitled *The Age of Reason* that Tom Paine demoralized half the Christian world. You forget too that men are *rational only*, not reasonable creatures. Have you never read the *Posthumous Works* of Frederick the II of Prussia? You will there find that great statesman as well as warrior says, 'Reason never did any great[2] in human affairs.' And have you never read the story of an Englishman who was so dissatisfied with the expenses and follies of the British government, in which everything was conducted by *passion*, that he set out to visit a country in Asia known by the name of the kingdom of Reason.[3] Upon being introduced to the prime minister of the king, he told him he had come from a great distance to do homage to a government and a people that were governed wholly by reason, and that he intended to end his days among them. 'O! sir,' said the minister, 'you will repent the exchange you have made of your country for ours. In your country, we are told, men who have lost an arm or a leg in a battle think themselves amply rewarded for their misfortune by having a blue or red ribbon hung over their shoulders, or the trifling monosyllables *Sir* or *Lord* attached to their names; but in our country our generals and officers laugh at those baubles and demand *reasonable* rewards for their services and sacrifices of their limbs, and these consist in large and splendid houses, extensive tracts of land, and pensions of many thousand pounds a year, by which our country is broken down and ruined by taxes, and instead of being the happiest, we are the most miserable nation upon the face of the earth.' But, Mr. President, in thus rejecting the empire of Reason in government, permit me to mention an empire of another kind, to which men everywhere yield a willing, and in some instances involuntary, submission, and that is the EMPIRE OF HABIT. You might as well arrest the orbs of heaven in their course as *suddenly* change the habits of a whole people. Even in little things they resist sudden innovations upon their ancient and general customs. Peter, the husband of the late Catharine of Russia, lost his life for an attempt to change a part of the dress of his subjects. The inhabitants of Madrid once rose in a mob to oppose an edict which was intended to compel them to use privies in order to prevent the accumulation of night soil in their streets. An hundred other instances might be mentioned of the fatal or mischievous consequences of opposing the settled habits and prejudices of nations and communities. Indeed, Mr. President, I am sorry to tell you, you are no more of a philosopher than you are of a politician, or you never would have blundered upon your spirit law. Let me advise you to retire from your present station and go back to your professor's chair and amuse your boys with your idle and impracticable speculations, or go among your patients and dose them with calomel and jalap ———" "Stop, stop, sir," said I. "What do you mean by thus insulting the first magistrate of your country? Here, John (calling to my servant), turn this man out of doors." The noise of John coming hastily into the council chamber, and the vexation I felt in being thus insulted, awoke me and made me happy in discovering that the whole of the scene I have described was nothing but a dream.

Do not suppose, my good friend, that I mean the least reflection by the contents of this letter upon any recent events in the administration of the government of the United States. I believe a republic to be the best possible government to promote the interest, dignity, and happiness of man. I believe the Embargo to be a wise, a just, and a necessary measure, and I believe simple water, molasses and water, and small beer to be the best ordinary drinks in the world; but if mankind will prefer a monarchy to a republic, commerce and war to an embargo, and drams, slings, grog, and toddy to the wholesome liquors above-mentioned, I can only testify my sorrow for the depravity of their political, moral, and physical inclinations by weeping over their folly and madness.

This letter must not be seen nor read out of your own house.

I shall endeavor to answer your acceptable favor of yesterday shortly. In the meanwhile believe me to be as usual ever yours,

BENJN: RUSH

MS: Adams Manuscript Trust, Boston.

[1] In *Old Family Letters*, *A*, p. 192-7.
[2] BR probably intended to write "anything great." Compare his use of the same quotation in letters to Adams of 11 July 1806 and 8 July 1812. Adams had quoted the French original in a

much earlier letter to BR, 4 Apr. 1790:
"La Raison n'a jamais fait grande chose"
(*Old Family Letters, A*, p. 56).

[3] This story was very likely borrowed
from one of the eighteenth-century
periodical essays.

To Louis Valentin[1]

My dear Friend,   Philadelphia, September 16, 1808

Your three letters of January 1st, July 4th, and June 9th have all been received with a cordial welcome. Accept of my thanks for the pamphlets which accompanied them. My old contemporary and ingenious friend Dr. Odier has done me great honor in translating my publication upon the functions of the spleen and liver into his native language.[2] Dr. Moreschi's theory of the spleen has been taught for some years by Dr. Haighton of London.[3] It does not militate against mine. The same viscera frequently perform many different and very important offices. I am much pleased with Dr. Vidal's essay upon "Animal Gas."[4] I have met with many phenomena in diseases which afford considerable support to his opinions. I have not yet received Dr. Petit's *Medicine dé Coeur*.[5] I admire everything that comes from his pen. The late revolutionary events in France seem to have given a new impetus to the French mind in all sciences and particularly in medicine. I read medical books in your language with more instruction and pleasure than any others. Your physicians are enslaved by no *one* system of medicine. They seem individually to think for themselves.

I shall profit by the hint you have given me respecting my publication upon the smallpox. I shall omit it altogether in the next edition of my works or do homage at its expense to vaccination. You will see in the next number of Dr. Coxe's *Museum* a strong argument in its favor in the history which I have there given of a second infection by the smallpox after *variolous* inoculation.[6]

I thank you for the friendly notice you have taken of my labors in your very elegant discourse upon the present status of the sciences in the United States.[7] I thank you likewise for my admission into the medical institution of Paris. My diploma is not yet arrived.

In answer to the two questions contained in your letter of June 9th, I shall briefly inform you that I have long considered the spasmodic asthma of Dr. Millar[8] as a *modification only* of the angina trachialis or trachitis of Professor Frank.[9] It is by no means a specific disease. Children are never or very rarely afflicted with the asthma. It belongs almost exclusively to adult life.

Trachiotomy for the cure of trachitis has never been performed in the United States. Our physicians despair of any benefit from it. The theory of the disease (which considers the *whole* system as affected in it) is opposed to it.[10]

I have lately met with a case of syphilis in which mercury excited a soreness and salivation on *one* side of the mouth *only*, and what is still more remarkable, it cured the sores upon one side *only* of the genital organs affected by the disease.

I have lately seen a pigeon affected in consequence of a wound upon one of its wings with an opisthotinos.[11] It was perfectly cured by taking four grains of opium at once by my advice.

Adieu! Continue to nourish me with your instructing letters and the publications of your friends.

Health, respect, and friendship from your brother in the republic of medicine,

BENJN: RUSH

Addressed: Dr: Louis Valentin Physician Marseilles.
MS: Bibliothèque Publique et Universitaire de Genève, Switzerland.

[1] Louis Valentin, M.D. (1758-1829), was trained at the University of Nancy, where he was for a time professor of military medicine; military physician in San Domingo during the early years of the French Revolution; made a miraculous escape from the burning city of Cap François, June 1793; spent the following five years in the United States, principally in Virginia, and then returned to France, where he practised successively in Marseilles, Lyon, and Nancy. Valentin was the author of numerous medical articles and treatises, particularly on croup and yellow fever; he announced Jenner's discovery in a *Traité* published 1799, and played an important role in introducing the technique of vaccination in France. He had been elected a member of the American Philosophical Society while still a resident of San Domingo, 1793, and after his return to France kept in intimate touch with medical developments in the United States, writing BR with great frequency for information and current publications. Unfortunately, very few of BR's letters to Valentin have been recovered. (Obituary notice in *Journal complémentaire du Dictionaire des sci-*

ences *médicales*, xxxiv [1829], 84-6; Surg. Gen. Off., *Index-Cat.*, 1st ser., xv, 556; Amer. Philos. Soc., *Early Procs.*, p. 212; Valentin's letters to BR, Rush MSS, XVIII, among which will be found all the letters acknowledged here by BR.)

[2] Louis Odier (1748-1817), of Geneva, Switzerland, obtained his M.D. at Edinburgh in 1770, and knew BR there (BR, *Autobiography*, p. 44). BR's "Inquiry into the Functions of the Spleen, Liver, Pancreas, and Thyroid Gland" had appeared in the *Phila. Medical Museum*, III (1807), 9-29. A much more extensive treatise on the spleen, in Italian and not mentioned by BR in his "Inquiry," had been published at Milan in 1803 by Alessandro Moreschi. Odier translated both works and published them together under the title of *Recherches sur les fonctions de la rate, &c.*, Geneva, 1807 (copy in Libr. Co. Phila.).

[3] John Haighton; see BR to John S. Dorsey, 23 May 1804.

[4] Barthélmi Vidal, *Essai sur le gaz animal considéré dans les maladies*, Marseilles, 1807 (Surg. Gen. Off., *Index-Cat.*, 2d ser., XX, 242).

[5] Marc-Antoine Petit (1766-1811) published an *Essai sur la médicine du coeur*, Lyon, 1806 (*Cat. Bibl. Nat.*).

[6] BR refers first to his early (1781) lecture on "The New Method of Inoculating for the Small-Pox," which he had allowed to stand in the second edn. of *Med. Inq. & Obs.*, 1805, I, 309-34. He then refers to his forthcoming article proving the unreliability of inoculation compared with vaccination: "An Account of a Case of Small-Pox after Variolous Inoculation," *Phila. Medical Museum*, v (1809), 183-7.

[7] That is, in Valentin's strangely entitled *Coup d'oeil sur la culture de quelques végétaux exotiques, dans les departemens méridionaux de la France, et Notice sur l'état présent des sciences physiques et naturelles aux Etats-Unis d'Amérique*, Marseilles, 1807 (copy in Libr. Co. Phila.). The *Notice* is a broad and highly interesting survey of American advances in education, agriculture, exploration, botany, paleontology, medicine, &c. BR's work in yellow fever and consumption is singled out for special praise.

[8] See John Millar (1733-1805), *Observations on the Asthma and on the Hooping Cough*, London, 1769; this was the Millar of "Millar's asthma," laryngismus stridulus (DNB; Surg. Gen. Off., *Index-Cat.*, 1st ser., IX, 309). BR had addressed one of his earliest medical tracts to Millar, namely, *A Dissertation on the Spasmodic Asthma of Children*, London: Cadell, 1770.

[9] Johann Peter Frank (1745-1821), professor at Vienna, was a prolific writer on medicine, best known as the founder of modern public hygiene (*Allgem. deutsche Biog.*). BR alludes specifically to his treatise *De curandis hominum morbis*, lib. II, Ticini, 1792, sect. 173, "Cyn. laryng. tracheal."

[10] By "trachitis" and "angina trachialis" (i.e., tracheitis and angina trache-

alis) BR means the disease which he elsewhere, following the Cullenian nosology, called cynanche trachealis; see his "Observations on the Cynanche Trachealis," *Med. Inq. & Obs.* [1], 1789, p. 120-5, revised and enlarged in the 2d edn., 1805, I, 167-75. "The vulgar name of this disease in Pennsylvania," BR wrote in the revised essay, "is HIVES. It is a corruption of the word *heaves*, which took its rise from the manner in which the lungs heave in breathing." It was also called croup; Valentin in his *Recherches historiques et pratiques sur le croup*, Paris, 1812, enumerated these and other names that had been used. But as BR's remark about spasmodic asthma suggests, these terms were used loosely and doubtless comprehended ailments ranging all the way from what we now call croup to diphtheria—a disease first identified and named by Valentin's compatriot Pierre Bretonneau in 1826. Until then there was extreme confusion in both nomenclature and treatment. "Trachiotomy" (i.e., tracheotomy) is of course incision of the windpipe. In a note on this passage, written on the address leaf, Valentin referred to an unsuccessful tracheotomy in Boston in 1810 or earlier, and quoted part of a letter from BR, 7 Feb. 1811, reporting a similar attempt, by Philip Syng Physick, in Jan. 1810. Bretonneau successfully performed this operation in 1825. (For help on technical points in this and other notes on the present letter, I am indebted to W. B. McDaniel, II, Librarian of the College of Physicians of Philadelphia, and to Professor Oswei Temkin of the Johns Hopkins Institute of the History of Medicine.)

[11] I.e., opisthotonos, defined in *Quincy's Lexicon* (N.Y., 1802) as a variety of tetanus in which "the body is rigidly bent backward."

To John Adams

My dear old and tried Friend, Philadelphia, September 22, 1808

The politics of our city are under the direction of three classes of

people: old tories, merchants, and brokers. They are neither anticipating nor retrospective animals. All their calculations are for the
present moment. They know nothing of treaties nor of the former
volcanic eruptions of the power and tyranny of France. The last
shower with them is always the heaviest. Why then do you ask
me "what our statesman think of the late events in Spain?"[1] Mr.
Clymer is almost the only citizen of Philadelphia with whom I
converse upon political subjects. His mind retains the texture which
the Revolution gave it. He is neither a Frenchman nor an Englishman and laments that Americans partake too much of the principles
of both. He is no advocate for Mr. Jefferson, but he boldly defends
the Embargo and acquits him of partiality to the French nation.
Your old friend Jos. Wharton, who is another citizen of Philadelphia to whose opinions I often listen in my medical visits to his
family, views the late events in Spain, not through the medium
of war or commerce or governments, but of the Book of Daniel and
the Revelations of St. John only. He sees the fulfilment of the
prophecies in every battle that is fought in that country. He talks
piously and learnedly upon the downfall of popery and Antichrist,
of the dragon, of the beast that came out of the sea and of his ten
horns, and has no doubt but Napolion is to be the instrument for
preparing the world for the righteous and peaceable government
of the Messiah over the nations of the earth. Here my information
respecting your question must end. I hasten from it to add that
from present appearances it is probable Mr. Ross will have a majority of votes for the chair of our state at the approaching election.
In our city this will not probably be the case, from the union that
has taken place between the Democrats and Quids, and from the
Embargo being much less felt by our citizens than by the country
part of the state, and this from the employment given to all classes
of mechanics by the building of above 600 houses, two churches,
and two shot manufactories, one of which is to be 160 feet in height.[2]
A gentleman who called to see me a few days ago intimated a
desire to know to which of the candidates for our government I
wished success. I answered him by telling him a story of Sir Richard
Steel,[3] who in traveling through Scotland stopped to ask a shepherd
whom he saw watching a flock of sheep what kind of weather it
would be the next day. "Just such weather, sir, as I please," said
the shepherd. "You mean," said Sir Richard (supposing him to be
mad from his answer), "just such weather as God pleases." "Well,
sir, what pleases him," said the shepherd, "pleases me." My blood
circulates now too slowly through my veins to expect any change

for the better in our affairs from the exertions of an individual, however well disposed he may be to accomplish it. The old game of "leapfrog" will be played over again should Mr. Ross be elected, and Snyder will not sacrifice the extensive powers our Constitution gives him by advising or consenting to a convention in order to change it.

Our papers teem with electioneering scandal. From all treason, sedition, conspiracies, and *party rage*, good Lord deliver us!—I have often heard when a boy of men's selling their souls to the Devil to relieve a pressing want of money. This practice is now in disuse, but we do the same thing in another way by selling our time, our talents, our tempers, our moral feelings and principles, and sometimes our *wills*, as well as our money, to a party. Under the constant pressure of the two powerful and opposite currents that divide our city, I am enabled to keep my feet. Sooner than float *after* either of them, I would quit my country and go where human folly and madness had exhausted themselves and where the extremity of despotism had left nothing to fear. I would in other words end my days in Constantinople or Paris.

Could the absurdities and contradictions in principle and conduct of our two great parties for the last 12 years be laid before the world in a candid and dispassionate manner, we should be ashamed to call ourselves MEN. The disputes of children about their nuts and gingerbread have less folly and wickedness in them.

From a dozen instances of what I allude to, I shall select but two. When the Spaniards shut the port of New Orleans against our vessels, the cry of the whole Federal party was for war and the acquisition of Louisissiana[4] by force. Its immense resources in West and East India produce were enumerated in long, sensible, and eloquent speeches and pamphlets. When that country was purchased by Mr. Jefferson, the same party condemned his conduct, depreciated the trade, soil, and people of that country, and represented it as a millstone about the neck of the United States. In the year 1798 the Democrats opposed the election of Mr. Ross upon the ground of his being a Deist. The Federalists either denied it or said his religious tenets had nothing to do with his qualifications for governor. In 1799[5] the Federalists opposed the election of Mr. Jefferson upon the ground of his being a Deist. The Democrats denied it, or said his infidel principles had nothing to do with his qualifications for President!!! "Non aula non eclesia, solum—sed totus mundus *histrionem* agunt."[6]

The Scriptures speak of nations being *drunk* and of all the individuals of the human race being *mad*. What *sober* man or what man in his *senses* would think of walking in company or reasoning with either of them?

In reviewing my attempts to regulate the winds or, in other words, in reviewing my political life, which, with the intervals of some years, ended with the establishment of the general government, I often wish, in the words of King Henry before one of his battles in France, for one ten thousand of those (not brave men) but *hours* that did no work for God, nor man, nor myself, nor family during the time I have mentioned. "What profit has the world or my country had from those things," to use the words of an apostle, "whereof I am now ashamed?"[7] None, none, none. Dr. Jebb used to say, "No good effort is lost." If this be true, let us console ourselves with the hope that our labors (like the conversations of the people in winter at the North Pole described by Mr. Addison, which froze as they came out of their mouths and thawed in the spring)[8] will in like manner be thawed by time and produce their fruits in knowledge and happiness in centuries to come.

When I took up my pen I expected to fill but a page or two with its contents, but my imagination has run away with it. Adieu! Adieu! With respects as usual, I am, dear sir, ever yours,

BENJN: RUSH

MS: Adams Manuscript Trust, Boston.

[1] See Adams' letter of 8 Sep. 1808 (*Old Family Letters, A*, p. 198).

[2] In 1807 a 142-foot shot tower was erected on Jones (now Carpenter) St. between Second and Front, the earliest such structure in the United States; in 1808 a 166-foot shot tower was erected at Twenty-first and Cherry Streets (Jackson, *Encyclo. of Phila.*, IV, 1086-7). Note their appearance in BR's allegory in a letter to Adams, 20 Feb. 1809.

[3] I.e., Steele, the famous essayist and dramatist (DNB).

[4] Thus in MS.

[5] This date appears to have been written over the date 1800, which is a more correct date.

[6] See BR's earlier use of this quotation in a letter to Adams of 6 Jan. 1806.

[7] Paraphrased from Romans 6:21.

[8] I have not located this fable attributed to Addison.

To Robert Davidson

Dear Sir,   Philadelphia, October 7, 1808

I am much pleased to hear of the election of Dr. Miller to be the head of our College. He has talents, learning, industry, good temper, and a laudable ambition to be eminent and useful in life. He is moreover an *American*, and will not sport with our national government and character at the expense of the interests of the College. Have you any reason to expect he will accept of the appointment? From the tenor of his letter to me which I sent to Mr. Montgomery, there is more to fear than to hope upon this subject.

I have happily succeeded in purchasing a complete and elegant air pump from a private gentleman in this city. It is now packed up and ready for transportation. Agreeably to your hint, I will offer *more* to a wagoner to take it and the other boxes than is commonly given for loads of merchandise. The air pump cost 150 dollars.[1]

The account of the commencement and of the election of Dr. Miller shall be published in our Philadelphia papers.

You have deserved well of our College. To your labors chiefly we are indebted for its present existence. You must not desert us. With such an auxiliary as Dr. Miller, you will I hope soon place our College upon a footing with the most popular colleges in our country.

I shall not pay the postage of this letter. As we shall be obliged to exchange many others hereafter upon the business of our College, it will be best to keep an account of the postage paid by us and charge the trustees with it. From, dear sir, yours sincerely,

BENJN: RUSH

Addressed: The Revd: Robert Davidson Professor of Nat: Philosy: Carlise,[2] Pennsylvania.
MS: Dickinson College Library.

[1] These arrangements were carried out about a week later (BR to Davidson, 13 Oct. 1808, Dickinson College Library).
[2] Thus in MS.

To Samuel Miller

My dear Sir,   Philadelphia, October 8th, 1808

After the positive manner in which you declined being a candidate for the chair of Carlisle College, in your letter addressed to me last summer,[1] which letter I sent to the trustees of the College, I was much surprised to hear of your election to that high and honorable situation by a *large* and *unanimous* vote. The Reverend Mr. Davies when elected president of the College of New Jersey wrote to his friend Dr. Gibbons[2] in London that "his congregation saw the hand of God in it and *did not dare to oppose it.*" The same thing may be said of your election. The hand of heaven is conspicuously evident in it. I hope therefore neither you nor your congregation will oppose it.

A wide field of usefulness will now be opened to you. You will become the patriarch of the western churches of the United States. You will have the honor of introducing a system of education into our country accommodated to the form of our governments and to our state of society and manners. You will be able to abolish customs and studies in the College of monkish origin and which have nothing but antiquity to recommend them. The present depressed state of the College will serve to administer fuel to your reputation. The difficulties you will encounter at first will give a vigor to your mind that will last through life. Be not discouraged in viewing them. "Hoc est periculum par animo Alexandri."[3] You are more than equal to them.

To your salary, Mr. Cathcart[4] informs me, will be added 2 or 300 dollars a year from the church in Carlisle, together with some perquisites from the students. An addition will be made to your salary with the increase of the College in students and in resources, and you may have 3 or 4 boarders in your family at any price you please.

Think among other things of the *air* of New York so unfriendly to weak lungs.

Your name will draw many pupils from Philadelphia. The fallen character and low state of the French College at Baltimore[5] promises a large increase of students from Maryland and the western parts of Virginia.

A large addition is now making to the philosophical apparatus, and a vote of the trustees has lately appropriated 1,000 dollars for the purchasing of popular *modern* books.

The temper and conduct of Dr. Nesbett rendered all efforts to serve the College abortive. With Dr. Miller at the head of it, there will be a revival of zeal and industry among its trustees and friends to promote its interest and reputation which cannot fail of adding to your interest and happiness.

Recollect the text chosen by Mr. Davies for his funeral sermon: "No man liveth to himself."[6] You are called, not to the chair of the President of the United States, not to a throne, but to a station above both of them—to rank with Edwards, Burr, and others of the greatest and best men who have lived in our country—to form young men for time and eternity, to raise up pillars for the Church as well as for the State, and to be no longer a star but a sun in the great system of science, morals, and religion in our country.

My best respects to Mrs. Miller and your brother. May they both as well as your congregation be endowed with the submissive spirit of Mr. Davies' congregation.——From, dear sir, your sincere friend,

BENJN: RUSH

Addressed: The Revd: Dr: Samuel Miller New York.
MS: Princeton University Library.

[1] Miller's letter was dated 16 July 1808; see BR to Miller, 5 July 1808. Despite his formal election and despite even the present letter, Miller did not accept the principalship.

[2] Thomas Gibbons, D.D. (1720-1785), independent clergyman and hymn-writer; honorary M.A., College of New Jersey, 1760 (DNB).

[3] "This is a danger fit for the spirit of Alexander." Source unknown.

[4] Robert Cathcart (1759-1849), Presbyterian pastor of churches at York and Hopewell, Penna.; trustee of Dickinson College, 1794-1833 (Sprague, *Annals*, III, 559-62; Dickinson College, *Alumni Record*, p. 12).

[5] BR probably had in mind St. Mary's College at Baltimore, which existed from 1799 to 1852 as a preparatory school for St. Mary's Seminary, a Sulpician institution established under the patronage of Bishop John Carroll; St. Mary's College at first admitted only French and Spanish boys (B. C. Steiner, *History of University Education in Maryland*, Johns Hopkins Univ. Studies in History and Political Science, IX [1891], pt. 3, p. 32-3).

[6] Paraphrased from Romans 14:7.

To John Adams

My dear Friend,   Philadelphia, October 21, 1808

The election in Pennsylvania has issued in a manner totally unexpected by the Federalists and beyond the expectations of the Democrats. I was deceived, in the opinion I gave you in my last letter, by some of my Federal friends who pretended to know the disposition of the interior and frontier counties of the state. Mr. Snyder will be returned governor by a majority of nearly 30,000 votes. This will be favorable to the stability of our government and the repose of the state. The largeness of the majority will admit of strife and division among them, and thus prevent the evils their opponents have expected from the success of their ticket.

Your view of the possible influence of the present war in Spain upon our country is I believe a correct one.[1] The issue of their struggle is still doubtful. The whole power of France will soon be directed against them.

General Wilkinson[2] is now in our city receiving daily marks of homage from our militia such as General Washington used to receive in his occasional visits to our city during the war. He is visited and entertained chiefly by the citizens of the Democratic party.

[988]

My brother, Judge Rush, lately visited the place in which we both received our academical education in Cecil County in Maryland. In wandering over the neighborhood, he met with a man of 70 years of age whom he recollected when a schoolboy. This man settled at 20 upon a farm which his father gave him, and has lived on it ever since without any other inmates but a cat and dog. He plowed, sowed, and reaped his fields alone, but he delighted chiefly in grazing. From contemplating the evils money did in the world, he resolved never to handle it, and hence he purchased all his clothing and farming utensils by bartering cattle for them. Gold and silver have never touched his fingers since he retired to his agricultural monastery. He read but one book, and that was the Bible. He appeared healthy and happy. My brother asked him whether he was satisfied with his situation; he said, "Perfectly so," and added that if he had to live his life over again, he would choose the life he had lived. Where is the politician or the man that has lived *in* the world or *with* the world that can make the same declaration at the same age?

Adieu. From, my dear and venerable friend, ever yours,

BENJN: RUSH

Addressed: John Adams Esqr: Woolaston Quincy near Boston.
MS: Adams Manuscript Trust, Boston.

[1] See Adams' letter of 8 Sep. 1808 (*Old Family Letters*, *A*, p. 197-9).
[2] James Wilkinson (1757-1825), military commander at New Orleans, who had first collaborated with Aaron Burr and then betrayed him (DAB).

To Mathew Carey

Dear Sir,   November 24, 1808

I have read the papers you sent me with great pleasure. Everything that enables me to think well of all sects of Christians is highly gratifying to me. The fact is new to me that Lord Baltimore taught Wm. Penn his sublime lesson of religious toleration.[1] It is certain, according to Dr. Robertson, that Oveido, a Spanish monk, first wrote in favor of it in South America.[2] What Tacitus says of the vices of lawyers, viz., "vitium *hominum*, non oratorum,"[3] should be said of the faults of all the different sects and professions of men. They belong to human nature.

From, dear sir, yours very respectfully,

BENJN: RUSH

MS: Historical Society of Pennsylvania, Society Collection.

[1] Carey had evidently sent BR a copy of the Act concerning Religion, proposed by the first Lord Baltimore, the Catholic proprietor of Maryland, and passed by the Assembly of that province in April 1649. Now usually called the "Toleration Act," it prohibited "the inforceing of the conscience in matters of Religion." See Gerald W. Johnson, *The Maryland Act of Religious Toleration: An Interpretation*, Baltimore, 1949, a brochure containing a facsimile of the Act; and the same author's "Landmark on the Road to Religious Freedom," *N.Y. Times Magazine*, 17 Apr. 1949, p. 13+; also Anson Phelps Stokes, *Church and State in the United States*, N.Y., 1950, I, 189-94.

[2] Gonzalo Fernandez de Oviedo y Valdès (1478-1557) was an important administrator and chronicler in the early Spanish settlements in the New World. His *Historia general de las Indias* (Seville, 1535—Valladolid, 1557) is one of the great repositories of information on its period. See Winsor, *Narr. and Crit. Hist.*, II, 209, 343-6, 563, with references there. The Scottish historian William Robertson, in his *History of America* (London, 1777), drew heavily on Oviedo, but I have not found the passage alluded to by BR.

[3] "It is their fault as *human beings* rather than as orators." Tacitus, *Dialogus de oratoribus*, xxv.

To John Adams

My dear Friend,   Philadelphia, December 14, 1808

Has your right hand forgotten its cunning from pain or sickness? Or have you ceased to contemplate the present interesting crisis of your beloved country? Or have you become fearful of committing your apprehensions of her future destiny to paper? If none of these events have come to pass, why am I not favored with answers to my two last letters?[1]

Say, my dear and venerable friend, what is to be done to preserve and perpetuate the result of the labors and solicitude of your life? Or in the language of the prophet, "Watchman, watchman (for such you have always been of the best interests of your country), what, O! what of the NIGHT?"[2] How long will its darkness continue, and how extensive will the evils be which have been engendered by it?

This hasty effusion from a heart that loves you is written under the pressure of business and duties that allow me time only to add that I am with great respect and affection and gratitude ever yours,

BENJN: RUSH

Addressed: John Adams Esqr: Quincy near Boston Massachussets.
MS: Adams Manuscript Trust, Boston.

[1] Adams had begun a letter on 10 Oct. which he did not finish until 20 Dec. 1808 (*Old Family Letters, A*, p. 203-8). He had read through Voltaire's works in the interval (same, p. 211-12).
[2] Isaiah 21:11.

VI.

Last Years of

A Republican Physician

1809-1813

1809-1811. James Rush at Edinburgh and London.

1809 Aug. 29. Marriage of Richard Rush to Catherine Murray.

1809. Publishes third edition of *Medical Inquiries and Observations*.

1811 May. Makes plea for temperance reform before General Assembly of Presbyterian Church.

1811. Publishes *Sixteen Introductory Lectures*.

1811 Nov.-Dec. Richard Rush appointed comptroller of the United States and moves to Washington.

1811-1812. Effects reconciliation between Ex-Presidents Adams and Jefferson.

1812. Publishes *Medical Inquiries and Observations, upon Diseases of the Mind*.

1813 Apr. 19. Dies at Philadelphia; buried in Christ Church Burial Ground.

Part VI. *Last Years of A Republican Physician*

1809-1813

To John Adams

My dear Friend,   Philadelphia, January 13, 1809

In a situation such as you have seen a sea captain in a gale of wind, I sit down to acknowledge the receipt of your two last instructing letters. Present events will justify your opinion of the present measures of our rulers. Your account of the pernicious influence of a belief in the *time* in which the prophecies are to be fulfilled is so much opposed to the system of the divine government adopted by my friend Mr. Wharton that I did not dare to read it to him.[1] He is happy in his creed. I thought it a pity to lessen in any degree his confidence in it or his high opinion of your judgment and character. For wise purposes it has pleased God to conceal from us the *precise times* in which the prophecies are to be accomplished. The attempts of bad men to defeat them and of good men to accelerate them would probably have increased in a great degree the miseries of our world from human ambition and folly.

In the clamors which have been excited lately against commerce, I have been led to consider the absurdity of deriving human depravity from any other source than that recorded in the Bible. It has been ascribed not only to commoners, but to kings, to different forms of government, to the clergy, and by Ruisseau and some members of the legislature of Pennsylvania to science and to colleges. Legislation founded upon any one of these opinions must necessarily be erroneous and productive of misery. In the Bible alone man is described as *he is*. He can be governed of course only by accommodating law to his nature as developed in that sacred book.

Strange changes are taking place in the offices in Pennsylvania! A gentleman remarked in my hearing a few days ago that Governor McKean had given a correct character of the citizens of our state when he called one part of them "Traitors, tories, apostate whigs, and British agents," and the other "Fools, Geese, and Clodhoppers."[2] As many true words are spoken in jest, so it was remarked

[993]

these words of the Governor, though spoken in anger, were strictly true.—Our Constitution will I believe be safe. Our new Governor too I believe aims well. But if, as you once told me George the 3rd is not King of Great Britain but ruled by a varying aristocracy, how can we expect Simon Snyder to be an independent governor of Pennsylvania?

It would seem as if there was but *two* vices in the United States— and that is the *vice* of Federalism and the *vice* of Democracy. My worthy brother has given great offense to the ruling powers by voting for Mr. Ross. The judiciary system of the state, it is said, is to undergo a change. If so, he may probably expiate his vote by a change in his situation.—With love to your fireside, I am, dear sir, ever yours with gratitude and affection,

BENJN: RUSH

MS: Adams Manuscript Trust, Boston.

[1] Adams' delightful letter of 22 Dec. 1808, on the futility of applying the Biblical prophecies to current events, is in *Old Family Letters, A*, p. 208-13.

[2] BR is quoting McKean's famous outburst on the occasion of a conference, 21 Mch. 1805, with a deputation of Democrats who favored revision of the state Constitution (Peeling, "Governor McKean," p. 338-9; Scharf & Westcott, I, 520).

To John Adams

Philadelphia, February 20th, 1809

My dear and excellent Friend,

Soon after the receipt of your last letter, in which you advise me to shake off my retired habits and prejudices and to come forward in support of the petitions of my fellow citizens for a repeal of the Embargo laws,[1] I went to bed at my usual hour and dreamed that I had yielded to your advice, and in consequence of it determined to appear at a Federal town meeting which was to be held the next day in company with my worthy friend and only surviving colleague in subscribing the Declaration of Independence, Mr. George Clymer. I thought I had agreed to speak in favor of the measures that were to be proposed by the meeting, and for that purpose prepared a speech which was amply larded with the Federal phrases of "the immortal Washington, the disciples of Washington, the ghost of Washington, &c., &c." At the proposed hour of the meeting (which was at 11 o'clock in the forenoon) I imagined I set off for the State house yard, and that on my way my attention was drawn to a small frame house between 4th and 5th Streets in Chesnut Street in which I saw a number of men busily employed in a manner which excited my curiosity to a very high degree. I begged permission to sit down in the room in which they were assembled. This was readily granted. Never did I witness such a scene. The man nearest to the door was engaged in placing a number of wheels within wheels. I was told he was attempting to find out perpetual motion. On one side of the fireplace I saw a man surrounded with crucibles with a small furnace before him. I was told that he was endeavoring to change a piece of copper into gold. On the opposite side of the fireplace I saw a man shaking a bottle in which were infused a number of rare gums and roots. He said he was preparing an elixir, a teaspoonful of which taken every morning in a tumbler of cold water would prevent the pains and all the deformities of old age and restore man to his original antediluvian longevity. In a corner of the room sat a meager-looking young man covered with goose down, with a basket of feathers on each side of him. I asked what he was about to do with those feathers. He said he was making a pair of wings with which he intended to amuse the citizens of Philadelphia shortly by flying from the top of the newly erected shot manufactory upon Schuylkill to the one lately erected in South-wark upon the Delaware. In another corner of the room sat a little squat fellow with a table before him upon which he was trying to make an egg stand upon one of its ends. In the middle of the floor I saw a stout man with a flushed face standing with both his feet upon a stick, with his two hands grasped round each end of it, straining with all his might to lift himself from the floor. "What! What means all this?" said I. "I am certainly in a madhouse." After this declaration I rose suddenly from my seat and walked towards the door. "Stop!" said a little old man who appeared to be the master of the house, "and tell me where are you going." "To the town meeting," said I. "You are at it already," said he. "What! in this receptacle of madmen?" said I. "Yes," said he, "they are an epitome of all public bodies, whether assembled in town meetings, state legislatures, congresses, conventions, or parliaments, and of all the statesmen and philosophers, whether at courts or in a closet, who expect to produce by their labors, *wisdom, justice, order,* and *stability* in human governments." Struck with the good sense of this speech, I instantly returned to my house, strongly impressed with a sense of my obligation to the little old man who *thus* as I thought saved me from adding to the list of the follies of my political life. While congratulating myself upon this escape, a midnight rap at my door awoke me and confirmed my pleasure by satisfying me that my *relapse* into the vices of party and the vexations of public life was nothing but a DREAM.

Adieu! All my fireside salutes you and yours! From your affectionate and grateful friend,

BENJN: RUSH

MS: Adams Manuscript Trust, Boston.

[1] In a letter of 23 Jan. 1809, Adams had urged BR to write publicly against the Embargo and in favor of naval construction (*Old Family Letters, A*, p. 214).

To John Adams

My dear and venerable Friend,   Philadelphia, March 2nd, 1809

Your favor of the 19th of February[1] was alike acceptable with all your former letters. The papers will inform you that our government is about to yield to the clamors of your part of the United States against the Embargo laws. Had our legislators been better historians, they would have promptly saved their honor and preserved the peace of our country. Augustus repealed a law to compel bachelors to marry as soon as he discovered that it could not be carried into effect. One of the kings of Spain issued an edict to oblige the citizens of Madrid to build and make use of privies in order to defend the streets of that city from the ordure which covered them every morning. This edict was resisted and repealed, and the inhabitants of Madrid continue to this day to enjoy in their old and filthy habit the triumph of their ancestors over the despotism of their government. From the scarcity and high price of wood in Vienna, Joseph the 2nd issued an order to the citizens of his capital to bury their dead in linen or woolen cloth. The order was disobeyed, and in consequence thereof repealed, with this declaration by the Emperor: "Let my subjects rot in the ground in any way they please."

Our new governor has begun his administration by a rupture with the general government which will possibly end in bloodshed.[2] The newspapers will inform you of its cause. His Excellency is said to be a well-disposed man, but he is said to be under the influence of a new sect of Democrats called "Quadroons." A Mr. Binns,[3] an active and intelligent printer, is at the head of them. The offices in the gift of the Governor have been confined chiefly to this sect. The old Democrats, of whom Duane and Leib are the heads, begin to complain of him. The Quids, of whom Mr. Dallas is considered as the head, have no influence over him.

The 22nd of last month, the birthday of General Washington was celebrated with great festivity in our city.

We are advised to eat onions in order to prevent our being offended with the breath of persons who have eaten them. Is there no method of infecting persons with madness in order to prevent their being offended and distressed with the madness of their friends and the public? Nat. Lee the poet[4] was asked in a cell in Bethlehem hospital "what brought him there." He answered, "He had said the world was mad, but that the world had said the same thing of him, and that he had been *outvoted*." Do and say what we will, we shall I fear always be *outvoted* by the fools and knaves and madmen of our country.

Tomorrow I expect to close my lectures. The subject of my last lecture will be "the diseases of the *eyes* and *ears*." Difficult as they are to cure in the human body, they are far less so than when they affect those two senses in public bodies. How blind have the former been to the drafts upon the Treasury in favor of ———,[5] and how deaf have the latter been to the cries of the sailors and others who have suffered by the Embargo!

Adieu! Ever yours,

BENJN: RUSH

Addressed: John Adams Esqr: Quincy near Boston.
MS: Adams Manuscript Trust, Boston.

[1] In *Old Family Letters*, *A*, p. 217-18 (dated 20 Feb. 1808).
[2] The "Fort Rittenhouse" affair; see BR's letter of 1 Apr. 1809.
[3] John Binns (1772-1860), Irish-born journalist, orator, and radical, had formerly conducted a newspaper in Northumberland, Penna., where he ac- quired large political influence in the back-country counties; published the *Democratic Press* in Philadelphia from 1807 (DAB).
[4] Nathaniel Lee (1653?-1692), writer of verse tragedies, spent five years in Bethlehem Hospital (DNB).
[5] Unidentified.

To John Adams

My excellent Friend,   Philadelphia, March 13th, 1809

When a young man I read Sidney upon Government.[1] In one of his chapters he agitates the following question, "Whether a civil war or slavery be the greatest evil?" and decides in favor of the latter. In revolving that subject in my mind, I have been led to suppose there are evils more afflicting and injurious to a country than a foreign war. The principal evil of war is death. Now vice I believe to be a greater evil than death, and this is generated more by funding systems, banks, embargoes, and nonintercourse laws than by war. Dr. Price calculates the perjuries in Great Britain from the excise and customs at three millions annually. What do you suppose was the number of the false oaths produced by our late Embargo? And what will be the number of the same crimes from the operation of our present nonintercourse law?[2] Greater probably than the amount in number and in enormity of all the crimes that are perpetrated by the *fighting* part of an army in twenty years, and even by its quartermasters, commissaries, and directors of hospitals in half that time.

We have had two gala days since the 1st of March in our city— one a procession on the 4th of March in honor of the elections of Mr. Madison and our governor; the other a dinner in honor of some of the Federal members of Congress from New England on the 10th instant. The latter was intended chiefly as a mark of respect to Colonel Pickering, but he did not arrive in time from Washington to receive it.

I was much pleased with the friendly disposition manifested by Mr. Madison to your son.[3] The unsuccessful issue of his attempt to honor him will not I hope prevent his recollecting at a future day the claims of his father as well as of himself to the gratitude of his country.

You have properly distinguished the two great parties which divide your state into French and English. The history of Massachussets is the history of all the states in the Union as far as it respects political zeal and party principles. We are not "all Federalists and all Republicans," but we are (with the exception of a few retired and growling neutrals) all Frenchmen or all Englishmen. The men of both those nations have immense advantages over you and me. By not eating of the onions of either of them, we are constantly exposed to the offensive breath of them *both*.

Adieu, my ever dear and valuable friend. From yours sincerely,

BENJN: RUSH

P.S. All my fireside as usual salutes yours.

Addressed: John Adams Esqr: Woolaston Quincy near Boston.
MS: Adams Manuscript Trust, Boston.

[1] Algernon Sidney, *Discourses concerning Government*, London, 1698; a handbook of whiggism throughout the eighteenth century.

[2] The Nonintercourse Act, which on 1 Mch. 1809 succeeded the Embargo,

prohibited trade only with Great Britain, France, and their possessions (McMaster, *Hist.*, III, 335-6).

³ Madison had nominated J. Q. Adams

as minister to Russia (J. Q. Adams, *Writings*, ed. W. C. Ford, N.Y., 1913-1917, III, 291).

The Medical Faculty of the University of Pennsylvania to President Madison[1]

Sir,   Philadelphia, March 29th, 1809

The medical professors of the University of Pennsylvania beg leave to address you upon a subject highly interesting to the honor and interest of the United States.

It has been the practice of the professors, ever since the establishment of the University, to give certificates to the students who have required them, of their having attended their respective lectures. These certificates are not intended to convey an idea of the young gentlemen's qualifications to practise physic or surgery. They are nothing more than testimonials of their diligence and punctuality in attending the lectures. We take the liberty respectfully to wish that this information may have its full force when those certificates are presented to the boards of war as recommendations for commissions in the Army and Navy of the United States, and we hope we shall not give offense when we add that we conceive great advantages will accrue to our country from limiting those commissions *exclusively* to gentlemen who are graduates in medicine in some respectable university in the United States or in any foreign country, or who have been examined by some of the boards lately instituted in most of the states for the purpose of preventing incompetent persons' exercising the profession of medicine. By adopting this measure, the same rank in point of qualification and character will be given to the medical staff in the United States which it possesses in the armies and navies of European nations.[2]

We have the honor, sir, with the greatest respect to subscribe ourselves your most obedient servants,

BENJN: RUSH
CASPAR WISTAR JUNR.
JAMES WOODHOUSE
B. S. BARTON
PHILIP SYNG PHYSICK
JOHN SYNG DORSEY

MS (in BR's hand): National Archives, Record Group 107 (Records of the Office of the Secretary of War), Letters Received and Sent.

[999]

¹ This letter was transmitted by Madison to the Secretary of War (William Eustis), but with what result does not appear.

² The explanation of this appeal lies in the fact that a great many students matriculated in the medical school without any thought of taking degrees. Their intention was doubtless "to get a smattering of medical knowledge that would enable them to set up as practitioners in backward communities with the claim that they had studied at a great medical school" (Cheyney, *Hist. Univ. Penna.*, p. 209). Cheyney mentions several attempts by the medical faculty to remedy this condition.

To John Adams

My dear and venerable Friend,   Philadelphia, April 1st, 1809

It would be well if legislators were taught before they begin to legislate that there are certain things which elude the power of government as certainly as a stone when thrown into the air falls to the ground. In addition to those subjects which have been mentioned in our letters, I will add "the dictates of conscience, religious and philosophical opinions, the current prices of goods, and tavern bills." Of the two last we saw memorable proofs in the year 1776 in several of the states.

In your letter of the 23rd of March¹ you mention Cicero as a precedent for a man's doing justice to his services to his country. You might have added the conduct of St. Paul for the same purpose. The calumnies of the Jews and the ingratitude of his pagan converts compelled him to enter into a long detail of his sacrifices, sufferings, and exploits in advancing the glory of his Master and the interests of his gospel. There is, it is true, great difficulty in a man's speaking or writing of himself so as to avoid giving offense. The King of Prussia in his *Posthumous Works* says this difficulty is so great that even a public justification for supposed offenses should be avoided, inasmuch as it cannot be made without some self-praise; but this opinion is by no means a correct one. A reverence for religion and a regard for truth, liberty, family honor, and the interests of society may make it indispensably necessary for a man who has been wronged by the country or the age in which he has lived to appeal to the world at large and to posterity for an acquittal of the follies or crimes with which he has been charged. Knowing that you feel your obligations to all these² objects, and your desire to maintain a fair and just character, I have formerly suggested to you to employ the evening of your life in writing "the history of your own times" as far as you were an actor in them. Let it be published by your sons after your death. It will be more than a patent of nobility to your descendants to the end of time. I shall follow the advice I am now giving you as far as it relates to volumes of scandal that have been printed against me for my medical opinions and practice since the year 1793, to no one of which I have ever replied even by a single paragraph in a newspaper. My sons expect this act of justice to them with more solicitude than they would an independence in property, were it possible for me to bequeath it to them.[3]

Mr. Bins, whose name I mentioned to you in my last letter, is an exiled Irishman. He has been 14 years in our country. Our governor and the party most attached to him are said to be wholly under his influence. When a young housekeeper, I well recollect a servant girl who lived with me had a quarrel with a mulatto man in the neighborhood. She called him by several scurrilous names, one of which was "a *no nation* son of a bitch." Does not this character apply to the citizens of Pennsylvania? We are Englishmen, Frenchmen, Irishmen, and Germans. The accent of an American tongue can scarcely be heard among them. We are in short "no nation sons of ———." You may fill up the sentence with anything you please.

Our legislature has exhibited prodigies of folly and madness. They have passed an arbitration law which is to supersede if possible trials by jury. They have made several attempts to sweep the benches of the state of federal judges.[4] In all of them they have failed, and from a secession of men of their own party. My worthy brother has escaped their fury. He has been heard and honorably acquitted by 2/3rds of the lower house. Judge of their hostility to commerce and civilized manners by the following fact. A member of the Senate, in the course of a debate in which the prosperity of Philadelphia was spoken of, said, "He should be glad to hear that the whole city was reduced to ashes and that those ashes were conveyed by the four winds to every part of the world, that not a single vestige of the spot where the city stood might remain." Similar feelings govern many of the members of both houses of our legislature.

O Liberty! liberty! I have worshipped thee as a substance.—But —but—but—"Where are my shoes and stockings?"—Where is my lancet?—Where are my gallipots?

I have lately been daily in the family of Major Butler, who has been much indisposed with the gout. Your name has been occasionally mentioned by him to me in the most respectful terms. "An honester man than John Adams," he says, "he believes never lived."

Upon my telling him we were in habits of corresponding, he begged me the next time I wrote to you to present his compliments to you. The Major has assumed new ground in politics. He views both parties through your and my spectacles. In the year 1800 I stood nearly alone in refusing to be led by either of the two parties that were then contending for the power of our country. This is not the case now. Hundreds of our citizens now think and act with me, more especially the whigs of the Revolution. The most active men of both parties were brought into life by the sunshine and safety of the peace of 1780 or by the prosperity or poverty which have been produced by it.

A state guard parades constantly before the doors of Mr. Rittenhouse's daughters.[5] Should the general government persist in the attempt to take them, blood will certainly be shed. The moderate Democrats, that is, the Quids and Duanites, have in vain united their strength to obtain a repeal of the exceptionable law and the payment of the money due to the United States. It is impossible to tell where and when this business will end. I foresee in it the seeds of the dissolution of the Union. Alas for the only surviving hopes of mankind! What has become of the tribunal of Reason? It would seem as if the history of our country would furnish new proofs that men are to be governed only by the Bible or the bayonet.

Are the labors and virtues of the patriots and heroes of 1774, 1775, and 1776 to perish without bringing forth any other fruit than what we have gathered from the transient duration of our general government? Or are their sleepless nights, their midnight addresses to the power and justice of Heaven for their oppressed and injured country, their sacrifices of time and property, and their "cruel mockings" (often worse than bodily sufferings) to be rewarded only in "another and a better world"? Let us believe

————————— the firm patriot *there*,
Who made the welfare of mankind his care,
Though here with envy and with faction tost,
Shall find the generous labor was not lost.[6]

Adieu. Always yours most sincerely, affectionately, and gratefully,

BENJN: RUSH

P.S. Since writing the above, we have heard that our legislature will *probably* consent to pay the money demanded by the U. States, and thus end the alarming contest between them.

MS: Adams Manuscript Trust, Boston.

¹ See *Old Family Letters, A*, p. 226-7.

² MS: "the."

³ Alluding probably to the section in BR's *Autobiography* (p. 78-109) dealing with his professional history.

⁴ This had long been a favorite scheme of the "Snyderites." See Elizabeth K. Henderson, "The Attack on the Judiciary in Pennsylvania, 1800-1810," PMHB, LXI (1937), 113-36.

⁵ BR alludes to "the Fort Rittenhouse affair," or Olmstead Case, a *cause célèbre* not susceptible to brief summary. It was a conflict between federal and state authority arising from many years' litigation over shares in a prize ship, the *Active*, taken during the Revolution. As treasurer of Pennsylvania, David Rittenhouse had had custody of the share originally adjudged by a state court to belong to the State of Pennsylvania; in 1803 his heirs—two widowed daughters named Elizabeth Sergeant and Esther Waters—had been obliged by legislative action to pay over the sum in question to the State. However, a suit against the state was still in progress in the federal courts (which had succeeded to admiralty jurisdiction under the Constitution), and the suit at length was decided against Pennsylvania. But the Act of 1803 had pledged protection to Rittenhouse's heirs, so that when, in Mch. and Apr. 1809, the United States marshal moved to arrest the two widows he was resisted by a force of state militia. No blood was shed, and Pennsylvania eventually paid over the sum required by the federal court, but not until after high feelings and grave fears had been aroused. (Scharf & Westcott, I, 540-1.)

⁶ Source not found.

To Thomas Jefferson

Dear Sir,   Philadelphia, May 3rd, 1809

Though late, I hope I am not among the last of your friends in congratulating you upon your *escape* from the high and dangerous appointment which your country (to use the words of Lord Chesterfield) *inflicted* upon you during the last eight years of your life. Methinks I see you¹ renewing your acquaintance with your philosophical instruments and with the friends of your youth in your *library*, a place in which Voltaire has happily said "every man's humor is subject to us," and, of course, the reverse of a public situation in the world, "in which we are subject to every man's humor."

Accept further of my congratulations upon the auspicious issue of your firm and protracted negotiations with Great Britain.

My 3rd son, who has lately graduated as doctor of medicine, requests your acceptance of a copy of his inaugural dissertation.²

I was much pleased to hear that your grandson had returned to Philadelphia to prosecute the study of medicine.³ After nearly 50 years spent in this study and in all the laborious duties connected with its practice, I can truly say they are both more agreeable to me than any other pursuits, and when it shall please God to cut the *last* of the few threads which remain of my life, I shall suffer nearly as much pain in being torn from my profession as from the common attachments of blood and friendship. I was about to conclude my letter by expressing a wish that we could, in a long evening, review the *early* and *late* political events of our country together, and trace the influence of the same principles under different names upon each of them—but, no, we would not waste a moment in conversing upon such *little* subjects. We would dismiss them to unite with the speculations upon alchemy and perpetual motion, and dwell only upon those topics of science and literature which are calculated to increase the agricultural, domestic, and moral happiness of our fellow citizens.

Adieu! my dear sir, and be assured of the respect and affection of your old and sincere friend of 1775,

BENJN: RUSH

MS: Library of Congress, Jefferson Papers.

[1] This word omitted in MS.

[2] *An Inquiry into the Use of the Omentum*, Phila., 1809 (Surg. Gen. Off., *Index-Cat.*, 1st ser., XII, 400). On James Rush's plans, see the following letter.

[3] Thomas Jefferson Randolph (1792–1875), Jefferson's favorite grandson, later an eminent figure in the politics and business affairs of his state and community (see DAB), was introduced by Jefferson to BR in a letter of 13 Oct. 1808 (L.C., Jefferson Papers). Jefferson's plan was to have Randolph study natural history, botany, anatomy, and surgery, not with a view to professional practice but "to the care of a family when he shall have one."

To John Adams

Dear Sir,   Philadelphia, May 5th, 1809

I am much pleased with the specimen you have given of the use of *your wings* upon a certain subject in your last letter.[1] Your publications in the newspapers show still further how important to the public, to posterity, and to your family honor are the words you have preserved of your political life. Your defense of the rights of our seamen[2] is much admired. It discovers, with the experience and wisdom of 70, the fire and eloquence of five-and-twenty. The *place* from which[3] it was dated induced me to read it. It is many years since I have read a political essay of half its length. It inspired me with the feelings of 1774 and 1776. Happily for my interest and peace of mind, those feelings soon subsided, for were I to cherish them with the just and noble principles from which they are derived, I should soon find myself *not* in a foreign but in an enemy's country, for our British, *not* monarchists (that is too flattering a title for them), but our British *subjects*—that is, the men who wish for the return of the jurisdiction of the British King, Lords, and Commons over our country, and who still consider the American Revolution as a rebellion—these men I say outroyal in toryism the British nation, the British ministry, and even the British king himself. From these men your publications receive no quarter, and they hold in a degree the balance, if not of power, certainly of fashion and character in our city.

I enclose you the inaugural dissertation of my 3rd son, James Rush, who has lately graduated in medicine in our University with credit to himself and satisfaction to his father. His talents and manners promise consideration in his profession. He will sail in a few weeks for Edinburgh, where and in London he expects to complete his medical education, after which it is my wish to establish him in Philadelphia. I pray God to prosper our united efforts for this purpose!

My son Richard has taken a sudden and great start in business. You know him. I shall only add that he continues to be a most indefatigable student, and in politics stands upon the broad basis of the Declaration of Independence.

Adieu. Yours—yours—yours,

BENJN: RUSH

I repeat again and again my wish that the hasty effusions of my heart contained in my letters be not read out of your family.

P.S. Some of your tory enemies in Boston have endeavored to prove that your country has canceled the immense debt it owes you by drafts upon the Treasury of the United States. They forget that the obligations due to patriots, heroes, and other benefactors of mankind can never be canceled by millions of dollars, especially when that acknowledgement of their services is opposed by calumny, falsehood, and persecution. The proper and the dearest compensation for the labors, sacrifices, and achievements of public spirit is *justice to character*. Everything short of this is nothing but Shakespear's purse—"all trash."[4]

MS: Adams Manuscript Trust, Boston.

[1] In Adams' letter of 12 Apr. 1809 are specimen extracts of an autobiographical apologia (*Old Family Letters*, A, p. 228-32).

[2] *The Inadmissible Principles of the King of England's Proclamation of October 16, 1807, Considered*, originally published in the Boston *Patriot*, then as a pamphlet, and to be found in Adams' *Works*, IX, 312-30.

[3] MS: "when."

[4] See *Othello*, III, iii, 158.

To Mrs. Rush

My dearest Julia,   Philadelphia, July 7th, 1809

Your letters from Albany, Ball town, and Skeenborough all came safe to hand.[1] We rejoiced in the protection you had experienced on your journey from a kind providence. By this time we hope you are happy in the society of your dear girls and their respective families.

On Tuesday, being the anniversary of the Declaration of Independence, most of our family, that is, Sam, Wm., Emely Anners, and Mrs. McDougal[2] in the carriage, and James and I in the chair, fled from the noise of the city to our customary and delightful retreat on the banks of Skuylkill, where we spent a pleasant afternoon. Wm. took his fishing tackle with him and amused himself on the side of a boat in fishing. On Wednesday Miss Pearce[3] called upon us about 7 o'clock to inform us that Mr. Levy[4] had written to his sister that he had seen you at Ball town.[5] We pressed her to come in and to make tea for us. She complied readily with our request, and we passed a pleasant hour together. Martha Levy charms and surprises all her connections with her letters. She is an uncommon child, as good as she is sensible. Her worthy parents I hope will enjoy much comfort in her.

The election for a successor to Dr. Woodhouse is to take place on Monday. In consequence of the medical professors' having said in answer to a letter from a committee of the trustees that a "physician is necessary to discharge all the duties of the chemical chair," it *is supposed* Mr. Hare will not be the successful candidate. Dr. Coxe's friends are more sanguine than they have yet been, but the issue of the election is still doubtful. Dr. Sybert is powerfully supported, and he has acknowledged merit.[6]

[*Three sentences have here been heavily scored out, presumably by Mrs. Rush.*] Richard is completely settled and much pleased with his new office. James sails on Monday or Tuesday next. His friends have loaded[7] him with letters. With love to all the two families (not forgetting my old friend Maria, now Mrs. R——),[8] in which all the family join, I am, my dear, dear, dear old friend, ever yours,

Benjn Rush

Addressed: Mrs: Julia Rush at Ross Cuthbert Esqr: Three Rivers Lower Canada.

MS: Josiah C. Trent, M.D., Durham, North Carolina. (On the last page are eighteen lines in rhyming couplets entitled "William Rush to his beloved Mother in Canada," copied in BR's hand.)

¹ Mrs. Rush was on her way to visit her two married daughters, Mrs. Cuthbert and Mrs. Manners, in Canada. A circumstantial record of her trip will be found in her letters to BR in the Rush MSS, XXXIV—the only group of her letters to her husband known to survive.

² Evidently nursemaids or governesses; see BR to James Rush, 1 May 1810.

³ Not identified.

⁴ Presumably Moses Levy (1757-1826), recorder of the city of Philadelphia and later a judge, in whose office Samuel Rush studied law; or possibly Samson Levy (1761-1831), brother of Moses, also a well-known Philadelphia lawyer (Morais, *Jews of Philadelphia*, p. 38-41, 409-10; *The Jewish Encyclopedia*, N.Y. and London, 1901-1906; *Inscriptions in St. Peter's Church Yard*, p. 207). On Martha Levy, mentioned below, I have no reliable information.

⁵ Ballston or Ballston Spa was an early health resort in Saratoga co., N.Y., about twenty-five miles north of Albany (H. G. Spafford, *Gazetteer of the State of New-York*, Albany, 1824).

⁶ James Woodhouse, professor of chemistry at the University, died 4 June 1809; Dr. John Redman Coxe was elected his successor. The unsuccessful candidates were Dr. Adam Seybert (1773-1825), scientist and politician; and Robert Hare (1781-1858), the brilliant experimenter who in turn succeeded Coxe, 1816 (DAB, under Seybert and Hare). On Hare, see also BR to George Clymer, 25 Nov. 1809. Charles Caldwell asserted that BR had forced Coxe into a post for which he was ill-qualified, in order to defeat the wishes of Wistar, whose candidate was Seybert (Caldwell's *Autobiography*, p. 306-8).

⁷ MS: "loadned."

⁸ Not identified.

To James Cheetham¹

Sir,   Philadelphia, July 17th, 1809

In compliance with your request, I send you herewith answers to your questions relative to the late Thomas Paine.

He came to Philadelphia about the year 1772,² with a short letter of introduction from Dr. Franklin to one of his friends. His design was to open a school for the instruction of young ladies in several branches of knowledge which, at that time, were seldom taught in the female schools of our country.

About the year 1773 I met him accidentally in Mr. Aitkin's bookstore and was introduced to him by Mr. Aitkin.³ We conversed a few minutes, when I left him. Soon afterwards I read a short essay with which I was much pleased, in one of Bradford's papers, against the slavery of the Africans in our country, and which I was informed was written by Mr. Paine.⁴ This excited my desire to be better acquainted with him. We met soon afterwards in Mr. Aitkin's bookstore, where I did homage to his principles and pen upon the subject of the enslaved Africans. He told me the essay to which I alluded was the first thing he had ever published in his life. After this Mr. Aitkin employed him as the editor of his *Magazine*⁵ with a salary of fifty pounds currency a year. This work was well supported by him. His song upon the death of General Wolfe and his reflections upon the death of Lord Clive gave it a sudden currency which few works of that kind have since had in our country.

When the subject of American independence began to be agitated in conversation, I observed the public mind to be loaded with an immense mass of prejudice and error relative to it. Something appeared to be wanting, to remove them, beyond the ordinary short and cold addresses of newspaper publications. At this time I called upon Mr. Paine and suggested to him the propriety of preparing our citizens for a perpetual separation of our country from Great Britain by means of a work of such length as would obviate all the objections to it.[6] He seized the idea with avidity and immediately began his famous pamphlet in favor of that measure. He read the sheets to me at my house as he composed them. When he had finished them, I advised him to put them into the hands of Dr. Franklin, Samuel Adams, and the late Judge Wilson, assuring him at the same time that they all held the same opinions that he had defended. The first of those gentlemen saw the manuscript and I believe the second, but Judge Wilson being from home when Mr. Paine called upon him, it was not subjected to his inspection. No addition was made to it by Dr. Franklin, but a passage was struck out, or omitted in printing it, which I conceived to be one of the most striking in it. It was the following: "A greater absurdity cannot be conceived of, than three millions of people running to their seacoast every time a ship arrives from London, to know what portion of liberty they should enjoy."

A title only was wanted for this pamphlet before it was committed to the press. Mr. Paine proposed to call it "Plain Truth." I objected to it and suggested the title of "Common Sense." This was instantly adopted, and nothing now remained but to find a printer who had boldness enough to publish it. At that time there was a certain Robert Bell, an intelligent Scotch bookseller and printer in Philadelphia, whom I knew to be as high-toned as Mr. Paine upon the subject of American independence. I mentioned the pamphlet to him, and he at once consented to run the risk of publishing it. The author and the printer were immediately brought together, and *Common Sense* burst from the press of the latter in a few days with an effect which has rarely been produced by types and paper in any age or country.

Between the time of the publication of this pamphlet and the 4th of July, 1776, Mr. Paine published a number of essays in Mr. Bradford's paper, under the signature of "The Forester,"[7] in defense of the opinions contained in his *Common Sense*.

In the summer and autumn of 1776 he served as a volunteer in the American army under General Washington. Whether he received pay and rations, I cannot tell. He lived a good deal with the officers of the first rank in the army, at whose tables his *Common Sense* always made him a welcome guest.

The legislature of Pennsylvania gave Mr. Paine 500*l.* as an acknowledgment of the services he had rendered the United States by his publications.

He acted as clerk to the legislature of Pennsylvania about the year 1780. I do not know the compensation he received for his services in that station. He acted for a while as secretary of the Secret Committee of Congress, but was dismissed by them for publishing some of their secrets relative to Mr. Dean.

Mr. Paine's manner of life was desultory. He often visited in the families of Dr. Franklin, Mr. Rittenhouse, and Mr. George Clymer, where he made himself acceptable by a turn he discovered for philosophical as well as political subjects.

After the year 1776 my intercourse with Mr. Paine was casual. I met him now and then at the tables of some of our whig citizens, where he spoke but little but was always inoffensive in his manner and conversation.

I possess one of his letters written to me from France upon the subject of the abolition of the slave trade.[8] An extract from it was published in the *Columbian Magazine*.

I did not see Mr. Paine when he passed through Philadelphia a few years ago. His principles avowed in his *Age of Reason*[9] were so offensive to me that I did not wish to renew my intercourse with him.

I have thus briefly and in great haste endeavored to answer your questions. Should you publish this letter, I beg my testimony against Mr. Paine's infidelity may not be omitted in it. From, sir, yours respectfully,

BENJN. RUSH

Printed: James Cheetham, *The Life of Thomas Paine*, New York, 1809, p. 34-40.

[1] James Cheetham (1772-1810) was an English radical who came to the United States in 1798 and engaged in political journalism in the interest of the Clintons in New York (DAB). He had once admired Paine, but found both his company and his ideas as an old man distasteful. His *Life of Thomas Paine*, N.Y., 1809, is a distorted and hostile biography. BR, however, approved it;

see his letter to Cheetham of 6 Jan. 1810. (Cheetham's letter of inquiry to BR has not been found.)

[2] Paine did not arrive in Philadelphia from Europe until Nov. 1774 (DAB).

[3] Robert Aitken (1734-1802) was an industrious Scot who opened a bookshop in Philadelphia in 1769 and eventually branched out into all phases of the book trade (DAB).

[4] Paine's "African Slavery in America" appeared in Bradford's *Pennsylvania Journal*, 8 Mch. 1775 (Paine, *Complete Writings*, ed. Philip Foner, N.Y., 1945, II, 15). Thus BR must have met Paine early in 1775, not in 1773.

[5] Paine edited the *Pennsylvania Magazine* from Feb. 1775 to May 1776 (F. L. Mott, *History of American Magazines*, Cambridge, 1939, I, 87, note). For his literary efforts prior to BR's acquaintance with him, see Foner's list in *Complete Writings*, I, xlvii; and for those mentioned by BR immediately below, see the same, II, 22, 1083.

[6] With the following account of the composition of *Common Sense* compare that in BR's *Autobiography*, p. 113-15, which, though substantially the same, varies in a number of particulars.

[7] Paine's four "Forester's Letters," arguing for American independence in reply to Dr. William Smith's "Cato" letters, appeared in the *Pennsylvania Journal* during Apr.-May 1776.

[8] The remarkable letter alluded to, which is dated 16 Mch. 1790 and is now in the Library of Congress, informs BR, *inter alia*, that Paine is taking the key of the Bastille to London to transmit to George Washington as a gift from Lafayette. Omitted from Foner's edition of Paine's *Complete Writings*, it was published in L.C., *Quart. Jour. of Acquisitions*, I (1943-1944), 17-22, and during 1948 was aboard the Freedom Train.

[9] Published in Paris and London, 1794-1795.

To Mrs. Rush

My dearest Julia,   Philadelphia, July 21, 1809

"How blessings brighten as they take their flight!"[1] The truth of this line is verified daily by your absence. There is a chasm in the family which nothing but your presence can fill, and there is a constant uneasiness in my mind which nothing but your company and your friendship can remove. I do not wish by this introduction to my letter to hurry you home. Spend the remains of the summer if you please in Canada. The traveling will be more agreeable in September than in the hot month of August. In the meanwhile I will endeavor to substitute, for your company, study and business. We have as yet received no Cape letter from James but expect one daily.[2] He left the Bay on Tuesday last. Richd. sets off tomorrow for Maryland.[3] His absence will render our house still more solitary. Sam and Wm. are everything to me that boys of their age are capable of being. I have brought Sam under fresh obligations to me by a present of a handsome gold watch. His manner of thanking me for it was truly elegant. We may say of him what Tristram Shandy says of his Uncle Toby, that "nature stamped gentleman upon him at his birth." His frown is the only exception in his conduct to the correctness of this remark.

The weather during the last four or five days has been very rainy and unusually cool for the season. Fires have been common in many houses. The harvest it is said has suffered very much from the rain. While our farmers are feeling the afflicting hand of Heaven in one way, our citizens are feeling it in another. The late news of the rejection of Mr. Erskine's convention with our government by the British Court has spread universal distress and resentment among all classes of citizens.[4] *How, when,* and *where* this business will end, it is impossible to tell. In addition to this unexpected and calamitous event, an alarm of yellow fever has this day spread through every part of the city. Several persons have died with it, and young Richd. Durdon[5] it is feared will not survive an attack of it. He is tenderly nursed by his mother and sister. Dr. Caldwell is his physician. I attend in consultation with him. Should the disease increase, I shall send Ben, Sam, and Wm. into the country. Mrs. McDougall and all the servants have agreed to remain with me. Our house and garden afford nearly as safe an asylum from it as a common farmhouse. I give you this information that you may not be terrified with vague reports respecting the state of our city and with unnecessary fears respecting your family. It is highly probable there will be no more, or but few more, cases of this fever. It never has spread in a summer so cool as the present has been.

All the family join in love to you and our dear children. All your friends inquire affectionately after you. Judge Peters speaks of your journey as an enterprise worthy of and equal only to yourself. Adieu! thou faithful companion of the adversities and blessings of my life. May God make us alike thankful for them both! I have left no room for a poetical nor prose postscript from either of our boys. But be assured they all tenderly remember and love you. Again adieu. Ever yours,

BENJN: RUSH

July 22nd. Poor Mr. Durdon is near his end! Alas! for his distressed mother and sister! I have just left them overwhelmed with grief.

Addressed: Mrs: Julia Rush at Ross Cuthbert Esqr, Three Rivers Lower Canada.

MS: Josiah C. Trent, M.D., Durham, North Carolina.

[1] Edward Young, *The Complaint* (1742), Night II.
[2] A "Cape letter" was one sent from Cape Henlopen, Del., where the pilot was dropped; see BR to Thomas Bradford, 2 Sep. 1766.

³ On 29 Aug. 1809 Richard married Catherine Elizabeth Murray, daughter of Dr. James Murray of Annapolis (Powell, *Richard Rush*, p. 8; DAB). The date of the wedding was unexpectedly moved forward, for Richard's mother wrote to BR from Albany on 30 Aug. that she had intended at all costs to be present (Rush MSS, XXXIV).

⁴ BR refers to an agreement proposed to our government by David Erskine, the British minister, in April, that the Nonintercourse Act, so far as it applied to Great Britain, be lifted in exchange for repeal of the orders in council of Nov. 1807. For a time there was great rejoicing in the seaport towns, but in July came word that Erskine's proposal had been disavowed by the British government and that he himself was recalled (McMaster, *Hist.*, III, 339-49).

⁵ Richard Haycock Durdin (1790?-1809), A.B., College of New Jersey, 1807; he died the following day. His father, Richard, and mother, Frances, were well-to-do immigrants from Ireland; his sister Frances died in 1812. (*Inscriptions in St. Peter's Church Yard*, p. 94-5; Princeton Univ., *Gen. Cat.*, 1908.)

To John Adams

[. . .]¹ Friend,   Philadelphia, July 26th, 1809

I enclose you three numbers of Duane's papers, that you may see in what manner the late news from St. James's has operated upon one class of our citizens.

Your communications continue to excite attention.² A general wish prevails among those who read them that they may be preserved and perpetuated in the form of a pamphlet or of a larger work.

My wife and youngest daughter left me on the 8th of June last in order to visit my daughters in Canada, one of whom, Mrs. Manners, with her husband and two children, were to sail from Quebec for England on the 10th of this month. My 3rd son, James (who graduated in medicine last spring in our University), sailed for Scotland on the 14th of this month, where and in London he will, I hope, spend 18 or 20 months in completing his studies in his profession. He is said to be very promising. He passed his examinations in our University much to the satisfaction not only of his father but of all the professors.

My eldest son, John, since his unfortunate duel, has lost his health and with it his reason, and is now on his way from New Orleans to his father's house.³ I feel this affliction in the most sensible manner.

My son Richard is rising into respectable business in the law. He is to be married shortly to an excellent woman and is to live next door to us. We now occupy the house in which you visited us in 1794 and which was afterwards occupied by Judge Shippen, to whom it belonged and who died in April 1807.⁴ Excuse this intrusion of domestic events upon your time, and believe me to be ever yours,

BENJN RUSH

P.S. Love as usual to all [who surrou]nd[5] your table. I rejoice in your son's mission to Petersburgh. He deserved it.

MS: Adams Manuscript Trust, Boston.

[1] MS torn; two or three words missing.

[2] Letters and documents defending Adams' conduct as President, communicated to the Boston *Patriot*, reprinted in other papers, and collectively published as *Correspondence of the Late President Adams*, Boston, 1809; printed in part in Adams' *Works*, IX, 241-311.

[3] This was premature. See the following letter; also note on BR's letter to Adams, 15 Dec. 1807.

[4] On the Shippen house, see BR to Mrs. Rush, 27-28 Oct. 1793. The Rushes had returned there in 1806 and remained there until BR's death.

[5] MS torn.

To John Adams

My dear old Friend,   Philadelphia, August 14, 1809

I send you herewith some more of Colonel Duane's papers. You will perceive in one of them proposals for republishing your letters in a pamphlet. It was from a conviction that you saw things with other eyes than most of the persons that cooperated with you in establishing the independence of the United States, and that your opinions and conduct would bear the scrutiny of posterity at that eventful time, that I have so often urged you to bequeath to your country memoirs of your life, or the history of your own times. Suppose you take up the state of the public mind with respect to that great measure in 1774, 1775, and 1776, and the private and public part you took in it. I once heard you say the *active* business of the American Revolution began in Philadelphia in the act of her citizens in sending back the tea ship, and that Massachussets would have received her portion of the tea had not our example encouraged her to expect union and support in destroying it.[1] Perhaps you have never heard that Colonel Bradford first suggested to General Mifflin the necessity of opposing landing of the tea in an accidental interview they had at the old man's door. The General received the proposition coolly and said it would be impossible to awaken our citizens to a sense of the importance of such a measure. The old man said, "Leave that business to me. I will collect a few active spirits at my house tomorrow evening. Do you be one of them, and we will soon set the city in motion." The next evening six or eight citizens (of whom I was one) met at his house. A number of resolutions were drafted. A town meeting was called a few days afterwards. Dr. Cadwallider[2] (an aged and highly respected whig) was applied to, to preside at it, which he cheerfully agreed to do. A large meeting was held. The business was conducted with prudence, spirit, and unanimity. The flame kindled on that day soon extended to Boston and gradually spread throughout the whole continent. It was the first throe of that convulsion which delivered Great Britain of the United States.

J. Cheetham is now employed in writing the life of Thos. Paine. He applied to me for the history of the origin of his *Common Sense*. In reply to his letter I informed him that Mr. Paine wrote that pamphlet at my suggestion and that I gave it its name. I did not suggest a single idea contained in it, and I believe Dr. Franklin's head and hand were equally distant from the author while he wrote it. Mr. Cheetham intends to do Paine justice. He will expose his errors and crimes as well as extol his talents and services to our country.

The young people of our country born since the year 1774, and who compose a majority of our citizens, would receive everything that came from your pen upon the subject of American independence with great avidity. The history of the prejudices and fears that were gradually written and spoken down before that measure took place would form an interesting view of the human mind in its relation to liberty and government. One thing would be very striking in the history of the time alluded to, and that is the sameness of the prejudices and fears of a certain class of our citizens with respect to the ministry, the government, the commerce, and the power of Great Britain.

We have had some cases of yellow fever in our city, but at present we are perfectly free from it.

I have great pleasure in informing you that my son John has recovered from his late attack of insanity and is now doing duty in the navy. A gloom still, I have heard, hangs upon his spirits. This I fear must be the case as long as memory and friendship retain their places in his mind. The young man who fell by his hand was as dear to him as a brother.

A safe passage to both our sons across the ocean! With love to all who still surround your table, I am, dear sir, your affectionate and obliged friend,

BENJN: RUSH

P.S. Do you recollect your once telling me Colonel Laurence [*Laurens*] told you that in a conversation he had with George Grenville, just before he left England after the war began, that it was not a war to enforce taxes but to restrain our commerce and "that we spread too much canvas upon the ocean"?[3] You concurred in this opinion.

MS: Adams Manuscript Trust, Boston.

[1] See BR to William Gordon, 10 Oct. 1773. Though the tea ship at Philadelphia was not turned back until 27 Dec., and the Boston Tea Party had occurred on 16 Dec., the resistance at Philadelphia had been thoroughly organized in the preceding October. See Scharf & Westcott, I, 287.

[2] Thomas Cadwalader, M.D. (ca. 1707-1799), eminent practitioner and man of property in both Philadelphia and Trenton; he had been active in opposition to the Stamp Act (DAB).

[3] On this anecdote, see BR to James Madison, 30 Jan. 1806, and BR to John Adams, 27 and 30 June 1812.

To James Rush

My dear Son,   Philadelphia, August 17th, 1809

The rejection of Mr. Erskine's convention with our government by the British ministry, and the consequent revival of the nonintercourse law with Great-Britain, will cut off all intercourse between you and your family except through the medium of packets and public ships. This letter is intended to go to New York, where I shall request my friend Dr. Miller to put it into the bag of a British vessel of war that is to sail on the 19th of this month for Liverpool. I lament this commercial hostility between two countries that ought to be friends and to unite in opposing the usurpations of Bonaparte. I greatly fear it will not end in nonintercourse laws and orders of council. The clamors against the late conduct of Great Britain are universal. I sincerely wish Mr. Jackson[1] may arrive with an olive branch in his hand and thus prevent an appeal to arms.

From several letters from your mother and sister Julia, we learn that your sister Mary with her family sailed for Plymouth in the ship *Dorset* on the 10th of last month. Your mother and sister Julia are much pleased with their jaunt. They speak in raptures of the magnificent scenes which surround the city of Quebec, and with veneration of the heights and plains on which French, British, and American heroes have fallen in defense of their respective countries. They met the Governor of Lower Canada on a tour through the providence with all his suite of generals and aides at Mr. Cuthbert's, and were treated with great politeness by them. We expect their return about the 10th of next month.

Our city continues to be alarmed by sporadic cases of yellow fever. Time only will determine whether it will be epidemic. As yet there have been no flights from the city.

Your brother Richard sets off on the 24th instant for Piny Grove in order to complete his business with Miss Murray. Your brother Sam is to accompany him and to act as his groomsman. His bride is to pass her time between Captain Murray's at Pomona[2] and our house until your mother and sister return.

It will be unnecessary I hope to hint to you that the utmost prudence will be required to avoid giving offense upon the subject of the present controversy between Great Britain and the United States. The Reverend Mr. Wm. Tennent[3] called his son John back after he had bidden him farewell when he went to Edinburgh, and said to him: "Hark, my son—if the wind blow, let it blow, and if it rain, let it rain," meaning thereby that he might as well attempt to regulate the weather as change the minds of men upon political subjects. Remember the speech of David Sproat[4] to his friend who jumped up from his table upon hearing one of the company defend Negro slavery, "Hut, hut, mon, sit down and sup your broth—you conno' put the world to rights, do what you will."

I hope you are by this time comfortably settled in pleasant lodgings and dividing your time between study and the agreeable and enlightened society of Edinburg. What would I not give, to pass a month, a week, or even a day in that city! "O! mihi praeteritos, referat si Jupiter annos!"[5] But [this is][6] impossible. If you are happy there, I shall enjoy the wishes of my heart over again.

I was glad to find from a late Edinburg publication that Mr. Creech[7] is still living. Present my cordial respects to him. Have you met with any of the daughters of Mr. Thos. Hogg?[8] The name of the eldest was Chrishey, of the second (my pet) Molly. Find them out and do homage to them and their parents' memories, in the name of your father.

All your brothers send their love to you. Adieu, my dear James. To the protection and mercy of the Great Preserver of men I commend you! Again and again adieu! From yours affectionately,

BENJN: RUSH

P.S. Write by every packet upon single sheets of large folio paper. Tell me everything you *see*, *hear*, and *feel*.

Addressed: Dr: James Rush Edinburg Scotland. By the Maida via Liverpool.

MS: Library Company of Philadelphia, Rush MSS.

[1] Francis James Jackson (1770-1814) succeeded Erskine as British minister to the United States; he brought no olive branch, and his mission was doomed to failure before his arrival (DNB; McMaster, *Hist.*, III, 349-57).

[2] Alexander Murray (ca. 1754-1821), of Maryland, Catherine Murray's uncle; naval officer in the Revolution and the Tripolitan War; naval commandant of Philadelphia, 1808-1821 (DAB). Pomona was his country seat, but I have not discovered its location.

[3] William Tennent, 2d (1705-1777), of the "New Light" family of clergymen, was pastor at Freehold, N.J. (Sprague, *Annals*, III, 52-5); his son, John Van Brugh Tennent (1737-1770), was a graduate of the College of New Jersey, 1758, and M.D., Edinburgh, 1764 (Packard, *Hist. of Med. in U.S.*, II, 974, 1126; Princeton Univ., *Gen. Cat.*, 1908).

[4] David Sproat (ca. 1716-1799), a Scot who came to Philadelphia in 1760 and dealt in clothing and other goods; a loyalist, he became British commissary of prisoners in New York and at the close of the war returned to Scotland. BR had been his physician. (*Hist. Cat. St. Andrew's Soc. Phila.*, II, 155-6; Rush MSS, Account Books.)

[5] "O! if Jupiter would but restore to me the years that are gone!" Virgil, *Aeneid*, VIII, 560.

[6] MS torn.

[7] Presumably William Creech (1745-1815), a leading Edinburgh publisher (DNB).

[8] On the Hogg family, of whom BR knew three generations, see letter to Jonathan B. Smith, 30 Apr. 1767, and BR's *Autobiography*, p. 47. Of "Chrishey" I know nothing further. "Molly" (Mary) married her cousin William Scott Moncrief (BR to James Rush, 4 Sep. 1809).

To James Rush

My dear Son,   Philadelphia, September 4th, 1809

I sit down at a late hour to write you a few lines, knowing how much your anxiety to hear from your friends will be increased by your distance from them.

I was this day made happy by taking into my arms your brother Richard's bride, who arrived with him from Maryland about 12 o'clock. She is a most charming woman and will I hope add much to the happiness of all our family.[1]

By a letter which I received this morning from your Mama, I think it probable she is this evening in New York. As your brother Ben is unusually engaged in his master's business, I have prevailed upon Edward Ingersoll[2] to set off early tomorrow morning for New York in order to escort her and your sister to Philadelphia. They are both highly delighted with their excursion to Canada.

Our city continues to enjoy an exemption from the yellow fever. The last sporadic victim to it was our inoffensive neighbor Samuel Rutter.[3] He had inhaled the seeds of it at his store in Water Street.

They were excited into action by his exertions at a fire near Dock Street soon afterwards.

My labors continue to be incessant in revising the press of the several publications[4] which are to appear if possible before the meeting of the classes in November. The edition of Dr. Cleghorn is finished and will be advertised in a few days. The edition of Dr. Sydenham is advancing, and all the volumes of my *Inquiries* are in the hands of different printers. Many additions will be made to them which I hope will add support to the principles maintained in them.

I have lately heard that an old friend of mine, Mr. Robert Scott Moncrief, is still living in Edinburg, and that his son William[5] is married to my former pet when a child, Miss Mary Hogg. Should you meet with them, tender them the homage of my gratitude and affection. Mr. Moncrief is one of the best of men. I love his very name.

Adieu! my dear son. Recollect often the advice I gave you in writing. You are now I hope surrounded with an atmosphere of knowledge. Inhale it in every act of inspiration. "Observe, read, think, record, converse, and compose." By so doing only, you will profit by your residence in the most rational and perhaps the most enlightened city in the world.

Mr. Jackson is arrived in our country from the Court of Great Britain—I hope with an olive branch in his mouth. We are all heartily disposed to peace with Britain, and sincerely rejoice in the checks that have lately been given to the Corsican usurper.

Your brother and his bride, Ben, and all the family now at home join in love to you with your affectionate father,

BENJN: RUSH

Addressed: Dr James Rush Edinburg Scotland. By the Windsor packet Capt: Sutton.

MS: Library Company of Philadelphia, Rush MSS.

[1] But see BR's letter to Adams of 9 Dec. 1811.

[2] Edward Ingersoll (1790-1841), a graduate of the University of Pennsylvania, 1808; lawyer and author of legal and poetical works (Univ. of Penna., *Biog. Cat. of Matriculates*).

[3] Samuel Rutter, grocer, had a store at the corner of Water and Walnut Streets; his residence was at 113 Walnut (*Phila. Directories* for 1807, 1810).

[4] The word "press" in this phrase means "printing," as elsewhere in BR's writings (see letter to Lettsom, 2 June 1786). The publications in question were as follows: 1. An edition of George Cleghorn's *Observations on the Epidemical Diseases of Minorca*, Phila.: Nichols, Fry and Kammerer, 1809. 2. *The Works of Thomas Sydenham, M.D., on Acute and Chronic Diseases. . . . With Notes, Intended to Accommodate Them to the Present State of Medicine, and to the Climate and Diseases of the United*

States, by Benjamin Rush, Phila.: B. &
T. Kite, 1809. 3. BR's *Medical Inquiries
and Observations,* 3d edn., Phila., 1809;
at least eight Philadelphia publishing
houses participated in issuing this four-
volume edition, and the imprints of the

sets therefore vary.
⁵ On Robert Scott Moncrief, see BR
to John Morgan, 20 Jan. 1768; since
he had married a sister of Thomas
Hogg, his son William married his own
first cousin.

To John Adams

My dear Friend,   Philadelphia, September 6th, 1809

Although for many years past I have read nothing but books upon medicine on weekdays and upon religion on Sundays, and have expected to continue to do so as long as I lived, yet you have almost persuaded me to read Fox's *History of James the Second.*¹ Your praise of it is enough for me, for I know how much your habits of reading and thinking qualify you to judge of the merit of books that describe the interior of courts and the political recesses of the human heart.

Have you seen Bishop Gregoire's letter to Mr. Barlow upon the subject of the frontispiece of the late edition of his *Columbiad?*² It is a masterly performance and exposes with great eloquence the folly and madness of infidelity.

You wonder how Parson Caldwell³ became possessed of certificates! He acted as a deputy quartermaster in the army at a time when purchases were made *only* with that species of paper money, and when the pay of quartermasters was a commission upon all purchases made with them.

Have you never observed a passion for going abroad to attend a guilty conscience? The jolting of a carriage and the company of strangers seem to act as opiates upon it. The gentleman who lately visited you from New Jersey,⁴ with the largest house in Burlington and everything in and about it to make it comfortable, cannot stay a week at home. New York, New Ark, Princeton (not Philadelphia often latterly) are the usual places of his resort, but the noise and variety of these places it seems have not been sufficiently soporific for the pain of his mind. Hence his late excursion to Boston. Home is generally the only resting place to a man at 70 who has preserved his innocence in his journey through life.

You charge me with the feelings of *patriotism.*⁵ I grant that man is naturally a domestic, a social, and a political or national animal, and that Horace's line is in general true, "naturam expellas furca, tamen usque recurrit."⁶ But those trible⁷ passions have been and may be subdued. There are political as well as social and domestic monks. Happy the man that in the present state of our country has put on the hood and that can look upon a newspaper and the history of town meetings as an old friar looks upon a blooming young woman. If I have not attained to this felicity, I have in a great measure deserved it, for I generally hear and read with the same indifference of the proceedings of the leaders of both the great parties that now agitate and divide our country.

My son Richard brought home from Maryland a few days ago his charming bride. We are all delighted with her. She possesses a highly cultivated understanding, gentle manners, and the whole circle of domestic accomplishments.

I am now busily engaged in revising the proof sheets of an edition of the celebrated Dr. Sydenham's *Works*, with notes, and the 3rd edition of my *Medical Inquiries*. To the latter I have made considerable additions. They will both be published I hope sometime in November. Such is the physical and moral influence of a man's constant employment upon his body and mind, that it is said in England "a button maker becomes a button and a buckle maker a buckle in the course of his life." Do not wonder then if you should hear of my habits of bookmaking having converted me into proof sheets and calfskin, or of my habits of feeling pulses into a pulse glass or a stop watch. I exist almost wholly in those two employments.

Adieu. From ever yours,

BENJN: RUSH

Addressed: John Adams Esqr: Quincy near Boston.
MS: Adams Manuscript Trust, Boston.

[1] Charles James Fox, *A History of the Early Part of the Reign of James the Second*, London, 1808, highly praised by Adams in his letter of 1 Sep. 1809 (*Old Family Letters*, *A*, p. 241).

[2] *The Columbiad*, by Joel Barlow, an allegorical epic in some 7,000 lines, was issued in a massive volume at Philadelphia and Baltimore, 1807. The pamphlet referred to by BR was *Critical Observations on the Poem of Mr. Joel Barlow, The Columbiad*, by M. Grégoire [i.e., Henri Grégoire, Bishop of Blois], Washington, 1809. Grégoire objected to the irreverent treatment given certain emblems of the Catholic faith in the engraved frontispiece. Barlow replied at length in a letter printed by his biographer (Charles B. Todd, *Life and Letters of Joel Barlow*, N.Y., 1886, p. 221-3).

[3] A question posed by Adams in his letter of 1 Sep. The person referred to was James Caldwell (1734-1781), a graduate of the College of New Jersey, 1759, and Presbyterian clergyman of Elizabeth, N.J., who served as a commissary in the Revolution and was accidentally killed by an American sentinel (Sprague, *Annals*, III, 222-8).

[4] Elias Boudinot. His interesting MS journal of his New England tour of this summer is now in the Princeton Univ. Libr. He had visited John Adams on 26 July.

[5] See *Old Family Letters*, *A*, p. 240.

⁶ Naturam expelles furca, tamen usque recurret: "Though you drive out nature with a fork, it will incessantly return."

Horace, *Epistles*, I, x, 24.
⁷ Thus in MS. BR meant "triple" or possibly "tribal."

To John Adams

My dear Friend,   Philadelphia, October 17, 1809

Who were the ancestors and posterity of Homer, Demosthenes, Plato, and Aristotle? Who were the ancestors and posterity of Cicero, Horace, and Virgil? Were any of them philosophers, orators, or poets? Who were the ancestors and posterity of Walsingham, Sully, Malborough, and Wolfe? Were any of them statesmen, generals, or heroes? I do not ask whether they were descended from gentlemen or whether they left gentle sons behind them. I ask, were their ancestors GREAT in the same elevated walks in life as themselves? I believe history and common observation will furnish many more instances of the truth of Lord Bacon's remark[1] than of the reverse of it.

I send you herewith a new edition of my *Lectures upon Animal Life*,[2] extracted from the third edition of my *Medical Inquiries* now in the press. It contains a number of new facts in support of the doctrine I have advanced. Should the perusal of them render an autumnal evening less gloomy to you, I shall be highly gratified.

"What book is that in your hands?" said I to my son Richard a few nights ago in a DREAM?[3] "It is the history of the United States," said he. "Shall I read a page of it to you?" "No, no," said I. "I believe in the truth of no history but in that which is contained in the Old and New Testaments." "But, sir," said my son, "this page relates to your friend Mr. Adams." "Let me see it then," said I. I read it with great pleasure and herewith send you a copy of it.

"1809

"Among the most extraordinary events of this year was the renewal of the friendship and intercourse between Mr. John Adams and Mr. Jefferson, the two ex-Presidents of the United States. They met for the first time in the Congress of 1775. Their principles of liberty, their ardent attachment to their country, and their views of the importance and probable issue of the struggle with Great Britain in which they were engaged being exactly the same, they were strongly attracted to each other and became personal as well as political friends. They met in England during the war while each of them held commissions of honor and trust at two of the first courts of Europe, and spent many happy hours together in reviewing the difficulties and success of their respective negotiations. A difference of opinion upon the objects and issue of the French Revolution separated them during the years in which that great event interested and divided the American people. The predominance of the party which favored the French cause threw Mr. Adams out of the Chair of the United States in the year 1800 and placed Mr. Jefferson there in his stead. The former retired with resignation and dignity to his seat at Quincy, where he spent the evening of his life in literary and philosophical pursuits surrounded by an amiable family and a few old and affectionate friends. The latter resigned the Chair of the United States in the year 1808, sick of the cares and disgusted with the intrigues of public life, and retired to his seat at Monticello in Virginia, where he spent the remainder of his days in the cultivation of a large farm agreeably to the new system of husbandry. In the month of November 1809, Mr. Adams addressed a short letter to his friend Mr. Jefferson in which he congratulated him upon his escape to the shades of retirement and domestic happiness, and concluded it with assurances of his regard and good wishes for his welfare. This letter did great honor to Mr. Adams. It discovered a magnanimity known only to great minds. Mr. Jefferson replied to this letter and reciprocated expressions of regard and esteem. These letters were followed by a correspondence of several years, in which they mutually reviewed the scenes of business in which they had been engaged, and candidly acknowledged to each other all the errors of opinion and conduct into which they had fallen during the time they filled the same station in the service of their country. Many precious aphorisms, the result of observation, experience, and profound reflection, it is said, are contained in these letters. It is to be hoped the world will be favored with a sight of them when they can neither injure nor displease any persons or families whose ancestors' follies or crimes were mentioned in them. These gentlemen sunk into the grave nearly at the same time, full of years and rich in the gratitude and praises of their country (for they outlived the heterogeneous parties that were opposed to them), and to their numerous merits and honors posterity has added that they were rival friends."[4]

With affectionate regard to your fireside, in which all my family join, I am, dear sir, your sincere old friend,

BENJN: RUSH

MS: Adams Manuscript Trust, Boston.

[1] To the effect that great men have neither ancestors nor posterity (Adams to Rush, 8 Oct. 1809; *Old Family Letters, A*, p. 243). I have not located this saying attributed to Bacon.

[2] Originally published as *Three Lectures upon Animal Life, Delivered in the University of Pennsylvania*, Phila.: Dobson, 1799. They constitute BR's most important contribution to formal philosophy.

[3] In the passage that follows, BR made his principal plea to Adams to make an effort toward reconciliation with Jefferson. That pains were taken in composing the plea is shown by an autograph draft of the letter, dated *16* Oct. in Hist. Soc. Penna., Gratz Coll. In the draft BR originally wrote, and then crossed out, the following introduction to his dream history: "What would [you *omitted*] think of some future historian of the United States concluding one of his chapters with the following paragraph?" The greater verisimilitude of the revision adds much to the effectiveness of this remarkable letter.

[4] Adams in reply, 25 Oct. 1809, exclaimed: "A Dream again! I wish you would dream all day and all Night, for one of your dreams puts me in spirits for a Month. I have no other objection to your Dream, but that it is not History. It may be Prophecy" (*Old Family Letters, A*, p. 246). And so, about two years later, it proved; see L. H. Butterfield, "The Dream of Benjamin Rush: The Reconciliation of John Adams and Thomas Jefferson," *Yale Review*, XL (1950-1951), 297-319.

To George Clymer

Dear Sir,   November 25, 1809

During the first years of the establishment of the Medical School of Philadelphia, it was required that every student who had not graduated in some college should be obliged to attend a course of lectures upon natural philosophy previously to his being admitted to an examination for a medical degree in our University. This rule was imperfectly complied with during the greatest part of Dr. Ewing's provostship, but has been neglected for several years, to the great injury of our Medical School and of medical science in our country.[1]

Permit me to suggest to you the necessity of appointing a professor of natural philosophy *for the express purpose* of teaching that important branch of science to students of medicine in the extensive way in which it is taught in European universities. Such a course of lectures will not interfere with the instruction in natural philosophy given to candidates for degrees in the arts by the Provost of the University. They will be addressed to persons of a more advanced age and will embrace many objects specifically necessary and useful to students of medicine. Should such a professorship be instituted, there will be no difficulty in filling it. Mr. Robert Hare's extensive knowledge in natural philosophy and all its collateral subjects points him out as a most suitable person for that purpose. His splendid talents and ardor in scientific pursuits I have no doubt would add greatly to the reputation of our Medical School and to the honor of our city and state.

Should you think proper to propose the professorship I have mentioned, suppose you add to it at the same time a professorship of rural economy?[2]

From, dear sir, yours very respectfully,

BENJN: RUSH

MS: University of Pennsylvania, Edgar Fahs Smith Memorial Collection.

[1] Provost Ewing had died in 1802 and was not succeeded until 1806, when John McDowell (1750-1820), recently appointed professor of natural philosophy, became provost. BR's plea, which was directed to Clymer because he was a trustee of long standing, was not successful. Robert Hare, who was BR's candidate, was elected to the chair of natural philosophy in 1810 but declined it; in 1819 he accepted the chair of chemistry. (Cheyney, *Hist. Univ. Penna.*, p. 435, 215; DAB, under McDowell and Hare.)

[2] Clymer was vice-president of the Philadelphia Society for Promoting Agriculture (DAB). This proposal by BR likewise came to nothing at the time.

To James Rush

My dear Son,   Philadelphia, November 29th, 1809

Your letters from Greenock, Glasgow, and Edinburg, the last dated Sept. 7, came safe to hand.[1] They diffused universal joy through our whole family. To me they were peculiarly acceptable. The gratitude and affection of children are among the most cordial stimuli of old age. God grant that they long, very long, be applied to my body and mind.

I fancied when I read your last letter that I witnessed[2] your first interview with the excellent and venerable Mr. Hogg and the worthy Mr. Scott Moncrief. I realized the pew in which I usually sat in the Tolbooth Church when you described your first visit to it. I hope you became acquainted with Mr. Davidson,[3] the minister of that church. He parted with a *great name* for the one he now holds. His father, the Reverend Mr. Randall,[4] was one of the first men I met with in Scotland. I now possess a copy of a letter he wrote to Dr. Wetherspoon when he was invited to Princeton, in which he discovers a view of the obligations and duties of a Christian and a clergyman that indicates an extent of mind rarely to be met with in modern times. On his way from London about the year 1767 I saw him in Edinburg at Mr. John Caw's. He had never seen the metropolis of the British empire before. He was much struck with its splendor, its business, its amusements, its follies, and its crimes. Upon a review of them I heard him say, "I have often heard of the vanity of the world—I have often read of it—I have even preached upon it, but I never saw it—never believed it until I visited London."

I feel extremely grateful to Dr. Stewart[5] for his services to you, and sincerely sympathize with him in his late domestic affliction. I estimated the intensity of his grief by looking at your dear sister Julia and asking myself what would be my grief, should it please God to afflict me in the same manner. Present my most affectionate regards to the Doctor and his excellent lady. I well remember her in her father's family.

I refer you to your Mama and sister's letters for family news. Under the pressure of my usual winter labors, it pleases God to continue to me my usual health. My class this day amounts to exactly 300 pupils, in which are included the usual proportion of perpetuals, doctors of medicine, and clergymen. Among the last is your friend Dr. Stoughton.[6] Dr. Coxe's *lectures* are highly satisfactory, but his *experiments* by no means so much so as his friends expected. He wants an able assistant, for he unfortunately has employed one not so capable as himself.

Dr. Stewart[7] died in October last with a sporadic case of yellow fever.

Adieu! my dear son. My prayers ascend daily to the God of our family for your welfare. Think of the duties that await you in life, and study and act accordingly. You have many friends in Philadelphia who wait with impatience for your return. Dr. Green speaks highly of you in all the circles of his extensive congregation. I hope to see you one of the fat lambs of his flock. Again adieu! Ever yours,

BENJN: RUSH

P.S. I have just read Allan Burns' treatise upon the diseases of the heart, &c.[8] He speaks highly of a Dr. Grapengiessier's book upon inflammatory or plethoric dropsies[9] noticed in Dr. Duncan's *Annals of Medicine* for the year 1798, in which bleeding is recommended as a new and an effectual remedy for them. The same theory and mode of cure were established and advised by me in the year 1792[10] in the first edition of the 2nd volume of my *Inquiries*. My new doctrine of animal heat was well received. *All* agreed in the conclusiveness of my objections to Dr. Black's theory of the decomposition of air in the lungs. I will give you the outlines of my doctrine in a future letter.

Addressed: Dr James Rush at the University of Edinburgh Scotland.
MS: Library Company of Philadelphia, Rush MSS.

[1] James' letters to his family from Edinburgh are in Rush MSS, Box 11.

[2] MS: "witned."

[3] Thomas Davidson (1747-1827), Scottish clergyman; minister of the Tolbooth Church, Edinburgh, from 1785; his family name was Randall, but it was changed to Davidson upon his succeeding to the estate of an uncle (DNB).

[4] On Rev. Thomas Randall, see BR to Witherspoon, 29 Dec. 1767.

[5] Probably Charles Stewart, M.D., of Nicholson Square (*Edinburgh Directory*, 1790). The address on BR's letter to James, 1 May 1810, suggests that James stayed with Dr. Stewart during at least a part of his sojourn in Edinburgh.

[6] William Staughton (1770-1829), Baptist clergyman, educator, and classical scholar; D.D., College of New Jersey, 1801; at this time he was minister of the First Baptist Church in Philadephia (DAB). Staughton was an intimate friend and admirer of BR's, and wrote a valuable *Eulogium in Memory of the Late Dr. Benjamin Rush*, Phila., 1813.

[7] James Stuart; see BR to Mrs. Rush, 28 Sep. 1798.

[8] Allan Burns, *Observations on Some of the Most Frequent and Important Diseases of the Heart*, Edinburgh, 1809 (Surg. Gen. Off., *Index-Cat.*, 1st ser., II, 551).

[9] Carl Johan Christian Grapengiesser, *De hydrope plethorico*, Göttingen [1795]; a dissertation (same, V, 553).

[10] Error for 1793.

To John Adams

My dear Friend,   Philadelphia, December 5th, 1809

I picked up some time ago a magazine in which I met with a revival of the old controversy concerning the divine origin of Episcopal and Presbyterian ordination carried on by Dr. Hobart and Dr. Mason of New York.[1] After reading a few pages of it, I threw down the magazine with disgust and committed the enclosed thoughts upon that subject to paper. The partiality you have been pleased to express for some of my dreams has induced me to send you a copy of it. It may perhaps afford some amusement to your parish minister after he has drunk his glass of wine and smoked his segar at your table.

I have great pleasure in informing you that my son who sailed from Philadelphia for Glasgow on the 15th of July, and my daughter, who with her husband and children sailed from Quebec on the 10th of July for Plymouth, both arrived at their wished port on the same day, August 29th, the day on which their brother was married to one of the most amiable and accomplished women in this country. A rare coincidence on *one* day of family blessings, for which I desire to be devoutly thankful! My son has been well received in Edinburgh and is much pleased with everything he has seen and heard in that part of the world.

I send you herewith a few numbers of the *Aurora*.

Excuse the shortness of this letter. For some weeks past, my lectures, the Hospital, and my private practice have occupied every moment of my time. My class amounts to 300, 260 of whom are students of medicine. The rest are graduates in medicine, clergymen, and private gentlemen.

With love to your fireside, in which my dear Mrs. Rush joins, I am, dear sir, ever yours,

BENJN: RUSH

P.S. Has the prophecy (as you called it) contained in my last letter as yet become history?

ENCLOSURE

The claims of the Episcopal and Presbyterian Churches to the divine origin of their respective modes of ordination proved to be just: extracted from a manuscript copy of T. E.'s "Travels into the East."[2]

"In passing through a part of Asia Minor, I came to a village where the first thing I heard of was a controversy between two TAILORS which engaged the attention of all its inhabitants. One of them contended that he was the descendant of Dorcas, who possessed from the twelve Apostles a patent for the exercise of his business, and that he had an exclusive right to make all the clothes that were worn in the village. His name was Peter. Another, whose name was John, contended that he had that right exclusively, and that he could show the patterns of coats, breeches, and pantaloons cut out by his ancestor Dorcas with her own hands. The contest between these two Tailors was carried on with great acrimony and fury. They branded each other with opprobious names. Peter called the clothes made by John 'dish-clouts,' while John insisted upon it that all the clothes made by Peter were composed of 'old rags' that had belonged to a noted prostitute known by the name of the Whore of Babylon. Such was the rancor with which they disputed about their exclusive patent for their respective trades, that they would neither eat nor drink with each other nor enter into each other's houses. Peter did not even acknowledge John to be one of the craft, but always spoke of him by the name of the 'Dish-clout maker.' Besides these two Tailors, there were several others who worked at the trade, who did not pretend to be the heirs or successors of Dorcas, but who by long practice had become as neat workmen as Peter and John. These persons were treated with the same contempt and obloquy by Peter that he treated John. I remarked, notwithstanding all the Tailors said against the ancient rights and skill of each other, that the inhabitants of the village were all clad in a manner equally comfortable and decent, although the clothes of some of them were a little more costly than others. In contemplating the dispute between these two Tailors and their[3] unhappy consequences, I could not help thinking how much more the widows that wept over the corpse of Dorcas would have deplored her *life* than her *death*, had they foreseen the evils that the exercise of her trade would have brought upon this part of the world: and thou venerable saint! little didst thou think thy charities would have become the source of so much discord among thy followers, and that a monopoly of a trade intended for the benefit of the whole human race should have been claimed by any one of them. Descend, gentle Spirit of Beneficence, from thy blest abode where thou are now enjoying the rewards of thy liberal and pious labors, and heal by thy presence and advice the divisions that have taken place among the votaries of the scissors and the thimble, and teach them that thy art was not entailed in thy family, and that every article of dress which completely covers those parts of the body which were intended to be concealed from the public eye and which protects it from the inconveniences of heat and cold is perfectly agreeable to the patterns by which thou didst make the coats and garments for the poor of Joppa!"

MS: Adams Manuscript Trust, Boston.

[1] This controversy was conducted by two learned polemical writers of New York City in 1806: John Mitchell Mason (1770-1829), of the Scots Presbyterian Church, and John Henry Hobart (1775-1830), rector of Trinity Church and later bishop of New York (DAB, and Allibone, *Dict. of Authors*, under both names). On Mason see also BR to James Rush, 22 Dec. 1809.

[2] BR's indebtedness in the following parody to Swift's *Tale of a Tub* (1704) is not acknowledged but would have been obvious to John Adams.

[3] Thus in MS.

To John Kingston[1]

Sir,   December 5, 1809

I am much flattered by your intention to give my humble name a place in your Biographical Dictionary, but I can by no means consent to furnish you with a single material for that purpose; and I take this method of imploring you to spare me the pain I shall feel in seeing an account of my life in a work destined to preserve the characters[2] of men with whom I am not worthy of being ranked in the records of history.

My opinions upon many subjects and my innovations in the practice of medicine have so much divided my fellow citizens upon the subject of my talents and character, that it will be impossible for many years to decide the controversy respecting either of them. Those who come after me (if my works should survive my interment) will be the best judges whether I have added by them to the knowledge and happiness or to the errors and miseries of my fellow citizens.

Should you think a justification necessary[3] of your omission of the account of my life which you have promised in your Dictionary, I have no objection to your publishing this letter in the place of it.[4]

From, sir, very respectfully yours,

B RUSH

MS (draft): Library Company of Philadelphia, Rush MSS.

[1] In the Rush MSS, XXV, immediately preceding the present draft letter, is a printed prospectus of "The New American Biographical Dictionary," to be issued by John Kingston of Baltimore. On the blank side of the prospectus is a letter from Kingston to BR, 1 Dec. 1809, appealing for information for the notice of BR to appear in the announced work. The work duly appeared as *The New American Biographic Dictionary; or, Memoirs of Many of the Most Eminent Persons That Have Ever Lived in This or Any Other Nation . . .*, by J. Kingston, Baltimore: Printed for John Kingston, and Sold at his Book and Stationery Store, 164, Market Street, 1810. It was reissued in 1811. The compiler, born in England in 1769, had been a Methodist missionary in the West Indies and had married Jane Branwell, aunt of the famous Brontë children, before setting up in Baltimore as a publisher about 1808; he later moved to New York and died there in 1824 (Fannie E. Ratchford, "John Kingston, Baltimore Publisher," Univ. of Texas, *Library Chronicle*, III [1947-1948], 10-26). Miss Ratchford lists twenty-four of Kingston's Baltimore imprints, nearly all of them religious or didactic in nature.

[2] BR first wrote "memories"; he then wrote "characters" above it but crossed out neither word. The printed text (see note 4, below) has "characters."

[3] This word omitted in draft; supplied from printed text.

[4] This was done, and Kingston added: "The author would gladly say much more on a character so justly and so highly valued in England, France, and America; but he must now leave Dr. Rush's letter to eulogize the man who is a rare instance of the modesty of merit" (*New American Biographic Dictionary*, p. 242-3).

To James Rush

My dear Son,   Philadelphia, December 22nd, 1809

I acknowledged the receipt of your letter by the packet dated September 29th a few days ago by a Mr. Buchannan,[1] who was to sail for England by the way of Baltimore but who has not yet left our city. I hope you will continue to write by every packet. A long letter upon a large sheet of paper will satisfy our whole family. We shall write to you in the same way except when we are so happy as to meet with private opportunities.

I suggested to you in a former letter to procure a small blank pocket memorandum, in which I requested you to get persons of distinction, kind friends, and worthy fellow students to write their names with such additions to them of texts of Scripture, lines of poetry, or expressions of regard as they may think proper. Books of this kind are common in the universities of Germany. They are called "Remembrancers." They are preserved with care and reviewed with pleasure in every subsequent period of life.

Do not fail of bringing home with you everything you hear worthy of being remembered in all the lectures you attend, particularly Monroe's,[2] Duncan's, and Gregory's.[3] Their facts (if they repudiate theory) can be incorporated with our principles.

I have this day delivered my lecture upon the unity of disease, with some additions to it, to a crowded and attentive class. A native of Mexico[4] who does me the honor to attend my lectures urged me to publish it as we came out of the room together, and promised to translate it immediately afterwards into the Spanish language. But it is not yet fit for the public eye. Take care of the copy of it you carried to Edinburgh. Do not suffer it to pass long enough out of your hands to be transcribed, or even to have an extract made from it. Dr. Caldwell's opposition and hostility to me have met with a severe check. In consequence of his saying "the students would attend his lectures, were they not afraid of old Rush blackballing them when they were examined for degrees," the whole class met and expressed their indignation against him and at the same time passed a very flattering vote in favor of your father.[5] The next day he was publicly hissed in Dr. Coxe's lecturing room, and the day afterwards (for his impudence is equal to his vices) he was refused admittance into the lecturing room by the janitor of the University.

The Reverend Dr. Mason dined with us yesterday. He has an uncle in Edinburgh, an intimate friend of Dr. Stewart's, with whom he wishes you to be acquainted. He has promised to write to him to attend to you. The Doctor charmed us with his eloquence and good sense upon all subjects. Your uncle and Mr. Hopkinson,[6] who were part of our company, objected only to his funny stories, which, they hinted, detracted somewhat from the dignity of his character. It is remarkable that men otherwise great sometimes derange the order established by Sir Wm. Temple for pleasing in conversation.[7] This order, he says, consists in truth, good sense, good humor, and wit. The last, which is the *least* necessary to command durable attention and character, is too often placed *first* in attempts to please, not only in conversation but in writing. It was the bane of Dr. Nesbitt's conversation and letters. He seemed to live only to make people laugh or angry. It was, I believe, from viewing the unfortunate propensity to ill-timed and indiscriminate wit in Dr. Nesbitt when a young man, that Dr. Wetherspoon said "he would almost as soon whip a boy for wit as for lying."

In your letters to Dr. Miller avoid any communications that can lessen the reputation of the University of Edinburgh. All will be safe that you deposit in my bosom upon that subject.

The College of Carlisle is reviving under the care of their new principal, Mr. Atwater.[8] It now bids fair, for the first time, to be a nursery for Church and State. I rejoice in its present state and future prospects. It was once to me a Benoni or "son of sorrow" from the persecutions to which it exposed me from Dr. Ewing. It is now an Isaac or "child of laughter" to my heart.[9]

My respect to all your and my Edinburgh friends. Thank them in my name for their civilities to you. I almost envy you the society of good Mrs. Hogg. With what pleasure would I view the influence of time and age upon the uncommon virtues she exhibited in the prime of life. I will mention a proof of one of them. A lady in her company once spoke disrespectfully of a gentleman who had lived unhappily with and afterwards separated from his wife. "Do you know that gentleman?" said Mrs. Hogg. "No," said the lady. "Perhaps if you did," said Mrs. Hogg, "you would not blame him— there may be faults on the part of his wife as well as himself. It is best to be silent upon such subjects." Sir John Pringle sat by and heard this conversation. When it was ended, he took her by the hand and said (irreverently), "If you, madam, were to judge the world at the last day, I am sure injustice would be done to no one." What a compliment to her candor and Christian temper!

My respects to Dr. Fuller.[10] Beg him to write *often* to his Uncle Butler.

From, my dear James, ever yours,

BENJN RUSH

P.S. Your dear sister Mary complains in her letters of the expenses of England. I have sent her £50 sterling to help her out, and your Mamma has advised her to hasten back to Canada. Such drafts upon my resources should command economy in all my children. You say nothing of the sum that will be necessary for a year's support in Edinburgh, nor what the expenses will be of spending 6 or 9 months in London. Think of your studies. I will think of the means of enabling you to pursue them, and faithfully (by God's blessing upon my labors) as well as cheerfully comply with your wishes and my engagements to you.

[*In Mrs. Rush's hand*:]

December 26th. Your father has written you so long a letter, and left me so little room, that I shall merely tell you that you are affectionately remembered by your mother and by every member of your family. Yesterday being Christmas day, we had a family party as usual, in addition to which we invited several of the young gentlemen of the shop. As soon as the cloth was removed, Mr. Van Brachel[11] filled his glass and begged to give Dr. James Rush as his toast. He expresses the greatest regard for you but said he feared you had forgotten your fellow pupils, for that you had promised to write to him. A letter from your friend Mr. Drinker[12] accompanies this. He will no doubt have given you all the anecdotes of your acquaintances that will be worth your knowing, therefore the less is necessary from me at this time. Your brother Richard would have written by this packet if he had known of it sooner. He says you must write to him. He begs remembrance to you—so does his wife. Julia, Ben, Sam, and Will all love you and talk of you in the most affectionate manner. Adieu, my ever dear son. Remember your poor sister Mary, and believe in the constant affection of your mother, JULIA RUSH.

[*In Mrs. Richard Rush's hand*:]

Will you allow your sister Catherine to offer her affectionate love to her brother James?

[*In Mary Stockton's and Mrs. Richard Rush's hands*:][13]

My dear James—Mary Stockton (who is now sitting by and trimming a dress for Hannah Emlen's[14] party this evening) desires her love to you and to say by the next packet she will write you a folio letter in answer to yours which she had the pleasure to receive. She says she was very much obliged to you for it and would have answered it before she left home, had she known where to direct. She says she regrets extremely and feels *most sensibly* your absence.

[*In BR's hand*:]

"Neither a borrower nor a *lender* be." I suffered by the latter *while* in Edinburgh. BR.

Addressed: Dr: James Rush at the University of Edinburgh Scotland.
MS: Library Company of Philadelphia, Rush MSS.

[1] Not identified.

[2] Presumably Alexander Monro, secundus, BR's old teacher; see BR to John Morgan, 16 Nov. 1766. However, Monro's son, Alexander, tertius (1773-1859), had been joint professor of anatomy and surgery with his father since 1800. (DNB.)

[3] James Gregory, M.D. (1753-1821), son and successor of John Gregory, BR's professor of medicine at Edinburgh; published medical writings (DNB).

[4] This was Joseph Roxas (dates unknown), a political exile from Mexico

and an enthusiastic disciple of BR's, who at one time styled himself "late Professor of Subterranean Geometry in the School of Mines, at Mexico." Dr. Corner has brought together considerable information on Roxas in a note on an entry pertaining to him in BR's Commonplace Book (*Autobiography*, p. 287).

⁵ This testimonial is in Rush MSS, XXXI; a blank page was used by BR for a draft letter of thanks to his class for their support, dated 18 Dec. 1809. Caldwell had been giving private medical lectures; it was his expectation, encouraged (according to Caldwell) by BR, that a post on the medical faculty would be offered him. When BR informed him that there was no prospect of an appointment, an angry exchange ensued. See Caldwell's letters in Rush MSS, XXIX, and also his *Autobiography*, p. 289-91.

⁶ Doubtless Joseph Hopkinson (1770-1842), son of BR's friend Francis Hopkinson; an able lawyer, he was one of BR's counsel in the Cobbett suit, but he is best remembered as the author of "Hail Columbia," 1798 (DAB).

⁷ "The first ingredient in conversation is truth, the next good sense, the third good humour, and the fourth wit" ("Heads of an Essay on Conversation," Temple's *Works*, London, 1814, III, 543). Compare BR's advice to Rebecca Smith in his letter of 1 July 1791.

⁸ Rev. Jeremiah Atwater (1773-1858), a graduate of Yale, 1793, and tutor there, 1795-1799; first president of Middlebury College, Vt., 1800 to 1809, when he accepted the call to Dickinson College (Dexter, *Yale Graduates*, 5th ser., p. 54-6). Morgan's *Dickinson College* gives a full account of his difficult administration. Atwater's letters to BR are in Rush MSS, XLII.

⁹ See Genesis 35:18; 21:3. BR has given the literal signification of the Hebrew names.

¹⁰ Thomas Fuller, Jr. (d. 1865); M.D., University of Pennsylvania, 1809; he accompanied James Rush to Europe and afterwards practised in Beaufort, S.C. (Univ. of Penna., *Gen. Alumni Cat.*; BR to Daniel Rutherford, 4 July 1809, Libr. Co. Phila., James Rush MSS, Yi2/7404/F; BR, *Autobiography*, p. 280).

¹¹ Samuel H. Van Brakle, of St. Croix, W.I.; M.D., University of Pennsylvania, 1810; afterwards studied in London and Edinburgh (Univ. of Penna., *Gen. Alumni Cat.*; Van Brakle letters in Rush MSS, XVIII).

¹² John Drinker, Jr., who was admitted to the bar in 1805 and had an office at 133 South 2d St., wrote chatty letters to James in Edinburgh, 1809-1810 (Martin, *Bench and Bar*, p. 264; *Phila. Directory* for 1810; Libr. Co. Phila., James Rush MSS, Yi2/7276/F).

¹³ This paragraph seems to be in two different hands. Probably begun by Mary Stockton, it was continued, following "trimming a dress," by Mrs. Richard Rush. This Mary Stockton (1790-1865) was the daughter of Mrs. Rush's brother Richard, the senator, and hence James' cousin; she later married William Harrison (Stockton, *Stockton Family*, p. 77).

¹⁴ Not further identified.

To James Cheetham

Sir,   Philadelphia, January 6, 1810

Accept of my thanks for the copy of the *Life of Thomas Paine* which you have done me the favor to send me.¹ I have read it with great satisfaction and consider it as a specimen of biography which, if more general, would be more useful than the ⟨common records of the lives of⟩ posthumous eulogiums upon distinguished men ⟨which contain the history of their virtues only, and thus render *the life of one man a mold in which a writer may fabricate a thousand similar impressions*). Doctor Franklin used to say, "The maxim of not speaking evil of the dead should be reversed. We should speak evil *only* of the dead, for in so doing we can do them no harm. We hurt the living only by exposing their vices."

Your account of the last illness and death of T. Paine is the best refutation of his *Age of Reason* that has been published. Christians in all countries will owe you a debt of gratitude for it.

With wishes for your happiness I am, sir, very respectfully yours,

BENJN: RUSH

MS (draft): Library Company of Philadelphia, Rush MSS.

[1] See BR's earlier letter to Cheetham, 17 July 1809.

To John Adams

My dear and excellent Friend, Philadelphia, February 1, 1810

With this letter you will receive a bundle of *Auroras* and another of the same size by the post of the next day. They are filled very much of late with our state politics, but you will find many columns still filled with complaints against Great Britain. So my son Richard tells me, for I assure you I have not read a column in any one of them this six months. My wife asked me a few days ago what was the object of Macon's bill.[1] I could not tell her. I have, however, since seen an epitome of it in one of our daily papers. Of its design and tendency I can say nothing. But let our rulers do what they will, I shall patiently submit to them.

Do we not, my friend, mistake the nature of government and the business and rank of the men who rule us? Was not government one of the causes of the fall of man? And were not laws intended to be our chains? Of course. Are not our rulers who make and execute those laws nothing but jailers, turnkeys, and Jack Ketches of a higher order? We give them titles, put them into palaces, and decorate them with fine clothes only to conceal the infamy of their offices. As labor, parturition, and even death itself (the other curses of the Fall) have been converted by the goodness of God into blessings, so government and rulers have in some instances become blessings to mankind. But this does not exempt them from the charge which I have brought against them. Let us do what we will to meliorate our government and to choose wise rulers, we cannot frustrate the designs of heaven. The former will always carry in their construction marks of their being other forms only of jails, stocks, whipping posts, cells, and dungeons, and the latter will always exhibit, notwithstanding the disguise of their titles, palaces, and dresses, the insignia of the offices I have already ascribed to them.

I thank you for your letter of the 17th of January.[2] Your short but sublime description of the objects and nature of Christianity delighted me. I care not whether you are Calvanist or Arminian or both, for both believe the truth, and a true system of religion I believe can only be formed from a union of the tenets of each of them. But after all that has been said of doctrines, they only "who *have done good* shall come forth to the resurrection unto life, and they only who *have done evil* to the resurrection of damnation."[3]

Next to my Bible I find the most satisfaction in reading the works of Dr. Hartley upon both doctrinal and practical subjects. His morality is truly evangelical. His posthumous letters to his sister[4] show him to have been a saint of the first order.

Adieu! Ever yours affectionately,

BENJN: RUSH

MS: Adams Manuscript Trust, Boston.

[1] "Macon's Bill No. 1," introduced by Nathaniel Macon of North Carolina, passed the House of Representatives at the end of Jan. 1810 but was unacceptable to the Senate. Known as "the American Navigation Act," it proposed the repeal of the Nonintercourse Act of Mch. 1809 but required that all goods carried to or from France and Great Britain should be carried in ships built and owned in America. (McMaster, *Hist.*, III, 357-60.)

[2] An error for 21 Jan.; see *Old Family Letters*, A, p. 250.

[3] John 5:29.

[4] This work, perhaps in a periodical, has not been identified.

To James Rush

My very dear Son,   Philadelphia, February 7th, 1810

The long delay of the packet which bore my last letter to you, at New York, has created a much longer interval between the times of writing to you than has been agreeable to me. This letter I hope will have a more speedy passage to your hands. It leaves all your family in good health except your brother John, who arrived from New Orleans by the way of Washington (from whence he was brought by your brother Ben and black William) on the 3rd instant in a state of deep melancholy. Neither the embraces nor tears of your mother, father, sister, nor brothers could obtain a word nor even a look from him. His countenance is pale and discovers no marks of his disease being induced by any *other* cause than the death of his friend by his hand in the duel of 1807. This evening we conveyed him to the Hospital, where all its officers vied with each other in offers and promises of kindness to him. To your parents this sight and this close and intimate union with his woes have been truly distressing. Your mother mourns, but it is with the resignation of a Christian. I do not despair, with the medical resources of the Hospital, of his recovery.

Nothing new has happened in the medical events of our city since my last letter. Dr. Caldwell has abdicated his chair. His name is never mentioned by the students but with contempt and detestation.

A number of cases have occurred in the Hospital in the course of the winter very favorable to the new system of medicine. Several maniacs have been cured by the same remedies that cure rheumatism. I have called mania a rheumatism in the brain, and rheumatism mania in the joints in my clinical remarks upon those forms of disease. Blisters to the *joints* continue to afford great and sudden relief in the rheumatism. A dropsy of the thorax, abdomen, and lower limbs has been completely cured by 15 bleedings and an artificial diarrhoea. A leprosy of 10 years' standing has been nearly cured by the internal use of arsenic and the external use of an ointment composed of equal parts of sulphur and hog's lard. An intermittent of 6 months' continuance has been cured by two bleedings. The blood in both instances was sizy. A pulmonary consumption of two years' standing has been completely cured by a salivation, and another has been nearly cured by tonic diet and remedies.

As soon as the lectures are over, I purpose to commit to the press 13 introductory lectures and the two lectures upon the pleasures of the senses and of the mind which compose a part of my physiology.[1]

Dr. Physick requests you would procure and send to him a copy of the oath taken by the graduates in medicine in Edinburgh. Suppose you accompany it with a respectful and grateful letter to the Doctor and with a short account of the state of surgery in the city and University of Edinburgh.

I hinted in a former letter at the necessity of your dissecting a dead body in London. At the same time spread your sails to every wind that can convey to you new facts and opinions in surgery. It will be necessary for you to practise it in order to assist you in getting into business. It will enable you moreover to keep your business when acquired. I have lost many families by declining it.

Dr. Pinkard has treated your sister and [Captain][2] Manners with neglect, for which reason it will not be worth your while to deliver your letter to him. Mr. Jno. Penn of London[3] will receive you kindly. If possible, I will get a letter conveyed to him in your favor before you go to London. If not, wait upon him and only mention your name to him. He is prepared to be your friend.

Visit all public and humane institutions, particularly maniacal ones. Pry into their interior, as far as diet, dress, regimen, and expense are concerned. Record everything useful, especially where *numbers* are concerned, in your journal. They will be choice raw materials to work upon in promoting the happiness of your fellow citizens when you return.

The public mind is in a state of suspense with respect to peace and war. We wait the pleasure of the British Court upon hearing the news of Mr. Jackson's dismission.[4] All the family join in affectionate love to you. Take care of your health. Take care of your morals. Take care of your soul. Remember the price, the high price, paid for the last. Adieu! my beloved son!

BENJN: RUSH

P.S. Your brother Richard and his excellent wife, also Mary Stockton, send their love to you. Remember me affectionately to my Edinburgh friends, the same as if named. All our domestics send their respects to you. I mentioned in my two last letters that I had sent £200 sterling to be passed to your credit by Messrs. Harrison & Latham of Liverpool.

Addressed: Dr: James Rush Nicholson Street Edinburgh Scotland. By the British packet.
MS: Library Company of Philadelphia, Rush MSS.

[1] This work appeared as *Sixteen Introductory Lectures, to Courses of Lectures upon the Institutes and Practice of Medicine. . . . To Which are Added, Two Lectures upon the Pleasures of the Senses and of the Mind, with an Inquiry into Their Proximate Cause*, Phila.: Bradford and Inskeep, 1811. An enlargement of the *Six Introductory Lectures* of 1801, it is still a readable work and at least partially explains BR's great popularity as a lecturer.

[2] MS torn by seal.

[3] John Penn, the younger (1760- 1834), of Stoke Park, Buckinghamshire, son of Thomas and grandson of William the founder. He had remained in America for some years after the Revolution, residing at "Solitude," on the site of the present Philadelphia zoo; published volumes of verse and erected the monument to Thomas Gray at Stoke Poges. (DNB; H. M. Jenkins, *The Family of William Penn*, Phila. and London, 1899, p. 173-83.) See also BR's letter to Robert Barclay, 9 May 1810.

[4] For the circumstances, see McMaster, *Hist.*, III, 349-57.

To James Rush

My very dear Son,   Philadelphia, March 19, 1810

Your letters of November 26th and December 25th came safe
to hand by the January packet. The details contained in them were
highly satisfactory to me. However wishfully you may cast your
eyes across the Atlantic and long for a seat at your father's fireside,
be assured you will often lick your fingers in reviewing the days
and hours you are now spending in the highly cultivated society of
Edinburgh. Perhaps there is at present no spot upon the earth where
religion, science, and literature combine more to produce moral
and intellectual pleasures than in the metropolis of Scotland. What
a contrast between an evening at Mrs. Hamilton's or Mrs. Fletch-
er's,[1] or a seat at the tea table of the venerable Mrs. Hogg, or a
chair next to Miss A. Hogg[2]—and the convivial dinners and insipid
tea parties of Philadelphia! Had I known that either of the two
last ladies had been living when you left us, I should have solicited
their attention to you by letters to each of them. Do homage in
my name to their goodness, and thank them over and over for
their kind remembrance of me. I cannot think of Heaven without
seeing them near the throne of our common Saviour. To Lady Jane
Steuart and her noble brother[3] say everything for me that gratitude
and friendship ought to dictate from a heart that still loves and
venerates them. Tell Mr. Scott Moncrief, Dr. Steuart, and Mr.
Creech that they have renewed my lease of affection and obligation
to them by their civilities to my son. Tell good Mr. Innis[4] and his
family that I recollect with pleasure the Sabbath I spent with them
at his glebe near the Marquis of Twedale's. Present my grateful
respects to the kind and good Lord and Lady Buchan.[5] But I must
stop the career of my pen, or the pleasing subjects and objects now
before my imagination would exclude every other topic from my
letter. I pass from them reluctantly to medicine.

Dr. Patterson[6] in a letter to his father gives nearly the same account of the practice of physic in Paris that you have given of it in
Edinburgh. I have concealed the details of your letters upon that
subject from everybody except Dr. Physick, and for reasons that
must be obvious to you. In what manner do you propose to go to
London? If by land, wait upon Mrs. Cappe, the widow of a celebrated dissenting minister at York,[7] and present my respects to her.
She is one of my most estimable correspondents. In London you
must be guided by public opinion in the choice of hospitals and
lectures. It will be necessary for you to dissect at least one body to

perfect yourself in anatomy and in the use of the knife. Dr. Peirson's lectures upon the practice of physic must be valuable from the texture of his syllabus.[8] By all means gain access to the *interior* of Bethlem and St. Luke's Hospitals. For this purpose obtain introductions to their physicians from some of your London friends, and obtain from them a knowledge of the *internal* government of the houses under their care. Visit if possible some one of the private madhouses near London, and pry into everything that relates to the management both of the bodies and minds of the patients that are confined in them. Visit likewise the lunatic asylum at York if you pass through that city. It is under the care of Dr. Hunter,[9] to whom the late Dr. Edwards made me known. Present my respectful compliments to him. While in London, suppose you make a short excursion to Oxford. It will scarcely be reputable to overlook in your travels that renowned seat of learning. It will be easy to obtain introductions to some of the professors in the University from some one of the physicians in London. I will add enough to your resources to defray the expense of this excursion. By the next packet I shall remit a sum to your bankers in Liverpool that will enable you I hope to meet all your new and pressing demands in London. They will I presume give you a credit in London, as they have done in Edinburgh. I sent them, I informed you, £200 sterling by the last packet but one.

The late Dr. Edwards informed me that Dr. Wetherspoon had mentioned when in Scotland that no tombstone had been placed over the grave of Captain Leslie, notwithstanding I had informed his sister, Lady Jane Steuart, that it had been done by me at the close of the war. I even sent her a copy of the inscription upon it. Perhaps Dr. W. meant only that no stone was erected to perpetuate his memory at *Princeton*, where he fell. This is true. His body after he fell was thrown into his baggage wagon and conveyed to Pluckmamin,[10] 40 miles from Princeton, where it was buried by our army with the honors of war in consequence of a letter being found in his pocket from me in which I addressed him, though a military enemy, as a personal friend. I have seen his grave and conversed with a person who has seen the tombstone and read the epitaph which is inscribed upon it. Mention [this][11] matter delicately and circuitously to Dr. Steuart or to [Mrs.?] Hogg. Speak of it as an act never contradicted, but if necessary give the above explanation of the business.

Dr. Chapman has republished Burns' *Midwifery* with notes and a pompous dedication to Dr. Barton.[12] He has omitted the notice

Mr. Burns has taken of Dr. Dewees' discovery of copious venesection in parturition in the American edition. I wish you to ascertain whether Dr. Hamilton of Edinburgh[13] ever advised copious venesection to [...][14] in parturition or even in ecclampsia.[15] He says nothing of this practice in his *Midwifery*. Chapman ascribes it to Hamilton. Find out, if you can, who translated the extract from Pinel's treatise upon madness[16] which was published in the *Medical Journal* or *Review* of Edinburgh some years ago. Dr. Chapman says he was the author of it.

Dr. Caldwell finished his lectures with a most intemperate phillipic against my system of medicine. In an oration he delivered in honor of the birthday of General Washington on the 22nd of February he delivered an equally vehement phillipic against the Democrats. This drew from the Democratic presses a detail of his crimes. Our citizens were shocked with them. They have already affected his practice, but I have not heard how he is affected by them. I have refused all intercourse with him. We are now busily engaged in examining candidates for degrees. We expect to graduate between 60 and 70 of them. Your poor brother John is I hope a little better. I repeat again that I do not despair of his recovery.

Do not fail when you leave Edinburgh to present some memorials of your gratitude to the children of the families in which you have been entertained. They may be cheap but rendered valuable by the *time* and *manner* in which they are presented. A knife, a breast pin, or a pencil given under appropriate circumstances are truly estimable and will serve to preserve your name until a 3rd generation of your father's family may visit Edinburgh. Your mother and sister write by this conveyance. Their letters will be enclosed by Mr. Bond to his friend in London. Your friend Dr. Poyntell[17] is comfortably established in London under the patronage of an uncle. Inquire first for him when you arrive in the great metropolis of the nation. Five of your fellow students, viz., Coxe, Mitchell, Murray, Rice, and Van Breckel,[18] have passed their examination. The last with great credit. Adieu! To the protection and blessings and mercies of the God of your fathers I commend you. "Pray without ceasing," and "in all things give thanks."[19]

BENJN: RUSH

Addressed: Dr: James Rush Nicholson Street Edinburgh Scotland. By the British packet Eliza Capt: Sansom.
MS: Library Company of Philadelphia, Rush MSS.

[1] Not further identified.
[2] Anne Hogg, daughter of William

and sister of Thomas Hogg, described in BR's Scottish Journal as a maiden lady of remarkable literary knowledge.

³ I.e., the former Lady Jane Leslie and her eldest brother, Alexander, who had succeeded in 1802 to the earldom of Leven and Melville.

⁴ Quite possibly the same as the Rev. Mr. Ennis, mentioned in BR's Scottish Journal, husband of Mary Hogg, another of William Hogg's daughters whom BR had known in Edinburgh.

⁵ The Countess of Buchan was the former Margaret Fraser (d. 1819), a cousin of her husband (DNB, under her husband's name).

⁶ Robert Maskell Patterson (1787-1854); A.B., 1804, and M.D., 1808, University of Pennsylvania; studied further in London and Paris; professor of natural philosophy and mathematics, University of Pennsylvania, 1813-1828; president, American Philosophical Society, 1845-1853 (University of Pennsylvania, *Biog. Cat. of Matriculates*).

⁷ Catharine (Harrison) Cappe (1743-1821), widow of Newcome Cappe, a Unitarian clergyman of York; she was active in support of various charitable foundations, edited her husband's sermons, and wrote on philanthropic subjects (DNB, under her husband's name). Her *Memoirs* were published in London and Boston, 1822, but contain no BR letters; there are two letters from her to BR in Rush MSS, III.

⁸ George Pearson, M.D. (1751-1828), physician to St. George's Hospital, London, published *Outlines of Lectures on the Practice of Physic*, London, 1789-1792 (DNB; Surg. Gen. Off., *Index-Cat.*, 1st ser., X, 591).

⁹ Alexander Hunter, M.D. (1729-1809), who practised at York for many years and wrote on medical and agricultural subjects, had founded the York Lunatic Asylum in 1777 (DNB).

¹⁰ I.e., Pluckemin, N.J.

¹¹ MS torn by seal.

¹² *The Principles of Midwifery*, by John Burns, M.D., of Glasgow, was first published in 1809 and was widely reprinted and translated (DNB); Chapman's edition was published in 1810.

¹³ Alexander Hamilton (1739-1802), professor of midwifery at Edinburgh, 1780-1800, published several treatises on this subject between 1775 and 1784 (DNB; Surg. Gen. Off., *Index-Cat.*, 1st ser., V, 807).

¹⁴ Illegible; perhaps "100 oz."!

¹⁵ Thus in MS.

¹⁶ Phillippe Pinel (1745-1826), famous for his humane reforms in the care of the insane, published his *Traité médico-philosophique sur l'aliénation mentale, ou la manie*, Paris [1801] (A. Deutsch, *The Mentally Ill in America*, Garden City, 1937, p. 88ff.; Surg. Gen. Off., *Index-Cat.*, 1st ser., XI, 317).

¹⁷ George Poyntell (1786?-1812), M.D., University of Pennsylvania, 1808 (Univ. of Penna., *Gen. Alumni Cat.*; *Inscriptions in St. Peter's Church Yard*, p. 44).

¹⁸ Swepson Coxe, of South Carolina, an apprentice of BR's in 1809; Edward Mitchell, who died at Charleston, S.C., 1855; George W. Murray, on whom I have no further information; John Rice, d. 1868; and Samuel H. Van Brakle, previously identified (Univ. of Penna., *Gen. Alumni Cat.*; BR's MS List of Apprentices).

¹⁹ I Thessalonians 5:17; Ephesians 5:20.

To John Adams

Dear Sir,   Philadelphia, April 26, 1810

In one of my letters written some time ago, I informed you that my eldest son had killed a brother officer and a friend in a duel at New Orleans. The distress and remorse which followed this event deprived him of his reason and threw him into the Marine Hospital, where he has been nearly ever since the duel. In the month of

February last he arrived in Philadelphia in a state of deep melancholy and considerable derangement. His appearance when he entered his father's house was that of the King of Babylon described in the Old Testament.[1] His long and uncombed hair and his long nails and beard rendered him an object of horror to his afflicted parents and family. No entreaties could induce him to utter a word to any of us. After three days spent in unsuccessful attempts to alter his appearance, we sent him to the Pennsylvania Hospital, where he has been ever since. From the authority of the officers of the Hospital and medical advice properly administered, he is much improved, not only in his appearance but in the health of his mind. Though still gloomy, he submits to be shaved and dressed, and walks out daily in the garden of the Hospital. At times he converses in the most lucid and agreeable manner. It is possible he may recover, but it is too probable he will end his days in his present situation. Could the advocates for duelling and the idolaters of the late General Hamilton peep into the cell of my poor boy, they would blush for their folly and madness in defending a practice and palliating a crime which has rendered a promising young man wretched for life and involved in his misery a whole family that loved him. But enough of this distressing subject. I have introduced it chiefly as an apology for my long neglect in answering your last letter.

I send you herewith a few of Duane's papers. The character of J. Randolph is well drawn and I believe just.[2] I have long considered him as a mischievous boy with a squirt in his hands, throwing its dirty contents into the eyes of everybody that looked at him. A kicking or a horsewhipping would be the best reply that could be made to his vulgar parliamentary insolence. It is only because the body which he insults *is what it is* that he has been so long tolerated. In the Congress of 1776 and 1777 he would soon have fallen and perished with his brother insects upon the floor of the house.

I am glad to find the Anglo-American spirit of Massachussets has received a check. I wish the Gallo-American spirit of our legislature may meet with a similar fate next October.

Adieu! All my family join in love to you and yours with, my dear sir, ever yours,

BENJN: RUSH

MS: Adams Manuscript Trust, Boston.

[1] See Daniel 4:33.
[2] An article hostile to Randolph, signed "Nepos," in the *Aurora* of this day.

To James Rush

My dear Son,   Philadelphia, May 1st, 1810

Your letters of January 28th and 31st and of the 1st of March came safe to hand yesterday by the February and March packets. We were all much gratified in reading every part of them except that which related to your sickness. I hope no cough has followed it. I tremble for your lungs when I think of the cold and damp weather of a Scotch spring. Take care of them. Avoid the night air, go to bed early, and above all protect your feet from the cold.

As your proposal to return next fall originated in a wish to lessen the expense of your excursion to Europe, I am happy in being able to assure you that it will be *perfectly convenient* to me to support you till next spring in London. I shall remit to your bankers in Liverpool £200 sterling by the next packet, and more shall be sent if necessary to defray the expenses of your voyage home. I shall write to you again upon the subjects of purchasing clothes, instruments, and medicines in London. In the meanwhile I shall only hint that they may all be had nearly at the sterling price in Philadelphia.

I did not expect you would be pleased with the principles of medicine taught in Edinburgh. But I am sure you will always look back with pleasure upon the winter you have spent in that city. Recollect the man, the scholar, and the gentleman should be cultivated, as well as the physician, in a person destined to act a high part in the profession of medicine. In London you will learn much, not only from lectures and dissections, but from hospitals and a familiar intercourse with physicians. That great city is an epitome of the whole world. Nine[1] months spent in it will teach you more by your "eyes and ears" than a life spent in your native country. I shall send you by Mrs. Coxe,[2] who sails for Liverpool in a few weeks, letters of introduction to Dr. Blagden[3] and Dr. Reynolds.[4] They were both my fellow students in Edinburgh. The latter is one of the King's physicians. I wish you to see the physicians of the Bethlehem and St. Luke's Hospitals. Dr. Dunston[5] of the latter and Mr. Halsam[6] of the former can furnish you with many facts upon the treatment of madness. During the summer an excursion to Oxford will be useful to you, also to Bath and Liverpool unless you conclude to embark in the spring from the latter place for Philadelphia. Dr. Jardine[7] has requested me to beg you to accept of a bed in his house while you remain in Liverpool. He will make you acquainted with

Mr. Roscoe, Dr. Bostock,[8] and the other distinguished men of that city.

Should this letter find you in Edinburgh, pray tender my affectionate regards to the worthy ladies and gentlemen who have treated you with so much kindness and friendship. Tell them we will repay their goodness in similar acts to their friends, should any of them visit Philadelphia, but if this pleasure be denied to us, we will endeavor to show our gratitude to them by prayers to Almighty God for their temporal and eternal happiness.

Your Mamma and sister write by this packet. Their letters will be addressed to the care of your sister Mary, who will send them to you or deliver them into your own hands according to circumstances. Should they be detained, I shall anticipate their contents as far as they relate to domestic matters by barely mentioning that Robert Field died last week at White-hill, resigned, penitent, and we hope in peace with his God. Your mother enjoys unusual good health. Your brother John is much better, though still depressed in his spirits. We expect shortly to remove him from the Hospital to a country situation near Darby, where he will have pure air, rural exercises, and pleasant domestic society. Your sister Julia is still the delight of her family. Richard thrives in business, Ben is very popular with his master, Sam goes to an excellent new school lately opened by Dr. Grey and Mr. Wiley, and William is at last a senior in Mrs. Watson's school.[9] All the domestics love and inquire after you. Mrs. McDougall has left us in compliance with the death-bed request of Mrs. Anners to take charge of her children as housekeeper to Mr. Anners. Wm. has called a 4th son James after you. Adieu! my dear, very dear son. From your affectionate father, who addresses you in behalf of all your family,

BENJN RUSH

P.S. We created 65 doctors of medicine on the 19th of last month in our University. Your friend Van Breckle graduated with great honor. Messrs. Harrison & Latham have acknowledged the receipt of the bill for £200 sterling I sent them last winter, and passed it to your credit.

Addressed: Dr: James Rush to the care of Dr: Charles Steuart Physician Edinburgh. By the Montrose packet.
MS: Library Company of Philadelphia, Rush MSS.

[1] This word was written over by BR and may be "Some."

[2] The former Sarah Redman (1752-1843), wife of Daniel Coxe and mother of John Redman Coxe (Alexander Du-Bin, "Coxe," p. 14-15, in *Old Philadelphia Families*, Phila., 1939). In a letter to Ashbel Green, 2 June 1810

(Boston Public Libr.), BR solicited the prayers of Green's congregation for Mrs. Coxe's safe voyage to England. See also BR's *Autobiography*, p. 272.

[3] Sir Charles Blagden (1748-1820); M.D., Edinburgh, 1768; for many years a medical officer in the British army (DNB).

[4] Henry Revell Reynolds (1745-1811) studied at Edinburgh; M.D., Cambridge, 1773; physician-in-ordinary to George III, 1806 (DNB; see also BR to James Rush, 8 June 1810).

[5] Not further identified.

[6] John Haslam, M.D. (1764-1844), apothecary at Bethlehem Hospital, 1795-1816; published works on insanity and medical jurisprudence (DNB).

[7] Lewis J. Jardine, evidently an English-trained physician and a political radical, came to the United States in 1794 and settled at Richland, Bucks co., Penna. (part of Pennsbury Manor); returned to England, ca. 1802, and corresponded with BR from Liverpool until the latter's death (Jardine's letters in Rush MSS, VIII; Drinker, *Journal*, p. 260-1). BR's letters to Jardine have not been found. Jardine was the author of a scarce and interesting pamphlet called *A Letter from Pennsylvania to a Friend in England, containing Valuable Information with Respect to America*, published without the author's knowledge at Bath, 1795 (Sabin 35785). In touring the Pennsylvania frontier he said he felt "a peculiar state of the air, which has invariably kept my spirits higher and more comfortable than I can describe" (*Letter*, p. 25-6).

[8] John Bostock, the younger (1773-1846), M.D., Edinburgh, 1798; eminent in several sciences; son of BR's much-admired fellow student at Edinburgh of the same name (DNB; BR, *Autobiography*, p. 45-6).

[9] The *Phila. Directory* for 1811 lists Grey and Wylie's "Hebrew seminary" at 306 High (Market) St. Mrs. Watson, teacher, is listed in the same at 138 North Third St.

To John Coakley Lettsom

Dear Sir,   Philadelphia, May 3, 1810

In the last letter which I had the pleasure of receiving from you, you expressed a wish to know whether our American yellow fever could be taken more than once.[1] To this question I am able to answer in the affirmative. More than an hundred instances have occurred of its having been twice taken in Philadelphia, and a few of its having been taken twice and three times, and one in which a young woman died of a fourth attack of it. In this respect it partakes of the character of the common bilious fever, of which it is only the *highest* grade. In this opinion I am supported by 19-20ths of the physicians of the United States, as well as by the respectable authorities of Dr. Hillary, Dr. Lind,[2] and Dr. Huck. The testimony of Dr. Huck is to be seen in a note in Sir John Pringle's *Treatise upon the Diseases of the British Army*.[3]

I have a son now in Edinburgh, who purposes to visit London in the course of the present or of the next month. I have directed him to do homage to his father's friends in London, and particularly to Dr. Lettsom. He is very dear to his family and much respected by all who know him. I have a daughter likewise at or near Barnet, twelve miles from London, with her husband, a Captain Manners of the British Army, and two children. I have given her a letter of introduction to you. By the antiquity and uniformity of our friendship, let me beg your attention to her. She complains in her letters of her solitary situation. Her father's house has been opened for forty years to British strangers. I hope she will meet with that kindness from you which you have often, nay more, *always*, showed to the natives and citizens of the United States. In case of sickness in her family, I beg you may be her physician as well as her friend.

Vaccination continues to triumph over prejudice and ignorance in every part of our country.

I have lately published editions of Dr. Sydenham's and Dr. Cleghorn's *Works*, with notes intended to accommodate them to the climate, diet, manners, and diseases of the inhabitants of the United States.

Adieu! from, dear sir, yours truly and respectfully,

BENJAMIN RUSH

Printed: Pettigrew, *Lettsom*, III, 202-4.

[1] This inquiry is in Lettsom's letter to BR of 1 May 1809 (Rush MSS, XXVIII).

[2] James Lind, M.D. (1716-1794); discoverer of lemon-juice as a specific for scurvy; author of *An Essay on Diseases Incidental to Europeans in Hot Climates*, London, 1768 (DNB). BR undertook to prepare an American edition of Lind's *Essay* but did not complete it (letter to James Rush, 10 May 1810).

[3] BR was at this time preparing an American edition of this standard work; it was published later this year in Philadelphia, Boston, Baltimore, and Petersburg, Va., under the title of *Observations on the Diseases of the Army*. The first English edition had been issued at London in 1752. As late as 1871 Allibone could say of it, in terms worthy of BR himself, that it "should be in the hands of every soldier, until the happy day when both physic and soldiers are unknown" (*Dict. of Authors*, II, 1690). See BR to James Rush, 10 May 1810, and especially to William Eustis, 4 June 1812.

To Robert Barclay[1]

Sir,   Philadelphia, May 9th, 1810

A tall and widespreading elm tree, eight feet[2] in diameter at its base, has long stood the object of the admiration of four or five successive generations near the Delaware at Kensington, a mile from Philadelphia.[3] Under this tree Wm. Penn held that treaty with the native Indians which Voltaire says[4] was the only treaty that ever was made without the formalities of pen, ink, paper, parchment, or an oath, and the only treaty that never was broken.[5] During the last winter a severe gale of wind prostrated this venerable tree to the ground.[6] From a limb of it I have caused a small bowl to be turned which I have now the honor of presenting to you, not doubting from your partiality to your native state of its being acceptable to you. It is contemplated from the trunk of the tree to carve a statue of the illustrious Mr. Penn and to place it upon a pedestal to be erected on the hollow spot left by the root of this tree.[7]

MS (draft): Library Company of Philadelphia, Rush MSS.

[1] Robert Barclay (1751-1830), great-grandson and namesake of the Quaker Apologist, was born in Philadelphia but was sent to England in 1763, where he remained except for the period 1771-1773, when he was in Philadelphia and presumably became acquainted with BR. He had large business interests and bought the great Thrale brewery in Southwark in 1781. Barclay lived at Bury Hill, near Dorking. (Charles W. Barclay and others, *A History of the Barclay Family*, London, 1924-1934, pt. iii, p. 273-7.) A notation on the draft of this letter states that other copies of it were addressed to John Penn and Benjamin West.

[2] BR should have said yards, not feet, if we are to accept the testimony of Roberts Vaux, who devoted himself to setting up a monument to mark the site of the treaty. Vaux further stated that the age of the tree when it fell was determined to be 283 years. ("A Memoir on the Locality of the Great Treaty . . . in 1682," Hist. Soc. of Penna., *Memoirs*, I, pt. i [1826], p. 96.)

[3] Kensington, now part of the city, was earlier known as Shackamaxon. The Treaty Elm stood near the intersection of present Beach Street and East Columbia Avenue (Jackson, *Encyclo. of Phila.*, IV, 1143). Its appearance is well known from the superb view of the river and the city, from the bank nearby the tree, by Thomas Birch in 1801; see illustration facing p. 781.

[4] What Voltaire wrote was: "C'est le seul traité entre ces Peuples [the Indians] & les Chrétiens qui n'ait point été juré, & qui n'ait point été rompu" (*Lettres Philosophiques* [Amsterdam, 1734], Quatrième Lettre, "Sur les Quakers," ed. G. Lanson, Paris, 1909, I, 48). This work, under the title *Letters concerning the English Nation*, had appeared first in an English translation, London, 1733.

[5] It is now generally agreed that Penn's "Great Treaty" as depicted in Benjamin West's famous painting (executed in 1771 for Thomas Penn, owned by the Pennsylvania Academy of the Fine Arts, and permanently exhibited in Independence Hall) was a largely legendary event. Specific details about the Treaty do not antedate Thomas Clarkson's *Memoirs of the Private and Public Life of William Penn*, London, 1813, the author of which derived his information from West himself. Yet it cannot be denied that the artist, drawing equally on local traditions and his own imagination, brilliantly dramatized on his canvas the whole history of Penn's relations with his forest neighbors. The Shackamaxon Treaty and the accuracy of West's rendering of it were discussed throughout the nineteenth century. A recent article, splendidly illustrated, supersedes all earlier discussions: Ellen S. Brinton, "West's Painting of Penn's Treaty with the Indians," Friends' Historical Assoc., *Bulletin*, XXX (1941-1942), 99-189.

[6] The tree fell during the night of 5-6 Mch. during a "tremendous gale" (Philadelphia *True American*, 7 Mch., and *Poulson's American Daily Advertiser*, 8 Mch.). The newspaper accounts are disappointingly brief.

[7] This plan was not carried out, but in 1827 the Penn Society placed a small marble obelisk on the site, the inscrip-

tion on which is given by Watson, *Annals*, I, 138. Many keepsakes were carved from the wood of the tree. Thus in 1811 BR sent inkstands to Governor Snyder and Lord Buchan (draft letter in Commonplace Book, p. 313-14, Amer. Philos. Soc.; see also BR to Buchan,

8 July 1811, below); and a little later he was himself the recipient of no inconsiderable souvenir, in the form of a chair made from the Treaty Elm (BR to Mary Pritchett, 21 Oct. 1811, copy in Hist. Soc. Penna., John F. Watson Papers).

To James Rush

My dear Son,   Philadelphia, May 10th, 1810

The bearer, Mr. James West,[1] your fellow citizen, to whom I beg your particular civilities, will deliver to you copies of the 3rd edition of my *Medical Inquiries* and of my edition of Dr. Sydenham's *Works*. After having looked over them, present them to that medical friend in London or Edinburgh to whom you owe most obligations and that will think them worthy of being perused. Perhaps a bookseller would thank you for them in order to republish them in London, and perhaps he may give you a trifle for the copyright of them. Do what you please with them, and I shall be satisfied.

Dr. Miller,[2] a graduate in our University in 1808, has just returned from London. He speaks in high terms of Mr. Horne's[3] lectures upon surgery. By the last packet I informed you of my wishes for you to spend next winter in London and of the perfect facility with which I can enable you to do so. During the summer you may visit Oxford and Bath. Take Liverpool in your way home. Perhaps you may hear of some of the descendants of your paternal ancestors in the neighborhood of Oxford. They lived at a place called Hornton.[4]

I have sent you herewith a letter of introduction to Mr. John Penn. He has lately written to me in a manner so polite and friendly as to authorize the liberty I have thus taken in making you known to him.

I have this day purchased a bill of £200 sterling to be remitted to Messrs. Harrison & Latham by the present conveyance and passed to your credit.

Find out Dr. Dunston, the physician of St. Luke's Hospital. He is eminent for his knowledge of the diseases of the mind. I am about to introduce a chair into our Hospital to keep the maniacs in the inflammatory stage of their disease in a perpendicular position so as to save the head from the impetus of the blood as much as possible. Mention this fact to the Doctor. The head will be so fixed as not to move in any direction. The patient will sit over a close stool half filled with water to suffocate the fetor of his evacuations.[5]

Your mother, sister, and all your brothers unite in love to you. Your brother John is nearly well. Richard is advancing in business, and Ben is growing in the esteem and confidence of his master.

I am now preparing notes upon Sir John Pringle's *Diseases of the Army* and Lind's treatise upon the diseases of warm climates, for which I am to receive a liberal compensation. Such publications serve as vehicles for my principles in medicine.

Adieu! my dear son. God bless you and preserve you from all evil!

From your affectionate father,

BENJN: RUSH

MS: Library Company of Philadelphia, Rush MSS.

[1] This being a common name in Philadelphia, it is not possible to identify its possessor with certainty. It is certain, however, that this James West, a Quaker with both mercantile and literary interests, wrote from London an interesting and circumstantial account of his travels thus far (letter to Roberts Vaux, 26 Aug. 1810, Hist. Soc. Penna., Vaux Papers).

[2] Robert Miller, M.D., University of Pennsylvania, 1807, not 1808 (Univ. of Penna., *Gen. Alumni Cat.*).

[3] Not further identified.

[4] I.e., probably, Horley-with-Hornton. See Dr. Corner's note in BR's *Autobiography*, p. 24.

[5] BR is describing his celebrated, or notorious, "Tranquillizer," which he described in more formal terms in a communication to Dr. John R. Coxe, 5 Sep. 1810, q.v.

To Josephus Bradner Stuart[1]

Dear Sir,   Philadelphia, May 24th, 1810

Since my settlement in Philadelphia I have known a great number of cancer-doctors who have for a while succeeded in curing cancerous sores, but who have uniformly depreciated in character and fortune from their numerous failures or from a return of the sores which were said to have been cured by them.[2] I have observed further that most of those cancer-doctors pretend to have obtained their remedies from the Indians of our country, and that they consist wholly of vegetables. The improbability of this being the case appears from cancers being unknown among the Indians and from so small a number of vegetables retaining a corrosive or strongly irritating power when they are dry. I suspect arsenic to be the basis of all those cancer powders which do not destroy sound as well as morbid flesh. It was the active medicine in the late Dr. Martin's powder, although he pretended it was obtained from a root which grew only in the neighborhood of Pittsburg.

Should you *succeed* in the cure of cancers by the remedy you have mentioned, you would derive but a small profit from your labors, for a majority of the persons afflicted with them are poor people. Should you *fail* in all or most cases, you would lose the fair and respectable character you have gained by your extensive education and honorable graduation in medicine.

With best wishes for your health and prosperity, I am, dear sir, yours very respectfully,

BENJ'N. RUSH

Addressed: Dr. Josephus B. Stuart, Physician, Albany, State of New York.
Printed: Medical News, LX (1892), 498.

[1] Josephus Bradner Stuart, M.D., University of Pennsylvania, 1810 (Univ. of Penna., *Gen. Alumni Cat.*). There are a number of letters on medical matters from Stuart to BR in Rush MSS. XVI; see also BR's letter to Stuart of 24 Aug. 1811, below.

[2] For BR's interest in cancer, see his letter to Elisha Hall, 6 July 1789, and notes there.

To James Rush

My very dear Son,   Philadelphia, June 8th, 1810

Herewith you will receive a duplicate of a credit upon the house of Puschell & Screiber of London for £200 sterling, to be used in case there should occur any failure or difficulty in obtaining supplies from your merchants in Liverpool. It is not probable this will be the case. A part of it may notwithstanding be necessary to bring you home.

I refer you to my former letters for instructions how you are to employ your time in London. See! and examine everything curious in that great metropolis of the arts of the world during the summer. Visit Oxford and (if the excursion be not very expensive) Bath, also the palaces in the vicinity of London before the winter. Cultivate an acquaintance with physicians, apothecaries, and surgeons, and subsidize them for knowledge in their respective professions. Obtain if possible an introduction to Dr. Dunstan of St. Luke's Hospital and Mr. Halsam [*Haslam*] of Bethlehem, and collect all the facts from them upon the subject of insanity that you can. "Be all eye, all ear, all grasp" in your intercourse with the citizens of London of all descriptions. Recollect the nobleman, the commoner, the country gentleman, the tenanted farmer, the merchant, the shopkeeper, the mechanic, the manufacturer, the bookseller, the book-maker, the lawyer, the divine, the physician, the apothecary, the surgeon, the soldier, the sailor, the porter, the footman, the waiter, the stage driver, the watchman, the waterman, and the beggar are all specifically different characters and require a peculiar and specific attention to know them. Sir Wm. Temple ascribes this variety in the English character to English liberty.[1] It is certain no such variety obtains in other European countries. The history of one French-man, whether a nobleman, a cook, or a hairdresser, is the history of the whole nation. Nearly the same remark applies to all the other nations in Europe. Even in Scotland and Ireland there seems to be but one species of character pervading all ranks and classes of people.

I regret that I did not request you to obtain a copy of young Dr. Duncan's lectures upon medical jurisprudence[2] while you were in Edinburgh. At a future day that science I hope will be taught in the University of Pennsylvania. I purpose making the state of mind which is proper to legalize testimony, wills, and crimes the subject of my next introductory lecture.[3]

Mr. Silliman's *Travels* through England and Scotland[4] are read with great avidity in our country. They are an excellent model for a journal. I presume they are or will be reprinted in London. Mr. James West carried a copy of them with him to England. While I thus wish to direct your attention to everything that can improve the gentleman, the philosopher, and the man of the world so as to qualify you to mix with all those classes of people who are to be your patients to advantage, always recollect that your first duties will be to the sick, and that the physician and surgeon should pre-dominate over all other human attainments in your character. For which purpose let the anatomical theater, the dissecting room, and hospitals, together with such lectures upon medicine as are valuable, occupy your first attention. A short course of natural philosophy with experiments would be useful to you. I formerly advised you against buying books. But this is not to prevent your stepping now and then into a second-hand book store, or stopping at a stall in the street, and picking up at a *low price* a rare and valuable book. Could you obtain a complete copy of Bacon's *Works* or of Baxter's in theology[5] in this way, they would be a great acquisition to our library.

Dr. Reynolds, one of the physicians to the British king, was my contemporary in the University of Edinburgh. He once advised one of his patients to consult me should he visit Philadelphia, from which I infer he has not forgotten me. Suppose you pay your respects to him with my kind remembrance of him and best compliments to him. Perhaps you may obtain an introduction from some of your medical friends.

I have lately contrived a chair and introduced it into our Hospital to assist in curing madness. It binds and confines every part of the body. By keeping the trunk erect, it lessens the impetus of the blood toward the brain. By preventing the muscles from acting, it reduces the force and frequency of the pulse, and by the position of the head and feet favors the easy application of cold water or ice to the former, and warm water to the latter. Its effects have been truly delightful to me. It acts as a sedative to the tongue and temper as well as to the blood vessels. In 24, 12, 6, and in some cases in 4 hours, the most refractory patients have been composed. I have called it a *Tranquillizer*. I shall shortly add to it a box in which all the above effects will I hope be produced more promptly by keeping the patients in a standing posture.

Through divine goodness I continue to enjoy good health amidst all the numerous and complicated duties and labors of my profession. I consider this as a great act of kindness and mercy to my family from the hand of God, for which I hope they will unceasingly give thanks. Adieu! Adieu! Ever yours,

BENJN: RUSH

P.S. Your brother John is still in the Hospital, but much better. He is deranged at present upon but one subject only. He fancies himself to be possessed of a great estate in New Orleans.[6]

Addressed: Dr. James Rush to the care of Mr: Leonard Street Coxe Mercht: No 40 Lime Street London. By the Princess Amelia packet.

MS: Library Company of Philadelphia, Rush MSS.

[1] "Liberty begets stomach or heart, and stomach will not be constrained. Thus we come to have more originals, and more that appear what they are; we have more humour [i.e., individuality of character], because every man follows his own, and takes a pleasure, perhaps a pride, to shew it"—Temple's essay "Of Poetry," *Works*, London, 1814, III, 438.

[2] Andrew Duncan, the younger (1773-1832), was first professor of medical jurisprudence and medical police at Edinburgh, 1807-1819 (DNB).

[3] Delivered 5 Nov. 1810 and published in BR's *Sixteen Introductory Lectures* as Lecture XVI, "On the Study of Medical Jurisprudence." It was a pioneer American contribution to this important field.

[4] *A Journal of Travels in England, Holland and Scotland . . . in the Years 1805 and 1806*, N.Y., 1810, by Benjamin Silliman (1779-1864), professor of chemistry and natural history at Yale, 1802-1853 (DAB).

[5] Richard Baxter (1615-1691), English Presbyterian divine, was the author of the perennially popular *Saint's Everlasting Rest*, 1650, and more than a hundred other works (DNB; Allibone, *Dict. of Authors*).

[6] An additional paragraph of four lines has been heavily scored out.

To James Hamilton

Dear Sir,   Philadelphia, June 27th, 1810

The trustees of our College are at liberty to apply my donation to it to the finishing of the hall[1] or to any other purpose they may judge proper. I request only—nay, I *insist* upon—no notice public or private being taken of it. Should I hear of my unworthy name being stained upon any of your walls, I shall employ a person to deface it. Tell Mr. Atwater I demand his interference to prevent it. The dread of seeing a record so calculated to feed vanity will forever keep me from fulfilling my promise to pay one more visit to Carlisle in order to pronounce my parting blessing upon our College before I depart hence and am no more.

I am prepared to execute the wishes of the trustees in laying out their fund for purchasing an apparatus as soon as that fund comes into my hands.

All the instruments necessary to perform the experiments you allude to have already been sent to the College. Could the gentleman who is to exhibit those experiments spend one week in Philadelphia, he might be taught gratis all that he wishes to know to enable him to perform them with success. One of my chemical friends has promised to be his teacher.

I wish very much the price of tuition to be raised in our College. Let a *learned* education become a luxury in our country. The great increase of wealth among all classes of our citizens will enable them to pay for it with more ease than in former years when wealth was confined chiefly to cities and to the learned professions. Besides, it will check the increasing disproportion of learning to labor in our country. This suggestion is not intended to lessen the diffusion of knowledge by means of reading, writing, and arithmetic. Let those be as common and as cheap as air. In a republic no man should be a voter or a juror without a knowledge of them. They should be a kind of sixth or civil sense. Not so with *learning*. Should it become *universal*, it would be as destructive to civilization as universal barbarism.[2]

From, dear sir, yours very respectfully,

BENJN: RUSH

Addressed: James Hamilton Esqr: Carlisle Pennsylvania.
MS: Historical Society of Pennsylvania, Hamilton Collection.

[1] I.e., West College, begun in 1803 and completed in 1810-1811; see BR to Montgomery, 30 May 1803, note 1, and illustration facing p. 113.

[2] This is a decidedly different view from that expressed toward the end of BR's letter on Franklin College (to Mrs. Stockton, 19 June 1787), q.v.

To John Adams

Dear and venerable Friend,   Philadelphia, July 4th, 1810

I have no objection to your knowing that by the "great hammer of the earth" I meant Napoleon. George the 3rd I believe to be the great hammer of the ocean. I consider them both as the scourges of the human race, and, in the language of the souls under the altar,[1] I feel disposed to cry day and night, "How long—how long," O Lord, will thou suffer them to trample upon the rights of individuals and nations, and to fill our world with widows and orphans, with poverty and misery, and with tears and crimes?

And is this the 4th of July? What a group of ideas are associated with those words! Patriots and heroes rise before me, some of them just emerging from their graves. They ask the news of the day. They hear of British and French insults and aggressions and of our dismantled navy and unprotected commerce. They inquire into the conduct and characters of the members of the present Congress. They visit the extensive arbor under which several hundred of the Federal citizens of Philadelphia are now assembled to celebrate the anniversary of the day which announced our independence. They listen to the orator appointed by them to commemorate the great events connected with it.[2] They hear with astonishment that he has quietly acquiesced in the charges made in a public newspaper of having committed fraud and forgery, and having exposed one of his illegitimate children at the door of a respectable citizen of Philadelphia. They recover the paleness of death in hearing the details of the degeneracy and depravity of the country for which they toiled or bled. Their looks indicate a mixture of grief and indignation. Behold, they tread back their steps and descend with haste and pleasure to their graves, now become agreeable and welcome to them inasmuch as they conceal from their view the base and inglorious conduct of some of their contemporaries and of all their posterity.

I thank you for the friendly interest you take in the welfare of my family. My son Richard is now in business of 4,000 dollars a year, and much respected by all parties in politics. My son James is now I hope prosecuting his studies in London. My eldest daughter has removed with her family to Quebec, where her husband now holds a respectable appointment under the government and enjoys much of the confidence of the Governor. My 2nd daughter is in England with her husband. My 3rd daughter is now upon an excursion of pleasure in Maryland with her brother Richard's wife. My 4th son is in a counting-house, where he stands high in the good opinion of his master.[3] My two youngest boys are at school. My poor son John is still in the Hospital and still alienated in his mind upon one or two subjects. But happily for him and his parents, he now suffers no pain either of body or mind. I send you herewith two publications extracted from Dr. Coxe's *Museum*.[4] Present one of them to your family physician, and read the other, that is, the "Charge" (if you think it worthy that honor), to your family circle, to all of whom my wife and son Richard desire to be remembered with respect and affection.

Adieu! adieu! from yours sincerely and affectionately,

BENJN: RUSH

P.S. You expressed a wish for an epigram. I shall add to my letter a hasty performance of that kind, written upon seeing the ground under the Presbyterian Church in Arch Street, in which the Reverend Gilbert Tennent (formerly minister of that Church) was buried, converted into a cellar to be let for a grocery store for the benefit of the Church.

> The trumpet sounds; the waking dead arise;
> And Tennent's spirit quits its native skies.
> To his own church it wings its joyful way,
> And seeks reunion with its kindred clay.
> "Where is my body?" cries the reverend saint.
> "Behold it here, good sir." "No, no. It a'nt.
> My body rested under my church floor;
> *That* body rises from a grocery store."[5]

MS: Adams Manuscript Trust, Boston.

[1] See Revelation 6:9-10.

[2] The celebration referred to took place at Peter Evans' near the Permanent Bridge on the bank of the Schuylkill. The orator of the day was BR's old pupil and intermittent foe, Dr. Charles Caldwell. I have found no evidence relative to the charges mentioned by BR in the following sentence. Caldwell's *Oration Commemorative of American Independence, Delivered before the American Republican Society, on the Fourth of July, 1810*, which was promptly published by Bradford and Inskeep, was strongly anti-French and anti-administration in tone, as were the toasts at the banquet. (*United States Gazette, True American*, and *Relf's Philadelphia Gazette*, 6 July 1810.)

[3] Ben's master was the Quaker merchant William Waln (1775-1826); see BR's *Autobiography*, p. 270.

[4] BR's "Charge, Delivered in the University of Pennsylvania, to the Graduates in Medicine, April 19th, 1810," *Phila. Medical Museum*, new ser., I (1811), 115-21; and, presumably, his "Pathological and Practical Remarks upon Certain Morbid Affections of the Liver" (same, p. 87-93).

[5] This doggerel is entered in BR's Commonplace Book under the date 8 Aug. 1809 (*Autobiography*, p. 284).

To James Rush

My dear James,   Philadelphia, July 5th, 1810

Two packets have arrived without a line from our dear son, and a letter from Mary by the last packet without mentioning your name in it. These circumstances, added to an account of your being in bad health about the 1st of May communicated by Mr. Liston to Mr. Bond, have very much distressed all your family. Should your silence be the effect of indisposition, and that indisposition be seated in your breast, let me beg of you to quit the climate of Great Britain and return as soon as possible to your native country. Another winter in Britain, and especially if passed in London, would fix a disease in the lungs beyond the power of a sea voyage or of native air to remove it. If my fears are ill-founded, as I trust they are, you will pursue the course of study recommended in my former letters. We shall all hail your return in the spring of 1811, and we all sincerely hope and pray in good health and rich in useful knowledge of every kind.

At a meeting of the trustees of our University last week, Dr. James was chosen professor of midwifery, and Robert Hare professor of natural philosophy. Dr. James was a few days before appointed to take charge of the midwifery ward in the Hospital. Dr. Jos. Hartshorn[1] has succeeded him as one of the surgeons of the Hospital.

My business continues to increase, but I daily retrieve a few hours from it for the purpose of copying my lectures so as to prepare them for your use or for publication after my death.

Your brother Richard's business is now equal he tells me to 4,000 dollars a year. His industry and his obliging manners have contributed no less than his talents to his rapid establishment in his profession.

Your brothers Saml. and Wm. passed the 4th of July with me yesterday on the banks of the Schuylkill. Wm. spoke of your sufferings from the toothache in the same place and on the same day with a good deal of feeling. While the boys were amusing themselves on the banks of the river, I strolled into the house of an old widow of 81 years of age and heard the story of her life from her. It was interesting. The most instructing part of it was that she had been afflicted with a disease in her kidneys for two years, one of which she passed in her bed; that physicians could do nothing for it; that "God Almighty put it into her head to take an infusion of garlic in mint water for it"; and that it relieved her in three weeks and finally cured her.

Your Mama and brother Richard spent yesterday at Farley, where a large circle of friends attended the christening[2] of a child lately added to Mr. Izard's family.[3]

Your brother John continues stationary. He still believes himself to be a man of great estate and is still cold in his behavior to all the members of his family. We are however consoled with a belief that he is now free from all suffering both of body and mind.

Adieu! my dear son. All the family join in love to you with your affectionate father,

BENJN: RUSH

Addressed: Dr James Rush to the care of Mr Leonard Street Coxe No 40 Lime Street London. By the Clothier Hamilton.
MS: Library Company of Philadelphia, Rush MSS.

[1] Joseph Hartshorne (1779-1850), M.D., University of Pennsylvania, 1805, had been resident apprentice and apothecary at the Pennsylvania Hospital, 1801-1805, and served on the staff from 1810 to 1821 (Morton, *Hist. Penna. Hospital*, p. 500-1).

[2] Thus in MS.

[3] The family of George Izard (1776-1828), of South Carolina, who had had a military career that was later resumed; his wife was Elizabeth Carter (Farley) Banister Shippen, her second husband having been Thomas Lee Shippen, son of BR's colleague and adversary, William Shippen, Jr.; the Izards were living at Farley, Bensalem twp., Bucks co. (DAB, under Izard; *So. Car. Hist. Mag.*, II [1901], 222-4; *Inscriptions in St. Peter's Church Yard*, p. 351).

To David Hosack[1]

Dear Sir, Philadelphia, August 15th, 1810

I shall this day put into the hands of Mr. Humphreys[2] the Spanish translation of my *Account of the Yellow Fever in 1793*, and a manuscript copy of Dr. Mitchill's letter on the yellow fever accompanied with a letter from Governor Colden upon the same subject.[3] They were found among the papers of my old master, the late Dr. Redman, and were given to me by his daughter since his death. The copy from which Dr. Coxe printed an extract of Dr. Mitchill's letter perished in the printing office to which it was sent for publication. I beg you would return the copy herewith sent with the Spanish translation which accompanies it. I thank you for the liberal manner in which you have dissented from my opinions upon the subject of your present inquiries. In the laudable attempts which are now making to improve the condition of mankind, I wish a society could be formed to *humanize* physicians. General Lee once said: "Oh! that I were a dog, that I might not call man a brother!" With how much more reason might I say, "Oh! that I were a member of any other profession than that of medicine, that I might not call physicians my brethren!"

I have lately treated a case of anthrax with bark and other cordial remedies, agreeably to your practice, with success. The inflammatory action in the blood vessels in that disease partakes too much of the soap-bubble to admit of the common antiphlogistic remedies.

Our city is unusually healthy. My wife and daughter are now in Jersey. Were they here, I am sure they would unite in cordial respects to you and your excellent lady with, dear sir, yours sincerely,

BENJN. RUSH

Printed: A. E. Hosack's memoir of David Hosack, in Gross, *Lives of Physicians and Surgeons*, p. 313-14.

[1] David Hosack (1769-1835), a graduate of the College of New Jersey, 1789, studied under BR briefly, and obtained his M.D. at Edinburgh, 1793; he was at this time professor of botany and materia medica at Columbia and was establishing the *American Medical and Philosophical Register*; he later held other important academic posts, wrote voluminously on medicine and allied subjects, and was a very influential figure in the cultural life of his day (DAB; Princeton Univ., *Gen. Cat.*, 1908). There is a long series of letters from Hosack to BR in Rush MSS, XXVII; their tone, as well as the few surviving letters from BR to Hosack, reveals the warmth of the friendship that subsisted between the two men. It was Hosack who in 1812 engaged Thomas Sully to execute the best-known portrait of BR (Hosack to BR, 23 Apr. 1812); and he was also the author of *An Introductory Discourse, to a Course of Lectures on the Theory and Practice of Physic: Containing . . . a Tribute to the Memory of the Late Dr. Benjamin Rush,* N.Y., 1813—one of the most perceptive of the numerous eulogies.

[2] Not certainly identifiable.

[3] On Dr. John Mitchell's account of the yellow fever in Virginia, see BR to J. R. B. Rodgers, 3 Oct. 1793. It had originally been addressed to Cadwallader Colden (1688-1776), lieutenant governor of New York from 1761, and eminent colonial scientist. Colden wrote two important letters on the yellow fever; see list of his medical writings in DAB article.

To John Redman Coxe

Dear Sir,   September 5, 1810

In attending the maniacal patients in the Pennsylvania Hospital, I have long seen with pain the evils of confining them, when ungovernable, by means of what is called the mad shirt or straight waistcoat. It generally reduces them to a recumbent posture, which never fails to increase their disease. In this state they often lie whole days and nights, and sometimes in a situation which delicacy forbids me to mention. The straight waistcoat moreover renders it impracticable to feel their pulses or to bleed them without taking off the greatest part of it. To obviate these evils and at the same time to retain all the benefits of coercion, I requested, by permission of the sitting managers of the Hospital, Mr. Benjamin Lindall, an ingenious cabinetmaker in this city,[1] to make for the benefit of the maniacal patients a strong armchair, with several appropriate peculiarities as noticed in the drawing which I have herewith sent you for your *Museum*.[2] From its design and effects I have called it a Tranquil-lizer.

It has the following advantages over the straight waistcoat:

1. It lessens the force of the blood in its determination to the head by opposing its gravity to it; and by keeping the head in a fixed and erect position, it prevents the interruption of the passage of the blood to and from the brain by pressure upon any of its blood vessels.

2. It produces more general muscular inaction and of course acts more powerfully in weakening the force of the blood vessels in every part of the body.

3. It places the patient in a situation in which it is possible, without any difficulty, to apply cold water or ice by means of a bladder to the head, and warm water to the feet at the same time.

4. It enables a physician to feel the pulse and to open a vein without relieving any other part of the body from its confinement but a single arm. It enables him likewise to administer purgative medicines without subjecting the patient to the necessity of being moved from his chair or exposing him afterwards to the fetor of his excretions or to their contact with his body.

5. The body of the patient in this chair, though in a state of coercion, is so perfectly free from pressure that he sometimes falls asleep in it.

6. His position in this chair is less irritating to his temper, and much less offensive to the feelings of his friends, than in a straight waistcoat.

I have hitherto employed this chair only as an auxiliary remedy for the cure of the violent state of madness; but I have no doubt it might be employed with advantage in other diseases in which a recumbent posture of the body has been found to be hurtful, particularly in epilepsy, headache, vertigo, wakefulness and sleepiness, and from too much fullness of the blood vessels of the brain. The back of the chair for such cases might be made to fall back at the pleasure of the patient or to suit the grade of his disease.

I subjoin to the account I have given of the Tranquillizer letters from two of the medical officers of the Hospital, viz., Dr. Vandyke and Mr. Moore,[3] who have faithfully attended to its effects upon a number of maniacal patients.

From, dear sir, yours very respectfully,

BENJAMIN RUSH

Printed: The Philadelphia Medical Museum, new series, 1 (1811), 170-2.

[1] Benjamin Lyndall, cabinetmaker, is located by the *Phila. Directory* for 1810 at 104 Lombard Street.

[2] The drawing was executed by J. J. Barralet and engraved by B. Tanner; it appears with BR's letter in Coxe's *Museum,* facing p. 169. On p. 169 is the following printed "Explanation of the Plate of the Tranquillizer":

"1. The Chair. 2. A piece of board which is so fixed to the back of the chair as to be made to rise and fall with the height of the patient. To the end of this board is fixed: 3. A wooden frame lined with stuffed linen, in which the patient's head is so fixed that it cannot fall backward nor forward nor incline to either side. 4, 5. Breast and belly bands, which are made of flat pieces of strong leather and which confine the body in the chair. 6. Bands which confine the arms and hands of the patient to the arms of the chair. 7. Pieces of wood which project from the chair, in which the patient's feet are so confined as to prevent their moving in any direction. 8. A close-stool-pan, half filled with water, so fixed as to be drawn out behind the chair and emptied and replaced without removing or disturbing the patient. The chair is confined to one spot by means of staples fixed in the floor."

See illustration facing p. 956.

[3] These communications, dated 27 Aug. and 4 Sep. 1810, from Frederick A. Vandyke and John Wilson Moore, respectively, were printed in the *Museum* at p. 172-6, but are omitted here. Vandyke obtained his M.D. at the University of Pennsylvania in 1810, and Moore, at this time an apprentice in the Hospital, obtained his M.D. at the University in 1812 (Univ. of Penna., *Gen. Alumni Cat.;* Morton, *Hist. Penna. Hospital,* p. 503).

To John Adams

My dear Friend,   Philadelphia, September 8th, 1810

Mr. Denny[1] is the principal writer in the *Port Folio.* He is precluded from introducing politics into it by its proprietor, Mr. Saml. Bradford, but not from traducing the works of whig and American authors. One of his coadjutors is a Dr. Chapman, a former pupil of mine and who owes me many, very many obligations. He is the son of a Virginia tory. After failing in getting into business and suspecting probably that his former connection with me was a bar to his success with that class of people in our city who possess patronage in everything but power, he began to calumniate me.

For this he has been cherished by all our physicians who are opposed to my system of medicine, for "parties," as General Gates used to say, "like armies, receive all able-bodied men." He has publicly renounced my medical principles and said all that I have ever written "is fit only to rot upon a dunghill." I am not moved by this instance of ingratitude, for I am accustomed to much greater; nor can I think so lowly of my writings as he now does, when I look around me and see every practitioner of medicine in Philadelphia, even my most implacable enemies among them, obsequiously adopting my modes of practice; nor am I disposed to renounce my principles in medicine by the censure the Edinburgh Reviewers have uttered against them.[2] My son James, who passed last winter in Edinburgh, treats the lectures given there with great contempt, as do all the young men who have studied there after studying in Philadelphia. They all, I should suppose from what I have heard from them, believe "there would be no great diminution of medical knowledge if that University were annihilated." I have sometimes amused myself by enumerating the different kinds of hatred that operate in the world. They are the "odium theologicum," the "odium politicum," the "odium philologium," and the "odium medicum." It has been my lot—I will not call it my misfortune—to be exposed to them all. The divines hate me for holding tenets that they say lead to materialism and that are opposed to the rigid doctrines of Calvin. The politicians hate me for being neither a democrat nor a monarchist, neither a Frenchman nor an Englishman. The philologists hate me for writing against the dead languages; and the physicians for teaching a system of medicine that has robbed them by its simplicity of cargoes of technical lumber by which they imposed upon the credulity of the world. The last I believe is the most deadly hatred of them all. Cobbett acknowledged when he left Philadelphia that he was not my enemy; he even spoke well of me and said that all he had written against me was dictated to him by three physicians. The publications thus dictated against me in the year 1797 were compared by a clergyman in the Delaware State to the "mouth of hell being opened against me."

It would be criminal in me to close my letter without an offering of gratitude and praise to that BEING who has preserved me from the rage and malice of all the classes of enemies that I have mentioned, and even caused me in many instances to triumph over them. "Non nobis, non nobis," shall be my song during the few remaining years of my life, if years be allowed me; and let all my family and all my friends who believe in the power and goodness of God say, Amen.

I return to one of the subjects of your letter. Mr. Walsh[3] is the son of an Irish Catholic in Baltimore. He was educated in the college lately established at Baltimore by some refugee Catholic French priests. He went to England as private secretary to Mr. Pinkney, and after spending some time in England, Scotland, and France, returned highly accomplished to his native country. He married the only daughter and child of Jasper Moylan,[4] Esquire, a worthy Catholic lawyer of this city, and has since become a citizen of Philadelphia. My son Richard, who has read and who admires the ingenuity and eloquence of his pamphlet, says "it ought to be answered, but that there is but one man in the United States capable of doing it, and that is John Quincy Adams."[5] I agree with you in your opinion of your son's *Lectures.*[6] They will add to your family name, in our country as well as abroad, when the names and scribblings of all his enemies will be unknown.

I know nothing of Mr. Bristed.[7]

I am just about to commit a volume of introductory lectures to the press. They will give employment to the critics in Edinburgh as well as in Philadelphia. I forgot to mention before that a student of medicine in the University of the former city wrote to his friend and fellow citizen in Virginia, "if he came to Edinburgh never to mention the name of his friend Rush, for that his doctrines were scouted from the University in that place." I shall send you a copy of the lectures as soon as they are published. Some of them may possibly amuse Mrs. Adams.

In the catalogue of hatreds to which I have been exposed, I neglected to mention the "odium mercatorium" and the "odium sanguiphobium." The former has rendered me so obnoxious to our merchants that some of them have proposed to drown me or drive me out of the city. My offense against them was deriving the yellow fever from domestic sources. The "odium sanguiphobium" has rendered me an object of more than hatred—of horror—to many of our citizens. Some have said they felt fainty at the sight of my carriage, and others have left sick rooms as soon as I entered them to avoid my company. This species of hatred against me has abated very much in Philadelphia in consequence of the practice which provoked it having become general. I am now the physician of a family, the mistress of which has since confessed that she had often left company as soon as I came into it, only because my presence gave her pain. I was her "raw head and bloody bones."[8]

But where am I? and with what have I stained my paper? Alas! with a worthless subject—that is, myself—but away with me. With love and respects as usual, in which the faithful companion of my persecutions and triumphs joins me, I am, dear sir, ever yours,

BENJN: RUSH

P.S. I send you herewith the second part of the Backerawash of Captain O'Brien.[9]

MS: Adams Manuscript Trust, Boston.

[1] Joseph Dennie (1768-1812) was a Harvard graduate, 1790, who in 1801 had established in Philadelphia the *Port Folio*, the leading American literary magazine of its day (DAB).

[2] Adams in his letter of 1 Sep. 1810 had alluded to the prejudice shown by the Scottish and English reviewers toward American authors generally (*Old Family Letters, A*, p. 260-1).

[3] Robert Walsh (1784-1859), Philadelphia journalist, had attended St. Mary's College, Baltimore, and had served briefly as secretary to William Pinkney, U.S. minister in London (DAB).

[4] Jasper Moylan (ca. 1758-1812) was admitted to the bar in 1782 (Martin, *Bench and Bar*, p. 296).

[5] Walsh's pamphlet was *A Letter on the Genius and Dispositions of the French Government*, Phila., 1810; it was strongly pro-British.

[6] J. Q. Adams' *Lectures on Rhetoric and Oratory*, Cambridge, 1810.

[7] Adams had presumably referred to John Bristed (1778-1855), writer of a bulky treatise entitled *Hints on the National Bankruptcy of Britain*, N.Y., 1809 (*L.C. Cat.*).

[8] "Why does the nurse tell the child of Raw-head and Bloody-bones? To keep it in awe." John Selden, "Priests of Rome," *Table-Talk* (1689).

[9] Part of a series of satires on Pennsylvania politics by Richard O'Brien (ca. 1758-1824), a sea captain famous for his long captivity in Algiers, later a diplomat, and at this time a member of the state legislature (DAB).

To the Managers of the Pennsylvania Hospital

Gentlemen,   September 24th, 1810

When our late illustrious fellow citizen Dr. Franklin walked out from his house to lay the foundation stone of the Pennsylvania Hospital, he was accompanied by the late Dr. Bond and the managers and physicians of the Hospital. On their way Dr. Bond lamented that the Hospital would allure strangers from all the then provinces in America. "Then," said Dr. Franklin "our institution will be more useful than we intended it to be."[1] This answer has been verified in a remarkable manner, and particularly in the relief our Hospital has afforded to persons deprived of their reason from nearly all the states in the Union. As great improvements have taken place in the treatment of persons in that melancholy situation within the last thirty years, I beg leave to lay an account of them before you as far as I have been able to obtain them from the histories of asylums for mad people in foreign countries, as well as from my own experience during five and twenty years' attendance upon that class of patients in the Pennsylvania Hospital. By adopting them, we may extend the usefulness and reputation of the Hospital, and thus contribute to add to the high character our city has long sustained for wise and benevolent institutions. The improvements which I wish respectfully to submit to your consideration are as follow:

1. That small and solitary buildings be erected at a convenient distance from the west wing of the Hospital for the reception of patients in the high and distracted state of madness, in order to prevent the injuries done by their noises to persons in the recent or convalescent state of that disease, and to patients in other diseases by depriving them of sleep or by inducing distress from sympathy with their sufferings.

2. That separate floors be appropriated for each of the sexes.

3. That certain kinds of labor, exercise, and amusements be contrived for them which shall act at the same time upon their bodies and minds. The advantages of labor have been evinced in foreign hospitals, as well as our own, in a greater number of recoveries taking place among that class of people who are employed in the ordinary work of the Hospital than in persons elevated by their rank in life above the obligations or necessity of labor. Exercise and amusements should be the substitutes for labor in such persons. The amusements should be swinging, seesaw, riding a hobby horse or in what are called flying coaches, playing at chess and checkers, listening to the music of a flute or violin, and in making short excursions into the city or country. Perhaps kinds of labor might be discovered for every class of mad people of such a nature as to afford a small addition to the funds of the Hospital.

4. That an intelligent man and woman be employed to attend the different sexes whose business shall be to direct and share in their amusements and to divert their minds by conversation, reading, and obliging them to read and write upon subjects suggested from time to time by the attending physicians. While we admit madness to be seated in the mind, by a strange obliquity of conduct we attempt to cure it only by corporeal remedies. The disease affects both the body and mind, and can be cured only by remedies applied to each of them.

5. That no visitor be permitted to converse with or even to see

[1064]

the mad people (the managers and officers of the Hospital excepted) without an order from the attending physician, unless he depute that power to one of the resident apothecaries. Many evils arise from an indiscriminate intercourse of mad people with visitors, whether members of their own families or strangers. They often complain to them of the managers, officers, and physicians of the Hospital, and at times in so rational a manner as to induce a belief that their tales of injustice and oppression are true. Madness, moreover, which might have been concealed in individuals and in families is thereby made public. Nor is this all. The anticipation of being exposed as a spectacle to idle and sometimes to impertinent visitors is the chief reason why our Hospital is often the last instead of the first retreat of persons affected by madness. "I would rather die," said a young gentleman of respectable connections in our city a few years ago who felt the premonitory signs of that disease, "than to be gazed at and pitied in the cell of a hospital." To prevent this poignant evil, he discharged a musket ball through his head a few days afterwards.

6. That a number of feather beds and hair mattresses, with an armchair, be provided for the use of the cells of all those persons who pay a liberal price for their board and whose grade of madness is such as not to endanger any injury being done to those articles.

7. That each of the cells be provided with a close-stool with a pan half filled with water in order to absorb the fetor from their evacuations. The inventor of this delicate and healthy contrivance (Dr. Clark of New-Castle in England)[2] deserves more from humanity and science than if he had discovered a new planet. Figure to yourselves, gentlemen, the sufferings of persons in a small room from inhaling the fetor of their stools for hours after they have discharged them into a chamber pot! Contrast the difference of this situation with that in which those persons passed days and nights of sickness and confinement in their own houses! But other and greater evils have followed the use of chamber pots in the cells of our Hospital. A Mr. Searle of Salem in Massachussets lost his life in the year 1794 in consequence of the mortification of a wound upon his buttock brought on by one of them breaking under him, and there is good reason to believe that the malignant fever of which George Campbell[3] died in the month of August last was induced by his being constantly exposed to the exhalations from the feces of mad people in emptying their chamber pots and cleaning their cells.

I am aware that it will be impracticable to carry into effect all the matters suggested in this letter in the present state of the funds of our Hospital, but the comfort of the mad people and the reputation of the institution are inseparably connected with the immediate adoption of some of them. There is a great pleasure in combatting with success a violent bodily disease, but what is this pleasure compared with that of restoring a fellow creature from the anguish and folly of madness and of reviving in him the knowledge of himself, his family, his friends, and his God! But where this cannot be done, how delightful the consideration of suspending by our humanity their mental and bodily misery! Degraded as they are by their disease, a sense of corporeal pleasure, of joy, of gratitude, of neglect, and of injuries is seldom totally obliterated from their minds.

I shall conclude this letter by an appeal to several members of your board to vouch for my having more than once suggested most of the above means for the recovery and comfort of the deranged persons under your care long before it pleased God to interest me in their adoption by rendering one of my family an object of them.[4]

I am, gentlemen, with great respect and esteem, your sincere friend and servant,

BENJN: RUSH

MS (in an unidentified hand, but with interlineations by BR and signed by him): Pennsylvania Hospital, Philadelphia.

[1] For Franklin's account of the founding of the Pennsylvania Hospital, see his *Autobiography* (*Writings*, I, 376-9); BR's anecdote is apparently not elsewhere recorded.

[2] John Clark, M.D. (1744-1805), medical writer and founder of the Newcastle Dispensary (DNB).

[3] Not further identified.

[4] See, for example, BR's letter to the Managers of the Pennsylvania Hospital, 11 Nov. 1789, and to Samuel Coates, 30 Apr. 1798. The present letter is an epitome of the humane reforms advocated in BR's *Diseases of the Mind*, 1812.

To John Adams

My dear Friend,   Philadelphia, October 2nd, 1810

Hate on, and call upon all the pedagogues in Massachussets to assist you with their hatred of me, and I will after all continue to say that it is folly and madness to spend four or five years in teaching boys the Latin and Greek languages.[1] I admit a knowledge of the Hebrew to be useful to divines, also as much of the Greek as will enable them to read the Greek Testament, but the Latin is useless and even hurtful to young men in the manner in which it is now taught. We do not stand in need now of Greek and Roman poets,

[1066]

historians, and orators. Shakespear, Milton, Thompson, Pope, Hume, Robertson, Burke, Curran, Fenelon, Bourdeloue, and a dozen others that might be named *more* than fill their places.[2] Were every Greek and Latin book (the New Testament excepted) consumed in a bonfire, the world would be the wiser and better for it. All of them that are good for anything are translated into modern languages. Even their beauties and fine thoughts are to be met with in an *improved* state in modern books. A passion for what are called the Roman and Greek classics may be compared to a passion for their coins. They are well enough to amuse the idle and the rich in their closets, but they should have no currency in the modern pursuits and business of mankind. The fate of Rome has been peculiar with respect to her empire. She once governed the world by her arms, afterwards by her religion, and she now governs the most civilized part of it by her language. Her empire is not less unjust in the last than in the two former instances. "Delenda, delenda est lingua Romana" should be the voice of reason and liberty and humanity in every part of the world.

Our election comes on next week. Both parties are active. Federal and Democratic principles and measures are the *ostensible* objects of contention. But the true objects of strife are a "mercantile bank" by the former and a "mechanics' bank" by the latter party.[3] I have seen this spirit pervade and govern our elections ever since the establishment of the funding system, and hence I have been unable to give a vote for either party since that event so inauspicious! to the morals and liberties of our country. Were I to compose an epitaph for the latter, it should be as follows.

Here lie interred
the liberties of the United States.

They were purchased with much treasure and blood, and by uncommon exertions of talents and virtues. Their dissolution was brought on by the cheapness of suffrage in some of the states, by a funding system which begat banks and lotteries and land speculations, and by the removal of Congress to the city of Washington, a place so unfriendly to health, society, and instructing intercourse, and so calculated to foster party and malignant passions, that wise and good men considered a seat in it as a kind of banishment, in consequence of which the government fell into the hands of the young and ignorant and needy part of the community, and hence the loss of the respect and obedience due to laws, and hence one of the causes of the downfall of the last and only free country in the world.

While writing the above, the venerable Chas. Thompson [*Thomson*] called to take a family dinner with me. He is now in his 81st year. He walks erect, is animated and full of anecdote in his conversation, and speaks of the affairs of his country and of the world as if he did not belong to either of them. He mentioned the name of your excellent lady with uncommon respect. On the characters and conduct of public men he was silent. While dining, he looked around him and said he had supped in the room in which we sat 60 years ago with Ed. Shippen, the first owner of the house. How few men can say the same thing of meals in houses not their own!

My son Richard has in vain sought in our city for a copy of your son's strictures upon Ames' *Works*.[4] Can you furnish him with one of them? He has read and admires them, and now wishes to possess them.

Adieu! ever yours,

BENJN RUSH

P.S. I have now a letter in my possession from General Lee, written immediately after the fall of Fort Washington in the year 1776, in which he says, "I pray you to exculpate me from having had any hand in that dirty business."[5] I exculpate you, with the same readiness[6] that I did General Lee, from having had any hand in the dirty business of the funding system and in removing Congress to the city of Washington.

MS: Adams Manuscript Trust, Boston.

[1] See Adams' letter of 16 Sep. (*Old Family Letters, A*, p. 262).

[2] In this hasty but interesting list, perhaps only two names call for annotation: John Philpot Curran (1750-1817) was an Irish patriot and lawyer celebrated for his eloquence (DNB); Louis Bourdaloue (1632-1704) was a famous pulpit orator in the age of Louis XIV (*Encyclo. Brit.*, 9th edn.). "Thompson" is of course James Thomson, author of *The Seasons*.

[3] On the bank rivalry in Philadelphia at this time, see Scharf & Westcott, I, 546.

[4] A pamphlet by J. Q. Adams entitled *American Principles. A Review of the Works of Fisher Ames*, Boston, 1809. For BR's enthusiastic approval of this resounding rebuke to the extreme Federalists, see his letter to John Adams of 10 Jan. 1811.

[5] Lee's letter, dated 20 Nov. 1776, is printed in the *Charles Lee Papers*, II, 288-9.

[6] MS: "readily."

To James Rush

My very dear Son,   Philadelphia, October 4th, 1810

Your two letters from Edinburgh dated in July gave great pleasure to all the members of your family. We all unite in felicitating you upon the pleasure and improvement you have derived from spending a summer as well as a winter in Scotland. I hope you did not neglect to obtain the names of all your valuable friends in that country in a little book entitled "a remembrancer" which I advised you to procure for that purpose in one of my letters last winter. Do not fail to present it to your London friends, when you leave them, for the inscription of their names with the year and month in which it was done. You will review a book of this kind with great pleasure when you return, and will be able to make your family and friends happy with a sight of it.

Dr. Fuller informs me that you did not attend a course of lectures upon natural philosophy in Edinburgh. By all means attend one in London, if you can obtain leisure for that purpose from your medical pursuits.

By all means pay your respects to Sir Jos. Banks.[1] Dr. Garthshore[2] can introduce you to him. Attend, if possible, his conversation parties. They are I have heard attended by the most respectable scientific gentlemen in London.

Dr. Fuller confirms your account of the dissensions of the Edinburgh physicians. The father of the present Dr. Gregory used to say "that nothing could exceed the malice of rival authors except the rancor of rival physicians." The history of my life would furnish a melancholy illustration of the truth of this remark. I have ascribed this peculiar professional depravity chiefly to physicians' so generally neglecting public worship. By meeting together once a week in the presence of God, they would feel their near relationship to each other by the ties of creation and redemption; and by hearing the precepts of candor, forbearance, gentleness, and forgiveness inculcated by the Gospel every Sunday, they would learn to exercise them, or at least cease to exercise the vices that are opposed to them. There never was and there never can be any real and permanent friendship or harmony between medical nor any other professional characters without religion. It is no less necessary to "peace with all men" than it is to our present and future happiness.

I am now preparing an introductory lecture upon the study of medical jurisprudence, in which I shall endeavor to show its usefulness by selecting as the principal subject of the lecture those states of intellectual and moral derangement which should prevent persons from disposing of their property, bearing testimony in a court of justice, and exempt them from punishment for a breach of the criminal laws of their country.

Messrs. Harrison & Lathem have lately informed me that Messrs. Smith & Robertson's draft in your favor for £200 sterling has been duly honored. £600 *in all* have now been deposited in their hands for your use. If that sum should not be sufficient to bring you home, avail yourself of Messrs. Smith & Robertson's credit in your favor upon his[3] London correspondent. It will not be safe for you to embark before April. Calculate therefore your expenses accordingly. What say you to returning with your sister by the way of Quebec, or all coming together to Philadelphia or New York? Inflammatory and mild remittents and intermittents give me constant employment. They yield to depletion and bark. I have lost three patients only with them, and all with melena[4]—that is, an hemorrhage of black, dissolved blood from the liver. I have called it the black vomit of that viscus. It seems to depend upon the same cause as the black discharges from the stomach in the yellow fever, that is, a secretion of blood. Adieu! Ever yours,

BENJN RUSH

P.S. Don't fail of writing to Dr. Miller of New York. Give him all the medical news of London, &c., &c. He is very much your friend.

Addressed: Dr: James Rush To the Care of Mr Leonard Street Coxe No 40 Lime Street London.

MS: Library Company of Philadelphia, Rush MSS.

[1] Sir Joseph Banks (1743-1820), eminent student of natural history; president of the Royal Society from 1778 until his death (DNB).

[2] Maxwell Garthshore, M.D. (1732-1812), writer on obstetrics and physician to the British Lying-In Hospital (DNB).

[3] Thus in MS.

[4] "*Melaena, Melaina*, black bile, or the disease the matter of which is black bile" (*Quincy's Lexicon*, N.Y., 1802).

To John Adams

Dear Sir, Philadelphia, October 8th, 1810

I enclose you a small publication[1] which contains an account of a new auxiliary or palliative remedy for madness. It will perhaps be acceptable to some of your medical friends. You will, I have no doubt, amuse yourself and your fireside by wishing that it could be applied for the relief of Napolion, George the third, and all the mad Federalists and Democrats in our country.

From, dear sir, ever yours,

BENJN RUSH

MS: Adams Manuscript Trust, Boston.

[1] Doubtless the letter to John Redman Coxe of 5 Sep. 1810 describing the tran-quillizing chair, q.v.

To Samuel Bayard

Dear Sir,   Philadelphia, October 23rd, 1810

The bearer of this letter, the Reverend Mr. Gloucester,[1] an or-dained minister of the Presbyterian Church, visits your town in order to obtain pecuniary aid to enable him to purchase the freedom of his wife and children, for which the extravagant sum of 1,500 dollars has been demanded by their master and mistress. The friends of religion and of the poor Africans in Philadelphia have sent 500 dollars to them for that purpose and have subscribed liberally to-wards building him a church. At present he preaches to crowds of his African brethren in a schoolhouse every Sunday, and to great acceptance. The prospects of his usefulness to them are very great. Perhaps the best mode of obtaining a contribution for the emancipa-tion of his family will be to invite him to preach in your church, and, after he has finished his sermon, for your minister to appeal to the Christian sympathy of the congregation in favor of Glouster's wishes.

From, dear sir, yours truly,

BENJN: RUSH

P.S. Subscription books are now in circulation in our city for build-ing three more African places of worship besides the one for Mr. Gloucester. By the present census it appears that the blacks in our city will amount to more than 12,000 souls. Their late great increase is from migration from the southern states. It will be much cheaper to build churches for them than jails. Without the former, the latter will be indispensably necessary for them.

The late excellent Mr. Thornton[2] of London bought churches and livings for evangelical Episcopal ministers. Let us if possible exceed him by purchasing evangelical ministers and their families for our churches.

Addressed: Samuel Bayard Esqr: Princeton New Jersey. In his absence to be opened by the Revd Mr Skenk.[3]

MS: Historical Society of Pennsylvania, Dreer Collection.

[1] John Gloucester (1776?-1832), was in 1812 minister to the Negro Presbyterian Church at Seventh St. below Shippen (Gloucester to BR, 11 Jan. 1812, with BR's endorsement, Rush MSS, VI); one of his sermons was published in 1839 (Dorothy A. Porter, "Early American Negro Writings," Bibliog. Soc. of Amer., *Papers*, XXXIX [1945], 232).

[2] John Thornton (1720-1790), philanthropist and friend of William Cowper, who describes Thornton in his poem *Charity* (DNB, under his son Henry Thornton).

[3] Rev. William C. Schenck (ca. 1788-1818), who had been installed as pastor of the Presbyterian Church at Princeton in the preceding June (Hageman, *Hist. of Princeton*, II, 105-15).

To James Madison

Dear Sir,   Philadelphia, October 29th, 1810

I have the honor to send you herewith the 4th *Report of the Directors of the African Institution* in London[1] and an adjudication of an appeal connected with the African trade, both of which appear to contain matter highly interesting to the national honor of the United States.

Can nothing be done to wipe away the stain that has been brought upon our moral and national character by the infamous practices alluded to in the *Report*?

Health, respect, and friendship! from, dear sir, yours sincerely,

BENJN: RUSH

MS: Library of Congress, Madison Papers.

[1] This *Report*, read at the annual meeting in London in March, and then printed, particularly deplores "the contraband American Slave Trade" conducted by American vessels sailing under foreign flags.

To John Adams

My dear Friend,   Philadelphia, December 21, 1810

We read of hurricane months in the West Indies. Men of business are exposed to them no less than the West India islands. I am now in the height of mine. For a few minutes only, I have torn my eyes from the tumultuous scenes that surround me and turned them towards Woolaston in Massachussets. I see you in your armchair, surrounded by your family. How do you do? And you! good madam, the faithful companion of the honors and persecutions of your husband's life, how is your health? Do the wheels move gently that convey you down the declivity of age? Peace and comfort from past, present, and future enjoyments to you both! In this wish my dear wife, who is now looking over my shoulder, and all my fireside most cordially unite.

You have made no impression upon me by your arguments in favor of the dead languages.[1] Napoleon would have been just what he is had he never read a page of ancient history. Rulers become tyrants and butchers from instinct much oftener than from imitation. As well might we suppose the human race would have been extinct had not Ovid bequeathed to modern nations his "arte amandi,"[2] as suppose that modern villains are made by ancient examples. Royal crimes, like yellow fevers, spring up spontaneously in similar circumstances in every country and in every age. The adoption of the former from antiquity is as contrary to truth and reason as the importation of the latter from foreign countries.

A bank mania pervades our city. I know not what is proper with respect to the Bank of the United States, but I am sure our country banks are preparing our citizens for a new form of government. They are everywhere drawing into their vortex farms and houses, and thus converting independent freeholders into obsequious and venal electors. The funding system was the "pomum Adami" of all the evils which now threaten the liberties and happiness of the United States. It created our canine appetite for wealth. It reduced regular industry and virtuous economy to the rank of sniveling virtues, and rendered "enterprise and successful speculation" the only mark of civic worth in our country. I would have filled my paper, but my better half begins to nod in her chair and tells me 'tis time to subscribe myself yours truly and affectionately,

BENJN: RUSH

MS: Adams Manuscript Trust, Boston.

[1] See Adams' letter of 13 Oct. 1810 (*Old Family Letters*, *A*, p. 265-8), wherein, among other things, Adams says that BR should be put into his own "Tranquillizer" long enough to cure him of his "Fanaticism against Greek and Latin."

[2] That is, Ovid's *Ars Amandi*, or (as it is more commonly called) *Ars Amatoria*.

To Thomas Jefferson

Dear Sir,   Philadelphia, January 2nd, 1811

Soon after I received your last and affectionate letter, I have been visited by a deep domestic affliction. My eldest son was brought home to me from New Orleans in a state of melancholy derangement induced by killing a brother naval officer, who was at the same time his most intimate friend, in a duel. Ragged clothes, disheveled hair, long nails and beard and a dirty skin, with a dejected countenance accompanied with constant sighing and an unwillingness to speak or even to answer a question, and an apparent insensibility to the strongest expressions of parental and fraternal affection, constituted the object that was introduced into my family. Judge of the distress of every member of it! For some time I was in a degree unfitted by it for study or business. In this depressed state of mind I was unable to discharge my usual epistolary obligations to my friends. Time has lessened the distress I have described, and I have again resumed my intercourse with them. My son is better. He has become attentive to his dress, now and then opens a book, converses with a few people, but still discovers, with a good deal of melancholy, alienation of mind upon several subjects, particularly those which associate with the cause of his derangement. He is now in a cell in the Pennsylvania Hospital, where there is too much reason to believe he will end his days. Could he have been seen, in the state I have described him when he was introduced first into his father's house, by the Assembly of your state when they deliberated upon the punishment for duelling, they would have classed it with the first of crimes and decreed a long, long season of confinement and labor to expiate it.

Pardon the length of this introduction to my letter, and forgive its relating wholly to myself. You are a father ⸺

I am now engaged in publishing a volume of introductory lectures to my courses of lectures upon the institutes of medicine. They will be 18 in number. Two will be subjoined to them upon the pleasures of the senses and the mind, delivered every year after considering the senses and mind. I shall request you to accept of a copy of them as soon as they are published. They are upon subjects that will be interesting I hope to private gentlemen as well as to students and practitioners of medicine. One of them is upon that part of medical jurisprudence which decides upon the state of mind which should disqualify a man from being a witness in a court of law, making a will, and which should exempt him from punishment for criminal or felonious acts.

I send you herewith a draft of a chair I have lately introduced into the Pennsylvania Hospital to aid in the cure of madness.

Have you found leisure to look into Dr. Hartley's *Observations upon the Frame, Duties, and Expectations of Man* since your retirement to Monticello? I envy the age in which that book will be relished and believed, for it has unfortunately appeared a century or two before the world is prepared for it. The Scotch philosophers of whom Dugald Stewart[1] has lately become the champion abuse it in intemperate terms, but it is because they are so bewildered in the pagan doctrines of Aristotle and Plato that they do not understand it. Its illustrious author has established an indissoluble union between physiology, metaphysics, and Christianity. He has so disposed them that they mutually afford not only support but beauty and splendor to each other.

Your and my old friend Mr. Adams now and then drops me a line from his seat at Quincy. His letters glow with the just opinions he held and defended in the patriotic years 1774, 1775, and 1776. In a letter which I have this day received from him, there is the following paragraph. "The banking infatuation pervades all America. Our whole system of banks is a violation of every honest principle of banks. There is no honest bank but a bank of deposit. A bank that issues paper at interest is a pickpocket or a robber. But the delusion will have its course. You may as well reason with a hurricane. An aristocracy is growing out of them that will be as fatal as the feudal barons if unchecked in time. Think of the number, the offices, stations, wealth, piety, and reputations of the persons in all the states who have made fortunes by the banks, and then you will see how deeply rooted the evil is. The number of debtors who hope to pay their debts with this paper, united with the creditors who build palaces in our cities and castles for country seats by issuing this paper, form too impregnable a phalanx to be attacked by anything less disciplined than Roman legions."[2]

When I consider your early attachment to Mr. Adams, and his to you; when I consider how much the liberties and independence of the United States owe to the concert of your principles and labors; and when I reflect upon the sameness of your opinions at present upon most of the subjects of government and all the subjects of legislation, I have ardently wished a friendly and epistolary intercourse might be revived between you before you take a final leave of the common object of your affections. Such an intercourse will be honorable to your[3] talents and patriotism and highly useful to the course of republicanism not only in the United States but all over the world. Posterity will revere the friendship of two ex-Presidents that were once opposed to each other. Human nature will be a gainer by it. I am sure an advance on your side will be a cordial to the heart of Mr. Adams. Tottering over the grave, he now leans wholly upon the shoulders of his old Revolutionary friends. The patriots generated by the funding system, &c., are all his enemies. Adieu! my dear friend, and believe me to be yours truly and affectionately,

BENJN: RUSH

MS: Library of Congress, Jefferson Papers.

[1] Dugald Stewart (1753-1828), for many years professor of moral philosophy at Edinburgh and a correspondent of Jefferson's, was one of the most influential, if not original, thinkers of his age (DNB).

[2] Quoted from the second of two letters Adams wrote BR on 27 Dec. 1810 (*Old Family Letters, A*, p. 272).

[3] This word omitted in MS.

To John Adams

Philadelphia, January 10th, 1811

My venerable and dear Friend,

I thank you for your son's pamphlet.[1] Much as I loathe political discussions of all kinds, I was induced by your request and my great respect for the genius of its author to read it. I thank you for the pleasure I derived from it. It is a masterly performance, overflowing with argument and eloquence. He places Mr. Ames where he ought to have stood in the meridian of his political glory. He seems to have died if not *of*, certainly *with*, the same kind of monarchical mania which raged with so much violence in the year 1776 as to carry off many of our citizens to Nova Scotia, Canada, and other parts of the British empire. My son has given you his opinion of your son's pamphlet from under his own hand. He continues to speak of it in the highest terms.

I was much struck with your strictures upon banks. They have long governed all our state legislatures. A few weeks will determine whether the general government has strength enough to resist the power of one of them.[2] Is there any difference in point of criminality between bribing public bodies and individuals? The funding system was carried by bribing both. The assumption of the state debts seduced the former, and many of the latter were seduced by certificates previously purchased at 2/6 in the pound. Among these Mr. Boudinot and Mr. Ames were so conspicuous that your friend characterized their speeches in defense of the funding system in one of our newspapers in the following lines:

"Pay the poor soldier! He's a sot,"
Cries our grave ruler, Boudinot.
"No pity from us now he claims,"
In artful accents echoes Ames.
"A soldier's pay are rags and fame.
A wooden leg, a deathless name.
To specs, both in and out on Cong,
The three and six percents belong."

How many other members of Congress were seduced by certificates put into their hands for the purpose of obtaining their votes I know not, but the following fact makes it probable that this was the case. I attended the late General P. Muhlenberg in his last illness.[3] During my visits to him he told me that while the issue of the funding system was in suspense, a gentleman came to him and offered him two hundred thousand dollars at 10/ in the pound upon a credit of one year without interest for his single note, without an endorser. Mr. M. instantly rejected the offer. The certificates in the course of that year rose to and sold for 25/ in the pound. With the knowledge of this and many similar instances of corruption soon after the organization of our government, I became so disgusted that I have ever since considered it as *prostituted*. The present legislature of the United States may be innocent, but they are the offspring of vice. They are sons of ————. I will not name their mother.

You say an attention to the dead languages has revived in Europe. This is true, and Napoleon is at the head of the junto confederated to restore and establish them. It is one among many other of his acts that are calculated and perhaps intended to bring back the darkness and ignorance of the 14th and 15th centuries. Cardinal Richlieu created and diffused a love for music, dancing, and other amusements among the people of France on purpose to divert them from prying into the machinations and oppressions of the government of Lewis the XIV. The study of the Latin and Greek languages will serve the same purpose to Napolion and George the third.

Adieu! Ever yours—yours,

BENJN: RUSH

P.S. You say you read novels with pleasure. The late Dr. Gregory informed me when a student in Edinburgh that the celebrated Mr. McLaurin,[4] the contemporary and friend of Sir Isaac Newton, was constantly appealed to for the character of all the novels that were published in his day in Great Britain.

MS: Adams Manuscript Trust, Boston.

[1] J. Q. Adams' critique of Fisher Ames' *Works*; see BR to John Adams, 2 Oct. 1810.

[2] In Feb. 1811 Congress was to debate the question of rechartering the Bank of the United States. The proposal of a new charter was defeated by the partisans of the state banks. See Henry Adams, *History of the United States*, v, 332-7.

[3] Peter Muhlenberg died on 1 Oct. 1807 at his home near Gray's Ferry on the Schuylkill (DAB).

[4] Colin Maclaurin (1698-1746), professor of mathematics at Aberdeen (DNB).

To Thomas Jefferson

Dear Sir,   Philadelphia, February 1st, 1811

I was much gratified in reading the confidential communication made to me in your letter. After reading the correspondence which accompanied it, I acquit you, in your refusal to renew it, of the least impropriety of temper or conduct. On the contrary, I was delighted with the kindness, benevolence, and even friendship discovered in your answers to Mrs. Adams' letter. I believe they were the genuine effusions of your heart, for they exactly accord with the expressions of regard and the opinion of the integrity of Mr. Adams which I have heard you utter a hundred times in our familiar intercourse with each other during the four last winters you passed in Philadelphia.[1]

I was induced to make the proposal to you of reviving a farewell intercourse with Mr. Adams before you meet in another world, in consequence of his having reverted back to the opinions and feelings of his early life upon several interesting subjects of government, and of his having in one of his letters expressed favorable sentiments towards you and a decided approbation of one of the unpopular acts of your administration.

Many are the evils of a political life, but none so great as the dissolution of friendships and the implacable hatreds which too often take their place. Mr. Adams' letters to me contain many affecting proofs of his sufferings from this quarter. The talents, integrity, and present conspicuous station of his son have lately soothed his mind under these sufferings. Have you seen the young man's strictures upon Ames' *Works*? They are a masterly performance, rich in republican sentiments and overflowing with eloquence. In addition to the comfort Mr. Adams derives from the character and worth of his son, he tells me he finds great pleasure in reading some of our late novels. Entertainment from this source is not new to great minds. The celebrated Mr. Mclaurin, the contemporary and friend of Sir Is. Newton, was so devoted to this species of reading that he was generally appealed to to decide the character of every novel and romance that issued from the press during the period of his greatest intellectual fame. Mr. Adams tells me further that he has lately read several of the ancient historians and philosophers, and some of them I believe in their *original languages*, for which he is a most strenuous advocate. He even gives Bonaparte credit for reviving the study of the Greek and Roman authors.

I have lately subscribed for a commentary upon the Bible which is publishing in numbers in our city.[2] The author, an Englishman of the name of Clark, professes uncommon qualifications for such a work. He is a naturalist, a philosopher, a chemist, an anatomist, well read in geography and travels, and a profound oriental scholar. In his commentary upon the 24th verse of the 1st chapter of Genesis, he has the following remarks. "In beasts also God shows his wondrous skill and power: in the vast elephant, and still more the *colossal mammoth* or *megalonyx*, the whole race of which seems to be extinct, a few skeletons only remaining. This animal is an astonishing effect of God's power. He seems to have produced him merely to show what he could do, and after suffering a few of them to propagate, he extinguished the race by a merciful providence that they might not destroy both man and beast. The mammoth, or megalonyx, is a *carnivorous* animal, as the structure of the teeth proves, and of an immense size. From a considerable part of a skeleton which I have seen, it is computed that the animal to which it belonged must have been nearly *twenty feet* high and *sixty* in length. The bones of one toe are entire. The toe upwards of *three* feet in length. Few elephants have ever been found to exceed eleven feet in height. How wondrous are the works of God!"

I shall make no remarks upon this quotation. It cannot fail of being gratifying to you.[3]

Mr. Adams continues to deplore the evils which impend our country from the increase of banks. He considers them as fraudulent institutions and so incorporated with the interests and prejudices of our citizens as to be an overmatch for the power of our governments. They are creating dependence, idleness, and extravagance among our farmers in all the villages in which they are established in the United States.

Adieu! my dear sir, and believe me to be yours truly and affectionately,

BENJN: RUSH

MS: Library of Congress, Jefferson Papers.

[1] In answering BR's letter of 2 Jan. 1811, Jefferson had reviewed the history of his relations with John Adams in the fullest and most confidential manner (letter of 16 Jan. 1811, in *Writings*, ed. Lipscomb and Bergh, XIII, 1-9). Among other things, Jefferson related how he had attempted in 1804, when Mrs. Adams had sent condolences on the death of Maria Jefferson Eppes, to heal the breach between himself and the Adamses. Several exchanges had followed (without John Adams' knowledge), but Mrs. Adams' feelings were not to be mollified, and Jefferson was at length obliged to give up. The entire correspondence of 1804 was sent for BR's perusal, and it is of this that BR speaks. Mrs. Adams' letters are available in *Letters of Mrs. Adams*, ed.

Charles Francis Adams, 2d edn., Boston, 1840, II, 247-60; Jefferson's in his *Writings*, ed. Lipscomb and Bergh, XI, 28-30, 42-5, 49-53.

[2] BR refers to *The Holy Bible . . . with a Commentary and Critical Notes*, by the Methodist scholar Adam Clarke (1762?-1832); this was a work of great bulk and learning published 1810-1826, and highly esteemed throughout the century (DNB; Allibone, *Dict. of Authors*).

[3] Jefferson was deeply interested in vertebrate paleontology. See BR's letter to him dated 4 Feb. 1797; also George G. Simpson, "The Beginnings of Vertebrate Paleontology in North America," Amer. Philos. Soc., *Procs.*, LXXXVI (1942-1943), 130-88.

To John Adams

Dear Sir,   Philadelphia, February 4th, 1811

All the coins are in readiness and subject to your order.[1] At present no opportunity of sending them to Petersburg offers from our city. Shall I send them to you by the post, put up in such a manner as to be mistaken for a small book, or will you request any one of your friends now in Congress to call for them on his way to Massachussets next month?

I have no objection to the *reading* the dead languages being still taught in our schools. Dr. Franklin used to say the acquisition of a language might be divided into ten parts, *five* of which only were necessary to read it, *seven* to speak it, and the whole *ten* to write it. By thus saving the time spent in teaching the *speaking* and *writing* of Latin and Greek, much time would be saved at school which might be employed in communicating the knowledge of *things* instead of the sounds and relations of *words*. Never will man walk erect until this is more generally the case. The human intellects are brutalized by being stuffed in early life with such offal learning.

It is the more necessary to banish it from our schools since the late wonderful increase of knowledge in all useful arts and sciences.

You will probably perceive by the papers that my son Richard has lately been appointed attorney general of our state.[2] The office was both unsolicited and unexpected on the part of himself and his family, nor has it been earned by the least sacrifice of principles or conduct to the voting powers of Pennsylvania. He acquired their confidence by his honest zeal in reprobating the outrage of the British navy upon the *Chesepeake.*

Six banks it is said are to be incorporated in our state, four in New Jersey, seven in New York, and ten in Virginia. Is it right for our state governments to possess this power of licensing companies to coin money? Should the charter of the Bank of the United States be renewed? *Where, where* will the emissions of paper money end? Is retribution to take place by the evils of its depreciation occurring in the hands of the rich to punish them for robbing the poor soldiers, the widows, and the orphans of our country of the original sources of their wealth?

Adieu! From, my dear sir, yours truly and affectionately,

BENJN RUSH

P.S. My son Richard has lately had another addition to his domestic happiness in the birth of a son, to whom he has given my Old Testament name.[3]

Addressed: John Adams Esqr: Quincy near Boston.
MS: Adams Manuscript Trust, Boston.

[1] Adams had requested a set of United States coins for his son J. Q. Adams, who wanted them for a collection in Russia (Adams to BR, 18 Jan. 1811; *Old Family Letters, A*, p. 277-9).

[2] Richard had been appointed to this office on 26 Jan. 1811, doubtless upon the recommendation of his friend John Binns, Philadelphia publisher and an adviser to Gov. Snyder (Martin, *Bench and Bar*, p. 27; Powell, *Richard Rush*, p. 7-10).

[3] Benjamin, son of Richard, was born 23 Jan. 1811; graduated from the College of New Jersey, 1829; chargé d'affaires, U.S. Legation, London, 1837-1841; married Elizabeth Simpson of Pittsburgh, 1849; lived most of his life in England, and died in London, 1877 (Biddle, *Memorial*, p. 249; Princeton Univ., *Gen. Cat.*, 1908; Rush Family Papers, deposited in Princeton University Library).

To Francisco de Miranda

Dear Sir,   Philadelphia, March 27th, 1811

"Per varios casus et tot discrimina rerum"[1] you have at length arrived at that situation for which your talents and wishes have destined you. To lead the van of a revolution in favor of liberty, to remove mountains of political and ecclesiastical rubbish from the human mind, and to make men of mere machines—these, sir, are the sublime labors for which you have panted for thirty or forty years and to which by a wonderful concurrence of unexpected events you have been called. May your success in these noble enterprises equal your merit, and may your name be dear to the friends of liberty in all ages and countries![2]

After thus felicitating you and your native country upon the accomplishment of your patriotic wishes, permit me to solicit your patronage and good offices to Mr. Curwen,[3] the bearer of this letter, who visits your country upon important business to himself and friends. He is worthy of your attentions. Beloved and respected, he carries with him the good wishes of hundreds of his fellow citizens for his success in the object of his voyage. It will give me great pleasure to hear him hereafter acknowledge his obligations for services rendered to him by the old and steady friend of, dear sir, yours very respectfully and sincerely,

BENJN: RUSH

MS (draft or copy): Library Company of Philadelphia, Rush MSS.

[1] "Through various chances and so many dangerous hazards." Virgil, *Aeneid*, I, 204.

[2] Napoleon's conquest of Spain further relaxed Spanish power in the Americas and presented another opportunity to the South American patriot Miranda (on whom see BR to Madison, 3 Dec. 1805). He returned to Venezuela at the close of 1810, acquired dictatorial power, and set up an independent regime; but in 1812 he was captured by royalist forces and spent his last years in prison. (William S. Robertson, *Life of Francisco de Miranda*, Chapel Hill, 1929, II, ch. XVIII ff.)

[3] Doubtless Joseph Curwen, merchant at 21 Dock St.; he was an international agent for Stephen Girard's financial enterprises (*Phila. Directories*, 1808-1811; Kenneth L. Brown, "Stephen Girard's Bank," PMHB, LXVI [1942], 31).

To James Monroe

My dear Sir,   Philadelphia, June 1st, 1811

An uncommon pressure of business both upon Dr. Physick and myself prevented your receiving the enclosed answer to your letter on an earlier day.[1]

Receive from me the most grateful acknowledgements for your expressions of regard. Be assured it is reciprocal. In every situation in which the suffrages of your fellow citizens or the executives of the United States have placed you, I have sincerely rejoiced; and when I have beheld you assailed by the malice of party spirit, I have uniformly borne a testimony (too feeble for your worth from my humble and limited sphere of life) in favor of your integrity and talents. I can never forget your early and firm opposition to that paper system of corruption which originated in New York in the 2nd Congress and which has produced most of the evils which have since distressed and dishonored our country.

With cordial respects for Mrs. Monroe[2] and best wishes for the recovery and permanent health of your amiable daughter (of which I entertain but little doubt), I am, dear sir,

Your sincere old Revolutionary friend,

BENJN: RUSH

MS: Massachusetts Historical Society, Washburn Papers.

[1] Monroe had written on 26 May requesting a consultation between Drs. Rush and Physick on the case of Mrs. George Hay, Monroe's daughter (*Biddle Papers*, pt. ii, No. 208). Their enclosed professional recommendation is missing.

[2] The former Eliza Kortright of New York City (DAB, under her husband's name).

To John Adams

June 13th, 1811

ACT I, SCENE I.

MR. ADAMS' STUDY.

Mr. A: Who is there?

Dr. R: A friend.

A: Walk in. Ah! Rush, is that you? Where have you been these two months? You seem to have forgotten your old friend Adams.

R: Forgotten my old friend Adams! No, sir, that is impossible. I owe more to your friendship than I ever owed to any human being except to my excellent mother and to my beloved and faithful wife.

A: What is the news in Philadelphia?

R: None, sir.

A: What do your citizens say of the battle between Captain Rodgers and the British sloop of war?[1]

R: They were at first much pleased with the conduct of Captain Rodgers, but ever since they have seen the motions of the United States fuglemen in the town of Boston, they have generally condemned it.

A: That is strange indeed!

R: Yes, sir, but it is no less strange than truth. The citizens of Philadelphia have long been in the habit of giving up the right of thinking for themselves. When the British treaty was first made public, all parties condemned it in strong terms, but no sooner did General Washington ratify it than a majority of our citizens defended it, and I well recollect hearing a respectable merchant who was uncommonly clamorous against it when he first read it abuse the rabble who objected to it as soon as he heard General Washington had approved of it. This conduct of our citizens was humorously exposed some weeks afterwards by Thomas Leiper.[2] In a large company in which he dined and where he met with Saml. Chase,[3] he was asked what he thought of a certain measure of the British or French government. "I have no opinion to give upon this subject as yet," said Mr. Leiper; "I will wait and hear what General Washington says about it, and then I will answer your question."

A: What are our rulers doing in Washington?

R: I don't know. I have no political correspondent there, and I believe nothing that our papers say of the conduct or secrets of the cabinet of the United States.

A: What do you think of Governor Gerry's late speech?[4]

R: I have not read it.

A: Not read it! Why, you want not only public spirit but curiosity. Don't you recollect Mr. G. was our companion in the labors and dangers of 1776?

R: So was General Washington's white horse, and so were General Lee's dogs, and what then? But don't suppose I mean any mark of disrespect to our friend Gerry by these allusions. I allude only to the equality in rank and fame of the patriots of 1776 (General Washington and Colonel Hamilton excepted) with those Revolutionary animals. I have not only a regard for Mr. Gerry but the highest opinion of his political integrity, and *this* I once heard you say "was the rarest virtue in the whole world." Tell him when you see him how sincerely I esteem him and how much I rejoice in his prosperity and honor.

A: Are your citizens making any preparations to celebrate the 4th of July?

R: Many of them are preparing to celebrate the praises (not of the men who subscribed the Declaration of Independence with ropes round their necks) but of General Washington and Colonel Hamilton on that memorable day.

A: Enough—enough, my old friend, upon this subject. Let us descend to more pleasant matters. How is your family?

R: I thank you, sir, for your kind inquiry after them. Through divine goodness they are all well except my poor son John, who continues in a deranged state in our Hospital but without any mixture of the distress in his disease which first induced it.

A: Where is your son the Doctor now?

R: About embarking or on his voyage to New York, Canada, or Philadelphia. He has spent a winter and spring in London much to his satisfaction, in a constant succession of the company of physicians, chemists, and philosophers of all grades and characters.

A: What has become of your son who went into a counting-house?

R: He is still at his master's writing desk and upon his wharf, but so correctly has he behaved that his master is about to send him out as supercargo of one of his vessels in the course of the summer, and upon a voyage that will separate him from his family for 18 months or two years.[5]

A: How is Richard and his family?

R: All well and doing well, and now, my good friend, permit me to ask how is the dear and venerable companion of all the good and evil of your life? How is your son Thos. B. Adams and his family? Where and how are Mrs. Smith[6] and her children? When do you expect the return of your son Jno. Q. Adams from Petersburgh? And though last not least in respect and affection, how do you do? How is your appetite? Do you sleep well at nights? Do grasshopper burdens of body or mind affect you? Do you still enjoy a chair in this study? Do glasses still supply the place of natural vision? How is your hearing? An answer to each of these questions will afford great pleasure not only to your old friend R., but to the whole of his family. And now, my dear and excellent friend, I must bid you adieu! Goodbye, sir! Expect another visit from me shortly. I had like to have forgotten to thank you for the kind things you have said of my *Introductory Lectures*. You appreciate them and their author too highly. Again adieu! *R. retires bowing, takes a seat in a hack which conveys him to Boston, from where he returns in the stage to his home in Philadelphia.*[7]

Addressed: John Adams Esqr: Quincy near Boston.
MS (unsigned): Adams Manuscript Trust, Boston.

[1] Commodore John Rodgers (1773-1838), in command of the *President* frigate, engaged and inflicted heavy damage upon the British naval sloop *Little Belt* off Cape Henry, 16 May 1811; the victory won wide acclaim for Rodgers (DAB).

[2] Thomas Leiper (1745-1825), Scottish-born merchant, manufacturer, banker, and public-spirited citizen, was long influential in Democratic-Republican circles and was a close friend and adviser of President Jefferson (*Hist. Cat. St. Andrew's Soc. Phila.* [1], 218-

21; Simpson, *Eminent Philadelphians*; MS correspondence in L.C., Jefferson Papers).

³ Samuel Chase (1741-1811), Maryland signer of the Declaration of Independence, had been appointed in 1796 to the United States Supreme Court, where he continued a somewhat turbulent career (DAB).

⁴ Elbridge Gerry, who had recently been reelected governor of Massachusetts on the Republican ticket, early in June

denounced Federalist protests against the Nonintercourse Act as treasonable (DAB; McMaster, *Hist.*, III, 420-2).

⁵ Ben did not sail until the end of the year; see BR to Adams, 9 Dec. 1811 and 11 Sep. 1812.

⁶ Mrs. William Stephens Smith, John Adams' daughter; she was living on a farm in central New York (Roof, *Col. William Smith and Lady*, p. 277ff.).

⁷ Italics supplied by the editor.

To John Adams

June 28, 1811

ACT I, SCENE 2ND.

*Mr. Adams alone in his study. Enter B. Rush.*¹

A: Aye, Rush, is that you? What is that paper you hold in your hand?

R: A summary VIEW of the physical, moral, and immoral effects of certain liquors upon the body and mind of man and upon his condition in society.² Permit me, sir, to request your acceptance of it.

A: What must I do with it?

R: Send it to the parson of your parish, but if he is "too good to do good," send it to any other person that you think will republish it and cause copies of it to be pasted upon the doors of your school and court and meeting houses in different parts of the state.

A: I am afraid your labor will be lost in this business. The same chain that binds our citizens to banks and lotteries, binds them to taverns and grogshops and to their bottles in their chimney corners.

R: I lament the truth of your remark, but let us remember one of your old friend Dr. Jebb's sayings—"No good effort is lost." The seeds of truth upon all subjects are imperishable. While some of them yield their increase suddenly; others, like the acorn, require centuries to bring them to perfection. The seeds of the reformation of which Luther and Calvin reaped the fruits in ecclesiastical fame were sowed by Wicklif and Jerome,³ and the seeds of all the liberty that now exists in England and the United States were sowed by Hampden, Ludlow,⁴ and others 160 years ago in Great Britain. The booksellers tell us that books that command an early and general sale seldom outlive the generation in which they are printed. The same thing may be said of opinions. The more profound they are and the more interesting they are to human happiness, the more

[1086]

slowly they come to maturity. Posthumous fame is perhaps the only fame that is well earned. Great men are tried by their peers only after the clamor against their opinions and actions has subsided, and after the *increase* of knowledge has prepared their posterity to form a correct judgment of each of them.

A: Stop—stop, Doctor. Your imagination is running away with you. But we will change the subject. What do your citizens say of Robt. Smith's publication?[5]

R: "Where are my shoes and stockings?" said Sancho when he was asked how he liked his government. Where is my pestle and mortar? William (*to his servant*), bring my horse and chair. It is time to take my evening tour among my patients. Good day, sir! *Exit Rush. In retiring he says*: May peace and joy and every form of domestic happiness be the portion of every tenant of this venerable mansion!

Addressed: John Adams Esqr: Quincy near Boston.
MS (unsigned): Adams Manuscript Trust, Boston.

[1] Italics supplied by the editor for stage directions here and below.

[2] This was evidently a revival of the "Moral Thermometer" device BR had contrived many years earlier; see letter to Belknap, 31 Jan. 1789. Adams in his acknowledgment calls it a "Table of Cyder and Health and Poison and Death" (letter of 31 July, *Old Family Letters*, *A*, p. 342). Unfortunately no copy of this handbill, sent also to Jefferson in a letter of this date, has been located. It is to be noted that in the previous month BR had presented to the Presbyterian General Assembly, then sitting in Philadelphia, a thousand copies of his *Inquiry into the Effects of Ardent Spirits* for free distribution (BR to Eliphalet Nott, 21 May 1811, printed in BR's *Autobiography*, p. 296). This may be considered the beginning of the organized temperance movement in the United States.

[3] Jerome of Prague (d. 1416), disciple of Wycliffe and collaborator of John Huss (*Encyclo. Brit.*, 9th edn.).

[4] Edmund Ludlow (d. 1692), Puritan regicide and author of important *Memoirs* relating to the Great Rebellion (DNB).

[5] *Robert Smith's Address to the People of the United States*, Baltimore, 1811, written by Smith to justify his conduct as secretary of state, an office he had just been obliged to resign because of differences with Secretary of the Treasury Gallatin on commercial restrictions (DAB; McMaster, *Hist.*, III, 400-1; *L.C. Cat.*).

To Thomas Jefferson

Dear Sir,   Philadelphia, June 28th, 1811

I enclose you another attempt[1] to combat a greater enemy to the prosperity and liberties of the United States than the fleets of Britain and the armies of Bonaparte. It is intended to catch the eye of the common people upon the doors of schoolhouses, courthouses, and churches. For this purpose suppose it were republished in your state. Bishop Madison[2] would I have no doubt concur in it, for I know him to think humanely and piously upon this subject.

Health and friendship! from, dear sir, yours truly.

MS (unsigned): Massachusetts Historical Society, Jefferson Papers.

[1] The temperance handbill mentioned in the preceding letter to Adams; see note 2 there.

[2] James Madison (1749-1812), cous-in of President Madison, first bishop of the Protestant Episcopal Church in Virginia and president of the College of William and Mary (DAB).

To the Earl of Buchan

My Lord,   Philadelphia, July 8th, 1811

I have the honor to acknowledge your lordship's polite letter, accompanied with sundry copies of your lordship's *Address* to the Americans in Edinburgh on the anniversary of the birthday of General Washington, all of which have been and shall be sent to the persons to whom they are directed.[1] The interest your lordship continues to take in the honor and prosperity of the United States continues to endear your name to our citizens of every description. We deeply lament that the principles of liberty and just government which have actuated every part of your lordship's conduct have so feeble an operation upon the British Court in their conduct towards the United States. We revere the country of our ancestors for what she has done and what she is now doing to check the progress of that formidable power which has attempted the subjugation of Europe, but we deplore at the same time her imitating that power so much as to refuse to do us justice. Liberty, humanity, science, and religion unite in calling upon us to combine our forces and our prayers in their defense. Terrible and destructive to each of them will be a war between our respective countries! Be assured, my lord, it is deprecated by a great majority of our citizens; and in spite of all that British and some American newspapers say to the contrary, permanent peace, friendship, and commerce with Great Britain upon equal and honorable terms is the wish of nine-tenths of the inhabitants of the United States.[2]

My son in all his letters from Scotland mentioned your lordship's name with great respect and gratitude. Accept of the thanks of both his parents and of a large family of children for your civilities to him. They have rendered your lordship's name very dear to us all.

I did myself the honor of requesting your lordship's acceptance of an inkstand (made of a piece of the elm tree upon the banks of the Delaware near Philadelphia under which William Penn held his first treaty with the Indians in the year 1682) from the hands of P. Bond, Esquire, who sailed for England a few weeks ago and who kindly promised to deliver it to your lordship in your own house in Scotland.[3]

In a former letter[4] I mentioned to your lordship that the much-valued box made from the tree that sheltered the illustrious Sir William Wallace, which you addressed to me and committed to the care of Dr. Chapman, was lost by him on his way from New York to Philadelphia.

Receive, my lord, from the subscriber and from every member of his family, fresh assurances of respect, gratitude, and attachment.

BENJN: RUSH

P.S. The sons of your friend Mr. Palmer of Kelso, whom your lordship recommended to me some years ago, are now becoming wealthy. They own a large printing establishment and are deservedly esteemed by all who know them. One of their sisters is the wife of a respectable silversmith—the other is the widow of a respectable clergyman. The latter, with one child, lives[5] with her eldest brother.

Addressed: The Right Honble: The Earl of Buchan Dryburgh Abbey North Britain.
MS: Maine Historical Society, Fogg Collection.

[1] Under a covering letter dated 25 Mch. 1811 (Rush MSS, XXIII), Buchan had sent BR several copies of *The Earl of Buchan's Address to the Americans at Edinburgh, . . . February 22d. 1811,* n.p., n.d. (copy in Princeton Univ. Libr.). The tract pays tribute to Washington and to the United States as a nation where "the perfection of society" has been nearly attained.

[2] On the cover of BR's letter Buchan wrote the following memorandum: "The contents of this letter in relation to the general sentiments of the United States seemed to me so interesting that I sent a copy of that part of it which relates to Politics to The Prince Regent."

[3] BR's draft of a letter presenting the inkstand, dated June 1811, is in his Commonplace Book (Amer. Philos. Soc.). On the Treaty Elm, see BR to Robert Barclay, 9 May 1810, and notes there.

[4] Letter of 22 Oct. 1806.

[5] MS: "live."

To John Adams

Dear old Friend,   Philadelphia, July 20th, 1811

The 4th of July has been celebrated in Philadelphia in the manner I expected. The military men, and particularly one of them, ran away with all the glory of the day. Scarcely a word was said of the solicitude and labors and fears and sorrows and sleepless nights of the men who projected, proposed, defended, and subscribed the Declaration of Independence. Do you recollect your memorable speech upon the day on which the vote was taken?[1] Do you recollect the pensive and awful silence which pervaded the house when we were called up, one after another, to the table of the President of Congress to subscribe what was believed by many at that time to be our own death warrants? The silence and the gloom of the morning were interrupted, I well recollect, only for a moment by Colonel Harrison of Virginia, who said to Mr. Gerry at the table: "I shall have a great advantage over you, Mr. Gerry, when we are all hung for what we are now doing. From the size and weight of my body I shall die in a few minutes, but from the lightness of your body you will dance in the air an hour or two before you are dead." This speech procured a transient smile, but it was soon succeeded by the solemnity with which the whole business was conducted.[2]

Of the farewell addresses you mention in your letter[3] it is hardly safe to speak, they are so popular in our country; but I cannot help mentioning a remark I heard made by one of our Democrats a day or two after the last of them was published. "He has treated us as a master would do his slaves, were he about to transfer them to a new master. As a *servant* of the public, he should have been more modest."

How is it that the old tories love him exclusively of all the whigs of the Revolution? The names of the Adamses, Hancock, the Lees, and Franklin are all more or less disliked or hated by them. One of them a few years ago, in viewing the statue of Dr. Franklin in a niche over our City Library door,[4] said with a malignant sneer, "But for that fellow, we should never have had independence."

There was a time when these things irritated and distressed me, but I now hear and see them with the same indifference or pity that I hear the ravings and witness the antic gestures of my deranged patients in our Hospital. We often hear of "prisoners at large." The majority of mankind are *madmen at large*. They differ in their degrees of insanity, but I have sometimes thought the most prominent in this general mental disease are those men who by writing and reasoning attempt to cure them.

I visited the late Reverend Mr. Marshall of this city in his last illness. A few days before his death he thanked me affectionately for my services to him and his family, and afterwards said some kind and flattering things to me upon the pursuits and labors of my life. I replied to the latter by saying that I had aimed to do all the good I could to my fellow citizens, but that I had been so much thwarted and opposed that I did not know that any of my labors had ever been attended with success. "Well, well," said this dying saint, "remember your Saviour at the day of judgment will not say, 'Well done, thou *successful*, but well done, thou *faithful* servant.' You have been 'faithful,' Doctor, and that is enough."

Let us, my dear friend, console ourselves for the unsuccessful efforts of our lives to serve our fellow creatures by recollecting that we have aimed well, that we have faithfully strove to tear from their hands the instruments of death with which they were about to destroy themselves, that we have attempted to take off their fancied crowns and royal robes and to clothe them with their own proper dresses, and that we have endeavored to snatch the poisoned bowl from their lips and to replace it with pleasant and wholesome food. We shall not I hope lose our reward for these well-intended labors of love. "She did all that she could,"[5] was once both the acquittal and the praise of a pious woman in the New Testament, and pronounced too by those lips which must finally decide the merit and demerit of all human actions. They are full of consolation to those who have aimed well.

Adieu! my dear old friend, and believe me to be, with unabated respect and affection, yours truly,

BENJN: RUSH

MS: Adams Manuscript Trust, Boston.

[1] See Adams' "Autobiography," *Works*, III, 54ff.

[2] This facetious speech by Benjamin Harrison (1726?-1791), an influential member of the Continental Congress and afterwards governor of Virginia, is given in John Sanderson's *Biography of the Signers* . . . , Phila., 1820-1827, VIII, 147, in these words: "When the hanging scene comes to be exhibited, I shall have all the advantage over you. It will be over with me in a minute, but you will be kicking in the air, half an hour after I am gone." Gerry himself confirmed the truth of the anecdote; see BR to Adams, 4 Sep. 1811.

[3] Adams in his letter of 21 June had observed of Washington that "if he was not the greatest President he was best Actor of Presidency we have ever had," as was shown by his farewell speeches to the army, to Congress, and to the nation (*Old Family Letters, A*, p. 287).

[4] This was a statue of the founder presented by William Bingham to the Library Company of Philadelphia and placed over the door of the old building at Fifth and Chestnut Streets (Austin K. Gray, *Benjamin Franklin's Library*, N.Y., 1937, p. 34).

[5] Mark 14:8.

To John Adams

My dear old Friend,   Philadelphia, August 6, 1811

You may tell your friend Mr. Cranch[1] that I included my correspondent among the men who were so preeminent in madness as to undertake the cure of the madness of mankind by appeals to their reason. I have been a fellow laborer with you in this irrational business. But we will console ourselves with the comfortable reflection that we have aimed well. Were we to live our lives over again and engage in the same benevolent enterprise, our means should be not reasoning but bleeding, purging, low diet, and the tranquillizing chair.

I did not hear your celebrated speech on the 2nd of July in opposition to Mr. Dickinson's, but I heard it spoken of in the highest terms by the whigs of that Congress that concurred in the vote of independence.

Your account of the state of parties in New York and Pennsylvania at that memorable period I believe is chiefly just, and your remark referred to in one of your early letters to me has been verified in a thousand instances in our country. You have forgotten part of it. It was—"the whigs have done too much, suffered too much, and succeeded too well ever to be forgiven."

It is scarcely safe to mention Dr. Franklin's name with respect in some companies in our city. An old Quaker tory in walking by his statue which stands over our Library door a few years ago gave the true reason for the hostility to his name which I have mentioned, in the following words: "But for *that* fellow, we never should have had independence."

Do you think my lancet and mercury would have filled Fenno's and Porcupine's papers with volumes of scandal against me if I had not subscribed the instrument which separated our country from Great Britain? I *continue* to feel the malice of the people you have alluded to. Not more than a dozen families among them have ever been my patients at one time since the peace. During the war many of them permitted me to feel their pulses, but it was only to secure my influence with the whigs to save them from banishment and the worse evils that impended them. The services I rendered them by that influence is I believe another cause of their hostility to me. Thank God, I am in a condition not to feel any injury from their unforgiving and ungrateful conduct to me. I live peaceably with *all* of them and in the most friendly intercourse with some of them who, with all their prejudices against the Revolution, are among the worthiest citizens of Philadelphia.

Dr. Franklin's son-in-law, Richard Bache,[2] died a few days ago and has left an estate of 530,000 dollars to his children, 400,000 of which were left to him by the Doctor. The rest were added from the interest of the principal. This immense estate has accumulated chiefly from lots and houses owned by the Doctor *before* the American war. At the time of his death, Mr. Hill, one of his executors, said his whole estate amounted only to £50,000, Pennsylvania currency. Adieu! Ever yours,

BENJN: RUSH

MS: Adams Manuscript Trust, Boston.

[1] Richard Cranch (1726-1811), of Quincy; Mrs. Adams' brother-in-law and a conversational companion of John Adams (Abigail Adams, *New Letters*, genealogical chart of the Cranch family).

[2] Richard Bache (1737-1811), English-born merchant of New York and Philadelphia, had married Sarah Franklin in 1767 (DAB). BR scaled down the size of Bache's fortune in a later letter to Adams, 9 Dec. 1811.

To John Adams

My dear old Friend,   Philadelphia, August 19th, 1811

It is possible Dr. Franklin's estate when sold in order to be divided may not produce the sum mentioned in my last letter. It consists chiefly of real property, purchased in the early part of his life. The improvements in our city have given it its present immense value. It is said the million of livres committed to him to be employed in secret services to his country were divided equally between the late Queen of France and Count de Vergennes. This fact it is said was discovered by Govr. Morris, who was instructed by General Washington to make an inquiry after it.[1] This information was given to me lately in a manner and from a person so capable of knowing its correctness that I am disposed to believe it. The Doctor was a rigid economist, but he was in every stage of his life charitable, hospitable, and generous. In his private intercourse with his fellow citizens he was honest even above suspicion, and from all I have ever seen and known of him I believe he was strictly upright and correct as a servant of the public. I recollect he once told me that a large sum of money passed through his hands for the purchase of stores for the British army during the last French war in America. When he settled his accounts with the quartermaster of the army, he said to him, "I wait now for my commissions." "Commissions," said the quartermaster. "Why, have you not paid yourself?" "No, sir, you see from the statement of my accounts I have not," said the Doctor. "I am sorry for it," said the quartermaster; "I have no power to allow you anything. You ought to have taken care of *yourself*."[2]

I have no hesitation in expressing a general want of belief not only in tradition but in recorded history and biography. The events of the American Revolution opened my eyes upon these subjects. A few nights before the capture of the Hessians at Trenton, Colonel Saml. Griffin with a company of volunteer militia from Philadelphia alarmed a regiment of Hessians at Mount Holly.[3] A reinforcement was sent from Trenton to support them. After the capture of the Hessians, this mode of weakening the enemy was ascribed to the consummate military skill of General Washington. Colonel Griffin to my knowledge acted without any concert with the General. It was altogether a volunteer piece of business.

What do you think of Colonel Jos. Read's name not being mentioned in the histories of our Revolution as the person who suggested the retreat and escape of our army by the Quaker road after the second battle at Trenton?[4] That wise measure gained the victory at Princeton, saved our army from annihilation, and perhaps, considering the desponding state of the public mind at that time, it saved our country.

Time and chance happen to all things as they appear to shortsighted mortals. Fame like money *seems* to be given with an undistinguishing hand. But all is just as it should be. Infinite wisdom and justice direct all the affairs of the children of men. In rejecting history and biography, I wish always to except the events and characters recorded in the Old and New Testaments. They are true because they are natural, for they ascribe the former to a divine hand, and they never fail to mention the weaknesses and vices of the latter. There is not a single Washington among all the heroes of the Bible. Not one (the Saviour of the World excepted) of whom it is said, "To us a son is born," who is styled "a cloud by day and a pillar of fire by night," also "our guide on earth, our advocate in heaven." And who is said to have "disciples." Lay not this iniquity, O! Lord! to the charge of our *whole* country.

When Nat. Lee was asked in Bedlam what brought him there, he said he had called the world mad, and the world called him so, and that he had been "outvoted." That was my fate in the year 1793 when I first introduced the use of mercury and bleeding for the cure of the yellow fever. I lost my character for sanity by being *outvoted* by my brethren, but since they have universally adopted those remedies, I have been permitted to resume my reason. This is literally true. The son of an old tory said some time ago at our coffeehouse that he "believed I had come to my senses" only because the clamor of my brethren had subsided against my remedies.

There is not a single instance of a discovery or improvement in any art or science made by a tory that I know of in any part of the United States. Their prejudices are as cartilaginous or bony upon all subjects as they are upon the subject of government.

Adieu! Ever yours,

BENJN: RUSH

P.S. There was scarcely a single deceased person that was active in our Revolution that has not died poor in Pennsylvania. Witness Read, Mifflin, Morris, Wilson, and many others of less note.

MS: Adams Manuscript Trust, Boston.

[1] Gouverneur Morris (1752-1816), who had been in France for several years, was appointed minister in 1792 (DAB). Adams in his reply of 25 Aug. flatly denied BR's story about secret service money (*Old Family Letters*, *A*, p. 347-8).

[2] Franklin recounts this incident, in his own inimitable way, in his *Autobiography* (*Writings*, I, 429-30).

[3] Samuel Griffin (d. 1810), a Virginia officer and later member of Congress, made a diversion with a body of

"associators" against the Hessian outposts near Mount Holly, N.J., in Dec. 1776 (Stryker, *Battles of Trenton and Princeton*, p. 74; *Biog. Dir. Cong.*).

[4] BR, who was in an excellent position to know, and who had no love for Joseph Reed, elsewhere assigned Reed the credit for proposing the "Quaker Road" route (*Autobiography*, p. 128; see also Stryker, *Battles of Trenton and Princeton*, p. 271-5; A. H. Bill, *The Campaign of Princeton*, Princeton, 1948, p. 92-3).

To John Adams

My dear old Friend,   Philadelphia, August 20th, 1811

The time cannot be very distant when you and I must both sleep with our fathers. The distinguished figure you have made in life and the high offices you have filled will render your removal from the world an object of universal attention. Suppose you avail yourself while in health of the sensibility which awaits the public mind to your character soon after your death[1] by leaving behind you a posthumous address to the citizens of the United States, in which shall be inculcated all those great national,[2] social, domestic, and religious virtues which alone can make a people free, great, and happy. You will not be suspected of insincerity nor of selfishness in this address, for no one can suspect you of sinning in the grave nor of aiming at any honor or profit by it. In such a performance you may lay the foundation of national happiness *only* in religion, not by leaving it doubtful "whether morals can exist without it," but by asserting that without religion morals are the effects of causes as purely physical as pleasant breezes and fruitful seasons. Under this head may be included public worship and the observance of the Sabbath, with which national prosperity has³ always been intimately connected. Recollect here your definition of a New Englander given to one of your friends in Amsterdam. It was: "He is a meeting-going animal." This is strictly true of the whole human race. Man is naturally as much a praying or worshiping animal as he is a social or a domestic animal, and the same perversion of the natural state of his mind takes place when he ceases to worship a being or an object of some kind as when he lives in solitude or in a state of celibacy. Next to the duties nations owe to the Supreme Being may be inculcated the influence of early marriage and fidelity to the marriage bed upon public happiness. Much may be said to discourage the use of ardent spirits and to lessen the number of taverns and grocery stores, both of which are sapping the virtue of our country. The influence of female education upon morals, taste, and patriotism should not be passed over in silence. In exposing the evils of funding systems and banks, summon all the fire of your genius as it blazed forth on the 2nd of July in the year 1776 upon the floor of Congress. The benefits of free schools should not be overlooked. Indeed, suffrage in my opinion should never be permitted to a man that could not write or read. I have only hinted at a few of the subjects that an address such as I have mentioned should embrace. Be assured it will be well received. You stand nearly alone in the history of our public men in never having had your *integrity* called in question or even suspected. Friends and enemies agree in believing you to be an honest man. I fancy I hear a cry for a sight⁴ of your voice from the tomb such as was excited by Mark Anthony for the reading of Caesar's will. I behold the venerable patriots of 1776 bedewing it with tears of gratitude and affection, while their descendants, old and young, male and female, Federalists and Democrats, all unite in honoring and admiring their early, their uniform, their upright, and their posthumous father and friend.

Perhaps the less that is said about *forms* of government the better. It may be sufficient barely to declare that the virtues recommended are indispensably necessary to the existence of a REPUBLIC, and that the vices that are opposed to them necessarily lead to anarchy, monarchy, and despotism.

Excuse the liberty I have taken in the subject I have chosen for this letter. Your name and fame have always been dear to me. I wish you to survive yourself for ages in the veneration, esteem, and affection of your fellow citizens and to be useful to them even in the grave. None but those persons who knew you in the years 1774, 1775, and 1776 will ever know how great a debt the United States owe to your talents, knowledge, unbending firmness, and intrepid patriotism. Adieu! Ever yours,

BENJN: RUSH

MS: Adams Manuscript Trust, Boston.

[1] Both the thought and structure of this passage are confused. BR first wrote: "the sensibility of the public mind to your character. . . ." He perhaps meant: "the keen interest with which the public will await a posthumous statement by you," but he seems to have become entangled in several related ideas.

[2] So punctuated by BR, but the comma should probably be omitted, because "national" evidently qualifies all three adjectives that follow and is not parallel with them.

[3] MS: "have."
[4] Thus in MS.

To Josephus Bradner Stuart

Dear Sir, Philadelphia, August 24th, 1811

Ancient history informs us that a certain great conqueror, after having planned schemes for subduing several of his neighboring nations, was asked what he intended to do afterward. "Sit down," said he, "and enjoy life." "Why can't you do that now?" said his friend. You say you are a partner in a business which brings in between 7 and 8,000 dollars a year. What can you expect or wish for beyond that income after all the supposed spoils in knowledge which the battles and hospitals of Spain and Portugal might afford you?[1] Sit down *now*, my friend. Enjoy the establishment God has given you, and be thankful and happy.

Were your situation less agreeable and your business less respectable, I would advise you against your contemplated enterprise. The practice of surgery in the British hospitals I believe is altogether empirical. Much as you would see there, you would probably learn but little. Besides, you would be considered by the British surgeons as an interloper, and probably be treated by them with neglect or contempt, for it is now a part of the British national character to hate an American. Your notes of Dr. Physick's lectures probably contain more knowledge than you would acquire, even under the most favorable circumstances in which you could visit the present theater of war, in the course of two or three years.

All your communications upon medical subjects afford me pleasure. Adieu!

Health, respect, and friendship from, dear sir, yours truly,

BENJ'N RUSH

Printed: Medical News, LX (1892), 498.

[1] In a letter of 20 Aug. 1811, Stuart had asked advice on his proposal to serve for a time in the British military hospitals in Portugal and Spain (Rush MSS, XVI).

To Thomas Jefferson

My dear old Friend,   Philadelphia, August 26, 1811

I sit down thus early to answer your pleasant and friendly letter from your Forest with a desire to administer to your relief from your present indisposition.[1] There shall not be a single theory in my prescriptions, and what will be more grateful to you, all of them shall be derived from the resources of empiricism.—The following remedies have been found useful in similar cases. I shall begin with the most simple and apparently the most feeble, and afterwards mention such as are of a more active nature.

1. A piece of calico or small bodies of cotton worn constantly upon the affected parts. 2. Bruised rolls of sulphur quilted into pieces of muslin and used in like manner. 3. Friction upon the parts affected, with a *dry* hand, or 4. with a flesh brush or a piece of coarse linen or woolen cloth. Or 5. drawing an iron comb, or three or four forks over the parts affected so as gently to irritate the skin. This is not a substitute for Perkins' points,[2] but preferable to them. 6. Bathing the affected parts twice a day with a liniment composed by adding two ounces of scraped Castile or Venice soap, an ounce of camphor, half an ounce of opium, and two drams of solid volative salt to a quart of spirit of any kind; or 7. with a pint of spirit of any kind in which a tablespoonful of Cayenne pepper has been mixed; or 8. with equal parts of the spirit of hartshorn and sweet oil; or 9. equal parts of the spirit of turpentine and sweet oil. 10. The warm bath. These applications may all be used with safety in the order in which they are mentioned.

The famous Admiral Wager[3] was once indisposed with a fever. His naval surgeon prescribed bathing his feet in warm water and some other *external* remedies, and then proposed sending him a dose of physic. "No, no," said the Admiral. "Doctor, you may batter my hulk as much as you please, but you shan't board me." If you have no objection to being "boarded" by medicine, I will add to the remedies that have been mentioned two or three to be taken internally. 1. From ten to thirty drops of the spirit of turpentine three times a day in a little syrup or molasses. Increase them gradually. 2. From one to three teaspoonsful of the volatile tincture of gum guajacum[4] in the same vehicle as the turpentine. 3. A quart of a tea made of the sassafras root taken in the course of a day. They may be taken in succession and rotation.

I fully agree with you in your opinions upon the subject of the coincidence of decay in the mental faculties with the bodily organs. It is to be lamented that the former is not as perceptible as the latter, and that we are so apt to mistake the continuance of *early* memory for correct reason. I wait only for the arrival of my 3rd son, whom I expect with every tide from Europe where he has spent two years in completing his studies in medicine, to retire to the background of my profession. I have two beacons constantly before my eyes to warn me to quicken my steps to the shade of life. These were two physicians of this city who lived to a great age and who made the ears of their patients sore with their details of the exploits of their children and grandchildren. I think I have observed that the infirmities of old age do not unfit a man so much for study as for company or business. There is time in writing for the tardy powers of the mind to act with their usual vigor and correctness, which is not the case in the former situations. Under the influence of this belief, I have begun to prepare my lectures for publication.[5] I have several motives for leaving a copy of these lectures to the public. One of them is to justify myself from the imputations which have been so liberally cast upon me from partial and imperfect views of my system of medicine. When read in toto, they will I hope vindicate my name from the calumnies which the malice of my brethren and the revenge of the tories have heaped upon it. "The whigs have done too much, suffered too much, sacrificed too much, and succeeded too well," says Mr. Jno. Adams in a letter I lately received from him, "ever to be forgiven." Hence the revenge of the tories to which I have alluded.

Our country has twice declared itself independent of Great Britain, once in 1776 and again in 1800. In the former year the legislatures, the bench, the bar, and the clergy were nearly all *united* in producing that event. In the latter year the legislatures, the bench, the bar, and the clergy were nearly all *opposed* to it. It was effected chiefly by the people, without concert, without system, and in many places without leaders. Are we upon the eve of a declaration of our independence upon G. Britain being repeated a third time, not by the pen or by a general suffrage, but by the mouths of our cannon?—But whither am I hurried? Away—away with the loathsome subject of politics! I was surprised into it by mentioning one of the motives for spending the old age which it has pleased God to give me in preparing my lectures for the press.

Adieu! my dear old friend of 1775. May health and peace be your portions during the residue of your life! and Heaven your happiness to all eternity. From yours truly and affectionately,

BENJN: RUSH

P.S. Recollect—all the remedies I have prescribed for your rheumatism are founded upon your saying it is *without* fever.

MS: Library of Congress, Jefferson Papers.

[1] Jefferson had written to BR on 17 Aug. from Poplar Forest, his retreat near Lynchburg; the letter contained general observations on old age, and particular ones on a rheumatic complaint Jefferson was suffering from (*Writings*, ed. Lipscomb and Bergh, XIII, 74-7).

[2] This is the sole reference by BR I have noted to perhaps the most famous quack device in American medical history. "Perkins' Patent Tractors" were the invention of Elisha Perkins (1741-1799), of Connecticut, who first brought them forward in 1795 and who enjoyed, with his son Benjamin, phenomenal success in selling them here and abroad as a galvanic cure for a great variety of disorders (DAB; Oliver Wendell Holmes' first lecture on "Homoeopathy and Its Kindred Delusions," 1842, in *Currents and Counter-Currents in Medical Science*, Boston, 1861, p. 73-101).

[3] Sir Charles Wager (1666-1743), who achieved fame and wealth in England's wars against France and served as first lord of the admiralty, 1733-1742 (DNB).

[4] The resin of the West Indies guaiacum tree or lignum vitae; for its medical uses in BR's time, see Coxe's *Amer. Dispensatory*, 1825, p. 308-9.

[5] This project was never carried to completion.

To John Adams

My dear Friend,   Philadelphia, September 4, 1811

I am two letters in your debt. To the last I shall reply first.

I am not satisfied with any one of your objections[1] to my proposal of a posthumous address from you to the citizens of the United States. The "good that men do lives after them"; the evil they have done, or the evil that has been unjustly imputed to them, generally descends into the grave with them. I have lately met with a most furious attack upon the character of the celebrated Mr. Baxter written too immediately after his death. This libel has died a natural death without affecting the real character of Mr. Baxter with posterity. He is justly considered as one of the greatest and best men England ever produced. His creed in religion embraced both the Calvanist and Arminian principles. Even the great and good Dr. Sydenham did not escape the envy and malice of his contemporary physicians. Their writings have perished. His name will live to the end of time. A library might be composed of the books written against Luther, Calvin, Whitefield, and Westley [*Wesley*]. Where are those books *now*? And who presumes at this day to call in question the integrity or the great achievements of those men in reforming and benefiting the world? Who now opposes to their benevolent exploits the infirmities of their tempers or trifling indiscretions in their conduct? I have heard booksellers say that a book which is well received when it is first published seldom commands a durable sale, and that *stock* books, as they call them, generally lie for years upon the shelves before they become known, after which they acquire a fame and currency which grow with time. The same remark may be applied to public men. Washington is probably the only exception to it that is to be met with in common times. He was devoured as soon as he came from the press, and he will probably descend like a stock book with increasing reputation to the latest posterity. Titus, Trajan, and Alfred have been equally dear to their contemporaries and to subsequent generations in ancient times. Perhaps it was because they were rather *good* than *great*, for great virtues are less envied and hated than great talents, and seldom stand in the way of the pretensions of contemporaries to public stations and fame.

No hand but your own must compose your voice from the tomb. Your style is bold, original, occasionally brilliant, and at all times full of nerve. There is not a redundant word in it. It is the artillery of language. Your son when he returns may review your address and give it the touches of modern grammar and order, but with all his genius and taste in composition, in which he is unrivaled in our country, he will not be able to render it more impressive upon your fellow citizens.

Had the scribblers who now fill the Boston prints with abusive publications against you known you in 1774, 1775, and 1776; had they heard you unfold the secret causes and the certain consequences of the American Revolution, and particularly *one* of its causes, viz., the monopoly of commerce and the future empire of the ocean by

G. Britain; had they heard your uniform testimony in favor of republican forms of government, and that long before your letter to Mr. Wythe[2] was published; had they heard the moderation with which you treated both the foreign and domestic enemies of our country, and that at a time too when you were preeminently obnoxious to both of them; had they heard your bold and eloquent speeches in favor of independence; and did they trace all their present liberty, their superb city houses, their splendid villas, and their bank and insurance stock in part to those exploits of your wisdom and patriotism, they would blush at their ingratitude and implore your forgiveness before you were removed forever from their sight.

Now for your first letter.[3] The memoirs of your life as far as they relate to your property have been read with great interest by all my family. A Mr. Richardson[4] from Charleston visited me a few days ago. He spoke with great delight of a day he spent at your house at Quincy a few weeks ago, and gave you great credit for your cheerfulness, and many pleasant anecdotes of the eventful years of the Revolution. He told me among other things that Governor Gerry, who introduced him to you, acquiesced in the correctness of B. Harrison's speech to him upon their subscribing the Declaration of Independence. Mr. Richardson mixed with both parties in Boston, and assured me that with all the complaints he heard from one party against your present conduct he did not hear a whisper unfavorable to your integrity in public or private life. On the contrary, he often heard you pronounced to be "one of the honestest of men." He added further that both friends and enemies agreed that you were certainly possessed of an estate that was valued from 80 to 100,000 dollars. All my family heard this with very great pleasure.

On the 26th of last month, Mr. Thos. Fitzsimons added a unit to the catalogue of our departed Revolutionary worthies. He died of a broken heart, induced not so much by great losses as by the unkindness of the persons by whom he sustained them. He lent 160,000 dollars to the late Robt. Morris, not a dollar of which was ever repaid. It was my affliction to see the gradual decay of his body and mind. I loved him sincerely and have deplored his death, for he was my uniform friend. In my last visits to him he now and then spoke of you, and always with a tribute of homage to the purity of your intentions in all the public acts of your life.

Not a word must be said of the military anecdotes of Colonel Griffin and Colonel Reed mentioned in one of my late letters to you

—no, not even to your brother-in-law Mr. Cranch, nor to any other of your public or private friends.

What a striking comment upon military history are the two letters of Commodore Rodgers and Captain Bingham![5] A similar comment may be seen in Sully's account of the immense difference in the details of a battle fought by Henry the 4th of France with Henry the 3rd which were communicated to the former by his officers after his retreat from the field in consequence of being wounded in the early stage of the battle.

I have read Mr. Cranch's letter to Mr. Norton[6] and have since put it into the hands of Mr. Wharton at your request. Mr. Cranch's theory is ingenious, but my friend Wharton I am sure will not adopt it. He has long considered London as the headquarters of Antichrist.

Adieu! my dear friend. With love to all who daily surround your pleasant and hospitable board, in which all my family join, I am, dear sir, your grateful and affectionate friend,

BENJN RUSH

P.S. I think I have observed that *integrity* in the conduct of both the living and the dead takes a stronger hold of the human heart than any other virtue. It is placed before mercy by the name of *justice* in the Scriptures, and *just* men are in many parts of the inspired writings placed upon very high ground. It is right it should be so. The world stands in more need of justice than charity, and indeed it is the want of justice that renders charity everywhere so necessary. The opposite vice to integrity is like the fly in the pot of ointment. It spoils a host of virtues. By integrity I mean not only justice as to matters of meum et tuum, but veracity, fidelity to promises, and a strict coincidence between thoughts, words, and actions.

MS: Adams Manuscript Trust, Boston.

[1] As set forth in Adams' remarkable letter of 28 Aug. 1811 (*Old Family Letters*, *A*, p. 352-8), which should be read entire in connection with BR's appeal. Adams, who pronounced BR's letter of 20 Aug. "the most serious and solemn one I ever received in my life," gave fifteen reasons why he could not compose an address to his countrymen, and ended by urging BR to compose such an address *for* him.

[2] *Thoughts on Government*, 1776; see BR to Adams, 21 Feb. 1789.
[3] Dated 25 Aug. 1811 (*Old Family Letters*, *A*, p. 347-51).
[4] Probably John Smythe Richardson (1777-1850), at this time attorney general of South Carolina and afterwards for many years a judge (*Lamb's Biographical Dictionary of the United States*, Boston, 1900-1903).
[5] I.e., the reports by the opposing

commanders in the affair of the *President* and the *Little Belt*; see BR to Adams, 13 June 1811.

[6] Richard Cranch Norton (1790-1821), grandson of Richard Cranch and

grandnephew of the Adamses (*Old Family Letters, A*, p. 295, 398; Abigail Adams, *New Letters*, genealogical chart of the Cranch family).

To John Adams

My dear Sir,   Philadelphia, September 20th, 1811

I shall begin my letter by replying to your daughter's. I prefer giving my opinion and advice in her case in this way. You and Mrs. Adams may communicate it gradually and in such a manner as will be least apt to distress and alarm her.[1]

After the experience of more than 50 years in cases similar to hers, I must protest against all local applications and internal medicines for her relief. They now and then cure, but in 19 cases out of 20 in tumors in the *breast* they do harm or suspend the disease until it passes beyond that time in which the only radical remedy is ineffectual. This remedy is the knife. From her account of the *moving* state of the tumor, it is now in a proper situation for the operation. Should she wait till it suppurates or even inflames much, it may be too late. The pain of the operation is much less than her fears represent it to be. I write this from experience, having about two years ago had a tumor of perhaps a larger size cut out by Dr. Physick from my neck. I was surprised when the Doctor's assistant told me the operation was finished, and could not help saying after Caesar when he had finished his conquests, "And is this all?" I repeat again, let there be no delay in flying to the knife. Her time of life calls for expedition in this business, for tumors such as hers tend much more rapidly to cancer after 45 than in more early life. I sincerely sympathize with her and with you and your dear Mrs. Adams in this family affliction, but it will be but for a few minutes if she submit to have it extirpated, and if not, it will probably be a source of distress and pain to you all for years to come. It shocks me to think of the consequences of procrastination in her case.

And now for your letter. It is like all your others. My son has just now snatched it from before me and taken it next door to read it to his wife, who feasts upon all your letters. I have good reason to believe as you do of Mr. Whitefield's sensibility to scandal, notwithstanding the speech your friend told you he made when interrogated upon that subject. I once mentioned to him a reflection Lord Hillsborough[2] had the day before made upon him and the

Methodists to Mr. Deberdt when I was in London. He instantly started from his chair, walked hastily up and down his room, and showed other marks of great emotion. "What does the man mean," said he, "by saying the Court has treated me with neglect? Have they not encouraged Foot to expose me upon the stage?[3] Is not this persecution? Yes, they have done everything to injure me that the laws have permitted them to do." In my occasional visits to him, I perceived other marks of his feeling for honor and character besides the one I have mentioned. I well recollect too that he now and then spoke of the men that had opposed and injured him as other folks write of their political and medical enemies. If this does not justify, it may serve at least to palliate their conduct, for with all Mr. W.'s infirmities of temper, I have always believed him to be a truly good man.

I am sorry your income is not equal to Mr. Richardson's account of it, but I am glad to find it is derived from terra firma. Our banks have not only depreciated gold and silver, but many of them by their failures and counterfeits have injured hundreds of our citizens. The stock of the Bank of the United States, which sold a few months ago at 148, is now dull at 90, nor has any interest been paid upon it for nearly a year past. Widows, orphans, aged citizens, and public institutions suffer greatly by this event. It is to be lamented the losses and distress thus incurred have not fallen upon the projectors and *original* stockholders in that bank. I know of but one of that class of people who has been injured by it, and that is Mr. Boudinot. His loss amounts upon the fall of his stock, he says, to 20,000 dollars, a small deduction from an immense estate made out of the rags and bellies and blood of the soldiers of the American Revolution and for which he worships the names of Washington and Hamilton.

"The world," says Dr. South, "was made for the bold." This was the case formerly. It seems now to be the portion of the *artful* as well as the bold.

Adieu. Ever yours,

BENJN: RUSH

MS: Adams Manuscript Trust, Boston.

[1] In his letter of 12 Sep. Adams had enclosed a letter from his daughter Abigail (Mrs. W. S. Smith). A tumor she believed cancerous had caused her to return to Quincy from her home at Chenango, N.Y. Having read BR's essay on cancer in *Med. Inq. & Obs.*, she determined to consult him; and the present letter enabled her to overcome her fear of surgical treatment. In a letter of 13 Oct. 1811 her father wrote a full account of the operation, which

was performed by Dr. John Warren, Sr. By the summer of 1812 she seemed wholly well, but she died in Aug. 1813 (Mrs. Smith's letter, Sep. 1811, Rush MSS, XV; Roof, *Col. William Smith and Lady*, p. 302-16; *Old Family Letters*, *A*, p. 363-4).

[2] Wills Hill, 2d Viscount Hillsbor-ough and 1st Marquis of Downshire (1718-1793), was secretary of state for colonies, 1768-1772 (DNB).

[3] Samuel Foote (1720-1777), celebrated satirical dramatist and actor, caricatured Whitefield in his comedy called *The Minor*, 1760 (DNB).

To John Adams

My dear old Friend, Philadelphia, October 18th, 1811

All my family rejoice with yours in the happy issue of the operation performed upon Mrs. Smith's breast.[1] The enclosed letter[2] is intended as an answer to hers to me and to serve the further purpose of exciting in her a belief that her cure will be radical and durable. I consider her as rescued from a premature grave.

Since my last letter to you it has pleased God to make all my family very happy in the return of my 3rd son, Dr. James Rush, and my 2nd daughter, Mary Manners, with her two children, from England, where they have spent two years and some months. Their passage was long and extremely dangerous. *This* has increased our gratitude to heaven and our joy for their return. My son has spent his time profitably. He has brought home a mass of useful information, not only in medicine but upon many other subjects. I expect to be very much relieved from some of my labors by him. His amiable and unassuming manners had recommended him to my patients before he went abroad. *These* he has brought back with him with a stock of practical knowledge in his profession. My daughter's husband will follow her in the spring. His regiment is still in Canada.

Adieu, my dear sir. With love and congratulations to all your family, I am ever yours,

BENJN: RUSH

MS: Adams Manuscript Trust, Boston.

[1] See the preceding letter and note 1 there. [2] Not found.

To James Monroe

Dear Sir,   Philadelphia, November 8th, 1811

I thank you for the copy of the President's message[1] you were so kind as to enclose to me. I am so ignorant of the nature and events of the controversies between our country and the two nations that are now treating us[2] with injustice and hostility, that I dare not rely upon my own opinion of it, but I can with great pleasure inform you that I have seldom known an act of any part of our government give more general satisfaction. It is said to be firm, spirited, temperate, and conciliatory. I have not in my intercourse with my fellow citizens heard a single person speak of it but with approbation. All parties are pleased with it. The complaints against France have extorted praise of it even from the tories in our city. When you see Mr. Madison, please to tell him how dear his honor and character are to his and your sincere old Revolutionary friend,

BENJN: RUSH

MS: Library of Congress, Monroe Papers.

[1] Madison's third annual message to Congress, 5 Nov. 1811, in which he vigorously pointed out "the duty of putting the United States into an armor and attitude demanded by the crisis" created by the unfriendly measures of France and Great Britain (J. D. Richardson, ed., *A Compilation of the Messages and Papers of the Presidents*, n.p., n.d., under date).
[2] This word omitted in MS.

To John Adams

Dear Sir,   Philadelphia, December 9th, 1811

You have touched me in a sore place in your letter of the 4th instant.[1] My son Richard has accepted of the office of comptroller general and is about to remove with his family to Washington in the course of this month.[2] Both his parents, all his brothers and sisters, his Uncles Rush and Richard Stockton, and all his professional and personal friends remonstrated against it. I painted to him in as strong colors as I was able the folly of giving up his present office and business in Pennsylvania, now equal to nearly 4,000 dollars a year. I held up to him the high standing he had acquired in his native state (the asylum of his ancestors, who accompanied William Penn to it in 1683) and the high station to which his fellow citizens had destined him in a few years. I pointed out the vexations, dangers, and poverty of political and official life, and mentioned the distress and obscurity in which many old patriots and servants of the public were now ending their days in many parts of our country, and that the acceptance of the office now offered to him would be an act of suicide to his family. Lastly I implored him by my affection for him, by my age, by my gray hairs, by the prospect of my death, which must according to the course of nature take place in a few years, and of the importance of his presence and patronage to his mother and to my young children when I shall be called from them. But alas! all these arguments and importunities were employed to no purpose. There was one insurmountable objection to them. His wife's connections live near Washington, and *her wishes* were to be near them. There are two classes of female tyrants—termagants and sirens. My son's wife belongs to the latter class. She is a most fascinating woman and ardently beloved by her husband, and "Where love enters," you know, "he will rule alone, And suffer no co-partner in his throne."[3]

Don't you think, my friend, there is a transposition and an error in the latter part of the 16th verse of the 3rd chapter of Genesis? "Unto the woman he said I will greatly multiply thy sorrows and thy conception. In sorrow shalt thou bring forth children and *thy desire shall be to thy husband, and he shall rule over thee.*" Should not the latter part of this verse have been placed at the close of the 19th verse, and the persons reversed in it, as a part of the curse inflicted upon Adam? "And thy *desire* shall be to thy *wife*, and *she shall rule over thee.*"

My son James, the young doctor to whom I shall now transfer the rank and privileges of primogeniture, is an excellent young man, well informed upon most subjects as well as in medicine, and will I have no doubt shine in his profession. But how little patronage does this "mute art" (as Ovid calls it when he speaks of Apollo being condemned to exercise it)[4] afford to a young family compared with the profession of the law, especially when it is exercised by splendid talents and accompanied with a fair character?

You have nothing to fear from Duane's threat.[5] Long before this time he has forgotten it. This is the manner of the man.

I was made happy by the account you gave me in your last letter but one that the clouds which hang over your house had dispersed, and that health and cheerfulness had again been restored to your family.

You say nothing of Mrs. Smith's breast. I hope it is perfectly and radically healed.

I am so closely employed in discharging my numerous and complicated winter duties that I have scarcely time to read what I have thus hastily scrawled.

With love to your fireside, in which mine joins, I am, dear sir, ever—ever yours,

BENJN: RUSH

P.S. My 4th son, Ben (a promising young merchant of about 21 years of age), sails in a few days for Smyrna, from whence he expects to sail for England and afterwards to Petersburgh as super-cargo and agent for his master, one of the wealthiest merchants in our city and very much the friend of my son. I have taken the liberty to commend him to the advice and good offices of your son at Petersburgh.

Dr. Franklin's estate has been divided among his grandchildren and does not amount to nearly the sum I formerly mentioned to you.[6]

Addressed: John Adams Esqr: Quincy near Boston.
MS: Adams Manuscript Trust, Boston.

[1] *Old Family Letters, A*, p. 364-5.
[2] Richard was appointed comptroller of the treasury by President Madison on 22 Nov. 1811. For the political circumstances and significance of the appointment, see Powell, *Richard Rush*, p. 12-17. The strength of BR's disapproval of Richard's acceptance is suggested by the fact that he promptly cut off his son's inheritance, but it is not altogether easy to explain why he felt so strongly. See, however, the following letters to Adams and Jefferson and also a remarkable passage in BR's *Autobiography* (p. 162), in which he reviews his own public service and concludes:

"To my sons I bequeath a father's experience, and I entreat them to take no public or active part in the disputes of their country beyond a vote at an election. If no scruples of conscience forbid them to bear arms, I would recommend to them rather to be soldiers than politicians, should they ever be so unfortunate as to live in a country distracted by a civil war. In battle men kill, without hating each other; in political contests men hate without killing, but in that hatred they commit murder every hour of their lives."

Though BR's letters to Richard have not survived among the papers inherited by Richard's descendants, there is abundant evidence in Richard's letters to his father (Rush MSS, XLIV), and in BR's letters to Adams published in the present collection, that father and son remained on good terms and that BR derived much secret satisfaction from Richard's rapidly rising prestige in government circles.

[3] Source not known.
[4] I have not found this passage in Ovid, but there is a closely parallel passage in the *Aeneid*, XII, 396-7, concerning Iapyx, a favorite of Apollo, who

scire potestas herbarum usumque medendi
maluit et mutas agitare inglorius artis.

In "Observations on the Duties of a Physician," a lecture delivered in 1789, BR observed: "It was in Rome, when medicine was practised only by slaves, that physicians were condemned by their profession 'mutam exercere artem' " (*Med. Inq. & Obs.*, 2d edn., 1805, I, 392).

[5] See *Old Family Letters, A*, p. 365.
[6] See BR's letter of 6 Aug. 1811.

To John Adams

My dear old Friend, Philadelphia, December 16, 1811

Mr. Jefferson and I exchange letters once in six, nine, or twelve months. This day I received a few lines from him in which he introduces your name in the following words.[1] After mentioning the visit paid to you by his two neighbors the Messrs. Coles[2] last summer, he adds, "Among other things he [Mr. Adams][3] adverted to the unprincipled licentiousness of the press against myself," adding, "*I always loved Jefferson and still love him*. This is enough for me. I only needed this knowledge to revive towards him all the affections of the most cordial moments of our lives. It is known to those who have heard me speak of Mr. Adams that I have ever done him justice myself and defended him when assailed by others with the single exception as to his political opinions, but with a man possessing so many estimable qualities, why should we be separated by mere differences of opinion in politics, religion, philosophy or anything else? His opinions are as honestly formed as my own. Our different views of the same subjects are the results of the difference in our organization and experience. I have never withdrawn from any man upon that account. Although many have done it from me, much less should I do it from one with whom I had gone through, with hand and heart, so many trying scenes. I wish therefore for an apposite occasion to express to Mr. Adams my *unchanged affection* for him. There is an awkwardness which hangs over the resuming a correspondence so long discontinued unless something should arise which should call for a letter. Time and chance may perhaps generate such an occasion, of which I shall not be wanting in promptitude to avail myself."

And now, my dear friend, permit me again to suggest to you to receive the olive branch which has thus been offered to you by the hand of a man who still loves you. Fellow laborers in erecting the great fabric of American independence!—fellow sufferers in the calumnies and falsehoods of party rage!—fellow heirs of the gratitude and affection of posterity!—and fellow passengers in a stage that must shortly convey you both into the presence of a Judge with whom the forgiveness and love of enemies is the condition of acceptance!—embrace—embrace each other! Bedew your letters of reconciliation with tears of affection and joy. Bury in silence all the causes of your separation. Recollect that explanations may be proper between lovers but are *never* so between divided friends. Were I near to you, I would put a pen into your hand and guide it while it composed the following short address to Mr. Jefferson:

"Friend and fellow laborer in the cause of the liberty and independence of our common country, I salute you with the most cordial good wishes for your health and happiness.

John Adams."

Excuse the liberty I have taken, and be assured of the respect, affection, and gratitude of yours truly,

BENJN: RUSH

MS: Adams Manuscript Trust, Boston.

[1] Jefferson's letter, dated 5 Dec. 1811, is printed in his *Writings*, ed. Lipscomb and Bergh, XIII, 114-17. In copying the passage quoted in the present letter, BR made discreet omissions from Jefferson's text.

[2] The brothers Edward and John Coles of Albemarle co., Va. Edward Coles (1786-1868), who was at this time secretary to Pres. Madison and later governor of Illinois (see DAB), left an exceedingly interesting account of the visit to Adams and the conversation relative to Jefferson. This was in the form of a letter to Henry S. Randall in 1857 and was printed in Randall's *Life of Jefferson*, III, 639-40.

[3] Brackets in MS.

To Thomas Jefferson

My dear old Friend,   Philadelphia, December 17th, 1811

Yours of December 5th came to hand yesterday.[1] I was charmed with the subject of it. In order to hasten the object you have suggested, I sat down last evening and selected such passages from your letter as contained the kindest expressions of regard for Mr. Adams and transmitted them to him. My letter which contained them was concluded as nearly as I can recollect, for I kept no copy of it, with the following words.

"Fellow laborers in erecting the fabric of American liberty and independence!—fellow sufferers in the calumnies and falsehoods of party rage!—fellow heirs of the gratitude and affection of posterity! —and fellow passengers in the same stage which must soon convey you both into the presence of a Judge with whom the forgiveness and love of enemies is the only condition of your acceptance!— embrace—embrace each other. Bedew your letters of reconciliation with tears of affection and joy. Let there be no retrospect of your past differences. Explanations may be proper between contending lovers, but they are never so between divided friends. Were I near to you, I would put a pen into your hand and guide it while it wrote the following note to Mr. Jefferson:

[1111]

" 'My dear old friend and fellow laborer in the cause of the liberties and independence of our common country, I salute you with the most cordial good wishes for your health and happiness.

John Adams.' "

I sincerely hope this my second effort to revive a friendly intercourse between you by letters will be successful. Patriotism, liberty, science, and religion would all gain a triumph by it.[2]

How cold the feelings! and how feeble the expressions of indignation in Congress against the outrages committed by G. Britain upon our rights, compared with what they were in 1774 and 1775 against outrages of a less degrading and insulting nature! Randolph seems to have composed his speeches from the fragments of the tory publications of those memorable years, with which his opponents seem to be shamefully unacquainted. But all I hope will yet end well.

Mr. Madison has inflicted a sore blow upon my whole family by taking my son Richard from us. He has been my friend and counselor for many years, and he relinquishes great political as well as professional prospects in his native state by accepting the office lately given to him under the general government. His talents and acquirements qualify him for active and professional pursuits, and his manners for popular favor. They will all be lost to his country and family in an office in which the mind can have no employment and in which a merchant or the cashier of a bank would be more respectable than even a Burke or a Fox.

I once said to Hamilton Roan,[3] whom I met in company at the time when Porcupine was amusing and gratifying the tory citizens of Philadelphia with his publications against me, that "I lived like himself in a *foreign* country." "No, sir, you do not," said he. "You live in an *enemy's* country." This has been strictly true ever since the restoration of the tories to their ante-Revolutionary rank by the officers of the general government upon the removal of Congress from New York to Philadelphia. Previously to that time, I was courted and employed by them, but it was with a view of protecting themselves by means of my influence from the rage of the insulted and triumphant party of which I was then a member; nor did they sue for my services in vain. I constantly advised forgiveness and clemency to be exercised towards them.[4] Often did I supplicate the executive council and judges of our state in their favor, and, from my attempts to serve them, as often incurred the censure of my whig friends. By one of them whom I was chiefly instrumental in saving from banishment or perhaps a worse fate, I was publicly abused and betrayed in the year 1800. I need not name him to you. He has been called in one of our papers a "traitor by instinct." From this detail of my situation in Philadelphia, living only with my patients and pupils, judge how severely I feel the loss of the society and the friendship of my son Richard! My 3rd son, James, who lately returned from Europe and who assists me in my business, is very amiable and promising, but what can eminence in the "mute art" of medicine (as Ovid calls it) do to protect a young and persecuted family, compared with eminence at the bar and a popular political character?

These fireside communications I am sure will be felt by you, for you are both a father and a friend. All their sensibilities are familiar to you.

As my son has quitted professional for official life, and state for national prospects, I hope he will be remembered in some future arrangments of office by Mr. Madison.

Health, respect and friendship! from, my dear sir, your sincere old friend,

BENJN: RUSH

P.S. A state of nature has been called a state of war. May not the same thing be said of civilized and even of the most polished societies? They fight only with different weapons. Judge of the disposition of the class of our citizens which I have described towards the old whigs by the following fact. An old tory in passing by the public library room some time ago pointed to the statue of Dr. Franklin which is placed in a niche in the front part of it, and with an acrid sneer said to a person who was walking with him, "But for that old fellow, we never should have had independence."

MS: Library of Congress, Jefferson Papers.

[1] See the preceding letter and note.

[2] For the result of BR's dual appeal, see his letter to Jefferson of 11 Feb. 1812.

[3] Archibald Hamilton Rowan (1751-1834), United Irishman; imprisoned for patriotic activities, but escaped and spent the years 1795-1800 in America, principally at Wilmington, Del. (DNB; Harold Nicolson, *The Desire to Please: A Story of Hamilton Rowan and the United Irishmen*, N.Y., 1943, especially ch. XI). BR tells this anecdote more circumstantially in the following letter to Adams.

[4] BR makes a similar assertion in his *Autobiography*, p. 117. The evidence to substantiate these assertions is scattered but plentiful. In the Revolutionary Papers in the Pennsylvania State Archives at Harrisburg are at least six, and perhaps more, original petitions signed by BR in behalf of banished or attainted persons between 1780 and 1785. (One of these, at XL, 27, dated 23 Oct. 1780, is in behalf of Dr. Adam Kuhn.) See also BR's letters to Mrs. Ferguson, 24 Dec. 1777, 25 Dec. 1787.

To John Adams

My dear old Friend,   Philadelphia, December 26th, 1811

During the time Cobbett was abusing me in his newspaper, to the great joy of a number of our tory citizens, I met Hamilton Roan [*Rowan*] in a family in which I was called to see a patient. We had met before at Major Butler's table. He took me by the hand in the most cordial manner. "Our situation," said I, "Mr. Roan, is a good deal alike in Philadelphia. We are both in an *enemy's* country." "No, sir," said he, "I am in a *foreign* country only," alluding to the avidity with which the scandal published against me had been devoured by the class of citizens above mentioned. It is true the papers no longer pour forth weekly and daily calumnies against me, but I am still in an *enemy's* country. My patients and my pupils (with a few exceptions) are my only friends out of my own family. Do you wonder then at my complaining of my son Richard for deserting me? Independently of his affection and kindness to me, his office kept libelers of my reputation in awe. But what have you done to render your fellow citizens so hostile to you? I answer, my *first* offense was keeping company with the Messrs. Adams and Jno. Hancock in the year 1774 and afterwards subscribing the Declaration of Independence. My *second* offense (of far less magnitude than the first) was opposing the wheelbarrow Constitution of Pennsylvania in 1776 and the men who supported it, particularly Jos. Read [*Reed*], which acts are still remembered with resentment by some of our old Constitutional, now Democratic, citizens. My *third* offense was writing down the old sanguinary criminal law of our state, by which I made many Old Testament divines and saints my enemies. My *fourth* offense was writing against monkish learning, commonly called the Latin and Greek languages, by which I produced a confederacy of pedagogues against me. My *fifth* and last offense was teaching a new system of medicine, part of which consisted in the use of remedies that did violence to the feelings and common sense of our citizens, and in inculcating a belief that our yellow fever was of domestic origin. "These were the most unkindly cuts of all." They armed a host of malignant and ruthless passions against me. They placed my reputation in the hands of between 20 and thirty physicians, each of whom brought into the field against me his circle of patients and family connections. Were I to detail to you the many acts of unkindness, ingratitude, treachery, malice, and cruelty I have received from the last class of

[1114]

enemies I have mentioned, you would wonder how I have survived them. There are several species of hatreds, such as the odium politicum, the odium theologicum, the odium philologicum, and the odium medicum. I have felt, severely felt, the effects of them all. The last has been by far the worst. It has been the hatred not of men but of beings actuated by a spirit truly demoniacal. In reviewing my conduct towards all the classes of enemies that I have enumerated, I cannot see much cause to complain of myself. Now and then I have yielded to the natural irritability of my temper under the sudden pressure of an injury, and used my lips unadvisedly against them; but in general I have been silent and always disposed to repay their injuries with kindness and forgiveness. Not a paragraph has ever found its way from my pen to a newspaper in defense of my innocence or to expose the folly, ignorance, falsehoods, and malice of my enemies.[1] While I thus open my heart to my dear old friend in complaints against many of my fellow citizens, do not suppose that my life has been made completely miserable by them. The good I have enjoyed in Philadelphia since the year 1774 has far, very far, exceeded the evil I have suffered. I have been blessed with an excellent wife and affectionate as well as intelligent and worthy children. I have had the constant and faithful attachment and support of half a dozen powerful and popular citizens (several of whom are of the old school in politics) against the malice of my medical brethren. One of them[2] opened his purse to me at the time when the publications against my practice reduced the income from my business £400 below the expenses of my family. In addition to these sources of enjoyment and comfort, I have derived from my studies and professional duties a large share of intellectual and moral pleasure. The midnight cry of "past twelve o'clock" has often found me insensible to the cold of winter and the heat of summer while I have been engaged with ineffable delight in forming a new arrangement of facts in order to derive from them new principles and new modes of treating diseases. For these and all God's other mercies to me, I desire to be truly, sincerely, and forever thankful.

My dear wife, who has been the faithful companion of my pains and pleasures, has sometimes told me she found no character in biography more like mine than Luther's—ardent in all my pursuits, fearless of the consequences of attacking old prejudices, and often hasty in my manner of speaking of my enemies. To the defects in the temper and the conduct of the illustrious reformer I heartily subscribe, but I think there is a character in the Old Testament which more nearly accords with mine. It is that of the prophet Jeremiah. I shall give it to you in his own words. "Woe is me, my mother, that thou hast borne me, a man of *strife* and a man of contention to the whole earth. I have neither lent on usury nor have men lent to me on usury, yet every one of them doth curse me." Jere. 15, 10.

I proceed now to the second part of your letter.[3] I do not consider my son as having been called upon to share in the honors of the general government, nor do I believe the office to which he has been appointed will satisfy the claims or appease the jealousy of Pennsylvania as you have supposed. You will say perhaps, what can she mean by asking for a larger representation in the honors of the general government? Is not Mr. Gallatin a Pennsylvanian?[4] I once heard a servant girl who quarreled with a mulatto fellow servant and called him "a no nation son of b——h." Many of our citizens who would blush to apply such low and indelicate language to any man, do not hesitate to say Mr. Gallatin is "a *no state* man" and that he belongs as much to the Union as to Pennsylvania.

I sincerely rejoice in Mrs. Smith's complete recovery. Please to present my congratulations to her and the compliments of the season to your excellent Mrs. Adams, in which all my family join. Health, friendship, and respect, from dear sir, yours affectionately,

Benjn: Rush

P.S. I forgot to mention a *6th source* of hostility to me from a part of my fellow citizens. It was brought on by my concurring in establishing a College at Carlisle in this state. Dr. Ewing, who wished to be at the head of all the learning of the state, opposed it with all his might and had the address to unite the Presbyterians in the city with him, who in consequence thereof became my enemies —and that to such a degree as to oblige me for a while to separate from them. From more just views of Dr. Ewing's character, they have since forgiven me and become my friends. The College at Carlisle, now in the hands chiefly of the Presbyterians, is a flourishing institution. Its president, a Dr. Atwater from Connecticut, has given it great celebrity.

MS: Adams Manuscript Trust, Boston.

[1] BR has overlooked his newspaper controversies with Dr. Shippen following the latter's court-martial in 1780 and with Provost Ewing concerning Dickinson College in 1785; some of his public communications on the yellow fever in 1793 were also polemical.

[2] Not identified; possibilities are Samuel Coates, Richard Peters, and George Clymer.

[3] This is a very puzzling reference, unless a letter written by Adams be-

tween 4 and 19 Dec. 1811 is missing (which seems quite improbable), or unless BR meant "your second letter [about Richard's appointment]"—that is, Adams' letter of 19 Dec., which is almost entirely devoted to comforting BR on this score (*Old Family Letters*, *A*, p. 366-7).

[4] Albert Gallatin (1761-1849), secretary of the treasury, 1801-1813, was a native of Switzerland (DAB).

To John Adams

My dear old Friend,   Philadelphia, January 15th, 1812

"Arma, cestusque, *parmamque* repono,"[1] upon the offensive subject of one of my late letters to you.

I sincerely rejoice in the successful issue of the operation upon Mrs. Smith's breast.

I would reciprocate your expressions of pleasure upon the appearances of a resuscitation of the spirit of 1774 at Washington, did I believe they would terminate in anything but in speeches, embassies, negotiations, and a repetition of insults and injuries. The army of 25,000 cannot be raised in our country in the present thriving state of our agriculture and manufactures. Double that number of men might more easily be obtained to man a navy in the present reduced state of our commerce. The independence of the United States must be defended, and what is more, the empire of the globe must be decided only upon the ocean. Posterity will do you justice for your opinions and conduct upon this subject.

All is bustle and intrigue we are told at Washington upon another subject—that is, who shall be the next President. My poor son Richard has no doubt of Mr. M.'s reelection. Should it be otherwise, he will realize the predictions of his father when he exchanged the rank of a warrior for the occupation of a cornplanter, to borrow an allusion from the language of the Indians of our country. His conduct is deplored and condemned not only by his family, but by every man, woman, and child in our city that knew him. Few men succeed in undertakings that are opposed by two such currents. His removal has been to me, under all the circumstances that attended it, one of the most distressing events of my life.

The bank mania is now epidemic in our state. There are at present about 20 petitions for banks, besides the one from the trustees of the Bank of the United States, for charters before our legislature. The issue of them is doubtful. The U. States have bid high for *theirs*.

[1117]

Adieu! my dear old friend, and be assured of the unabated respect and gratitude of yours affectionately,

BENJN: RUSH

P.S. We complain here of Governor Gerry's speech embracing too many objects and of its being too long.[2] He should have "left off when he was done." Great and good thoughts suffer by being too much diluted.

Addressed: John Adams Esqr: Quincy near Boston.
MS: Adams Manuscript Trust, Boston.

[1] "I lay aside my arms, gauntlets, and shield." Doubtless an echo of the *Aeneid*, v, 484: "Hic victor caestus artemque repono." The "offensive subject" alluded to was no doubt BR's assertion in the preceding letter that he lived "in an *enemy's* country." In his reply of 8 Jan., Adams had administered to BR a characteristic rebuke:
"Such are the Terms upon which an honest Man and real Friend to his Country must live in times such as these we have been destined to witness. . . . In my opinion there is not in Philadelphia a single Citizen more universally esteemed and beloved by his Fellow Citizens than Dr. Benjamin Rush. There is not a man in Pensilvania more esteemed by the whole State. I know not a man in America more esteemed by the nation. There is not a Citizen of this Union, more esteemed throughout the litterary, Scientifical, and Moral World in Europe, Asia and Africa. Such in my opinion is the enemies Country and enemies World in which you live and will die" (*Old Family Letters, A*, p. 369-70).

[2] In a long and intemperate harangue to the Massachusetts legislature on 8 Jan. 1812, Gov. Gerry designated the pro-British Federalists as "royalists" and "disciples of Bute, . . . the author of a plan to enslave these states" (John S. Barry, *The History of Massachusetts. The Commonwealth Period*, Boston, 1857, p. 367).

To Thomas Jefferson

Dear Sir,   Philadelphia, February 11th, 1812

Few of the acts of my life have given me more pleasure than the one you are pleased to acknowledge in your last letter.[1]

I wish in your reply to Mr. Adams' letter you had given him the echo of his communications to you respecting his daughter Mrs. Smith and her husband. The former has been saved from certain death by a painful operation, and the honor and interest of the latter lie near his heart. I wish he could be provided for in the new army. He possesses, with a fine martial appearance, military talents and knowledge. I well recollect, upon his return to America after visiting the Continent of Europe, being much struck with his details of the improvements in the art of war with which he had taken pains to make himself acquainted during a residence of some weeks at Berlin.[2]

It will give me pleasure to hear of a frequent exchange of letters between you and Mr. Adams. I associate the idea of your early friendship for each other, founded upon a sympathy of just opinions and feelings, with every retrospect I take of the great political, moral, and intellectual achievements of the Congresses of 1775 and 1776.

Health, respect, and friendship! from, dear sir, yours truly and affectionately,

BENJN: RUSH

MS: Library of Congress, Jefferson Papers.

[1] In answer to BR's appeal of 16 Dec. 1811, Adams wrote BR on Christmas Day, saying, "I perceive plainly enough, Rush, that you have been teasing Jefferson to write to me, as you did me some time ago to write to him. . . . Of what use can it be for Jefferson and me to exchange letters? . . . Time and chance, however, or possibly design, may produce ere long a letter between us" (Adams, *Works*, X, 10-12). Whereupon, on 1 Jan. 1812, Adams addressed a short letter to Jefferson expressing good wishes and saying he was sending him, as "a friend to American Manufactures, . . . two Pieces of Homespun lately produced in this quarter" (*Correspondence of John Adams and Thomas Jefferson*, ed. Paul Wilstach, Indianapolis, 1925, p. 31-2). Without waiting for the parcel of "homespun" which turned out to be J. Q. Adams' two volumes of Boylston *Lectures*, Jefferson graciously replied on 21 Jan. 1812, commending home manufactures and saluting Adams "with unchanged affection and respect" (Jefferson, *Writings*, ed. Lipscomb and Bergh, XIII, 122-5). Jefferson enclosed this answer, to be read and forwarded, in a letter of the same date to BR (L.C., Jefferson Papers; partly printed in Jefferson, *Writings*, ed. Ford, IX, 332). This was done, and on 10 Feb. Adams informed BR: "Your dream is out, and the Passage you read in the History that Richard was reading is come to pass, notwithstanding you said you believed no History but the Bible" (*Old Family Letters, A*, p. 453). Four letters had already passed between Quincy and Monticello, the earliest in a long and splendid series that is to be published, for the first time in its entirety, in an edition being prepared by the Institute of Early American History and Culture at Williamsburg.

[2] William Stephens Smith's career was wrecked by his trial for complicity in the Miranda expedition. Despite his military experience he was unable to obtain a post in the new army; he did, however, serve briefly in Congress, 1813-1815 (DAB; Roof, *Col. William Smith and Lady*, p. 312ff.).

To John Adams[1]

Dear Sir,   Philadelphia, February 12th, 1812

I did not require the anecdote you have communicated to me in your letter of last month to know that I had incurred the hatred of General Washington.[2] It was violent and descended with him to the grave. For its not being perpetuated in the history of his life, I am indebted to the worthy and amiable Judge Washington.[3] I will give you a history of its cause in as short a compass as possible.[4]

During the session of Congress in Philadelphia in the year 1774 I met Mr. Washington at the coffeehouse at the time he was generally spoken of as commander in chief of the American army, and informed him that his appointment would give universal satisfaction to the citizens of Pennsylvania and hoped he would not decline it. I had reason to believe that he considered this opinion ever afterwards as an expression of attachment to his military character never to be canceled, and that a subsequent change of that opinion was an evidence of insincerity. The sequel of this letter will show that I was not singular in this respect.

In the summer of 1775 or thereabouts I dined in company with General, then Colonel, Stevens[5] on his way from Virginia to the camp. I sat next to him. In a low tone of voice he asked me who constituted General Washington's military family. I told him Colonel J. Reed and Major Thos. Mifflin. "Are they men of talents?" said he. "Yes," said I. "I am glad to hear it," said the General, "for General Washington will require such men about him. He is a *weak man*. I know him well. I served with him during the last French war."

After the defeats and retreats of our army in the year 1776, I went out as a volunteer physician to General Cadwallider's corps of Philadelphia militia. During this excursion I rode with Colonel J. Reed from Bristol to Head Quarters on the Delaware nearly opposite to Trenton.[6] On our way he mentioned many instances of General Washington's want of military skill and ascribed most of the calamities of the campaign to it. He concluded by saying "he was only fit to command a regiment." General Gates informed me in March 1777 that Patrick Henry of Virginia had said the same thing of him when he was appointed commander in chief.

A little later than this time, General Mifflin told me[7] "he was totally unfit for his situation, that he was fit only to be the head clerk of a London counting-house," and as a proof of his assertion mentioned the time he wasted with his pen, and particularly noticed his having once transcribed a letter to Congress of three sheets of paper only because there were two or three erasures in the original.[8]

The brilliant affair at Trenton in January 1777 dissipated all the impressions which those opinions and anecdotes of General Washington had excited in my mind, notwithstanding I received them from men who knew him intimately, both in the cabinet and in the field, and who were his personal friends.

In April or May 1777 I accepted of the appointment of physician general of the military hospitals of the United States under the direction of Dr. Shippen. Here I saw scenes of distress shocking to humanity and disgraceful to a civilized country. I can never forget them. I still see the sons of our yeomanry brought up in the lap of plenty and domestic comforts of all kinds, shivering with cold upon bare floors without a blanket to cover them, calling for fire, for water, for suitable food, and for medicines—and calling in vain. I still hear the complaints they utter against their country. I hear their sighs for their fathers' firesides and for a mother or sister's care. Their dying groans still pierce my ears. I see them expire.—While hundreds of the flower of the youth of our country were thus perishing under the most accumulated sufferings, Dr. Shippen, the director general of the hospitals, whose business it was to provide all the articles necessary for their comfort, was feasting with the general officers at the camp or bargaining with tavern-keepers in Jersey or Pennsylvania for the sale of madeira wine from our hospital stores, bought by him for the use of the sick. Nor was this all. No officer was ever sent by General W. to command or preserve discipline in our hospitals (a practice universal in Euro-pean armies), in consequence of which many of our soldiers sold their blankets, muskets, and even clothing for the necessaries of life or for ardent spirits. In this situation of our hospitals, I ad-dressed two letters to General W.—the one complaining of the above abuses and pointing out their remedies, the other impeaching Dr. Shippen of malpractices.[9] I expected a court-martial would be ordered to inquire into Dr. Shippen's conduct in consequence of my second letter. In this I was disappointed. Both my letters were sent to Congress, and a committee was appointed by them to hear my charges against the Director General. On my way to York town, where the Congress then sat, I passed through the army at Valley forge, where I saw similar marks of filth, waste of public property, and want of discipline which I had recently witnessed in the hospi-tals.[10] General Sullivan (at whose quarters I breakfasted) said to me, "Sir, this is not an army—it is a mob." Here a new source of distress was awakened in my mind. I now felt for the safety and independence of my country as well as for the sufferings of the sick under my care. All that I had heard from General Stevens, Colonel Reed, Mr. Mifflin, and some others was now revived in my mind. At York town I found alarm and discontent among many members of Congress. While there I wrote a short account of the state of our hospitals and of the army to Patrick Henry, and concluded my letter by quoting a speech of General Conway's unfriendly to the talents of the Commander in Chief. This letter Patrick Henry transmitted to General W———, and hence the *cause* and *only* cause of his hostility to me.[11]

My charges against Dr. Shippen were soon dismissed by the Committee of Congress, in consequence of which I resigned my commission of physician general.[12]

In the year 1779 [*i.e., 1780*] Dr. Morgan dragged Dr. Shippen before a court-martial at Morristown, agreeably to an order of Congress, where I was summonsed as a witness. During the trial several members of the court were changed—a thing I believe never done in such courts, nor in juries except in cases of sickness and death. The Doctor was acquitted but *without* honor, and by a majority of but *one* vote. Soon after this cold and bare acquittal, he resigned. General W. afterwards gave him a certificate approving of his conduct while director general of the hospitals,[13] which the Doctor published in one of our newspapers about the year 1780.

The state of the hospitals at the time I left them may easily be conceived from the following fact. Mr. Morris informed me that the expenses of the medical department were five millions of dollars during the last year Dr. Shippen presided over them. The year after his resignation they amounted only to one million, estimating both funds in gold and silver coin. The state of the army when I passed through it may be conceived from the declaration of Baron Stuben,[14] who passed through it a few weeks after me. He said that more clothes were destroyed in it than would be sufficient for the largest army in Europe.

Feeling no unkindness to G. Washington during the years of the war after 1777 and after the peace, I cordially joined in all the marks of gratitude and respect showed to him from time to time by the citizens of Philadelphia. I *first* pointed the public attention to him as the future President of the United States in several of our newspapers while the Convention was sitting which framed the Constitution, at the same time that I mentioned your name as Vice-President.[15] These acts were the effects of a belief that the counsels of Stuben, Green [*Greene*], and Hamilton, aided by his own experience, had qualified him for his station, and of a conviction that he always acted honestly and faithfully to promote the first interest of his country. In addition to my uniting in public acts of respect to him, I entertained him while he presided in the Convention, and treated him with the utmost respect while he was President of the United States.[16] At no time after the year 1777, however, did

I believe him to be the "first in war" in our country. In addition to the testimonies of Stevens, Reed, and Mifflin, I had *directly* or *indirectly* the testimonies of Green, Hamilton, Colonel Tilghman,[17] your son-in-law, and of many other of the most intelligent officers who served under him to the contrary. Nor have I ever dared to join in the profane and impious incense which has been offered to his patriotism and moral qualities by many of our citizens. Were I to mention all that I have heard of his "heart," and from some of his friends too, it would appear that he was not possessed of all the divine attributes that have been ascribed to him. But enough of this hateful subject! Help me to blot the knowledge and recollection of everything connected with it from my memory.

The venerable Charles Thompson [*Thomson*], now above 80 years of age, now and then calls to see me. I once suggested to him to write secret memoirs of the American Revolution. "No, no," said he, "I will not. I could not tell the truth without giving great offense. Let the world admire our patriots and heroes. Their supposed talents and virtues (where they were so) by commanding imitation will serve the cause of patriotism and of our country." I concur in this sentiment, and therefore I *earnestly request* that you will destroy this letter as soon as you read it. I do not even wish it to be known that General W. was deficient in that mark of true greatness which so preeminently characterized Julius Caesar, Henry the 4th of France, and Frederick the 2nd of Prussia—*the talent to forgive.*[18]

Brutus said near the close of his life, "I early devoted myself to my country, and I have ever since lived a life of liberty and glory." Your correspondent early devoted himself to the cause of humanity. He has lived in a constant succession of contests with ignorance, prejudice, and vice, in all which his only objects were to lessen the miseries and promote the happiness of his fellow men, and yet he has lived a life constantly exposed to malice and persecution. "Blessed are they who are persecuted for righteousness' sake."[19] I have derived great comfort and support from this passage of Scripture, for I believe it applies to all those persons who suffer from their zeal (whether successful or not) in the cause of truth, humanity, and justice in the present world.

When Calvin heard that Luther had called him "a child of the devil," he coolly replied, "Luther is a servant of the most high God." In answer to the epithet which G. Washington has applied to me, I will as coolly reply, "He was the highly favored instrument whose patriotism and name contributed greatly to the establishment of the independence of the United States."

Adieu! my dear friend. I repeat again, or rather I entreat again, that you will destroy this letter as soon as you have read it.

From your ever affectionate and grateful friend,

BENJN RUSH

P.S. March 9th. In your letters to me which are to follow the receipt of this, take no notice of anything that is contained in it beyond an expression of your satisfaction or dissatisfaction with my defense of my conduct in the above affair. This must be done without mentioning names. My reason for this request is, all my family have descended with the multitude down the stream created by the homage paid to GW., and I have taken no pains to bring them back again. He is welcome to their praises and admiration. They know only that I am not one of his idolaters, and that I ascribe the success of our Revolution to an illustrious band of statesmen, philosophers, patriots, and heroes. They know likewise from your history of G. W.'s ten talents in one of your letters[20] that we agree in ascribing honor to all to whom honor is due, and not to any one citizen or soldier of the United States.[21]

I hope the chain which now connects Quincy with Monticello continues to brighten by every post.

MS: Adams Manuscript Trust, Boston.

[1] In a letter of 8 Jan. Adams observed that "absurd and ridiculous stories" are told about all great men. He instanced BR himself, of whom Adams had lately heard the story, at about third hand, that Washington had once described BR as "the most black hearted scoundrel he had ever known" (*Old Family Letters*, *A*, p. 370-1). Adams discounted the story, but it opened an old wound in BR's mind, and he sat down to compose the fullest explanation he ever rendered of his conduct toward Washington. It is noteworthy that, though he enjoined Adams to burn the letter at once, BR kept two copies of it among his own papers, and that they were in turn left among the papers bequeathed by James Rush to the Library Company of Philadelphia. For related documents and commentary, see BR to Patrick Henry, 12 Jan. 1778; to John Marshall, 5 Sep. 1804; and Appendix 1, below.

According to his letter of 17 Feb. 1812, BR began the present letter about 3 Feb., but he did not finish and send it until 9 Mch., the date of the postscript. His difficulty in composing this apologia is further attested by the existence of three versions. The undated rough draft is in Rush MSS, XXIX, 137; its text is heavily scored out and interlined. Having gotten well in mind what he wanted to say, BR began anew, on sheets he evidently intended to send to Adams; this version, begun as a fair copy, is in the same volume of the Rush MSS at fol. 136. Writing with only moderate difficulty, BR rejected some matter in the rough draft but added a greater amount of new matter. At some point during the weeks he kept it by him, he decided he would retain this version as his own copy (and he so docketed it), thus converting it into a second draft. The version finally sent, now among the Adams MSS, is longer than either draft, but it lacks interesting matter found in both of them, most strikingly a paragraph near the close, printed as note 18, below. Because of the unusual psychological and textual interest of the letter, the principal variant passages in the drafts, both those deleted and those still standing, are added in the notes below. A complete variorum text would require elaborate apparatus and has not been attempted.

2 The first draft begins: "I forgot, in the history of the hatreds with which I have contended, to mention not only the odium nigrotyrannum but the odium Washingtonium."

3 Bushrod Washington; see BR to John Marshall, 5 Sep. 1804.

4 A paragraph follows in the first draft that reads: "In the year 1774 I published the note from Mr. Davies' *Sermon* in which he predicted the future services Major W. should render to this country." The reference is to a famous sermon by Samuel Davies, *Religion and Patriotism the Constituents of a Good Soldier*, Phila., 1755, in which Davies spoke of "that heroic Youth, Col. *Washington*, whom I cannot but hope Providence has hitherto preserved in so signal a Manner for some important Service to his Country" (p. 9, note). BR's "1774" is probably an error for 1775; see Appendix 1, below.

5 I.e., Adam Stephen; see BR to R. H. Lee, 21 Dec. 1776, note 7.

6 This incident is told in BR's *Autobiography*, p. 124. It must have occurred one or two nights before the surprise attack on Trenton. Washington's headquarters were at William Keith's farmhouse, on the road from Brownsburg to the Eagle Tavern (Baker, *Itinerary of Washington*, p. 61).

7 First draft: "said in a company in my presence."

8 Deleted in first draft: "His presenting Congress at the close of the war with a large quarto containing an account of all his receipts and expenditures of money *written with his own hand* would seem to favor this general idea." Washington, who was nothing if not meticulous in financial affairs, kept his accounts as commander in chief, 1775-1783, in duplicate in his own hand. The copy he retained has been published in facsimile, ed. J. C. Fitzpatrick, Boston and N.Y., 1917; the copy submitted to the government, which won the admiration of the treasury clerks, is now in the National Archives and was exhibited on the Freedom Train in 1947-1948.

9 Letters of 26 Dec. 1777 and 25 Feb. 1778, qq.v. Here again BR mistakenly supposes (as in his letter to John Marshall, 5 Sep. 1804, q.v.) that *both* these letters were written before his resignation at the end of Jan. 1778.

10 This visit occurred on 3 Jan. 1778. BR left vivid and unflattering notes on conditions at the American encampment in 1777-1778 (printed by S. Weir Mitchell in PMHB, XXVII [1903], 147-8). He undoubtedly drew on these notes when composing the present letter.

11 In the first draft this passage continues as follows: "which I am well informed continued till his death. It was inflamed, I have reason to believe, from time to time by Dr. Shippen, for whom the General ever afterwards cherished an attachment. He [*Shippen*] was the brother-in-law of his [*Washington's*] friends the Lees."

12 In the second draft this paragraph reads: "Dr. Shippen was acquitted by the Committee of Congress, of which Dr. Wetherspoon was chairman. The Doctor had witnessed the sufferings of the sick soldiers at Princeton, but he was notwithstanding the friend of Dr. Shippen upon this occasion. Disgusted with the issue of this business, I resigned my commission and retired to private life."

13 In the first draft the remainder of this paragraph reads as follows (the portion here italicized having been scored out in the draft): "and saying 'that the distresses of the sick in the hospitals were inseparable from the new and peculiar situation of our country.' *The Doctor attended the General's family while Congress sat in Philadelphia. I attended the Doctor's son soon afterwards, who mentioned some anecdotes to me of General W., communicated to him by his father, which showed the Doctor to be as deficient in gratitude*

to *his protector as he had been in faithfulness to his country.*" This precious gossip has happily not survived. For BR's attendance on Thomas Lee Shippen, see letter to Ashton Alexander, 21 Dec. 1795.

[14] Baron von Steuben (1730-1794), the former Prussian staff officer who served as inspector general of the Continental army from Apr. 1778 (DAB).

[15] The first draft has an added sentence: "I even composed at the request of Dr. Ramsay that paragraph in his *History* in which he is described as returning to Mount Vernon after the toils and horrors of the war were over." See David Ramsay's *History of the American Revolution*, Phila., 1789, II, 333-4.

[16] In the second draft a new paragraph begins here and reads as follows: "From the statement I have given you, I hope you are convinced that the epithet he applied to me as far as it related to my conduct to him was not merited. He cherished in his family and honored with his confidence several persons who treated his character with a disrespect very different from that which was conveyed by my quoting a speech of General Conway's concerning him. Your son-in-law, Colonel Smith, informed me that he had heard one of his secretaries call him a 'd——d fool.' I have heard an officer who often did business at headquarters say 'he was a greater impostor than Mahomet.' A gentleman of high rank who traveled through the United States soon after the conclusion of the war informed me that he had heard General Hamilton say 'that he had no heart, that he was a stone, that he was no general, and that he had never read anything upon the art of war except Sims' [*Simes'*] *Military Guide.*' I have heard Major Edwards say that he has heard General Green (to whom the Major was aide-de-camp) say 'that the world was deceived in his character—that' ——— But enough, enough of this hateful subject. Help me to blot the knowledge and recollection of such speeches from my memory." (Maj. Edwards is not clearly identifiable.)

[17] Lt. Col. Tench Tilghman (1744-1786), of Maryland, aide-de-camp to Washington, 1776-1783 (DAB).

[18] In the first draft there is an added paragraph which was retained with only slight alterations in the second draft: "I thank God my destiny in the world of spirits is not to be determined by slaveholders, old tories, Latin and Greek schoolmasters, judges who delight in capital punishments, Philadelphia physicians, profligate or infidel clergymen, nor yet by General W.—all of whom I have offended only by attempts to lessen the ignorance and misery of my fellow citizens."

[19] Matthew 5:10.

[20] See *Old Family Letters, A*, p. 168-70.

[21] BR's son Richard, it may be pointed out, published late in life a group of Washington's private letters, with connecting commentary, under the title *Washington in Domestic Life*, Phila., 1857. Profits from the book were to be contributed to the Washington Monument Fund. In replying to the present letter John Adams intimated that BR had taken Adams' anecdote (the genesis of this long and intensely earnest apologia) much too seriously; see Adams' letter of 19 Mch. 1812 (*Old Family Letters, A*, p. 372).

To John Adams

Dear Sir,   Philadelphia, February 17th, 1812

I began a long and confidential letter[1] to you two weeks ago upon the subject of one of your late letters, but an unusual pressure of business has prevented my finishing it. Judge of the nature and extent of my engagements when I add that after lecturing twice, visiting my usual number of patients this day, and entertaining some of my pupils at tea, I have since written six answers to letters for medical advice and to persons who have applied to me for recommendations for appointments in the new army.

Mr. Norton called upon us on his way to Washington. We consigned him to the good offices of our son Richard.

I rejoice in the correspondence which has taken place between you and your old friend Mr. Jefferson. I consider you and him as the North and South Poles of the American Revolution. Some talked, some wrote, and some fought to promote and establish it, but you and Mr. Jefferson *thought* for us all. I never take a retrospect of the years 1775 and 1776 without associating your opinions and speeches and conversations with all the great political, moral, and intellectual achievements of the Congresses of those memorable years.

I admire, as do all my family, the wonderful vivacity and imagery of your letters. Some men's minds wear well, but yours don't appear to wear at all. O! king, live forever, said the Eastern nations to their monarchs! Live—live, my venerable friend (to use a less extravagant Spanish salutation), a thousand years, to make your family and friends around you happy and to instruct and delight with your letters.

Yours truly and affectionately,

BENJN RUSH

P.S. Expect the letter begun two weeks ago shortly.

MS: Adams Manuscript Trust, Boston.

[1] The letter immediately preceding.

To Thomas Jefferson

Dear Sir,   Philadelphia, February [*i.e., March*] 3rd, 1812[1]

In a letter which I received a few days ago from Mr. Adams, he informs me, with a kind of exultation, that after a correspondence of five or six and thirty years had been interrupted by various causes, it had been renewed, and that four letters had passed between you and him. In speaking of your letters, he says, "They are written with all the elegance, purity, and sweetness of style of his youth and middle age, and with (what I envy more) a firmness of finger and steadiness of chirography that to me are lost forever."

It will give me pleasure as long as I live to reflect that I have been in any degree instrumental in effecting this reunion of two souls destined to be dear to each other and animated with the same dispositions to serve their country (though in different ways) at the expense of innumerable sacrifices of domestic ease, personal interest, and private friendships. Posterity will do you both justice for this act. If Mr. Adams' letters to you are written in the same elevated and nervous style, both as to matter and language, that his letters are which he now and then addresses to me, I am sure you will be delighted with his correspondence. Some of his thoughts electrify me. I view him as a mountain with its head clear and reflecting the beams of the sun, while all below it is frost and snow.

Health, respect, and friendship! from, dear sir, yours truly and affectionately,

BENJN: RUSH

MS: Library of Congress, Jefferson Papers.

[1] The letter from Adams mentioned in the first line was that dated 10 Feb. 1812 (*Old Family Letters, A*, p. 453-5). Jefferson endorsed the present letter from BR as received 19 *Mch*.

To Nathan Benjamin[1]

Sir,   April 15, 1812

The following remedies appear to me to be proper in your case.[2]

1. Garlic taken in *substance*—that is, a bruised clove three times a day, or in *infusion*—that is, eight or ten cloves bruised and put into a pint of peppermint tea, of which a wineglassful should be taken three times a day.

2. The oil of amber, of which from 10 to 15 drops should be taken three times a day in a tablespoonful of molasses.

3. A mixture composed of tar, molasses, lime or lemon juice, and old spirit of any kind, of each one gill intimately united by simmering for a few minutes over the fire. A teaspoonful of this medicine should be taken three times a day.

The above three medicines should be taken in succession and rotation in the order in which they are mentioned. A month or more may be interposed between the use of each of them.

4. A perpetual blister about the size of a French crown should be opened upon your left arm between the shoulder and elbow. It should be kept open until your disease is removed.

5. Receive frequently into your lungs the vapor of a quart of boiling water poured upon a gill of tar in a mug, through a funnel placed over the mug.

6. Take as many drops of laudanum every night as will compose your cough. Continue to take laudanum in the morning. A pill of a grain or two grains of opium may be taken at bedtime if the ordinary dose of laudanum should lose its effect.

7. Go to bed early. Sleep upon a mattress in summer and a featherbed in winter.

8. Wear flannel next to your skin in winter, and muslin in summer. Continue your former diet and drinks.

9. Use gentle exercise daily, especially that kind of exercise which employs the arms.

10. Carefully avoid the early morning and evening air, also fatigue from all its causes.

11. Should your pulse at any time, from taking cold or any other cause, become *tense* or *full*, and your cough be more troublesome than usual, lose eight or ten ounces of blood and abstain from animal food and from the use of the first *three* medicines recommended to you, until your pulse be restored to its ordinary strength. If one bleeding do not reduce your pulse, repeat it until it is reduced.

12. Spend the last month of next autumn, all the winter months, and the first and part of the second month in the spring in a large room warmed by a close stove. Not only eat and drink and sit during the day in this room, but sleep in it. Exercise or gentle labor of any kind may be used in it. Its temperature should be uniformly between 65 and 70 degrees. This remedy is to be used only in case you are not much better before the 1st of November.

13. Should the above remedies fail of relieving you in three months, recourse should be had to a salivation, after which resume them all. Should your family physician advise it, the salivation may be resorted to as soon as you reach home and before you begin to take any of the medicines herein prescribed except such as are intended to relieve your cough.

BENJN: RUSH

MS: New York Academy of Medicine.

[1] Not further identified than from what appears in a memorandum in an early hand on page four of the letter: "Letter of Benjamin Rush M D to Na- than Benjamin on return from the South (whither he had [*sic*] for his health) to his Family residing in Cattskill N Y."

[2] Benjamin evidently suffered from a

respiratory ailment. The treatment recommended under No. 12 in the series of instructions is like that which BR prescribed later this year for a granddaughter of Charles Carroll of Carrollton who had a bad cold. She was to stay in a room heated to a temperature of 70°-75° and to "use constant exercise, particularly playing battledore and jumping the rope" (letter to Mrs. Richard Caton, 5 Nov. 1812; Anderson Auction Co., Sale Catalogue No. 1119, N.Y., 1915, lot 239).

To David Petrikin[1]

Dear Sir,   Philadelphia, April 21, 1812

The facility with which a medical education is acquired in our country has multiplied physicians to such a degree that I do not know of a spot in the United States in which you could fit yourself with more advantage than in the one you now occupy. Competition and slow pay are now the conditions of a medical life everywhere.

My advice to you is to remain where you are. You will grow with the growth of the settlement. Purchase if possible and upon credit a small farm. A little debt will make you industrious and furnish you with an excuse to send in your bills as soon as your patients recover. Employ the leisure which a healthy season will give you in agricultural labors. The more you obtain in this way, the more independent you will be of your patients, and of course the more you will be courted by them. Happiness does not consist in wealth. A competence, books, "alternate labor and ease," to use the words of the poet Thompson,[2] a good wife, a few friends, vicinity to a church, and a conduct regulated by the principles of the Gospel, constitute the sum total of all the happiness this world is capable of giving, and these may all be possessed and enjoyed in your present situation.

From, dear sir, yours truly and affectionately,

BENJN: RUSH

MS: University of Pennsylvania, Medical School Library.

[1] Dr. David Petrikin addressed an appeal to BR for advice on where to settle, in a letter dated 14 Apr. 1812 from Danville, Northumberland co., Penna. (Rush MSS, XIII).

[2] The quotation is an approximate one from Thomson's Seasons, "Spring" (1728), line 1160.

To Thomas Jefferson

Dear Sir,   Philadelphia, April 26th, 1812

Your favor of the 20th instant came safe to hand, but *not* accompanied with the pamphlet you have mentioned in it.[1] I have read your letter to Mr. Adams[2] with pleasure, and shall put it into the post office tomorrow agreeably to your wishes.

The daughters of the late Wm. Lyman[3] and his only son arrived in this city a few weeks ago from London. Two of them are now members of my family. The eldest of them, a most accomplished woman in point of mind, is now at Washington, where she has probably communicated some anecdotes to Mr. Monroe relative to the noted Mr. Henry (whom she knew in London) that may serve to extend the views of the Executive of the mischief intended by him.[4]

I have often heard of the great respect of your daughter Mrs. Randolph for religion.[5] I beg you will present her with the excellent little work which accompanies this letter in defense of the object of her faith and affections. It will be invaluable in the hands of her children.

Health, respect, and friendship! from, dear sir, yours very affectionately,

BENJN: RUSH

P.S. I am now preparing for the press the result of the reading, experience, and reflections of fifty years upon all the forms of madness and upon all the other diseases of the mind.[6]

MS: Massachusetts Historical Society, Jefferson Papers.

[1] A retained copy of Jefferson's letter to BR of 20 Apr. 1812 is in L.C., Jefferson Papers; the pamphlet accompanying it was Jefferson's learned brief on the celebrated "Batture Case": *The Proceedings of the Government of the United States in Maintaining the Public Right to the Beach of the Mississipi, Adjacent to New Orleans*, N.Y., 1812.

[2] Also dated 20 Apr. 1812; printed in Jefferson's *Writings*, ed. Lipscomb and Bergh, XIII, 141-4.

[3] William Lyman (1755-1811), of Massachusetts; a Yale graduate, 1776; Jeffersonian member of Congress, 1793-1797; U.S. consul at London, 1805-1811 (Dexter, *Yale Graduates*, III,

619-20). His eldest daughter, Jerusha, later Mrs. Jackson Kemper, died in 1818 (DAB, under Kemper).

[4] This was the Canadian-American John Henry, a self-appointed secret British agent with whom Timothy Pickering and other New England Federalists had dealt in 1808 in an effort to have the Embargo repealed and to prevent a war with England. When the British government refused to buy Henry's papers, he sold them (Mch. 1812) to the United States government and fled to France. (McMaster, *Hist.*, III, 285-7, 444-7.)

[5] Martha Jefferson (1772-1836), wife of Thomas Mann Randolph

(Dumas Malone, *Jefferson the Virginian*, Boston, 1948, p. 434). The "excellent little work" sent her was one of the numerous religious tracts written by Beilby Porteous, Bishop of London (BR to Jefferson, 15 Mch. 1813).

[6] This work was duly published in the fall of 1812 as *Medical Inquiries and Observations, upon the Diseases of the Mind*, Phila.: Kimber & Richardson. BR provided the best statement of his aim in this book when he wrote John Adams, 4 Nov. 1812, presenting him with a copy: "They [the *Inquiries*] are in general accommodated to the 'common science' of gentlemen of all professions as well as medicine. The subjects of them have hitherto been enveloped in mystery. I have endeavored to bring them down to the level of all the other diseases of the human body, and to show that the mind and body are moved by the same causes and subject to the same laws." BR's application of this truth, it is generally agreed, forms the starting-point of psychiatric science in this country. His treatise at once became the standard American guide in its field and remained without a rival for many decades. A second edn. was brought out in 1818, a third in 1827, a fourth in 1830, and a fifth in 1835; a German translation, *Medizinische Untersuchungen und Beobachtungen über die Seelenkrankheiten*, was published in Leipzig, 1825. The originality and soundness of some of BR's ideas on this subject, together with his unusually readable presentation of them, have won high praise from later authorities. See Charles K. Mills, *Benjamin Rush and American Psychiatry*, N.Y., 1886; Deutsch, *The Mentally Ill in America*, ch. VIII; articles by C. B. Farr, Adolf Meyer, and R. H. Shryock in *Amer. Jour. of Psychiatry*, C-CI (1944-1945); Fritz Wittels, "The Contribution of Benjamin Rush to Psychiatry," *Bull. Hist. Med.*, XX (1946), 157-66.

To John Adams

My dear old Friend of 1774,   Philadelphia, May 5, 1812

I return you the copies of your letters to the Messrs. Smith and their answer, with my advice (as you have done me the honor to ask it) *by no means to publish them*.[1] "Scandal," Dr. Wetherspoon used to say, "will die sooner than you can kill it." I can subscribe to the truth of this assertion of our old Scotch Sachem from my own experience. Not a paragraph or even a line did I ever publish in reply to the volumes of scandal and falsehoods that filled our papers against me for more than three months in the year 1797. They have all perished, and I am still permitted to live with as much or more reputation than I deserve in the very city in which those publications were devoured like hot rolls every morning and evening by thousands of my fellow citizens. Be assured, my venerable friend, that your character does not require such an appeal to the public. Were it to be made, perhaps not more than twenty persons in the United States would recollect the idle and improbable tale the testimony of the Messrs. Smith was intended to refute. Time and posterity will do you justice, and your children will enjoy the fruits of your well-earned reputation. Posterity, did I say, will do you justice? It will not be necessary for your children to wait for that satisfaction. Read the enclosed letters from your and my old enemy Cobbett to the Prince of Wales. There you will see your opinions upon the subject of the impressment of American seamen ably defended, together with a just tribute to your services to your country.

Colonel P. mentioned probably the same things in the family of Mr. Henry Drinker, formerly a respectable Quaker of our city, some years ago that he communicated to you respecting your *man of ten talents*.[2] They were retailed to me by his son and who appears to believe them.[3]

You are mistaken in supposing General Green [*Greene*] was one of his idolaters, or that he was at all times discreet in speaking of him. His aide-de-camp Major Edwards informed me that this was far, very far, from being the case. He thought and spoke of him as you have often heard your son-in-law Colonel Smith, who knew him better than most men. But enough of this hateful subject. We will dismiss it forever.

I am now busily engaged in preparing for the press a volume of medical inquiries and observations upon madness and all the other diseases of the mind. The ancient Roman sculptors and painters always inscribed upon their works, when they had completed them, "facie*bat*" and "pinge*bat*." I shall inscribe the same declaration of *im*perfection upon my work.[4] It has been extorted from me by my pupils. It will I hope serve to excite more attention to the subject than has hitherto been bestowed upon it by physicians.

The issue of the application for loans will probably check the military spirit at Washington. The tide of the passions of our nation for war has nearly spent itself. In Pennsylvania it is daily becoming more and more unpopular. I well recollect in opposing Mr. Dickinson's proposal for deferring the Declaration of Independence until we were more numerous and more powerful than we were in 1776, you said to me that time by increasing our numbers and wealth would increase our ties to Great Britain. Late events show that this is the case. The tories have increased four or five-fold by ordinary population, and an immense accession has been made to them of British emigrants and apostate whigs who have become wealthy by successful speculations in certificates and banks.

A declaration of war against France as well as against England would probably unite us and fill the Treasury of the United States. It would do more: it would render a war wholly defensive, it would make both nations feel our importance, and it would produce such a reaction in domestic manufactures and internal commerce as would soon make us a great and independent nation. But why have I suffered my pen to run away with me? I know nothing of the subject which, alas! now so generally agitates and divides our country. I shall however venture to risk one question before I finish my letter. Do you think if the declaration of war against England had been made last fall, and the public mind thereby been instantly excited and inflamed to the *war point,* that so much clamor would have existed at this time against embargoes, loans, and taxes?

Adieu! Ever your truly grateful and affectionate friend,

BENJN RUSH

MS: Adams Manuscript Trust, Boston.

[1] Late in 1811 Timothy Pickering charged in one of his frequent polemical publications that Adams as president had made an unethical bargain with two influential Maryland politicians, Robert and Samuel Smith, to turn Pickering out of office as secretary of state. The correspondence relative to this controversy is in Adams' *Works*, x, 4-9.

[2] I.e., Washington. "Colonel P." is Pickering. See Adams to BR, 22 Apr.

1812 (*Old Family Letters, A,* p. 378-81).

[3] BR was from time to time the Drinkers' family physician. There were two sons in the family, William and Henry. See Drinker, *Not So Long Ago,* p. 4; Elizabeth Drinker, *Journal, passim.*

[4] One of BR's few attempts at a pun: the Latin verbs are in the *imperfect* tense.

To John Adams

Philadelphia, May 19th, 1812

My dear Friend of 1774 and 1812,

Your two letters of yesterday and today[1] have made me serious. They discover a profound knowledge of time past, present, and to come. I have directed one of my daughters to copy two sentences from your letter of this day to be sent to my son Richard at Washington, who, poor fellow! is swamped in a belief of the infallibility and perpetuity of the "powers that are."[2] I know he reveres your judgment. Perhaps the extracts from your letters may remove his delirium. I do not wish to see any of the men you have named in Mr. M.'s place, but if that event should happen, I sincerely hope his first act will be to send my son back again to Philadelphia and to his profession. All Jersey is becoming disaffected. A change will certainly take place in the elections in our state next fall, but how far it will extend I know not. The Embargo is the chief cause of the dissatisfaction in the country, the Nonintercourse law in our city. Stephen Gerard, who has lately bought the banking house of the

United States, and who is to open a private bank in it upon a capital of a million and a half dollars on the 1st of June, has refused to subscribe to the loan.[3] He even openly complains of the "people at Washington." His high standing as a Democrat I presume is known to you.

There are at present not less than 1,000 houses empty in Philadelphia.

Nations seem to be created as necessarily subject to war as individuals come into the world predisposed to the smallpox and measles. No plans of a general peace, no embargoes, no negotiations, no *Wasps*, nor *Hornets*, nor Pinckneys, nor Barlows,[4] nor appeals to the tribunal of reason, ever have or ever will prevent them while man is *man*. Peace has its evils and its sufferings as well as war, but from the greater share the passions have in enabling us to support the latter, they are borne with more patience and fortitude than the former.

I admit your reasonings upon the subject of a war with France as well as England. I mentioned it as the only consistent measure of the present *Chinese* system of resisting foreign aggression.

You are mistaken in supposing I have not read your *Defence*.[5] The first American edition of the 1st volume of it was printed by my advice in Philadelphia. The facts contained in it may be considered indeed as the history of the present times in the United States.

I write in great haste. Expect a sequel to this scrawl in a few days. Yours truly,

BENJN RUSH

P.S. Mr. Gerry is agreed upon at Washington as successor to Mr. Clinton.[6] So says Duane.

MS: Adams Manuscript Trust, Boston.

[1] Dated 13 and 14 May, respectively (*Old Family Letters*, *A*, p. 456-9, 382-5).

[2] Adams' letter of 14 May was a searching but sympathetic critique of Madison's administration. At a hazard, the two sentences sent by BR to Richard may have been: "The Republican Party are now split into four or five Factions, exactly as the Federal Party was in 1799, and by the same causes and the same means. . . . When a party grows strong and feels its power, it becomes intoxicated, grows presumptuous and extravagant, and breaks to pieces."

[3] Stephen Girard (1750-1831), the well-known Philadelphia merchant and financier, bought the first United States Bank after its charter expired and reopened it as the Bank of Stephen Girard (DAB; Kenneth L. Brown, "Stephen Girard's Bank," PMHB, LXVI [1942], 29-55). See also BR's sketch of Girard in the following letter to Adams.

[4] The *Wasp* and *Hornet* were American sloops of war that were to win

fame in the War of 1812 (DAH). William Pinkney had failed as minister to England to obtain fair treatment for United States shipping (DAB). Joel Barlow was currently on a mission to Napoleon for the same purpose, but failed likewise and died before the end of the year (same).

[5] *Defence of the Constitutions of Government of the United States . . .* , London, 1787-1788; see BR to Price, 2 June 1787.

[6] That is, as vice-president.

To John Adams

My dear old Friend,   Philadelphia, June 2nd, 1812

Stephen Gerard came to Philadelphia from France about thirty years ago in the capacity of a sailor. Having had some education and possessing a strong mind, he soon became a master of a vessel, afterwards a merchant, by which employment he has amassed an estate of five millions of dollars, one million of which was in stock of the late Bank of the United States; the rest is in houses, lots, ships, and in the hands of European merchants and bankers. His character is as singular as his prosperity has been extraordinary. In the year 1793 he acted as a superintendent of the yellow fever hospital at Bush hill, and even performed many of the humble offices of a nurse for the sick. With this great stock of voluntary humanity to strangers, he has lately refused to see a sister with several helpless children who were allured from France by the fame of his wealth in hopes of being assisted by him. To his carpenters, captains, sailors, and supercargoes he is always just and sometimes generous, but so despotic that he once dismissed one of his captains for bringing a present of a gown or cloak for his mistress after he had sold his privilege to the owner of the ship. While receiving an increase of his wealth by hundreds of thousands yearly, he sits down weekly and settles with a tenant of a small farm in the neighborhood of Philadelphia for fivepenny pieces and cents. You may judge of his religion when I tell you he has had two ships called by the names of the *Helvetius* and the *Voltaire*. In politics he has been uniformly Democratic. He is, however, unfriendly to the present measures of Congress. His bank went into operation yesterday. It is said it will soon consist of a capital of three millions of dollars. It possesses universal and unlimited confidence, founded alike in a belief of his resources, his abilities, and his integrity. He is the Robert Morris of the years 1779 and 1780.

Wm. McCorkle[1] came to Philadelphia years ago and set up a Democratic paper. He soon afterwards became a *Quid* and has gradually veered round to the Federal party. He is zealous, intelligent, and has a large subscription.

I have no doubt of the truth of Mr. Malcom's[2] account of Cobbett's character of you. He said to a gentleman who asked him why he was so much my enemy that he had abused me at the request of three physicians whom he named, but added "he had no enmity to me, and that he believed me to be as honest a man as may be in our country." He spoke likewise to another person very respectfully of my opinions in medicine, particularly of my belief in the domestic origin of the yellow fever, and yet he abused me in some of his papers for holding and propagating that belief. This was done to please his good friends the tories, who were preeminent in their opposition to that opinion and hostility to me for maintaining it.

Accounts from Washington say war will be declared in a few days[3] *in spite of the opposition* of printers, brokers, and tavern-keepers (who govern the public mind) in all the states.

I lament that Mr. Gerry was not the candidate for the Vice-President's chair, and fully concur with you in the high and correct character you have drawn of him. You have probably mentioned the *real* cause of Mr. Langdon's being preferred to him.[4] "Great events from little causes" will be reversed, should he be chosen. It will be a *little* event (compared with the election of Mr. Gerry) from a GREAT cause.

Dr. Logan of our city has been indefatigable in circulating petitions against war in and near Germantown. A petition from the Federalists is now handing about for the same purpose in our city. It is intended to counteract our late town meeting at which Captain Wm. Jones[5] presided, a man who has lately become the head of that section of the Democratic party which has adhered most closely to Governor Snyder. He possesses a powerful mind, dignified manners, and one of the ten talents you formerly ascribed to General Washington—that is, a "fine person."

I am sorry to find from your letter that your excellent son will not return as soon as you expected, to take his seat by the side of the cradle of his venerable parents. But don't despair of seeing him. Were I to judge of the vigor of your body, by the activity and force of your understanding, and the brilliancy of your imagination as manifested in your letters, I should suppose you are far, very far, from the close of life. In the language of the East, my whole heart says, Live, O! live forever, much esteemed and invaluable friend!

Adieu! Ever yours,

BENJN: RUSH

MS: Adams Manuscript Trust, Boston.

[1] William McCorkle was editor and publisher of the *Freeman's Journal* from 1804 to 1824 (Scharf & Westcott, III, 1981-2).

[2] Samuel B. Malcom had been secretary to John Adams during part of the latter's presidency (Adams, *Works*, X, 21, note; see *Old Family Letters*, *A*, p. 390-1).

[3] Madison had sent his war message to Congress on 1 June, but it was not until 18 June that it was approved by both Houses of Congress and signed

(Henry Adams, *History of the United States*, VI, 221-9).

[4] The vice-presidential nomination had been tendered by a Congressional caucus to John Langdon (1741-1819), former governor of New Hampshire; he declined it, and Gerry accepted it (DAB, under both names).

[5] William Jones (1760-1831), sailor and soldier in the Revolution; member of Congress, 1801-1803; secretary of the navy, 1813-1814 (DAB; see also BR to Adams, 22 Jan. 1813).

To John Adams

My dear Friend,   Philadelphia, June 4th, 1812

In spite of the speech made by my wife a few days ago, "that you and I corresponded like two young girls about their sweethearts," I will not be outdone by you in the number and promptness of my letters.

The General Assembly of the Presbyterian Church have just finished a long and interesting session. Among other things done by them, they have addressed a petition to Congress praying that the post offices may not be opened on the Sabbath day. A vote was lost in the Assembly for petitioning the President to appoint a national fast. It was objected to only because a majority believed it would not be attended with success. Are we not the only nation in the world, France excepted, whether Christian, Mohamidan, pagan, or savage, that has ever dared to go to war without imploring supernatural aid, either by prayers, or sacrifices, or auspices, or libations of some kind? How few men know that man is naturally a "go-to-meeting animal," to use your definition of a New England-man, or in other words that he is as naturally a *praying* as he is a breathing animal. Sailors, soldiers, Indians, nay more, Deists and Atheists, all pray by an unsubdued instinct of nature when in great danger or distress. How differently did the Congresses of 1774, 1775, and 1776 begin and conduct the war with Great Britain that ended in the establishment of the liberties and independence of our country! They appealed to the God of armies and nations for support, and he blessed both their councils and their arms. Do you recollect the rebuke you gave Mr. Jefferson in Congress upon this subject?[1]

Our papers teem with publications against the *horrors* of war. They remind me of an amendment which Mr. Saml. Adams told me he had moved in a proclamation by the first convention that sat in Boston.[2] It was to strike out the word "horrors" and to substitute in its room the "calamities" of a civil war. The latter word he said would alarm less than the former; and war he believed at that time to be both inevitable and necessary for the safety of his country.

It is curious to observe how exactly the sentiments and language of a certain class of citizens upon the subject of a war with G. Britain accord with the sentiments and language of their ancestors in politics in the years 1773 and 1774. There is nothing new under the sun in the feelings, opinions, and conduct of parties, whether in or out of power. Your view of them in your *Defence of the American Constitutions* might pass for a history of the whigs and tories and of the Federalists and Democrats of the United States.

I believe with you that all men who affect to despise public slander are hypocrites. Sir Thomas Brown, a learned and pious physician of the 17th century, says in his *Religio Medici* that "he would rather be exposed to the stroke of a fiery basilisk than of an angry pen,"[3] and yet anger and malice had nothing to feed upon in his excellent character. General Washington I have heard felt public abuse in the most sensible manner. Mr. Jefferson told me he once saw him throw the *Aurora* hastily upon the floor with a "dam" of the author, who had charged him with the crime of being a slaveholder. It is even said that paper induced him to retire from the President's chair of the United States.

Physiologists teach us that sensations originally painful sometimes become pleasurable from repetition. In this way only can scandal give pleasure to an innocent mind. From experience I can say this to be the case. I review the volumes of calumnies published against me by my brethren with more than pleasure. They are permanent memorials that the opinions and modes of practice which I introduced, and which my enemies have since adopted, were correct, and that thousands have owed their lives to them.

I need not add that it is now a time of uncommon health in our city or I should not intrude upon your leisure by such long and trifling letters. With respect and love to all who surround your table, I am, dear sir, ever yours,

BENJN: RUSH

MS: Adams Manuscript Trust, Boston.

[1] See BR to Adams, 27 June 1812.   Jan. 1769.
[2] The Convention of Sep. 1768; see   [3] Approximately quoted from pt. 2,
BR to an unidentified addressee, 26   sect. 3.

To William Eustis

Dear Sir,   Philadelphia, June 4th, 1812

An American edition of Sir John Pringle's invaluable treatise upon army diseases has lately been published in this city.[1] Permit me, sir, to ask whether a copy of this work would not be an useful and important article in the furniture of every medical chest for the army of the United States. I am the more disposed to ask this question from my knowledge of the inability of many of the young surgeons to purchase it, and from my recollection of the sufferings of the soldiers of the American Revolution from the ignorance of their surgeons of the contents of that book. Pardon the liberty I have taken, and believe me to be with great respect, dear sir, your friend and humble servant,

BENJN: RUSH[2]

MS: National Archives, Record Group 107 (Records of the Office of the Secretary of War), Letters Received and Sent.

[1] The American editor was BR himself; see letter to J. C. Lettsom, 3 May 1810.

[2] In a reply dated 8 June 1812, Secretary Eustis stated that orders had been issued "to purchase a number of the late Edition of Dr. Pringle sufficient to be distributed to the medical Staff" (National Archives, Record Group 107, Military Books, No. 5).

To Maxwell McDowell[1]

Dear Sir,   Philadelphia, June 11th, 1812

Your letter gave me pleasure, first because it gave me a proof that I was still remembered by you, and secondly because it contained an account of your being united with me in an attempt to remove the distressing and obstinate disease of Mr. Norris.[2] I received a letter from him a few days ago in which he gives me the same account of the state of his health that you have done. I have advised him to use the water of the Warm Springs in Virginia, both internally and externally, and to continue his bland and simple diet.

My best wishes attend your Medical School![3] I am not acquainted with Dr. Davage,[4] but I have heard that he is determined to prostrate the new doctrines in medicine taught in the University of Pennsylvania. Success to him!—if his opinions are more calculated to lessen the empire of pain and death than ours.

Give my compliments to your pastor, Dr. Inglis.[5] He charmed a numerous and respectable audience by his elegant and ingenious missionary sermon during the session of the General Assembly. A few objected to his text *only*, as not according with the design of the sermon.

I am now preparing for the press my lectures upon the diseases of the mind. They will, I hope, be published in the course of a few months.

Adieu, my dear sir. Health, respect, and friendship from yours sincerely,

BENJN: RUSH

Addressed: Dr: Maxwell McDowell Physician Baltimore.
MS: New York Public Library, Miscellaneous Papers.

[1] Maxwell McDowell (1771-1848), a graduate of Dickinson College, 1792, studied under BR at an unspecified time; first practised at York and came to Baltimore in 1810; professor of the institutes of medicine at the University of Maryland, 1814-1833, and honorary M.D., 1818 (Dickinson Coll., *Alumni Record*; E. F. Cordell, *University of Maryland, 1807-1907*, N.Y. and Chicago, 1907, I, 194; McDowell's letters to BR in Rush MSS, XI).

[2] William Norris, of Baltimore; several letters from Norris are in Rush MSS, XII.

[3] The College of Medicine of Maryland, founded 1807 and from 1812 the medical department of the University of Maryland (Packard, *Hist. of Medicine in the U.S.*, II, 737-9).

[4] John Beale Davidge (1768-1829), M.D., Glasgow, 1793; a principal founder of the College of Medicine of Maryland, in which he held the chairs of anatomy and surgery (DAB).

[5] Rev. James Inglis (1777-1820), pastor of the First Presbyterian Church, Baltimore; D.D., College of New Jersey, 1811 (Sprague, *Annals*, IV, 278-84).

To David Hosack

My dear Friend,   June 20th, 1812

Our Philosophical Society meets but once a month in summer. They met last evening. Their next meeting will be on the *third* Friday of next month, which is I think on the 17th of the month, on which day, or before it, I shall expect to have the pleasure of taking you by the hand as my guest.[1] All my family unite with me in requesting you to make our house your home while you remain in Philadelphia. Let us show the world that a difference of opinion upon medical subjects[2] is not incompatible with medical friendships; and in so doing, let us throw the whole odium of the hostility of physicians to each other upon their competition for business and money. Alas! while merchants, mechanics, lawyers, and the clergy live in a friendly intercourse with each other, and while even the brutes are gregarious, and

"Devil with devil firm concord holds,"

to use the words of Milton,[3] physicians, in all ages and countries, riot upon each other's characters! How shall we resolve this problem in morals?

With love to Mrs. Hosack and Miss Mary, in which all my family join, I am, dear sir, your friend and brother in the republic of medicine,

BENJN. RUSH

Printed: A. E. Hosack's memoir of David Hosack, in Gross, *Lives of Physicians and Surgeons*, p. 314-15.

[1] On 17 July 1812 the Philosophical Society met, and "Dr. Hossac [a clue to the correct pronunciation of the name] of New York read a paper on the laws governing the communication of contagious diseases" (Amer. Philos. Soc., *Early Proceedings*, p. 435-6). The attendance records do not indicate BR's presence; see letter to Vaughan, 22 Oct. 1806.

[2] Hosack held, in opposition to BR, that yellow fever was imported and that it was contagious. Thus, like BR, he was fifty percent right.

[3] Approximately quoted from *Paradise Lost*, II, 496-7.

To Vine Utley[1]

Dear Sir,   Philadelphia, June 25th, 1812

Did you know how much folly and ignorance cleave to the character of the person whose history you have required of his physical habits, you would not have thought it of any consequence to know them.

It will not be in my power to answer all your questions. I shall barely inform you that from necessity I conformed to the Spanish proverb of "being *old* when I was young, that I might be *young* when I was old," by living temperately. This necessity was imposed upon me at the age of eighteen, at which time I was affected with a pulmonary complaint which continued, with occasionally a spitting of blood at longer or shorter intervals, until I was about forty years of age. During that long period I lived chiefly upon vegetables, tea, coffee, and a small quantity of animal food. When most free from my disorder, I drank malt liquors and wine and took bark with advantage.

In the paroxysms of my disease, whether induced by cold or any other cause, I lost blood and reduced my diet, which generally relieved me in a few days.

I have had several severe attacks of acute diseases, particularly pleurisy and bilious fevers. I have suffered likewise for months with vertigo and headache, since as well as during[2] the period before mentioned.

Since my 58th year I have enjoyed uninterrupted health, with the exception of now and then a catarrh, such as is common to persons of all ages in our country.

I am now in my sixty-eighth year, and through divine goodness possess the same facility in doing business and the same pleasure in study that I did when I was a young man. I generally sleep about seven hours in the four-and-twenty, and spend from three to seven hours at my desk every day, according to the greater or less hurry of my business. I continue to prefer tea and coffee with their usual accompaniments to all other kinds of aliment. At dinner, but at no other time, I eat sparingly of animal food, with the common garden vegetables of our country, and generally drink one glass or a glass and a half of old Madeira wine after them. I never drink ardent spirits in any way nor at any time. I see well with spectacles, and my hearing is unimpaired. I appreciate the continuance and perfection of these two senses at 100,000 dollars a year. Blessed be God for them; without them life would be a living death.

I have been employed for several years in preparing for the press a work to be entitled "Rules for the preservation of health, accommodated to the climate, diet, and present state of society and manners of the inhabitants of the United States."[3] It will include all my opinions and most of my practices upon the subject of your letter.

I am, dear sir, yours very respectfully,

BENJ. RUSH

Addressed: Dr. Vine Utley, Fellow of the Medical Society of Connecticut.

MS (copy by Utley, enclosed in a letter from Utley to Thomas Jefferson, 18 Feb. 1819): Massachusetts Historical Society, Jefferson Papers.

[1] Utley's first letter to BR, dated from Lyme, Conn., 2 June 1812, transmitted the preface to a medical work on which he desired BR's advice. The writer hoped to present the completed work to BR in person, for he wished to behold "one of the greatest Philosophers in America." A second letter, of 15 June, acknowledged a reply (now lost) from BR which evidently disapproved Utley's plans for authorship but evoked from the latter a request for information so that "I may learn a little further, how you keep your body in health, and intellects in a state of such regular excitement, as to write with such correctness

at all times." (Both of Utley's letters are in Rush MSS, XVIII.) To this BR replied in the revealing letter here printed, which would probably not have been preserved if Utley had not sent a copy of it enclosed in a later letter making similar inquiries of Jefferson. Jefferson's reply, 21 Mch. 1819, is printed in his *Writings*, ed. Lipscomb and Bergh, XV, 186-8. Little has been discovered concerning Utley beyond what is revealed in the letters mentioned. He was evidently an ardent Re-

publican. He appears interestingly in a medical document printed in the Connecticut Historical Society, *Bulletin*, XII (1947), 31-2. This is a certificate, signed by Utley in May 1805, pledging to pay all medical expenses for any member of the Brainard family of Colchester, Conn., who shall come down with smallpox after Utley's vaccinating eleven of them at this time.

[2] This word omitted in Utley's transcript.

[3] See BR to Adams, 24 Aug. 1808.

To John Adams

My dear Friend,   Philadelphia, June 27th, 1812

Don't complain of my wife.[1] You have not a better friend nor a greater admirer in the United States. She devours your letters. The reflection you have noticed was aimed, not at the *subjects*, but at the *frequency* of our letters. It was uttered with an air of pleasantry, such as you have often admired in your excellent Mrs. Adams.

The anecdote I alluded to respecting the fast day is as follows. Upon a motion for such a day, Mr. Jefferson not only opposed it but treated it with ridicule, and hinted some objections to the Christian religion. You rose and defended the motion, and in reply to Mr. Jefferson's objections to Christianity you said "you were sorry to hear such sentiments from a gentleman whom you so highly respected and with whom you agreed upon so many subjects, and that it was the only instance you had ever known of a man of sound sense and real genius that was an enemy to Christianity." You suspected, you told me, that you had offended him, but that he soon convinced you to the contrary by crossing the room and taking a seat in the next chair to you.[2]

My son, I perceive by the papers, is to deliver an oration on the 4th of July at Washington.[3] I sent him the following fact which you communicated to me from Colonel Henry Laurens a few days after he took his seat in Congress, with a view to direct the attention of my son's audience to the importance of the navy. When the Colonel left London, he called to take leave of Mr. Greenville [*Grenville*]. The subject of conversation was the taxation of America. Colonel L. said the amount of the taxes was not worth the controversy and war which existed and hung over both countries. "You mistake the cause of the present controversy with your country," said Mr. Greenville. "*You spread too much canvas upon the ocean. We must clip it.*"[4] The late depredations of G. Britain upon our commerce and the present war are striking illustrations of the truth of Mr. Greenville's confession.

I extracted those parts of your letters that related to the character, sacrifices, and sufferings of Mr. Gerry in the cause of his country, and sent them to my son at Washington. From his activity and zeal in the measures of the government and of the ruling party, I am disposed to believe they were made use of in favor of Mr. G.'s occupying the place of Mr. Langdon in the Democratic ticket.

The declaration of war has produced a suspension of political hostilities in our city, but no change has been induced in the minds of the persons who were opposed to it. They look forward to the next election for new rulers who shall restore peace and trade with Great Britain and make war upon France. Perhaps the increase of the power and influence of the ruling party from military commissions and appointments connected with them may disappoint them. Alas! what dead weights are banks, whiskey distilleries, and the funding system in the opposite scale to that which contains the patriotism, the justice, and honor of our country! We are indeed a bebanked, a bewhiskied, and a bedollared nation.

Our wise men and women look back to the administration of Washington as the golden age of our country, without recollecting that the seeds of all the disputes which now divide our citizens, and of the controversy with France, were sown in it. I say the controversy with France, for this began in consequence of the offense given to her by the British treaty. But not only the seeds of political disputes but of our vices were sown during the same administration, by the funding system and the passion for banks which was created by the profits of script and of the immense interest of the Bank of the United States.

The capital now vested in banks in the city of New York is seventeen millions five hundred thousand dollars. There are twelve hundred whiskey distilleries in Lancaster county *only* in Pennsylvania. There have been 300 bankruptcies in our city since last April, and 700 more are expected, all of which have been produced chiefly by the two evils that have been mentioned, viz., banks and distilleries.

Adieu. Ever yours,

BENJN: RUSH

MS: Adams Manuscript Trust, Boston.

[1] See *Old Family Letters, A*, p. 391.
[2] Adams remembered "the little Flirt between Jefferson and me" as arising out of a motion for Congress to sit on a Sunday (same, p. 298).
[3] BR need not have learned of his son's honor from the newspapers, for Richard consulted with his father through every stage of the composition of the oration, which was delivered in the House Chamber and was a great success (Powell, *Richard Rush*, p. 34-5). It was published as *An Oration, Delivered by Richard Rush, on the 4th of July, 1812* [Washington, 1812] (*L.C. Cat.*).
[4] On this anecdote, see BR to Madison, 30 Jan. 1806.

To John Adams

My dear Friend,   Philadelphia, July 8th, 1812

It is now a time of uncommon health in our city, insomuch that I spend six or seven hours of every day, including the evenings, at my desk. I mention this fact to apologize for the promptness with which I reply to your letters.

I sent your letter of yesterday morning[1] to my son Richard in order that he may correct from it the mistake I made in the name of the British minister whose jealousy of our canvas upon the ocean I had mentioned in a letter to my son after I saw his name announced as the orator of the 4th of July. He can correct it in the oration when it issues from the press.

You are most probably right in the anecdote of the little good-natured sparring between you and Mr. Jefferson in Congress.

We are much alarmed at the news our papers daily contain of the opposition to the general government in your state. Massachussets has long and justly been considered as the right arm of the Union. Your physical force equals that of our state, but in *mental* force you tower much above us, nor will the physical force of Pennsylvania be brought into full operation upon the present occasion. Alas! our poor country! Even the powers delegated to carry on the war are divided. This has been seen during the whole of the last session of Congress, and lately in the refusal of Congress to comply with Mr. Madison's request to increase the number of general officers.

The organization of the medical department is incomplete.

Among the national sins of our country that have provoked the wrath of Heaven to afflict us with a war, I ought to have mentioned in my last letter the idolatrous worship paid to the name of General Washington, by all classes and *nearly* all parties of our citizens, manifested in the impious application of names and epithets to him which are ascribed in Scripture only to God and to Jesus

Christ. The following is a part of them: "our Saviour," "our Redeemer," "our cloud by day and our pillar of fire by night," "our
star in the east," "To us a Son is born," and "our guide on earth,
our advocate in heaven." With the sin of these epithets is connected
two other sins: 1st, Ingratitude to all other Revolutionary servants
of the public in the cabinet or the field, Alexr. Hamilton only excepted; and 2ly, a total unbelief in the divine talents and virtues
ascribed to him by most of his companions in arms and contemporaries in the Revolution, more especially by the citizens of Boston,
New York, and Philadelphia who submitted to the British army
during the American war. What an ocean of political turpitude has
been wiped away by the ten letters that compose his name!

"The whigs have done too much, suffered and sacrificed too much,
and succeeded too well ever to be forgiven" by their *Bebritished*
fellow citizens.

Few men have more reason to deplore the present war than I
have. One of my daughters with her two children are now with
me, and if Canada should be invaded, my other British daughter
with her three children will follow her, and all of them remain
with me, perhaps without any pecuniary intercourse with their
husbands until the war is over. Besides, my 4th son is now probably
on his way from Smyrna to Petersburg, where his capture by the
British is inevitable, and in his capture will be involved considerable
losses. But "sic Deo visum est."[2] I will notwithstanding stand or
fall with the government of the United States.

Many calculations are made daily of the comparative wickedness
of France and Britain and of the comparative injuries each has
done us. I resolve the questions thus in *my own family*. France has
thrown off all the restraints of religion, natural law, and national
justice, and professes to be governed only by convenience and self-
interest. Britain professes to be a *Christian* nation and the defender
of the religion, liberty, and even civilization of the world. Their
crimes are the same, but in which of them are they most aggravated?
Again France takes and burns our property *only*; Britain robs us
of our citizens on the high seas, murders our women and children
on our frontiers, as well as robs us of our property. Which of them
has done us the most injury? All this is between ourselves. I *think
aloud* only in my own house and when I write to you.

With all the clamors against war with England *only*, and the
destruction it is to bring upon our country, how will the minority in
the Senate justify their voting for war with both England and
France?[3] Its evils must have been double if not fourfold. Alas!

the *madness* of party spirit! Where—where is my tranquillizer?

I sent your list of *small majorities*[4] to my son Richard while he was composing his oration. He has probably used them to defend the declaration of war. But I am far from thinking from *present* appearance that it is acceptable to even a small majority of our citizens. With the black list of taxes hanging over our states for next year, I think there is reason to expect a large majority next October for peace and no taxes.

From the view of our war and its consequences, I am led to see more and more of the hand of heaven in it. "Behold I will send *divisions* among you."[5] What greater punishment for moral and political evil can be inflicted upon a nation?

One of the most necessary ingredients in the apparatus of war is still wanting in our country. I mean *war passions*. No person appears to feel them as we felt them in 1774, 1775, and 1776. Even the friends to war talk of it with apathy. Without an *inflammation in our passions*, nothing effective can be done in the mighty contest before us. Reason cannot be substituted for it, "for what did Reason ever do that was great in human affairs?" says Frederick the 2nd of Prussia. He must have meant chiefly in military affairs.

The Philadelphia bar, with the exception of two or three young lawyers, are the friends of peace. I send you an oration of one of those young men delivered on the 4th of July.[6] He has openly and decidedly taken part with the friends of war with Great Britain. I enclose you likewise a short account of the manner in which my son's oration was received in Washington.

If this long and heterogeneous letter lessens the pressure of the heat upon your venerable limbs for a few minutes, or makes you forget for half an hour the unkindness and ingratitude of friends and the malignity of enemies, I shall be highly gratified.

Adieu! Ever yours,

BENJN: RUSH

MS: Adams Manuscript Trust, Boston.

[1] Dated 3 July 1812 (*Old Family Letters, A*, p. 297-300). For the correction made by Adams, see BR's letter to the Editor of the *Pennsylvania Journal*, 4 July 1782, note 3.

[2] "Thus God has decided." "Visum est" in this sense is a common phrase, but the source of BR's quotation (if it is one) has not been found.

[3] The Giles faction of rebellious Re- publicans delayed action on Madison's war message for twelve days by urging, instead of a declaration of war on England, the issuance of letters of marque and reprisal against both England and France (James Schouler, *History of the United States under the Constitution*, rev. edn., N.Y., 1894-1913, II, 393-4).

[4] See *Old Family Letters, A*, p. 393-4.

⁵ Not located; probably misquoted.
⁶ The oration was by Charles Jared Ingersoll (1782-1864), then a brilliant young Philadelphia lawyer and author, afterwards a national political figure and historian (DAB). BR presumably sent a newspaper text.

To Edward Harris[1]

Dear Sir,   July 11, 1812

The following remedies appear to me to be proper in your case:

1. From twenty to sixty drops of the spirit of turpentine (increasing from the smaller to the greater number gradually) in a tablespoonful of molasses every morning, *fasting*. Nothing is to be eaten after it for an hour or longer.

2. If you are not relieved by the above medicine in one month, mix two ounces of iron filings[2] with the same quantity of common salt, and take a teaspoonful of it every morning in molasses or syrup, *fasting* as before directed. Should that dose be offensive to your stomach, take *less*; if it be not offensive to your stomach, take a larger dose of it.

3. Use sea-bathing for two or three weeks, and drink at the same time from a gill to half a pint of salt water[3] two or three times a day upon an empty stomach. If that quantity should not purge you, take more of it; if it do, take less.

Carefully avoid fatigue from all its causes, also costiveness by taking occasionally a little rhubarb.

From, dear sir, yours very respectfully,

BENJN: RUSH

Addressed: Mr Edward Harris near Moorestown New Jersey.
MS: University of Pennsylvania Library.

[1] Not further identified.
[2] Coxe's *American Dispensatory*, 1825 (p. 285-6), has this to say about the medical use of iron filings:
"The general virtues of this metal, and the several preparations of it, are, to constringe the fibres, to quicken the circulation, to promote the deficient secretions in the remoter parts, and at the same time to repress inordinate discharges into the intestinal tube. After the use of them, if they take effect, the pulse is very sensibly raised; the colour of the face, though before pale, changes to a florid red; the alvine, urinary, and cuticular excretions are increased. . . . Iron is given in most cases of debility and relaxation."
[3] The same authority states (p. 92): "Sea water is well known to be purgative, and forms at sea, an excellent clyster. It is taken to the amount of about a pint in the morning, as a cathartic, at two doses, with an interval of half an hour."

To John Adams

My dear Friend,   Philadelphia, July 13th, 1812

Will you bear to read a letter that has nothing in it about politics or war?—I will, without waiting for an answer to this question, trespass upon your patience by writing you one upon another subject.

I was called on Saturday last to visit a patient about nine miles from Philadelphia. Being a holiday, I took my youngest son with me to drive me instead of my black servant. After visiting my patient, I recollected that I was within three or four miles of the farm upon which I was born and where my ancestors for several generations had lived and died.[1] The day being cool and pleasant, I directed my son to continue our course to it. In approaching it I was agitated in a manner I did not expect. The access to the house was altered, but everything around it was nearly the same as in the days of my boyhood, at which time I left it. I introduced myself to the family that occupied it by telling them at once who I was and my motives for intruding upon them. They received me kindly, and every branch of the family discovered a disposition to satisfy my curiosity and gratify my feelings. I asked permission to conduct my son upstairs to see the room in which I drew my first breath and made my first *unwelcome* noise in the world. My request was readily granted, and my little son seemed to enjoy the spot. I next asked for a large cedar tree which stood before the door, that had been planted by my father's hand. Our kind host told me it had been cut down 17 years ago, and then pointed to a piazza in front of the house, the pillars of which he said were made of it. I stepped up to one of those pillars and embraced it. I inquired for an orchard planted by my father. The owner of the house conducted me to an eminence behind it and showed me a few large, straggling apple trees that still bore fruit, to each of which I felt something like the affection of a brother. The house, which is of stone, bore marks of age and decay. On one of the stones near the front door I discerned with difficulty the letters J.R. Before the house flows a small but deep creek[2] abounding with pan fish. The farm contains 90 acres, all in a highly cultivated state. I knew the owner of it to be in such easy circumstances that I did not ask him his price for it, but requested, if he should ever incline to sell it, to make me or my surviving sons the offer of it, which he promised to do. While I sat in his common room, I looked at its walls and reflected how often they had been made responsive by my ancestors to conversations about wolves and bears and snakes in the first settlement of the farm—afterwards about cows and calves and colts and lambs, and the comparative exploits of reapers and mowers and threshers, and at all times with prayers and praises and chapters read audibly from the Bible, for all who had inhabited it of my family were pious people and chiefly of the sects of Quakers and Baptists.[3] On my way home I stopped to view a small family graveyard[4] in which were buried three and part of four successive generations, all of whom were descended from Captain John Rush, who with six sons and three daughters followed William Penn to Pennsylvania in 1683 in the 60th year of his age and died in 1702. He commanded a troop of horse under Oliver Cromwell, and family tradition says he was personally known to him and much esteemed by him as an active enterprising officer. When a young man, I was sometimes visited by one of his grandsons,[5] a man of 85 years of age who had lived many years with him when a boy and often detailed anecdotes from him of the battles in which he had fought under Cromwell, and once mentioned an encomium upon his character by Cromwell when he supposed he had been killed. The late General Darke of Virginia and the present General James Irvine of our city, now a venerable Revolutionary officer, are a part of his numerous posterity. As the successor to the eldest sons of the family, I have been permitted to possess his sword and watch.[6] In walking over the graveyard I met with a headstone with the following inscription:

"In memory of
James Rush
who departed this life March 16th, 1727
aged 48 years.

I've tried the strength of death,
And here lie under ground,
But I shall rise above the skies,
When the last trump shall sound."

This James Rush was my grandfather. My son the physician was named after him. I have often heard him spoken of as a strong-minded man and uncommonly ingenious in his business, which was that of a gunsmith. The farm still retains the marks of his boring machine. My father inherited both his trade and his farm.

While standing near his grave and recollecting how much of my kindred dust surrounded it, my thoughts became confused, and it was some time before I could arrange them. Had any or all my ancestors and kinsmen risen from their graves and surrounded me in their homespun and working dresses (for they were all farmers or mechanics), they would probably have looked at each other with some surprise and said, "What means that *gentleman* by thus intruding upon us?"—"Dear and venerable friends! Be not offended at me. I inherit your blood, and I bear the name of most of you. I come to claim affinity with you and do homage to your Christian and rural virtues. It is true my dress indicates that I move in a different sphere from that in which you passed through life, but I have acquired and received nothing from the world which I prize so highly as the religious principles I inherited from you, and I possess nothing that I value so much as the innocence and purity of your characters."

Upon my return to my family in the evening, I gave them a history of the events of the day, to which they listened with great pleasure and partook at the same time of some cherries from the limb of a large tree (*supposed* to have been planted by my father) which my little son brought home with him.

Mr. Pope says there are seldom more than two or three persons in the world who are sincerely affected at hearing of the death of any man, beyond the limits of his own family.[7] It is I believe equally true that there are seldom more than two or three persons in the world who are interested in anything a man says of himself beyond the circle of his own table or fireside. I have flattered myself that you are one of those two or three persons to whom the simple narrative and reflections contained in this letter will not be unacceptable from, my dear and much respected friend, yours very affectionately,

BENJN: RUSH[8]

MS: Adams Manuscript Trust, Boston.

[1] BR's birthplace still stands, at the end of a short lane off Red Lion Road near its intersection with Academy Road and not far from the center of the present suburban community of Torresdale. The early settlement, known as Byberry, was twelve or more miles up the Delaware from the city of BR's day, but it is now within the bounds of the city and county of Philadelphia. A photograph of the Rush homestead is reproduced in Goodman's *Rush*, facing p. 4. The original building, erected before 1700, was probably a square one-story structure, but by BR's time it had a second story, and possibly the ground plan had also been enlarged by a stone addition. Various wooden extensions are of more recent construction. BR lived there until he was six, when his father died and his mother set up a shop in Philadelphia. The house and farm were sold in 1765 to Jonathan Parry, whose descendants still retain possession. (BR to Adams, 8 Aug. 1812; Goodman, *Rush*, p. 3-4; information from Mrs. Samuel H. McKenty, the present resident, who courteously showed the editor through the Rush homestead in 1947.) Reminiscences of the Rushes and their neighbors, and of life and manners in early Byberry are available in Martin-

dale's *Hist. of Byberry and Moreland,* one of the most charming books of its class.

[2] Poquessing Creek (variously spelled); its course is the northeastern boundary of Philadelphia co., dividing it from Bucks co.

[3] BR's own genealogical notes state that John Rush "embraced the principles of the Quakers in 1660. . . . In 1691 he and his whole family left the Quakers and became Keithians. In 1697 they became Baptists" (Biddle, *Memorial,* p. 223).

[4] This graveyard, much overgrown, may still be seen on Red Lion Road between the Rush homestead and Red Lion Tavern. See also Martindale, *Hist. of Byberry and Moreland,* p. 30-1, 145-51.

[5] I.e., Thomas Rush, "who lived to be eighty-four years of age and died about the year 1770. He passed the first fourteen years of his life with his grandfather John Rush, and has often related anecdotes to Benjamin Rush and others, of the battles, skirmishes, etc., of the old captain which he received from his own lips" (BR's genealogical notes, in Biddle, *Memorial,* p. 234).

[6] Now in the possession of Mr. Benjamin Rush of Devon, Penna., a direct descendant.

[7] I have not located this saying attributed to Pope.

[8] A copy of this letter was retained by BR and sent, upon request, to David Hosack (see letter to Hosack, 25 Sep. 1812). Hosack subsequently communicated the letter to the New York *Mirror* at an unknown date, whence it was reprinted in Biddle, *Memorial,* p. 1-4, and from the *Memorial* in turn by Goodman, *Rush,* p. 355-8. It is therefore deservedly well known.

To John Adams

My dear Friend,   Philadelphia, July 18th, 1812

During the Revolutionary War I kept notes and preserved pamphlets with a view to write memoirs of it. From the immense difference in my facts and opinions from those that were current and popular, I was sure if I had published them they would not have been believed, and would moreover have exposed me and my posterity to persecution. I therefore burnt all my notes (the characters of the gentlemen who subscribed the Declaration of Independence excepted) and gave my pamphlets to my son Richard, who has carried them with him to Washington.[1] This I hope will be a sufficient reason for my not being one of the judges of the histories you have wished to have written.[2] But, my friend, why blot paper with any more records of the folly and wickedness of man? Were I compelled to write a history of any of the human race, it should be of my lunatic patients in the Hospital. There I should find *folly* only, for most of them are innocent and some of them amiable. There is not a French Jacobin, nor a visionary Democrat, nor an Essex Junto man, nor a priest deranged with Federalism or Democracy, nor a governor compounding praying and fasting with party politics, among them all.

Wars I believe are not only inevitable and necessary, but sometimes *obligatory* upon nations. "Nil Dei mortalibus sine" (not only
"labore") but "sine bello."[3] We rise in society and we preserve our
property, our names, and our standing in it, nay more, our lives,
by means of war. The weapons employed in this war are lawsuits,
doors, and locks and bolts. To neglect to employ these weapons
is to forfeit those blessings. Nations in like manner can exist with
all the prerogatives of nations only by war. It is the condition by
which they navigate the ocean and preserve their territory from
incursion. To neglect to contend for both by arms is to forfeit their
right to them. The ocean has been called the highroad of nations.
It might be called God's gift to all nations. Not to maintain the
exercise and enjoyment of this gift is (I hope I do not say too much
when I add) ingratitude and disobedience to him that gave it. To
expect perpetual peace therefore among beings constituted as we
are, is as absurd as to expect to discover perpetual motion. I have
read no other state paper upon the subject of our war but Mr. Madison's message to Congress recommending a declaration of war,
but from my knowledge of the authors and subscribers of the addresses you allude to,[4] I am prepared to believe all you say of them.
Some of them or of their leaders I know cursed Mr. Jefferson
some years ago for his cowardice for not doing exactly what Mr.
Madison has done.

I blush for the selfishness, ignorance, and party spirit of our
citizens, and in thinking of them have often applied to them the
words of Jugurtha that you have quoted in your letter.[5] Is our
nation *worth* a war? Would it not have been more correct, and more
in unison with our habits and principles, had Congress instead of
declaring war sent an advertisement to be published in all the newspapers in Europe drawn up in some such form as the following?

"For *Sale*
to the highest bidder.
The United States of America.

Terms of payment—A bank in every village in the country
composed of five houses, and a dozen in every city; commerce
with the whole world; a whiskey distillery on every farm; and
a charter conveying to the whole nation and to every individual
in it the title of 'Disciples of Washington.' Inquire of Messrs.
———— in Boston and of Messrs. ———— in New York and
Philadelphia."

I lament with you the manner in which our rulers have begun the war. But—but, my friend. Non est "fas mihi audita loqui."[6] There are empirics in all professions as well as in medicine. The world will not bear principles in *practical* sciences. In seeking the "faults" you allude to, I have made enemies or scoffers of all my medical brethren.

You are mistaken in supposing that I think our executive too strong. I wish it were wholly independent of the Senate in all its appointments. I wish further that the President should be chosen for 7, 9, or 11 years, and afterwards become ineligible to that or any other station or office, with a salary of 2 or 3 thousand dollars a year to compensate for that disability and to enable him to support the expenses to which his having filled the office of President would expose him in subsequent life. This would give him an independence as the first magistrate of the nation that would obviate one half the evils of our government.

Adieu! From, dear sir, ever yours,

BENJN: RUSH

P.S. I permitted Miss Lyman to read one of your late letters to me. She accorded with all your opinions and was delighted with the force and brilliancy of your style. When she returned it, she said, "This gentleman is too great an object to be fully seen and known while he *is so near us*. Such minds require the distance of centuries to be perfectly understood and fully appreciated."

July 20. I have just seen my son's *Oration*. I fear it contains too many indigestible and inebriating truths for the weak stomachs and heads of *most* of our citizens. He informs me that he intended to send you a copy of it. Our old friend Saml. Adams used to say "nations were as free as they deserved to be" and that "even enslaved nations were free when they preferred slavery to liberty, inasmuch as freedom consisted in possessing the objects of our predilection." Alas! For what have you thought and read and wrote and spoke and negotiated? They have taken away my gods, they have taken away the profits of our banks and whiskey distilleries, and reduced the price of our grain. What! what! have we left?— Yes, the last has been taken away for a *time* only, that you may enjoy a high price for it forever. Happy[7] would it be for our country if the two former were taken away forever.

Addressed: John Adams Esqr: Quincy near Boston.
MS: Adams Manuscript Trust, Boston.

[1] This was evidently an extensive collection. Richard Rush told Jared Sparks in 1828 that these pamphlets and related papers had been "preserved till recently, when they were lost by accident" (Herbert B. Adams, *Life and Writings of Jared Sparks*, Boston and N.Y., 1893, II, 49).

[2] See Adams' list of historical works, such as "the best History of the Friendship and Benevolence of Great Britain towards America from 1600 to 1774," for which he said he intended to offer prizes; BR was to be one of the judges (letter of 7 July 1812; *Old Family Letters*, A, p. 401).

[3] "The gods have given nothing to mortals without (not only labor) but without war." Apparently adapted from Horace, *Satires*, I, ix, 59-60: "Nil sine magno Vita labore dedit mortalibus."

[4] From Massachusetts and Connecticut towns opposed to the war (*Old Family Letters*, A, p. 403).

[5] Adams in his letter of 10 July (*Old Family Letters*, A, p. 302) had quoted Jugurtha's denunciation of Rome ("Urbem venalem," &c.) from Sallust; see BR's earlier use of this passage in his letter to Adams of 13 June 1808.

[6] "It is not 'right for me to say what I have heard.'" Approximately quoted from the *Aeneid*, VI, 266.

[7] MS: "Happily."

To John Adams

Dear Friend,   Philadelphia, August 8th, 1812

The paternal farm which I visited on the 11th of last month lies *two miles* further from Philadelphia than the cottage where you once did me and my brother the honor to take a family dinner with my dear and venerable mother. She purchased and retired to it after she gave up business in Philadelphia. I had seen my native place but once since I was six years old, and that but for a few minutes on a winter's day five-and-thirty years ago, a time when war and news and politics occupied my mind so entirely as to exclude all moral and domestic reflections. The impressions made by my visit to that beloved and venerated spot have not passed out of my mind. I hope to revisit it and shall try by every honest effort to purchase it from its present owner. Many anecdotes of the American progenitor of our family have been reviewed in my memory by association since the day I stood upon his dust. I shall mention two of them which will give you an insight into his character. In one of his reconnoitering excursions during Cromwell's Wars, he came to a farmhouse where he was kindly received and waited upon by a pretty young girl of 17 years of age. The whole family were Roundheads. When he left the house, he thanked the family for their civilities to him, and particularly the young woman who had been so attentive to him, and in parting with her said, "When the war is over I will come back again and court this pretty little maiden." This he did, according to his extempore and perhaps unmeaning promise, and married her.[1] She was the mother of all his children and accompanied him to Pennsylvania, where she survived him several years. There is a record of her baptism in the books of a Baptist church in the neighborhood of the place where she lived after she was 80. She had been before that time a Quaker.

When the Old Trooper left England, one of his relations entreated him to leave one of his grandchildren behind him. "No—no," said he, "I won't. I won't leave even a *hoof* of my family behind me." He had been persecuted for his religious principles and left his native country in a fit of indignation at its then intolerant government. His name is mentioned in Fox's *Journal*.[2]

The "retaliation" as you have called it, or the history of your ancestors,[3] has given great pleasure to my family. They were men of whom England was not worthy. How much greater the achievement to subdue a wilderness such as you say they found at Braintree, than to conquer a province! You are indeed "well born," for all men are so who are descended from a long line of pious ancestors. I agree with you that the pleasure we derive from the respect and homage we pay to our forefathers, and from visiting the spots where they worked or walked or prayed, is a proof of *disinterested* benevolence, and I agree further with you that it shows the principle you allude to in all nations and individuals to be a natural one, and to be implanted in us for wise purposes. I possess Butler's *Sermons*, also his *Analogy*,[4] and have read them over and over and marked and selected passages from each of them. They are monuments of the strength of the human understanding. I feel in reading them as if I were in company with a visitor from another planet, alike elevated above ours in size and in the intellect of its inhabitants.

Here I would willingly lay down my pen, but I cannot take leave of you without heaving a sigh over our beloved country. "A blacker cloud" (to use the words of the Bishop of St. Asaph[5] in speaking of the probable issue of the Boston port bill) "never hung over our nation." *Black* from the disaffection of New England to the war, *black* from the *time* (too *late* or too *soon*) in which it was declared, and *blackest* of all from the manner in which it *has been, is,* and *will be* conducted. It has been called a "reelection war," also "a dramatic war." Alas! it has none of the properties of the war of 1775.[6]

You have misapprehended me in supposing that I believe the government of France to be more profligate than that of England. On the contrary, considering the high pretensions of Britain to piety and morality, I believe her conduct to be more criminal towards the whole world than that of France, for she adds to her wickedness the crime of hypocrisy. My friend Geo. Clymer, who is true to the principles of 1776, says, "Britain has lately become very devout, that is, she has *fled* to religion, but it was only to get *further* from France." Have you ever attended to the Prince Regent of England being the only monarch in Christendom who now unites ecclesiastical and civil power in his person? The Emperors of France and Austria have not imitated Henry the 8th. Secular power in an ecclesiastic died with the Pope, for which reason one of my patients who is a great reader of the Scriptures, particularly of the book of Revelation, has repeatedly said to me and others that "the monarchy and government of Britain is now *the only Antichrist.*"

Ah! What do I see? The Bishop of London running to the Archbishop of Canterbury with a New England proclamation in his hand, and hastily crying out: "See!—see here, please your Grace. This impudent Yankee calls his Congregational religion the *same as ours.* Why, the canting fellow has forgotten that we drove his ancestors from this country for having *no religion at all.*" "*Their* religion the same as *ours!* What! extempore praying and preaching, and presbyterian ordination, *Religion!*" "No—no—no, please your Grace—there is but one religion in the world, and that is the religion of the Church of England." "True—true, my Lord Bishop, the fellow has not profited by the line in the fable, 'See! how we apples swim.' "[7]

I began my letter with the subject of attachment to the names and tombs and property of our ancestors, and of the beneficial effects derived from it to individuals and communities. A gentleman who had returned from France about the year 1802 dined with me soon after his arrival in this country. He said he had dined with Tallerand in a large company in Paris, and heard him say he had met with but one American while in the United States who was not willing to sell everything he possessed, whether farm, house, horse, carriage, or watch. The exception was in a sportsman who refused at any price to sell his terrier. A citizen of New York who sat at my table and heard the above anecdote confirmed it by saying "there was but one man in New York who lived in a house owned by his father, and he was very anxious to sell it." It is too high an honor to call us a nation of shopkeepers. It would be more proper to call us a nation of peddlers. The funding system, founded in rapine and fraud, begat universal speculation, speculation begat banks, and banks have ruined our country. A city in flames kindled by the hand of war is not so melancholy a sight as a whole nation absorbed in the love of money, nor is a field of battle covered with dead bodies so awful a spectacle as a nation deliberately preferring slavery to liberty, and peace and commerce to national independence.

I recollect Saml. Adams once told me that in the publications of the first convention of Massachussets the words "*horrors* of a civil war" were often deprecated in strong terms. The old gentleman, well knowing the influence of words upon feelings and principles, moved that the word "calamities" might be substituted to the word "horrors." This was done, and probably some evil was prevented by it. A list of more lenient vocables for many unpopular words would be very useful at the present day.

I received my academical learning at the school of the Reverend Dr. Finley, who married my mother's sister. He lived in Cecil county, Maryland. While a schoolboy I well recollect his preaching a sermon upon these words from the Proverbs: "Madness is in their hearts while they live."[8] This sermon was printed. The title of it was "On the madness of mankind."[9] The present times have added many facts in support of his position.

Yours truly,

BENJN: RUSH

MS: Adams Manuscript Trust, Boston.

[1] Her name was Susanna Lucas, according to BR's genealogical notes (Biddle, *Memorial*, p. 223).

[2] The *Journal* of George Fox (1624-1691), founder of the Society of Friends (see DNB), was published in 1694 and frequently reissued. BR was mistaken about the John Rush therein mentioned, for *this* John Rush died in Warwick Gaol (Fox's *Journal*, ed. Norman Penney, Cambridge [England] and Phila., 1911, I, 199, 434).

[3] In Adams' letter of 19 July (*Old Family Letters*, *A*, p. 411-13).

[4] Bishop Joseph Butler (1692-1752) published *Fifteen Sermons*, 1726, and *The Analogy of Religion, Natural and Revealed*, 1736, the latter remaining highly esteemed for a century and a half (DNB).

[5] Jonathan Shipley (1714-1788), Bishop of St. Asaph, a friend of Benjamin Franklin and the champion of America in Parliament (DNB).

[6] Adams characteristically rebuked BR for taking so gloomy a view; see his letter of 17 Aug. (*Old Family Letters*, *A*, p. 420-1).

[7] Used by Swift and others, this phrase, as applied to apples in a rapid stream, appears to have been proverbial (Burton Stevenson, *The Home Book of Quotations*, N.Y., 1934, p. 90). BR's handling of quotation marks in the dialogue above is, as frequently, ambiguous, and the passage has necessarily been repunctuated.

[8] Ecclesiastes 9:3.

[9] *Madness of Mankind, Represented in a Sermon Preached in the New Presbyterian Church in Philadelphia* . . . , Phila. [1754].

To John Adams

My dear Friend, Philadelphia, August 20th, 1812

My son Ben sent me a quarter-cask of old muscat wine as a present from the isle of Samos. The vessel on board of which it was sent, to avoid capture put into Boston, where her cargo is to be sold. I have requested Messrs. Walley & Foster, merchants of Boston, to deliver it to your order free of all costs. I beg your acceptance of it as a small mark of the gratitude and friendship of, dear sir, your sincere old friend,

BENJN: RUSH

P.S. I enclose you the letter from the gentleman by whose order the wine was shipped to me.[1]

MS: Adams Manuscript Trust, Boston.

[1] This enclosure, dated from "Vathi of Samos," 11 Apr. 1812, and signed by David Offler, is present in the Adams MSS. It reads as follows: "At the request of your son Benjamin Rush Jr., Esq., I have shipped on board the ship John Adams one cask of wine marked BR to the Address of Messrs. Hathaway & Scule [i.e., Scull] of your city desiring them to have delivered you [*sic*]. This wine is here esteemed the best muscat made on the Island being from the vineyard of the convent of St. Centram." A letter from Walley & Foster, Liberty Square, Boston, 22 Aug. 1812, is also present, notifying John Adams that the cask has been landed and will be delivered according to Adams' order.

To John Adams

My dear Friend, Philadelphia, August 21st, 1812

Your letter of August 1st[1] is still unanswered. It is full of truth and useful information and reflections. I regret that my son did not state the impressment of seamen being in 1807 an *act* of the British government. It would have obviated one of the objections to the war by the minority in Congress.

Our country is divided into two great parties called Federalists and Democrats. The former are subdivided into *British* Federalists, *tory* Federalists, and *American* Federalists. The latter are divided into *French* Democrats, *Irish* Democrats, and *American* Democrats. They all hold different speculative opinions in government and different views of the proper mode of conducting public affairs. Suppose a ship to be manned by sailors of six different nations, and suppose no one of them to understand the language of the other. Suppose the ship to be overtaken by a storm, and the captain and mates to be able to speak the language of but one class of the sailors. What do you suppose would be the fate of that ship? Is not this the exact situation of our country? Can Captain Madison and his cabinet mates under such circumstances bring her into port?

It is one of the laws of epidemic diseases that when two or three of them appear at the same time, the most powerful one chases away the weaker ones or compels them to do homage to it by partaking of some of its symptoms. British and tory Federalism have had that effect upon *American* Federalism. It wears their livery everywhere —that is, it adopts a part of their principles. French Democracy has had the same effect upon American Democracy, so that we rarely see a pure unsophisticated American Federalist or American Democrat. We are not *all* Federalists and *all* Republicans. We are nearly all British Federalists or French Democrats. The former are more numerous and powerful than the latter. Our ancient habits, our commerce, our language, and even our family connections favor this preponderance in our country.

I have often regretted that your son-in-law has been overlooked in the late military appointments. He has courage and talents, but alas! you say he is still his own enemy.

I rejoice to hear that the cure of your daughter's breast has been complete.

I think aloud when I write to you. Light your segar therefore I beseech you with my thoughts.

From, dear sir, your ever grateful and affectionate friend,

BENJN: RUSH

P.S. My work upon the diseases of the mind is *now* in the press. I hope to send you a copy of it in November.

MS: Adams Manuscript Trust, Boston.

[1] In *Old Family Letters*, *A*, p. 414-18.

To John Adams

My dear Friend,   Philadelphia, September 11, 1812

I will say of the wine which you have done me the favor to accept, what you said to me when I called to thank you for the appointment you gave me at the Mint: "You have not more pleasure in receiving it than I had in giving it to a faithful old Revolutionary whig." I hope the wine is of a good quality and that it will assist the influence of the present times in invigorating your body and mind so as to prolong your life for many years to come.

I convene in all the sentiments contained in your letters of September 4th and 6th.[1] The thoughts upon a navy I had anticipated and written them to my son. Captain Hull's success[2] strongly points out to us that the ocean, not Canada, should be the theater of our war. The Chinese system, so dear to philosophers and so repugnant to our habits, to good sense, and apparently to the will of heaven, I fear will ruin our country. I shall not wonder nor even *complain* of a Northern Confederacy if a change in measures should not take place after the next election. Our state it is said will support Madison and Gerry. Had the proposed taxes and a nonexportation of flour followed the declaration of war (as they honestly ought to have done), there would have been a total change in the representation from Pennsylvania.

The *English* and *tory* Federalists who deny that we have any cause of war, and who justify all the aggressions of Great Britain, form a bond of union to the Democrats. Did they condemn the conduct of Britain and object only to the manner in which the war has been and is likely to be conducted, they would carry a great body of the Democrats with them at the next election.

I am much struck with Colonel Smith's letter.[3] Time has verified his predictions. I lament that such talents should not be employed in the present alarming state of our country. But—but—but—you can guess the rest. Did you ever hear him speak of W———'s [*Washington's*] military talents? I never heard any person speak of them with more contempt. He illustrated his opinion of him by anecdotes. Can this be an objection to him? I think not; otherwise Armstrong[4] would never have been in his present situation.

My son Ben is now war-bound at Smyrna. *When* and *how* he will return, we know not—most probably by the way of England or Halifax. He *feels* that he treads on classic and apostolic ground. His letters give us great pleasure. He is very dear to his parents and family. His success in business has exceeded *our* expectations. The property he has sent home amounts to between 8 and 10,000 dollars.

I have not broken my head unnecessarily by meddling with the controversy about madness being a demoniacal disease in my work now in the press. Sir Jno. Pringle and Shakespeare thought very differently from your friend Farmer[5] upon that subject.

Adieu! with love as usual, I am ever yours—yours—yours,

BENJN: RUSH

[1162]

MS: Adams Manuscript Trust, Boston.

[1] In *Old Family Letters, A*, p. 423-8.

[2] The victory of the *Constitution*, Captain Isaac Hull (1773-1843), over the *Guerrière*, 19 Aug. 1812 (DAB, under Hull).

[3] Enclosed in Adams' letter to BR of 6 Sep. Adams contemplated publishing it, and BR apparently returned it. Adams believed that the reason Smith could not obtain a command was that "he is my Son in Law, and that is a sentence of eternal damnation against him in the Creed of all Parties" (*Old Family Letters, A*, p. 428).

[4] John Armstrong (1758-1843), who in 1783 had antagonized Washington by writing the "Newburgh Letters," was commissioned brigadier general in July 1812 (DAB).

[5] Adams had mentioned the interest with which he had read an *Essay on the Demoniacs of the New Testament*, London, 1775, by Hugh Farmer, who was, according to Allibone's *Dict. of Authors*, "a dissenting divine of great learning."

To David Hosack

Dear Sir,   Philadelphia, September 25th, 1812

Accept of my thanks for your letter and the interesting pamphlet which accompanied it.[1] I have read it with pleasure and instruction. The author discovers great research in collecting so many facts upon the subject of his inquiries. I cannot however accord with him in his conjectures respecting the origin of the fortifications and other marks of civilized ingenuity and labor which have lately been met with in different parts of our country. I have supposed that they are the works of the ancestors of our Indians, whom I have supposed to have been civilized, and that their posterity have become savages in consequence of their having lost the use of letters or written characters and the knowledge and habits of religion they brought with them to this country, without both of which nations seldom or perhaps never become civilized or preserve their civilization. The extent of our country, and the facility of subsistence by fishing and hunting and the spontaneous fruits of the earth, would naturally accelerate the progress of the descendants of the first settlers of our country to the savage state. [I think it probable that America was settled from some Eastern country[2] in which elephants of one sex only were employed in war, that the first settlers brought those animals with them for protection or conquest, and this I suppose may account for their extinction in our country.][3] I throw these opinions out in a crude state, without adducing some facts in their[4] favor which would be more proper for an essay than a friendly letter. You may communicate them with my respectful compliments and thanks to Mr. Clinton.

I enclose you the copy of my letter to Mr. Adams[5] agreeably to your request.

My volume of *Medical Inquiries and Observations on the Diseases of the Mind* will be published in a few weeks.

I have chosen for the subject of my next introductory lecture—"the duties of physicians to each other, and the causes of their dissensions in all ages and countries."[6]

Mrs. Rush and Mrs. Manners are now at Princeton. All who surround my table at home join in love to you and yours. Yours, &c.,

BENJN RUSH

MS (draft): Josiah C. Trent, M.D., Durham, North Carolina.

[1] Hosack's letter, dated 20 Sep. 1812, is in Rush MSS, XXVII. The pamphlet he sent was DeWitt Clinton's *Discourse Delivered before the New-York Historical Society*, N.Y., 1812; reissued in N.Y. Hist. Soc., *Colls.*, II (1814), 37-116. A classic account of the Iroquois, the *Discourse* also advances the view that the celebrated mounds in the Mississippi basin were constructed by a civilized but vanished race that preceded the Indians on this continent. BR's speculations on prehistoric America resemble his speculations in other non-medical fields in their compound of sense and nonsense. Since the late nineteenth century the accepted view has been that no distinct lost race built the mounds (Winsor, *Narr. and Crit. Hist.*, I, 397-402;

Henry C. Shetrone, *The Mound-Builders*, N.Y. and London, 1930, ch. I). But BR's "elephants of one sex only" are figments of his imagination, doubtless inspired by the current interest in paleontological discoveries. The "mammoth" fad, in its serious and lighter aspects, has been described with full and colorful details in Sellers, *Peale*, II, 125ff.

[2] BR first wrote "China."

[3] Brackets in MS, perhaps indicating that BR omitted this passage in the fair copy sent to Hosack.

[4] MS: "its."

[5] Of 13 July 1812; see note 8 there.

[6] This lecture was unfortunately not published; see, however, BR to John Adams, 4 Nov. 1812.

To John Adams

My dear Friend,   Philadelphia, November 4th, 1812

Herewith you will receive a copy of my *Medical Inquiries and Observations upon the Diseases of the Mind.* I shall wait with solicitude to receive your opinion of them. They are in general accommodated to the "common science" of gentlemen of all professions as well as medicine. The subjects of them have hitherto been enveloped in mystery. I have endeavored to bring them down to the level of all the other diseases of the human body, and to show that the mind and body are moved by the same causes and subject to the same laws. For this attempt to simplify the "medicina mentis" I expect no quarter from my learned brethren. But time

I hope will do my opinions justice. I believe them to be true and calculated to lessen some of the greatest evils of human life. If they are not, I shall console myself with having aimed well and erred honestly.

Pray furnish me with the details of the intrigues that led to the permanent establishment of Congress in Washington, and mention the circumstances that led H. to threaten W. with writing the history of his battles and campaigns.[1]

The Democrats of our city begin at last to think that the ocean is the theater upon which the Americans must defend their independence. In the year 1778 I published several numbers under the signature of Leonidas in favor of a navy in Bradford's paper.[2] I have never for a moment changed my opinion upon the subject of its importance to our country. It is the *safest* defense of a nation. It is its *cheapest* defense. It can be managed only by men of *some education*. Illiterate men of all professions and occupations may make brave and popular colonels and majors of an army, but they can neither navigate or fight a ship of war. A navy upon this account will always command the *best resources* of our country in talents and character. It will become the depot of supernumerary sons of all the wealthy families in the United States. It is less destructive to *human life* by diseases than an army, and far less so *to morals*. There are no taverns nor brothels in ships of war. All this is inter nos. For I dread above all things having my name connected in any way with a political or military opinion of any kind.

Yesterday I began my annual labors by delivering an introductory lecture upon the "Duties which physicians owe to each other and the causes of their dissensions." I ascribed the latter to their being less *gregarious* than the members of the other learned professions, and recommended, as a remedy for them, frequent social and convivial meetings. To enforce this advice, I entered extensively into a consideration of the influence of what Sir Thomas Brown calls "commensality"[3] upon morals, manners, knowledge, and happiness.

I rejoice to hear that Paul's and Homer's wine is so acceptable to the ladies of your family.[4] If it serve to [...][5] a single pain or a moment's care in them, [...][6] my dear old friend, it will afford great pleasure to yours truly and sincerely,

BENJN: RUSH

P.S. From the great extent of our seacoast, from the immense number of bays, rivers, and deep creeks which intersect our country, all of which are covered for 8 months in the year with shallops and market or ferry boats, and from the heat of our climate disposing our boys to bathe and swim 6 months in the year, our citizens are a kind of amphibious animals, alike at home and in their element on water and land. By this early and universal familiarity with the water and the arts of commanding it and surviving its fatal influence upon life, our citizens know nothing of the water-phobia so common and natural to nations otherwise situated and educated, and *hence* their greater aptness or predisposition to be sailors and soldiers at sea than the natives of even Great Britain herself; and hence in yielding to the cry for a navy, we yield to the voice of nature manifested in the physical circumstances of our country.

[*In margin of first page*:] My bookseller has disappointed me in not sending me a copy of my book which I intended for you. It shall follow this letter in a day or two.

Addressed: John Adams Esqr: Quincy near Boston.
MS: Adams Manuscript Trust, Boston.

[1] Adams furnished the details concerning the establishment of the capital in his letter of 14 Nov. 1812, but pointed out that BR himself had first told the anecdote of Hamilton's threat to Washington (*Old Family Letters*, *A*, p. 429-31; see BR to Adams, 6 Jan. 1806).

[2] BR's "Leonidas" papers on the American navy and other topics appeared in 1782; one of them is printed above under date of 4 July 1782.

[3] Defined in OED as "commensal state; habit of eating at the same table,"

and exemplified by a quotation from Browne's *Pseudodoxia Epidemica*, 2d edn., 1650, p. 142: "Being enjoined or prohibited certain foods . . . to avoid community with the Gentiles upon promiscuous commensality."

[4] See Adams' letter of 18 Sep. 1812 (*Old Family Letters*, *A*, p. 306). Adams said among other things that the wine would "increase [his] love of Greek and Latin more than [his] Patriotism."

[5] MS torn; one word missing.

[6] Two or three words missing.

To John Adams

My dear Friend,   Philadelphia, November 17th, 1812

Gibbon tells us in his *Life* that he studied anatomy and chemistry on purpose to furnish himself with new allusions for the style of his *History*.[1] You seem to have studied natural history for the more important purpose of furnishing your memory with new precedents for industry and foresight in human affairs, and particularly for the conduct of governments. But what avail reading, reflection, experience, and American birth in the present state of our country? It would seem as if we had read history not to avoid but to imitate the blunders of those who have gone before us. A

night or two after receiving your last letter,[2] I fancied in a dream
that I was elevated upon a bench in our Hospital yard surrounded
by between 60 and 70 of my lunatic patients. Deeply impressed
with the contents of your letter, I addressed them upon the subject
of a navy. While I was speaking, one man came up to me and said,
"I am Solon," a second said he was Wm. Penn, a third said he was
Numa Pompillius, and all of them asked me how I dared to attempt
to instruct them upon the means of defending our country. A 4th
spat in my face, a 5th hissed me, a 6th called me a fool, a 7th said
I was crazy, an 8th took up a stone and threw it at me. In an effort
to avoid it I awoke, satisfied that such would have been my treatment in the House of Representatives in Washington, had I addressed them upon the same subject and had they not been restrained by the habits of civilized life.

The American States consist of three districts. The Northern,
Southern, and *Western*, all of which are divided by different interests, habits, manners, and principles. In the midst of them is a
gas more powerful than steam in its repulsive nature. A despotic
stopper might keep it from exploding, but kept together as those
districts are by voluntary association, the gas must operate, and a
separation of them must take place unless a conformity to mutual
interests should speedily prevent it. Canada is likely to become to
us what Flanders and Hanover have been to England, the slaughter-
house of generations of our citizens, and for no one purpose but
such as are of a selfish nature. Admit that we have conquered it.
As a republic we cannot hold it as a vassal province; and as a member of the Union, what can be expected from a representation in
Congress composed of Englishmen and Frenchmen? When the news
of the surrender of Quebec and all its dependences reached Philadelphia, Joseph Galloway, Jos. Fox,[3] and a Dr. Evans[4] rode out
in great haste to Fairhill, the seat of Isaac Norris, then speaker of
our Assembly, and told him the news with great exultation. "I
am sorry to hear it," said the Quaker Sachem. "Farewell now to
the liberties of America." The Stamp Act in 1765 showed the
wisdom of this remark. Should the subjugation of Canada, or her
union with us in Congress take place, with equal propriety might
we not say, "Farewell to the Union of the American republics"?
A man's evil passions help to keep him alive no less than his good
ones. Individual enemies help to make men wise, prudent, and
successful in life. Britain and France have been made equally great
in national character by their hereditary and perpetual hostility
to each other. A circumambient pressure of England on the north

and east, and of Spain, France, and Indians on the south and west, would probably have kept our states together for many centuries to come. It is somewhat remarkable that in none of the works of the primitive fathers or reformers do we find plans for perpetual and universal peace. They knew too well what was in man to believe it possible in his *present weak* and *depraved* state. Such plans have been suggested chiefly by infidels and atheists, who ascribe all that is evil in man to religion and bad governments. The Quakers it is true are advocates for universal and perpetual peace. But examine their disposition to other sects. Do they breathe love or peace to any of them? Look at their conduct in politics. Are they more under the influence of Christian principles than other people? Let the immense proportion of Porcupine's subscribers to his paper when in Philadelphia answer this question.

Adieu! From, dear sir, yours truly and sincerely,

BENJN RUSH

P.S. I spent a few minutes in Mr. Geo. Clymer's company this morning. He *feels* as we do for our country, and he *thinks* as we do of the necessity of its being defended by a navy. He remarked that every ship of war we built would call for two from Britain to watch it, and that in a few years we should draw a large portion of the British navy from her own coast and thus expose her to her European enemies.

MS: Adams Manuscript Trust, Boston.

[1] See Gibbon's *Memoirs*, ed. G. B. Hill, London, 1900, p. 200-1.
[2] Dated 7 Nov. 1812 (*Old Family Letters, A*, p. 314-17).
[3] Joseph Fox (ca. 1709-1779), speaker of Penna. Assembly, 1764-1765, 1768 (W. W. Hinshaw, *Encyclopedia of American Quaker Genealogy*, II, Ann Arbor, 1938, p. 364; *Penna. Archives*, 2d ser., IX, 637).
[4] Cadwalader Evans (d. 1773), eminent early Quaker physician (Morton, *Hist. Penna. Hospital*, p. 489).

To John Adams

Philadelphia, December 14th, 1812

My venerable and dear old Friend,

You have so far outdreamed me in your last letter[1] that I shall be afraid hereafter to let my imagination loose in that mode of exposing folly and vice. My whole family was delighted in contemplating you upon your rostrum in the Garden of Versailles and in witnessing the effects of your speech upon your hairy, feathered, and scaly audience. Let is not be said, "De republica America fabula narratur."[2]

I thank you for your kind reception and favorable opinion of my book upon the diseases of the mind.[3] It has been well received by many of my fellow citizens and particularly by some of the gentlemen of the bar, several of whom have spoken in the most flattering terms of it, but not a single physician in our city (one young man excepted) has taken the least notice of it in any of my interviews with them since its publication. I doubt much whether more than the young doctor before mentioned has[4] purchased or read it. My old friend Judge Peters called to see me some time ago and remarked that I now seemed to live at peace with all my brethren. "Yes," said I, "they do not fill the papers with calumnies against me as formerly, but I still have no friends among them." "Leave off writing books, Doctor," said the Judge, "and they will cease to be your enemies."

It is a curious but not a singular fact that those of them who owe me most obligations are the most hostile to me.

In spite of their malice, aided by all the disadvantages to which my whig principles and conduct during the Revolutionary War have exposed me from the tories, it has pleased God to crown the labors of the evening of my life with such abundant success that I am now in easy circumstances. My excellent wife says, "We have enough," and urges me to retire to our little farm in the neighborhood of the city and leave our son James the inheritor of my business. We have now a competent and regular income, chiefly from well-situated real property, and we do not owe a dollar upon note, bond, or mortgage in the world. I would follow my wife's advice by retiring, did not the probable changes in the expenses of my family render it improper. My 2nd daughter and her two children are still with me, and should her husband fall in battle (which is, alas! not improbable, for he is now at Queenstown[5] or in the neighborhood of it with his regiment, the 49th), his whole family would remain with me for life with but a scanty inheritance from him.

I am now visiting Mr. Clymer, who is indisposed. I read your dream to him yesterday. He was delighted with it. "What an imagination," said he, "the old gentleman possesses!"

Captain Decatur's victory[6] has produced a navy ardor in our city such as I never witnessed before. I wish it may excite equal enthusiasm for a navy in Washington.

Adieu! Yours—yours—yours,

BENJN RUSH

Addressed: John Adams Esqr: Quincy near Boston.
MS: Adams Manuscript Trust, Boston.

[1] Dated 29 Nov. 1812 (*Old Family Letters*, *A*, p. 317-21).

[2] Adapted from Horace; see an earlier letter to Adams, 23 Mch. 1805, note 4.

[3] *Diseases of the Mind* had confirmed Adams' opinion that BR's writings had done more good for mankind than Franklin's.

[4] Thus in MS.

[5] Queenston, on the Niagara River, was the scene of an unsuccessful invasion attempt by Gen. Stephen Van Rensselaer in Oct. 1812 (Lossing, *Field-Book of the War of 1812*, ch. XIX).

[6] Stephen Decatur, in the *United States*, defeated and captured the British frigate *Macedonian* near Madeira, 25 Oct. 1812 (DAB; see also BR to Adams, 8 Jan. 1813).

To John Adams

My dear Friend,   Philadelphia, December 19, 1812

Better and better! Dream on, my venerable friend! In one of the King of Prussia's poetical letters to Voltaire written immediately after reading his *Henriade*, he tells him that he had dreamed that he had visited Elysium, where he saw Homer and Virgil walking with dejected countenances. They were on their way, they said, upon asking them what was the matter, to Minos, to ask permission to return for a short time to the earth in order that they might burn their respective epic poems now become obsolete and dishonored by the superior merit of the *Henriade*. Could I obtain permission from my patients and my pupils, I would visit Quincy, and there search in your desk for all my dreams in order that I might burn them (if you have not in kindness to me done it already) to prevent their being disgraced by your speech in a dream in the Garden of Versailles and your subsequent dream of events and scenes in Washington.[1]

I recollect the last verse of a song which a British lieutenant with whom I crossed the ocean on my return from England in 1769 used to sing to the cabin passengers every Saturday night. It was composed in honor of Prince Ferdinand and the Marquis of Granby after the celebrated victory of Minden.[2] In describing the restraint imposed upon the valor of the Marquis, whom he compares to a lion, the chorus concludes with "While Sackville held him by the tail." Say, my friend, who is the Sackville that holds the patriotism and valor of our country by the tail? Who is it that has clipped the wings of the American Eagle in order to prevent her spreading them upon the ocean? Who has broken her bill in order to prevent her picking out the eyes of the British Lion? But I hasten from this painful subject to pay my respects to Mr. Hobby.[3] "Tread gently and safely, highly favored beast, while your master bestrides your back. Shake every blood vessel of his body, and gently agitate every portion of his brain. Keep up the circulation of his blood for years to come, and excite aphorisms and anecdotes and dreams for the instruction and amusement of his friends by the action of his brain upon his mind. Be assured, Mr. Hobby, your master will not be ungrateful to you for your services. He will not send you to vendue *and sell you for 75 dollars*[4] after the painful and disinterested labors of your life are over. He will reward your *vigilant* eye and *sure* feet in carrying him over rough and stony roads at night without stumbling, and your strength in conducting him through quack-mires[5] and streams of water during the day, by a warm stable and soft food suited to thy toothless gums in winter, and by luxuriant pasture in summer; and when you pay the debt of nature, he will not permit your carcass to furnish a repast for weeks to buzzards and other birds of prey, but decently inter you beneath the shade of one of the ancient and solitary oaks of his fields, and say of you as he turns his back upon your grave: 'Alas! my Hobby!—but you have done your DUTY, and this is more than can be said of most of the heroes and philosophers of ancient or modern times.' "

Our city is divided into parties upon the supposed discovery of perpetual motion by a certain Mr. Redheffer at German town.[6] These parties consist of *Believers, Doubters,* and *Unbelievers.* I have been educated in the unbelief of the philosopher's stone, of an elixir that shall restore the antediluvian age, of a panacea or a single medicine that shall cure *all* diseases, of the omnipotence of human reason, and of the perfectibility of governments composed of imperfect materials; but if the discovery of perpetual motion be a *real* one, I will renounce my infidelity upon all the above subjects and believe in them all. I have supposed that there is but one[7] self-moving Being in the Universe, that all motion is the effect of his hand imposed upon matter, and all volition the effect of his will imposed upon mind. Weights and springs, and wind and water and steam are substitutes only to an ever-existing, ever-acting, and omni-present power. This is the uniform language of Revelation. There are no such words as the "laws of nature" in the Bible. It speaks constantly of creation and preservation being the same thing. Did I believe in a machine that possessed a perpetual and independent power of moving itself, I should be disposed to consider it as a little ――――― I cannot utter upon paper the awfully profane idea.

From, dear sir, your sincere and faithful old friend,

BENJN. RUSH

MS: Adams Manuscript Trust, Boston.

[1] See Adams' letter of 8 Dec. 1812 (*Old Family Letters*, *A*, p. 322-5). His dream dramatized the need for increased American naval power.

[2] A victory over the French in 1759 by Prussian and British forces under Prince Ferdinand of Brunswick and the Marquis of Granby. Disobedience to orders by Lord George Sackville (1716-1785) prevented total destruction of the enemy. Sackville, under the name Germain, became secretary of state for colonies and directed British military operations during the Revolution (Lecky, *Hist. of England*, II, 432; DNB, under Germain).

[3] A horse, fancifully supposed by Adams to inspire his dreams; see *Old Family Letters*, *A*, p. 322.

[4] A guarded allusion to Washington; see BR's letter of 8 Jan. 1813.

[5] Thus in MS.

[6] This "discovery," by Charles Readheffer (variously spelled), of Chestnut Hill, was announced in the papers in September, brought well-paying crowds to Readheffer's house, and was taken so seriously that a committee of the Philadelphia City Council was appointed to determine whether the machine might not be used to operate the municipal waterworks. According to Readheffer, his invention worked by the principle of "quiescent momentum," but he never allowed qualified persons to examine it, and it was soon dismissed as a fraud. (Scharf & Westcott, I, 561-2; Jackson, *Encyclo. of Phila.*, IV, 1041-3, with a drawing of the machine reproduced from the *Port Folio*, Feb. 1813; BR to Adams, 22 Jan. 1813; Robert Patterson to Thomas Jefferson, 30 Nov. 1812, L.C., Jefferson Papers; and Jefferson's reply, 27 Dec. 1812, printed in his *Writings*, ed. Lipscomb and Bergh, XIII, 191-3.)

[7] This word omitted in MS.

To the Managers of the Pennsylvania Hospital

Gentlemen,   December 26th, 1812

Permit me, with all the respect which is due to your personal characters and faithful services to the Pennsylvania Hospital, to address you again in behalf of the sick committed to your care.

Intimately connected with health and life is a uniform and pleasant temperature of the air; hence the longest-lived and healthiest inhabitants of our globe are to be found in those latitudes in which that temperature of the air most generally prevails.

In many diseases, and particularly in such as are of a chronic nature, this uniform and pleasant temperature of the air is so much more necessary than in health. To obtain it, it is indispensably necessary that the temperature of sick rooms should be the same in the night as in the day. *One* reason why more deaths occur among sick people in the night than in the day is because they are exposed in a debilitated state to a reduced temperature of the air.

The whole body frequently feels this change, but it produces its hurtful effects chiefly through the medium of the lungs. From an experiment recently made, it appears that the pulse descends five strokes in a minute in its frequency in those cases in which every part of the body except the lungs is protected from the action of cold air. Not only consumptions, but rheumatism, dysenteries, low fevers, and all other diseases when accompanied with a *feeble action* of the blood vessels, are necessarily made worse by this diminution in the force and frequency of the pulse.

For this reason I beg leave to suggest to you the appointment of an officer whose business shall be to renew the fires in all the wards during the night as often as it shall be necessary. Perhaps he might be made further useful by acting as a watchman over the property of the Hospital during the night.

2ndly. Warm and cold baths are admitted by all physicians to be remedies of the greatest importance in chronic diseases such as usually occur in hospitals. From the distance of the baths in the Pennsylvania Hospital[1] from the wards, it is impossible to make use of them in cold weather without exposing the patients to taking cold in passing, under the cover of a blanket only, to and from them, and from the small size of the bathroom it is impossible for patients to undress or dress in them or to remain long enough in them to accommodate their systems to the external atmosphere after they come out of the baths, for which reasons I beg leave to recommend the enlargement of the bathroom in such a manner as to your wisdom may seem most proper to obviate the above-mentioned evils and to render the baths as useful in public as they are in private practice.

From, gentlemen, yours very respectfully,

BENJN. RUSH[2]

MS (copy, only partly in BR's hand): Library Company of Philadelphia, Rush MSS.

[1] This word omitted by the copyist.   [2] The name is in the copyist's hand.

To Ashbel Green

Dear Sir,   Philadelphia, December 31, 1812

I have heard from time to time with *great pleasure* of the auspicious circumstances that have attended your entrance upon your new situation, and with *great pain* of the late outrage upon decency that has taken place in the College. I rejoiced in the punishment that has been inflicted upon the offenders.[1]

There appears to me to be but one mode of preventing such gross violations of the laws of the College in future, and that is to prevent or abolish the obligation the students enter into not to inform of each other. This obligation is founded in a deep-seated immoral principle. It is an association to protect folly and vice. It is contrary to the letter and spirit of divine and human laws, both of which consider the persons who conceal offenses of a public nature and injurious to society as partakers of them. Young men educated under the habitual influence of such an obligation as I have mentioned cannot fail of losing all moral sensibility, and of carrying into the world with them principles and habits better calculated to make them accomplished members of a confederacy of highwaymen or swindlers than citizens of a civil and religious community. I am unable to suggest a remedy for the evil of which I am complaining, but unless it be prevented in future, I shall consider our College as an *additional* nursery for vice and infidelity in our country. Alas! how extensive has been the influence of Godwin's works in the United States! We see them in every *new* folly and vice that rises among us.

This letter does not require an answer. Keep your precious time for other and more useful purposes. My present duties will only permit me[2] to serve the interests to which you are devoted by my advice and prayers. Whenever a thought occurs to me that can in any way contribute to them, you shall hear in this way from, dear sir, your truly affectionate friend,

BENJN RUSH

Addressed: The Revd Dr Green President of the College at Princeton.
MS: Pierpont Morgan Library, Signers Collection, Series III.

[1] The election of Ashbel Green as president of the College at Princeton in 1812 sprang from misguided efforts by the trustees to reestablish the pious regime of earlier generations; see BR's letter to Green of 9 Dec. 1802 and note 2 there. Green's first years in office were marked by frequent rebellious gestures on the part of the students, whose favorite prank was setting off "crackers" of gunpowder in the small hours of the morning. Green's diary duly records the long series of incidents and the dismissals that followed them (Green, *Life*, N.Y., 1849, ch. XIX-XX; see also Wertenbaker, *Princeton, 1746-1896*, ch. V). The specific "outrage" alluded to by BR was a typical one and had resulted in the dismissal of three students on 18 Dec. (Faculty Minutes, Secretary's Office, Princeton Univ.).

[2] This word omitted in MS.

To John Adams

My dear Friend,   Philadelphia, January 8th, 1813

Having just now gotten my task, that is, revised my lecture, and added to it the results of my reading and observations during the last year, I now sit down to acknowledge the receipt of your three last very pleasant and entertaining letters.[1]

I shall begin my answer to them by wishing you a happy new year!

I was much gratified with your account of your conversations at two late public dinners. But I was more struck with the wonderful health and spirits which you discover in being able at 77 to occupy a chair at a large convivial board, to take an active part in the subjects that are usually discussed in such companies, and afterwards to ride 12 miles in the dark or by moonlight to Quincy. It was said of Dr. Johnson after he published his *Lives of the Poets* that, "like *tin*, he was bright to the last." To unite study, business, and company in middle life falls to the lot of but few men. Lord Bolingbroke, it is said, possessed talents for them all in an eminent degree, but he exercised them only in early life. You seem to have united the durable luster of Johnson with the versatility of mind of Bolingbroke at an advanced stage of life in a degree which I have seldom met with in the histories of public men.

I feel for Dr. Waterhouse.[2] He possesses talents, knowledge, and great worth. Can nothing be done for him at Washington? He would make an excellent purveyor to a military hospital. The medical department of our navy and army requires amendment. It is a faithful and absurd copy of what it was under the administration of Dr. Shippen.

You have given the true reason for the hostility to a navy at Washington. Were the resources of our country which are now thrown away on the borders of Canada concentrated in a navy, very different would be the situation of the United States. The finger of heaven points to the ocean as the theater on which America must again contend for her independence. Your anecdotes of the laborious birth of our little navy in the beginning of the Revolutionary War are truly interesting. You may add to them what I once saw from the pen of Paul Jones and heard from the lips of Commodore Barry. In the journal of the former are the following words: "My hands first hoisted the American flag." The latter with equal exultation once said to me, "The British naval flag first struck to me," alluding to his having taken the first British sloop of war. The following lines, which I cut out of the *Aurora* a few days ago, will, I hope, no doubt accord with your feelings upon the present subject:

FOR THE AURORA.
IMPROMPTU
On hearing of the capture of the MACEDONIAN *by the* UNITED STATES, *commanded by captain* DECATUR.

"Said Neptune to Britain, 'No more shall you reign,
The mistress and tyrant of my wide domain.
The decree is confirmed, as proclaimed by the fates,
My mistress hereafter is the United States.' "

Remember me most gratefully to my friend Hobby, and thank him for his admirable letter. Read my lecture to him on the veterinary art, and tell him of my regard for his whole species. I admire nothing more in the character of Howard than the provision he made for all his superannuated horses. I was charmed in hearing of the affection of Burke for this noble animal. In walking through one of his fields at Beaconfield, he suddenly left his company and ran towards a horse which he embraced and kissed. "This horse," said he to his company when they came up to him, "was rode by my deceased son." A physician died in this city about 20 years ago and left a horse on which he had visited his patients for many years. His son declared he should never be rode nor worked again. He sent him to a farmer in the neighborhood of Philadelphia, where he was well fed and lived and died agreeably to the declaration of the heir of his master. After these facts, what shall we say of an officer of high rank in the American army who sold his charger, on which he had rode during the greatest part of the Revolutionary War, for 75 dollars? This officer, I was told, was a rich man. For the honor of our country we must conceal his name.[3]

Our excellent Revolutionary friend Mr. Clymer is I fear in the last stage of a disease which too generally in old people resists the power of medicine. A great mass of genius, knowledge, and patriotism, without the least portion of party spirit, will descend with him to the grave. He is one of those few citizens of the United States who admits the outrages and dreads the power of *both* France and Britain.

Yours truly and affectionately,

BENJN RUSH

MS: Adams Manuscript Trust, Boston.

[1] Dated 21, 27, and 29 Dec. 1812 (*Old Family Letters, A*, p. 325-8, 432-6, 328-31).

[2] Waterhouse had been dismissed from the Marine Hospital in 1809 (for reasons not known to me) and from the Harvard medical faculty in 1812 (for his opposition to the removal of the medical school from Cambridge to Boston). Adams had appealed for help, and BR did his best, but, as his letter of 8 Feb. 1813 indicates, he was not hopeful. Waterhouse did, however, obtain an appointment in the military service later that year and held it until 1821. (Sources cited in notes on BR's letter to Jefferson, 28 Nov. 1807, q.v.)

[3] I have not discovered any facts relating to this charge against Washington; it was probably circulated in Democratic-Republican newspapers. See Adams' comment in his letter of 15 Jan. 1813 (misdated 1812) in *Old Family Letters, A*, p. 292.

To John Adams

My dear Friend,   Philadelphia, January 22nd, 1813

The letter from Colonel Smith to which you have alluded was not received with yours of this day.[1] Was it withheld, or was it lost by the way? I was much pleased in seeing his name upon record among the successful candidates for a seat in Congress from the State of New York. The air, the society, and the great objects which will occupy his mind in Washington will resuscitate him and show his country the difference between modern and Revolutionary patriots and soldiers. I beg he may always take us in his way to the headquarters of our government. We feel related to all your family.

Captain Jones meant only that the American flag was hoisted first on board a *national* ship by his hands, and Captain Barry meant only that a British *national* ship struck first to his *national* flag. Captain Manly[2] I believe commanded only a private ship of war and captured only British merchantmen and transports—more, I believe with you, to the benefit of our country and the annoyance of our enemy than anything that was done by any one naval officer in the service of the United States.

I feel with you for our friend Dr. Waterhouse. Perhaps something may be obtained for him from one of the two new secretaries? I will second and support a recommendation from his friends in and near Boston for a situation in the marine and military hospitals which shall not separate him from his family. The cause of his dismission from office by Mr. Madison must be noticed in his recommendation, and its falsehood exposed if possible. I am wholly ignorant of it.

Our excellent friend Mr. Clymer is still living, but a day or two it is expected will close the scenes of his useful life.[3] In one of my visits to him in the early stage of his disease, he put a few lines of poetry into my hands, of which the following is a copy:

> "At first the affair of *Chesapeake*.
> Hull sorely did our Yankees pique.
> For then the honor of the nation,
> Stood foremost in their estimation;
> Indeed so valued they that prize,
> E'en codfish to't they'd sacrifice.
> But as things often change about,
> And patriotism may wear out,
> So let them now put both in scale
> And see which of them would prevail.
> I dare to say, tho' strange it seem,
> *Codfish makes honor kick the beam.*"

Our legislature appointed a committee to examine Redheiffer's perpetually moving machine. Yesterday was appointed by him for that purpose. But he declined submitting it to their inspection. This event with many others have opened the eyes of our citizens, and Mr. R is now generally believed to be an impostor. All the imitations of his machine made as to the number of wheels, proportion, or size by several ingenious mechanics have failed of exhibiting the phenomenon of self-motion.

Captain Wm. Jones, who succeeds P. Hamilton[4] as secretary of the navy, is up to the patriot of Quincy in his zeal to extend, protect, and properly employ a navy. He is a man of a bold and original mind, but well drilled for his office by a practical education as a naval officer in the Revolutionary War and as a sea captain and merchant ever since the war. A letter from you I am sure would animate him to carry his plans for rendering the United States a naval power into execution.

But one of the physicians of Philadelphia, formerly my pupil, has at last mentioned my late publication to me. This fact enhances my obligations to your female friends and to your medical neighbor for the honor they have done me in reading it. I live in a beehive, and save myself from being stung to death only by being as passive and apparently as lifeless as an old dead tree.

Adieu! from, dear sir, yours truly,

BENJN: RUSH

MS: Adams Manuscript Trust, Boston.

¹ That is, Adams' letter erroneously dated 15 Jan. 1812 (*Old Family Letters, A*, p. 291-4).

² Adams had disputed the claims of John Paul Jones and John Barry (see preceding letter) and had given precedence to Capt. John Manley (ca.

1734-1793), a Massachusetts naval hero (DAB).

³ Clymer died two days later.

⁴ Paul Hamilton (1762-1816), of South Carolina, secretary of the navy, 1809-1812 (DAB).

To the Trustees of
the University of Pennsylvania

Gentlemen,   January 30, 1813

In the last letter which I had the honor to address to you upon the subject of medical education,¹ I took the liberty of suggesting the propriety of all the candidates for degrees in medicine spending three winters in our University and attending a course of lectures on natural and experimental philosophy before they were examined for degree. Permit me to trespass a few minutes upon your time while I lay before you a few additional reasons for the above suggestions.

Most of the young men who study medicine in our University have been but superficially instructed in academical learning. A few of them only are graduates in the arts. They all pay fees to country or city physicians for the benefit of seeing their private practice, but so constantly are they employed in attending four or five lectures daily in the winter, and in transcribing copies of them in the spring and summer in order to qualify themselves for an examination upon them, that few of them can be prevailed upon to attend to the practice of their preceptors. This is so generally the case that several physicians in this city have declined taking private pupils from a conviction that they can derive no benefit from their services nor confer any advantage upon them by sending them to visit sick people. Without these advantages it is as impossible to make a physician as it would be to teach a boy to swim by means of lectures or books without taking him into the water; and from the neglect of these advantages, there is good reason to believe some young men have obtained degrees in our University who did not know how to spread a common plaster, to dress a sore, to perform the operation of bleeding, and who were even ignorant of the sensible qualities of many of the most common medicines of our shops. Should it be asked—Why were such candidates approved of and recommended by the medical professors to the trustees for degrees? I answer—From their constant exercises in *"grinding,"* that is, examining each other, they fill their memories with the subjects of the lectures of the professors to which their examinations are wholly confined, so as to answer the questions proposed to them in a satisfactory manner. Of the physicians thus educated and thus graduated, not more than one fourth for several years past, Dr. Wistar informed a committee two years ago, were qualified to practise medicine.

Should it be said—By increasing the time and objects of study we shall lessen the number of graduates in our University, I answer —We shall increase the honor of our degrees proportionably and the respectability and usefulness of our graduates. Should it be said —We shall diminish the number of students in our University, I answer—So much the better. In every part of the country physicians have increased far beyond the demands of its population. This is evident from the great number of them who crowd our cities, villages, and country places that are wholly unemployed. The loss to the agriculture and arts of the United States by the abstraction of their labor, and the evils to society to be dreaded from their idleness, are too obvious to be mentioned. In Edinburg an attendance upon medical lectures for three winters is required before a student can offer himself as a candidate for a degree in medicine. Most of their candidates have been previously instructed in modern and ancient languages and in general science. The lectures in the University of Edinburg each season continue six months, so that a student spends eighteen months in attending them in the whole course of his medical education. The lectures in our University continue but four months in each season, so that a student according to the present regulations spends but eight months in order to qualify him for a degree. This immense difference in the time of acquiring a medical education in the two universities cannot surely be defended by a supposed superiority of intellect in the American student nor by the less value of human life in the United States than in Great Britain.

By requiring an attendance upon the lectures upon natural philosophy and midwifery (the last of which is indispensably necessary to a physician who intends to practise medicine in the United States) as a condition for a degree, an attendance in the University for three years will be more patiently submitted to, inasmuch as it will multiply the studies of candidates beyond the possibility of their being grasped in two years. It will moreover afford them time to become acquainted with diseases in hospitals and in private practice, and to acquire a knowledge of such branches of academical learning as they are deficient in when they come to the University.

I shall conclude this long letter by mentioning a fact somewhat foreign to its subject, to which the attention of the trustees is earnestly solicited.

In consequence of the diplomas of the Medical Society (which like the diplomas of the University are written in the Latin language) being subscribed by one of the medical professors as its president, three instances have been communicated to me of their having been imposed upon the public as diplomas from the University. It is probable similar frauds have been practised in the same way that have not as yet been detected. It belongs exclusively to the trustees of the University to devise a method of preventing in future such fraudulent substitutes to the medical honors.[2]

From, gentlemen, with great respect, your most obedient servant,

BENJN. RUSH

MS (copy, with the date and a few interlined words in BR's hand): Library Company of Philadelphia, Rush MSS.

[1] Probably BR's letter of 15 May 1811, covering some of the same ground as the present one (draft in Rush MSS, XXXI). See further, BR's letter to the Trustees dated 1 Mch. 1813, below. [2] For a protest against a similar abuse, see letter of 29 Mch. 1809.

To John Adams

My dear Sir,   Philadelphia, February 8th, 1813

It was wholly unnecessary to bring forward the respectable testimony of Mr. Langdon in order to rectify the mistake into which Captain Barry's communication and Captain P. Jones' journal had led me.[1] You do me great injustice in supposing I possess a single Pennsylvania or anti-New England prejudice. I know my native state too well. It is a great exchange filled with men of all nations who feel no attachments to each other from the ties of birth, education, and religion, and who from that circumstance are incapable of a *state* character. From that small number of our citizens with whom ancient English blood and the principles of our ancestors *ought* to have united me, my whig principles and conduct have *wholly* separated me. Had it not been for what are called newcomers and strangers, I could not have retained my standing in Philadelphia. With a few exceptions they have been my most steady personal and professional friends. Before the Revolution we had two aristocracies in our city—the Friends,[2] and the officers of the proprietary government. For more than 60 years they were enemies to each other, but the Revolution united them. They are now all-powerful in all our monied institutions except one, in our Library, Hospital and University, and possess universal professional, mercantile, maritime, and mechanical patronage. The principles which produced their union must necessarily lead them to expatriate a man who subscribed the Declaration of Independence. In the city of London or Constantinople I should not feel myself more a foreigner than I do in the city of Philadelphia. I do not mention these facts as matters of complaint, but to convince you how little disposed I am to absolve my Pennsylvania fellow citizens from the charges you have made against them. There have been times when I have been ready to say of my native state what Dr. Swift said of Ireland, "I am not of this vile country," and with the Grecian general, "Ossa mea non habebis."[3] But these times have been transient in their duration, and the hectic produced by them has soon passed away. My *habitual* feelings to my parent state dispose me to say to it with Father Paul, "Esto, esto perpetua."[4]

Your remarks upon Redheffer's machine pleased and diverted my family.

The share which Pennsylvania now holds of the executive power of the general government is calculated, as you have supposed, to preserve her *colonial* dependence upon the rulers of our country and to ensure her loyalty for years to come.

Dr. Waterhouse's situation in Philadelphia, with his whig principles, would have been worse than mine, for he has more whig fire to provoke hostility than I ever possessed. Even his more splendid talents would not have placed him in a higher rank in his profession than he now occupies. I have read and admired his *Botanist.*[5] I hope your influence will procure something for him from Washington. I shall heartily cooperate with you.

Alas! Another defeat![6] and another source of care to our country! Have you read the corrected edition of Mr. Quincy's speech?[7] It is a masterly performance. I subscribe to everything he has said of the folly, madness, and cruelty of the Canada war.

Adieu! Ever yours,

BENJN: RUSH

P.S. We have lately heard from our son Ben. He narrowly escaped capture by the Algerines in his voyage from Smyrna. He was to sail from Cadiz to the United States in January.

Addressed: John Adams Esquire Quincy near Boston.
MS: Adams Manuscript Trust, Boston.

¹ See Adams' letter of 3 Feb. (*Old Family Letters*, *A*, p. 337).

² This word is not capitalized in the MS, and BR almost always used the term Quakers rather than Friends; but it is clear from what follows that he meant "Friends" here.

³ "Thou shalt not have my bones." Source not traced.

⁴ See BR's letter of 20 Oct. 1773 and note 2 there.

⁵ Waterhouse's lectures on natural history were published in a volume called *The Botanist*, Boston, 1811.

⁶ The defeat and capture of Gen. James Winchester (1752-1826) at Frenchtown (Monroe, Mich.), 22 Jan. 1813, was followed by the massacre of the American wounded by Indian allies of the British (DAB; Lossing, *Field-Book of the War of 1812*, p. 353-60).

⁷ Speech of the Massachusetts congressman Josiah Quincy against the current war plans and particularly against the proposed enlisting of minors without the consent of their parents or masters (McMaster, *Hist.*, IV, 204-5).

To John Adams

My dear Friend,   Philadelphia, February 15th, 1813

I am now attending a daughter of Mr. Mathew Carey's. In one of my visits to her, I mentioned your opinions to him upon the subject of a navy and your documents upon the subject of its origin in the United States. He requested a sight and copies of your letters containing those opinions and documents for a publication which he expects shortly to issue from his press.¹ I said I could not comply with his request without your consent. Should you yield to his wishes, I will take care to furnish him with nothing unconnected with the subject of the navy. Perhaps you would prefer dilating those subjects into a sheet or two of paper and addressing them to Mr. Carey from under your own hand.

I enclose you a letter to Dr. Waterhouse which you will please to send to him.² The situation he wishes for is the one which he formerly held in the Marine Hospital near Boston.

The defeat of General Winchester has produced, it is said, a great deal of sensation at Washington. "We must command the navigation and possess the dominion of the ocean," says Great Britain. "We must have no hostile nation contiguous to us," says Bonaparte, and "We must have the navigation and empire of the Lakes, and tolerate no hostile province near to us," say the United States. One of the prophets speaks of the "nations being drunk."³ Which of the above three nations exhibits the strongest signs of intoxication?

Adieu! Yours—yours—yours,

BENJN: RUSH

P.S. I have promised to cooperate with you, Governor Gerry and Mr. Gray[4] in an application to Captain Jones in favor of Waterhouse's wishes to be reinstated in the Marine Hospital, provided that measure meets your approbation. There will probably be no staff appointments in the medical department until we have blundered a little longer as we did during the Revolutionary War. How faithfully do our scholars at Washington imitate us in wasting money and lives! Histories and memoirs amuse, but was there ever a nation or an individual the wiser or better for reading them?

Addressed: John Adams Esquire Quincy near Boston.
MS: Adams Manuscript Trust, Boston.

[1] I have not identified this contemplated work, and it was evidently not published, though see BR to Adams, 10 Apr. 1813.
[2] This letter has not been found.

[3] See Jeremiah 51:7.
[4] William Gray (1750-1825), merchant, shipowner, and currently lieutenant governor of Massachusetts (DAB).

To the Trustees of the University of Pennsylvania

Gentlemen, March 1st, 1813

With great respect I beg leave once more to address you upon the subject of the present mode of education in the Medical School of Pennsylvania.

In support of the facts mentioned in my former letters in favor of three winters' study in order to become a candidate for a medical degree, permit me to refer you to a petition subscribed by all the medical professors except Dr. Barton a few years ago. All the reasons that dictated that petition continue to operate, and with more force *now* than when it was subscribed. The number and subjects of our lectures have been increased, and the insufficiency of two years' instruction was evinced last year by the rejection of six of the applicants for degrees. One of those who answered to our satisfaction, and who afterwards graduated, applied to a practitioner of physic in this city to be taken into his shop as an apprentice, declaring at the same time he was unacquainted with diseases except from the histories of them in books and lectures, and that he had never compounded a medicine in his life.

In favor of an attendance upon the lectures upon natural philosophy as a prerequisite for a degree, I beg leave to state that it is impossible for a student of medicine who is unacquainted with it

[1184]

to understand the lectures upon the institutes of medicine, without which he cannot be a physician.

In favor of making an attendance upon the lectures upon midwifery necessary to a degree, permit me to mention that that branch of medicine embraces an extensive view of the diseases of women and children, and that an attendance upon it is made necessary to a medical degree in all the medical schools in the United States.

In addition to an attendance upon lectures upon the two branches of science that have been mentioned, an attendance upon the lectures upon botany would be highly useful. A knowledge of it is required in the University of Edinburgh in all applicants for medical degrees. A physician cannot be completely educated who is not more or less acquainted with it. Most of our medicines are obtained from the objects of that science. To facilitate the study of it, a botanical garden has been established by the medical schools of Boston and New-York. It is an appendage to all the medical colleges in Europe. The University of Pennsylvania would derive both reputation and benefit from such an institution.

It has been said by increasing the time and expenses necessary for obtaining a degree we shall drive students to other colleges. This has never occurred in the College of Edinburg, with four medical schools in its neighborhood; nor can it occur in Philadelphia until the opportunities of instruction in our rival colleges exceed ours, in which case they will be preferred in spite of all that can be done to prevent it.

Pardon me, gentlemen, while I ask a single question. Would you cross the ocean in a ship built by a carpenter who had heard lectures only upon shipbuilding for two years without ever having handled an ax or hammer in the course of his life? The danger to life is the same in trusting a sick person to a doctor of medicine whose knowledge is derived exclusively from lectures and books and who has not been familiar for several years with diseases and medicines.

I have the honor to be, gentlemen, with great respect, your most obedient servant,

BENJN. RUSH

MS (copy, with the date and a few corrections in BR's hand): Library Company of Philadelphia, Rush MSS.

To Thomas Truxtun[1]

Dear Sir,   Philadelphia, March 5th, 1813

It will only be necessary to send your Negro woman to the Hospital and to subscribe an obligation to pay for her board, &c., in order to have her admitted. Tomorrow is the day for admitting patients. The managers of the Hospital and physicians attend at the Hospital on *Saturdays* and *Wednesdays* between 10 and 12 o'clock for that purpose. The price of your servant's board will be not more than four dollars per week, perhaps less. I enclose you a certificate of her disease, to be subscribed by you. Please to mention her name in it. Although my time of attendance has expired at the Hospital, I will attend there tomorrow on purpose to facilitate her admission, and shall not fail of recommending her to the particular attention of my successor, Dr. Parke.

I thank you for the kind expressions contained in your letter, and beg leave to reciprocate them in the most cordial and respectful manner.

From, dear sir, your old friend and Revolutionary fellow citizen,

BENJN: RUSH

March 6h. Your servant may be sent on *any* day, but the enclosed paper must be first subscribed by a manager of the Hospital. Jos. Lownes and Saml. W. Fisher[2] are now acting managers.

Addressed: Thomas Truxton Esquire Wood-Lawn.
MS: Historical Society of Pennsylvania, Dreer Collection.

[1] Thomas Truxtun (1755-1822), naval officer and privateersman in the Revolution and naval hero of the Quasi-War with France, was at this time living in retirement on his farm, Wood Lawn, near Moorestown, N.J. (DAB; Eugene S. Ferguson, *Commodore Thomas Truxtun* [Research Bulletin of the Free Library of Philadelphia], 1947, p. 22-3).

[2] Joseph Lownes, goldsmith, served as manager of the Hospital, 1804-1820; Samuel W. Fisher, merchant, served 1812-1817 (Morton, *Hist. Penna. Hospital*, p. 405-6; *Phila. Directory* for 1813).

To Thomas Jefferson

My dear Sir,   Philadelphia, March 15th, 1813

Soon after I became the advocate of domestic animals, as far as related to their diseases, in the lecture of which I sent you a copy, Mr. Carver applied to me to become his advocate with our citizens for the purpose he has mentioned in his letter to you.[1] His proposition at first struck me as humane and praiseworthy, but in a short time afterwards it appeared to me in the same light that it does to you. I gave him a trifle to assist in paying for his passage, and obtained for him a passport from Mr. Monroe. Here my services to him ended. After this information your line of conduct will be an obvious one. He is an Englishman and has parents in England whom he has not seen for many years. All this is inter nos.

Alas! for the divided state of our citizens and the distracted state of the councils of our country! While I have uniformly considered the war we are engaged in as *just*, I have lamented the manner in which it has been conducted. The attack upon Canada appears to involve in it too much of the conquering spirit of the Old World and is contrary to the professions and interests of republicans. Admit that we have conquered it—shall we hold it as a province? or give it a representation in our national legislature? If the latter, by what means shall we eliminate British principles and habits from the representatives that will be sent by that British state to our Congress? Have we not evils enough to contend with already from those principles and habits? Why then should we increase them? But further—is not the perpetuity of our Union and of our republican institutions intimately connected with our being constantly under the pressure of circumambient monarchical states?

In favor of defending our rights of sovereignity upon the ocean exclusively, I have thought that, as the outrages committed upon our national interests were upon the ocean, they ought to be vindicated there only; that on the ocean the resentments of our citizens had arisen to the *war point*, but *nowhere else*; that our citizens, from the number of our bays, rivers, and creeks, and their habits of living by arts that render them familiar with the means of managing the water, and by their general knowledge of swimming and climbing, were better prepared for a sea than a land war; that our ships could be manned by volunteers only and never by drafts from the farmers and mechanics of our country, nor by soldiers enlisted in a fit of intoxication; that our inability to meet the force of Britain upon the ocean would lessen every year, and that every ship we built would require two or three ships of equal force to watch her, and that in this manner we might weaken the naval strength of Britain in the European and East India seas without giving her an opportunity to lessen ours; that in the winter months we could convoy our trade to and from our shores in spite of the whole navy of Britain, and that even this transient protection to our imports would supply our treasury with the means of defraying the ex-

penses of our navy; and lastly, that a navy would never be dangerous to liberty and that it would transfer the vices of war from our
farmers and prevent women and children from sharing *directly* in
its calamities.

Our naval victories are presages of what may be done by a free
and incensed nation contending for the gift of God to all the inhabitants of the globe. The year 1812 will be memorable in the
history of the world for having witnessed the first checks that have
been given to the overgrown pride and power of France on land
and of Britain on the ocean. Many of the crimes of Great Britain
that remain yet "unwhipt by justice," to use the words of Shakespeare,[2] were perpetrated in America. Our country was settled by
them. The jails and prison ships of New York, which were the
theaters of others of her crimes during the Revolutionary War,
have cried for more than thirty years to Heaven for retribution.
Those cries have been echoed over and over by the sailors who have
been dragged from our merchantmen and compelled to shed their
blood in fighting against nations against whom they felt no hostility
and in some instances against their own countrymen. Perhaps the
time for punishing all those crimes is now come, and as the navy
of Britain has been the principal instrument of those crimes, perhaps
the long and much injured United States may be the means employed by a just Providence of setting bounds to the power of that
navy and thereby of rendering the ocean the safe and common high-
way of all nations. Such an event would create a jubilee in all the
maritime nations in the world. Humanity and justice would forever
triumph in it.

But whither has an attempt to reply to the latter part of your
letter carried me? As an apology for it, I shall only add that I
am now in my 69th year, that I seldom read anything in a newspaper but articles of intelligence, and that I loathe political controversies above all things. From these declarations you have a right
to infer that I have filled my paper with nothing but the "babblings
of a second childhood."[3]

I have lately published a volume of inquiries upon the diseases
of the mind. They have been well received by the public. If you
wish to look into them, I shall do myself the pleasure of sending
you a copy of them.[4]

The few sands that remain in my glass urge me constantly to
quicken my labors. My next work will be entitled "Hygiene, or
Rules for the preservation of health accommodated to the climate,
diet, manners, and habits of the people of the United States." All

the imperfections of both these publications must be ascribed to a conviction that my time in this world must necessarily be short. Had they been kept to the "novum annum," they would have had fewer faults.

I enclosed in my last letter to you a small book written by Bishop Porteus as a present to Mrs. Randolph's children. As you have not acknowledged the receipt of it in your letter, I fear it has not been received by you.

Mr. Adams still does me the honor of favoring me now and then with a letter. In his last he mentions your name with kindness and speaks with surprise of the correctness of your style, of the steadiness of your hand evidenced in your writing, and of your exploits on horseback at your advanced stage of life.

From, dear sir, your sincere old friend of 1775,

BENJN: RUSH

P.S. From the present complexion of affairs in our country, are you not disposed at times to repent of your solicitude and labors and sacrifices during our Revolutionary struggle for liberty and independence? Have you not been disappointed in the conduct of both tories and whigs? Have not the former increased in number, not only by population but by the accession of Englishmen and the apostasy of many Revolutionary whigs? Are not the sons of tories Nerone Neronior?[5] Have not our funding system and its offspring, banks, like so many Delilahs robbed the whigs of their Revolutionary strength and virtue? War has its evils; so has a long peace. A field of battle covered with dead bodies putrefying in the open air is an awful and distressing spectacle, but a nation debased by the love of money and exhibiting all the vices and crimes usually connected with that passion, is a spectacle far more awful, distressing, and offensive. Hinc, hinc lacrymae rerum![6]

MS: Library of Congress, Jefferson Papers.

[1] See Jefferson's letter to BR, 6 Mch. 1813 (*Writings*, ed. Lipscomb and Bergh, XIII, 222-3). BR had permitted James Carver, a young Anglo-American, to use his (BR's) name in soliciting funds to enable Carver to attend a veterinary school in London. A letter from Carver describing his plans, 12 Oct. 1812, is in the Rush MSS, III.

[2] "Unwhipped of justice," *Lear*, III, ii, 53.

[3] Source not found.

[4] Jefferson in reply, 8 Apr. 1813, asked for a copy of the book, saying, "I read with delight every thing which comes from your pen, and the subject of this work is peculiarly interesting"; he also acknowledged the work by Bishop Porteus, mentioned below (Mass. Hist. Soc., Jefferson Papers).

[5] "More Nero-like than Nero." Source unknown.

[6] "Hence are there tears for things!" Probably a reminiscence of the *Aeneid*, I, 462; but the phrase in variant forms was common in Latin verse.

To John Adams

My dear Sir,   Philadelphia, March 16, 1813

The enclosed letter to Dr. Waterhouse contains the welcome intelligence that his son has passed his examination for a degree in our University with great honor, and that he will in a few weeks be created Doctor of Medicine.[1]

The documents you sent me relative to the origin of the American navy are now in the hands of Mr. Carey, who is heartily disposed to do ample justice to the early, uniform, and zealous advocate of that important part of the defense and honor of our nation.

I have spent 4 hours in the day since Thursday sennight in examinating[2] candidates for degrees, and expect to spend the same number of hours in the same dull, mechanical, and fatiguing business for more than a week to come. This employment has reduced the hours I usually devoted to your instructing and delightful correspondence. Oh! worse and worst—omnia in pejus ruunt.[3] The blunders, disasters, and disgraces of 1774 and 1775 and 1776 are poor apologies for similar events in 1812 and 1813.

Count Saxe says three things are requisite to make a general, viz., courage, genius, and *health*. Three of our generals are above *sixty*, a time of life in which the employments inseparable from a camp and military duty seldom fail of deranging the body and mind. Each of those generals has been laid up with sickness since their appointment, and two of them nearly in sight of the enemy.

Alas! the abortive issue of the new loan! I possess notes of a speech you made in Baltimore upon the question of raising the interest to be given by Congress upon money from 4 to 6 percent. Richd. Henry Lee opposed it—you defended it. Your words were, "Unless, Mr. President, we accommodate our measures to the *interest* of the tories as well as the feelings of the whigs, we shall never be able to govern this country." I wish this aphorism were inscribed over the doors of both houses of the present legislature of the United States. Yours—yours—yours,

BENJN: RUSH

[1] John Fothergill Waterhouse, who had graduated at Harvard, 1811, died at Charleston, S.C., 1817 (Univ. of Penna., *Gen. Alumni Cat.*). BR's letter to his father has not been found.

[2] Thus in MS.

[3] "Everything rushes to destruction." A more or less proverbial expression; the source of this precise form of it has not been found.

To William Graydon[1]

Dear Sir,   Philadelphia, March 24th 1813

I put your letter requesting a supply of Bibles into the hands of Mr. Ralston,[2] the worthy president of our Society.[3] Unhappily our stock is nearly exhausted. A few copies however, with double the number of New Testaments, will be sent to you by one of the wagons that goes to or passes through Harrisburgh. A large and elegant edition of the Bible, printing from stereotypes, is now in the press.[4] As soon as it is published, you may depend upon receiving a supply of them sufficient for all the poor and destitute families in your town.

May the great HEAD OF THE CHURCH prosper your pious efforts to spread the knowledge of his glorious name through our country by means of the history of what he has done and suffered for the human race!

From, dear sir, yours affectionately,

BENJN: RUSH

Addressed: Mr William Graydon Harrisburgh Pennsylvania.
MS: Mr. Lloyd W. Smith, Madison, New Jersey.

[1] William Graydon (1759-1840), brother of Alexander Graydon the memoirist, practised law in Harrisburg from 1786 and compiled several legal handbooks (W. H. Egle, ed., *Notes and Queries, . . . Chiefly Relating to Interior Pennsylvania*, 1st and 2d ser., reprint, Harrisburg, 1894, I, 331; *L.C. Cat.*).
[2] Robert Ralston (1761-1836), a merchant well known for his philanthropies; he had been BR's collaborator in organizing the first African Church (Simpson, *Eminent Philadelphians*, p. 825-6;

BR, *Autobiography*, p. 202).
[3] I.e., the Philadelphia Bible Society, founded in Dec. 1808 for the purpose of distributing free Bibles; BR was a charter manager and vice-president (BR, *Autobiography*, p. 275; *The First Report of the Bible Society Established at Philadelphia*, Phila., 1809).
[4] This Bible, "Stereotyped for the Bible Society by T. Rutt, Shacklewell, London, 1812," was an early example of the stereotyping process (*L.C. Cat.*, from a copy in the Huntington Library).

To John Adams

My dear Friend,   Philadelphia, April 10th, 1813

I put the papers you sent me into the hands of Mr. Carey. Some of them will be published in an appendix to his history of the rise and progress of the American navy.[1] They shall all be returned to you in a few days.

I rejoice with you in the 5th naval victory of our country.[2] The year 1812 will I hope be immortal in the history of the world for having given the first check to the overgrown power and tyranny of Britain and France. Russia and the United States may now be hailed as the deliverers of the human race.

The loan is filled. Two gentlemen, Mr. Parrish,[3] an Englishman, and Mr. Gerard, a Frenchman, subscribed for the whole of the deficient sum a few days ago. It would be nothing new in the history of wars if it should be discovered years hence that a part or the whole of the money thus subscribed was the property of British subjects and of the French government. I do not however think this probable. Both the gentlemen are immensely rich and possess respectable public and mercantile characters. They moreover, it is said, represented many of the *Federal* citizens of New York and Philadelphia who were afraid of being disowned by their party had they subscribed in their own names.

Is the present a war for the liberty of the ocean between Britain and the United States, or for the power of the Union between the southern and eastern states? It is, alas! conducted and opposed as if this were the case.

My son Ben returned to us last week by the way of New York in good health and fine spirits, much pleased with his voyages and grateful for his escapes from the plague in Smyrna, from Algerine pirates and British cruisers, as well as from the dangers of the sea. His details of what he has seen and heard form every day the pleasantest part of the repasts of our table.

Adieu! my dear old friend. Yours truly,

BENJN: RUSH

P.S. Knowing that my time is short and that the night of imbecility of mind or of death is fast approaching, I have sat down to prepare two small tracts for the press which have long been called for by my pupils. One of them will contain the outlines or elements of my specific opinions in medicine as far as they relate to the nature of diseases.[4] It will be accommodated to *all* classes of readers.

Addressed: John Adams Esquire Quincy near Boston.
MS: Adams Manuscript Trust, Boston.

[1] See BR to Adams, 15 Feb. 1813, and note 1 there.
[2] Doubtless alluding to the victory of the *Hornet*, Capt. James Lawrence, over the *Peacock* in the South Atlantic, 24 Feb. 1813 (Lossing, *Field-Book of the War of 1812*, p. 698-9).

[3] David Parish, or Parrish, an English-born financier concerning whom there is little information except that, with Stephen Girard and John Jacob Astor, he subscribed for the deficiency of the loan and, after the war, resumed his banking business in Europe (J. B.

McMaster, *Life and Times of Stephen Girard*, Phila. and London, 1918, II, 248-52, 313; Kenneth L. Brown, "Stephen Girard's Bank," PMHB, LXVI [1942], 41-2).
[4] Not completed.

To Samuel Miller

My dear Sir,   Philadelphia, April 13th, 1813

I have more than *read*—I have *devoured* your account of the life of our excellent friend Dr. Rodgers.[1] It is what the epicures call a titbit in biography. You have given an importance to the most minute incidents in his life by your reflections upon them. In doing so, you have happily imitated the manner of Tacitus. Mrs. Rush has been equally delighted with myself with your history of her much-beloved friend. She says it has the variety and animation of a novel, with all the dignity and instruction of real history. I was particularly pleased with your having given so correct a view of the Apostolic Age of the Presbyterian Church in America. The names of the Tennents, Dickinson, Burr, the Blairs, Finley, Smith, Roan, Wilson, and Allison[2] have been translated by your pen from their long repose in their graves to the skies, where they form a splendid constellation which I hope will never cease to command the admiration and affection of their descendants in the same church. I was pleased still further in observing that you ascribe their preeminence in scriptural knowledge and scriptural preaching to their familiarity with the writings of Baxter, Charnock,[3] Howe,[4] and other illustrious divines and saints who adorned the 17th century. They formed the Apostolic Age of the Christian Church in Great Britain.

I wish you had mentioned the names of Waddle, Kirkpatrick, Hunt, Caldwell, and Strain[5] among Dr. Finley's pupils in West Nottingham. They were excellent and useful ministers of the Gospel. Mr. Strain was a great man. In eloquence, as far as it consists in sublime conceptions and expressions, he was not inferior to Mr. Whitefield. He was so truly a "burning and shining light" that he consumed himself. He died prematurely from the vehemence of his labors, particularly in the pulpit, in which at times, unhappily, he rather *roared* than spoke. I will give you a specimen of the sublimity of his eloquence. In a sermon upon these words, "In him dwelleth all the fullness of God,"[6] delivered in Pine Street Church in our city, after mentioning most of the attributes of God which dwell in and were exercised by the Son, he added: "Above all, the fullness of the LOVE of God dwells in him. And here what shall

I say?———Help me, Gabriel—help me, Michael—help me, Ithuriel, with your celestial eloquence to do justice to the BOUNDLESS of the love of the Son of God." Here, with his eyes elevated towards the ceiling of the church, he paused for half a minute. A solemn stillness instantly pervaded the audience—then with a voice a little reduced and slow he cried out: "See! they droop their wings, unable even to comprehend the mighty theme."

There was great force in the word BOUNDLESS used as a substantive instead of an adjective.

May we both be enabled to follow the examples of these great and good men who are now through faith inheriting the great and precious promises of the Gospel!

Adieu! From, my dear sir, yours truly and affectionately,

BENJN: RUSH

P.S. My last work upon the diseases of the mind is not worth a place in a clergyman's library, but it contains some facts connected with morals that might be useful to you in your ordinary studies and duties. It will be easy to obtain a sight of it by applying to Dr. Hosack. Yours as above, B R.

MS: Princeton University Library.

[1] *Memoirs of the Rev. John Rodgers, D.D., Late Pastor of the Wall-Street and Brick Churches in the City of New-York*, N.Y., 1813. BR contributed to this volume a long letter on Rodgers' character, dated 7 June 1811 and printed by Miller at p. 291-7.

[2] All but two of these Presbyterian stalwarts—those teachers who had formed BR's views in early life and whom he had revered all his life—have been identified earlier. Jonathan Dickinson (1688-1747), minister for forty years at Elizabeth, N.J., was the first president of the College of New Jersey (DAB). John Roan (ca. 1716-1775), Irish born, after missionary labors in Virginia, was minister to several congregations in Lancaster co., Penna. (Sprague, *Annals*, III, 129-30).

[3] Stephen Charnock (1628-1680), Puritan divine; his *Sermons* were published, London, 1682 (DNB).

[4] John Howe (1630-1705), Cromwell's chaplain and a prolific theological writer; his *Works* were collected and published, London, 1724 (DNB; Allibone, *Dict. of Authors*).

[5] James Waddel (1739-1805) as a young man assisted Samuel Finley and Robert Smith in their Presbyterian schools, and afterward preached for many years in Virginia (Sprague, *Annals*, III, 235-42). William Kirkpatrick (d. 1769), a graduate of the College of New Jersey, 1757, preached at Trenton and Amwell, N.J. (same, p. 263, note). James Hunt (d. 1793), also a graduate of the College of New Jersey, 1759, preached and kept a school at Bladensburg, Md., from 1773 or earlier (Alumni Records, Secretary's Office, Princeton Univ.). David Caldwell (1725-1824), College of New Jersey, class of 1761, preached and kept a school in North Carolina (Sprague, *Annals*, III, 263-7). John Strain (d. 1774), College of New Jersey, class of 1757, had a congregation in York co., Penna.; according to one of Sprague's informants, Strain had a picturesque habit of "unexpectedly shooting aside of his subject, and taking his hearers unaware with a frightful or a rapturous exclamation" (same, p. 215-16).

[6] Colossians 2:9.

Appendices

APPENDIX I:

RUSH AND WASHINGTON

UNFORTUNATE and unseemly as Rush's quarrel with Washington was, there is nothing very mysterious about it. If one can rid one's mind of certain traditions of Revolutionary history, long standard but not well supported by evidence, the basic cause of the quarrel stands out clearly: Rush was given to reckless criticism, and Washington was extremely sensitive to any kind of criticism. Both men had justification for their mutual resentment, though neither fully understood the causes of the other's feeling. The incident reflects little credit on Washington and still less on Rush, who was, however, to pay a far greater penalty than his indiscretion merited.

The charge or insinuation that Rush lacked patriotism, repeated for a century after the appearance of the Rush-Henry-Washington correspondence in an appendix to Sparks' fifth volume of Washington's *Writings*, is absurd. Rush's notorious unsigned letter to Henry was the product of super-patriotism. Over and over again, Rush's letters, notes, and speeches during the Revolution (and, for that matter, all through his life) betray an overconfidence in his own judgment. In the Revolution *he was determined to win the war himself*. He was full of suggestions from the outset as to just how this was to be done. Consider only the series of letters written to R. H. Lee in Congress while Rush was serving in the campaign on the Delaware in December and January 1776-1777. He proposes a scheme for forcing the acceptance of Continental notes, and another for raising an army of seventy or eighty thousand men; he virtually orders the promotion of certain army officers; he insists that several thousand pounds in hard money be instantly sent to General Washington for espionage purposes; he proposes the appointment of a commissary of prisoners to ensure adequate supplies for captured American troops; he submits a plan for reforming the Continental medical service. And so on. Moreover, "Let not this matter be debated and postponed in the usual way for two or three weeks; the salvation of America, under God, depends upon its being done in an *instant*" (30 Dec. 1776). Some of Rush's manifold suggestions were excellent, and one or two were adopted. Obsessed by reforming zeal, Rush of course could never understand why his suggestions were not all carried out at once. Anyone who objected, who urged caution, or was indifferent to his proposals, was an enemy to the liberties of America. This is the psychological basis of Rush's controversy with Dr. Shippen, which led directly to the quarrel with Washington.

Brought up amid Quaker influences, Rush was an anti-militarist on principle, but he admired George Washington from the moment of his first meeting with him in the fall of 1774.[1] He was present at the dinner in celebration of Washington's appointment as commander in chief in the following June and left a moving account of it.[2] One of the handsomest tributes anyone paid to the new commander was sent by Rush in a letter to his friend Ruston, in London, 29 Oct. 1775: "You would distinguish him to be a general and a soldier from among ten thousand people. There is not a king in Europe that would not look like a valet de chambre by his side." (This letter, it may be observed in passing, was unsigned.) During the campaign around Trenton at the close of 1776 Rush served with Washington's forces and saw his chief repeatedly.[3] His opinion at this time is reflected in his urgent suggestion to R. H. Lee that Washington be invested with dictatorial powers, "or we are undone" (30 Dec. 1776). In 1777 the physician and his commander exchanged several letters on inoculation and other health measures.

The beginning of the rift between them may be traced to Rush's observations during his earliest service in the field. Though struck with the brilliance of the Trenton-Princeton campaign as a military feat, he here first witnessed and pointed out the woeful inadequacies of the army hospital arrangements. During the second battle of Trenton (2 Jan. 1777), Rush and Dr. John Cochran were in charge of the military hospital temporarily established in that town. When Washington withdrew during the night to march to Princeton and north Jersey, no word was left with the surgeons, who had many wounded on their hands, and apparently no medical officers accompanied the main army northward.[4] To latter-day readers this may appear one of the heroic elements in a celebrated achievement, but it could not have favorably impressed those responsible for the health of the troops. In a letter to R. H. Lee of 14 Jan. 1777, written after observing the enemy's care for his wounded at Princeton, Rush delivered his first attack upon the Continental medical organization, or, rather, upon the want of one. Though he did not mention Washington specifically, Rush found "our generals" remarkably indifferent to the medical needs of their men.

On 8 Apr. 1777 Rush made the following revealing entry in his pocket notebook:

"I think it more than probable that General Washington will not

---

[1] At Thomas Mifflin's house, probably (as Dr. Corner points out) on 17 Oct. 1774; Washington dined at BR's house next day (BR, *Autobiography*, p. 111; Washington, *Diaries*, II, 168).

[2] *Autobiography*, p. 112-13.

[3] Same, p. 124, 126.

[4] Same, p. 128. Thomas Rodney, captain in the Delaware regiment, tells in his *Diary* of his having to dress the wounds of his men on this march because the surgeons had been left behind (Hist. Soc. of Del., *Papers*, VIII [1888], 39).

close the present war with G. Britain. 1. Because in ordinary revolutions different characters always appear in their first and last stages. 2. Because his talents are better fitted to unite the people of America into one body than to give them afterwards a national complexion. 3. Because his talents are unequal to those degrees of discipline and decision which alone can render an army finally successful. 4. Because he is idolized by the people of America and is thought to be absolutely necessary for us to enable us to carry on the war."[5]

Of the four reasons given for his opinion, Rush's first is a hoary platitude that in this instance was to prove completely wrong. The second, since no evidence is given for it, is not clear. The third shows that Rush had been talking with some of the numerous informants he was to name in later explanations of the affair—persons who were supposed to know Washington intimately and who therefore, supposedly, knew weaknesses in him that were carefully screened from the public eye. The best and the worst commanders in all wars have been subjected to this kind of gossip by "insiders." Rush listened to these wagging tongues and was credulous enough to believe what he heard even before a personal grievance inclined him more eagerly to do so.

The fourth reason in Rush's list—popular idolatry of Washington—reflects the mingled fear and jealousy with which the civil leaders of the new nation regarded the growth of a great military reputation. These self-conscious republicans knew Roman history well and hence knew what this could portend. Years earlier, in his maiden flight as a political philosopher, Rush had criticized Mrs. Macaulay's proposed constitution for Corsica because it allowed generals and admirals to vote in the legislature:

"Men who have fought in defense of their country and have endured the hardships of war, naturally claim superiority over the rest of their countrymen. They feel their own importance, they know how necessary *they* are to the support of the state, and therefore assume more to themselves than is consistent with a free government. Should they ever be provoked to it, their knowledge in arms and their popularity with the soldiers and common people would give them great advantages over every other citizen, and would render the transition from democracy to anarchy, and from anarchy to monarchy, very natural and easy." (Letter to Catharine Macaulay, 18 Jan. 1769.)

In the perspective of our national history, observations like these may appear empty clichés. But the statesmen of the Revolution, who had a different perspective, devoted much of their eloquence to the dangers of

[5] "Notes on Continental Congress, &c.," vol. 2.

military domination over civil power.[6] The course of events in Europe during their later lives confirmed rather than lessened their conviction.

A few days after setting down his skeptical thoughts on Washington as commander in chief, Rush was appointed surgeon general of the Continental middle department, that is to say, of Washington's army. He entered upon his duties in the most idealistic and zealous spirit. Within a fortnight he had compiled and printed a code of military hygiene that was to prove serviceable in our armies as late as the Civil War. (See his letter to the Officers of the Army, 22 Apr. 1777.) That summer and fall he spent with the army, being nearly captured at Brandywine Creek in September, and witnessing the gallant but fruitless defense of Fort Mifflin on the Delaware in November. For the troops as fighters and as men he came to have a high regard; toward the military and administrative leadership of the army he developed a growing distrust. His immediate superior, Dr. William Shippen, Jr., director general of hospitals in the middle department, displayed, it seemed to Rush, the worst qualities of the lazy and complacent bureaucrat, while the men with whose care Shippen was charged died by the thousands in the hospitals. In circumstances like these Rush was incapable of silence. The ample record of his protests will be found in his letters of the fall and winter of 1777. Those to John Adams in Congress, written following a visit to the well-ordered British camp after the battle of Brandywine, epitomize Rush's sense of outrage and frustration:

"The wounded whom we brought off from the field were not half so well treated as those whom we left in General Howe's hands. . . . It would take a volume to tell you of the many things I saw and heard which tend to show the extreme regard that our enemies pay to discipline, order, economy, and cleanliness among their soldiers. [On the other hand] The present management of our army would depopulate America if men grew among us as speedily and spontaneously as blades of grass. The 'wealth of worlds' could not support the expense of the medical department alone above two or three years." (To Adams, 1 Oct. 1777.)

Since he was writing confidentially to a friend, Rush did not confine his criticisms to his own department. He questioned whether such a ragged and undisciplined mob as he saw, panting after its repulse at Germantown early in October, could ever become an effective army. Washington pondered the same question himself during the terrible months that followed, and so it is not surprising that many onlookers did. Congress,

---

[6] See the speeches of BR and John Adams in the debates on referring the appointment of three major generals to the general officers of the army, 19 Feb. 1777. These were recorded by BR in his notebook and are printed in Burnett, *Letters of Members*, II, 262-3. There is a full discussion of this republican dogma in Miller, *Triumph of Freedom*, p. 238-44.

which had fled to York after Washington's failure to hold Philadelphia, was rife with doubts and questions. It will not do to say that the criticism of Washington in the winter of 1777-1778 was the work of a little group of scheming congressmen, principally Massachusetts men, who wished to seize control of the army and to place their creatures—Gates, Mifflin, and Conway—in command.[7] There is plentiful evidence to show that those most deeply disturbed by the failures of Washington's army were the public leaders in Pennsylvania and New Jersey who had found the protection of that army inadequate. Two of the severest condemnations of Washington's strategy in the campaign around Philadelphia were uttered by Elias Boudinot, commissary general of prisoners, and Jonathan Dickinson Sergeant, attorney general of Pennsylvania, neither of whom has yet been associated by historians with the "Conway Cabal," though perhaps they will be hereafter.[8] There was in fact a movement in Pennsylvania at this time to take matters to some extent out of Washington's hands, not by replacing him but by organizing what might be called a "people's army" to wrest Philadelphia from British control.[9]

Rush fell in wholeheartedly with this plan, for it would confirm (he believed) his theorem that professional armies are unnecessary for the defense of a republic. As early as 1 Oct. he had observed to Adams that Stark's militia at Bennington had "cast a shade on everything that has been done by regulars since the beginning of the war" and had shown "what wonderful qualities are to be called forth from our countrymen by an active and enterprising commander." He ventured to assert that the militia would end the war that they had begun. "I should despair

[7] This interpretation is developed at great length by John C. Fitzpatrick in *George Washington Himself*, Indianapolis, 1933, ch. XLVIII, "The Conway Cabal." Fitzpatrick's lurid account of the "Cabal" was an attempt to set history back more than a century. Even John Marshall in 1804 conceded that the "machinations" of Washington's critics were carried on "possibly with good intentions" (*Life of George Washington*, Phila., 1804-1807, III, 338). Fitzpatrick's characterization of John Adams in the role of Washington's spiteful rival is perhaps the grossest caricature—or libel—invented since the days of Adams' presidency.

[8] Their letters, dated 23 Sep. and 20 Nov. 1777 respectively, are quoted by Knollenberg in *Washington and the Revolution*, p. 195, 194.

[9] In December the Pennsylvania Council and Assembly presented a formal remonstrance to Congress "against the Propos'd Cantonment of the Army of the United States" west of the Schuylkill, and on 2 Jan. the same bodies communicated a petition from forty-four citizens of Lancaster county "proposing the calling out of the whole strength of this State against the Enemy." The letter of transmittal stated that other petitions "of like import are circulating in different parts of the State; and we have reason to believe they contain the sense of a large number of our constituents." *Penna. Archives*, 1st ser., VI, 104-5, 109, 111, 153-4; *Penna. Colonial Records*, XI, 386, 394, 464.

of our cause if our country contained 60,000 men abandoned enough to enlist for 3 years or during the war."[10]

Militia forces had played a substantial part in the campaign that ended at Saratoga; the Saratoga campaign was the one redeeming feature of an inglorious American record during 1777; and the victor at Saratoga was Rush's very good friend Horatio Gates. There is no doubt about the fact that Rush would have liked to see Gates replace Washington as commander in chief, for he said as much time and again that winter. Nor would Rush have stopped there. He wanted a sweeping reformation among the general officers of the main army because he believed Washington had often accepted bad advice from incompetent subordinates. In this latter view Rush was in agreement not only with those who have been associated by various historians with a dark conspiracy against Washington, but with others whose personal loyalty to Washington has never been questioned, among them Henry Laurens, Anthony Wayne, and Johann Kalb.[11] Mr. Knollenberg concludes his chapter on the Conway Cabal by quoting the one clear bit of evidence he has found for a plot to remove Washington, to wit, certain sentences in Rush's unsigned letter to Patrick Henry. His comment is that "it takes more than one to form a conspiracy."[12] This is true, but it is also true that, if criticism is to be regarded as conspiracy, Rush had a great many fellow conspirators in 1777-1778. The Conway Cabal was less than the commonly received accounts have made it; but it was also more. It was a great deal of complaining talk, some of it loose and some more thoughtful, by men of all sorts who sensed that American affairs were at a crisis. Some of the critics were undoubtedly disgruntled and ambitious, but most of them were simply wondering if a change in the command might not be necessary. Washington's explanation that it all sprang from a little knot of personal rivals and enemies was incorrect. But this was a very human explanation, and was perhaps necessary to enable him to hold fast to his great purpose.

Affairs in Rush's own department came to a crisis that winter. Finding

---

[10] BR probably discussed the plans for a Pennsylvania army with George Bryan, vice-president of the state, in Jan. 1778. Their conversation in Lancaster, which dealt with Washington's "slackness" and the need for "some heroic action," was partially recorded by Christopher Marshall in his *Diary*, p. 159. Writing Gates a month later, BR proposed Mifflin for the command of the army of citizens forming to drive Howe out of Philadelphia (4 Feb. 1778). Evidently the Yorktown campaign did not alter BR's conviction about professional armies. In his letter to the Ministers of All Denominations, 21 June 1788, he restated his views with great emphasis.

[11] See letters of Laurens, 16 Oct. 1777; of Wayne, 21 Nov. 1777; and of Kalb, 7 Jan. 1778, quoted in K. R. Rossman, "Thomas Mifflin—Revolutionary Patriot," *Pennsylvania History*, xv (1948), 17-18.

[12] *Washington and the Revolution*, p. 77.

the hardships, the mortality, and what would now be called the morale among the men in the hospitals he supervised rapidly passing beyond his control, he addressed letters to Shippen, to Congressman William Duer, and at length to Washington himself asking for effective action. The letter to the Commander in Chief (26 Dec.) is a model statement and plea of its kind, and it was supported by a letter to the same effect from Governor Livingston of New Jersey. Washington answered Livingston's letter promptly (31 Dec.) and communicated both letters to Director General Shippen. Rush's letter undoubtedly gave Shippen offense, for it hinted that, though Shippen's hands were more than full, he would depute no part of his authority to the medical officers actually in the hospitals. This was an issue which Washington perhaps thought he could not meddle with, for the hospital regulations had been established by Congress, with Rush as a leading participant. Yet much harm might conceivably have been prevented if Rush's letter had received a prompt and conciliatory reply. As it was, Washington, who was shouldering other burdens, did not answer until the very day (12 Jan. 1778) when Rush sat down and wrote his letter to Patrick Henry.[12a]

It is not easy to divine just what Rush expected to accomplish by writing Governor Henry. He suggested publication of the direful circumstances he described, but the newspapers were as available to him as to Henry. Primarily he seems to have been thinking out loud in order to relieve his mind. Rather than sounding Henry out, Rush simply assumed a sympathetic listener, and wrote in a vein almost as confidential as he did to his wife in a more optimistic letter three days later. But he mistook his listener. In due time Henry transmitted the letter to Washington, and Washington, who recognized Rush's hand and who was still smarting from the Conway affair, bitterly denounced Rush's duplicity.[13]

[12a] In note 1 on BR's letter to Patrick Henry (p. 184, above), it is said that no evidence has been found to show that BR remained in touch with Henry after the latter left Congress in 1775. But after these volumes were in proof an important letter from BR to Henry, written from Philadelphia, 16 July 1776, came to light. Listed in the Parke-Bernet Galleries' catalogue of *American Historical Autographs*, sold 9 Jan. 1951, lot 129, this 4-page A.L.S. is a typically bold and patriotic outpouring by BR on American prospects as he saw them during the interesting interval between the adoption of the Declaration of Independence and the formal signing of it, in which he was himself to partici-

pate. The letter was acquired by the American Philosophical Society and will be published, with a commentary, in the Society's *Proceedings* for 1951.

[13] Henry to Washington, 20 Feb. and 5 Mch. 1778; Washington to Henry, 27 and 28 Mch. 1778; Washington, *Writings*, ed. Sparks, v, 512-15. It may be pointed out here that the period of BR's stay in York for hearings on the hospital department was perhaps the only time when the several major "conspirators" against Washington could have conspired together: Lovell, Gates, Conway, and Mifflin were apparently all in York more or less continuously during the latter part of Jan. 1778. This has been thought to provide an explana-

APPENDIX I

The mistake that Rush made in his free-swinging criticism (which embraced Congress as well as the high command) was in getting off the firm ground of his own department. Even if we disregard everything Rush himself said, the evidence seems overwhelming that the medical service in Washington's army was woefully, if not criminally, inadequate; and there appears to be very little evidence to show that Shippen extended himself to improve it. Full substantiation of these statements, particularly of the second, must await a definitive history of the Continental medical services. With respect to Shippen's conduct it may be pointed out, first, that for months at a time—and during very bad times—he reported nothing out of the ordinary either to Congress or to Washington.[14] Second, that Rush's charges of neglect and incompetence on the Director General's part were supported fully and with grim examples by Dr. James Tilton, a very reputable witness, in sworn testimony at Shippen's court-martial.[15] Third, that Congress, though accepting Rush's resignation when his superior officer forced a choice between them, promptly effected a general reform of the hospital department. The reform made the changes that Rush had called most loudly for: separation of administrative and purveying functions; wider authority for the officers in direct charge of the hospitals; a clear instruction that the director frequently visit the hospitals; improved methods of financial accounting and of returning the sick and dead; and so on.[16] Fourth and finally, Shippen won only the barest acquittal when he was at length brought before a court-martial. His judges, indeed, though finding the evidence for the second charge (speculating in and selling hospital stores) not sufficient to convict, declared they were "clearly of opinion, that

tion for the paper called "Thoughts of a Freeman," which was mysteriously conveyed to President Laurens and was by him transmitted to Washington. The paper expressed views very similar to some held by BR, but its style is decidedly not his, and it is inconceivable that a major general or a member of Congress would expect anything from such a childish device. The paper is printed by Sparks, v, 497-9, presumably from the copy made by R. H. Harrison now in L.C., Washington Papers. Patterson, in his *Gates* (p. 207), says flatly that BR was the sponsor and principal author of the paper: "Several quills doctored its style and pointed its meaning here and there. Beyond that, the document was Rush's brain child." This is unconvincing without the original MS before

one, and Patterson does not make clear that he has seen the original. (The text assigned by him to the Gates Papers in the New-York Historical Society has not been located after repeated searches.)

[14] Statement based on Shippen's letters in the Papers of the Continental Congress and in the Washington Papers, L.C.

[15] Tilton's evidence is printed in the *Penna. Packet*, 14 Oct. 1780; it provides one of the most comprehensive and harrowing accounts of the Continental hospitals available.

[16] *Jour. Cont. Cong.*, X, 128-31 (6 Feb. 1778). A broadside version of this report is in L.C., Papers of the Continental Congress, No. 78, XXII, 567; Evans, *Amer. Bibl.*, No. 16413.

doctor Shippen did speculate in and sell hospital stores, THAT IS, stores proper for hospitals, whilst he was purveyor general: which conduct they consider highly improper, and justly reprehensible."[17] If Shippen did not live like a wastrel, as Rush charged, he did sell sugar and Madeira wine for his private profit while director general, and admitted doing so.[18]

In view of these plain facts it is not surprising that Rush considered Shippen's triumph in 1778 another proof of the demoralization of the republic. Congress had dealt the blow—the Congress that has been supposed by historians to be full of intriguers against the Commander in Chief.[19] But it was approved by Washington, who did not answer Rush's letter setting forth his reasons for resigning (25 Feb. 1778). Instead, he showed it to Shippen and, after nearly a month, sent it on to Congress with a comment more or less implying he agreed with Shippen that Rush was merely a trouble-maker.[20] Three years later, upon retiring from his post under renewed criticism, Shippen asked Washington for a testimonial on his conduct as director general. His commander replied that he was quite satisfied with Shippen's conduct and that, so far as he was capable of judging, "I believe no hospitals could have been better administered."[21] Shippen published this testimonial, and Rush naturally resented it. The opinion of one highly qualified student of the Revolution is that in respect to the Continental medical service Washington "was badly advised . . . and did not know the facts."[22] The available evidence strongly supports this judgment.

In time, Washington's bitterness of feeling toward Rush subsided. Early in 1780 he made magnanimous use of an opportunity that presented itself to renew friendly relations with Rush by inviting him to dine at Headquarters.[23] This was at Morristown, where Rush was attending the court-martial of Shippen. Rush reported of the dinner: "The General uncommonly cheerful—talked of affairs in Ireland."[24] No doubt Rush talked with equal liveliness on subjects equally remote. It is not possible to say whether Rush knew at this time that Washington had read the unsigned letter to Henry. He knew this for certain in 1788, upon the

---

[17] *Penna. Packet*, 25 Nov. 1780.
[18] Same.
[19] James Lovell, a sharp and persistent critic of Washington and therefore often pointed out as a leader of the "Cabal" in Congress, was particularly hostile to BR in the hearings before the medical committee at York; see BR to Morgan, June? 1779.
[20] To the President of Congress, 21 Mch. 1778; *Writings*, ed. Fitzpatrick, XI, 125.

[21] Letter of 13 Feb. 1781; *Writings*, ed. Fitzpatrick, XXI, 218.
[22] Randolph G. Adams, "Benjamin Rush, the Doctor in Politics," *Journal of the Michigan Medical Society*, XXIX (1930), 806.
[23] Washington to BR, no date [19 Mch. 1780]; MS owned by Josiah C. Trent, M.D.
[24] BR, "Notes on Continental Congress, &c.," vol. 2.

publication of Gordon's *History*,[25] but meanwhile he enjoyed an increasingly pleasant, if formal, relationship with Washington. The two men exchanged letters from time to time; Washington dined in the Rush home while attending the Federal Convention; and Rush expressed repeated satisfaction with the popular assumption that the former commander in chief would "drive our new wagon"—that is, become first President of the United States.[26]

All this was natural enough in view of Rush's ardent Federalism, but his ardor scarcely outlasted the launching of the new government. In the Federalist ascendancy of the 1790's he saw a repetition of some things he had not liked in the late war. Washington, surrounded by a cluster of ambitious and unscrupulous advisers (as Rush believed), was once more a popular idol whose fiat it was heresy to question. Surely this was not a healthy condition in a republic! After Washington's retirement, it served the old-guard Federalists' purposes to foster the legend of Washington's infallibility. The indignation expressed by Rush (as well as by the Adamses, Jefferson, and others) over public tributes to Washington is seriously misunderstood if thought disrespectful to the first President. It was directed principally at those whom Rush called the "old tories," who had draped themselves in the mantle of Washington and were using his name for political purposes. Senator William Plumer, a Federalist, said in 1805 that the celebration of Washington's birthday had become "a mere party festival"; and John Adams observed several years later that these "Feasts and Funerals" were "mere hypocritical Pageantry to keep in Credit, Banks, Funding Systems and other Aristocratical Speculation."[27]

Yet there is undeniable spitefulness in Rush's allusions to Washington in the letters of his last years. One cause of this was the publication of John Marshall's *Life of Washington*, a huge textbook of idolatry, in the third volume of which were printed Rush's unsigned letter to Patrick Henry and the correspondence between Henry and Washington relating thereto.[28] Despite the fact that Rush's name was suppressed by the printer,

[25] See notes on BR's letter to Henry, 12 Jan. 1778.

[26] Washington, *Diaries*, III, 229; BR to Pickering, 30 Aug. 1787. BR sent Washington inscribed copies of his own publications during this period (A. P. C. Griffin, comp., *Catalogue of the Washington Collection in the Boston Athenaeum*, Boston, 1897, p. 176); and Washington sought BR's advice regarding books on education (Washington to Clement Biddle, 10 Sep. 1787, *Writings*, ed. Fitzpatrick, XXIX, 272).

[27] William Plumer, Jr., *Life of William Plumer*, Boston, 1856, p. 326. Adams to BR, 14 Mch. 1809 (*Old Family Letters*, *A*, p. 223). See also two remarkable letters by Abigail Adams to her sister, Mary Cranch, 15 and 28 Feb. 1798, on the first celebration of Washington's birthday in Philadelphia after Washington became a private citizen (*New Letters of Abigail Adams*, p. 133, 136-7).

[28] See the notes on BR's letter to John Marshall, 5 Sep. 1804.

well-informed persons could supply it, and the incident caused him acute distress. (The book was being read in his own family.) In the following year (1805), Rush and John Adams resumed their long-interrupted correspondence. Never an idolater, and never one to mince words, Adams had complained to Rush as early as 1790 about the growing Washington legend:

"The History of our Revolution will be one continued Lye from one end to the other. The essence of the whole will be *that Dr. Franklins electrical Rod, smote the Earth and out sprung General Washington. That Franklin electrified him with his rod—and thence forward these two conducted all the Policy, Negotiations, Legislatures and War.* These underscored Lines contain the whole Fable Plot and Catastrophy. If this Letter should be preserved, and read an hundred years hence the Reader will say, 'the envy of this J.A. could not bear to think of the Truth! He ventured to scribble to Rush, as envious as himself, Blasphemy that he dared not speak when he lived. But Barkers at the Sun and Moon are always Silly Curs.' But this my Friend, to be serious, is the Fate of all ages and Nations. . . . No Nation can adore more than one Man at a time. It is an happy Circumstance that the object of our Devotion is so well deserving of it; that he has virtue so exquisite and wisdom so consummate. There is no Citizen of America will say, that there is in the World so fit a Man for the head of the Nation. From my soul I think there is not; and the Question should not be who has done or suffered most, or who has been the most essential and Indispensable Cause of the Revolution, but who is the best qualified to govern us?"[29]

A great part of what Rush and Adams had to tell each other in old age was naturally what they knew about the history of their time. Agreeing as they did that the Washington of the eulogists was not precisely the Washington of actuality, they took satisfaction in facts, real or supposed, discreditable to the popular hero. If this is not creditable to them, it is at least understandable. Rush's final word on the matter, in his long letter of 12 Feb. to 9 Mch. 1812, was evoked by a bit of gossip, passed on at third hand by Adams, to the effect Washington had once said: "He had been a good deal in the world and seen many bad Men, but Dr. Rush was the most black hearted scoundrel he had ever known."[30] Adams gave no credence to the anecdote. Indeed, he had quoted it in order to show how unfounded most such gossip is. But Rush, deeply wounded, overlooked this important point. After reviewing the whole history of his relations with Washington, he concluded as follows:

[29] 4 Apr. 1790; *Old Family Letters, A*, p. 55-6.

[30] Adams to BR, 8 Jan. 1812; *Old Family Letters, A*, p. 371.

"When Calvin heard that Luther had called him 'a child of the devil,' he coolly replied, 'Luther is a servant of the most high God.' In answer to the epithet which G. Washington has applied to me, I will as coolly reply, 'He was the highly favored instrument whose patriotism and name contributed greatly to the establishment of the independence of the United States.' "

Here the defense rested in 1812, and here it may be allowed to rest for good.

APPENDIX II:

JOHN ADAMS' APPOINTMENT OF RUSH
AS TREASURER OF THE MINT

Rush's appointment as treasurer of the Mint in Nov. 1797 was a turning point in his life, and it provides at the same time a highly interesting example of appointment policy under President Adams.

An entry in Rush's Commonplace Book for 9 Apr. 1795 states that "This day Tench Coxe called upon me to know whether I would accept of the Directorship of the Mint with a salary of £750 a year in the room of Dav. Rittenhouse, who was about to resign. I declined the offer on the steps of my door without deliberating one moment upon it." The reasons for his declining were both financial and professional: the salary would not compensate him for his loss of time, and he wished to devote himself to the establishment of his "new System of Physic."[1] The post was afterwards accepted by Mrs. Rush's uncle, Elias Boudinot.

Two years later Rush felt differently. The income from his practice had remained stationary since 1793, and his family had been increasing. With the reappearance in 1797 of the yellow fever—in a more virulent form, as he believed, than previously—Rush applied his bloodletting therapy more rigorously than ever before, and thereby brought a torrent of criticism upon himself. Many hints show that his nerve came close to snapping that fall. He tried to find a teaching post in New York, and he contemplated giving up medical practice altogether. Immediately following the death of Nicholas Way, treasurer of the Mint since 1794, Elias Boudinot wrote to Secretary of State Pickering to announce that fact and to say: "I have seen Dr. Rush, whose Mind is greatly clouded by the present appearance of the disorder. He seems determined if he should live thro' this Visitation of the City, to retire from the City, and I suspect would gladly accept the Office of Treasurer of the Mint."[2] It is not clear from this letter, or from Rush's mention of the incident in his *Autobiography*,[3] whether Rush asked for this recommendation before Boudinot offered it.

Adams knew full well that Rush had openly sympathized with the Jeffersonian party in the election of 1796. Nevertheless, on 15 Sep. he wrote from Quincy to Secretary of the Treasury Wolcott: "Many applica-

[1] *Autobiography*, p. 233-4.
[2] 4 Sep. 1797; National Archives, Record Group 59 (General Records of the State Department), Applications and Recommendations for Office. This letter covered another of the same purport to President Adams.
[3] Page 102.

APPENDIX II

tions have been made to me for the place of Dr. Wray [Way]. . . .[4] These are all respectable characters; but all things considered, my judgment inclines to Dr. Rush, on account of ancient merits and present abilities. Of his integrity and independence I have a good opinion."[5] To Pickering, Adams wrote much the same, adding that he had "known, esteemed, and loved [Rush] these three and twenty years," and directing Pickering, if he concurred in Adams' choice, to make out a commission.[6]

Pickering, at Trenton, sought the opinion of Judge Richard Peters, a staunch Philadelphia Federalist who had known Rush long and intimately. Peters' response was—and is—illuminating. He wrote:

"If Dr Rush wishes for the Place he ought to have it. His Talents are equal to it & his Exertions, formerly at least, deserve Reward. All I know of his Politics is unfavorable. But I believe he has meddled very little in public Affairs for some Time past. I find him frequently entirely unacquainted with public Occurrences which convinced me of his Inattention to political Movements. He was very much Mr Jefferson's Friend at the last Election, but took no active Steps to help him mount the Ladder. He always speaks in the most friendly Terms of Mr Adams. On some political Questions I have found his Sentiments *shabby*; but he did not appear to me to take much Interest in either Side, tho' if he had any Lean it was to what we think the wrong Side. He met with some Disappointment during the Washington Administration. The old Affairs of Shippen stuck to him & I believe he was disgusted by the President employing Shippen in his Family. His Talents might *be enlisted* by due Notice being taken of him. I lament his Want of Stability, for he certainly has great Merit, unshaken Integrity & eminent Talents. I do not believe he can or will abandon his Business, but wishes this Office supplementary to it. . . . Rush has a large & expensive Family to whom he is very indulgent. As to the present Depression of his Business I think Nothing of it & am sorry he gives Way to Resentment or Chagrin on that score. His Patients are mostly among opulent People & Strangers who are generally out of Town. He should not have shewn himself irritated or hurt by the Newspaper Abuse thrown on him. His suing Fenno & Porcupine is a foolish Thing & only gratifies his Enemies. I admire his Abilities, lament his Foibles, & with them all sincerely love him, therefore I cannot but wish him gratified."[7]

[4] Both BR and Adams stated that there were some forty applicants for the post (BR, *Autobiography*, p. 102; Adams to BR, 30 Sep. 1805, *Old Family Letters, A*, p. 84).
[5] George Gibbs, *Memoirs of the Ad-ministrations of Washington and John Adams*, N.Y., 1846, I, 562.
[6] 18 Sep. 1797; Pickering and Upham, *Pickering*, III, 457.
[7] 7 Oct. 1797; Mass. Hist. Soc., Pickering Papers.

Rush's commission as treasurer of the Mint, dated 27 Nov. 1797, was sent to him by Pickering under a covering letter of the same date.[8] The appointment perfectly exemplified the policy that Mrs. Adams attributed to her husband in a letter to Mary Cranch a few months later: "The P[resident] has said, and he still says, he will appoint to office merit, virtue & Talents, and when Jacobins possess these, they will stand a chance, but it will ever be an additional recommendation that they are Friends to order and Government."[9] What party regulars thought of the appointment is disclosed in two letters of William Loughton Smith, of South Carolina, then United States minister to Portugal. On 25 Feb. 1798 Smith wrote to Oliver Wolcott:

"I have been much amused in reading over some files of American papers by the last vessel. I see the old dispute revived with great violence for [i.e., over] bleeding for fever and ague, and that Dr. Rush is charged with bleeding many hundreds to death. . . . I was not very much surprized at this charge, but I confess I was surprized to see him appointed treasurer of the mint. I hope he won't bleed that to death also."[10]

Smith's remarks somehow came to the notice of President Adams, who resented them. On 19 June 1798 Smith wrote asking Pickering to explain to Adams that "my observation respecting Dr. R's appointment arose altogether from my warm regard for the President, to whose election I have the best evidence that the said Dr. was strongly opposed, and I confess that, with that knowledge, I could not see without some disrelish the appointment to the office in question, more especially as I have reason to believe that he is a warm admirer of the V[ice] P[resident] and is a man of whimsical and unsettled opinions in government."[11]

There is no evidence that the appointment influenced Rush's political opinions by so much as a feather's weight, but it made him grateful to John Adams to his dying day. Years later he told Adams that between 1797 and 1807 he had lost an estimated $30,000 in his professional income because of his stand during the epidemics. "Had it not been for the emoluments of the office you gave me . . . , I must have retired from the city and ended my days upon a farm upon the little capital I had saved from the labors of former years" (letter of 24 Aug. 1808).

In the summer of 1812 Rush grasped an opportunity to present to Adams a quarter-cask of wine from Samos. Answering Adams' warm acknowledgment, Rush said: "I will say of the wine which you have

[8] The commission, on parchment, is in Hist. Soc. Penna., Society Miscellaneous Coll.; a retained copy of Pickering's letter is in Mass. Hist. Soc., Pickering Papers.

[9] Feb. 1798; *New Letters of Abigail Adams*, p. 127.

[10] George Gibbs, *Memoirs of the Administrations of Washington and John Adams*, N.Y., 1846, II, 55.

[11] *South Carolina Magazine of History and Genealogy*, XXV (1924), 58-9.

done me the favor to accept, what you said to me when I called to thank you for the appointment you gave me at the Mint: 'You have not more pleasure in receiving it than I had in giving it to a faithful old Revolutionary whig'" (11 Sep. 1812). To this Adams replied in a wonderfully characteristic passage in his next letter:

"When you thanked me [for the appointment], in strict propriety you was in error. You did wrong. I gave you nothing. I was Trustee for our Country. Had I known a Man more fit, more deserving, you would not have been selected. You have given me your own. I have accepted your own. I ought therefore to give you ten thousand, thousand Thanks, and you ought to have given me none at all. You have a head metaphisical enough to discern, and an heart suscescible [sic] enough to feel these nice distinctions: and therefore to be convinced that I ought not always to lay under the Weight of this great obligation."[12]

[12] 18 Sep. 1812; *Old Family Letters, A*, p. 306-7.

APPENDIX III:
THE COBBETT-RUSH FEUD

THE public announcement by Rush on 2 Oct. 1797 (q.v.) that he had begun suits for libel against John Ward Fenno and William Cobbett was his answer to the increasing streams of abuse poured out upon him in the *Gazette of the United States* and *Porcupine's Gazette*, the two high-flying Federalist newspapers of Philadelphia. Some specimens of Fenno's invective are given by Nathan Goodman,[1] but Rush soon found Cobbett a much more formidable assailant and dropped the suit against Fenno in order to concentrate on "Peter Porcupine."[2]

William Cobbett (1766-1835), the English writer, politician, and agriculturist who twice sojourned in the United States, was one of the most colorful figures of his own era, and in his genius for savage journalistic satire remains perhaps without a rival in any era. Arriving in the United States in 1792, he stumbled almost by accident upon a public eager to buy and devour the coarse brand of fare he could purvey.[3] For several years he was the principal mouthpiece of the Federalist conservatives—those who hated and feared "French principles," a term broad enough to include everything from the policies of Talleyrand to the ideas of Thomas Jefferson. When the Federalists themselves divided, during John Adams' administration, and the country turned toward Jeffersonianism, Cobbett's occupation was gone. But in his heyday his influence was potent indeed. Joseph Priestley, who was one of Cobbett's principal victims, admitted that Peter Porcupine was "by far the most popular writer in this country, and, indeed, one of the best in many respects."[4] The President's wife, a woman of sound taste, was an avid reader of Cobbett's newspaper. "Peter says many good things," Mrs. Adams wrote her sister, "and he is the only thorn in Baches side [Franklin Bache published the Democratic-Republican *Aurora*]. . . . I have a great curiosity to see the Creature." And again: "*that Man is* a very extraordinary creature. . . . His shafts are always tipt with wit, and his humour is such as frequently to excite more of good than ill."[5] A very different estimate

---

[1] *Rush*, p. 215-16.

[2] Cobbett asserted, no doubt with a measure of truth, that the action against Fenno was dropped because it would be much more difficult to obtain damages for libel from an American citizen than from an alien; see *Porcupine's Works*, London, 1801, XI, 144, 382, note.

[3] On this point, see William Reitzel's excellent analysis of Cobbett's brief popularity: "William Cobbett and Philadelphia Journalism, 1794-1800," PMHB, LIX (1935), 223-44, especially p. 234.

[4] Letter of 1800, quoted in Mary E. Clark, *Peter Porcupine in America: The Career of William Cobbett, 1792-1800*, Phila., 1939, p. 166.

[5] 13 Mch. and 7 May 1798; *New Letters of Abigail Adams*, p. 143, 169.

was given of him by a fellow newspaper proprietor, Benjamin Russell. Russell was a Boston Federalist but, like the Jeffersonians, he considered Cobbett a hireling.

"Cobbett [he wrote] was never encouraged and supported by the Federalists as a solid, judicious writer in their cause; but was kept merely to hunt Jacobinic foxes, skunks, and serpents. The Federalists found the Jacobins had the AURORA, ARGUS, and CHRONICLE, through which they ejected their mud, filth, and venom, and attacked and blackened the best characters the world ever boasted; and they perceived that these vermin were not to be operated on by reason or decency. It was therefore thought necessary that the opposite party should keep, and feed a suitable beast to hunt down these skunks and foxes; and 'the fretful Porcupine' was selected for this business. This imported, or transported beast has been kept as gentlemen keep a fierce bull Dog, to guard his house and property against thieves, Jacobins and Frenchmen, and as such he has been a good and faithful dog, and has been fed and caressed accordingly."[6]

Such was the antagonist Rush faced in one of the greatest fights of his career. Cobbett had publicly castigated Rush's *Eulogium on Rittenhouse* as "silly sans-culottish" stuff early in 1797;[7] and with the renewal of the fever and of Rush's pronouncements on the efficacy of bleeding, he came forward to rescue the citizenry from the great republican quack. A series of squibs and parodies on the "preposterous puffs" of "the Philadelphia phlebotomist" began to appear in *Porcupine's Gazette* in mid-September, and they merely increased in trenchancy after Rush's notice that he was suing Cobbett.[8] For example, on 7 Oct. appeared the following narrative of Rush's conduct in the crisis of the 1793 epidemic:

"So much was the Doctor about this period possessed with the notion that he was the only man of common sense existing, that he not only refused to consult with any but his former pupils who submitted to obey his dictates, and rudely intruded his advice upon other people's patients. He also appointed two illiterate negro men, and sent them into all the alleys and bye places in the city, with orders to bleed, and give his sweating purges, as he empirically called them, to all they should find sick,

---

[6] Quoted without date from the *Boston Centinel*, in Robert W. Jones, *Journalism in the United States*, N.Y., 1947, p. 161-2.

[7] In the *Political Censor*, VIII (Jan. 1797); reprinted in *Porcupine's Works*, IV, 361-2; see also *Rush-Light*, No. III, p. 150.

[8] The passages on which the suit was grounded were reprinted in *A Report of an Action for a Libel, Brought by Dr. Benjamin Rush, against William Cobbett, in the Supreme Court of Pennsylvania, December Term, 1799. . . . [Taken in Shorthand by T. Carpenter]*, Phila., 1800, unpaged. Extracts are given in Goodman, *Rush*, p. 216-17.

without regard to age, sex, or constitution; and bloody and dirty work they made among the poor miserable creatures that fell in their way.

"That his mind was elevated to a state of enthusiasm bordering on frenzy, I had frequent opportunity of observing; and I have heard from popular report, that in passing through Kensington one day, with his black man on the seat of his chaise along-side of him, he cried out with vociferation, 'Bleed and purge all Kensington! drive on, boy!' "[9]

On 16 Oct. Cobbett printed a passage from *Gil Blas*, in which Dr. Sangrado of Valladolid, "a *tall, pale, hungry-looking fellow*, who had kept the shears of Clothos employed for forty years at least," is quoted as saying (after drawing six porringers of blood from a patient and ordering six more to be drawn in three hours), "It is a gross error to suppose that blood is necessary to the conservation of life."[10] From this time forth, Cobbett's favorite name for Rush was "Sangrado." On 24 Oct., under the caption "Rush and his Patients," Cobbett inserted this notice: "Wanted, by a physician, an entire new set of patients, his old ones having given him the slip; also a slower method of dispatching them than that of phlebotomy, the celerity of which does not give time *for making out a bill*."[11]

Rush writhed under these assaults but remained silent—at least in public. Some conception of their virulence is essential to explain his attempt, recorded in his letters of October and November 1797, to move to New York. Cobbett of course got wind of this. A New York newspaper paragraph mentioned Rush's possible appointment at Columbia and concluded with the observation that "He is a man born to be useful to society." Cobbett reprinted the paragraph, adding: "And so is a *musquito*, a *horse-leech*, a *ferret*, a *pole cat*, a *weazel*: for these are all *bleeders*, and understand their business full as well as Doctor Rush does his."[12]

As appears from various hints about retirement in Rush's letters of this period, Cobbett very nearly succeeded in driving his victim out of business. Certain it is that Rush went through a grave emotional as well as professional crisis in the fall of 1797. He had to have revenge on his persecutor, and, despite advice from more than one quarter, he persisted in the legal action he had begun. Rush *v.* Cobbett came on before the state supreme court in Dec. 1797 but was delayed for one reason or another for two years. Then, as Cobbett tells it, the case was tried before a packed bench and a packed jury immediately after Cobbett moved to New York early in Dec. 1799. The testimony, the speeches of the several attorneys on each side, and the charge to the jury by Judge Shippen (the

[9] *Porcupine's Works*, London, 1801, VII, 234.
[10] Same, p. 243.
[11] Same, p. 254.
[12] Same, p. 288-9.

latter highly favorable to the plaintiff) may be read in the printed *Report of an Action for Libel.* "The Jury, after an absence of two hours, brought in a verdict in favor of the Plaintiff of *Five Thousand Dollars.*" Most authorities have agreed that the trial was in some respects unfair and that the damages were excessive.

Whether fair or unfair, the verdict whetted Cobbett's appetite for vengeance in his turn, and the upshot was to bear out the worst predictions of Rush's advisers. Upon learning of the judgment, Cobbett wrote his close friend Edward Thornton, a member of the staff of the British legation:

"Nothing provokes me but the thought of such a whining republican rascal putting the 5,000 dollars in his pocket. Why the pauper never saw so much money before, not even in his *mint.* Mr. L[iston] hinted something about *softening* Rush. I hope in God it will not be attempted. I would sooner beg my bread from door to door. The villain shall not enjoy his prize in peace. I shall find the means of reaching him be I wherever I may."[13]

In a farewell number of *Porcupine's Gazette* issued at New York on 13 Jan. 1800, Cobbett began to make good this threat. Declaring that his sole motive had been to expose the menace to Philadelphians' lives that lay beneath Rush's "sleek-headed, saint-looking" appearance, Cobbett, with his usual resourcefulness, capitalized on a recent event much in the public mind. Quoting an official medical report, he pointed out that *on the very day* when a Philadelphia court had imposed damages of $5,000 upon Cobbett for opposing Rush's depleting methods, George Washington had expired at Mount Vernon under treatment "in precise conformity to *the practice of Rush.* . . . On that day the victory of RUSH and of DEATH was complete."[14]

The dragging in of the Washington case must have seemed like the last twist of the knife to Rush, but there was much more in store for him. Shortly afterward Cobbett gave notice that he would issue a periodical work devoted exclusively to Rush, the "Rushites," and their iniquities. So far Porcupine had merely taken journalistic pot shots; he would now release some broadsides. The first *Rush-Light* appeared in the middle of February, its principal content being a comic biographical sketch of

[13] *Letters from William Cobbett to Edward Thornton . . . 1797-1800,* ed. G. D. H. Cole, London, &c., 1937, p. 25.

[14] *Porcupine's Works,* London, 1801, XI, 150. Cobbett later learned and announced with great satisfaction that Elisha Dick, one of the physicians who had signed the report on Washington's death, had been a pupil of BR's (*Rush-Light,* No. II, p. 81-6). Dr. Corner, who has reviewed and cited the medical literature relating to Washington's last illness, observes that while "there is no doubt that the doctors bled too freely," BR's pupil Dr. Dick "was opposed to the later venesections in this case" (BR's *Autobiography,* p. 249, note).

Rush and an analysis of his writings that would have done honor to
Swift or Smollett. The havoc it wrought in the Rush household is evidenced in Rush's agitated letter to Brockholst Livingston of 5 Mch. 1800.
That day Richard Rush had knocked down a Philadelphia physician
who had abetted Cobbett, and John Rush had left on the New York
stage to assault Porcupine himself. In subsequent issues Cobbett kept his
readers abreast of these developments, which greatly added to his fun
and that of the public. To private friends who advised his departure for
England, Cobbett said he was enjoying himself too much to leave the
United States. Besides, he was making money. He told Thornton in
April that "the Rush-Light has surpassed in circulation any publication
ever before issuing from my press." Twenty-five hundred copies of the
first two numbers and 3,000 of the third and fourth were not meeting
the demand. Cobbett expected to be able to carry home about $10,000
with him when he finally embarked.[15] Rush's suit had made Cobbett rich!

Like all great satirists, Cobbett decorated—or one should perhaps say
disfigured—the truth only a little. A shrewd observer of human foibles,
he had a perfect target for ridicule in the Messianic side of Rush's per-
sonality. Furthermore, as Professor Shryock has pointed out, Cobbett
the layman must be credited with a suggestion of scientific importance
that never seems to have occurred to Rush the physician—or for that
matter to any of his professional colleagues for another generation or so.
In *Rush-Light*, No. II, Cobbett examined Rush's claims of cures by
depletion as set forth in *An Account of the Yellow Fever in 1793*, and
correlated them with the daily bills of mortality in the city. It was easily
demonstrable that the more the bleeders bled, the more the victims died.
Since Rush had no list of successful and unsuccessful cases to submit,
his claims could not be credited. Whatever his motives, Cobbett in his
approach to clinical statistics proved himself a better epidemiologist than
Rush.[16]

The last number of the *Rush-Light* (No. v) appeared at the end of
April.[17] Another trial was coming up in which Cobbett knew he would

[15] 17 and 25 Apr. 1800 (*Cobbett-
Thornton Letters* [see note 13], p. 74,
87). BR in his *Autobiography* (p. 103-
4) confirms all this by saying that the
pamphlets "were purchased, lent, and
read with great avidity by most of the
citizens of Philadelphia, and my children were insulted with the contents of
them at School, and in the public
streets."

[16] *Rush-Light*, No. II, p. 65-71. See
Richard H. Shryock's article on BR in
DAB, and especially his *Development of*

Modern Medicine, N.Y., 1947, p. 138-
140.

[17] A sixth number, which had little
or nothing to do with BR, was issued
in London in August. *The Republican
Rush-Light* "by William Cobbet," called
Volume II, No. VII, and issued without a date or place, is a lame imitation of Cobbett from the opposite political camp. It was evidently published
in the United States after the election of
1800.

be the loser. On 1 June he sailed for England. He had been apprehensive during the preceding days that "some vile wretch or other" would start still another action that would detain him, but on the following day he wrote from off Sandy Hook that he was "in a fair way of losing sight, for ever, of the land of *liberty*."[18] (In this he proved quite wrong.) Speaking for the Jeffersonians, Philip Freneau exclaimed:

> O may the sharks enjoy their bait:
> He came such mischief to create
> We wish him not a better fate. . . .
>
> Alack, alack! he might have stay'd
> And followed here the scribbling trade,
> And lived without the royal aid.
>
> But democratic laws he hated,
> Our government he so be-rated
> That his own projects he defeated.[19]

As for Rush, the departure of Cobbett,[20] followed by the election of Jefferson and the decline of the annual attacks of yellow fever, in some degree restored his spirit. He turned with pleasure to writing his "Travels through Life" as a testament for his children. The self-justifying tone sometimes apparent in that work, as well as in many of his letters in the following years, must be partly attributed to the wounds inflicted by the barbed quills of Peter Porcupine. The protracted feud with Cobbett hastened Rush's retreat from public life and humanitarian causes toward the sequestration of his later years. He was more tranquil, but he was also more disillusioned. His unbounded optimism had given way to resignation tinged with embitterment. Full knowledge of the Rush-Cobbett feud is necessary to understand that embitterment.

[18] To Thornton, 27 May and 2 June 1800 (*Cobbett-Thornton Letters*, as cited in note 13 above, p. 98, 99).

[19] "On the Departure of Peter Porcupine for England" (*Poems*, ed. F. L. Pattee, Princeton, 1902-1907, III, 240-1).

[20] Cobbett left without paying the judgment against him in Rush v. Cobbett, but his attorneys finally settled with Rush's lawyer in 1801 for the amount of $4,250 (Brockholst Livingston to BR, 16 July 1801; Rush MSS, XXIX). It has been said that BR gave the money to charity (Joseph McFarland, in *Medical Life*, new ser., XXXVI [1929], 496; Goodman, *Rush*, p. 220). This would have been in character, but I have not seen the evidence for it, and it is not mentioned in BR's *Autobiography*.

List of Short Titles and Other Abbreviations

Abraham, *Lettsom*
> James Johnston Abraham, *Lettsom: His Life, Times, Friends and Descendants*, London, 1933.

Adams, *History of the U.S.*
> Henry Adams, *History of the United States of America* [1801-1817], New York, 1930; 9 vol. in 4.

Adams, *New Letters*
> *New Letters of Abigail Adams, 1788-1801*, edited by Stewart Mitchell, Boston, 1947.

Adams, *Works*
> *The Works of John Adams, . . . with a Life of the Author*, edited by Charles Francis Adams, Boston, 1856; 10 vol.

Allgem. deutsche Biog.
> *Allgemeine deutsche Biographie*, Leipzig, 1875-1912; 56 vol.

Allibone, *Dict. of Authors*
> S. Austin Allibone, *A Critical Dictionary of English Literature and British and American Authors*, Philadelphia, 1871; 3 vol.

Amer. Philos. Soc., *Early Proceedings*
> *Early Proceedings of the American Philosophical Society for the Promotion of Useful Knowledge, Compiled by One of the Secretaries, from the Manuscript Minutes of Its Meetings from 1744 to 1838*, Philadelphia, 1884.

Ann. Med. Hist.
> *Annals of Medical History.*

Annals of Congress
> *The Debates and Proceedings in the Congress of the United States* [1789-1824], Washington, 1834-1856; 42 vol.

Baker, *Itinerary of Washington*
> William S. Baker, *Itinerary of George Washington from June 15, 1775, to December 23, 1783*, Philadelphia, 1892.

Barratt, *Old St. Paul's*
> Norris Stanley Barratt, *Outline of the History of Old St. Paul's Church, Philadelphia, Pennsylvania*, n.p., 1917.

Biddle, *Memorial*
> *A Memorial containing Travels through Life, or Sundry Incidents in the Life of Dr. Benjamin Rush. . . . Written by Himself. Also Extracts from his Commonplace Book as Well as a Short History of the Rush Family in Pennsylvania*, ed. Louis Alexander Biddle, Lanoraie [i.e., Chestnut Hill, Penna.], 1905.

Biddle Papers
> Parke-Bernet Galleries, Inc., *The Alexander Biddle Papers: American Historical Autographs*, New York, 1943; 3 parts.

Biog. Dir. of Cong.
> *Biographical Directory of the American Congress, 1774-1927*, Washington, 1927.

Biog. Univ.

[J. F. and L. G. Michaud] *Biographie universelle, ancienne et moderne,* Paris, 1811-1847; 80 vol.

Blanton, *Medicine in Va. in the Eighteenth Century*

Wyndham B. Blanton, *Medicine in Virginia in the Eighteenth Century,* Richmond, 1931.

Boudinot, *Boudinot*

J. J. Boudinot, *The Life, Public Services, Addresses, and Letters of Elias Boudinot, LL.D.,* Boston and New York, 1896; 2 vol.

BR, *Account of the Yellow Fever in 1793*

Benjamin Rush, *An Account of the Bilious Remitting Yellow Fever, as It Appeared in the City of Philadelphia, in the Year 1793,* 2d edn., Philadelphia, 1794.

BR, *Autobiography*

The Autobiography of Benjamin Rush: His "Travels through Life," *Together with His Commonplace Book for 1789-1813,* edited by George W. Corner, Princeton, 1948.

BR, *Diseases of the Mind*

Benjamin Rush, *Medical Inquiries and Observations, upon Diseases of the Mind,* Philadelphia, 1812.

BR, *Essays*

Benjamin Rush, *Essays, Literary, Moral & Philosophical,* Philadelphia, 1798.

BR, *Med. Inq. & Obs.*

Benjamin Rush, *Medical Inquiries and Observations.* References in the present work are to the separate volumes of the first edn., [I] (1789) to v (1798); to the 2d edn., 1805, in 4 vol.; or to later edns. as indicated. All edns. were published in Philadelphia.

BR, MS List of Apprentices

List of his private pupils kept by BR, 1770-1812, in Rush MSS (see below), Notebooks, vol. 4, p. 204-8. The list has been printed by James E. Gibson in "Benjamin Rush's Apprenticed Students," Coll. Phys. Phila., *Trans.,* 4th ser., xiv (1946), 127-32.

BR, "Notes on Continental Congress, &c."

See below under Rush MSS, Notebooks.

BR, *Scottish Journal*

MS journal (115 p.) kept by BR during 1766-1768, while a student in Scotland; University of Indiana Library.

BR, *Sixteen Introductory Lectures*

Benjamin Rush, *Sixteen Introductory Lectures, to Courses of Lectures upon the Institutes and Practice of Medicine, with a Syllabus of the Latter,* Philadelphia, 1811.

Brigham, *Hist. and Bibliog. of Amer. Newspapers*

Clarence S. Brigham, *History and Bibliography of American Newspapers, 1690-1820,* Worcester, Mass., 1947; 2 vol.

Brit. Mus. Cat.

The British Museum Catalogue of Printed Books, 1881-1900, Ann

Arbor, Mich., 1946; 58 vol. Also: British Museum, Department of Printed Books, *General Catalogue of Printed Books*, 1931—.

Brown & Brown, "Directory of Book-Arts"

H. Glenn Brown and Maude O. Brown, "A Directory of the Book-Arts and Book Trade in Philadelphia to 1820 including Painters and Engravers." Published serially in New York Public Library, *Bulletin*, LIII-LIV (1949-1950). Also issued separately, 1950.

Brunhouse, *Counter-Revolution*

Robert L. Brunhouse, *The Counter-Revolution in Pennsylvania, 1776-1790*, Harrisburg, 1942.

Bull. Hist. Med.

Bulletin of the History of Medicine.

Burnett, *Letters of Members*

Letters of Members of the Continental Congress, edited by Edmund C. Burnett, Washington, 1921-1936; 8 vol.

Caldwell, *Autobiography*

Autobiography of Charles Caldwell, ed. Harriot W. Warner, Philadelphia, 1855.

Carey, *Short Account*

Mathew Carey, *A Short Account of the Malignant Fever, Lately Prevalent in Philadelphia*, 4th edn., Philadelphia, 1794.

Carrington, *Battles of the Amer. Rev.*

Henry B. Carrington, *Battles of the American Revolution, 1775-1781*, New York, &c., 1876.

Carson, *Hist. of the Medical Dept. of the Univ. of Penna.*

Joseph Carson, *A History of the Medical Department of the University of Pennsylvania*, Philadelphia, 1869.

Cat. Bibl. Nat.

Catalogue général des livres imprimés de la Bibliothèque Nationale: Auteurs, Paris, 1897—.

Centennial Memorial of the Presbytery of Carlisle

Centennial Memorial of the Presbytery of Carlisle: A Series of Papers, Historical and Biographical, Relating to the Origin and Growth of Presbyterianism in the Central and Eastern Part of Eastern Pennsylvania, Harrisburg, 1889; 2 vol.

Charles Lee Papers

New-York Historical Society, *Collections, Publication Fund Series*, IV-VII: *The Lee Papers*, 1872-1875.

Cheyney, *Hist. Univ. Penna.*

Edward Potts Cheyney, *History of the University of Pennsylvania, 1740-1940*, Philadelphia, 1940.

Cobbett, *Rush-Light*

The Rush-Light. . . . By Peter Porcupine, New York, 1800; Nos. I-V.

Coll. Phys. Phila.

College of Physicians of Philadelphia.

Collins, *Continental Congress at Princeton*

Varnum Lansing Collins, *The Continental Congress at Princeton*, Princeton, 1908.

Collins, *Witherspoon*

Varnum Lansing Collins, *President Witherspoon: A Biography*, Princeton, 1925; 2 vol.

Condie & Folwell, *Hist. of the Pestilence*

Thomas Condie and Richard Folwell, *History of the Pestilence, Commonly Called Yellow Fever, Which Almost Desolated Philadelphia, in the Months of August, September & October, 1798*, Philadelphia [1799].

Conyngham, "Reminiscences"

David Hayfield Conyngham, "Reminiscences," edited by Horace F. Hayden, Wyoming Historical and Geological Society, *Proceedings*, VIII (1902-1903), 181-291.

Cordell, *Med. Ann. Md.*

Eugene Fauntleroy Cordell, *The Medical Annals of Maryland, 1799-1803*, Baltimore, 1903.

Coxe's *Amer. Dispensatory*, 1825

John Redman Coxe, *The American Dispensatory, containing the Natural, Chemical, Pharmaceutical and Medical History of the Different Substances Employed by Medicine*, 6th edn., Philadelphia, 1825.

DAB

Dictionary of American Biography, edited by Allen Johnson and Dumas Malone, New York, 1928-1936; 20 vol.

DAE

A Dictionary of American English on Historical Principles, ed. Sir James Craigie and James R. Hulbert, 1938-1944; 4 vol.

DAH

Dictionary of American History, ed. James Truslow Adams and R. V. Coleman, N.Y., 1940.

DNB

Dictionary of National Biography, edited by Leslie Stephen and Sidney Lee, London, 1885-1912; 63 vol. and supplements.

Deutsch, *The Mentally Ill in America*

Albert Deutsch, *The Mentally Ill in America: A History of Their Care and Treatment from Colonial Times*, Garden City, N.Y., 1937.

Dexter, *Yale Graduates*

Franklin Bowditch Dexter, *Biographical Sketches of the Graduates of Yale College* [1701-1815], New York, 1885-1912; 6 vol.

Dickinson College, *Alumni Record*

Alumni Record Dickinson College, edited by George Leffingwell Reed, Carlisle, Penna., 1905.

Drinker, *Journal*

Extracts from the Journal of Elizabeth Drinker, from 1759 to 1807, A.D., edited by Henry D. Biddle, Philadelphia, 1889.

Drinker, *Not So Long Ago*

Cecil K. Drinker, *Not So Long Ago: A Chronicle of Medicine and Doctors in Colonial Philadelphia*, New York, 1937.

Dubbs, *Franklin and Marshall College*

Joseph Henry Dubbs, *History of Franklin and Marshall College*, Lancaster, Penna., 1903.

Duncan, *Medical Men in the Amer. Rev.*
> Louis C. Duncan, *Medical Men in the American Revolution, 1775-1783,* Carlisle, Penna., 1931.

Egbert, *Princeton Portraits*
> Donald Drew Egbert, assisted by Diane M. Lee, *Princeton Portraits,* Princeton, 1947.

Evans, *Amer. Bibl.*
> Charles Evans, *American Bibliography: A Chronological Dictionary of All Books, Pamphlets and Periodical Publications Printed in the United States of America* [1639-1799], Chicago, 1903-1934; 12 vol.

Flexner, *Doctors on Horseback*
> James Thomas Flexner, *Doctors on Horseback: Pioneers of American Medicine,* New York, 1938.

Force, *Archives*
> [Peter Force, compiler] *American Archives: Consisting of a Collection of Authentick Records, State Papers, Debates, and Letters and Other Notices of Publick Affairs,* Washington, 1837-1853; 9 vol.

Ford and Skeel, *Webster*
> Emily E. F. Ford and Emily E. F. Skeel, *Notes on the Life of Noah Webster,* New York, 1912; 2 vol.

Franklin, *Writings*
> *The Writings of Benjamin Franklin,* edited by Albert Henry Smyth, New York and London, 1905-1907; 10 vol.

Gibson, *Bodo Otto*
> James E. Gibson, *Dr. Bodo Otto and the Medical Background of the American Revolution,* Springfield, Ohio, and Baltimore, Md., 1937.

Good, *Rush*
> Harry G. Good, *Benjamin Rush and His Services to American Education,* Berne, Ind., 1918.

Goodman, *Rush*
> Nathan G. Goodman, *Benjamin Rush, Physician and Citizen, 1746-1813,* Philadelphia, 1934.

Gross, *Lives of Physicians and Surgeons*
> *Lives of Eminent American Physicians and Surgeons of the Nineteenth Century,* edited by Samuel D. Gross, Philadelphia, 1861.

Hageman, *Hist. of Princeton*
> John Frelinghuysen Hageman, *History of Princeton and Its Institutions,* 2d edn., Philadelphia, 1879; 2 vol.

Heitman, *Register*
> Francis B. Heitman, *Historical Register of Officers of the Continental Army during the War of the Revolution,* new edn., Washington, 1914.

Hist. Cat. St. Andrew's Soc. Phila.
> *An Historical Catalogue of the St. Andrew's Society of Philadelphia with Biographical Sketches of Deceased Members,* n.p., 1907-1913; 2 vol.

Inscriptions in St. Peter's Church Yard
> William W. Bronson and Charles R. Hildeburn, *The Inscriptions in St. Peter's Church Yard, Philadelphia,* Camden, 1879.

Jackson, *Encyclo. of Phila.*

Joseph Jackson, *Encyclopedia of Philadelphia*, Harrisburg, 1931-1933; 4 vol.

Jefferson, *Writings*, ed. Ford

The Writings of Thomas Jefferson, edited by Paul Leicester Ford, Letterpress Edition, N.Y., 1892-1899; 10 vol.

Jefferson, *Writings*, ed. Lipscomb and Bergh

The Writings of Thomas Jefferson, ed. Andrew A. Lipscomb and Albert Ellery Bergh, Washington, 1903-1904; 20 vol.

Jour. Cont. Cong.

Journals of the Continental Congress, 1774-1789, edited by Worthington Chauncey Ford and others, Washington, 1904-1937; 34 vol.

Keith, *Provincial Councillors*

Charles P. Keith, *The Provincial Councillors of Pennsylvania Who Held Office between 1733 and 1776, and Those Earlier Councillors Who Were Some Time Chief Magistrates of the Province, and Their Descendants*, Philadelphia, 1883.

Kelly & Burrage, *Dict. Amer. Med. Biog.*

Howard A. Kelly and Walter L. Burrage, *Dictionary of American Medical Biography: Lives of Eminent Physicians of the United States and Canada, from the Earliest Times*, New York and London, 1928.

Knollenberg, *Washington and the Revolution*

Bernhard Knollenberg, *Washington and the Revolution: A Reappraisal*, New York, 1941.

Lamb, *History of New York*

Martha L. Lamb, *History of the City of New York*, New York and Chicago, 1877; 2 vol.

L.C.

Library of Congress, Division of Manuscripts.

L.C. Cat.

A Catalog of Books Represented by Library of Congress Printed Cards, Ann Arbor, Mich., 1942-1946; 167 vol. Also: *Supplement* to the same, 1948; 42 vol.

Lecky, *Hist. of England*

William Edward Hartpole Lecky, *A History of England in the Eighteenth Century*, new impression, London, &c., 1913; 7 vol.

Libr. Co. Phila.

Library Company of Philadelphia, Ridgway Branch.

Life of Ashbel Green

The Life of Ashbel Green, V.D.M., Begun to Be Written by Himself. . . . Prepared for the Press at the Author's Request by Joseph H. Jones, New York, 1849.

Lossing, *Field-Book of the War of 1812*

Benson J. Lossing, *The Pictorial Field-Book of the War of 1812*, New York, 1868.

Lundin, *Cockpit of the Revolution*

Leonard Lundin, *Cockpit of the Revolution: The War for Independence in New Jersey*, Princeton, 1940.

Maclean, *Hist. Coll. N.J.*

John Maclean, *History of the College of New Jersey, from Its Origin in 1746 to the Commencement of 1854*, Philadelphia, 1877; 2 vol.

McMaster, *Hist.*

John Bach McMaster, *A History of the People of the United States, from the Revolution to the Civil War*, Philadelphia, 1883-1913; 8 vol.

McMaster and Stone, *Penna. and the Federal Constitution*

John Bach McMaster and Frederick D. Stone, *Pennsylvania and the Federal Constitution, 1787-1788* [Philadelphia], 1888.

Marshall, *Diary*

Extracts from the Diary of Christopher Marshall, Kept in Philadelphia and Lancaster, during the American Revolution, 1774-1781, edited by William Duane, Albany, 1877.

Martin, *Bench and Bar*

John Hill Martin, *Martin's Bench and Bar of Philadelphia, Together with Other Lists of Persons Appointed to Administer the Laws in the City and County of Philadelphia, and the Province and Commonwealth of Pennsylvania*, Philadelphia, 1883.

Martindale, *Hist. of Byberry and Moreland*

Joseph C. Martindale, *A History of the Townships of Byberry and Moreland, in Philadelphia, Pa.*, Philadelphia, 1867.

Mease, *Picture of Philadelphia*

James Mease, *The Picture of Philadelphia, Giving an Account of Its Origin, Increase and Improvements in Arts, Sciences, Manufactures, Commerce and Revenue*, Philadelphia, 1811.

Mettler, *Hist. of Medicine*

Cecilia C. Mettler, *History of Medicine*, edited by Fred A. Mettler, Philadelphia and Toronto, 1947.

Miller, *Nisbet*

Samuel Miller, *Memoir of the Rev. Charles Nisbet, D.D., Late President of Dickinson College, Carlisle*, New York, 1840.

Miller, *Triumph of Freedom*

John C. Miller, *Triumph of Freedom, 1775-1783*, Boston, 1948.

Mills, *Glimpses of Colonial Society*

Glimpses of Colonial Society and the Life at Princeton College, 1766-1773, by One of the Class of 1763 [William Paterson], edited by W. Jay Mills, Philadelphia and London, 1903.

Moon, *Morris Family*

Robert C. Moon, *The Morris Family of Philadelphia, Descendants of Anthony Morris*, Philadelphia, 1898; 3 vol.

Morais, *Jews of Philadelphia*

Henry Samuel Morais, *The Jews of Philadelphia: Their History from the Earliest Settlements to the Present Time*, Philadelphia, 1894.

Morgan, *Dickinson College*

James Henry Morgan, *Dickinson College: The History of One Hundred and Fifty Years, 1783-1933*, Carlisle, Penna., 1933.

Morton, *Hist. Penna. Hospital*

Thomas G. Morton, assisted by Frank Woodbury, *The History of the Pennsylvania Hospital, 1751-1895*, revised edn., Philadelphia, 1897.

New Jersey Archives

Archives of the State of New Jersey, First Series: Documents Relating to the Colonial History of the State of New Jersey, Newark, &c., 1880—. Also: *Second Series: Documents Relating to the Revolutionary History of the State of New Jersey*, Trenton, 1901-1917; 5 vol.

OED

A New English Dictionary on Historical Principles, edited by James A. H. Murray and others. Oxford, 1888-1933; 10 vol. in 15, and suppl.

Old Family Letters, A

Old Family Letters: Copied from the Originals for Alexander Biddle. Series A, Philadelphia, 1892.

Packard, *Hist. of Medicine in U.S.*

Francis R. Packard, *History of Medicine in the United States*, New York, 1931; 2 vol.

Patterson, *Gates*

Samuel White Patterson, *Horatio Gates, Defender of American Liberties*, New York, 1941.

Peeling, "Governor McKean"

James Hedley Peeling, "Governor McKean and the Pennsylvania Jacobins (1799-1808)," *Pennsylvania Magazine of History and Biography*, LIV (1930), 320-54.

Penna. Archives

Pennsylvania Archives. Selected and Arranged from Original Documents in the Office of the Secretary of the Commonwealth, Philadelphia and Harrisburg, 1852-1935; 119 vol. in 123.

Penna. Census, 1790

U.S. Bureau of the Census. *Heads of Families at the First Census of the United States Taken in the Year 1790: Pennsylvania*, Washington, 1908.

Penna. Colonial Records

Minutes of the Provincial Council of Pennsylvania, Minutes and Proceedings of the Council of Safety, and Minutes and Proceedings of the Supreme Executive Council of Pennsylvania, 1683-1790, Philadelphia and Harrisburg, 1851-1853; 16 vol. [Each volume has separate title, but the official collective title is *Colonial Records*.]

Pettigrew, *Lettsom*

Thomas Joseph Pettigrew, *Memoirs of the Life and Writings of the Late John Coakley Lettsom, M.D. . . . With a Selection from His Correspondence*, London, 1817; 3 vol.

Pickering and Upham, *Pickering*

Octavius Pickering and Charles W. Upham, *The Life of Timothy Pickering*, Boston, 1867-1873; 4 vol.

Pleasants, "Hall Family"

J. Hall Pleasants, "Hall Family of Tacony, Philadelphia County, Pennsylvania," *Wm. & Mary Quart.*, 1st ser., XXII (1913-1914), 134-9, 265-8.

PMHB

Pennsylvania Magazine of History and Biography.

Powell, *Bring Out Your Dead*

John H. Powell, *Bring Out Your Dead: The Great Plague of Yellow Fever in Philadelphia in 1793*, Philadelphia, 1949.

Powell, *Richard Rush*

John H. Powell, *Richard Rush, Republican Diplomat*, Philadelphia, 1942.

Princeton Univ., *Gen. Cat.*, 1908

General Catalogue of Princeton University, 1746-1906, Princeton, 1908.

Quincy's Lexicon (N.Y., 1802)

Quincy's Lexicon Physico-Medicum Improved: or a Dictionary of the Terms Employed in Medicine, and in Such Departments of Chemistry, Natural Philosophy, Literature, and the Arts, as Are Connected Therewith. . . . From the Eleventh London Edition, New York, 1802.

Ramsay, *Eulogium*

David Ramsay, *An Eulogium upon Benjamin Rush, M.D. . . . Written at the Request of the Medical Society of South Carolina*, Philadelphia, 1813.

Reed, *Reed*

William B. Reed, *Life and Correspondence of Joseph Reed*, Philadelphia, 1847.

Roof, *Colonel William Smith and Lady*

Katharine Metcalf Roof, *Colonel William Smith and Lady: The Romance of Washington's Aide and Young Abigail Adams*, Boston, 1929.

Ruschenberger

W. S. W. Ruschenberger, *An Account of the Institution and Progress of the College of Physicians of Philadelphia during a Hundred Years, from January, 1787*, Philadelphia, 1887.

Rush MSS

Correspondence and other papers of Benjamin Rush in the Library Company of Philadelphia, Ridgway Branch. References in the present work are to the following classes of material:

1. Correspondence, Volumes i-xliv, call numbers Yi2/7216/F to Yi2/7261/F. (Vol. ii is repeated, and there is an unnumbered volume between xl and xli.)

2. Notebooks, vol. 1-4, call numbers Yi2/7262/1-4; also three smaller notebooks in one slipcase labeled "Manuscript Notes on Continental Congress etc.," call number Yi2/71257/D.

3. Further correspondence, lecture notes, and miscellaneous papers, Boxes 1-20, call numbers Yi2/7394/F to Yi2/7413/F.

4. Account books and day books, 19 vol., uncatalogued. (Records of BR's professional practice.)

Sabin, *Bibl. Amer.*

Bibliotheca Americana. A Dictionary of Books Relating to America, from Its Discovery to the Present Time. Begun by Joseph Sabin, continued by Wilberforce Eames, and completed by R. W. G. Vail, New York, 1868-1937; 29 vol.

Sabine, *Loyalists*

> Lorenzo Sabine, *Biographical Sketches of Loyalists of the American Revolution, with an Historical Essay*, Boston, 1864; 2 vol.

Scharf & Westcott

> J. Thomas Scharf and Thompson Westcott, *History of Philadelphia, 1609-1884*, Philadelphia, 1884; 3 vol.

Sellers, *Peale*

> Charles Coleman Sellers, *Charles Willson Peale*, Philadelphia, 1947; 2 vol.

Selsam, *Constitution of 1776*

> J. Paul Selsam, *The Pennsylvania Constitution of 1776: A Study in Revolutionary Democracy*, Philadelphia, 1936.

Simpson, *Eminent Philadelphians*

> Henry Simpson, *The Lives of Eminent Philadelphians, Now Deceased*, Philadelphia, 1859.

Smith, *Smith*

> Horace Wemyss Smith, *The Life and Correspondence of the Rev. William Smith, D.D.*, Philadelphia, 1880; 2 vol.

Sprague, *Annals*

> William B. Sprague, *Annals of the American Pulpit; or Commemorative Notices of Distinguished American Clergymen of Various Denominations from the Earliest Settlement to the Year 1855*, New York, 1859-1869; 9 vol.

Stillé, *Dickinson*

> Charles J. Stillé, *The Life and Times of John Dickinson, 1732-1808*, Philadelphia, 1891.

Stillé, *Wayne*

> Charles J. Stillé, *Major-General Anthony Wayne and the Pennsylvania Line in the Continental Army*, Philadelphia, 1893.

Stockton, *Stockton Family*

> Thomas Coates Stockton, *The Stockton Family of New Jersey and Other Stocktons*, Washington, 1911.

Stryker, *Battles of Trenton and Princeton*

> William S. Stryker, *The Battles of Trenton and Princeton*, Boston and New York, 1898.

Surg. Gen. Off., *Index-Cat.*

> *Index-Catalogue of the Library of the Surgeon General's Office, United States Army*, Washington, 1880—; 4 series.

Thacher, *Amer. Med. Biog.*

> James Thacher, *American Medical Biography; or Memoirs of Eminent Physicians Who Have Flourished in America*, Boston, 1828; 2 vol.

Thomas, *Columbia Univ. Officers and Alumni*

> Milton Halsey Thomas, *Columbia University Officers and Alumni, 1754-1857*, New York, 1936.

Univ. of Penna., *Biog. Cat. of Matriculates*

> *University of Pennsylvania: Biographical Catalogue of the Matriculates of the College, . . . 1749-1893*, Philadelphia, 1894.

Univ. of Penna., *Gen. Alumni Cat.*
> General Alumni Catalogue of the University of Pennsylvania, Philadelphia, 1922.

Van Doren, *Franklin*
> Carl Van Doren, *Benjamin Franklin*, New York, 1938.

Van Doren, *Secret History*
> Carl Van Doren, *Secret History of the American Revolution*, New York, 1941.

Warren, *Making of the Constitution*
> Charles Warren, *The Making of the Constitution*, Boston, 1928.

Washington, *Writings*, ed. Fitzpatrick
> *The Writings of George Washington*, edited by John C. Fitzpatrick, Washington, 1931-1944; 39 vol.

Washington, *Writings*, ed. Sparks
> *The Writings of George Washington*, edited by Jared Sparks, New York, 1848-1852; 12 vol.

Watson, *Annals*
> John F. Watson, *Annals of Philadelphia, and Pennsylvania, in the Olden Time*, Philadelphia, 1884; 3 vol.

Webster's Biog. Dict.
> *Webster's Biographical Dictionary*, Springfield, Mass., 1943.

Wertenbaker, *Princeton, 1746-1896*
> Thomas Jefferson Wertenbaker, *Princeton, 1746-1896*, Princeton, 1946.

Wickes, *Hist. of Medicine in N.J.*
> Stephen Wickes, *History of Medicine in New Jersey, and of Its Medical Men, from the Settlement of the Province to A.D. 1800*, Newark, 1879.

Wilson, "Col. John Bayard"
> James Grant Wilson, "Colonel John Bayard (1738-1807) and the Bayard Family of America," *New York Genealogical and Biographical Record*, XVI (1885), 49-72.

Winsor, *Narr. & Crit. Hist.*
> *Narrative and Critical History of America*, edited by Justin Winsor, Boston and New York, 1884-1889; 8 vol.

INDEX

THE Index covers the notes, illustrations, Introduction, and Appendices as well as the texts of the letters here printed; but it is selective rather than exhaustive for everything but the letters. References in the Index to matter in the notes are not distinguished in form from references to matter in the text, with the single important exception that *all references to the principal identifying notes on persons are italicized and follow immediately the names of the persons identified.*

Adams, Mrs. John (Abigail Smith), *192*; on BR's epistolary indiscretions, lxv; invited to Philadelphia, 546-7; and Jefferson, 1078, 1080; her "air of pleasantry," 1144; on Washington's birthday celebrations, 1206; on her husband's appointment policy, 1211; on Cobbett, 1213; mentioned, 191, 243, 469, 508-9, 524-5, 890, 891, 893, 899, 903, 909, 912, 913, 917, 920, 922, 939, 961, 964, 972, 1062, 1068, 1072-3, 1085, 1104, 1116

Adams, John ("Master Adams," Phila.), 688, 701

Adams, John Quincy, *894*; visits BR, 893, 909, 910; *Inaugural Oration* as Boylston professor, 927; loses his Senate seat, 966, 967, 971; and Madison, 998; Russian mission, 1013; *Lectures on Rhetoric and Oratory*, 1062; *American Principles: A Review of the Works of Fisher Ames*, 1068, 1076, 1078; coins for, 1080; in Russia, 1085, 1137; mentioned, 892, 934, 1101

Adams, Mrs. John Quincy (Louisa Johnson), *894*, 893, 909

Adams, Randolph G., quoted, 1205

Adams, Samuel, *157*; opposes Federal Constitution, 449; traduced by Gordon, 534; and independence movement, 942, 949; and Paine's *Common Sense*, 1008; quoted, 1155, 1159; mentioned, 80, 148, 157, 165, 335, 443, 623, 768, 900, 1090, 1114, 1139

Adams, Thomas Boylston, *892*, 891, 1085

Adams Manuscript Trust, owners of Rush autograph letters, lxxv, lxxxi

Addison, Joseph, *Cato*, 102; quoted, 198; on Virgil, 852; story by, 985

"Address of the Representatives of the African Church," 609

Adet, Pierre-August, *783*, 782

deaths from, 843. *See also* BR, Writings

Continental army, strength of (Sep. 1776), 110; leadership criticized by BR, 121, 156-7; soldiers praised, 124, 163-4; British respect for, after Princeton, 126, 128; its good condition, 151; lack of discipline, 155ff.; BR proposes annual election of general officers, 164; a "mob," 183; Congress and, 185; depleted by abuses in hospitals, 198-9; improvements in, 252; "melted away into peaceable citizens," 330, 344; mentioned, 91-2, 123

Continental Board of War, orders publication of BR's tract on health of soldiers, 145, 195; membership of, 185

Continental Congress, BR meets Massachusetts delegates at Frankford (1774), 2; BR's sensations as a member, 103-4; BR speaks in, 105-6, 107; described, 108; affairs in, 109, 111, 114, 133-5; *"vis inertiae"* of, 123; at Baltimore, 130ff.; BR urges its return to Philadelphia, 133-4; speaks on question of conference with Lee, 135; weakness of, 182-3; handling of controversy in Continental medical department, 185, 187, 189, 191, 193-4, 196-7, 199-200, 204-5, 207, 210-11; reforms Continental medical department, 203, 207-8; counterfeit resolution printed, 213; and Saratoga campaign, 218; address to states on finance (1779), 223, 230; BR's "Speech" to Congress on inflation, 229-37; proposal to fix seat in Princeton, 245; and Shippen courtmartial, 249, 258-9; and "Sergeants' Revolt," 302, 305, 307-8; BR approves financial plan of, 307-8; expected to return to Philadelphia, 345; mentioned, 86, 91-2, 96, 255, 330

Continental hospitals, healthy, 153; disorder in, 156; deplorable state of, 161ff., 173-6, 183, 195, 209, 257-60; military inspectors required, 168-70, 181, 194-5, 203; BR reports to Washington on, 180-2; hearing on, before Congress, 193; affidavits concerning abuses in, 201-2, 204; summary of BR's observations in, 358-60. *See also* Continental medical de-

partment; health of soldiers; Shippen, William (Jr.)

Continental loan offices, 120, 134-5, 230, 233, 268

Continental medical (or hospital) department, reforms needed, 129-30; BR appointed physician general, middle department, 139; his service in, 154ff.; history of, 161; BR urges reforms, 165ff.; "a mass of corruption and tyranny," 175; remedies proposed, 181-2; controversy placed before Congress, 185ff.; reformation, 203, 207-8; BR's review of controversy over, 225-8; Shippen courtmartial, 247-9; and BR's quarrel with Washington, 1202-5. *See also* British military hospitals; Continental hospitals; health of soldiers; Shippen, William (Jr.); U.S. Army medical department

Continental money, BR's plan for forcing acceptance, 120; depreciation, 183, 212, 223-4, 350; BR's "Speech" on inflation, 229-37; "breathing its last," 239, 246; redemption (at 40 to 1), 252; evils of paper money, 261, 471. *See also* Continental loan offices; price regulation

Convention of Saratoga. *See* Saratoga Convention

conversation, nature of good, 436; American, 550; essential to mental health, 926; Sir William Temple on, 1030

Conway, Thomas, *159*; "the idol of the whole army," 158; on George Washington, 161, 183, 1120, 1126; praised, 164; banished from Headquarters, 185-6; and Lafayette, 196, 199; "sacrificed," 220, and the "Cabal," 1201, 1203

"Conway Cabal," as presented in Gordon's *History*, 185; BR and, 1201-3

Conyngham, David Hayfield, *810*, 604, 808

Conyngham, Mrs. David Hayfield (Mary West), *604*, 603

Conyngham, Redmond, 810

Conyngham. *See also* Cunningham

Coombe, Thomas, *80*, lxxv, 79

Coon. *See* Kuhn, Adam

Cooper, Astley Paston, 884

Cooper, Robert, *302*, 301, 343, 433, 878

Cooper, Samuel, *805*; describes BR's

also "gyrater"; insane patients; psychiatry; BR, Writings; tranquillizing chair
international arbitration, BR advocates, 473, 540
Ireland, "distractions" in, 409
Irish. *See* Scotch-Irish
iron filings, iron rust, prescribed by BR, 576, 577, 1149
Irvine ("Erwin"), James, *117*, 117, 1151
Irvine ("Erving"), William, *343*, 342, 363, 631
Isham, Ralph, 633, 635
Italian language, BR's knowledge of, 531
Italian Society of Arts and Letters (Florence), 976
Izard, George, *1057*, 1057
Izard, Mrs. George (Elizabeth Carter [Farley] Banister Shippen), 1057

Jackson, Francis James, *1017*, 1015, 1018, 1037
Jackson, Robert, *884*, 883
Jackson, William, *310*, 309
Jackson & Dunn (firm), *349*, 348
Jacobi-Kloest. *See* Kloest
jail fever, 143, 661-2, 697
jails. *See* prisons and prisoners; Walnut Street Jail
jalap. *See* "ten and ten" purging dose
James, Thomas Chalkley, *709*, 708, 775, 1056
James, Major (British officer), *19*, 18
James I (king of England), 9
Jardine, Lewis J., *1045*, 1043
Jarvis, Charles, 957
jaw-fall, 457, 459. *See also* tetanus
Jay, John, 242, 514, 906, 909
Jay's Treaty, 768-9, 773, 775, 1084
Jebb, John, *827*; quoted, 825, 985, 1086
Jefferson, Thomas, *548-9*; BR's conversation with (1790), 546; and cultivation of sugar maple tree, 587, 597-9; asked to manumit a slave, 613-14; contributes to African Church, 602; characterized, 779; *Notes on the State of Virginia*, 784; and presidency of American Philosophical Society, 785; "Memoir on the Discovery of Certain Bones of a Quadruped of the Clawed Kind," 785-6; "Syllabus of an Estimate of the Merit of the Doctrines of Jesus," 822, 864;

BR's reminiscences of their friendship, 826; praise of his First Inaugural, 831-3; and vaccination, 840-1; prescriptions for, 856-9, 863-4, 1098-9; and medical science, 864; "Life and Morals of Jesus of Nazareth," 886; appointment policy, 897; his following in Pennsylvania, 901; and Miranda, 910; and quarantine laws, 911; and Jacob Rush, 917; and Burr, 937, 938; on B. Waterhouse, 957; and public birthday celebrations, 961; difficulties as President, 964; George Clymer on, 983; Federalists and, 984; pamphlet on the Batture Case, 1131; and Vine Utley, 1144; BR's efforts to reconcile Adams and, 1021-2, 1075-6, 1078-80, 1110-12; reconciliation with Adams, 1118-19, 1124, 1127-8; on Washington, 1139; rebuked by Adams, 1138, 1144, 1146; BR supports in 1796 election, 1210; mentioned, lx, lxi, lxvi, lxviii, lxx, lxxi, 564, 623, 701, 781, 841, 843, 850, 928, 943, 1154, 1172, 1206, 1213, 1218
   Letters to, 10 July 1791, 587; 17 Jan. 1792, 612; 26 Mch. 1792, 613; 1 Mch. 1796, 771; 4 Jan. 1797, 784; 4 Feb. 1797, 785; 22 Aug. 1800, 819; 6 Oct. 1800, 824; 12 Mch. 1801, 831; 27 Nov. 1801, 840; 12 Mch. 1802, 847; 12 Mch. 1803, 856; 5 May 1803, 863; 11 June 1803, 868; 5 Aug. 1803, 872; 29 Aug. 1804, 886; 29 Apr. 1805, 894; 15 June 1805, 896; 6 Dec. 1805, 910; 28 Nov. 1807, 956; 3 May 1809, 1003; 2 Jan. 1811, 1073; 1 Feb. 1811, 1078; 28 June 1811, 1087; 26 Aug. 1811, 1098; 17 Dec. 1811, 1111; 11 Feb. 1812, 1118; 3 Mch. 1812, 1127; 26 Apr. 1812, 1131; 15 Mch. 1813, 1186
Jeffreys ("Jeffries"), George, Baron, *129*, 128
Jenkins ("Jinkins"), John, *578*, 578
Jenks, Phineas, *884*, 883
Jenner, Edward, tribute to, 845; mentioned, 67, 845
Jennerian Society, 917
Jerome of Prague, 1086
Jewish wedding, described by BR, 429-32
Jinkins. *See* Jenkins
Joel, Beesly Edgar, 263

U.S., 351-3, 355; reception at Carlisle, 356; favorable impressions of, 356-7; illness and complaints of, 361-2; decides to return to Scotland, 369-70; account of his conduct, 373-5; "insane," 376; salary, 379, 384, 398, 509, 866; "abdication," 381-3; "deranged" by fever, 389; attempted reconciliation with BR, 393; his "Present State of Dickinson College," 399; conduct injures College, 410-11, 537, 987; given a house, 416; portrait reproduced, facing p. 764; Federalist politics, 812, 813; BR's tribute to, 878; unrestrained wit of, 1030-1; mentioned, 320, 331, 332, 346, 358, 835, 967, 968
   Letters to, 5 Dec. 1783, 315; 19? Apr. 1784, 321; 15 May 1784, 334; 27 Aug. 1784, 335; 28 Nov. 1784, 344
Nisbet, Mrs. Charles (Anne Tweedie), 335; characterized, 361, 369, 373-4, 376, 384; mentioned, 335
Nisbet, Thomas, 370, 370, 374, 376
Noble, Arthur, 597-8, 588, 589, 590
Noel, Experience (Mrs. Garrat Noel), 15, 17
Noel, Garrat, 15, 13, 17, 19, 24, 68, 69
Nogel. See Nagel
Nonintercourse Act, 998, 1015, 1035, 1134
nonjurors, 340. See also test laws
Norris, Isaac, 301, 300, 1167
Norris, William, 1141, 1140
North, Frederick, Lord, 86, 91, 276, 545, 898
North Briton, Number XLV, 72
North Carolina, migration of Pennsylvanians to, 405-6
Norton, Richard Cranch, 1104, 1103, 1127
Notre Dame (church in Paris), 852
Nott, Eliphalet, 1087
Nottingham Academy. See Finley, Samuel

oaths, BR refuses oath to Pennsylvania Constitution, 289; John Howard on oaths, 526; BR opposes oaths, 527-8. See also test laws
O'Brien, Richard, 1063, 1063
O'Bryan, Michael Morgan, 439, 438
O'Bryan, Mrs. Michael, 438
Occom, Samson, 59
oculists, 251

Odier, Louis, 981, 980
Offler, David, 1160
Offley, Daniel, 709; dies of yellow fever, 708, 720
O'Hara, Charles, 210, 209
Ohio, "wilderness," 333; River, 367
old age, medical alleviations for, 870-1; reflections on, 1099. See also BR, Writings
Old Light (or Old Side) Presbyterians, 38, 296, 299, 336, 379
Old Mill Prison ("Mill Prison"), 275
"Olden Diary," 127
Olmstead Case. See "Fort Rittenhouse" affair
opisthotonos, 981
Ord, Miss (Phila.), 79
Oriskany, battle of, 666
Orrick, Rebecca?, 133, 132
Orton, Mr. (perhaps Azariah Horton), dies of yellow fever, 714
Otaheite (i.e., Tahiti), 443
Otis, James, 73, 72, 443, 534
Otis, Samuel A., 702
Otto, Bodo (Sr.), 260, 257
Otto, John Conrad, 775; introduced to John Warren, 850-1; mentioned, 260, 775, 778, 797, 801, 804
Ovid, unsuitable for schools, 535; quoted, 964, 1108, 1113; mentioned, 1073
Oviedo y Valdès, Gonzalo Fernandez, 989
Owen, John, 827, 825
Oxford, BR advises James Rush to visit, 1039, 1043, 1048, 1050

pacifism. See BR, Opinions
Paine, Robert Treat, 548, 546
Paine (sometimes "Payne"), Thomas, 95-6; his Common Sense, 95, 1008, 1014; his Crisis criticized, 209; at fête in honor of Dauphin, 280; Rights of Man, 583, 620; Age of Reason, 770, 978, 1009, 1034; his infidelity deplored, 854, 948; quoted, 898; biographical data furnished by BR on, 1007-9, 1014; Cheetham's Life, 1033-4; mentioned, 148, 244, 903
painting, in America, 550. See also medical illustrations
paleontological discoveries. See mammoths, mammoth bones
Paley, William, Principles of Moral and Political Philosophy, commended by

INDEX

BR, 436; *View of the Evidences of Christianity*, 820, 854, 878
Palloni, Gaetano, *897*, 896
Palmer, George, *931*, 930, 1089
Palmer, Thomas, *931*, 930, 1089
Palmer sisters, 1089
Palmyra, ruins of, 494
palsy, 843
Paoli, Pasquale, *72*, 70-1
paper money. *See* Continental money
Paris, BR at, 2, 852
Parish (or Parrish), David, *1192*, 1192
Parke, Thomas, *654*; in 1793 epidemic, 653, 658, 677, 687, 708; succeeds BR at Pennsylvania Hospital, 1186
Parliament, Houses of, BR's visit to, 68-9
Parry, Jonathan, 1152
Pascalis, Felix, 797, 945
Pasha Hamet Karamanli, 913
Patapsco River, 132
Paterson, John, *136*, 135
Paterson, William, 72
patriotism, BR's analysis of, 83-4
Patterson, Robert, *897*, 896, 969, 1038, 1172
Patterson, Robert Maskell, *1041*, 1038
Patterson, Samuel, on "Thoughts of a Freeman," 1204
Patterson. *See also* Paterson
Patteson, David R., *921*
    Letter to, 19 June 1806, 921
Paul, Mr. (near Philadelphia), 237
Payne, Mrs. (Baltimore), 132
Payne. *See also* Paine
peace with Great Britain, 152, 161, 264, 268, 285
Peacock (ship), 1192
Peale, Charles Willson, *244*, lvi, lvii, 244, 852
Pearce, Captain (sea captain), 26
Pearce, Miss, 1006
Pearson ("Peirson"), George, *1041*, 1039
Peggy (ship), 46
Peirson. *See* Pearson
Pemberton, Israel, *849*, 849
Pemberton, James, *622*, 621, 755
penal reform. *See* capital punishment; prisons and prisoners; public punishments; solitary confinement
Penick, S. B., & Co., 516
Penington, John, *658*; dies of yellow fever, 672; tribute to, 698; mentioned, 658

Penn, John (of North Carolina), *188*, 187, 207, 236
Penn, John (1729-1795, royal governor of Penna.), *632*, 631
Penn, John (1760-1834, of Solitude and Stoke Park), *1037*, 1037, 1047, 1049
Penn, Richard, *945*, 943
Penn, Thomas, 76, 1047
Penn, William (founder of Pennsylvania), and religious toleration, 989; his treaty with the Indians, 1046-7, 1089; mentioned, 405, 621, 825, 943, 1107, 1151
Penn, William (great-grandson of the founder), *945*; characterized, 943
Penn Society, 1047
Pennsylvania (province and state), BR's love for, 63, 186; BR's account of, furnished to Nisbet, 335-9; prediction of its future happiness, 367-8; "Account" of its progress in population, &c., 400-7; opportunities for immigrants in, 557-9; BR's mixed feelings toward, 1182.
Pennsylvania, University of. *See* University of Pennsylvania; University of the State of Pennsylvania
Pennsylvania Abolition Society, 417, 448, 529, 755-6
    Letters to, 14 Nov. 1788, 497; 1794?, 754; 14 Jan. 1795, 756
Pennsylvania Assembly, affairs in, 119; turns BR out of Congress, 130, 137; improved, 255; and Congress, 255, 302; and Dickinson College, 319, 345, 354, 377, 378, 379, 537; "drunk with power," 349; fiscal policy, 411, 412
Pennsylvania Coffee House (London), 69, 81
Pennsylvania Committee of Safety, 94, 107
Pennsylvania Constitution of 1776, criticized and denounced by BR, 114-15, 137, 148, 303-4, 333, 498; BR's tract against, 150; John Adams on, 240; evils produced by, 244; origin and history, 336-7; "our *Balloon* Constitution," 469; "Dr. Franklin's Constitution," 901; mentioned, 253, 290, 375, 502, 530, 532, 558, 1114
Pennsylvania Constitution of 1790, BR's part in projecting, 509-10; BR satisfied with, 530; Convention framing it, 531, 532; praised, 558; struggle

in, 656, state of health in, 811, 821,
823, 860, 886-7, 970, 1058, 1070,
1139, 1146; Center House (water
works), 816; State House, 816; shot
towers, 983, 995; State House Yard,
995. *See also* seat of government,
controversy over; yellow fever in
Philadelphia
Philadelphia, College of. *See* College of
Philadelphia
Philadelphia Almshouse, 804
Philadelphia Bible Society, 830, 1191
Philadelphia Committee (or Board) of
Health, and City Hospital, 804; and
Bölke's medicine, 815; and local ori-
gin of yellow fever, 816
Letter to, 13 Sep. 1794, 749
Philadelphia Dispensary, 318, 415, 448,
478, 610, 675
Philadelphia General Hospital, 804
Philadelphia Medical Museum, 980,
1055, 1059
Philadelphia Society for Alleviating the
Miseries of Public Prisons, 417, 441
Philadelphia Society for Promoting Ag-
riculture, 956
Phile, Frederick, *721*; dies of yellow
fever, 720
Phillips ("Philips"), Jonas, *432*; BR
attends wedding in home of, 429-32
Phillips, Mrs. Jonas (Rachel Machado),
432, 430-1
Phillips, Rachel (Mrs. Michael Levy),
432; marriage of, 429-32
phlebotomy. *See* bloodletting
phthisis pulmonalis. *See* consumption
Physick, Philip Syng, *709*; supports
BR in yellow fever controversy, 749,
750, 752; prospers, 753, 769; and
Kuhn, 759; exceeds BR in bloodletting, 765; president of Academy
of Medicine, 797; at City Hospital,
807, 814, 815; BR consults with,
880, 1082; and tracheotomy, 982;
signs letter with BR, 999; lectures,
1097-8; removes tumor from BR's
neck, 1104; mentioned, 708, 882,
1036, 1038
Pickering, Timothy, *188*; member
Board of War, 185; in Luzerne co.,
439; BR's queries to, concerning Indians, 580-1; and Dr. Bölke, 815;
and John Henry, 1131; and Washington, 1133; and BR's appointment
to Mint, 1209-11; mentioned, lxxi,
629, 707, 791, 967, 998, 1134

Letters to, 30 Aug. 1787, 439; 29
Jan. 1788, 449; 2 May 1791, 580;
24 Sep. 1799, 815; 30 Sep. 1799,
816; 2 Mch. 1808, 961
Pickering, Mrs. Timothy (Rebecca
White), *440*, 440, 449
Pickering, Timothy (Jr.), *815*, 815
Pickering, William, *962*, 961
Pigon (ship), 753
Pigou (*Pigon?*, ship), 611
Pilmore, Joseph, *609*, 608, 720, 733
Pinckard ("Pinkard"), George, *884*,
883, 1037
Pinckney ("Pinkney"), Thomas, *761*,
761, 771, 782, 785
Pinckney's Treaty (Treaty of San Lo-
renzo), 771, 773
Pinel, Philippe, *1041*; treatise on mad-
ness, 1040
Pinkard. *See* Pinckard
Pinkney, William, *1063*, 1062, 1135
Pintard, John, *107*, 106
Pintard, Lewis, *263*, 107, 263
Pintard, Mrs. Lewis (Susan, or Susanna,
Stockton, Mrs. Rush's aunt), *263*,
263
Pintard, Mr., 886
Pitt, William, the elder. *See* Chatham,
Earl of
Pitt, William, the younger, 912, 941
Pittsburgh, 309
place names in U.S., BR's proposals
regarding, 819-20
plague, in London, 746, 823; will be
conquered by medicine, 846; not im-
ported, 872-3; not contagious, 881
Plains of Abraham, 95, 1015
Plato, 1021, 1075
Pleadwell, Captain F. L., owner of
Rush autograph letters, 839, 863
Plearne, Mr., 188
Pluckemin ("Pluckamin," N.J.), 326,
1039
Plumer, William, on *Secret History . . .
of St. Cloud*, 924-5; on Washington's
birthday celebrations, 1206
Point-no-Point, trip to, 545, 548, 898
Poland, King of, 912
Polly (tea ship), 82-3
Pompey, 191, 544
Poor, Enoch, *136*, 135
Pope, Alexander, quoted and para-
phrased, 219, 285, 369, 374, 955,
1152; mentioned, 1067
Poplar Forest (Jefferson's home), 1098
Poquessing Creek, 1150

INDEX

RUSH, BENJAMIN (1746-1813, *writer of the letters here published, and referred to as* BR), chronological tables summarizing his life, 2, 90, 318, 626, 830, 992. (*For fuller chronological data, consult the* CONTENTS, *where a brief summary of each letter is given; and see also the chronological listing of* BR's Published Writings, *below*.)

CHARACTER, APPEARANCE, HABITS, DOMESTIC LIFE

compulsion to share his thoughts, lxiv; chronic indiscreetness in letters, lxv; ardor in social and philanthropic crusades, lxviii-lxix; righteousness and quarrelsomeness, lxx-lxxi; portraits (by Sully), lxx, 1058; (by Peale), reproduced, facing p. 3; (by Furst), reproduced, facing p. 780; talent for friendship, lxxi-lxxii; self-dedication to "the Good of Mankind," 3, 9, 10-11, 14-15; Hazard on BR's lack of stability and prudence, 6; dislike of solitude and attachment to family life, 96-7, 106, 306, 435-6, 438-9, 531, 535-6, 926; on his own appearance, 327; "that turbulent spirit Dr. Rush," 349; "as crazy as ever," 432; filial discipline and parental authority in the Rush home, 511-12, 601, 776-7; persecutions and calumnies endured (symptoms and expressions of a mild paranoia), 530, 531, 533-4, 685, 717, 725, 727-8, 741, 750, 752, 766, 767, 775, 791-6, 825, 836, 891, 931, 944, 1060-1, 1092, 1112-13, 1114-15, 1123, 1169, 1178; on his own perseverance, 531; self-characterization among sketches of Signers of Declaration of Independence, 535; accustomed to work and ashamed of idleness, 603, 933; enjoyment of natural scenery and rural life, 803, 836; love of study, 819, 1115; compares himself with Jeremiah, 1115-16; account of a busy day, 1126-7; account of his diet and regimen, 1142-3; R. Peters' letter on BR's character, 1210. *See also* BR, Opinions; BR, Health and Illnesses

OPINIONS

Literary: best models of style, 219, 524; on American magazines, 450-1; English style and American style, 492-3; Swift on style, 861; on poetry, 876-7;

932; modern authors superior to ancient, 1066-7. *See also* letter-writing, BR's advice on; *and the names of specific authors*

Political: dedicates himself to American cause, 54; on the elder Pitt, 68-9; criticizes Mrs. Macaulay's plan for Corsican constitution, 69-71; admires Wilkes, 72-4; writes patriotic propaganda, 82ff.; total repeal of all offensive acts of Parliament essential (1775), 91; denounces Pennsylvania tories, 101-2; on Declaration of Independence, 103, 108; urges emergency measures (Dec. 1776), 120ff.; denounces Pennsylvania Constitution, 148ff.; critical of military leadership, 156ff., 182-3; faith in America and the cause of independence, 192, 196, 198, 200; denounces British peace commission (1778), 213-14; on monarchical tendencies in U.S., 219-20; apostrophe to liberty, 221-2; Pennsylvania a "mobocracy," 244; despairs of reforming men by political means, 246; republican credo, 264, 265; indispensableness of union, 268; public opinion in a republic, 386; American Revolution has "just begun" (1786), 388; plan of regional confederacies, 408; the "continental wagon will overset our state dung cart," 439-40; evils of a "simple democracy," 454-5; "We have become a nation," 475; republicanism and monarchy compared, 522-3; revision of state constitution completes "his last political wish," 531; the funding law "a mighty act of national injustice," 539; blessings of American form of government, 556-7; America and world happiness, 561; republicanism and Christianity, 584, 820-1; holds fast to Revolutionary principles, 768; predicts extinction of "nobles and kings," 638, 785; indifference to, and ignorance of, politics, 768, 797, 1020; on the 1796 election, 779, 782; "the *New York* administration of our government" (1797), 784; on separation of church and state, 824-5; stands firmly committed to republicanism, 826, 831-2, 859; disapproves of politics as a career, 886, 891, 1109; disillusionment with political means of improving society, 892-3, 899, 995, 1090; regrets his own public efforts, 913, 941, 966-7, 985, 1189; on the coercive nature of govern-

RUSH, BENJAMIN (*continued*)

ment, 1034-5; epitaphs on the nation and its liberties, 1067-8, 1154; "a be-banked, a bewhiskied, and a bedollared nation," 1145; on the office of President, 1155; separatist tendencies in U.S., 1167-8. *See also* Constitutionalist party in Pennsylvania; Pennsylvania Constitution of 1776; Republican party in Pennsylvania

Religious: summary of BR's religious evolution, lxix; millennial belief, lxxii; early religious reflections and outbursts, 3, 6, 7, 10-11, 16, 20, 39; religion necessary to correct the effects of learning, 294; breach with Presbyterians and resignation from Arch Street Church, 304, 379-80, 433-4, 533; admires Pennsylvania German piety and church organization, 425-6; returns to Episcopalian fold and later retires from it, 533, 962; belief in universal salvation animates him in all his labors, 419; on conflict between Calvinism and philanthropy, 490; Universalism and republicanism, 583-4; on clergy who "are too good to do good," 600, 620-1; esteem for Methodist doctrine, 611; millennial predictions, 611-12, 620, 762, 834, 837, 919; how to combat infidelity, 783-4; disillusionment with politics and retreat to religion, 799; compares his own creed with Jefferson's, 864; composite nature of his later religious views 962-3. *See also* Bible; church attendance; Universalism

Miscellaneous: anti-militaristic and pacifist views, 70-1, 406, 462, 470-1, 492, 540, 542, 561, 621, 787, 840, 847-8, 871, 1197-9; Anglophobia, 215, 242, 268-9, 506, 513, 771-2, 779, 785; on Scotchmen, 393; primogeniture "founded in nature," 511; doubts truth of any history, 534; on the feebleness of human reason, 545; "no good effort is lost," 571; on the conjugal relationship, 616-18; scheme for honoring American patriots, 819-20; on the comparative force of reason and habit, 978-9; war not the worst of evils, and probably unavoidable, 997-8, 1135, 1154, 1168; plan of an address on national principles, 1096-7. *See also* capital punishment; education; science; slavery and the slave trade; temperance propaganda; public punishments

MEDICAL PRACTICE AND THEORY

BR's medical reputation at his death and after, lxi-lxiii; his medical correspondence, lxvii-lxviii; apprenticeship under Redman, 5, 11, 13, 24; studies at Edinburgh, 28-9, 40, 49, 50-1, 61-3; on fashions in medical theories, 41; career in state and Continental hospital service, 94, 125-30, 139-94; perpetual hurry, 109; resumes practice in Philadelphia, 218, 219, 222; reluctance to leave patients in others' hands, 248; advice to young doctors, 284, 1130; difficulties of practice in U.S., 311; summary of observations as physician general, 358-60; "still fond of voyages to Otaheite in medicine," 443; BR's medical system ("new theory of fever," or doctrine of "the unity of disease"), 571, 583, 584-5, 765, 791, 822-3, 915-16, 923, 1030, 1061, 1114, 1140-1; prescriptions for patients, 574-7, 631, 814, 856-9, 863-4, 870-1, 879-80, 921, 1098-9, 1128-9, 1149; describes a busy day, 603-4; medical use of balloons, 627; described by Hazard during 1793 epidemic, 702; case records, 764-5; described by Hodgdon during 1797 epidemic, 791-2; advice by mail order, 810; theory of epidemics, 816; medical "commonplace books," 863; "depleting remedies" more necessary in America than in Britain, 881-2; work in yellow fever and consumption praised in Valentin's *Notice*, 982; John Adams on BR's wide repute, 1118; "new doctrine of animal heat," 1025; on his own reputation as a physician, 1028; on proper accommodations for hospital patients, 1172-3; Cobbett on BR in 1797 epidemic, 1214-15. *See also* allergic phenomena; apprentices; bloodletting; epidemics; health of soldiers; inoculation; insane patients; medical education; medicine, profession of; Pennsylvania Hospital; psychiatry; pulse; quarantines; BR, Finances; BR, Teacher and Lecturer; BR, Writings; sanitarian, BR as; surgery; "ten and ten" purging dose; vaccination; *and the names of particular diseases and medicines*

TEACHER AND LECTURER

a pupil's tribute, lxi; popularity of his lectures, lxvi; relations with former

INDEX

RUSH, BENJAMIN (*continued*)
the United States," 542; "Account of the Influenza in 1789, 1790, and 1791," 566, 567; "Observations on the Symptoms and Cure of Dropsies," 573, 1025; lecture "On the Character of Dr. Sydenham," 700; *Medical Inquiries and Observations*, vol. II, 872, 1025; "Account of the State of the Body and Mind in Old Age," 873

1794: aids in preparing Samuel Magaw's *Discourse* in the African Church, 601; *Account of the Bilious Remitting Yellow Fever . . . in . . . 1793* (vol. III of BR's *Medical Inquiries and Observations*), 652, 670, 683, 732-3, 739, 748-9, 754

1795: *Syllabus of a Course of Lectures on the Institutes of Medicine*, 767

1796: "Defence of Blood-Letting," 751, 760; *Medical Inquiries and Observations*, vol. IV, 751, 759, 766, 774, 778, 780, 783; *Eulogium* on Rittenhouse, 782, 784, 793, 1214

1797: "Observations" on Negroes' skin color, 786

1798: "Observations upon the Influence of the Habitual Use of Tobacco," 527, 570; "Observations upon the Nature and Cure of the Gout," 780; *Medical Inquiries and Observations*, vol. V, 781; *Essays, Literary, Moral & Philosophical*, 626, 939

1799: *Observations upon the Origin of the Malignant Bilious, or Yellow Fever in Philadelphia*, 814, 816; *Three Lectures upon Animal Life*, 1021

1801: *Six Introductory Lectures, to Courses of Lectures, upon the Institutes and Practice of Medicine*, 839, 840

1804: *Inquiry into the Effects of Ardent Spirits upon the Human Body and Mind*, 273, 893, 1087; *Relacion de la calentura biliosa remitente amarilla . . .*, 945, 1057

1805: "Inquiry into the Cause and Cure of Pulmonary Consumption," 567; "Outlines of a Theory of Fever," 584; *Medical Inquiries and Observations*, 2d edn., 830, 886, 890, 899, 909, 911; *Inquiry into the Various Sources . . . of Summer and Autumnal Diseases. . . . To Which Are Added Facts Intended to Prove the Yellow Fever Not to Be Contagious*, 911

1806: lecture "On the Opinions and Modes of Practice of Hippocrates," 932; *Essays*, 2d edn., 940

1807: lecture "On the Means of Acquiring Business . . . in the Profession of Medicine," 285; lecture "On the Duty and Advantages of Studying the Diseases of Domestic Animals," 953-5, 1176, 1186; "Inquiry into the Functions of the Spleen, Liver, Pancreas, and Thyroid Gland," 980

1808: obituary notice of John Redman, 11, 964

1809: "Account of . . . Mrs. Elizabeth Ferguson," 179; "Account of a Case of Small-Pox after Variolous Inoculation," 980; *Medical Inquiries and Observations*, 3d edn., 992, 1018, 1020, 1021, 1048; American edn. of Cleghorn's *Observations on the Epidemical Diseases of Minorca*, 1018, 1046; American edn. of Sydenham's *Works*, 1018, 1020, 1046, 1048

1810: American edn. of Pringle's *Observations on the Diseases of the Army*, 1045, 1046, 1049, 1140; lecture "On the Study of Medical Jurisprudence," 1051, 1069-70, 1074; "Charge . . . to the Graduates in Medicine," 1055; "Pathological and Practical Remarks upon Certain Morbid Affections of the Liver," 1055; account of the "Tranquillizer," 1058-60, 1070-1

1811: American edn. of Hillary's treatise on *Epidemical Diseases of Barbadoes*, 700; *Sixteen Introductory Lectures, to Courses of Lectures upon the Institutes and Practice of Medicine*, 1036, 1062, 1074, 1085; handbill against spirituous liquors, 1086-8

1812: *Medical Inquiries and Observations, upon Diseases of the Mind*, lxix, 763, 847, 932, 933, 1131, 1132, 1133, 1141, 1161, 1164-5, 1169, 1178, 1188, 1194

1892: *Old Family Letters Relating to the Yellow Fever*, lxiv

1946: *Reminiscences of Boswell & Johnson*, 634

1948: *Autobiography* (see "Travels through Life" *among* Unpublished Writings, *above*)

1950: "Diary" of trip to Carlisle (1784), 320

See also public letters *in main body of this Index*

[1279]

Rush, Benjamin (BR's 5th son, died in infancy), *520*, 519
Rush, Benjamin (BR's 6th son), *629*; in infancy, 628; during yellow fever epidemic, 637, 642, 644, 673, 704, 705, 709, 720, 737-8, 746, 860; at Princeton College, 892; in William Waln's counting-house, 1017, 1044, 1049, 1055; voyage to the Mediterranean, 1085, 1109; sends cask of wine from Samos, 1160; at Smyrna, 1162; at Cadiz, 1182; returns home, 1192; mentioned, 1011, 1032, 1035
Rush, Benjamin (BR's grandson), *1081*, 1081
Rush, Benjamin, IV, 1153
Rush, Elizabeth (BR's daughter, died in infancy), *520*, 519

Rush, Emily, or Anne Emily ("Nancy," "Emely," "Emelia," BR's eldest daughter, later Mrs. Ross Cuthbert), *250*; characterized, 519, 535-6, 599; during 1793 epidemic, 713, 722; marriage, 783, 813; and Mary Rush's engagement, 861-2, 865; visits Philadelphia, 948, 951; moves to Quebec, 1054; mentioned, 224, 248, 306, 327, 436, 586, 601, 653, 869, 885, 890, 892, 1006, 1147
Rush, Jacob (BR's brother), *44*; recommended to Benjamin Franklin, 76; at Baltimore, 131; his home (Rush Hill), 139, 237; judicial career, 315, 916-17; visit to Nottingham School, 989; attempted impeachment of, 994, 1001; mentioned, lxxv, 41, 55, 62, 138, 157, 161, 237, 370, 701, 826, 1030, 1107, 1156
Rush, Mrs. Jacob (Polly Rench, or Wrench), 44
Rush, James (BR's grandfather), his epitaph, 1151
Rush, James (BR's 3d son), *385*; and BR's papers, lxii-lxiii; birth, 384; as a child, 396, 519, 684; during 1793 epidemic, 713; at Princeton College, 839ff.; commencement oration, 895, 896, 907; medical thesis, 1003; plans of, 1005, 1006; sails for Edinburgh, 1010, 1012, 1026; introduced to Lettsom, 1045-6; returns to U.S., 1085, 1099, 1106; and Earl of Buchan, 1088; succeeds Richard as BR's heir, 1108; mentioned, 306-7, 892, 928, 1051, 1054, 1061, 1169
Rush, Mrs. James (Phoebe Ridgway), lxii-lxiii, 385
Rush, John (founder of Rush family in America), *102-3*; a foe of tyranny, 102; BR's inheritance from, 825-6;

and Cromwell, 1151; courtship and marriage, 1156-7; mentioned, 117

Rush, Mrs. John (Susanna Lucas, wife of BR's first American forebear), *1159*, 1156-7

Rush, John (BR's father), 2, 1150, 1151, 1152

Rush, Mrs. John (Susanna [Hall] Harvey Rush Morris, BR's mother), *98*; characterized, 536; during 1793 epidemic, 641, 645, 670, 674, 686, 688, 691, 693, 701, 704, 705, 716, 723, 733, 740; BR's epitaph for, 782; his debt to, 1083; mentioned, 53, 54, 97, 138, 139, 1152, 1156

Rush, John ("Jack," "Jackey," BR's eldest son), *166*; as a child, 166, 178, 216, 237, 243, 306; to go to Edinburgh, 328; visits hospital with BR, 394-5; in Federal Procession, 469; how disciplined, 511-12; characterized, 519, 615-16, 618-19; BR's attachment to, 599, 600; denied use of gun, 601; sent to Princeton College, 613, 615-16; at Princeton, 619; withdrawn from College, 622; during 1793 epidemic, 638, 641, 642, 643, 693, 713, 722, 733; studies medicine, 766; sails for Calcutta, 776-7, 778; BR's "principal assistant," 791; in navy, 813, 815; affray with Cobbett, 817-18; resigns commission, 842, 847; medical student at University, 860; thesis, 882; goes to South Carolina, 890-1; reenters navy, 892, 923; opinion on Burr's enterprise, 940-1; kills Benjamin Turner in duel, 959; insane, 959-60, 1012; returns to duty, 1014; returns to Philadelphia and is committed to Pennsylvania Hospital, 1035-6; course of his case, 1040, 1041-2, 1044, 1049, 1052, 1055, 1074, 1085; mentioned, 139, 186, 187, 190, 192, 219, 224, 327, 431, 436, 535, 689, 842, 877, 928, 1066, 1217

Letter to, 18 May 1796, 776

Rush, Julia (BR's youngest daughter, later Mrs. Henry J. Williams), *714-15*; in infancy, 713, 722; characterized, 892; manual of conduct for, 929; at Princeton, 967; trip to Canada, 1012, 1015; trip to Maryland, 1054; in New Jersey, 1058; mentioned, 809, 928, 1025, 1032, 1044, 1049

Rush, Julia Williams. *See* Biddle, Mrs. Alexander

Rush, Mary (BR's daughter, later Mrs. Thomas Manners), *862*; during 1793 epidemic, 713; during 1797 epidemic, 793; engagement and marriage, 861-2, 865, 869, 883; visits Philadelphia, 948, 951; sails for England with her family, 1012, 1015; in England, 1026, 1031, 1032, 1037, 1044, 1046, 1054, 1070; returns to Philadelphia, 1106, 1147; at Princeton, 1164; with BR, 1169; mentioned, 307, 519, 601, 885, 890, 1006, 1056

Letter to, 1 Apr. 1803, 861

Rush, Nancy. *See* Rush, Emily, or Anne Emily

Rush, Rachel (BR's sister). *See* Montgomery, Mrs. Joseph

Rush, Rebecca (BR's sister). *See* Stamper, Mrs. Thomas

Rush, Rebecca (BR's niece), 645. *See also* "Becky"

Rush, Richard ("Dick," BR's 2d son), *306-7*; and BR's papers, lxi-lxii; as a child, 306, 327; characterized, 599, 601-2, 886; at school, 619; during 1793 epidemic, 637, 641, 642, 643, 670, 713, 722; sent to Frazer's school, 679; in New York, 788, 790; assists his father, 805; gardening at Sydenham, 808, 809; quarrel with Dr. Glentworth, 816; recommended to Madison, 841-2; as lawyer, 860, 891, 1005, 1006, 1044, 1049, 1054, 1056; and John Adams' letters, 903, 906, 942, 972, 1104, 1134, 1145, 1146, 1148; writes James' commencement oration, 907; and *Chesapeake* inquiry, 955; engagement and marriage, 1010, 1012, 1016, 1017, 1020, 1026; attorney general of Pennsylvania, 1081; comptroller general of U.S., 1107, 1112-13; cut off by BR, 1108, 1109; "desertion" of BR, 1114; Adams' opinion of his conduct, 1116, 1117; and George Washington, 1126; *Oration . . . on the 4th of July, 1812,* 1144, 1146, 1148, 1155; and BR's collection of Revolutionary pamphlets, 1153, 1156; mentioned, 431, 519, 535, 646, 688, 869, 894, 895, 898, 899, 902, 909, 913, 927, 943, 1021, 1032, 1034, 1037, 1055, 1057, 1062, 1068, 1076,

of dead, 195; charges against BR, 196; BR's charges against, 197ff.; investigation by Congress, 206, 210-11, 213; review of BR's relations with, 225-8; impending trial, 242-3; arrested, 246-7; court-martial, 247-9, 950-1, 1122; BR substantiates charges against, 256-60; his "Vindication," 260; and P. Garvey, 262-3; BR and Morgan protest his continuing as professor, 289; attachment to University of the State of Pennsylvania, 571; attends Mrs. Washington's grandson, 599; and 1793 epidemic, 642, 668, 712; maneuvers in medical school, 753, 766; reconciliation with BR before death, 971, 972; and the Lees, 1125; causes of BR's quarrel with, 1197, 1200, 1203-5; Washington's physician, 1210; mentioned, 41, 50, 62, 180, 194, 765, 888, 1117, 1175

Letters to, 2 Dec. 1777, 169; 1 Feb. 1778, 196; 18 Nov. 1780, 256

Shippensburg ("Shippen's Town," Penna.), 309, 381

Shippin, William, *127*, 126

Shryock, Richard H., 1217

Shultz. *See* Schultz

Sidney (or Sydney), Algernon, 73; *Discourses concerning Government*, 997; mentioned, 72

silk culture in America, BR recommends, 74

Silliman, Benjamin, *1052*; *Journal of Travels in England, Holland and Scotland*, 1051

Simes ("Sims"), Thomas, *Military Guide for Young Officers*, 952, 1126

Sims, Mr. and Mrs. B., 677

Sims, Wooddrop ("Woodruf"), *645*; dies of yellow fever, 644

Simson, Dr. (Birmingham, England), 881

Sinclair, Sir John, *907*; *An Essay on Longevity*, 872; *Code of Health and Longevity*, 873; anecdote of Adam Smith, 905

Sinclair (British deserter), his story, 186-7

Sinclair. *See also* St. Clair

Skenk. *See* Schenck

slavery and the slave trade, BR's attacks on, 76-8, 79, 81, 82, 286, 529, 541, 1072; revival of slave trade in southern states, 331; abolition of

slavery in Pennsylvania, 371, 460; progress of abolitionist cause, 939-40; and Federal Constitution, 446-7; diseases incident to slavery, 457-8; runaway slaves, 482, 489; slavery a deterrent to settlement in South, 504, 559; Franklin and, 564; sugar production by slaves, 592ff.; recommendations of the convention of abolition societies, 756-8; Thomas Paine on, 1007, 1009. *See also* Negroes; Pennsylvania Abolition Society; BR, Writings

Sloan, Sir Hans, 955-6, 952

Slough, Mathias, *341*, 340

smallpox. *See* inoculation; vaccination

Smiley (or Smilie), John, *385*, 384

Smith, Adam, saying of, 905

Smith, Datus C., Jr., lxxxiii

Smith, Edward Leffingwell, lvii

Smith, James (M.D., N.Y.), 22, 21

Smith, James (lawyer, York, Penna.), *315*, 314

Smith, John (Sr.), *680*; dies of yellow fever, 679

Smith, John (Jr.), *680*; dies of yellow fever, 679

Smith, John (theologian), *King Solomon's Portraiture of Old Age*, 778

Smith, John Blair, 377, *377*, 813

Smith, Jonathan Bayard, *43*; mentioned, 60

Letters to, 30 Apr. 1767, 39; 20 Apr. 1778, 211

Smith, Mrs. Jonathan Bayard (Susannah Bayard), 45

Smith, Lloyd W., owner of Rush autograph letters, 640, 836, 880, 1191

Smith, Nathan, 843

Smith, Rebecca (afterwards Mrs. Samuel Blodget, Jr.), *586*, 631, 681, 707, 715

Letters to, 1 July 1791, 585; May? 1792, 616

Smith, Richard R., 598

Smith, Robert (secretary of the navy), *848*, 842, 847, 1087, 1132

Smith, Robert (Rev.), 947, *947*, 1193

Smith, Samuel (Philadelphia merchant), *43*, 39

Smith, Samuel (Maryland politician), *1134*, 1132

Smith, Samuel Stanhope, *325*; presides over Princeton College, 325; characterized, 376; and principalship of Dickinson College, 377; mentioned,

lxxi, lxxv, 346, 427, 433, 654, 711,
716, 855, 895, 947
Smith, Mrs. Samuel Stanhope (Ann
Witherspoon), 325, 377
Smith, Sarah, 680; dies of yellow fever,
679
Smith, Thomas (trustee of Dickinson
College), 537-8
     Letters to, 26 Feb. 1790, 536; 14
     Mch. 1793, 631
Smith, Mrs. Thomas (wife of the preceding), 632; BR prescribes for, 631
Smith, Thomas (of South Carolina),
943
Smith, William (judge, N.Y.), 860,
22, 858
Smith, William (provost, College of
Philadelphia), 78; toryism, 101;
eulogy of Montgomery, 124-5; colleges founded by, 371; character,
393; eulogy of Franklin, 565; epigrams on Franklin and Rittenhouse,
851-3; "Cato" letters, 1010; mentioned, 77, 282, 289, 423, 537, 586
     Letter to, 10 Aug. 1802, 851
Smith, Mrs. William (Rebecca Moore,
wife of the preceding), 538; dies of
yellow fever, 715, 719-20; mentioned, 537, 586, 618
Smith, William (clergyman and schoolmaster, N.Y.), 952, 951
Smith, William Loughton, 945; on BR's
appointment to Mint, 1211; mentioned, 943
Smith, William Moore, 284; his ode to
the Dauphin, 282
Smith, William Stephens, 503; char-
acterized, 1118; and Miranda, 1119;
on Washington, 1123, 1126, 1133,
1162; John Adams on, 1163; in
Congress, 1177; mentioned, 192, 502,
920, 939, 940, 1161
Smith, Mrs. William Stephens. See
Adams, Abigail (daughter of John
Adams)
Smith, William Steuben, 920, 920, 923,
939, 940
Smith, William W., 203, 201
Smith & Robertson (firm), 1070
Smith, Wright, & Gray (firm), 28
Smyth, Leopold, 805; dies of yellow
fever, 804
Snow, Gideon, 911
Snowden, Captain, 616
Snyder, Simon, 900; election, 988; as
governor, 994, 996, 998, 1001; BR

presents Treaty Tree souvenir to,
1048; mentioned, 898, 901, 908,
967, 976, 984, 1137
Society for Promoting Political Enquir-
ies, 416
Socinianism (anti-Trinitarianism). See
Unitarianism
solitary confinement, preferable to other
forms of punishment, 511-12, 526,
527
Sommerville, Mr. (Scottish immigrant),
761
Sonnoni de Manoncourt, C.N.S., Travels in Upper and Lower Egypt, 821
South, Robert, 928; quoted, 925, 1105
South Carolina, its future prospects,
268; migration of Pennsylvanians to,
405
Spain, aid from, to U.S. likely, 136;
and Indians in South America, 539,
569; threat of war with U.S. (1806),
929-30; Napoleon in, 974, 983
Spalding, Lyman, 843
     Letter to, 9 Feb. 1802, 843
Spanish language, its prospective influence, 493; BR enjoys books in, 531
Sparks, Jared, lxxvi, 1156
Sparks, Mr. (sea captain), 338
Speakman, Townsend, 703; dies of yellow fever, 701
Spear. See Spier
speculation, the result of depreciation
of money, 232; denounced by BR,
538-9, 623; victims of, 781; mania
for, 966-7. See also banks; Funding
Act; script
Spencer, Mr. (Phila.), 718
Spier, Robert ("Spear"), 46, 45, 52
spirituous liquors, BR's public letter denouncing use of, 270-3; new settlers
fond of, 401, 402; harmful to morals and health, 462; "Antifederal,"
475-6; to be avoided even as medicines, 479-80; Princeton commencement speech on, 490; John Howard
and, 526. See also temperance propaganda
sprains, treatment of, 583
Sproat, Anne (or Nancy), 676; dies of
yellow fever, 675, 677, 717
Sproat, David, 1017, 1016
Sproat, James, 334; minister at Second
Presbyterian Church, 332, 434, 437,
440, 646, 690; dies of yellow fever,
716, 718; funeral, 720

343, 352, 377; financial straits, 449; and new constitution of Pennsylvania, 509; and chief justiceship, 514; and Paine's *Common Sense*, 1008; mentioned, 183, 350, 361, 412, 501, 1095
Wilson, Matthew, *947*, 947, 1193
Wilson, Sir Robert Thomas, *History of the British Expedition to Egypt*, 872, 912
Wilson, Miss (Phila.), 679
Wilson, Mrs. (roominghouse keeper), 672, 674
Winchester, Elhanan, *372-3*; BR and, lxix; success of his preaching, 372, 773; commended to Dr. Price, 432-3; *Lectures on the Prophecies*, 581-2, 602, 628; other works, 611; writings generally, 783
  Letters to, 11 May 1791, 581; 12 Nov. 1791, 611
Winchester, James, *1183*, 1183
Windsor (ship), 1018
Wingate, Paine, *574*, 573, 578
Wirt, William, 833
Wistar ("Wister"), Caspar, *572-3*; professor of chemistry in College of Philadelphia, 571; commended, 610; in 1793 and 1794 epidemics, 645, 648, 651, 653, 663, 675, 685, 687, 717, 720, 741, 752; charged by BR with desertion, 735-6; forced to adopt BR's remedies, 759, 775; and controversy over Dr. Way's death, 790; signs letter with BR, 999; on low standards in the Medical School, 1180; mentioned, 763
Wistar, Catharine (later Mrs. William Bache), 652
Wistar, Thomas, *721*, 720
wit, the least desirable of the social virtues, 585-6, 1030-1; effect of "morbid action on the blood vessels of the brain," 932
Witherspoon, Ann. *See* Smith, Mrs. Samuel Stanhope
Witherspoon, David, 123
Witherspoon (frequently "Wetherspoon"), John, *35-6*; urged to come to Princeton, 33-8, 45-9; his preaching, 41-2; arrangements for reception in America, 56-7; departure from Scotland, 58, 60; joy at his acceptance, 58-9; and the Rush-Shippen controversy, 194, 207, 226-7, 1125; mission to Europe (1784), 314; and founding of Dickinson College, 324, 338, 343; and Nisbet, 374, 384; praise of Madison as a student, 850; disapproval of wit, 1031; on scandal, 1132; mentioned, 19, 123, 322, 393, 452, 546, 1024, 1039
  Letters to, 25 Mch. 1767, 33; 23 Apr. 1767, 36; 1 Aug. 1767, 45; 29 Dec. 1767, 46; 30 Apr. 1768, 57
Witherspoon, Mrs. John (Elizabeth Montgomery), *38*; characterized, 56; "another Sarah," 59; mentioned, 37, 41, 46, 48-9
Witt, Christopher, *872*, 871
Woedtke ("Wotke"), Frederic William, Baron de, *112*, 112
Wolcott ("Walcot"), Oliver (Jr.), *702-3*, 701, 1209, 1211
  Letter to, 8 Oct. 1793, 708
Wolfe, James, 95, 143, 157, 1008, 1021
Wolford, Mr., 243
Wollstonecraft ("Woolstonecraft"), Charles, *638-9*, 638
Wood, Joseph, *116*, 114
Woodbridge, Mr., 526
Woodbury (N.J.) Academy, 619
Woodford, William, *136*, 135, 164
Woodhouse, James, *713*; in 1793 epidemic, 712, 714, 715, 717, 718, 720, 722, 723, 726, 729, 733; on medical faculty, 765; signs letter with BR, 999; mentioned, 1006
Woolman, John, *444*, 441
worms, cures for, 576-7; sugar as a preventive, 594
Wotke. *See* Woedtke
Wrench, Polly. *See* Rush, Mrs. Jacob
Wycliffe ("Wickliff," "Wicklif"), John, 442, 1086
Wynkoop, Benjamin, *762*; his device for ventilating ships, 761-2
Wynkoop, Gerardus, *510*, 510
Wyoming Valley, disputes in, 504

"X.Y.Z." affair, 807
Xenophon, 145
Ximenes (Jiménez de Quesada), 371

Yale College ("College of New-Haven"), 367, 867
Yard, Mrs. (roominghouse keeper), *900*, 898, 944
Yeates, Bartholomew, *129*, 127
Yeates, Jasper, *340*, 425
yellow fever, controversy over treatment of, 644, 648, 650-9, 673, 675, 678, 681, 683, 685-7, 693, 695-9,

ERRATA

Page 567, note 3, line 9 from end. *For* II [1793] *read* I [1789].

Page 982, note 5, line 2. *For* "*médicine*" *read* "*médecine.*"

Page 1040, lines 10-11. *For* phillipic *read* philippic.

Page 1041, note 16, line 1. *For* Phillippe *read* Philippe.